JOHN S. REYNOLDS

RECONSTRUCTION

IN

SOUTH CAROLINA

1865-1877

BY
JOHN S. REYNOLDS

NEGRO UNIVERSITIES PRESS
NEW YORK

F
274
.R46
1969

Originally published in 1905
by The State Co., Publisher, Columbia, S. C.

Reprinted 1969 by
Negro Universities Press
A DIVISION OF GREENWOOD PUBLISHING CORP.
NEW YORK

SBN 8371-1638-4

PRINTED IN UNITED STATES OF AMERICA

TABLE OF CONTENTS.

CHAPTER I.
The Provisional Government.

Conditions at the close of the Civil War. Military occupation and control. The negro troops. Reconstruction under President Johnson's plan. The Provisional Government. The Convention and the Constitution of 1865. Legislative proceedings.................. **Page.** 3

CHAPTER II.
Orr's Administration.

Complete establishment of the State Government. The "Black Code" and contemporaneous legislation. The President's policy continued. The Philadelphia Convention. Military interference. The Freedmen's Bureau. The Reconstruction measures of Congress. The rule of the military commanders. The negro enfranchised by Congress. The Reconstruction Convention. The new Constitution. Appeals and remonstrances of the white people. Congressional reconstruction completed. The campaign of 'sixty-eight......... 25

CHAPTER III.
Scott's First Term.

The new government organized. Elections in joint assembly. Notable legislation. Ignorance in official stations. The Civil Rights bill. A Congressman sells a West Point cadetship. A costly investigation. Some fruits of misgovernment. Governor Scott's campaign plans. The negro militia. The Union Reform movement. The campaign of 'seventy. Citizens arrested by soldiers. The State constabulary and their gang of roughs. A Republican victory. 106

CHAPTER IV.
Scott's Second Term.

Leaders in the new Legislature. The Governor's message. Elections in joint assembly. Notable legislation. The Taxpayers' Convention and the reforms suggested by that body. Scott's last message. Legislative expenses. Patterson and the Blue Ridge Scrip. Charges of a Republican committee................... 154

CHAPTER V.
The Kuklux Troubles.

Organization and characteristics of the Kuklux Klan. Arming of the negroes by the State Government. Murder and other outrages by militiamen. Raids by the Kuklux. Quiet restored. Action of Congress and the President. Martial law in several counties. Arrests by United States soldiers. The Kuklux trials in Columbia and Charleston.. 179

CHAPTER VI.
Moses' Administration.

Conditions after four years of Republican rule. The State Government sunk to a condition of weakness and disgrace. Frank Moses nominated for Governor. Failure of Republican opposition. Extravagance and corruption still prevalent. Patterson's election to the United States Senate. The State University a school for blacks. Social equality required in a State asylum. The State debt in a muddle. The funding scheme. The floating debt largely increased. Defaulting treasurers. County indebtedness. The school system a failure and a fraud. Extravagance and corruption supreme in the Legislature. The "Robber Governor" and his doings. A second convention of taxpayers. Their appeals to the President and to Congress disregarded. Reply of the Republicans to the taxpayers' charges. Chamberlain nominated for Governor. The opposition of independent Republicans. Results of the contest................. 218

CHAPTER VII.
Chamberlain's Administration.

The Governor's inaugural urges reforms. Notable legislation. The State Treasurer under charges. The Governor commended. Troubles in Edgefield. Failure of Hardy Solomon's bank. Prosecution of Ex-Treasurer Parker and other officials. Joseph Crews shot. The publishers of the *News and Courier* indicted for libel. The last legislative session under Republican rule. Whipper and Moses chosen to be circuit judges. Indignation and disgust universal. Chamberlain's high stand heartily commended. The extent of Republican reforms. The Legislature and its manner of working.. 286

CHAPTER VIII.
The Campaign of 'Seventy-six.

Reorganization of the Democratic party. The conventions in May and August. Differences and discussions as to policies. Bloodshed in Hamburg. Wade Hampton for Governor. The onset of the Red-shirt Democracy. "Hurrah for Hampton." The Republican conventions in April and September. Chamberlain renominated. The

Page.

lines sharply drawn. Republican weakness manifest. The Charleston riot. The Ellenton riot. The Cainhoy massacre. Chamberlain appeals to the President, who proclaims against "insurrection and domestic violence." Answers and remonstrances of the white people. No bloodshed on election day. Riotous negroes in Charleston. The election and the count. The Republican returning board. Proceedings in the Supreme Court. Its order nullified by a Federal judge.. .. ..· 337

CHAPTER IX.

THE DUAL GOVERNMENT.

Meeting of the General Assembly. Federal soldiers seize the State House. The Republicans organize a House of Representatives by excluding Democratic members-elect. The lawful House, organized by the Democrats with some Republicans, enter the hall, but afterwards retire. A bloody plot discovered and a conflict narrowly averted. The Federal commander breaks faith. The Democratic House adjudged by the Supreme Court lawful and constitutional. The court's judgment disregarded. Chamberlain's sham installation. Governor Hampton inaugurated. The struggle for possession. Contributions to the Hampton government. Hampton adjudged by the Supreme Court to be Governor. The contest carried to Washington. Memorials to Congress. The new President's Southern policy. He orders the removal of the troops from the State House. Chamberlain's farewell. The lawful government in full possession.. 408

CHAPTER X.

THE STORY OF THE FRAUDS.

The State debt. The Greenville and Columbia Railroad. The Blue Ridge Scrip, etc. Impeachment of the Governor and the Treasurer. Patterson's election to the Senate. The public printing. Supplies. Pay certificates. Miscellaneous frauds. The Land Commission. Corrupting a judge.. 463

CHAPTER XI.

REVIEW AND REFLECTIONS.

Conditions at the close of the Civil War. The action of Congress. The course of the whites. Characteristics of negro rule. Republican reforms. Attitude of the Federal Government. Conclusion.. 495

AUTHOR'S NOTE.

The matter of this book was first printed in weekly parts in *The State,* and to the enterprise and liberality of the publishers is due also its presentation in permanent form.

The chapters, as they appeared in the newspaper, have been rearranged. The whole has been carefully revised, in order to approach as closely to absolute accuracy throughout as is possible in view of the nature of many of the sources of information. Public records have been used wherever accessible. Statements about which there might be a question—especially those affecting the character of individuals—have been carefully verified by reference to such records or to other sources of equal authority. J. S. R.

Supreme Court Library.

CHAPTER I.

THE PROVISIONAL GOVERNMENT.

Upon the collapse of the Government of the Confederate States, following the dispersion of the armies of Lee and Johnston, there was but the semblance of civil authority in South Carolina. Governor Magrath did indeed direct that all district and municipal officers should exercise their functions for the maintenance of peace and order, but he was so soon sent as a prisoner to Fort Pulaski, Savannah, that even the appearance of any power save that of the army of the United States was altogether wanting. There was no organized State government, no central civil authority, no militia, to which the people might look for the protection of life or property. The district governments, whose functions were limited and whose powers were quite inadequate to meet existing difficulties, maintained an apparent authority, but how far, in the changed order of things, their powers really extended it might have been difficult to determine. The appearance of United States troops to garrison the different cities and towns evidenced the presence of constituted authority superior to that theretofore exercised.

Until the appointment of the "provisional governor," the Government of the United States, acting by its military officers, was in actual possession of the territory of South Carolina—in actual control of the entire population. The military authority extended to every act of the citizen in his relations to government. Courts-martial or military commissions or provost courts tried most questions formerly cognizable in the civil tribunals—their jurisdiction including all criminal offenses, from petit larceny to murder. Police regulations—the ordering of towns, the restriction of the sale of intoxicants, the subordination of the citizen to ordinances and rules of conduct—all these were administered by the military courts. The trial by jury not available, the question of guilt or innocence was decided by the post commander, or the provost marshal, or the provost court, or the military commission, according to the grade of the offense. There was harshness of administration, there was arbitrary use of power, there were instances of injustice. But, all this recognized, it may, after the lapse of so many years, be conceded that the presence of the troops conduced to the maintenance of peace.

The powers assumed by military commanders extended beyond the endeavor to enforce obedience to existing laws and ordinances, and even beyond the effort to protect those rights of the freedmen which, apparently incident to emancipation, had not yet been recognized in any declaration by the State Government or by the white people claiming exclusive citizenship.

In an order dated May 15, 1865, Maj.-Gen. Q. A. Gillmore, commanding the Department of the South, with headquarters at Hilton Head, declared that "the people of the black race are free citizens of the United States," whose rights must be respected accordingly. By another order all persons who should fail to inform the negroes on their lands (before a date stated) of the fact that such negroes were free were made liable to the pains and penalties of disloyalty, and their lands subject to confiscation under the act establishing the "Bureau for the Relief of Freedmen and Refugees," commonly called the "Freedmen's Bureau." By an order issued about the same time persons desiring to publish newspapers were required first to "obtain the consent of the major-general commanding."

One principal and really useful function of the military in those days was in promoting, formulating and supervising contracts between landowners and their former slaves. Emancipation became a recognized fact, by the negroes as well as the whites, about the 1st of June, 1865. It is easy to see what might have followed a general refusal of the negroes on the plantations to engage to work thereon. There were signs of restiveness on the freedmen's part, but this was steadily discouraged by the army officers. Numbers of negroes promptly assumed contractual relations with their late masters. Others, for different reasons, real or imaginary, were recalcitrant, and it was in these cases that the judicious intervention of an army officer was of wholesome effect. Nearly all the contracts were for shares of crops—one-third to the laborer being the accepted rule.

THE NEGRO TROOPS.

The garrisons were at first of white troops entirely. Soon, however, came negro soldiers—the use of which, essentially cruel, was likewise reckless in the extreme. Even after the lapse of forty years it is easy to understand that the presence of armed negroes wearing the uniform of the United States, representing the power of the conquering government, must have demoralized and even inflamed the blacks, just freed from slavery. The discipline of some of these negro troops was effective and satisfactory. Some of their officers were simply soldiers who felt that they could as legitimately command free negroes regularly enlisted as they could white men, whilst others, using the opportunity which the negro regiments or companies afforded for getting commissions, accepted these with the purpose to fight for the flag just as they might do—as some indeed had before done—in bodies of white troops. Many of these officers, however, of either class, resented the aversion which they and all others in like relations naturally excited in the white people, and were thus tempted to condone conduct on the part of their soldiers which should have been repressed. The negro soldiers were commonly arrogant, frequently impertinent, sometimes insulting. They were even lawless, brutish, in some instances murderous.

In the town of Chester there were stationed two companies of negro soldiers who became very annoying and offensive to the white citizens. At times a bloody riot seemed imminent. On one occasion these black soldiers clubbed and bayoneted an old gentleman, who died from the wounds thus inflicted. Other citizens were at other times injured, and the situation at last became so serious that the obnoxious troops were removed. As they moved out on their train they fired on the citizens, many of whom, fully armed, had assembled at the depot in response to the call that had been previously fixed.

In Abbeville a lady and a gentleman quietly using the sidewalk were approached by a negro soldier who had with him a negro woman, and were rudely informed that they must make way. The soldier's language was so abusive and his general bearing so threatening that the lady deemed it best to get a guard of white soldiers at her home for the night. While the sentinel walked his post in the hall he was killed by a shot from some negro soldiers who had appeared at the gate—the shot evidently intended for the gentleman whose rightful remonstrances had provoked insult in the afternoon. On the following morning the negro company was moved away.

A party of negro soldiers stopped at a house in Charleston, asking that they might stay until the rain was over. Permission was given, and they next asked for food—the family being then at dinner. This request was complied with, but later on the soldiers, taking offense at some fancied grievance, proceeded to act in a most outrageous manner. They felled the lady of the house to the floor, so that she was unconscious for a time and was severely hurt. They were about to smash the furniture on the premises when they were interrupted by the arrival of a squad of white soldiers, who, after something of a fight, arrested the rioters and carried them off.

At Newberry, Calvin Crozier, a paroled soldier of the Confederate army, who was on his way to his home in Texas, was in a railway car in company with two young ladies under his care. Leaving the car for a short time he found on his return a negro soldier in such offensive proximity to one of these ladies that he ordered the fellow out. The negro refusing to go, an altercation ensued, in the course of which he was cut in the neck. Going back to his regiment (which was at Newberry only en route to some other point), he soon returned with a squad of negro soldiers, under the command of a sergeant. Hunting for Crozier they arrested another gentleman by mistake and threatened to shoot him. Crozier very soon appeared and avowed that he was the man wanted. He was seized, taken to the camp, and a few hours later shot to death—the negro soldiers showing their brutish delight by dancing on his grave, while they swore vengeance on all "rebels." The colonel of the regiment, addressing his men, formally approved the murder. To the memory of Calvin Crozier the people of Newberry have built a handsome monument.

In Beaufort District a party of negro soldiers visited a house occupied by unprotected ladies, and there committed acts too horrible to relate. Two of the brutes were apprehended, tried by military court, sentenced to death and promptly hung—the authorities sparing no pains to visit that summary punishment upon the guilty scoundrels.

These instances may be taken as specimens, and to them might be added numerous cases of misconduct of lesser enormity, but none the less calculated to spread alarm in every community exposed to the misdoings of the negro troops.

The original purpose in thus using these troops was clearly to harry and insult the white people among whom they were sent. Whether that purpose was Andrew Johnson's or Secretary Stanton's cannot be safely asserted. Of Johnson, however, it must be said that he took early steps to rid the South of the presence of negroes wearing the army uniform, whilst Stanton made no sign of relenting in his hatred towards the Southern people or in his purpose to oppress them.

THEORIES OF RECONSTRUCTION.

The authority of the United States was promptly recognized and obeyed by the white people. They very generally took the oath of allegiance to the National Government—wherein also each affiant in terms disavowed all allegiance to "the so-called Confederate States," and promised obedience to President Lincoln's proclamation setting free the slaves. Negroes were neither invited nor expected to take the oath.

The Federal authority thus paramount, it was natural that some exponent of that authority should set about to reestablish civil order in the South and restore the States "lately in rebellion" to their proper relations to the Federal Union. What these relations should be, and what the process of restoration, were questions which had long engaged the attention of both the Executive and the Congress. Diverse views were entertained; and these should be stated in order to a sufficient understanding of the subsequent course of President Johnson, of Congress, and of the Southern people. Of the doctrines held by different leaders among the Northern people there were five that attained to special prominence in the debates in Congress in the earlier discussions of the "Southern question." These have been well stated as follows:

I. The Restoration Doctrine. This was based on the assumption that the acts of secession were essentially invalid and of no effect. No State, therefore, had seceded, or could secede; the State officers who were acting against the Federal Government were simply committing illegal acts which rendered them liable to punishment, but the States themselves were not destroyed nor their Constitutions abrogated, and so soon as their officers returned to their duty, or other officers took their places, the States would *ipso facto* resume their normal relations with the Union.

II. The Presidential Doctrine. This doctrine, which originated with President Lincoln, was of gradual development. Its essential feature was that prior to the restoration of the seceding States to their rights and privileges under the Constitution the President was empowered to dictate such terms as in his opinion seemed necessary to secure the Union from further peril. These terms were eventually defined to be the cessation of resistance, the appointment of a provisional governor, the taking of an oath of amnesty, proffered to all but certain specified classes of leading men, by at least one-tenth of the white voters of a State, the recognition and declaration of the permanent freedom of the blacks, and the formation of a new republican government by the State. But it was expressly announced that the admission of Senators and Representatives from the States lately in insurrection was a matter that rested not with the executive, but with the separate houses of Congress.

III. The Davis-Wade Doctrine. This plan was proposed by Henry Winter Davis, of Maryland, and Benjamin F. Wade, of Ohio, as a remedy for what they believed the defects of the Presidential policy. The latter, they complained, asked no security for the faithful performance of the terms of restoration, proposed no guardianship of the United States over the reorganization of the State governments, no law to prescribe who shall vote, no civil functionaries to see that the law be faithfully executed, no supervising authority to control and judge of the elections. Their plan, therefore, was to appoint provisional governors, who, through the aid of the United States marshals, were to administer the oath of allegiance to white citizens. When the citizens who had taken the oath constituted a majority, they were to hold a State convention, excluding, however, all Confederate officeholders and all who had voluntarily borne arms against the United States, and adopt a new constitution repudiating the Confederate debt, abolishing slavery and prohibiting the military and civil leaders of the Confederacy from serving in any official capacity. The provisional governor was then to notify the President, and when the latter had obtained the assent of Congress he was to recognize the new government by proclamation, after which Senators and Representatives were to be admitted.

IV. The Sumner Doctrine. This doctrine, formulated by Charles Sumner, of Massachusetts, and vehemently supported by a small band of his followers, directly combated the restoration theory, which the two last-named plans had merely sought to modify. According to Sumner the declaration of secession, although it was void as against the Constitution, was an abrogation by the State of its rights under the Constitution. It had ceased to exist as an integral element of national sovereignty, and its soil became a territory under the exclusive jurisdiction of Congress. For, as a territory became a

State by coming into the Union, so a State becomes a territory by leaving it. In other words, secession was State suicide. Therefore, it was the duty of Congress to establish republican forms of government in the vacated territory, taking care to provide for the protection of the persons who had recently been made free.

V. The Stevens Doctrine. This doctrine, fathered by Thaddeus Stevens, of Pennsylvania, reached the same results as the Sumner theory, by a different course of reasoning. Stevens held that the Constitution was suspended in any part of the country where the resistance to its execution was too strong to be suppressed by peaceful methods. It was absurd to say that the Constitution and the laws were in force when they could not be enforced. The termination of the suspension could be decided only by the victorious party. If the Civil War were successful the suspension would be permanent—if unsuccessful the suspension would continue until the war-making and law-making power should decide that the resistance had been honestly abandoned. Congress had omnipotent power, because the seceding States had repudiated the Constitution, and could no longer claim its advantages.

THE AMNESTY PROCLAMATION.

Mr. Johnson had early manifested his purpose to carry out the "Presidential" program. Pardon for past offenses being necessary to any action by the people held to have been in rebellion against the Government, looking to their restoration to full citizenship and their proper relations to the Union of States under the Constitution, the President proclaimed amnesty to those people upon stated terms and conditions. In his proclamation dated May 29, 1865, he indicated not only his ideas of the mode of restoration, but more particularly his conception of the different degrees of guilt among those whose past conduct was to be condoned. For this reason—in addition to considerations of historic value—that paper must be given in full:

Whereas, the President of the United States, on the 8th day of December, A. D. 1863, and on the 26th day of March, A. D. 1864, with the object to suppress the existing rebellion, to induce all persons to return to their loyalty and to restore the authority of the United States, did issue proclamations offering amnesty and pardon to certain persons who had, directly or by implication, participated in the said rebellion; and, whereas, many persons who had so engaged in said rebellion have, since the issuance of said proclamation, failed or neglected to take the benefits offered thereby; and whereas many persons who have been justly deprived of all claim to amnesty and pardon thereunder by reason of their participation, directly or by implication, in said rebellion and continued hostility to the Government of the United States since the date of said proclamation, now desire to apply for and obtain amnesty and pardon:

To the end, therefore, that the authority of the Government of the United States may be restored, and that peace, order and freedom may be established, I, Andrew Johnson, President of the United States, do proclaim and declare that I hereby grant to all persons who have directly or indirectly participated in the existing rebellion, except as hereinafter excepted, amnesty and pardon, with restoration of all rights of property, except as to slaves, and except in cases where legal proceedings, under the laws of the United States, providing for the confiscation of property of persons engaged in rebellion have been instituted, but on the condition, nevertheless, that every such person shall take and subscribe the following oath or affirmation, and thenceforward keep and maintain said oath inviolate, and which oath shall be registered for permanent preservation and shall be of the tenor and effect following, to wit:

"I, ..., do solemnly swear (or affirm), in the presence of Almighty God, that I will henceforth faithfully support and defend the Constitution of the United States and the Union of the States thereunder, and that I will in like manner abide by and faithfully support all laws and proclamations which have been made during the existing rebellion with reference to the emancipation of slaves. So help me God."

The following classes of persons are exempted from the benefits of this proclamation:

First. All who are or shall have been pretended civil or diplomatic officers or otherwise domestic or foreign agents of the pretended Confederate Government.

Second. All who left judicial stations under the United States to aid in the rebellion.

Third. All who shall have been military or naval officers of said pretended Confederate Government, above the rank of colonel in the army or lieutenant in the navy.

Fourth. All who left seats in the Congress of the United States to aid the rebellion.

Fifth. All who resigned or tendered resignations of their commissions in the army or navy of the United States to evade duty in resisting the rebellion.

Sixth. All who have engaged in any way in treating otherwise than lawfully as prisoners of war persons found in the United States service as officers, soldiers, seamen, or in other capacities.

Seventh. All persons who have been or are absentees from the United States for the purpose of aiding the rebellion.

Eighth. All military and naval officers in the rebel service who were educated by the Government in the Military Academy at West Point, or the United States Naval Academy.

Ninth. All persons who held pretended offices of governors of States in insurrection against the United States.

Tenth. All persons who left their homes within the jurisdiction and protection of the United States and passed beyond the Federal military lines into the so-called Confederate States for the purpose of aiding the rebellion.

Eleventh. All persons who have been engaged in the destruction of the commerce of the United States upon the high seas, and who have made raids into the United States from Canada, or been engaged in destroying the commerce of the United States upon the lakes and rivers that separate the British provinces from the United States.

Twelfth. All persons who, at the time when they seek to obtain the benefits hereof by taking the oath herein prescribed, are in military, naval or civil confinement or custody, or under bonds of the civil, military or naval authorities or agents of the United States, as prisoners of war, or persons retained for offenses of any kind, either before or after conviction.

Thirteenth. All persons who have voluntarily participated in said rebellion, and the estimated value of whose taxable property is over $20,000.

Fourteenth. All persons who have taken the oath of amnesty as prescribed in the President's proclamation of December 8, A. D. 1863, or an oath of allegiance to the Government of the United States since the date of said proclamation, and who have not thenceforward kept and maintained the same inviolate.

Provided, that special application may be made to the President for pardon by any person belonging to the excepted classes, and such clemency will be liberally extended as may be consistent with the facts of the case and the peace and dignity of the United States.

The Secretary of State will establish rules and regulations for administering and recording the said amnesty oath, so as to insure its benefit to the people and guard the Government against fraud.

THE PROVISIONAL GOVERNOR.

The Southern people were much at sea. They were particularly anxious for the displacement of the military authority—more especially because, as before stated, it was represented to some extent by negro soldiers. In South Carolina several meetings were held, in which the desire of the white people for a restoration of the State to her place in the Union, and, most earnestly, for the reestablishment of civil government, took the form of resolutions unanimously adopted. Committees appointed by some of these meetings went to Washington to lay before the President the condition of affairs and to ask the appointment of a "provisional governor," to the end that steps might be taken to accomplish the objects desired.

President Johnson was not averse to the enforcement of his own policy in South Carolina. On the arrival of the first of the committees in Washington he appeared to have had the subject already under consideration. Several gentlemen had been mentioned in connection with the post of provisional governor—among them ex-Governor William Aiken, of Charleston; William W. Boyce, of Fairfield, lately a prominent member of the Confederate Congress; ex-Governor John L. Manning, of Clarendon; Mr. Samuel McAlily, of Chester, and Col. Benjamin F. Perry, of Greenville. The last named was selected.

Benjamin Franklin Perry was born in Pickens District—in that portion now included in Oconee County—November 20, 1805. He worked on his father's farm and attended the country school alternately till he reached the age of sixteen, when he was sent to an academy of note in Asheville, N. C. He prepared to enter the South Carolina College, but changed his purpose—a mistake which he always regretted. Shortly after the completion of his sixteenth year he wrote an article in favor of John C. Calhoun for the presidency, and at nineteen delivered a Fourth of July oration in Greenville. Having read law in Greenville and Columbia, he was admitted to practice in 1827, and at once located in the former town. In 1832 he became editor of the *Greenville Mountaineer,* and in its columns boldly attacked the Nullification party—not sparing its then leader, Mr. Calhoun. The sturdy defense of his principles and his persistent warfare upon his opponents led to the formation of the Union party in South Carolina, and he was the leading spirit of its convention in 1832. In 1834 he ran for Congress from the district in which Mr. Calhoun resided, and was defeated by a majority of fifty votes in seven thousand—his opponent being Warren R. Davis, a gentleman of great popularity. In 1836 he was elected to the lower branch of the State Legislature, and there served till 1844, when he was sent to

THE PROVISIONAL GOVERNMENT 13

the Senate; and he sat in that body for twenty years. In 1850 he established the *Southern Patriot,* at that time the only Union paper in South Carolina. In the Legislature that year he spoke earnestly against secession. He was a member of the National Democratic Convention, which met in Charleston in 1860, and remained in the body when many of the Southern members had withdrawn—all of the South Carolina delegates having retired except Colonel Perry, Lemuel Boozer, of Lexington, and Arthur Simkins, of Edgefield.

In the excitement following Lincoln's election in November, 1860, Colonel Perry declared openly and earnestly his opposition to secession. But when South Carolina acted he went with his State. In the early part of 1861 there came an opportunity for him to show the sincerity of his declaration of the purpose to go with his people. There was lukewarmness, not to say disaffection, in the mountain section of Greenville District, where the Union sentiment had prevailed, and where Colonel Perry had a very large following. On the request of friends he went among those people and urged them to follow his example—to go with their State. From among those mountaineers there went into the Confederate army a body of the bravest and best of its soldiers.

Colonel Perry held the office of district judge of the Confederate States Court, and his allegiance to the government which he thus served was as constant as had been his devotion to the principles for which he earnestly fought before the controversy between North and South culminated in disunion. Elected to the Senate of the United States by the Legislature in 1865, he was never permitted to take his seat. He was sent as a delegate to the National Democratic Convention of 1876.

Governor Perry died at his home, "Sans Souci," near Greenville, December 3, 1886.

By a proclamation dated June 13, 1865, President Johnson appointed Benjamin F. Perry "provisional governor of the State of South Carolina, whose duty it shall be at the earliest practicable period to prescribe such rules and regulations as may be necessary and proper for convening a convention to be composed of delegates to be chosen by that portion of the people of the said State who are loyal to the United States, and no others, for the purpose of altering or amending the Constitution thereof, and with authority to exercise, within the limits of said State, all the powers necessary and proper to enable such loyal people of the State of South Carolina to restore said State to its constitutional relations to the Federal Government, and to present such a republican form of State government as will entitle the State to the guaranty of the United States therefor, and its people to protection by the United States against invasion, insurrection and domestic violence; provided, that in any election which may hereafter be held for choosing delegates to any State convention as aforesaid no person shall be qualified as an elector, or shall be eligible as a member of such convention, unless he shall have previously taken and subscribed the oath of amnesty, as set forth in the President's proclamation of May 29, A. D. 1865, and is a voter qualified as prescribed by the Constitution and laws of the State of South Carolina in force before the 20th day of December, A. D. 1860, the date of the so-called ordinance of secession; and the said convention when convened, or the Legislature that may be thereafter assembled, will prescribe the qualifications of the electors and the eligibility of persons to hold office under the Constitution and laws of the State—a power which the people of the several States composing the Federal Union have rightfully exercised from the origin of the Government to the present time."

Accepting this appointment, Governor Perry, by a proclamation dated July 20, 1865, directed that the civil officers of the State should resume their functions, that an election of delegates to a convention to carry out the purposes indicated in the President's declaration accompanying the same be held on the 4th day of September next ensuing, and that such convention assemble in Columbia on the 13th day of that month. All citizens were urged to take the amnesty oath, because that act would evidence their cooperation in the endeavors of the President to restore civil order, and because it was a condition precedent to the exercise of the right to vote. Citizens of the excepted classes mentioned in the President's proclamation of amnesty were urged to apply at once for pardon—the Governor expressing his desire to expedite action upon all applications.

Petitions for pardons were now sent on in very large numbers, and favorable consideration followed in each case, as a matter of course. The number of persons in the excepted classes in South Carolina, pardoned by the President, was 845, of whom 650 were of those having as much as $20,000 in property—the remainder con-

THE PROVISIONAL GOVERNMENT

sisting of those who had been Confederate treasury agents, tax-collectors, postmasters or blockade-runners.

As the day set for the meeting of the Convention approached there were fears lest some of the members-elect might not receive their pardons in time to take their seats on the opening day. Timely action by the Provisional Governor, seconded by the proper officers in Washington, prevented embarrassment on this score.

THE CONVENTION OF 1865.

The names of the delegates elected and commissioned were as follows:

Abbeville—David L. Wardlaw, Samuel McGowan, Thomas Thomson, W. A. Lee, J. W. Hearst.

All Saints—W. A. DeLettre.

Anderson—James L. Orr, John Wilson, Alexander Evins, W. S. Pickens.

Barnwell—A. P. Aldrich, J. J. Brabham, J. M. Whetstone.

Chester—James Hemphill, A. P. Wylie, C. D. Melton.

Chesterfield—John A. Inglis, Henry McIver.

Christ Church—A. T. Morrison.

Clarendon—James McCauley, John Peter Richardson.

Darlington—David C. Milling, J. H. Norwood, J. E. Byrd.

Edgefield—W. S. Mobley, George D. Tillman, R. G. Dunovant, F. W. Pickens, Paul F. Hammond.

Fairfield—James H. Rion, John Bratton, William R. Robertson.

Greenville—William H. Perry, James P. Boyce, T. C. Bolling, J. P. Latimer.

Horry—Joel B. Skipper.

Kershaw—A. D. Goodwyn, L. W. R. Blair.

Lancaster—R. M. Sims, J. L. Reed.

Laurens—C. P. Sullivan, William Mills, Jr., A. W. Moore, B. W. Ball.

Lexington—Lemuel Boozer, John Fox.

Marion—A. Q. McDuffie, William T. Wilson, R. H. Reeves.

Marlboro—T. C. Weatherly, C. W. Dudley.

Newberry—E. P. Lake, Henry Summer, R. Stewart.

Orange—J. H. Morgan, C. W. McMichael.

Pickens—Edward Herndon, L. B. Johnson, Alexander Bryce, Sr., James Lafayette Boyd.

Prince George, Winyah—Benjamin F. Dunkin, B. C. Fishburn.
Richland—F. W. McMaster, A. R. Taylor, William Wallace.
St. Andrew—William Izard Bull.
St. Bartholomew—A. Campbell, Hugo G. Sheridan.
St. Helena—James G. Thompson.
St. James, Goose Creek—W. M. Brailsford.
St. James, Santee—J. G. DuPre.
St. John, Berkeley—J. G. Gaillard.
St. George, Dorchester—W. A. Chisolm.
St. Luke—LeRoy F. Youmans.
St. Matthew—T. J. Goodwyn.
St. Paul—Isaac M. Dwight.
St. Peter—H. C. Smart.
St. Philip and St. Michael—Charles Macbeth, Alfred Huger, H. D. Lesesne, W. H. Gilliland, James Connor, William M. Martin, F. Melchers, P. C. Gaillard, John Schnierle, George W. Williams, James Rose, John A. Wagener, Charles H. Simonton, P. J. Coogan, A. O. Andrews, Edward Frost, William L. Henery, Henry Gourdin, William Ravenel.
St. Stephen—W. H. Cannon.
St. Thomas and St. Dennis—C. M. Furman.
Spartanburg—John Winsmith, John W. Carlisle, M. C. Barnett, James Farrow.
Sumter—John N. Frierson, Thomas M. Muldrow, F. J. Moses.
Union—William H. Wallace, Thomas N. Dawkins, William J. Keenan.
Williamsburg—J. A. James, Edward J. Porter.
Winyah—R. Dozier.
York—Cadwallader Jones, W. C. Beatty, W. C. Black, R. A. Ross.

Gen. Wade Hampton was elected from Richland, but, spending the summer at Cashiers Valley, N. C., he received notice too late to attend. Mr. William F. Hutson was elected from Prince William, but received information of the fact too late to attend.

The delegate from St. Helena was a Northern man who had come to this State with the Federal army, and who in later years edited *The Union-Herald* in Columbia.

The Convention met in the Baptist Church, Plain street, Columbia, on September 13, 1865. The Hon. David L. Wardlaw, one of the judges of the circuit courts, was elected president. and Col. John T. Sloan, of Pendleton, clerk.

The work of the Convention consisted of the framing of a Constitution and the passage of such ordinances as were necessary to put the State government in motion till the meeting of the Legislature. That instrument contained provisions intended to meet the new conditions induced not only by the failure of secession and the destruction of slavery, but by changes in the social and political relations of the different communities making up the new body politic.

Slavery was prohibited by a section declaring that "the slaves in South Carolina having been emancipated by the action of the United States authorities, neither slavery nor involuntary servitude, except as a punishment for crime whereof the party shall have been duly convicted, shall ever be reestablished in this State."

The qualifications of the voter were fixed as follows: "He shall be a free white man who has attained the age of twenty-one years, and is not a pauper, nor a noncommissioned officer or private soldier of the army nor a seaman or marine of the navy of the United States. He shall, for the two years next preceding the day of election, have been a citizen of this State; or for the same period an emigrant from Europe, who has declared his intention to become a citizen of the United States, according to the Constitution and laws of the United States. He shall have resided in this State for at least two years next preceding the day of election, and for the last six months of that time in the district in which he offers to vote." No person was eligible to any office unless possessed of the qualifications of an elector.

The single reference to the negro race, to be found in the instrument, is in the following provision in the judiciary article: "The General Assembly shall, as soon as possible, establish for each district in the State an inferior court or courts, to be styled 'The District Court,' the judges whereof shall be resident in the district while in office, shall be elected by the General Assembly for four years and shall be reeligible—which court shall have jurisdiction of all civil causes wherein one or both of the parties are persons of color, and of all criminal cases wherein the accused is a person of color, and the General Assembly is empowered to extend the jurisdiction of said court to other subjects."

The election of the Governor and the Lieutenant-Governor (each for the term of four years) was transferred from the Legislature to the people. The Governor was invested with the veto power, and the Lieutenant-Governor was made President of the Senate. The other State officers were made elective by the Legislature, each for the term of four years.

Ministers of the gospel and public preachers of any religious persuasion, while they should continue in the exercise of their pastoral functions, were declared not eligible to the office of Governor or Lieutenant-Governor or to a seat in the General Assembly—this because, in the language of the prohibition, "the ministers of the gospel are by their profession dedicated to the service of God and the cure of souls, and ought not to be diverted from the great duties of their functions." The Constitution of 1791 contained a like provision.

The legislative authority was vested in a General Assembly—the Senate to be composed of one member from each election district, except the election district of Charleston, to which were allowed two senators; and the House of Representatives, to "consist of 124 members, to be apportioned among the several election districts of the State, according to the number of white inhabitants contained in each, and the amount of all taxes raised by the General Assembly, whether direct or indirect, or of whatever species, paid in each." Thus was abolished the "parish system"—of which some further mention would seem to be proper.

In 1860 Beaufort District contained four parishes; Charleston, eight (St. Philip's and St. Michael's counted as one); Colleton, four; Georgetown, two; Orangeburg, two; Horry two—making twenty-one parishes, with twenty-two senators out of forty-five; and fifty-five representatives out of 124.

Referring to the parish system, Governor Perry, in his first message to the Convention, said:

The basis of representation in the Senate of this State, as you know, is entirely arbitrary and is founded on no just principles of property or population. At the time it was adopted—more than seventy-five years ago—it was no doubt fair and equal. But since that time the entire relative condition of the election districts has changed. The upper country, at the adoption of our State Constitution in 1790, was comparatively but newly settled, had a sparse population and had very little wealth. But since that time this portion of the State has increased in wealth and numbers in a much greater ratio than the lower country. Hence it is that the parish representation in the Senate is unequal and unjust. Twenty or thirty voters in one of the parishes, whose population and taxation combined entitle it to only one member of the House of Representatives, have the same representation in the Senate that three thousand voters have in Edgefield District, whose population and taxation entitle it to six members in the House. This is contrary to all republican principles of political justice and equality. In the early history of South Carolina the representation in the parishes was repeatedly changed, to equalize it amongst the respective election districts; but all such changes have been obstinately refused during the last seventy-five years. Now that slavery is abolished a reformation in this respect is imperative and must be adopted.

There had been opposition to the parish system even before the War of Secession. The late George D. Tillman was earnest and continuous in his protests, while Colonel Perry, Mr. Boyce, of Fairfield, Mr. McAlily, of Chester, and others were strongly in favor of a change. Even in the city of Charleston there were those who felt that, in justice to the up-country and for the purpose of promoting cordiality between that section and the lower districts, some concession was advisable.

The vote in the Convention in favor of the abolition of the system was decisive—97 to 9. Those voting against the change were: Messrs. Aldrich, of Barnwell; Campbell and Sheridan, of St. Bartholomew; Chisolm, of St. George, Dorchester; Goodwyn, of St. Matthew; McCauley, of Clarendon; Smart, of St. Peter; Wallace, of Richland, and Youmans, of St. Luke.

Charleston was divided into two election districts—one to consist of the late parishes of St. Philip and St. Michael, to be known as Charleston; the other to consist of the remainder of the territory of Charleston District, and to be known as Berkeley.

All voting by the Legislature was required to be viva voce—a vote by ballot having formerly obtained in elections in that body.

The Constitution was not submitted to the people.

By different ordinances the Convention formally repealed the ordinance of secession; declared that electors for President and Vice-President of the United States ought to be chosen by the people; declared of force the Constitution adopted by the people in convention at Charleston on the 8th day of April, 1861, except as altered or repealed; provided for the election of the General Assembly (ordered to meet in special session on October 25) and of Governor and Lieutenant-Governor; authorized incumbent officials to continue in office upon taking the amnesty oath; and divided the State into four congressional districts, as follows:

First—Lancaster, Chesterfield, Darlington, Marlboro, Marion, Horry, Georgetown, Williamsburg, Clarendon, Sumter, Kershaw.

Second—Charleston, Colleton, Beaufort, Barnwell, Berkeley.

Third—Orangeburg, Edgefield, Abbeville, Lexington, Newberry, Richland, Fairfield.

Fourth—Anderson, Pickens, Greenville, Laurens, Spartanburg, Union, York, Chester.

The Convention, by resolution, directed that "a commission consisting of two persons be appointed by his Excellency, the Provisional Governor, to prepare and report to the Legislature what laws will be necessary and proper in consequence of the alterations made in the fundamental law, and especially to prepare and submit a code for the regulation of labor and the protection and government of the colored population of the State."

Under that resolution Judge David L. Wardlaw and Mr. Armistead Burt, a prominent member of the Abbeville bar, were duly appointed.

The Convention adjourned sine die on September 27, 1865.

Pursuant to the ordinance of the Convention the election of Governor, Lieutenant-Governor, and members of the Legislature was held on Wednesday, October 18.

The vote for Governor was as follows: James L. Orr, 9,928; Wade Hampton, 9,185. General Hampton had positively refused to run, and had urged his friends all over the State not to vote for him.

For the office of Lieutenant-Governor, William D. Porter, of Charleston, received 15,072 votes.

The election of members of Congress was held November 22, and the following named gentlemen were chosen:

First District—John D. Kennedy, of Kershaw.

Second District—William Aiken, of Charleston.

Third District—Samuel McGowan, of Abbeville.

Fourth District—James Farrow, of Spartanburg.

LEGISLATIVE PROCEEDINGS.

In pursuance of the ordinance of the Constitutional Convention the General Assembly met in Columbia on Wednesday, October 25, 1865—the Senate using the library of the South Carolina College

THE PROVISIONAL GOVERNMENT

and the House the chapel in the campus. The Senate was composed as follows:

Abbeville—Thomas Thomson.
Anderson—John Wilson.
Barnwell—Benjamin W. Lawton.
Beaufort—R. J. Davant.
Berkeley—W. Pinckney Shingler.
Charleston, Henry Buist, William S. Henery.
Chester—James Hemphill.
Chesterfield—A. McQueen.
Clarendon—John L. Manning.
Colleton—Carlos Tracy.
Darlington—Edward W. Charles.
Edgefield—George D. Tillman.
Fairfield—John Bratton.
Georgetown—Richard Dozier.
Greenville—George F. Townes.
Horry—Joel B. Skipper.
Kershaw—J. B. Kershaw.
Lancaster—J. L. Reid.
Laurens—C. P. Sullivan.
Lexington—Lemuel Boozer.
Marion—A. Q. McDuffie.
Marlboro—J. C. Weatherly.
Newberry—J. H. Williams.
Orangeburg—John Townsend.
Pickens—W. S. Grisham.
Richland—E. J. Arthur.
Spartanburg—John Winsmith.
Sumter—F. J. Moses, Sr.
Union—Robert Beaty.
York—George W. Williams.

Senator Manning, of Clarendon, having resigned, John Peter Richardson was elected for the unexpired term. Under like circumstances Col. John N. Frierson, of Sumter, was elected to succeed F. J. Moses, Sr.

The roll of the House of Representatives was as follows:

Abbeville—A. C. Haskell, J. W. Hearst, W. A. Lee, R. A. Fair, D. Wyatt Aiken.

Anderson—B. F. Crayton, T. H. Russell, R. N. Wright, William H. Trescott.

Barnwell—J. J. Ryan, A. P. Aldrich, W. E. Flowers, Johnson Hagood.

Beaufort—LeRoy F. Youmans, Alfred M. Martin, William F. Hutson, Stephen Elliott.

Berkeley—J. M. Manigault, Henry S. Tew, T. P. Mikell, J. C. McKewn, John G. Gaillard, J. J. Williams, John Y. DuPre.

Charleston—John A. Wagener, F. Melchers, Charles H. Simonton, Thomas K. Ryan, Rudolph Seigling, Samuel Lord, Jr., John Hanckel, Benjamin Lucas, William J. Gayer, W. E. Mikell, P. J. Coogan, R. S. Duryea, James M. Eason, Theodore G. Barker, F. J. Porcher, J. T. Milligan, J. M. Mulvaney, James B. Campbell, F. D. Richardson.

Chester—W. A. Walker, T. C. House, T. A. Lipsey.

Chesterfield—S. W. Evans, J. H. Hough.

Clarendon—John Peter Richardson, H. L. Benbow.

Colleton—C. B. Farmer, David Gavin, Hugo G. Sheridan, William Stokes, B. Stokes.

Darlington—F. F. Warley, D. C. Miljing, J. L. Coker.

Edgefield—Luke Culbreath, M. C. Butler, M. L. Bonham, B. M. Talbert, Thomas Jones, J. Landrum.

Fairfield—James R. Aiken, William J. Alston, B. E. Elkin.

Georgetown—J. Harleston Read, A. J. Shaw, J. R. Sparkman.

Greenville—William H. Perry, J. H. Goodwin, H. D. Hammett, W. P. Price.

Horry—J. T. Walsh, F. J. Sessions.

Kershaw—William L. DePass, W. Z. Leitner.

Lancaster—B. R. Clyburn, William A. Moore.

Laurens—B. W. Ball, G. Anderson, R. P. Todd, M. M. Hunter.

Lexington—F. S. Lewie, E. S. J. Hayes.

Marion—W. S. Mullins, R. F. Graham, E. T. Stackhouse.

Marlborough—T. C. Weatherly, H. Covington.

Newberry—C. H. Suber, Ellison S. Keitt, A. C. Garlington.

Orangeburg—W. F. Barton, A. S. Salley, F. M. Wannamaker.

Pickens—W. L. Keith, W. K. Easley, Joseph J. Norton, R. E. Bowers.

Richland—William Wallace, William H. Talley, William K. Bachman, Edwin J. Scott.

THE PROVISIONAL GOVERNMENT 23

Spartanburg—John W. Carlisle, A. B. Woodruff, D. R. Duncan, Gabriel Cannon, Alexander Copeland.

Sumter—A. A. Gilbert, John T. Green, John S. Richardson, Jr.

Union—A. W. Thomson, Jr., Thomas N. Dawkins, Charles Petty.

Williamsburg—James F. Pressley, P. C. Dozier.

York—A. S. Wallace, J. W. Rawlinson, A. B. Springs, W. C. Black.

To fill vacancies afterwards caused by resignations, the following named gentlemen were later elected: J. J. Brown, of Barnwell, to succeed A. P. Aldrich; Edward Magrath, of Charleston, to succeed Henry D. Lesesne; John P. Thomas, of Richland, to succeed E. J. Scott; John A. Keels, of Williamsburg, to succeed James F. Pressley; James M. Carson, of Charleston, to succeed F. G. Richardson; D. L. DeSaussure, of Kershaw, to succeed W. Z. Leitner; Alexander McBee, of Greenville, to succeed William H. Perry; W. W. Waller, of Horry, to succeed J. T. Walsh; B. C. Fishburne, of Georgetown, to succeed A. J. Shaw; J. N. McElwee, Jr., of York, to succeed A. S. Wallace; Robert H. Reaves, of Marion, to succeed R. F. Graham.

Mr. F. J. Moses, Sr., of Sumter, was elected president pro tem. of the Senate, and Gen. William E. Martin, of Charleston, clerk. Mr. A. P. Aldrich, of Barnwell, was elected speaker of the House, and Col. John T. Sloan, of Pendleton, clerk. Before the close of the session Mr. Aldrich was elected circuit judge, and Col. Charles H. Simonton, of Charleston, was elected speaker.

Governor Perry sent the customary message outlining the legislation which he deemed proper.

In view of the fact that the Governor-elect would not be inaugurated until the meeting of the General Assembly in regular session, no acts were passed at the special meeting.

Benjamin F. Perry was elected senator of the United States for the long term, and John L. Manning for the short term.

The Thirteenth Amendment to the United States Constitution was duly ratified. The sufficiency of this act of the General Assembly organized under the Reconstruction scheme of President Johnson was recognized in the proclamation of the Secretary of State, dated December 18, 1865, wherein South Carolina was included in the necessary number of States which had ratified the amendment and thus made it a part of the Federal Constitution.

The Code Commissioners made their report, embodying statutes deemed necessary in view of the emancipation of the negro, but none of these was passed till the regular session commencing Monday, November 27.

The special session ended on November 13.

CHAPTER II.

ORR'S ADMINISTRATION.

The Governor-elect took the oath of office on November 27, 1865, the day on which the General Assembly met in regular session, and was inaugurated with the customary ceremonies.

James Lawrence Orr was born in Anderson District May 12, 1822. Graduated from the University of Virginia in 1842, he was afterwards admitted to the bar. He located at Anderson for the practice of his profession, and there established and edited the weekly *Gazette*. He served in the lower branch of the Legislature from 1844 to 1857, and in that body earnestly opposed nullification. He sat in Congress from December, 1849, till March, 1859. In December, 1857, he was elected speaker of the House. In the agitation over the questions of slavery and states' rights he opposed separate State action, while distinctly affirming the right of secession. These views he so strongly presented to the Southern Rights Convention, held in Charleston, in 1851, that the body refrained from passing the secession ordinance framed for its adoption. In 1854 he joined with Stephen A. Douglas and others in opposition to the Know Nothing party. In 1860 he opposed separate State action, but acquiesced in the decision of South Carolina and went actively with her people into the Civil War. In 1861 he raised a regiment of riflemen for the Confederate service and commanded it in the field until, in 1862, he was called to a seat in the Congress. He was a member of the Constitutional Convention of 1865, and his candidacy for the governorship was in response to the request of many of the leading men in that body. In 1868 he was elected judge of the Eighth Circuit, holding that office till his appointment, in December, 1872, as United States minister to Russia. In the summer of that year he had been sent as a delegate from South Carolina to the National Republican Convention.

Judge Orr died May 5, 1873—within two months after the presentation of his credentials to the Russian government.

The Hon. William D. Porter was duly installed as Lieutenant-Governor.

At this session there was the ordinary legislation for the support and operation of the State Government, and the vacant offices within the gift of the General Assembly were filled by elections. Especial pains were taken to pass an act organizing the State militia.

The choice of presidential electors was, by an act duly passed, given to the qualified voters of the commonwealth.

The General Assembly adjourned sine die on December 21. On that day Mr. Seward, Secretary of State, by direction of the President, notified Colonel Perry that he was relieved of the trust which had theretofore reposed in him as provisional governor of the State of South Carolina, and instructed him to deliver into Governor Orr's possession the papers and property relating to that trust. A communication was addressed to Governor Orr, advising him of this action of the National Executive, and tendering him the cooperation of the Government of the United States, "whenever it may be found necessary in effecting the early restoration and the permanent prosperity and welfare of the State."

Thus was effected the restoration of the State of South Carolina to her relations with the Federal Government, under the scheme of Reconstruction founded upon the "Presidential" doctrine held by Abraham Lincoln and sought to be enforced by Andrew Johnson.

On December 25, 1865, Governor Orr issued his first proclamation, in the course of which he stated his view of the relations between the State government and the civil and military authorities of the United States, as follows:

The order suspending the writ of habeas corpus, issued by the President, has not been modified or revoked in this State, and the military authority is therefore paramount in all such matters as they are instructed to take jurisdiction of, and as such will be respected by all orderly and law-abiding people.

The military claim jurisdiction in all cases of disloyalty to the Government and infractions of its laws; to preserve order and discipline in and near their garrisons; to adjudge and determine all controversies in which freedmen and whites are engaged, including violations of State laws by freedmen; in all cases of wrong or injury done to its officers and soldiers; and is an auxiliary in aiding treasury agents to recover United States property, and the Freedmen's Bureau in supervising contracts with freedmen. Whenever, therefore, a person is arrested by military authority on either of the above grounds, they have jurisdiction of the case, and are instructed not to obey any writ of habeas corpus for the release of such person.

In all controversies between citizens, arising out of wrongs or injuries done to person or property, and in all violations of the penal code by citizens, the laws are in full force, and the courts will be opened henceforth on every circuit to administer law and punish crime.

The people were admonished to avoid collisions with the military authorities. The colored people were advised to make contracts forthwith for the coming year, to be good citizens and to cultivate sobriety, industry, economy and honesty.

THE "BLACK CODE."

After the consideration of the report of the Code Commissioners provided for by the ordinance of the Convention, the General Assembly, at the regular session of 1865, passed certain laws intended to establish the relations of persons of color to the State government, and to the white race, as brought about by emancipation. These laws—called by the negro leaders and the Republican organs the "Black Code"—were as follows: An act preliminary to the legislation induced by the emancipation of slaves; an act to amend the criminal law; an act to establish district courts; an act to establish and regulate the domestic relations of persons of color and to amend the law in relation to paupers and vagrancy.

These statutes must be deemed to have embodied the views of the Legislature touching the status of the colored people in South Carolina, as established by emancipation and by the new relations of the State to the Federal Government; and as they were taken by the Radical leaders to be evidence of a purpose by the white people not to accept the rightful results of the freedom of their former slaves, a summary of the significant provisions should be given.

All free negroes, mulattoes and mestizos, all freedmen and freedwomen and all descendants through either sex of any of these persons were to be known as persons of color, except that every such descendant who might have of Caucasian blood seven-eighths or more should be deemed a white person.

Persons of color, though "not entitled to social or political equality with white persons," were to have the right to acquire, own and dispose of property, to make contracts, to enjoy the fruits of their labor, to sue and be sued, and to receive protection under the law in their persons and property.

All rights and remedies respecting persons or property, and all duties and liabilities under laws, civil and criminal, which applied to white persons were extended to persons of color—subject, however, to the modifications made by contemporaneous legislation.

The penalty of death was denounced upon any person of color who should commit any wilful homicide unless in self-defense, who should commit an assault upon a white woman with manifest intent to ravish her, or who should have sexual intercourse with a white woman by personating her husband.

For a servant to assault his master or employer or any member of his master's or employer's family, or any person authorized to direct and control him, was declared an aggravated misdemeanor, punishable by whipping or imprisonment.

It was made a misdemeanor for any person of color who should be in the employment of a master to sell any bacon, fresh meat or any product of a farm without having written evidence from such master or some person authorized by him, or from the district judge or a magistrate, that he had the right to sell such article.

It was made a misdemeanor for any person not authorized to write or give to a person of color a writing purporting to show evidence of the right of that person of color to sell any farm product which he was forbidden to sell without such evidence.

Persons of color were to constitute no part of the militia of the State, and no one of them should, without written permission from the district judge, be allowed to keep a firearm, sword or other military weapon—except that one of them who should be the owner of a farm might keep a shotgun or rifle, such as was ordinarily used in hunting, but not a pistol, musket or other firearm or weapon appropriate for purposes of war.

It was made a misdemeanor for a person of color to engage in the manufacture or sale of spirituous liquors.

It was declared unlawful for any person of color to migrate into and reside in this State, unless within twenty days after his arrival within the same he should enter into a bond of $1,000 with two freeholders as sureties, conditioned for his good behavior and for his support if he should become unable to support himself.

The district court was clothed with exclusive jurisdiction, subject to appeal, of all civil causes wherein any one of the parties should be a person of color, and also of all criminal cases wherein the accused should be a person of color.

The right of trial by jury was provided in the district court, except in the summary jurisdiction of "small and mean causes"—the grand jury consisting of eight persons and the petit jury of six.

An indictment against a white person for the killing of a person of color was triable in the circuit court, as was any other indictment in which a white person should be accused of a capital felony affecting the person or property of a person of color.

In every case, civil or criminal, in which a person of color should be a party, or which should affect the person or property of a person of color, persons of color should be competent witnesses—the accused in a criminal case and the parties in every civil case being also competent.

In reference to wills, executors and administrators, distribution of estates after payment of debts, the rights and remedies of legatees and next of kin, and all matters relating to testators and intestates, the same law which applied to white persons was extended to persons of color.

The relation of husband and wife amongst persons of color was established—those then living as such being declared to be husband and wife.

In the case of one man having two or more reputed wives, or one woman having two or more reputed husbands, the man was required, before the 1st day of April, 1866, to select one of his reputed wives, or the woman one of her reputed husbands, and the ceremony of marriage between the man or woman and the person so selected should be performed.

Every colored child theretofore born was declared to be the legitimate child of his mother and also of his colored father if he was then acknowledged by such father.

Persons of color desirous thereafter to become husband and wife should have the contract of marriage duly solemnized by a clergyman, a district judge, a magistrate, or any judicial officer, but cohabitation, with reputation or recognition of the parties, should be evidence of marriage in cases criminal and civil.

Marriage between a white person and a person of color was declared to be illegal and void.

The relations of parent and child, guardian and ward, and master and apprentice, were fully declared.

All persons of color who should make contracts for service or labor should be known as servants, and those with whom they should contract should be known as masters.

"On farms or in outdoor service the hours of labor, except on Sunday, shall be from sunrise to sunset, with a reasonable interval for breakfast and dinner. Servants shall rise at the dawn in the morning, feed, water and care for the animals on the farm, do the usual and needful work about the premises, prepare their meals for the day, if required by the master, and begin the farm or other work by sunrise. The servant shall be careful of all the property and animals of his master, and especially of the animals and implements used by him, shall protect the same from injury by other persons, and shall be answerable for all property lost, destroyed or injured by his negligence, dishonesty or bad faith.

"All lost time, not caused by the act of the master, and all losses occasioned by the neglect of the duties hereinbefore prescribed, may be deducted from the wages of the servant; and food, nursing and other necessaries for the servant while he is absent from work on account of sickness or other cause may also be deducted from his wages. Servants shall be quiet and orderly in their quarters and on the premises, shall extinguish their lights and fires and shall retire to rest at seasonable hours. Work at night, and outdoor work in inclement weather, shall not be exacted unless in case of necessity. Servants shall not be kept at home on Sunday, unless to take care of the premises or the animals thereon, and in such cases only so many shall be kept at home as are necessary for these purposes. Sunday work shall be done by the servants in turn, except in cases of sickness or other disability—when it may be assigned to them out of their regular turn. Absentees on Sunday shall return to their homes by sunset.

"The master may give to the servant a task at work about the business of the farm, which shall be reasonable. If the servant complain of the task the district judge or a magistrate shall have power to reduce or increase it. Failure to do a task shall be deemed evidence of indolence, but a single failure shall not be conclusive. When a servant is entered into a contract he may be required to rate himself as a full hand, three-fourths, half or one-fourth hand, and, according to this rate, inserted in the contract, shall be the task and the wages.

"Visitors or other persons shall not be invited or allowed by the servant to come or remain upon the premises of the master without his express permission.

"Servants shall not be absent from the premises without the permission of the master.

"The servant shall obey all lawful orders of the master or his agent, and shall be honest, truthful, sober, civil, and diligent in his business. The master may moderately correct servants who have made contracts and are under eighteen years of age."

The servant might for certain causes stated depart from the master's service, and when wrongfully discharged might recover wages for the whole period of service according to the contract.

The rules and regulations prescribed for master and servant were made applicable to persons in service as household servants, conferring the same rights and imposing the same duties, with certain modifications made necessary by the difference in the services.

Provision was made for the proper care of persons of color who should be paupers and for the punishment of those who should be adjudged by a jury of three freeholders, in a magistrate's court, to be vagrants.

The act to establish district courts provided that "the judges first elected under this act shall not be commissioned until the Governor shall be satisfied that they will be permitted to exercise the jurisdiction committed to them." The commissions were withheld accordingly.

In response to the proclamation of the Governor, the Legislature assembled in extra session on Tuesday, September 4, 1866—called for the purpose of "recommending such modifications of existing laws with reference to persons of color as will entitle the tribunals of this State to exercise jurisdiction over them in all cases, and such a reorganization of these tribunals as may be best adapted to this end."

On the Governor's suggestions, coupled with his statement that he had satisfied himself that the district courts would not be permitted by the military authorities to exercise jurisdiction over persons of color, the Legislature at this and the regular session following proceeded to amend the "code" in several important particulars.

By an act to amend the act to establish district courts the special powers given in relation to persons of color were abrogated, and these courts were made an inferior tribunal for the trial of certain causes, civil and criminal, without reference to the race or color of the parties. Changes of procedure, not necessary to mention, were made, and the judges were required to organize their courts immediately upon the passage of the act.

By an act to amend the act to amend the criminal law, all special provisions as to persons of color were repealed, and the statute was made applicable to all persons, without regard to race or color.

It was further enacted that "all persons hitherto known in law in this State as slaves or as free persons of color shall have the right to make and enforce contracts, to sue, to be sued, to be affiants and give evidence, to inherit, purchase, lease, sell, hold, convey and assign real and personal property, make wills and testaments, and to have full and equal benefits of the rights of personal security, personal liberty and private property, and of all remedies and proceedings for the enforcement and protection of the same, as white persons now have, and shall not be subjected to any other or different punishment, pain or penalty for the commission of any act or offense than such as are prescribed for white persons committing like acts or offenses."

The district courts were thereupon duly organized, the judges were commissioned, and these tribunals (sitting quarterly) proceeded to hear and determine the causes within their jurisdiction.

Governor Orr, in his message to the Legislature (November 28), informed that body that "the acts passed at the late extra session were transmitted to the military commandant of the Department of the Carolinas, at Charleston, and on the 1st day of October last, by general orders, he remitted all cases in which the inhabitants of this State were concerned, civil and criminal, to the civil authorities."

The Governor further stated: "Experience will demonstrate the wisdom of your enactment authorizing negroes to testify in all cases. It takes away the impunity which bad men have long enjoyed in tempting these ignorant people to perpetrate crime for the benefit of the tempters. The result of the experiment at the late fall terms of the courts has been entirely satisfactory, and most of the freedmen who have been called to the witness stand have manifested a highly creditable desire to tell the truth."

The relations of master and servant, as set forth in the "code," may be said not to have been established in any instance.

The second regular session of the General Assembly opened November 26, 1866, and adjourned December 21—being the last meeting of that body under the Constitution of 1865.

In his message Governor Orr informed the Legislature that he had been officially notified of the passage by Congress of the resolution proposing to the States the adoption of the Fourteenth Amendment to the Federal Constitution. Of this proposition the Governor said:

Do not its first and last sections, if adopted, confer upon Congress the absolute right of determining who shall be citizens of the respective States and who shall exercise the elective franchise and enjoy any and all of the rights, privileges and immunities of citizenship? The sections referred to not only do this, but they subvert the theory and practice of the Government by abrogating the right of fixing the elective franchise, conferred upon the respective State governments, and by giving the Representatives of Oregon or California in Congress the power to declare what shall constitute the measure of citizenship within the limits of Georgia or South Carolina. . . .

The third section, if its spirit were carried out, would not only disorganize the State government in all its departments, but would render it nearly impossible for the people of South Carolina at least to recognize a government until Congress by a two-thirds vote, in the case of each individual person, removes the disability. . . .

[The third section above mentioned reads as follows: "No person shall be a Senator or Representative in Congress, or elector of President and Vice-President, or hold any office, civil or military, under the United States or under any State, who, having previously taken an oath as a member of Congress or as a member of any State Legislature, or as an executive or judicial officer of any State, to support the Constitution of the United States, shall have engaged in insurrection or rebellion against the same, or given aid or comfort to the enemies thereof. But Congress may, by a vote of two-thirds of each house, remove such disability."]

There are other objections of a grave character which might be urged; and among these it may be mentioned that if the amendment is adopted we not only have no guaranties that our Representatives would be admitted to Congress, but there are unmistakable indications that they would still be excluded. It is unnecessary, however, to dwell upon a subject which has been so far decided by the public opinion of the people of the State, that I am justified in saying that if the Constitutional amendment is to be adopted let it be done by the irresponsible power of numbers, and let us preserve our own self-respect and the respect of our posterity by refusing to be the mean instruments of our own shame.

The Legislature shared with Governor Orr the feeling that the people of South Carolina could not honorably accept the terms proposed by Congress in the Fourteenth Amendment. Adverse action was taken by the Senate unanimously, and by the House with but one dissenting vote—that of Mr. P. J. Coogan, of Charleston.

At this session James B. Campbell, of Charleston, was elected Senator of the United States, for the long term, succeeding the short term for which the Hon. John L. Manning had been elected. Upon this action, the latter surrendered his credentials, and Mr. Campbell was elected for the short term also.

Judge Wardlaw submitted a "code" as a "substitute for the legislation induced by the emancipation of slaves," of which the House Committee on the Judiciary reported that "many sections of the bill would be impracticable at present, though the whole bill is full of useful suggestions for future legislation when time has reconciled labor and capital in their new relations." In order that "the labor and learning bestowed on the bill should not be lost," the committee suggested that "it ought to be preserved by being printed with the reports and resolutions of this session"—and this was accordingly done. Some of the sections of this "code" were enacted in the laws, already noted, making the changes suggested in the Governor's message submitted at the extra session.

THE PRESIDENT'S POLICY CONTINUED.

In April, 1866, a further step towards the restoration of South Carolina to full relations with the National Government was taken by the appointment of the Hon. George S. Bryan, of Charleston, to be judge of the United States District Court. John Phillips was made district attorney; Daniel Horlbeck, clerk; and J. P. M. Epping, marshal—all of Charleston.

Under the scheme of President Johnson there had been appointed a large number of Federal officials—customs collectors, internal revenue collectors and postmasters. With very few exceptions these appointees had to vacate because they could not take the required "test oath" (act of June 22, 1862), whereby each affiant had to swear in these words: "I do solemnly swear that I have never voluntarily borne arms against the United States since I became a citizen thereof; that I have voluntarily given no aid, countenance, counsel or encouragement to persons engaged in armed hostility thereto; that I have never sought nor accepted nor attempted to exercise the functions of any office whatever under any authority, or pretended authority, in hostility to the United States; and that I have not yielded a voluntary support to any pretended government, authority, power or constitution within the United States, hostile or inimical thereto."

In his message to Congress on the opening of its regular session, December 4, 1865, the President reported to that body his acts in relation to the Southern States, giving at length his views in support of his policy.

In a message to the Senate, delivered on December 19, the President said: "In reply to the message adopted by the Senate on the 12th, I have the honor to state that the rebellion waged by a portion of the people against the properly constituted authorities of the United States has been suppressed; that the United States are in possession of every State in which the insurrection existed, and that, as far as could be done, the courts of the United States have been restored, postoffices reestablished, and steps taken to put into effective operation the revenue laws of the country." Then followed a statement of the action of the several States "lately in rebellion" in their efforts towards a restoration of their relations with the Federal Union.

The President submitted at the same time General Grant's letter to him, written after his "tour of inspection" through some of the Southern States, in the course of which that officer said:

I am satisfied that the mass of thinking men of the South accept the present situation of affairs in good faith. The questions which have heretofore divided the sentiments of the people of the two sections—slavery and State rights, or the right of a State to secede from the Union—they regard as having been settled forever by the highest tribunal—arms—that man can resort to. I was pleased to learn from the leading men whom I met that they not only accepted the decision arrived at as final, but that now the smoke of battle has cleared away and time has been given for reflection, that this decision has been a fortunate one for the whole country, they receiving the like benefits from it with those who opposed them in the field and in council. Four years of war, during which law was only executed at the point of the bayonet throughout the States in rebellion, have left the people possibly in a condition not to yield that ready obedience to civil authority which the American people have been in the habit of yielding. This would render the presence of small garrisons throughout those States necessary until such time as labor returns to its proper channel and civil authority is fully established. . . . The presence of black troops, lately slaves, demoralizes labor, both by their advice and by furnishing in their camps a resort for the freedmen for long distances around. White troops generally excite no opposition, and therefore a small number of them can maintain order in a given district. . . . My observations lead me to the conclusion that the citizens of the Southern States are anxious to return to self-government within the Union as soon as possible; that, whilst reconstructing, they want and require that protection from the Government which they think is required by the Government, not humiliating to them as citizens, and that if such a course were pointed out they would pursue it in good faith.

By his proclamation of April 2, 1866, the President restored the writ of habeas corpus, which, as before stated, had been suspended, and abrogated the military power in civil matters—this in all the Southern States except Texas. By his proclamation of August 20, 1866, His Excellency took similar action in reference to that commonwealth, and as to the late rebellion declared "that the said insurrection is at an end, and that peace, order, tranquillity and civil authority prevail in and throughout the whole of the United States of America."

At a later stage of the Reconstruction period (September 7, 1867), President Johnson proclaimed amnesty to all those who participated in "the late rebellion" except persons of three classes—(1) those who held the chief executive offices or cabinet positions, or military rank above the grade of brigadier-general, or naval rank above the grade of captain; (2) those who had treated otherwise than as lawful prisoners of war persons who had been engaged in the military or naval service of the United States; (3) all persons in civil or military custody, and all persons engaged directly or indirectly in the plot to assassinate the late President of the United States.

By his proclamation of July 4, 1868, the President proclaimed "unconditionally and without reservation to all and to every person who directly or indirectly participated in the late insurrection, excepting such person or persons as may be under presentment or indictment in any court of the United States having competent jurisdiction, upon a charge of treason or other felony, a full pardon and amnesty for the offense of treason against the United States, or of adhering to their enemies during the late Civil War, with restoration of all rights of property, except as to slaves, and except also as to any property of which any person may have been legally divested under the laws of the United States."

On December 25, 1868, the President proclaimed full pardon and amnesty "to all and to every person who directly or indirectly participated in the late insurrection or rebellion."

[It is interesting to note that from the benefits of the proclamation of July 4, 1868, there was excepted Jefferson Davis, the President of the Confederate States of America, who before the issuance of the proclamation had been indicted for treason—this at the March term, 1868, of the Circuit Court of the United States for the District of Virginia, Chief Justice Chase and Judge Underwood presiding. The defendant pleaded that under Section 3 of the Fourteenth Amendment certain penalties and disabilities were fixed upon him for having engaged in rebellion after having taken the oath of a member of Congress in 1845, and that any other or further penalty was not admissible by the Constitution and laws of the United States. Upon the question thus made the Court were divided—the Chief Justice stating that in his opinion the objection of the prisoner was well taken. The amnesty proclamation of December 25, 1868, effectually disposed of the prosecution, and at a subsequent term of the court it was dismissed.]

THE PHILADELPHIA CONVENTION.

An assemblage which attracted notice all over the country and which had relation to the Reconstruction policy of President Johnson was the National Union Convention, which met in Philadelphia on August 14, 1866. The call for this convention was issued by Messrs. A. W. Randall and J. R. Doolittle, of Wisconsin, Mr. O. H. Browning, of Illinois, and Mr. Edgar Cowan, of Pennsylvania—these constituting the executive committee of the National Union Club—and was indorsed by Thomas A. Hendricks, of Indiana; Daniel S. Norton, of Minnesota; and J. W. Nesmith, of Oregon.

The objects of the convention were stated to be "to sustain the administration in maintaining unbroken the Union of the States under the Constitution which our fathers established—that Union of

States which is indissoluble and perpetual—and the laws of Congress, passed in pursuance thereof, to hold counsel together, as friends and brothers, upon the present condition of our national affairs, to take measures to avert possible dangers from the country, to affirm the perpetuity of the Union, the equality of the States, the abolition of slavery, and the right of the South to immediate representation in Congress"; and (in the language of Governor Orr, who was vice-president of the club for South Carolina,) "to join in an acknowledgment of the wisdom of that policy by which Andrew Johnson, President of the United States, has, in the midst of difficulties unparalleled in the history of any administration, maintained the integrity of the Constitution, identified the exercise of the executive power with the rules of strict justice and the spirit of mercy, and proved his legitimate right to succeed the great founders of the Republic as the Chief Magistrate of a common country which can be made and preserved as one nation only by the equal administration of just and equal laws."

The State Convention met in Columbia on July 31—all the districts being represented except Beaufort, Edgefield, Horry and York. The following officers were elected:

President—James L. Orr, of Anderson.

Vice-Presidents—Wade Hampton, of Richland; B. H. Brown, of Barnwell; C. W. Dudley, of Marlboro; Gabriel Cannon, of Spartanburg.

Secretaries—W. L. DePass, of Kershaw; F. J. Moses, Jr., of Sumter.

On motion of Gen. Samuel McGowan, it was resolved that "this convention approves the restoration policy of President Johnson, as opposed to the radical policy of Congress, and we accept the invitation to unite with the conservatives of the country in the national convention to be held in Philadelphia."

Delegates were then elected as follows:

State at Large—James L. Orr, James B. Campbell, B. F. Perry, John L. Manning.

Congressional Districts—First, Richard Dozier, of Georgetown; F. J. Moses, Sr., of Sumter. Second, Thomas Y. Simons, of Charleston; William P. Shingler, of Berkeley. Third, David L. Wardlaw and Samuel McGowan, of Abbeville. Fourth, Thomas N. Dawkins, of Union; James Farrow, of Spartanburg.

The National Union Convention duly assembled in Philadelphia, on the day appointed, there being about six hundred delegates in attendance.

Mr. A. W. Randall opened the proceedings by saying: "Gentlemen, I have to announce that the delegates from South Carolina and Massachusetts will now come, arm in arm, into this Convention."

"This announcement," according to the telegraphic report to the *Columbia Phoenix,* "was greeted with great applause. The entire audience rising at this moment, Major-General Couch, of Massachusetts, and Governor Orr, of South Carolina, at the head of their delegations, marched arm in arm—banners flying and music playing. Shout upon shout spontaneously rent the air, and tears filled the eyes of delegates and spectators."

Gen. John A. Dix, of New York, was made temporary chairman, and Mr. J. R. Doolittle elected president. Among the vice-presidents was Judge Wardlaw, of South Carolina.

C. L. Vallandigham, of Ohio, sent a letter expressing his entire sympathy with the objects of the Convention, and stating that he had declined to be a delegate because his action might expose the body to misconception or misrepresentation.

President Johnson sent a telegram saying: "I thank you for your cheering and encouraging dispatch. The finger of Providence is unerring and will guide you safely through. The people must be trusted, and the country will be restored. My faith is unshaken as to the ultimate success."

The Committee on Resolutions (on which was the Hon. B. F. Perry, of South Carolina) submitted a declaration of principles (which was unanimously adopted) and afterwards issued an address to the country. These papers stated *in extenso* the propositions contained in the call for the Convention.

A committee, of which the Hon. Reverdy Johnson was chairman and spokesman, reported to the President, in an appropriate address, the action of the Convention. The President received them cordially and made a suitable response.

MILITARY INTERFERENCE.

The extent of the restoration of South Carolina to her place in the Federal Union, considered independently of the action of Congress, was affected by the acts and proceedings of the military commanders still exercising authority, and also by the employment of the powers of the officials charged with the administration of the Freedmen's Bureau. As before stated the military authority was expressly recognized by Governor Orr in his proclamation issued in January, 1866.

On January 12, 1866, General Grant, as commanding general of the army, directed post commanders and others to protect persons from prosecution in State or municipal courts, when charged with offenses growing out of the enforcement of the military orders of the President, or other competent military authority; to protect from prosecution and penalties all occupants of abandoned lands and all persons holding property by the military authority of the President; and to protect colored persons from penalties not imposed on white persons.

On February 17 General Grant ordered his department commanders in the South to "transmit to headquarters, as soon as practicable, and from time to time thereafter, such copies of newspapers published in the department as contain sentiments of disloyalty and hostility to the Government, in any of its branches, and state whether such paper is habitual in its utterances of such sentiments"—the order further declaring that "the persistent publication of articles calculated to keep up the hostility between the different sections of the country cannot be tolerated, and this information is called for with a view to their suppression."

On July 13, 1866, certain civilians undergoing sentence for offenses committed in the "conquered territory" after the cessation of hostilities were, by authority of the President, ordered to be held in military custody.

On July 16, 1866, military officers on duty in any of the Southern States were, by order of General Grant, required to arrest persons charged with crime, if they should not have been apprehended by the civil authorities—this not in aid of the latter, but by virtue of the Federal authority acting independently.

Major-Gen. Daniel E. Sickles, having been assigned to duty in the department hitherto commanded by General Gilmore, formally assumed command by a general order dated January 1, 1866, whereby he not only indicated the relations of the military to the civil authority, but undertook to forbid certain acts theretofore authorized by the statute law of South Carolina. From this action on this line there very soon arose a conflict between the civil court and the Federal commander. The general order referred to, among other restrictions upon the law officers of the State, forbade the infliction of corporal punishment.

At the spring term, 1866, of the Circuit Court in Charleston, Judge A. P. Aldrich sentenced to be whipped a white man who had been convicted of larceny. On the day after the sentence a soldier appeared at the courthouse and inquired for the Judge. Not finding him, the soldier reported the fact to his superior. On the next day came a note from the post commander (Brigadier-General Bennett) asking the Judge to report at headquarters. The Judge respectfully declining, an officer called at his hotel and repeated the request. Thereupon the Judge, remarking, "I see I am under arrest," accompanied the officer into the General's presence. There was some colloquy about the case, the Judge firmly maintaining the authority of his court, and pointing out his inability to do anything to interfere with the execution of the sentence lawfully passed. A few days later the prisoner was taken by the military from the sheriff and discharged—this by an order of General Sickles, enforced in spite of the request of Governor Orr to the contrary. Judge Aldrich thereupon adjourned his court, and he refrained from holding any term until the apparent adjustment following the action of the Legislature, at the special session in September, in relation to the rights of the freedmen.

[The course of Judge Aldrich in declining to hold court while his judgments were subject to interference by the Federal military, was similar to that taken by the Justices of the United States Supreme Court, who until the summer of 1867 abstained from sitting in any of the "insurgent States," on the ground that "their process might be disregarded, and their judgments and decrees set aside, by military orders."]

In another case Judge Thomas N. Dawkins sentenced a prisoner to be whipped, and the commanding general interposed to prevent the enforcement of the judgment. Pending the correspondence between General Sickles and Governor Orr the prisoner was respited, but the time having expired, and that fact having apparently escaped the notice of both the executive and the military commander, the whipping was duly administered according to law.

In the latter part of 1865, while two citizens of Edgefield, standing in front of the courthouse, were discussing in an ordinary tone of voice some case about to come to trial, a white cavalryman, belonging to a company stationed in the town, stepped rudely and violently between them and pushed both backward with a threat. One of the citizens, having a stiff leg, fell to the ground, whereupon the soldier, evidently drunk, drew his pistol, got on top of the prostrate man, held him down and fired—the bullet passing under his neck into the ground. Some gentlemen standing a little distance off stepped up and remonstrated with the soldier. Refusing to release his hold, the soldier's conduct attracted a crowd whose evident purpose was to release the victim. Suddenly a young man stepped out in front of the crowd and deliberately fired upon the soldier—inflicting a wound from which he soon died. In a short while an infantry sergeant very excitedly marched his company to the public square, brandished his pistol and threatened vengeance upon the whole town. Gen. M. C. Butler informed him that if he did not cease his threats and march his company back to their quarters he and they must take the consequences—there being on the ground five or six hundred ex-Confederate soldiers who might not be longer restrained. The sergeant followed General Butler's advice, and quiet was soon restored. Both the citizen who had been maltreated and the one who had killed the soldier left the community. Several citizens of Edgefield, including Gen. M. W. Gary, were arrested on the charge of complicity in the killing of the trooper, huddled into an ambulance, taken to Columbia in the nighttime, and there incarcerated in the basement of the College chapel (outside the campus)—having for their fellow prisoners some of the most depraved and loathsome criminals in the country. To Gen. Adelbert Ames, the post commander, General Butler, who had promptly followed the ambulance, protested against this treatment of the accused gentlemen, whereupon that officer promptly had them transferred to comfortable tents in another part of the city. On hearing of this action, Maj. Alexander Moore, of General Sickles's staff, who had made the arrests, presented to General Ames a paper, "by order of General Sickles," directing that the accused be sent to Charleston. General Ames obeyed the order, and at once went in person to General Sickles—to whom it was thought he protested against the arrest and imprisonment of the parties accused. These were kept in Charleston, their prison guard being negro soldiers, but were after a time released. No charges were ever formulated and no trial was ever ordered.

In October, 1865, three soldiers of a Maine regiment, while guarding some cotton at Brown's Ferry, in Anderson District, were killed by unknown parties. Five men—four citizens of the district named, and one a resident of Georgia—were arrested on suspicion of complicity in the crime. The accused were first taken to Darlington and thence to Charleston, where they were tried by a military commission—Lieut.-Col. A. J. Willard (afterwards a justice of the State Supreme Court) representing the Government, and Gen. James Conner, of Charleston, with Mr. Armistead Burt, of Abbeville, appearing for the defense. Four of the defendants were found guilty of murder and sentenced to death. Application having been made to Judge Bryan, of the United States District Court, a writ of habeas corpus was issued, commanding General Sickles to produce the prisoners. That officer refused to obey the writ, declaring that the prisoners had been duly tried and convicted by a competent tribunal; that the case was before the President for review, and that the commanding general had no power by which he could in any manner interfere with the present disposition of the parties without the further order of the President. Thereupon, by the order of Judge Bryan, General Sickles was attached for contempt. He refused to be taken, writing on the writ these words: "In compliance with orders from superior authority I decline to be arrested." Shortly after this proceeding the sentence of the prisoners having been commuted by the President to life imprisonment on the Dry Tortugas, off the coast of Florida, they were removed from Castle Pinckney. Later they were transferred to Fort Delaware. Brought by habeas corpus before the Hon. Elisha Hall, judge of the United States Court for the District of Delaware, they were, on November 17, 1866, by him discharged from custody—this on the ground that the trial, conviction and sentence by military commission were contrary to the Federal Constitution, null and void. The accused were never prosecuted further.

On November 20, 1865, James Egan, a white citizen of Lexington, about eighty years of age, was tried by military commission on the charge of murder—the alleged killing of a negro boy—found guilty and sentenced to life imprisonment in the Albany penitentiary.

Taken before Associate Justice Nelson, of the United States Supreme Court, the prisoner was discharged on the ground that his trial and conviction had been without authority of law. In the course of his opinion Judge Nelson declared that, in pursuance of the appointment of the Provisional Governor of South Carolina, "a new Constitution had been formed, a Governor and Legislature had been elected under it, and the State was in the full enjoyment, or was entitled to the full enjoyment, of all her constitutional rights and privileges."

A decision similar to those above given was rendered by Judge Bryan in Charleston in February, 1867, when he discharged from prison a negro who had been convicted by a military court of assault and battery—this being the first effective assertion of the actual subordination of the military power to the civil authority since the occupation of the State by the Federal army.

There were numerous instances, of more or less enormity, of the employment of military force, represented by military courts, to punish accused parties for alleged violations of State laws, Federal statutes, military orders, or police regulations of post commanders. The cases cited must serve to indicate the condition of affairs.

THE FREEDMEN'S BUREAU.

On March 3, 1865, President Lincoln had approved the "act to establish a bureau for the relief of freedmen and refugees," by which there was committed to such bureau during the war, and for one year thereafter, the "management of all abandoned lands and the control of all subjects relating to refugees and freedmen from rebel States," and the custody, disposition and sale of confiscated property. On July 16, 1866, despite the veto of the President, Congress passed an act to "continue in force and amend" the act above noted, "and for other purposes." The new act, so far as it related to the Bureau, was continued in force for two years after its passage. The supervision and care of the bureau were extended "to all loyal refugees and freedmen so far as the same shall be necessary to enable them as speedily as practicable to become self-supporting citizens of the United States, and to aid them in making the freedom conferred by proclamation of the Commander-in-Chief, by emancipation, under the laws of States and by constitutional amendment, available to them and beneficial to the Republic." Various officials were provided, whose duty it should be to enforce the act; "and all persons appointed to service under this act and the act to which this is an amendment, shall be so far deemed in the military service of the United States as to be under the military jurisdiction and entitled to the military protection of the Government while in discharge of the duties of their office." Sales of certain lands in South Carolina, under the "act for the collection of direct taxes in insurrectionary districts within the United States" (June 7, 1862), and the act amendatory thereof (February 6, 1863), were confirmed, and other lands bid in by the United States were directed to be sold to the occupants in lots of twenty acres at $1.50 per acre. "School farms" in the parish of St. Helena were directed to be sold, and the proceeds to be invested in United States bonds as a fund for "the support of schools, without distinction of color or race, on the islands in the parishes of St. Helena and St. Luke."

The act further provided that "in every State or district where the ordinary course of judicial proceedings has been interrupted by the rebellion, and until the same shall be fully restored, and in every State or district whose constitutional relations to the government have been practically discontinued by the rebellion, and until such State shall have been restored in such relations and shall be duly represented in the Congress of the United States," the rights, remedies, and immunities conferred by the Civil Rights act, hereafter noticed, should be secured to and enjoyed by all the citizens of such State or district, without respect to race or color or previous condition of servitude. In such State or district the President was vested with power to "extend military protection and exercise military jurisdiction over all cases and questions concerning the free enjoyment of such immunities and rights" as were created or conferred by the act.

The bureau in South Carolina was under the management of Brig.-Gen. R. K. Scott, assistant commissioner, aided by a sufficient corps of subordinates. Vested by the act with military authority, these officials nevertheless appeared to occupy towards the State government the relations of independent civil functionaries deriving all their power from the Congress of the United States. Aside from the actual custody of lands held by the Government under color of title acquired through the enforcement of the direct tax or by seizure in the course of military operations, the bureau officers undertook to exercise a supervisory control in all matters affecting the freedmen or their rights consequent upon emancipation.

In the matter of contracts between landlords and tenants or between farmers and their laborers—where any party thereto was a person of color—the bureau established standards and regulations which, though put forth in the form of suggestions, were yet of sufficient force to cause the negroes to feel that the bureau was the authorized arbiter for the enforcement of their rights and the protection of their interests. Regulations made by the bureau were generally respected by the freedmen—and the white people had little choice in such matters.

In June, 1866, the assistant commissioner suggested the surrender of all lands occupied otherwise than by virtue of title to their true owners—a step which led to the ultimate restoration of the owners' rights. Shortly afterwards he ordered the arrest of all freedmen (including women) who should for any but lawful reasons have quitted the farms whereon they had been working and who, having broken their contracts, were idlers or vagrants. Trading in crops before division among the parties entitled to them and before they were ready for market was made an offense punishable by a fine varying from $50 to $500, in the discretion of the post commander—a repetition of the offense to be punished with imprisonment not exceeding six months.

In January, 1867, the jail at Kingstree was destroyed by fire—this, according to the newspaper accounts given at the time, caused by the act of some of the negro prisoners who thus endeavored to escape. Of those confined in the building nineteen colored men and two colored women were burnt to death—the single white prisoner getting out unharmed. General Scott issued a sort of proclamation charging the sheriff and his two deputies with criminal misconduct in not protecting the lives of the negro prisoners "while the single white prisoner was permitted to escape unharmed." The officers mentioned were on General Scott's order arrested by a squad of soldiers and taken to Castle Pinckney, where they were confined for a time, but were neither tried nor punished.

In Marion District in July, 1867, a negro was lawfully committed to jail on the charge of assault and battery, with intent to kill, upon the person of a white citizen. Two agents of the Freedmen's Bureau

—an army captain and a civilian—demanded of the clerk of the circuit court that the prisoner should be discharged on his own recognizance. The clerk refused—basing his action upon the State law and the standing orders of General Sickles. The officers replied that they had nothing to do with General Sickles, that they acted under General Scott, who was "the ruling power in this State," that they had orders from him directing that freedmen should not be required to give bail, that they recognized General Scott only, and that the negro should not give bail. The clerk still refusing to discharge the prisoner, the captain sent a message to the jailer with a peremptory order to release him. The jailer felt constrained to obey, and the prisoner was discharged.

There were thus, between the Federal occupation of territory in South Carolina and the appointment of the district commander under the Reconstruction acts hereafter noticed, at least three separate powers exercising authority over the people of this State—the civil government organized under the proclamations and directions of President Johnson; the military forces of the United States, acting in the apparent exercise of the right to control conquered territory, by express authority of Congress and with the apparent acquiescence of the President; and, lastly, the organs of the Freedmen's Bureau, deriving their quasi-military powers from the acts of the lawmaking branch of the Federal Government.

THE RECONSTRUCTION MEASURES.

The Thirty-eighth Congress adjourned March 3, 1865, and the President did not call an extra session of the Thirty-ninth. That body, composed of forty Republican senators and eleven Democratic, 146 Republican representatives and forty Democratic, met in regular session on December 4, 1865. The course of the President, together with the action of the Southern States in the adoption of his suggestions and the furtherance of his plan, had been much discussed by the press of the country and criticized by leading men in the Republican party. It was clear that the new congress would not acquiesce in the adjustments embodied in the Presidential scheme of Reconstruction.

The credentials of the Southern senators and representatives were severally ordered to lie on the table, pending the report of the joint committee on Reconstruction, which was composed of fifteen members, as follows: Senators W. P. Fessenden, of Maine; James W.

Grimes, of Iowa; Ira Harris, of New York; Jacob M. Howard, of Michigan; George H. Williams, of Oregon, and Reverdy Johnson (Dem.) of Maryland; Representatives Thaddeus Stevens, of Pennsylvania; Elihu B. Washburne, of Illinois; Justin S. Morrill, of Vermont; John A. Bingham, of Ohio; Roscoe Conkling, of New York; George S. Boutwell, of Massachusetts; Henry T. Blow, of Missouri; A. J. Rogers, of New Jersey (Dem.), and Henry Grider, of Kentucky (Dem.).

The Reconstruction committee was directed to inquire, ascertain and report what was the actual condition of affairs in the States "lately in rebellion," and also what were the relations of those States to the Federal Union. The "investigation" by the committee was long and laborious.

On January 10, 1866, the House of Representatives, by a vote of 94 to 37, adopted a resolution declaring that "in order to the maintenance of the national authority and the protection of loyal citizens of the seceded States it is the sense of this House that the military forces of the Government should not be withdrawn from those States until the two houses of Congress shall have ascertained and declared that their further presence there is no longer necessary." A declaration of the same purport was made by the Senate.

On February 20 the two bodies adopted a concurrent resolution declaring that neither the House nor the Senate would admit any representative from any of the seceded States until both houses should declare such State entitled to representation.

Next came the Civil Rights act—"an act to protect all persons in the United States in their civil rights and furnish the means of their vindication"—vetoed by President Johnson, and passed over the veto April 9, 1866. By the first section it was enacted that "all persons born in the United States, and not subject to any foreign power (excluding Indians not taxed) are hereby declared to be citizens of the United States, and such citizens, of every race and color, without regard to any previous condition of slavery or involuntary servitude, except as a punishment for crime whereof the party shall have been duly convicted, shall have the same rights in every State and territory in the United States to make and enforce contracts, to sue, be parties and give evidence, to inherit, purchase, lease, sell, hold and convey real and personal property, and to full and equal benefit of all laws and proceedings for the security of person and property, as is enjoyed by white citizens, and shall be subject to like punishment, pains and penalties, and none other—any law, statute, ordinance, regulation or custom to the contrary notwithstanding." Penalties were affixed for depriving any person of any right thus declared, because of race, color or previous condition of servitude, and of the offenses thus denounced the district courts of the United States were vested with jurisdiction, exclusively of the courts of the several States. Provision was made for the removal of causes wherein any right declared by the act was involved to the courts of the United States, and the duties of attorneys, marshals and commissioners were fully set forth.

By a resolution of Congress, passed June 16, 1866, the Fourteenth Amendment of the Constitution was submitted to the several States.

On June 18, 1866, the Reconstruction committee finally reported to Congress. The majority, after what was claimed to be an exhaustive and impartial review of the testimony submitted by the President and that otherwise taken by the committee, presented a series of accusations against the Southern people, of which the following may be taken as specimens:

From the whole mass of testimony submitted by the President it appears that in no instance in the Southern States was any regard paid to any other consideration than obtaining immediate admission to Congress under the barren form of an election in which no precaution was taken to secure regularity of proceedings or the assent of the people. . . .

Indeed, all feeling of conciliation on the part of the North has been treated with contempt. The bitterness and defiance against the United States have been unparalleled in the history of the world.

The burden rests upon the Southern people, before claiming to be reinstated in their former positions, to show that they ought to resume their federal relations. In order to do this they must prove that they have established, with the consent of the people, a republican form of government in harmony with the Constitution and laws of the United States—that all hostile purposes have ceased, and that they have given adequate guaranties against future treason and rebellion, which will be satisfactory to the Government against which they have rebelled and by whose army they were subdued." . . .

The committee further reported that the seceding States had deliberately severed their relations with the Union, renounced their right to representation and abolished their State governments so far as these connected them with the Union, but nevertheless that the

Federal Constitution and laws still remained binding upon the individuals who formed the State, and before the privileges which they had abandoned should be restored to them they must give such guaranties of future obedience as would be satisfactory to the law-making power which in 1861 had recognized the existence of obstruction.

Although neither the Reconstruction theory of Sumner nor that of Stevens was adopted by this report, it reached the same conclusion in placing the restoring or reconstructing power in the hands of Congress exclusively.

The minority of the committee—Messrs. Johnson, Grider and Rogers—submitted a report in which they substantially sustained the policy and the action of the President. They contended that the evidence adduced before the committee contained nothing to justify the denial of representation to the several Southern States in Congress, and especially urged that in no view could their admission to their rights in the Union be dangerous to any public interest. They disclaimed any purpose "to impute to President Johnson any design to extend the executive power, but cheerfully concede to him the most patriotic motives."

By the act of March 2, 1867, "making appropriations for the support of the army for the year ending June 30, 1868, and for other purposes" it was enacted that "it shall be the duty of the officers of the army and navy, and of the Freedmen's Bureau, to prohibit and prevent whipping or maiming of the person, as a punishment for any crime, misdemeanor or offense, by any pretended civil or military authority in any State lately in rebellion, until the civil government of such State shall have been restored and shall have been recognized by the Congress of the United States."

By the same act it was required that "all militia forces now organized or in service in either of the States of Virginia, North Carolina, South Carolina, Georgia, Florida, Alabama, Mississippi, Louisiana and Texas be forthwith disbanded, and that the further organization, arming or calling into service of the said militia forces or any part thereof is hereby prohibited under any circumstances whatever, until the same shall be authorized by Congress."

Following the report of the Reconstruction Committee and the debates in Congress upon the matters presented there were various schemes of restoration, and these were fully discussed as well by the press of the country as by the Senate and the House. The different ideas of Republican leaders were submitted, and the entire situation was duly considered by the President, his cabinet and his other advisers. Prominent men in the South held the opinion that it was best to reach some adjustment of the questions of citizenship and suffrage, which should be preferable to that embodied in the Fourteenth Amendment and which should not offend the Southern people by disfranchising a large part of their very best men.

In the early part of 1867 it was announced in the dispatches from Washington that there had been prepared a proposed substitute for the Fourteenth Amendment as submitted to the States by Congress, which, whilst declaring and protecting the civil rights of the freedmen, had certain provisions which would free it of some of the greatest objections taken to the amendment in its form as so submitted. On February 4 there was a conference in Washington, at which were present with other prominent gentlemen Governors Orr of South Carolina, Sharkey of Mississippi, Parsons of Alabama, and Marvin of Florida. The conference resulted in the suggestion by these Governors that the Legislatures of the Southern States, some of which were then in session, be notified of the conclusion reached—which was that for the Fourteenth Amendment as previously proposed there should be substituted and submitted to the several States an amendment (to be indicated as Article XIV) in terms as follows:

Section 1. The Union under the Constitution is and shall be perpetual. No State shall pass any law or ordinance to secede or withdraw from the Union, and any such law or ordinance shall be null and void.

Sec. 2. The public debt of the United States, authorized by law, shall ever be held sacred and inviolate. But neither the United States nor any State shall assume or pay any debt or obligation incurred in aid of insurrection or rebellion against the government or authority of the United States.

Sec. 3. All persons born or naturalized in the United States, and subject to the jurisdiction thereof, are citizens of the United States and of the State wherein they reside. No State shall make or enforce any law which shall abridge the privileges or immunities of citizens of the United States; nor shall any State deprive any person of life, liberty or property, without due process of law, nor deny to any person within its jurisdiction the equal protection of the laws.

Sec. 4. Representatives shall be apportioned among the several States according to their respective numbers, counting the whole number of persons in each State, excluding Indians not taxed. But when any State shall, on account of race, or color, or previous condition of servitude, exclude from voting at any election for the choice of electors for President or Vice-President of the United States, Representatives in Congress, members of the Legislature, or other officers, elective by the people, any of the male inhabitants of such State, being twenty-one years of age and citizens of the United States, then no part of the entire class of persons so excluded from the elective franchise shall be counted in the basis of representation. No State shall require as a property qualification for voters more than two hundred and fifty dollars worth of taxable property, nor as an educational qualification more education than enough to enable the voter to read the Constitution of the United States in the English language and write his own name.

In connection with this proposed amendment, and as part of the scheme to adjust fairly and satisfactorily the relations of the freedmen to the States, it was suggested that each State incorporate in its Constitution the following provision as to the suffrage:

Every male citizen who has resided in this State for one year, and in the county in which he offers to vote six months immediately preceding the day of election, and who can read the Constitution of the United States in the English language, or who may be the owner of two hundred and fifty dollars worth of taxable property, shall be entitled to vote at all elections for Governor of this State, members of the Legislature and all other officers elective by the people of the State: provided, that no person shall, by reason of this article, be excluded from voting who has heretofore exercised the elective franchise under the Constitution and laws of this State, or who, at the time of the adoption of this amendment, may be entitled to vote under said Constitution and laws.

How far the adjustments contemplated by the proposed amendments might have been acceptable to the white people of the South cannot be said—this because there was no opportunity for a presentation of them to the Legislatures of the Southern States or indeed for a discussion of them by the press of the country. The program of the Radical majority in Congress had been already settled, and their scheme of Reconstruction had been formulated in a bill then under discussion in the lower house. This bill, with others of like purpose, very soon became a law.

On March 21, 1867, Congress passed over the President's veto "an act to provide for the more efficient government of the rebel States"—the preamble setting forth that there was in such States no legal State government or adequate protection for life or liberty, and that it was "necessary that peace and good order should be enforced in said States until loyal and republican State governments can be legally established."

This act divided the "rebel States" into military districts—North and South Carolina constituting the second district. The President was directed to assign to the command of each district an army officer not below the rank of brigadier-general, and to furnish him with a military force sufficient to enable him to perform his duties and enforce his authority.

It was made the duty of the district commander to protect persons and property and suppress disorder, for which purpose he might "allow local civil tribunals to take jurisdiction of and try offenders," or for that purpose to organize military commissions or tribunals; and "all interference under color of State authority with the exercise of military authority under this act shall be null and void."

It was provided that all persons under military arrest by virtue of this act should be speedily tried, that no sentence affecting life or liberty should be executed until approved by the district commander, and that no death sentence should be executed without the approval of the President.

By the fifth section it was enacted "that when the people of any one of said rebel States shall have formed a constitution of government in conformity with the Constitution of the United States in all respects, framed by a convention of delegates elected by the male citizens of said State, twenty-one years old and upward, of whatever race, color or previous condition, who have been resident in the said State for one year previous to the day of such election, except such as may be disfranchised for participation in the rebellion or for felony at common law, and when such convention shall provide that the elective franchise shall be enjoyed by all such persons as have the qualifications herein stated for electors of delegates, and when such constitution shall be ratified by a majority of the persons voting on the question of ratification who are qualified as electors for delegates, and when such constitution shall have been submitted to Congress for examination and approval and Congress shall have adopted the same, and when said State by a vote of its Legislature elected under said constitution shall have adopted the amendment to the Constitution of the United States, known as Article Fourteen, and when said article shall have become a part of the Constitution of the United States, said State shall be declared entitled to representation in Congress, and Senators and Representatives shall be admitted therefrom on their taking the oath prescribed by law [meaning the test oath], thereupon and thereafter the preceding sections of this act shall be inoperative in said State: provided, that no person excluded from the privilege of holding office by said proposed amendment to the Constitution of the United States shall be eligible as a member of the convention to frame a constitution for any of said rebel States, nor shall any such person vote for members of such convention."

It was further enacted "that until the people of said rebel States shall be by law admitted to representation in the Congress of the United States, any civil government which may exist therein shall be provisional only and in all respects subject to the paramount authority of the United States at any time to abolish, modify, control or supersede the same, and in all elections to any office under such provisional governments all persons shall be entitled to vote, and none others, who are entitled to vote under the provisions of the fifth section of this act, and no person shall be eligible to any office under any such provisional government who would be disqualified from holding office under the provisions of the third article of said constitutional amendment."

On March 23, 1867, Congress passed over the President's veto "an act supplementary to an act . . . passed March 2, 1867, and to facilitate restoration." By this act registration was directed to be made of such male citizens (negroes, of course, included) of each State as were not disqualified under the provisions of the proposed Article XIV. It was further enacted that after such registration "an election shall be held of delegates to a convention for the purpose of establishing a constitution for such State loyal to the Union"—the number of delegates in the South Carolina body to be the number of members in the House of Representatives.

It was provided that if a majority of those voting should vote for a convention the same should be held upon the order of the district commander, within sixty days after the election—which convention when organized "shall proceed to frame a constitution and civil government according to the provisions of this act and the act to which it is supplementary, and when the same shall have been so framed it shall be submitted by the convention for ratification to the persons registered under the provisions of this act, at an election" to be held for that purpose; and if a majority of those voting should have voted for ratification, such constitution should be referred to Congress for its approval precedent to the admission of the State wherein the convention was held to representation in the Senate and House of Representatives.

Officers charged with the registration of voters and the conduct of elections were required to take the test oath prescribed in the act of July 2, 1862.

By the supplementary act of July 19, 1867, passed over the President's veto, the governments in the "rebel States," existing on March 2, 1867, were declared to be and to have been illegal, and if continued were to be continued "subject in all respects to the military commanders of the respective districts and to the paramount authority of Congress."

The district commander was authorized to suspend or remove any civil or military officer whenever in his opinion the proper administration of the Reconstruction acts required, and to appoint a successor—this subject to the approval of the general of the army, who was vested also with original power to suspend, remove and appoint.

It was further enacted that "no district commander or member of the board of registration or any of the officers or appointees acting under them shall be bound in his action by any opinion of any civil officer of the United States."

By the joint resolution of July 20, 1868, the States "lately in rebellion" were excluded from the electoral college unless the people thereof should since the 4th day of March, 1867, have adopted a Constitution and should have become entitled to representation in Congress under the provisions of the Reconstruction acts. In this instance also the President's veto was unavailing.

For the purpose of carrying into effect the several "acts for the more efficient government of the rebel States" Congress first appropriated $500,000, and later increased the amount to $1,000,000—such increase being enacted despite the President's veto.

These acts were passed only after a contest between Congress and the President, an outline of which may properly be given as indicating the temper and motives of the Radical majority.

In August, 1867, the President undertook to remove Mr. Stanton, the Secretary of War, and to appoint General Grant to that office.

At the meeting of Congress in September that body declared the removal of Stanton to have been contrary to the tenure-of-office law (act of March 2, 1867), thus replacing the secretary. Five months later Mr. Johnson again removed Stanton and appointed Maj.-Gen. Lorenzo Thomas in his place. The Senate thereupon resolved that "the President has no power to remove the Secretary of War and designate any other person to perform the duties of that office." On the day following the House, by a vote of 126 to 47, resolved that the President be impeached of "high crimes and misdemeanors." The articles of impeachment, eleven in all, recited many offenses, the principal of which were the removal of the Secretary of War, the public expression of contempt for the legislative branch of the Government, the declaration that the one in session was not a constitutional congress, and particularly the President's obstruction of the execution of the acts of that body. The main ground of defense was that Mr. Johnson's course in the work of Reconstruction was merely the continuation of a plan resolved upon by President Lincoln and the members of his cabinet. In the Senate sitting as a court of impeachment Andrew Johnson was acquitted as to nine of the articles and on the two remaining (contempt of Congress and removing Stanton) the vote stood thirty-five for conviction, nineteen for acquittal. Less than two-thirds of the Senate having voted for conviction the impeachment failed.

The breach between the President and Congress was thus widened, the feeling of the Radical majority against the Southern people intensified, and the Reconstruction policy of that majority thereafter enforced with greater harshness than had ever seemed possible.

There were earnest protests against the passage and later against the enforcement of the Reconstruction acts—many prominent men and leading papers in the "loyal" States sharing the opinion of the Southern people that these pretended laws were unconstitutional and void. Efforts were made to have the judgment of the United States Supreme Court upon the validity of these statutes and the right of the President to carry them into effect.

On behalf of the State of Mississippi a motion was made for leave to file a bill in the name of the State, praying the court perpetually to enjoin and restrain Andrew Johnson, a citizen of the State of Tennessee and President of the United States, and his officers and agents appointed for that purpose, and especially E. O. C. Ord, assigned as military commander of the district including the State of Mississippi, from executing or in any manner carrying out the Reconstruction acts.

Attorney-General Stanbery, appearing for the President, objected to the bill as containing matter not fit to be received—saying in the conclusion of his argument: "So far as this bill seeks to make the President a party I have said from the first that it was scandalous. I mean of course in legal language—that is to say, a suit not fit to be brought and which no court in the United States can sustain. Therefore it is that as *amicus curiae* or as law officer next the President I have felt bound, at the first motion made to file this bill, to attempt to keep so scandalous a thing from the records of this court. It is with the approbation, advice and instruction of the President that I appear here to make this objection. I should have felt bound to make it on my own motion, as the law officer of the Government. But although counsel in their bill have said that the President has vetoed these acts of Congress as unconstitutional, I must say in defense of the President that when the President did that he did everything he intended to do in opposition to these laws. From the moment they were passed over his veto there was in his estimation but one duty resting upon him—and that was faithfully to execute and carry out these laws. He has instructed me to say that in making this objection, it is not for the purpose of escaping any responsibility either to perform or to refuse to perform."

The motion for leave to file the bill was refused on the ground that the President of the United States cannot be restrained by injunction from carrying into effect an act of Congress alleged to be unconstitutional, and a bill for that purpose cannot be filed.

Subsequently, on behalf of the State of Georgia, a bill was filed in the Supreme Court against Edwin M. Stanton as Secretary of War, U. S. Grant as general of the army, and John Pope, assigned to the command of the third military district, consisting of Georgia, Florida, and Alabama, for the purpose of restraining those officials from carrying into execution the Reconstruction acts of Congress. Attorney-General Stanbery moved to dismiss the bill for want of jurisdiction, and the application was granted, on the ground that the bill called for a judgment on a question political in its nature— the court thus declining to consider on their merits the grave constitutional questions presented.

An application was next made to the Supreme Court, on behalf of the State of Georgia, for leave to file a bill against General Grant, General Meade and others, having the same objects as those of the previous bill, but stated to be not open to the objections thereto sustained by the court. The motion was docketed for argument, but before it could be reached the Reconstruction acts had been put in force in Georgia, injunction had become impracticable, and the complainants' case thus came to nought.

In November, 1867, William H. McCardle, a citizen of Mississippi, was arrested by the order of the military commander of that State, claiming authority under the Reconstruction acts, and was held for trial, by military commission, on the charges (1) of disturbance of the public peace, (2) of inciting to insurrection, disorder and violence, (3) of libel, and (4) of impeding the execution of the Reconstruction acts. The Circuit Court of the United States for the district of Mississippi, in habeas corpus proceedings, decided that the accused was lawfully in the custody of the military authorities. On appeal the Supreme Court, first considering the question of jurisdiction, held that the appeal was properly taken—this at the December term, 1867. The case was argued on its merits on March 9, 1868, and was taken under advisement. On March 27 Congress passed over the President's veto an act repealing the law which had given the right of appeal from the Circuit Court to the Supreme Court. Upon further consideration the Supreme Court decided that under the repealing act McCardle's appeal was no longer effective and must be dismissed.

Thus every effort to have a judicial inquiry into the constitutionality of the Reconstruction acts was defeated by the action of the Government's law officers or by the action of Congress, evidently taken with the purpose to prevent such inquiry. The constitutional questions involved are yet open.

On June 12, 1867, Attorney-General Stanbery, on the previous request of the President, wrote an opinion in which, after an exhaustive and discriminating analysis of the Reconstruction acts, he advised that those laws were beyond the scope of the legislative authority vested in Congress by the Constitution, and were therefore neither binding upon the President nor lawfully enforceable by the measures and agencies therein provided.

Upon this opinion the President took no action, but in that connection he showed a purpose to obey and execute these laws until by some competent proceeding in the Supreme Court their validity should be judicially considered and determined.

Soon after the publication of the Attorney-General's opinion General Sickles, commanding one of the military districts created by the Reconstruction acts, addressed to the President a communication asking to be relieved of his command, on the ground that "the declaration of the Attorney-General that the military authority has not superseded the so-called State governments, declared illegal by Congress, prevents the execution of the Reconstruction acts, disarms me of means to protect life, property or the rights of citizens, and menaces all interests in the States with ruin." General Sickles further asked for a court of inquiry, whereby to disclose the character of his enforcement of the acts of Congress and to vindicate himself. These requests were by order of the President refused and General Sickles was ordered to retain command in his district.

THE REPUBLICAN PARTY ORGANIZED.

The passage of the Reconstruction acts having introduced the negro vote as the dominant factor in restoring South Carolina to her place in the Federal Union, Republican politicians were not slow to take steps to organize the negroes under the direction and control of the party to which these agitators professed allegiance. A convention of the Union Republican party of South Carolina met in Charleston on May 9, 1867, but on the next day, without transacting any business or making any declaration, adjourned to meet in Columbia on July 24. On that day there assembled the following delegates:

Abbeville—H. J. Lomax, Henry Sager.

Anderson—Samuel Johnson, Henry Kennedy.

Barnwell—C. P. Leslie, Northern white man and Government employee; Charles Fisher, Smart Folk, Fred Nix, William Allen, E. P. Stoney.

Beaufort—R. H. Gleaves, Northern negro; W. J. Whipper, Northern negro; E. G. Dudley, Northern white man and Government employee; W. H. Langley, Northern negro; J. J. Wright, Northern negro.

Charleston—J. P. M. Epping, naturalized citizen and Government employee; Gilbert Pillsbury, Northern white man and Government employee; E. W. M. Mackey, native white man and Government employee; C. C. Bowen, Southern white man; W. J. McKinlay, James D. Price, R. C. DeLarge, Peter Miller, R. Howard, Jr., P. Wall, James N. Hayne.

Chester—M. Blackwell, J. Humphreys, Dublin Walker, Barney Burton.

Clarendon—Elias E. Dickson, native white man; William McDowell.

Colleton—Gilbert Reece.

Darlington—B. F. Whittemore, Northern white man and Government employee; Alfred Bush, John A. Barnes, Isaac Brokenton, E. J. Snetter.

Fairfield—W. W. Herbert, Southern white man; Sandy Ford, Samuel Greer.

Greenville—W. A. Bishop, Southern white man; James M. Allen, Northern white man; Wilson Cook.

Kershaw—J. K. Jillson, Northern white man and Government employee.

Lexington—Simeon Corley, native white man; James Rawl.

Marion—H. E. Hayne, Edward Inman, B. A. Thompson.

Newberry—B. Odell Duncan, native white man; Joseph Boston, James Anderson, Simon Young, Matthew Gray.

Orangeburg—T. K. Sasportas, Northern negro and Government employee; B. F. Randolph, Northern negro; E. J. Cain, Northern negro; Thomas Phillips.

Richland—Thomas J. Robertson, native white man; C. H. Baldwin, Northern white man; C. M. Wilder, William Myers, S. B. Thompson.

Sumter—Joseph White, James Smylie, W. E. Johnson, Northern negro; J. G. Burrows.

York—John W. Mead.

All not otherwise specified were Southern negroes.

Officers were elected as follows:

President—R. H. Gleaves.

Vice-Presidents—C. M. Wilder, Thomas J. Robertson, Gilbert Pillsbury, James N. Hayne.

ORR'S ADMINISTRATION

Secretaries—W. J. McKinlay, R. Howard, Jr., T. K. Sasportas, E. E. Dixon.

Chaplain—Rev. J. Brockenton.

The platform declared for universal suffrage, elections by the people (except in the case of the judiciary), reorganization of the courts, the division and sale of unoccupied lands among the poorer classes, the cautious restoration of the rights of those lately guilty of "treason," the enforcement of the Reconstruction acts in the Southern States, ad valorem taxes, liberal provision by the State for "the poor and destitute, those aged and infirm people, houseless and homeless and past labor, who have none to care for them"; the repeal of the tax on cotton, and steadfast loyalty to the Union Republican party.

A resolution offered by J. J. Wright, of Beaufort, was passed, declaring that the colored man should "be represented by one of his own race on the next Presidential ticket of the Republican party."

The State Executive Board was organized as follows: President, B. F. Whittemore; Vice-President, B. F. Randolph; Secretary, W. J. McKinlay; Treasurer, J. P. M. Epping.

The State Central Committee was appointed as follows: Abbeville, H. J. Lomax; Anderson, Samuel Johnson; Barnwell, C. P. Leslie; Beaufort, J. J. Wright; Charleston, Gilbert Pillsbury; Chester, Barney Burton; Chesterfield, H. L. Shrewsbury; Colleton, William M. Viney; Darlington, J. E. Brockenton; Fairfield, Samuel B. Clowney; Georgetown, Joseph H. Rainey; Greenville, Wilson Cook; Kershaw, J. K. Jillson; Lexington, John S. Hendrix; Marion, H. E. Hayne; Newberry, Matthew Gray; Orangeburg, J. K. Sasportas; Richland, C. M. Wilder; Sumter, William E. Johnston; York, John W. Mead.

Upon the adoption of the platform as above summarized, Mr. B. Odell Duncan, of Newberry, announced that he must withdraw from the Convention because he could not pledge loyalty to the party—this on account of the declaration as to the division of certain lands, which was in these words: "That as large land monopolies tend only to make the rich richer and the poor poorer, and are ruinous to the agricultural, commercial and social interests of the State, the Legislature should offer every practicable inducement for the division and sale of unoccupied lands among the poorer classes, and as an encouragement for immigrants to settle in our State."

Mr. Lemuel Boozer, who had been elected as a delegate from Lexington, sent a letter regretting his inability to attend and expressing his endorsement of the objects of the Convention.

Mr. W. J. Armstrong, who had been sent from Washington by the National Republican Committee "to visit this Convention," was elected an honorary member of the body.

The committee on finance reported that the expenses of the Convention were $36.25 and the collections $46.

THE UNION LEAGUE.

While the negroes in South Carolina were openly invited to join the Republican party they were secretly enjoined to unite with another organization—the Union League—which had a powerful influence upon them.

In 1862, when the repeated victories of the Confederate armies had caused apprehensions among the Northern people for the safety of the Union as contemplated by them, and when there was more or less "disloyalty" among them, there began a movement for the formation of "loyal leagues," the mission of which was to organize and cement the Unionists and at the same time crush out the doubting or disaffected. Thus was instituted the Union League of America, the object of which, as declared in its constitution, was "to preserve liberty and the union of the United States of America; to maintain the constitution thereof and the supremacy of the laws; to sustain the government and assist in putting down its enemies; to protect, strengthen and defend all loyal men, without regard to sect, condition or race; and to elect honest and reliable union men to all offices of profit or trust in National, State and local government; and to secure equal civil and political rights to all men under the government."

All loyal citizens of the age of eighteen years and upward (including aliens who should have declared their intention to become citizens) were eligible to membership. There was a National council, whilst each State had its council directing and controlling as many district councils thereunder as might be deemed necessary.

Upon initiation into a council the member was required, amid much form and ceremony, to take the following oath:

I do solemnly swear, in the presence of God and these witnesses, that I will never voluntarily bear arms against the United States while I am a citizen thereof; that I will support, protect and defend the Constitution and the Government of the United States and the flag thereof, against all enemies, foreign and domestic; that I will bear true faith and allegiance to the same; and that I will also defend this State against any invasion, insurrection or rebellion, to the extent of my ability. This I freely pledge without mental reservation or evasion. Furthermore, that I will do all in my power to elect true and reliable Union men and supporters of the Government, and none others, to all offices of profit or trust, from the lowest to the highest, in ward, town, county, State and general government. And should I ever be called to fill any office I will faithfully carry out the objects and principles of this League. And further, that I will protect, aid and defend all worthy members of the Union League, and that I will never make known in any way, to any person or persons not members of the Union League, any of the signs or passwords, proceedings, debates or plans of this or any other council under this organization, except when engaged in admitting new members into this League. [Place your right hand upon the Holy Bible.] And with my hand upon the Holy Bible, Declaration of Independence and the Constitution of the United States of America, under the seal of my sacred honor, I acknowledge myself firmly bound and pledged to the faithful performance of this my solemn obligation. So help me God. To defend and perpetuate freedom and the Union I pledge my life, my fortune and my sacred honor. So help me God.

In connection with the work of the Union League there were distributed by its agents among the negroes of the South a paper purporting to represent a dialogue between a "sound Radical Republican" and a newly enfranchised freedman seeking light upon the subject of his political duties. By this catechism it was enjoined upon the colored man that he should vote with the Union Republican party because that party made him free and gave him the right to vote; that the friends of the colored race in Congress belong to that party; that a Democrat was a "member of that party which before the rebellion sustained every legislative act demanded by the slaveholders, such as the fugitive slave law and the attempt made to force slavery upon the western territories"; that the Democratic party "resisted every measure in Congress looking to emancipation, and denounced the Government for arming colored men as soldiers"; that the Democratic party was otherwise known as "Conservative, Copperhead and Rebel, and under each name is still the same enemy of freedom and the rights of man"; that it was fair to presume that the Democrats would make slaves of the colored people if they could, and would not allow colored men to vote—having "tried to keep them in slavery and opposed giving them the benefit of the Freedmen's Bureau and Civil Rights bill and the right to vote"; that the Democratic party would disfranchise the colored people and if possible return them to slavery; that that party was composed of the "slaveholders and leaders of the rebellion"; that the colored men should vote with the Republican party and "shun the Democratic party as they would the overseer's lash and the auction block"; that if the colored men should vote with the Democratic party "the people of the North would think that they did not fully understand either their own rights or the duties devolving on them"; that the money which the colored people of the Southern States had paid as taxes had been used to establish schools for white children, to pay the expenses of making and executing laws in which the colored people had had no voice, and in endeavoring to have the Supreme Court set aside the law which gave the colored man the right to vote; and that the colored people ought to suffer or even starve to death rather than aid the Democratic party to enslave them.

The emissaries of the League went secretly but actively to work among the negroes in every part of South Carolina, so that upon the first opportunity of the whites to present public matters to the men of that race these had already become members of a secret, oath-bound organization wherein, as the members actually declared, they had solemnly sworn to vote the Republican ticket.

THE SICKLES ADMINISTRATION.

On March 21, 1867, Maj.-Gen. Daniel E. Sickles, U. S. A., by appointment of the President, acting under the provisions of the Reconstruction acts, formally assumed command of the second military district, including North and South Carolina. By that order the commanding general in terms assumed all the powers vested in him by those acts.

This State was divided into eleven military posts, each under the command of an officer of the army, as follows:

Post of Charleston—Berkeley, Charleston, Colleton.

Post of Hilton Head—Beaufort.

Post of Georgetown—Horry, Georgetown.

Post of Darlington—Williamsburg, Marion, Darlington, Marlboro, Chesterfield.

Post of Sumter—Clarendon, Sumter.
Post of Aiken—Barnwell, Edgefield.
Post of Columbia—Orangeburg, Kershaw, Richland, Lexington.
Post of Newberry—Newberry, Laurens, Abbeville.
Post of Anderson—Greenville, Anderson, Pickens.
Post of Unionville—Spartanburg, Union.
Post of Chester—York, Chester, Fairfield, Lancaster.

The whole number of troops employed to garrison these posts was nineteen companies averaging 100 men each, besides line and staff officers.

One of the first acts of General Sickles in the administration of his government was the issuance, April 11, 1867, of General Order No. 10, which excited much criticism at the time. By this order imprisonment for debt was abolished; execution was stayed for twelve months on all causes of action arising between December 19, 1860, and May 15, 1865; sales were suspended for a like period on all judgments recovered prior to December 19, 1860, unless the debtor should consent to execution; a homestead of twenty acres of land, together with $500 in personal property, was declared exempt from levy or sale for any debt; the death penalty for burglary and for horse-stealing was abolished, and imprisonment for a term of years substituted; whipping as a punishment for any crime or misdemeanor was prohibited; the carrying of concealed weapons was declared a crime; and the pardoning power was conceded to the Governor of the State, though resting concurrently in the district commander.

By subsequent orders, the remedy by distress for the collection of rent was abolished; common carriers were prohibited from making any distinction whatever on account of race, color or previous condition of servitude; the distillation of spirituous liquors was absolutely prohibited; quarantine of the several seaports was established under military supervision; all male persons assessed for taxes, without regard to race or color, were declared eligible as jurors, and the several judges were ordered to enforce this provision; sheriffs, chiefs of police, city marshals and town marshals were required to obey the orders of provost marshals, to report their own name, official position and date of commision to the district commander, and also to make to him a monthly report setting forth the arrests and commitments made by them, escapes and discharges, together with the condition of their jails or guardhouses.

By several special orders General Sickles illustrated and enforced his views of his own powers and of the purposes of the acts of Congress under which he proceeded.

On the occasion of the annual parade of the Charleston fire department (April 27, 1867), he ordered that the United States flag, attended by a color guard of two men from each company, should precede the procession (which had for years carried only the different company banners), and that on its arrival at the reviewing stand the flag should be saluted by each man in the several companies passing in front—each man being required to uncover when three paces from the flag and so remain till three paces beyond it. This order was duly carried out—the parade being delayed a few hours in order to procure a flag and arrange other details. Disobedience would have caused the instant arrest of the department chief with others to be selected by General Sickles, and their incarceration in his discretion. A young gentleman who, losing his temper under the provocation naturally given by the order of Sickles, cut with his knife a national flag used to decorate the hook-and-ladder truck, and not flying as colors, was arrested, confined without trial for a month, and then discharged with a reprimand published in an order.

The district court of Edgefield was abolished and in its place was created a special provost court composed of two military officers and one civilian, appointed by General Sickles.

By a "special order" issued August 7, 1867, General Sickles reviewed a decree of Chancellor Henry D. Lesesne in the case of the Bank of Charleston against the Bank of the State of South Carolina, and set it aside as "without jurisdiction, erroneous, irregular and a fraud upon the rights of the United States." The order contained a suggestion of a combination among certain of the lawyers engaged in the cause to conceal the proceedings from the Federal officials, who claimed that their Government had some interest in a part of the fund distributed by the decree, because that part was assets of the Confederate Government; and it appeared to impute connivance to the Chancellor himself. The order finally directed that the fund should be paid over to the receiver (a military officer), appointed by General Sickles, and remain in the receiver's hands until further orders. The money was afterwards distributed by military order.

It is safe to say that no act of any military commander in the South ever gave greater offense than this order of General Sickles did to every reputable citizen of South Carolina who was informed of the proceeding. The attorneys whom the military commander aspersed were of the highest character personally and professionally—William D. Porter, James Conner, Charles H. Simonton, Theodore G. Barker. These gentlemen set forth the facts of the case in statements in the press, whereby they pointed out the infamous character of Sickles's performance and showed that neither they nor the Chancellor could be open to suspicion or even to criticism. The aspersion upon the good name of the Chancellor was especially an outrage—for no life had been purer, no career had been more honorable, no man's character was higher, than that of Henry D. Lesesne. So great was the public disgust at this order of General Sickles that it was freely intimated that he himself had been corrupted or, at the best, influenced by unworthy persons actuated by corrupt motives.

By order of General Sickles the captain of a steamer plying between Charleston and Beaufort was tried by military commission on the charge of refusing a first-class passage to a mulatto woman of the name of Rollin—who, by the way, afterwards figured as a recipient of fraudulent pay certificates issued by F. J. Moses, Jr., Speaker of the House. Conviction followed as a matter of course and the captain was sentenced to a fine of $250.

On the occasion of the Union Republican Convention in Columbia there were in the city William J. Armstrong, already mentioned as the promoter sent by the National Republican Committee, and J. Q. Thompson, a correspondent of one or more newspapers of the Radical type. By their offensive behavior these men became involved in a personal difficulty with two citizens and were considerably worsted. Upon the warrant of a magistrate they were arrested and then released upon amply sufficient surety. By the advice of friends the accused expressed to the post commander at Columbia, and through him to the parties claiming to be aggrieved, their regrets at the occurrence. On the unsworn complaint of Thompson, General Sickles had the two citizens arrested, taken to Charleston and sentenced to six months' imprisonment in Fort Macon, N. C., where they were detained for the greater part of the term. The magistrate who had taken the gentlemen's recognizances was summarily removed, without opportunity for defense or explanation, on the alleged ground of having taken insufficient bail.

Early in his administration General Sickles took occasion to notify Governor Orr that all public officers, in whatever department of the State, district or municipal governments, held their places at the will of the district commander, who only was authorized to appoint a successor. Governor Orr made no sign of dissent from this determination, to which, of course, neither objection nor resistance would have availed anything. All appointees of the district commander were required to take the test oath.

Among the appointments made by General Sickles was that of Mr. William S. Hastie to be sheriff of Charleston, in the place of Col. John E. Carew, the incumbent. To test the military commander's right to make this appointment, proceedings were had before Judge Franklin J. Moses, Sr., of the circuit court, who sustained the act of the military authority. An appeal was taken from this decision but was not perfected—so that the questions made were never taken to the court of last resort. Various other appointments were made by General Sickles, simply carrying out his ideas of his powers under the Reconstruction acts.

By an order of the President, dated August 31, 1867, General Sickles was relieved of his command in the military district embracing the Carolinas—this because, by the enforcement of his General Order No. 10, he had unduly interfered with the process of the United States court in North Carolina. It was publicly stated at this time that General Sickles had in this State avoided a conflict with the Federal court (whose authority and mandates Judge Bryan had shown a decided purpose to enforce) by allowing the process and mandates of that tribunal to be enforced in disregard of General Order No. 10.

Upon the removal of General Sickles, Governor Orr wrote him a letter, expressing regret at the President's action, and also declaring that the General's administration in South Carolina had been marked by "wisdom and success—moderation and forbearance." Governor Orr especially commended the issuance and enforcement of the "relief" provisions of General Order No. 10. He further declared that but for the "wisdom, moderation and forbearance" of General Sickles a considerable number of troops would have been necessary to "preserve public records and insure the safety of sheriffs and other officials"—Governor Orr's reference here being to the really distressful condition of many of the debtor class, who had in fact sought relief at the hands of the Legislature, but who really had no purpose to resist process, to destroy public records, or in any way to interfere with the due execution of the laws.

The Legislature had indeed passed a stay law embodying provisions similar to those in General Order No. 10, but the court of errors—composed of all the appeal court justices, the law judges and the chancellors—had declared the exemption in favor of debtors to be contrary to certain provisions of the State and the Federal Constitution—a fact strongly suggestive of the extraordinary character of General Sickles's legislation.

THE CANBY ADMINISTRATION.

On September 5, 1867, Brevet Maj.-Gen. E. R. S. Canby, U. S. A., assumed command of the second military district.

Among the first of General Canby's orders was a modification of General Order No. 10—the new order directing that where sales of property should be made under decree or execution the sale should be postponed for three months unless the highest bid therefor should be a sum equal to two-thirds of the actual value. In other respects the Order No. 10 stood unchanged.

By an order dated September 13, 1867, General Canby directed that "all citizens assessed for taxes, and who shall have paid taxes for the current year and who are qualified and have been or may be duly registered as voters, are hereby declared qualified to serve as jurors," and that "any requirement of a property qualification for jurors, in addition to the qualification herein prescribed, as hereby abrogated." The judges were directed to revise the jury lists in conformity with the order—the effect of which was to make negroes eligible as jurors.

In charging the grand jury of Edgefield at the fall term, 1867, Judge Aldrich called attention to this order in relation to jurors and declared that he could not and would not obey it. The jury law of 1831, which Judge Aldrich held himself bound to obey, required that the juror in the circuit court must be a white male citizen, or an emigrant from Europe, who should have given notice of his intention to become a naturalized citizen, a resident of the State for one year and also a taxpayer on property held in his own right. General Canby's order, already noticed, explicitly abrogated certain of these qualifications.

At Barnwell, some days afterwards, Judge Aldrich, ready to open court as directed by the statute, received an order from General Canby, purporting to suspend him from the office to which he had been elected by the Legislature acting under the express authority of the State Constitution. After reading the order in open court, the judge announced that in forced obedience to the command of General Canby he would "lay down his office for the present." Then, laying aside his robe, he spoke as follows:

Gentlemen of the juries, for the present, farewell; but if God spares my life I will yet preside in this court, a South Carolina judge whose ermine is unstained. My brethren of the bar, be patient—be loyal to the Constitution—be true to yourselves. Mr. Clerk, as I am not permitted to perform any judicial act, you and the sheriff will issue to the jurors their pay certificates as if the judge had not attended. Mr. Sheriff, let the court stand adjourned while the voice of justice is stifled.

(Judge Aldrich's defiant prediction was verified by his election in 1878 to the circuit bench, where for twelve years he served as honorably as he had done before he was removed at the point of the bayonet.)

Judge Aldrich afterwards called General Canby's attention to his order directing the State Treasurer not to pay the salary provided by law. General Canby justified his order by referring to the Judge's retirement, caused by his refusal to comply with the order in relation to juries, and declined to recede. Judge Aldrich responded in a spirited letter, denouncing General Canby's course as an act of "monstrous tyranny." A few weeks later the Judge was formally removed and in his place General Canby appointed Mr. Zephaniah Platt, of New York, a well-meaning old gentleman of small abilities and moderate attainments, then wintering at Aiken.

By an order dated October 19, 1867, General Canby forbade the holding of the regular municipal election in Charleston. The incumbent council continued in the exercise of its functions until January 1, 1868, when the district commander, to fill a vacancy caused by the death of an alderman, appointed Niles G. Parker, who was afterwards conspicuous as chief among the robbers who, controlling the State government, defrauded the State in various ways.

Shortly afterward Mayor Peter C. Gaillard was removed and Col. W. W. Burns, U. S. A., was assigned to fill the place. Later Col. Milton Cogswell, U. S. A., was appointed, and finally Mr. George W. Clark, a Northern man, who held on until the election under an act of the Legislature of 1868. Constant changes were made in the board of aldermen, so that finally out of eighteen there remained but four who had been chosen by the people. General Canby's appointees included seven white men and seven negroes. No cause was assigned for any of the removals.

In some of the towns General Canby appointed the entire municipal force—intendant, wardens, clerk and marshal.

In a few districts, as occasion arose, sheriffs and magistrates were appointed. In Columbia, to succeed Magistrate J. T. Zealy, whose summary removal by General Sickles has been mentioned, General Canby appointed W. Beverly Nash, a black negro who was grossly incompetent, whose incendiary talks had caused friction between the races, and who a few years later was active among the minor Republican thieves who helped to rob the people of South Carolina.

By the order of General Canby taxes were levied and appropriations were made for the support of the different departments of the State Government—the collections and disbursements being committed to the several State and district officers holding under the Constitution of 1865 and the acts of "so-called" Legislatures.

It has already been stated that the session of 1866 was the last one of the General Assembly elected under the Constitution of 1865. The election of a new body should, by the mandate of the Constitution, have been held on the third Wednesday in October, and by the statute it was made the duty of the Governor to make the necessary appointment of managers and otherwise arrange for the election. Governor Orr having given no sign of a purpose to obey the Constitution and laws in this regard, the Hon. I. W. Hayne, Attorney-General of South Carolina, on September 10, 1867, addressed to his Excellency a letter calling his attention to the fact that, unless steps should be taken and instructions be given to the managers to hold an election at the proper time for members of the House of Representatives and for a portion of the Senate, the State would be left without any legislative authority. To that letter Governor Orr made no answer. It must be regarded as certain that had the Governor taken any steps along the lines stated by the Attorney-General the military commander would have interposed his authority to prevent the execution of the laws.

From a review of the "administrations" of Generals Sickles and Canby—whose policies were illustrated by numerous acts of oppression, other than those here noted—it will be seen that in the enforcement of the Reconstruction acts these military commanders exercised every power known to our system of government—whether resting in the people themselves, in the legislative assembly, in the executive, in the courts from the highest to the lowest, in the municipalities or in the ministerial officers holding under the statutes.

THE NEGRO ENFRANCHISED BY CONGRESS.

There were differences of opinion among the white people of South Carolina as to the acceptance of the terms which Congress in the Reconstruction acts had fixed as conditions precedent to the cessation of bayonet rule and the restoration of the State to her place in the Federal Union. On the one hand was the absolutism of the military authority, against which neither protest nor entreaty was of any avail, and which so disordered things that not only the liberties of the people, but their property rights and business interests, were seriously affected. Among those who, from the very inception of the Congressional scheme as embodied in the Reconstruction acts, earnestly, vehemently opposed any surrender to the requirements of the Radicals was ex-Governor Perry. In a series of letters to the press he analyzed the Radical program, pointed out its cruelty and infamy, and showed how its enforcement must bring ruin and dishonor alike upon the State. These articles went far to shape sentiment among the white people into the determination to reject the offers of peace as embodied in the measures of Congress and to submit to its mandates under coercion only. General Wade Hampton also, in response to a request for his views, urged that every white man register and then vote against the proposed convention. When, therefore, there arose a question whether the conqueror's terms of peace would be accepted, it was certain that such acceptance would be the separate act of the negro population aided by a very small body of white men—most of the latter being irresponsible and some of them disreputable.

By the orders of General Sickles, issued July 19 and August 1, 1867, there was a registration of the voters of South Carolina, in accordance with the terms laid down in the Reconstruction acts—the times and places to be fixed by the several post commanders—the commander being the superintendent of registration within his territory. In every district there were provided three boards of registration, each having three members, except that in some districts the number of boards was enlarged for special reasons. Every member of a board was required to take the test oath, and negroes, equally with whites, were eligible to membership.

Before being permitted to register every applicant was required to "solemnly swear (or affirm) in the presence of Almighty God" that he was qualified to vote under the provisions of the Reconstruction act and, with more particularity, in the following words: "That I have never been a member of any State Legislature, nor held any executive or judicial office in any State, and afterwards engaged in insurrection or rebellion against the United States, or given aid or comfort to the enemies thereof; that I have never taken oath as a member of the Congress of the United States or as an officer of the United States, or as a member of any State Legislature, or as an executive or judicial officer of any State, to support the Constitution of the United States, and afterwards engaged in insurrection or rebellion, or given aid or comfort to the enemies thereof; that I will faithfully support the Constitution and obey the laws of the United States and will to the best of my ability encourage others so to do."

The registration of voters was completed about the middle of October, and showed 46,346 whites and 78,982 blacks, distributed as follows:

Districts.	Whites.	Blacks.
Abbeville	1,722	3,352
Anderson	1,801	1,398
Barnwell	1,902	3,695
Beaufort	927	6,278
Berkeley	982	8,264
Charleston	3,452	5,111
Chester	1,222	2,198
Chesterfield	1,071	317
Clarendon	754	1,552
Colleton	1,370	3,870

Districts.	Whites.	Blacks.
Darlington	1,572	2,910
Edgefield	2,507	4,367
Fairfield	942	2,434
Georgetown	432	2,725
Greenville	2,077	1,485
Horry	1,065	466
Kershaw	859	1,765
Lancaster	983	881
Laurens	1,628	2,372
Lexington	1,480	975
Marion	1,837	1,737
Marlboro	961	1,207
Newberry	1,131	2,251
Orangeburg	1,645	3,371
Pickens	2,075	851
Richland	1,236	2,812
Spartanburg	2,690	1,462
Sumter	1,190	3,285
Williamsburg	800	1,725
Union	1,426	1,893
York	2,606	2,072

The vote on the calling of a State Convention was taken on November 19 and 20, and showed—for the Convention, 130 whites and 68,876 blacks; against the Convention, 2,801 whites. The total vote cast was only 71,087.

THE WHITE PEOPLE PROTEST.

At a meeting of "conservative (white) citizens," held in Columbia on September 21, 1867, it was resolved that "a committee of nine be appointed to invite a meeting in this city of delegates from the various districts of the State, to deliberate upon the present condition of our political affairs."

In response to this invitation the proposed Convention assembled in Columbia on November 6, there being delegates present from twenty districts—Anderson, Barnwell, Beaufort, Chester, Chesterfield, Colleton, Edgefield, Fairfield, Greenville, Kershaw, Laurens, Lexington, Marlboro, Newberry, Orangeburg, Pickens, Richland, Sumter, Union and York.

Officers were elected as follows:

President—James Chesnut, of Kershaw.

Vice-Presidents—Wade Hampton, of Richland; B. F. Perry, of Greenville; John A. Inglis, of Chesterfield; A. P. Aldrich, of Barnwell; John D. Kennedy, of Kershaw; John Bratton, of Fairfield; Simeon Fair, of Newberry; Joseph Daniel Pope, of Beaufort.

Secretaries—John T. Sloan and Felix G. DeFontaine, of Columbia.

The action of the Convention consisted only in the issuance of an address to the people of South Carolina, reviewing the situation and suggesting the course to be pursued by them. The purport of this address, so far as it related to pending political questions, may be gathered from the following extracts:

We desire peace for its own sake, for its holy Christian influence, and for the civilization and refinement which spring up in its path. Do the Reconstruction acts of Congress propose to give us this peace? No—they give us war and anarchy, rather. They sow the seeds of discord in our midst and place the best interests of society into the hands of an ignorant mob. They disfranchise the white citizen and enfranchise the newly emancipated slave. The slave of yesterday, who knew no law but the will of the master, is today about to be invested with the control of the government. In all popular governments the two great sources of power may be traced, (1) to the exercise of the ballot, (2) to the franchise of the jury box. Invest any people with these two great powers, and they have at once the government of the country in their hands. By the Reconstruction acts of Congress these powers are conferred upon the negro— he can make and unmake the Constitution and the laws which he will administer according to the dictates of others or his own caprice.

We are not unfriendly to the negro; on the contrary, we know that we are his best friends. In his property, in his life and in his person we are willing that the black man and the white man shall stand together upon the same platform and be shielded by the same equal laws. We venture the opinion that the people of South Carolina are prepared to adopt as their own the Constitution of any New England or other Northern State, wherein it is supposed that the civil rights of the negro are most fully and amply secured. But upon a question involving such grave and momentous issues we should be untrue to ourselves and unfair to our opponents were we to withhold the frank and full expression of our opinions. We, therefore, feeling the responsibility of the subject and the occasion, enter our most solemn protest against the policy of investing the negro with political rights. The black man is what God and nature and circumstances have made him. That he is not fit to be invested with these important rights may be no fault of his. But the fact is patent to all that the negro is utterly unfitted to exercise the highest functions of the citizen. The government of the country should not be permitted to pass from the hands of the white man into the hands of the negro. The enforcement of the Reconstruction acts by military power under the guise of negro voters and negro conventions cannot lawfully reestablish civil government in South Carolina. It may for a time hold us in subjection to a quasi-civil government backed by military force, but it can do no more. As citizens of the United States we should not consent to live under negro supremacy, nor should we acquiesce in negro equality. Not for ourselves only, but on behalf of the Anglo-Saxon race and blood in this country, do we protest against this subversion of the great social law, whereby an ignorant and depraved race is placed in power and influence above the virtuous, the educated and the refined. By these acts of Congress intelligence and virtue are put under foot, while ignorance and vice are lifted into power. . . .

We have shown that free negro labor, under the sudden emancipation policy of the Government, is a disaster from which, under the most favorable circumstances, it will require years to recover. Add to this the policy which the Reconstruction acts propose to enforce, and you place the South politically and socially under the heel of the negro. These influences combined would drag to hopeless ruin the most prosperous community in the world. What do these Reconstruction acts propose? Not negro equality merely, but negro supremacy.

In the name, then, of humanity to both races—in the name of citizenship under the Constitution—in the name of a common history in the past—in the name of our Anglo-Saxon race and blood—in the name of the civilization of the nineteenth century—in the name of magnanimity and the noble instincts of manhood—in the name of God and nature—we protest against these Reconstruction acts as destructive to the peace of society, the prosperity of the country and the greatness and grandeur of our common future.

The people of the South are powerless to avert the impending ruin. We have been overborne; and the responsibility to posterity and to the world has passed into other hands.

THE RECONSTRUCTION CONVENTION.

In obedience to General Order No. 160 of Brevet Maj.-Gen. E. R. S. Canby, U. S. A., dated December 28, 1867, the delegates elected to the "convention of the people of South Carolina" assembled in Charleston on January 14, 1868, "for the purpose of framing a constitution and civil government" according to the provisions of the Reconstruction acts of Congress. General Canby directed that "a copy of this order [No. 160] will be furnished to each of the persons hereinafter named and shall be the evidence of his having been elected a delegate to the aforesaid convention." The delegates present, accordingly, were the following:

Abbeville—John A. Hunter, B. Milford, white; H. J. Lomax, W. N. Joiner, Thomas Williamson, colored.

Anderson—William Perry, N. J. Newell, white; Samuel Johnson, colored.

Berkeley—M. F. Becker, D. H. Chamberlain, Timothy Hurley, Joseph H. Jenks, A. C. Richmond, white; William Jervey, Benjamin Byas, W. H. W. Gray, George Lee, colored.

Beaufort—J. D. Bell, R. G. Holmes, white; F. E. Wilder, L. S. Langley, W. J. Whipper, Robert Smalls, J. J. Wright, colored.

Barnwell—C. P. Leslie, Niles G. Parker, white; James N. Hayne, A. Middleton, C. D. Hayne, Julius Mayer, colored.

Charleston—A. G. Mackey, C. C. Bowen, Gilbert Pillsbury, white; F. L. Cardozo, William McKinlay, R. H. Cain, R. C. DeLarge, A. J. Ransier, colored.

Chester—Purvis Alexander, Barney Burton, Sancho Sanders, colored.

Chesterfield—R. J. Donaldson, white; H. L. Shrewsbury, colored.

Clarendon—Elias E. Dickson, white; William Nelson, colored.

Colleton—J. S. Craig, white; William M. Thomas, William Driffle, W. M. Vinery, colored.

Darlington—B. F. Whittemore, white; Isaac Brockenton, Jordan Lang, Richard Humbird, colored.

Edgefield—Frank Arnim, white; R. B. Elliott, Prince R. Rivers, John Bonum, David Harris, John Wooley, colored.

Fairfield—James M. Rutland, white; H. D. Edwards, Henry Jacob, colored.

Georgetown—Henry W. Webb, white; F. F. Miller, Joseph H. Rainey, colored.

Greenville—James M. Allen, J. M. Runion, white; Wilson Cook, W. B. Johnson, colored.

Horry—Henry Jones, A. R. Thompson, colored.

Kershaw—J. K. Jillson, S. G. W. Dill, white; John A. Chestnut, colored.

Lancaster—Albert Clinton, Charles Jones, colored.

Lexington—Lemuel Boozer, Simeon Corley, white.

Laurens—Joseph Crews, Y. J. P. Owens, white; Harry McDaniels, Nelson Davis, colored.

Marion—W. S. Collins, white; J. W. Johnson, H. E. Hayne, B. A. Thompson, colored.

Marlboro—Calvin Stubbs, George Jackson, colored.

Newberry—B. O. Duncan, white; James Henderson, Lee Nance, colored.

Orangeburg—E. W. M. Mackey, white; E. J. Cain, W. J. McKinlay, T. K. Sasportas, B. F. Randolph, colored.

Pickens—M. Mauldin, Alexander Bryce, L. B. Johnson, white.

Richland—Thomas J. Robertson, white; W. B. Nash, S. B. Thompson, C. M. Wilder, colored.

Spartanburg—J. P. F. Camp, J. S. Gentry, white; Rice Foster, Coy Wingo, colored.

Sumter—T. J. Coghlan, F. J. Moses, Jr., white; W. E. Johnston, Samuel Lee, colored.

Union—J. H. Goss, white; Abram Dogan, Samuel Nuckles, colored.

Williamsburg—William Darrington, white; C. M. Olsen, S. A. Swails, colored.

York—J. L. Neagle, William E. Rose, white; J. W. Mead, J. H. White, colored.

Three of the delegates elected failed to attend—F. A. Sawyer, white, Charleston; John K. Terry, white, Colleton; George D. Meddis, colored, Edgefield.

Of the 124 delegates elected, forty-eight were white and seventy-six colored. The white men classed as Republicans were about equally divided as natives or newcomers—in the vernacular of the times, "scalawags" or "carpetbaggers."

The following table gives the previous residences of the delegates:

Whites.		Negroes.	
South Carolina	23	South Carolina	59
North Carolina	3	Pennsylvania	2
Georgia	1	Michigan	1
Massachusetts	7	Georgia	1
Connecticut	1	Tennessee	1
Rhode Island	1	Ohio	1
New York	1	North Carolina	1

Whites.		Negroes.	
Other Northern States	5	Virginia	1
England	2	Massachusetts	2
Ireland	1	Dutch Guiana	1
Prussia	1	Unknown	6
Denmark	1		—
Unknown	1		76
	48		

Of the Barnwell delegation Niles G. Parker was an alderman of Charleston, and James N. Hayne a very recent resident of that city. E. W. M. Mackey moved up from Charleston to Orangeburg in order to represent the latter district, and immediately upon the adjournment of the Convention resumed his residence in the city. B. F. Randolph lived in Charleston while representing Orangeburg. R. B. Elliott lived in Charleston while representing Edgefield.

Of the white delegates twenty-three paid no tax whatever; of the total tax paid by the other whites ($761.62) one member, Mr. Perry, "Conservative," of Anderson, paid $508.85, leaving $252.76 paid by the remaining forty-six—or less than $6.00 each.

Of the colored delegates fifty-nine paid no tax at all; of the total tax paid by the colored members one, William McKinlay, of Charleston, paid $85.35—leaving the amount paid by the remaining seventy-three to be $32.58, or less than fifty cents each.

The total tax paid by the 120 Republican delegates present was $359.70—an average of less than $3.00 each.

Dr. Albert G. Mackey was elected president, and the office of secretary was given to Carlos J. Stolbrand, of Beaufort, lately a soldier in Sherman's army. A full complement of subordinate officers was provided for. Quite a discussion arose over the proposition to elect a chaplain, but it was finally decided to have each day's proceedings opened with prayer by a clergyman to be selected by the president. There were several preachers in the body.

The sergeant-at-arms first elected—a negro of the name of Edward Conway—was at once found to be incompetent and was summarily made to resign.

The pay of members was fixed at $11.00 a day, and 20 cents per mile for coming and going—these sums payable in "bills receivable," the scrip previously issued by the Legislature, worth eighty cents on the dollar. The per diem of attaches and employees ranged from $3.00 to $11.00, payable, of course, in bills receivable.

The policy, temper and ideas of this body may be judged by some of its proceedings in matters having no relation to the framing of a constitution.

The *Charleston Mercury* was violently denounced, and its reporters were excluded from the hall—this on the motion of D. H. Chamberlain.

A negro delegate from Richland—S. B. Thompson—offered a resolution demanding the summary removal of Maj. Thomas B. Lee, Superintendent of the State Penitentiary—this on the alleged ground of cruelty to convicts. An investigation by a military commission soon afterwards showed Thompson's charge to have been utterly false. By a later resolution General Canby was requested to remove Major Lee and appoint William E. Rose, of York.

Beverly Nash, of Richland, offered a section taxing uncultivated lands one per cent. higher than those under cultivation.

Congress was requested to lend the State $1,000,000 for the purchase of lands to be resold on long time to persons in South Carolina.

T. J. Coghlan, of Sumter, offered a section expunging from the vocabulary of South Carolina the words "negro," "nigger," and "yankee," and making the opprobrious use of any of those terms a misdemeanor punishable by fine and imprisonment.

By resolution General Canby was requested to order a further stay, for three months, of all executions and all sales of property for any debt whatsoever. The district commander issued his order accordingly.

By ordinance, contracts made for the purchase of slaves were declared void and the courts were prohibited from issuing process for their collection. General Canby was requested to issue an order to enforce this ordinance, but he forbore to act in the premises.

On motion of D. H. Chamberlain, General Canby was requested to abolish the district courts, dismiss their judges and declare vacant all offices incident to such courts. On this request General Canby took no action.

Congress was requested to donate to the State, for distribution among the freedmen, the land which had here been sold for non-payment of the direct tax—the value of such lands being estimated at $700,000.

A commission was appointed to frame and submit to the Legislature a scheme of "financial relief" for the people of the State.

The Convention adjourned *sine die* on March 18—after a session of fifty-three working days. The cost of the session was about $110,000.

The new Constitution contained many provisions which made that instrument materially different from the one adopted in 1865.

The paramount allegiance of the citizen was declared to be to the Constitution and Government of the United States, and the oath required of all officials contained the acknowledgment of that allegiance.

In indictments for libel the truth of the publication might be given in evidence—the jury being the judges of the law and the facts.

Offenses less than felony, in which the punishment should not exceed $100 fine or thirty days' imprisonment, were made triable without the intervention of a grand jury.

Imprisonment for debt was abolished, and a homestead exemption of $1,000 in lands and $500 in personalty was allowed to the head of every family.

Representation was apportioned according to population only.

The judicial districts were designated as counties, and Pickens district was divided into two counties—Pickens and Oconee.

The age of eligibility of Senators was fixed at twenty-five—the old Constitution fixing it at thirty. Members of either house must have resided one year in the State and three months in the county—the old Constitution having required in the case of the Senators a residence of five years and for the Representatives three years.

The regular meetings of the General Assembly were fixed for the fourth Tuesday in November of each year.

The pay of members of the Legislature was fixed at $6.00 per day, with 20 cents per mile of travel in going to and returning from the place of meeting—with leave to the body to reduce these figures.

The term of the Governor and Lieutenant-Governor was fixed at two years—each being eligible to reelection. The term of the Comptroller-General, Treasurer, Attorney-General, Adjutant and Inspector-General, Secretary of State, and Superintendent of Education was in each case four years, with the right to reelection.

The Supreme Court was constituted of three justices, to be elected by the Legislature for the term of six years; and no provision was made for the Court of Errors.

The circuit courts remained as they had been, except that the civil branch exercised both chancery and common law powers, that the judges were elected for a term of four years and were to be assigned to circuits territorially distinct. Masters and commissioners in equity were no longer to exist. The election of solicitors was committed to the people in the several circuits.

A court of probate was created for every county, with all the powers of the former ordinaries and some of those of the masters or commissioners in equity.

Justices of the peace were to be chosen by the qualified electors in each county.

There was provided in each county a board of three county commissioners, to be elected by the people and to have general charge of the fiscal administration.

The right of suffrage was conferred upon "every male citizen of the United States, of the age of twenty-one years and upwards, not laboring under the disabilities named in this Constitution, without distinction of race, color or former condition, who shall be a resident of this State at the time of the adoption of this Constitution, or who shall thereafter reside in this State for one year and in the county in which he offers to vote sixty days next preceding any election"—the "disabilities" mentioned being those arising under the provisions of the Reconstruction acts of Congress, and those having reference to prisoners, paupers, and lunatics.

It was provided that no property qualification should be necessary for an election to or holding of any office, and that no office should be created the appointment to which should be for a longer time than good behavior.

Presidential electors were required to be elected by the people.

Due provision in detail was made for the assessment, levy and collection of taxes upon real and personal property except such only as was in terms exempted—property used for religious, educational or eleemosynary purposes. The proceeds of the poll tax were specifically appropriated to the public school fund. Provision was made for the levy and collection of taxes by counties, townships, cities, towns, and school districts for corporate purposes.

The educational system was placed in charge of the State Superintendent of Education, aided in each county by a school commissioner to be elected by the people for the term of two years.

It was made the duty of the Legislature, so soon as there should be "a system of public schools thoroughly and completely organized," to require all children between the ages of six and sixteen to attend at either a public or private school for a term equivalent to twenty-four months at least.

It was required that "all the public schools, colleges, and universities of this State, supported in whole or in part by the public funds, shall be free and open to all children of this State, without regard to race or color."

Divorces from the bonds of matrimony were prohibited "except by the judgment of a court, as shall be prescribed by law."

The real and personal property of a married woman, held at the time of her marriage, or that which she might thereafter acquire, was declared not subject to levy or sale for her husband's debts, but should be held as her separate property which she might dispose of to the same extent as if she were unmarried.

All contracts, whether under seal or not, the consideration of which was for the purchase of slaves, were declared null and void and the courts of the State were prohibited from enforcing the same. (This section was by the State Supreme Court adjudged void, as violating that provision of the Federal Constitution which declares that no State shall pass any law impairing the obligation of contracts.)

It was provided that after the adoption of the Constitution any person who should fight a duel, or send or accept a challenge for that purpose, or be an aider or abettor in fighting a duel, should be deprived of holding any office of honor or trust in this State and should be otherwise punished as the law should prescribe.

The Convention ordained that the Constitution should be submitted to the people for ratification.

The State was divided into four Congressional Districts as follows:

First—Lancaster, Chesterfield, Marlboro, Darlington, Marion, Horry, Georgetown, Williamsburg, Sumter, Clarendon, Kershaw.

Second—Charleston, Colleton, Beaufort, Barnwell.

Third—Orangeburg, Lexington, Richland, Newberry, Edgefield, Abbeville, Anderson.

Fourth—Oconee, Pickens, Greenville, Laurens, Spartanburg, Union, York, Chester, Fairfield.

Following the ordinance of the Convention, General Canby, by an order dated March 13, 1868, directed that an election be held, commencing April 14 and ending April 16, at which all registered voters of South Carolina might vote "for constitution" or "against constitution," and also on the same ballot for State officers and members of the Legislature, for a member of Congress from each of the four Congressional Districts and for two members from the State at large. The provision for members at large was made in contemplation of an increase to that extent in the State's representation.

A DISGRACEFUL SCHEME FOILED.

Mention has been made of the attempt to attack the administration and character of Maj. Thomas B. Lee, the superintendent of the State penitentiary.

In the summer of 1867 a petition purporting to have been signed by thirty-one persons was addressed to Brig.-Gen. H. S. Burton, post commander at Columbia, charging that there had been "cruel and inhuman treatment of the colored prisoners in the State prison," and declaring that "their treatment would be a disgrace to any government, even in the Dark Ages, and they are made subject to punishments only such as might be expected from the Turks or cruel savage."

The petition having been referred to Governor Orr, he addressed a letter to General Burton, in which he fully stated actual conditions in the penitentiary, and closed by expressing his conviction that the charges brought against the prison officers were "unjust and false." There the matter ended until it was revamped in the Constitutional Convention.

Acting upon the resolutions adopted and sent to him, General Canby appointed as a commission to "examine into and report upon the charges of cruel and harsh treatment of convicts," preferred against Major Lee, the following named officers: Brevet Col. Henry B. Judd (retired), Brevet Col. Francis S. Guenther, Captain Fifth Artillery, and Brevet Capt. James Chester, First Lieutenant Third Artillery—the last named to act as recorder.

The commission, after publishing in the newspapers a notice of its meeting and a request that all persons having information as to the subject matter should appear and testify, met in open session in Columbia.

The first witness for the complainants was Thomas J. Robertson, one of the signers of the petition for Major Lee's removal on the ground of "harsh and cruel treatment" of negro convicts, who delivered himself as follows: "The principal cause [for signing the petition] was that I am a 'Jacksonian' in principle, believing that 'to the victors belong the spoils,' and that as the Republican party are in power in South Carolina their friends should hold the offices of the State. I know nothing personally of Mr. Lee's harsh treatment of the prisoners, only from hearsay." The witness further stated that upon the occasions of his visits to the penitentiary he "saw no evidence of dissatisfaction among the prisoners."

In his written defense Major Lee referred to Robertson's testimony thus: "One of those who would blacken my character has sworn that all he knew of the charges against me was hearsay, and that his principal reason for thus accusing me of harsh treatment and cruelty towards convicts was that those in authority might be induced to remove me and make room for one of his own party."

Beverly Nash, who had been loud in his abuse of Major Lee, and S. B. Thompson, who had introduced the resolution seeking his removal, each testified that he had acted upon rumor only or upon unsworn statements. Thompson confessed that he had gone to the penitentiary as one of a committee of the Union League, and that the prisoners were clean, orderly and generally healthy—though "some of them looked as if they had been treated roughly"—and that he "saw no distinction made on account of color."

The list of witnesses summoned having been called and no others answering to their names, the recorder invited anyone present who knew anything about the matter under consideration to come forward and testify. Three negro witnesses accordingly volunteered to testify to certain matters in the management of the prison, most of which had no relation to the acts of Major Lee.

After taking further testimony (the entire case consuming ten days) the commission repaired to the penitentiary and there closely examined into its condition and workings.

In their report the commission carefully reviewed the evidence and concluded as follows: "The commission have not failed to be impressed with the devotion, fidelity and skill with which in the midst of many embarrassments the present superintendent has labored in the performance of the various duties devolving upon him. The commission find that the charges of harsh and cruel treatment, made against him, are unfounded; and they regard the administration of Thomas B. Lee, as superintendent of the South Carolina penitentiary, as humane and efficient, and would consider any change in that important office at this time as fraught with danger to the people of the State and injurious to the interests and welfare of the institution and its inmates."

General Canby approved the findings of the commission, declared that no further action upon the petition for removal would be taken, and directed that a copy of the record be furnished the president of the Constitutional Convention.

While the investigation was in progress some of the parties (white and black) who had been pursuing Major Lee sent a man to him and offered to let him alone in his office if he would share with them the money appropriated for maintaining the penitentiary. The messenger was instantly ordered away. Later on a howling mob of negroes with a few whites, led by a white man, surrounded Major Lee's home in the nighttime and threatened him with violence—this, though in the house at the time were his wife and four young children. Fortunately for the rioters they lacked the courage to execute their threat.

The case of Major Lee is given thus somewhat at length because it shows how soon the corrupt purposes of the Republican party in South Carolina showed themselves. It is especially to be noted that some of those who took part in this disreputable affair had been members of the Constitutional Convention and were aspirants to still higher honors at the hands of their party.

PARTY NOMINATIONS.

At a convention held in Charleston during the last week of the Constitutional Convention the Republicans there assembled made the following nominations:

For Governor—Robert K. Scott, of Charleston.

For Lieutenant-Governor—Lemuel Boozer, of Lexington.

ORR'S ADMINISTRATION

For Secretary of State—Francis L. Cordozo (colored), of Charleston.
For Treasurer—Niles G. Parker, of Charleston.
For Comptroller-General—John L. Neagle, of York.
For Adjutant and Inspector General—Franklin J. Moses, Jr., of Charleston.
For Attorney-General—Daniel H. Chamberlain, of Charleston.
For Superintendent of Education—Justus K. Jillson, of Kershaw.

General Scott came from Ohio and was prominent as assistant commissioner of the Freedmen's Bureau in this State. Mr. Boozer was a respectable citizen and prominent lawyer of Lexington. F. L. Cardozo was a mulatto preacher, a man of some ability and of alleged culture. Niles G. Parker came from Massachusetts—a typical carpetbagger, with neither conscience nor character, who had turned up in this State in command of a company of negro troops and in that capacity, as the agent of the Government, had already been charged with official misconduct involving corruption. F. J. Moses, Jr., was without occupation—though nominally a lawyer—and had acquired notoriety chiefly by having raised the Confederate flag over Fort Sumter, when holding the office of private secretary to Governor Pickens. D. H. Chamberlain was a distinguished graduate of Yale College, and a student for one year in the Harvard Law School; lieutenant in a negro regiment of cavalry for the last year of the war; cotton planter on Wadamalaw Island, near Charleston, in 1866 and 1867—having, as he declared, come to South Carolina for the purpose of settling up the estate of a deceased friend who had lived in New Haven. John L. Neagle had been a farmer and merchant and was of very questionable reputation among his own neighbors. J. K. Jillson was a Massachusetts teacher who had come as an employee in the educational branch of the Freedmen's Bureau.

The character of the citizenship of these nominees of the Republican party for the high offices named may be estimated by the amount of property held by them in South Carolina. Of the eight nominees six paid no taxes at all. Moses paid a poll tax only. Mr. Boozer, a man of some property, was the only real taxpayer on the list.

The Republican nominees for Congress were as follows:
First District—B. F. Whittemore, carpetbagger, of Darlington.

Second District—C. C. Bowen, late of Georgia, recently arrived here and resident in Charleston—a tough character all through.

Third District—Simeon Corley, native, farmer in Lexington.

Fourth District—James H. Goss, native, farmer in Union.

State at large—J. P. M. Epping, United States marshal, Charleston; Elias E. Dickson, farmer, Clarendon.

As will be seen hereafter, Whittemore and Bowen soon became steeped in corruption. Corley and Goss were soon set aside for others more in sympathy with the schemes and standards of the party. Epping and Dickson never rose to any prominence.

Pursuant to a call previously issued "a general convention of delegates from the several Democratic clubs of this State" assembled in Columbia on the evening of April 2, 1868—the following districts being represented: Abbeville, Anderson, Barnwell, Chester, Colleton, Edgefield, Fairfield, Georgetown, Greenville, Kershaw, Laurens, Lexington, Marion, Newberry, Orangeburg, Richland, Spartanburg, Sumter, Union, York.

The following officers were elected:

President—Armistead Burt, of Abbeville.

Vice-Presidents—James Chesnut, of Kershaw; Benjamin F. Perry, of Greenville; John S. Preston, of Richland; James D. Blanding, of Sumter; Simeon Fair, of Newberry.

Secretaries—William K. Bachman and James G. Gibbes, of Richland.

All papers presented were referred without debate to the committee appointed to prepare business for the Convention.

At the next day's session that committee submitted a series of resolutions which were adopted—that the Democratic party of South Carolina do unite with the national Democratic party in the United States; that the people be urged to go to the polls and vote against the "constitution of the Radical faction, lately promulgated in Charleston, and (though protesting against the validity of the instrument) for good and true men for all offices within their gift," together with the following:

That under the action of the State of South Carolina, heretofore taken, we recognize the colored population of the State as an integral element of the body politic, and as such in person and property entitled to a full and equal protection under the State Constitution and laws; and that as citizens of South Carolina we declare our

ORR'S ADMINISTRATION

willingness, when we have the power, to grant them, under proper qualifications as to property and intelligence, the right of suffrage.

The following nominations were made:

For Governor—William D. Porter, of Charleston.
For Lieutenant-Governor—Thomas C. Perrin, of Abbeville.
For Secretary of State—Ellison Capers, of Greenville.
For Treasurer—William Hood, of Abbeville.
For Comptroller-General—S. L. Leaphart, of Richland.
For Adjutant and Inspector General—John P. Thomas, of Richland.
For Attorney-General—Isaac W. Hayne, of Charleston.
For Superintendent of Education—John A. Leland, of Laurens.

The District Conventions made the following nominations for Congress:

First—John N. Frierson, of Sumter.
Second—Johnson Hagood, of Barnwell.
Third—Samuel McGowan, of Abbeville.
Fourth—Samuel McAlily, of Chester.

Delegates to the National Democratic Convention to be held in New York on July 4 were named as follows:

State at Large—Benj. F. Perry, of Greenville; James Chesnut, of Kershaw; alternates, John A. Inglis, of Chesterfield; A. P. Aldrich, of Barnwell.

First District—W. S. Mullins, of Marion; alternate, J. B. Kershaw, of Kershaw.

Second District—Carlos Tracy, of Colleton; alternate, M. L. Bonham, of Edgefield.

Third—John S. Preston, of Richland; alternate, William B. Stanley, of Richland.

Fourth—Armistead Burt, of Abbeville; alternate, William D. Simpson, of Laurens.

The State Central Executive Committee was elected as follows: Wade Hampton, John P. Thomas, F. W. McMaster, Joseph Daniel Pope, of Richland; William M. Shannon, of Kershaw; Samuel McGowan, of Abbeville; S. P. Hamilton, of Chester.

Mr. Porter declined the nomination for Governor, and Colonel Hayne that for Attorney-General—each expressing the opinion that no nomination should have been made, and that the white people should simply vote against the proposed Constitution.

APPEALS AND REMONSTRANCES.

The Democratic convention issued and later its executive committee, by its authority, issued certain papers bearing upon the condition of affairs in South Carolina—of which brief summaries are here proper because they fairly expressed the sentiments of the white people of the State, and because they were prophetic of some of the results of the Reconstruction policy of Congress.

I. In "an address to the colored people of South Carolina" the relations of those people to the white race, politically, socially and industrially, were plainly set forth, and the following conclusions drawn:

Your present power must surely and soon pass from you. Nothing that it builds will stand and nothing will remain of it but the prejudices it may create. It is therefore a most dangerous tool that you are handling. Your leaders, both white and black, are using your votes for nothing but their individual gain. Many of them you have only known heretofore to despise and distrust, until commanded by your Leagues to vote for them. Offices and salaries for themselves are the heights of their ambition, and so that they make hay while the sun shines they care not who is caught in the storm that follows. Already they have driven away all capital and credit from the South; and while they draw $11.00 a day thousands among you are thrown out of employment and starve simply for lack of work. What few enterprises are carried on are only the work of Southern men who have faith that the present state of affairs is but temporary. The world does not offer better opportunities for the employment of capital than are to be found in the South; but will your Radical friends send their money here to invest? Not one dollar. They would just as soon venture on investments in Hayti or Liberia as commit their money to the influence of your legislation. Capital has learned to shun it as a deadly plague.

We therefore urge and warn you, by all the ties of our former relations still strong and binding in thousands of cases, by a common Christianity and by the mutual welfare of our two races, whom Providence has thrown together, to beware of the course on which your leaders are urging you in a blind folly which will surely ruin both you and them.

We do not pretend to be better friends to your race than we are to ourselves, and we only speak when we are not invited because your welfare concerns ours. If you destroy yourselves you injure us, and though but little as compared with the harm you will do yourselves we would if we could avert the whole danger.

We are not in any condition to make you any promises or to propose to you any compromises. We can do nothing but await the course of events—but this we do without the slightest apprehension or misgiving for ourselves. We shall not give up our country, and time will soon restore our control of it. But we earnestly caution you and beg you in the meanwhile to beware of the use you make of your temporary power. Remember that your race has nothing to gain and everything to lose if you invoke that prejudice of race which since the world was made has ever driven the weaker tribe to the wall. Forsake, then, the wicked and stupid men who would involve you in this folly, and make to yourselves friends and not enemies of the white citizens of South Carolina.

II. In another paper the white people were urged to vote against the adoption of the proposed Constitution and also induce as many negroes as possible to do the same; that instrument being declared to involve the menace of "negro rule and supremacy at the point of the sword and bayonet—the work of sixty-odd negroes, many of them ignorant and depraved, together with fifty white men, outcasts of Northern society, and Southern renegades, betrayers of their race and country, who have assembled in convention and framed a Constitution for the government of South Carolina."

The paper concluded thus:

We must unite cordially, heartily and actively with the National Democratic party, North and South, in their most vigorous efforts to prevent all this monstrous injustice and oppression and the subversion of the American republic.

We must unite among ourselves as one man, in South Carolina, to defeat this bogus Constitution, which is submitted for ratification on the 14th of April next and which if adopted will render our condition most ignominious and to manly spirits galling in the extreme. It provides not only for our government by the negroes, but that our sons and daughters shall be educated with their children, on terms of equality, and that they shall have the right of taxing our property *ad libitum* and spending the money as they please, whilst at the same time they contribute comparatively nothing to the treasury.

Specific objections to the proposed Constitution were set forth as follows:

1. Because in the name of liberty it was forced upon the white people by the sword, "prepared and imposed by strangers and adventurers ignorant of our conditions and our needs and in many cases not only indifferent to our welfare but actually inimical to it."

2. Because the whole machinery which produced it was illegal, revolutionary and unconstitutional.

3. Because its purpose was not to reconstruct the State, but to make South Carolina an ally and supporter of the Radical party.

4. Because it was a patchwork of contradictions—not made by the delegates who endorsed it, but abstracted from the constitutions of other States having different conditions and habits of thought from the people of South Carolina.

5. Because it contained many acts of mere legislation suited, perhaps, to conditions in New England and in other parts of the Union, but surely involving cost and trouble in South Carolina.

6. Because it was based upon the falsehood that white and black are the same—being thus cruel to the blacks in thrusting them into a political contact and competition with the whites.

7. Because "it destroys our admirable judiciary, introducing a new system which is repugnant to our customs and habits of thought," and which promises to increase expenses and encourage pernicious litigation.

8. Because it disfranchised a large number of the best citizens of the State.

9. Because that disfranchisement "is kept up by the mean whites, not for the good of the State, but to enable themselves to get and hold all the offices."

10. Because of "the stupendous school arrangement, requiring an enormous taxation, which is to be borne mainly by one class for the benefit of another, and which must be a fruitful source of peculant corruption"—because of the provision for "compulsory schooling, which is contrary to the genius and spirit of republican institutions and never accomplishes the purposes intended."

11. Because it contained a "snare and a deceit" in the shape of homestead exemptions which, inapplicable to debts contracted before its adoption, would not help the very class of debtors most needing relief.

12. Because "by numerous officers, many courts and expensive machinery the attempt is made to assimilate this small State, with an empty treasury and exhausted resources, to large and prosperous commonwealths; property, and property only, is made subject to taxes which must be enormous, and the hope of improvement is cut off by the subjection of those who have property to the rule of those who have none."

It was finally stated on behalf of the white people of South Carolina that they "would rather still live under a military government than to have the proposed Constitution established over them as the permanent fundamental law of the State."

The election to determine the acceptance of the new Constitution by the people of South Carolina was duly held April 14, 15, 16, 1868—the vote standing thus: For ratification, 70,758; against ratification, 27,288; not voting, 35,551; total vote, 133,598. A majority of the registered voters having voted to ratify the Constitution, General Canby notified Congress accordingly. The Republican nominees for Congress were all elected.

Against the acceptance and enforcement of this Constitution a formal remonstrance was submitted to Congress by the State Central Executive Committee of the Democratic party, the paper being carried to Washington by a subcommittee consisting of John P. Thomas, James G. Gibbes and L. D. Childs, all of Columbia. The grounds taken against the instrument were substantially those mentioned in the papers issued by the full committee prior to the election. The paper concluded as follows:

We have thus suggested to your honorable body some of the prominent objections to your adoption of this Constitution. We waive all argument on the subject of its validity. It is a constitution *de facto,* and that is the ground on which we approach your honorable body in the spirit of earnest remonstrance. The Constitution was the work of Northern adventurers, Southern renegades, and ignorant negroes. Not one per cent. of the white population of the State approves it, and not two per cent. of the negroes who voted for its adoption understood what this act of voting implied. That Constitution enfranchises every male negro over the age of twenty-one, and disfranchises many of the purest and best white men of the State. The negroes being in a large numerical majority as compared with the whites, the effect is that the new Constitution establishes in this State negro supremacy with all its train of countless evils. A superior race—a portion, Senators and Representatives, of the same proud race to which it is your pride to belong—is put under the rule of an inferior race; the abject slaves of yesterday, the flushed freedmen of today. And think you there can be any just, lasting reconstruction on this basis? The committee respectfully reply, in behalf of their white fellowcitizens, that this cannot be. We do not mean to threaten resistance by arms, but the people of our State will never quietly submit to negro rule. We may have to pass under the yoke you have authorized, but by moral agencies, by political organization, by every peaceful means left us, we will keep up this contest until we have regained the political control handed down to us by an honored ancestry. This is a duty we owe to the land that is ours, to the graves that it contains, and to the race of which you and we are alike members—the proud Caucasian race, whose sovereignty on earth God has ordained, and they themselves have illustrated on the most brilliant pages of the world's history.

The subcommittee having appeared before the Reconstruction Committee, Colonel Thomas, as the spokesman for the occasion, presented an argument in support of the remonstrance. He said that upon anlyzing the propositions embodied in the proposed instrument there were two objectionable features that stood out in bold relief—unqualified negro suffrage and the taxing power. He argued to show their disastrous effects upon both races. The proposed Constitution established taxation without representation. Those who have no property were to tax those who have all the property. Under this Constitution $2,000,000 might be raised in the way of taxes, $1,000,000 of which was for educational purposes, and yet these advantages were to be enjoyed by the blacks alone, as white children would not attend black schools. The State heretofore, even in its most prosperous days, had not been able to bear a tax of more than $500,000 annually. Colonel Thomas, in conclusion, said that he deemed it his duty to state to the committee that while the whites were willing to concede to the negro all of the legal rights and a qualified suffrage, yet the white race would never acquiesce in negro rule. "You may make us pass under the yoke," he said, "and we shall have to do so; but by every means which God and Congress have left us under the Constitution and laws we shall resist this domination of an inferior race. By peaceful means, by political efforts, by industrial agencies, we will carry on this political contest until we regain the control which of right belongs to the power of mind and the influence of virtue. Nor can you have prosperity in the South under your Reconstruction scheme. But give the South a fair showing, restore the States to the Union on a just basis, and again will our people return with willing hearts to the Union, and the same energy, the same self-sacrifice, the same valor which they gave to the 'Lost Cause' will they give now to the Union, provided you meet them in a spirit of just magnanimity and concede to them the rights to which they deem themselves entitled."

Subsequently there was submitted by the same committee "an appeal to the honorable the Senate of the United States, in behalf of the conservative people of South Carolina, against the adoption by

Congress of the new Constitution proposed for South Carolina," in which the committee said:

In spite of the respectful remonstrance submitted to the House of Representatives and the Senate we find that the former body have given to said instrument their approval. For the sake of all classes of our people, for considerations affecting the peace of society, in view of the substantial interests of the State, put in jeopardy by an organic law which may truthfully be characterized as a political abortion, the offspring of incapacity and prejudice and hate, we submit our case—the case of the conservatism of South Carolina—to the high court of last resort, the Senate of the country.

Although South Carolina is struggling for bread, yet observe how, under the new Constitution, the burdens of taxation have been increased:

Proposed now to be raised.................................$2,230,950
Before the war, amount about........................... 350,000
Proposed now to be levied on the real estate of the State.. 3 per ct.
Before the war.. ½ per ct.

But when there is taken into consideration the depreciation of the value of property since the war the difference is far greater. For illustration, take the case of a piece of property in a town, before the war worth, say.......................................$10,000
Levied on this, before the war ½ per cent.............. 50
Now at same valuation, it pays at 3 per cent........... 300

Thus the proposition stands as 1 to 6.
But—
The property value before the war at $10,000 has now a value of...$ 3,000
Before the war a tax of ½ per cent. levied on this would give 15
But to raise the $300 required now, demands a tax of 10 per cent... 300

Thus taking into consideration the value of real estate the proportion stands as 1 to 20, or the taxation provided for in the new Constitution is absolutely twenty times as great as before the war. But in the case of land, which has depreciated more in value than city property, the proportion is even greater than the one established above. In fact it is now a common thing to find large tracts of land sold by the sheriff for less than the taxes resting thereon.

The committee's estimate of the total amount required to run the new government for its first year included the following items:
Educational system complete.......................$ 994,000
Current expenses (Canby's tax)...................... 445,000
Five per cent. for collection.......................... 71,950
Interest on State debt ($6,000,000) July, 1866, to July, 1868.. 720,000

Total amount of taxes............................$2,230,950

The committee next showed the amount of taxes paid by all the members of the Constitutional Convention, and thence pointed out the non-representative and irresponsible character of that body.

The appeal closed thus: "In behalf, therefore, of justice and fair dealing, representing the just claims of the white citizens of South Carolina, without further comment we have the honor respectfully to submit the statistical argument herewith presented in exhibits, and to express the hope that it may appear to your honorable body weighty enough to induce the rejection, at your hands, of the Constitution proposed for South Carolina."

These remonstrances were unavailing, and the Constitution of South Carolina, framed and adopted in pursuance of the Reconstruction acts, was duly approved by Congress.

CONGRESSIONAL RECONSTRUCTION COMPLETED.

By the act of June 25, 1868, passed over the veto of President Johnson, it was enacted that South Carolina (with other States named) "shall be entitled and admitted to representation in Congress as a State of the Union when the Legislature of such State shall have duly ratified the amendment to the Constitution of the United States, proposed by the Thirty-ninth Congress, and known as Article XIV, upon the following fundamental conditions: That the Constitution of said State shall never be so amended or so changed as to deprive any citizen or class of citizens of the United States of the right to vote in said State who are entitled to vote by the Constitution thereof herein recognized, except as a punishment for such crimes as are now felonies at common law, whereof they shall have been duly convicted under laws equally applicable to all the inhabitants of said State; provided that any alteration of said Constitution may be made with regard to the time and place of residence of voters."

At its first session, in July, 1868, the Legislature assembled under the new Constitution, formally ratified the Fourteenth Amendment, and in due time the Senators and Representatives of the State were admitted to seats in the Congress of the United States. Thus, by the exercise of the military power of the Federal Government, executing the mandates contained in the acts of Congress, was Reconstruction according to the Radical or congressional theory consummated in South Carolina, as in the other Southern States. Thus was established that negro government which lasted only so long as it was supported by the same military force by which it had been organized and instituted.

Though the Constitutional Convention had ordained that the first meeting of the Legislature under the new instrument (if it should be ratified by the people) should be held on May 12, 1868, that meeting was postponed. By the order of General Canby, issued previous to that date, that officer directed that the meeting be postponed till Congress should declare its approval and acceptance of the new Constitution. It was further ordered that an election be held on June 2 and 3 for all county officers elective under the Constitution—sheriffs, clerks of court, probate judges, school commissioners, coroners and county commissioners.

By his General Order No. 120, June 30, 1868, General Canby revoked a previous order requiring the officers elected under the new Constitution to qualify by taking the test oath, and directed that upon the ratification of the Fourteenth Amendment by the Legislature they qualify by taking the oath prescribed by that Constitution. The order further directed:

That Governor Orr and Lieutenant-Governor Porter be removed, and that R. K. Scott be appointed Governor and Lemuel Boozer Lieutenant-Governor—these appointments to take effect June 6, on the meeting of the General Assembly.

That the records of the district courts (these tribunals having been abolished by the operation of the new Constitution) be transferred to the several clerks of the circuit courts.

That all the boards of county commissioners in the several counties—these superseding the several boards of commissioners in the old districts—should qualify by taking the proper oath, to be administered in each case by the ordinary.

That the new judges of probate perform the duties formerly devolving upon the ordinaries.

That each board of county commissioners appoint a treasurer, who should keep and disburse all county funds, for a compensation not to exceed two per cent. for receiving and two per cent. for disbursing, to be fixed by the board of commissioners.

That the circuit judges who should be chosen by the General Assembly should, until otherwise provided by law, exercise in suits in equity all the powers pertaining to chancellors.

By Special Order No. 140, dated June 19, 1868, General Canby removed Mr. Theo. Starke, mayor of Columbia, and assigned to the duties of that office Brevet Col. F. L. Guenther, captain Fifth Artillery. By the same order Aldermen T. W. Radcliffe, W. P. Geiger, A. M. Huntt, John Fisher, W. T. Walter and A. R. Taylor were removed, and in their places were appointed Mr. W. K. Greenfield, Dr. F. W. Green, Dr. Thomas J. Rawls, C. M. Wilder (colored), Joseph Taylor (colored) and William Simonds (colored). Dr. Green declined. All the appointees were required to take the test oath. No reason was given for these changes—the act of the district commander seeming to have been done in the mere indulgence of the spirit of tyranny and with the purpose to humiliate those with whose feelings and interests he had no sympathy and who, he must have learnt, had little respect for his motives or character. The white appointees were all gentlemen in good repute in the community.

By a later order, Mr. C. H. Baldwin, a business man of character and standing, was appointed mayor.

On July 24, 1868, General Canby issued his General Order No. 145, whereby he declared that "all authority conferred upon and heretofore exercised by the commander of the second military district under the aforecited law of March 2, 1867 [being the first of the Reconstruction acts] is hereby remitted to the civil authorities constituted and organized in the States of North Carolina and South Carolina, under the Constitutions adopted by the people thereof, and approved by the Congress of the United States."

Thus ended the rule of the military commander in South Carolina under Federal statutes, which subverted the lawful government of the State, which gave to that officer absolute power over every right of the citizen, which at every stage subordinated the civil authority to the military, which caused every mandate to be enforced at the point of the bayonet, and which, from first to last, constituted as brutish a tyranny as ever marked the course of any government whose agents and organs claimed it to be civilized.

FEELING AMONG THE WHITES.

The action of Congress in establishing the negro government in South Carolina was not in any sense a disappointment to the white people of the State; nor did it anywise cause them to abate anything of their resolution to assert their rights, their opposition to the new order of things and their feeling towards the men who had carried out here the wishes of the Radical majority in Congress. For the great mass of the negroes there was no feeling but kindness mixed with regret that they should have been made the instruments of wrongs against which the white people rebelled. The negro leaders as a rule very soon betraying their corrupt character and purposes, there was no tolerance for them. Of the carpetbaggers nothing had been expected but such things as might naturally proceed from unscrupulous adventurers. Towards the few native whites who had joined hands with negroes and aliens to place the State under black rule there was a feeling of bitter animosity.

That feeling had an illustration in the preamble and resolutions adopted on or about April 9, 1868, by the Euphradian Society of the South Carolina University. This paper, after setting forth in the preamble the principles to which the society had always been devoted and its hearty deprecation of any act of any individual in disregard of the same, proceeded as follows:

And whereas, in the eyes of the public generally, and more especially in the eyes of this society, Thomas J. Robertson and Franklin J. Moses, Jr., late regular members, have in all these respects lowered their dignity and station as true gentlemen of Carolina; and whereas, on this account the names of the said Thomas J. Robertson and Franklin J. Moses, Jr., are no longer an ornament to or a jewel in the honorary roll of this society, but, as it were, two black stains upon that otherwise unblemished roll as yet of brothers true and faithful to their vows; therefore

Resolved, That Thomas J. Robertson and Frank. J. Moses, Jr., be now expelled from this society, and that the immunities of entering the hall during session, or participating in the exercises of the society, be now and ever hereafter denied them.

Resolved, That a committee of three be appointed to inform the said Thomas J. Robertson and Frank. J. Moses, Jr., of their expulsion.

Resolved, That a copy of these resolutions be sent to the *Columbia Phoenix* and the *Charleston Mercury* for publication.

The single ground upon which the young gentlemen of the Euphradian Society thus proceeded consisted in the active and uncompromising adherence of the obnoxious individuals to the Radical party of South Carolina. No charge was suggested against the personal character of either. Whatever the doubts felt as to the society's jurisdiction of the particular matters upon which it thus strongly and publicly declared its judgment, it is safe to say that in the then existing state of sentiment among the white people of South Carolina quite ninety-nine per cent. of these heartily shared the feeling to which the paper gave expression. At the same time it must be stated, in view of the course of events in the eight years of negro rule in the State, that it would be very unfair to put Robertson in the same class with Moses.

Robertson was graduated from the college in 1843, and Moses was honorably dismissed from the freshman class in 1855.

THE CAMPAIGN OF 'SIXTY-EIGHT.

The enforcement of the new Constitution and the establishment of the State Government thereunder caused the white people to strengthen and extend the organization of the Democratic party, so as to enable it to make the best possible fight in the November election.

There were considerable differences of opinion touching the wisdom of holding the April convention, and its authority to speak or act for the Democratic party was openly called in question. In response to an invitation extended by the Democratic citizens of Edgefield District a convention of the party was held in Columbia, on June 10, 1868, the following "districts" being represented: Barnwell, Berkeley, Charleston, Chesterfield, Darlington, Edgefield, Georgetown, Orangeburg, Sumter, Williamsburg. The following officers were elected:

President—Charles H. Simonton, of Charleston.

Vice-Presidents—John L. Manning, of Clarendon; Thomas W. Glover, of Orangeburg; Charles M. Furman, of Charleston; F. D. Richardson, of Berkeley; M. C. Butler, of Edgefield; E. W. Charles, of Darlington; Dr. Mark Reynolds, of Clarendon; Alexander McQueen, of Chesterfield; J. G. Pressley, of Williamsburg.

Secretaries—A. A. Gilbert, of Sumter; Henry Sparnick, of Charleston.

The convention adopted a resolution expressing doubts of the propriety of the taking of any part by the white people of South Carolina in the National Democratic Convention—this because they would have no effective voice in the election of presidential electors—and submitting the matter to the action of that convention; also a resolution in effect declaring for "a white man's govern-

ORR'S ADMINISTRATION

ment"—this without any statement as to the negro's exercise of the suffrage when he should become qualified therefor.

Delegates to the National Convention were chosen as follows:

State at Large—Wade Hampton, of Richland; James B. Campbell, of Charleston; alternates, C. M. Furman, of Charleston; James P. Carroll, of Richland.

First District—John L. Manning, of Clarendon; alternate, Richard Dozier, of Georgetown.

Second District—Charles H. Simonton; alternates, John Hanckel, R. B. Rhett, Jr., all of Charleston.

Third District—M. W. Gary, of Edgefield; alternate, A. D. Frederick, of Orangeburg.

The Fourth District being unrepresented in the convention, no choice was made of a delegate therefrom.

The delegates thus chosen united, with those elected at the April convention, to form the State's delegation in the National Convention—the April body having overlooked the fact that the delegation was of double the number of our representatives in both branches of Congress.

The following additional members of the State Executive Committee were elected: William D. Porter, Theo. G. Barker, John E. Carew, Robert Adger, Charleston; Henry McIver, Chesterfield; A. A. Gilbert, Sumter; W. P. Finley, Marlboro.

By the action of this convention and the cooperation of the executive committee of the April convention harmony was established in the Democratic party of South Carolina.

On August 6 there was another meeting of the Democratic State Convention in Columbia—all the counties being represented. The following officers were elected:

President—Armistead Burt, of Abbeville.

Vice-Presidents—A. P. Aldrich, of Barnwell; W. W. Harllee, of Marion; John A. Wagener, of Charleston; Gabriel Cannon, of Spartanburg.

Secretaries—James G. Gibbes, of Columbia; James A. Hoyt, of Anderson; W. J. McKerrall, of Marion; J. C. Davant, of Beaufort.

The convention adopted resolutions indorsing the action of the National Democratic body, commending the course of the South Carolina delegates, and declaring the purpose to rely upon peaceful agencies only to win the fight.

The following nominations were made for presidential electors:

State at Large—John P. Thomas, of Richland; John D. Kennedy, of Kershaw.

First District—Robert F. Graham, of Marion.

Second District—B. H. Rutledge, of Charleston.

Third District—A. C. Haskell, of Abbeville.

Fourth District—E. C. McLure, of Chester.

The National Democratic Convention had assembled in New York on July 4, and had nominated for President, Horatio Seymour, of New York; and for Vice-President, Frank P. Blair, Jr., of Missouri.

The platform declared for universal amnesty and for the regulation of the suffrage by the States, denounced the Reconstruction acts as "usurpations, unconstitutional, revolutionary and void"—and further denounced in detail the general policy of the Republican party.

In the meantime the Republican party, in its convention at Philadelphia, had nominated Ulysses S. Grant for President, and Schuyler Colfax for Vice-President. The platform embodied substantially an outright indorsement of the Reconstruction policy of Congress.

The State Republican Convention met in Columbia on September 8, and remained in session three days. The following electoral ticket was nominated:

State at Large—D. H. Chamberlain, of Charleston; C. J. Stolbrand, of Beaufort.

First District—S. A. Swails (colored), of Williamsburg.

Second District—A. J. Ransier (colored), of Charleston.

Third District—B. F. Randolph (colored), of Orangeburg.

Fourth District—J. M. Allen, of Greenville.

The Democratic party set promptly and vigorously to work to oppose the negro party in the fight for electors, congressmen and solicitors.

Democratic clubs were formed in all the counties—the number depending upon population and upon considerations of convenience. Meetings were held all over the State, at which speakers presented the Democratic cause and appealed to the colored people to break away from their already apparent slavery to their party organization and party leaders. Especial efforts were made to get the colored people into Democratic clubs. The small number of that race who declared themselves Democrats suffered persecution at the hands of the men and women alike of their own race—extending to abuse, assault and grievous bodily harm. In some cases the killing of colored men was attributed—and fairly attributed—to the action of negroes who sought thus to dispose of obnoxious parties of their own race and to deter others from voting the Democratic ticket. The determination of the white men to protect negro Democrats from all harm was one thing that so affected the white Republican leaders, that though evidently in sympathy with the policy of abusing and frightening negro Democrats they yet counseled the utmost freedom of speech and action. Little or no impression could be made upon the colored people—this largely for the reason that their leaders had warned them that their oath in the Union League bound them to vote the Republican ticket.

The Republican managers evidently relied upon the power of the League to solidify the negroes against the whites—though they made speeches which frequently contained passionate appeals to the race feeling and sometimes language of a most incendiary character. The negroes had been secretly arming themselves, and in some of the counties—notably in Union—they were so demonstrative as to cause actual alarm for the safety of the white people in the country, apparently at their mercy. The coolness, firmness and wisdom of the whites, with little or no help from the Radical leaders, prevented race conflicts of a serious character.

The excited state of feeling did give rise to the killing of some colored leaders among the Radical party and of one white man, who was said to have used incendiary language to his negro hearers. This last mentioned person was S. G. W. Dill, of Kershaw, who was shot in his own house in the nighttime by unknown parties. B. F. Randolph, the colored preacher from Orangeburg, made speeches in the up-country which were calculated to inflame the negroes and equally calculated to cause a race conflict. He was shot to death in the daytime at Hodges depot in Abbeville County. James Martin, a colored member of the Legislature from Abbeville, was shot to death by unknown parties. Wade Perrin, a colored member from Laurens, suffered a like fate after the October election. There were other cases of homicide by unknown parties, the victims being negroes, but they were not really significant of the feeling aroused by the incendiary speeches of many of the Radical speakers. Governor Scott offered rewards ranging from $2,500 to $5,000 for the arrest of the guilty parties.

Extraordinary measures were taken in the employment of the State constabulary, organized under an act of the new Legislature, to arrest persons under suspicion. Men of the highest character—some at least selected solely because of their standing in the State—were arrested, taken to Columbia, and, after causeless confinement in the common jail, released for failure of proof. The constable was, in some cases, attended by a squad of United States soldiers under arms. No one of the parties thus arrested was ever brought to trial.

The Republican electoral ticket carried the day. The Republican congressmen at large were elected by about the same vote, but were not seated.

The Democrats elected J. P. Reed, of Anderson, over Solomon L. Hoge, of Richland, in the Third Congressional District, and William D. Simpson, of Laurens, defeated A. S. Wallace, of York, in the Fourth. Upon a contest in Congress both of the Democratic members were unseated. C. C. Bowen was elected from the Second District, defeating R. W. Seymour, of Charleston, and B. F. Whittemore, from the First, defeating Harris Covington, of Marlboro.

Solicitors were elected as follows: First Circuit, D. H. Chamberlain (Republican), of Charleston; Second, P. L. Wiggin (Republican), of Beaufort; Third, S. T. Atkinson (Democrat), of Georgetown; Fourth, A. J. Shaw (Democrat), of Marion; Fifth, William H. Talley (Democrat), of Richland; Sixth, William H. Brawley (Democrat), of Chester; Seventh, H. L. McGowan (Democrat), of Abbeville; Eighth, William H. Perry (Democrat), of Greenville. The number of Democrats thus chosen is explained by the scarcity of Republican lawyers.

The vote for electors was—Republican, 62,300; Democratic, 45,137; Republican majority, 17,163. The Democrats carried Abbeville, Anderson, Chesterfield, Greenville, Horry, Lancaster, Laurens, Lexington, Marion, Newberry, Oconee, Pickens, Spartanburg, Union, and York. The Republicans carried Barnwell, Beaufort, Charleston, Chester, Clarendon, Colleton, Darlington, Fairfield, Georgetown, Kershaw, Marlboro, Orangeburg, Richland, Sumter, and Williamsburg. There was no election in Edgefield—this because the Governor had not appointed election commissioners for that county.

On the day of the voting for congressmen and electors there were municipal elections in several cities and towns. These were without striking incidents, except in Charleston.

The white people of that city had nominated a "citizens' ticket" with Henry D. Lesesne for mayor and with gentlemen for aldermen whose character and conservatism were thought such as to invite the cooperation of the colored people. The canvass was a most exciting one. To meet the efforts of the Lesesne managers to get negro votes, the Radical leaders, white and black, resorted to disgraceful measures. Colored men who indicated a purpose to vote the "citizens' ticket" were abused, assaulted and subjected to other wrongs. One instance was seen in the treatment of Stephney Riley, a colored man who had a livery stable in the city. On the day of the election a mob of negroes assaulted Riley, and would have done him serious injury but for the vigorous interference of his white friends. Radical negroes, in bodies apparently organized for the purpose, then proceeded to injure (in one case to destroy) Riley's vehicles. After the election some of his friends among the white people raised a fund (considerably more than $600) and presented it to Riley to reimburse him for the losses he had suffered.

The Radical ticket, headed by Gilbert Pillsbury, an irresponsible carpetbagger from Massachusetts, was declared elected, and he, with a board of aldermen altogether unworthy, very soon took control of the city government.

CHAPTER III.

SCOTT'S FIRST TERM.

Pursuant to the call of Governor Scott and the order of General Canby, the General Assembly met in Columbia on July 6, 1868. The Senate was composed as follows:

Abbeville—Valentine Young, white. (Mr. Young was a Baptist clergyman, a gentleman of character and standing, who was elected against his wish and who, declining to serve, never qualified. James S. Cothran, Democrat, was afterwards elected in his place, defeating L. P. Guffin, white Republican, but the Senate declared the election void.)

*Anderson—John H. Reid, white.
Barnwell—C. P. Leslie, white.
Beaufort—J. J. Wright, colored.
Charleston—D. T. Corbin, white, R. H. Cain, colored.
Chester—Lewis Wimbush, colored.
Chesterfield—R. J. Donaldson, white.
Clarendon—E. E. Dickson, white.
Colleton—William R. Hoyt, colored.
Darlington—B. F. Whittemore, white.
Edgefield—Frank Arnim, white.
Fairfield—James M. Rutland, white.
Georgetown—Joseph H. Rainey, colored.
Greenville—James M. Allen, white.
*Horry—H. Buck, white.
Kershaw—J. K. Jillson, white.
*Lancaster—R. M. Sims, white.
Laurens—Y. J. P. Owens, white.
Lexington—E. S. J. Hayes, white.
Marlboro—H. J. Maxwell, colored.
Marion—Henry E. Hayne, colored.
Newberry—C. W. Montgomery, white.
*Oconee—D. Biemann, white.
Orangeburg—B. F. Randolph, colored, succeeded by Joseph A. Greene, colored.
*Pickens—T. A. Rodgers, white.

SCOTT'S FIRST TERM

Richland—W. B. Nash, colored.
*Spartanburg—Joel Foster, white.
Sumter—T. J. Coghlan, white.
Union—H. W. Duncan, colored.
Williamsburg—S. A. Swails, colored.
York—William E. Rose, white.

The number of white senators elected was twenty-one, and of colored, ten.

The counties marked * were Democratic.

The roll of the House of Representatives was as follows:

Abbeville—George Dusenberry, T. B. Milford, James Martin, white; R. M. Valentine, W. J. Lomax, colored.

*Anderson—John B. Moore, B. Frank Sloan, John Wilson, all white.

Barnwell—B. F. Berry, W. J. Mixson, white; C. D. Hayne, James N. Hayne, Julius Mayer, R. B. Elliott, colored.

Beaufort—C. J. Stolbrand, Charles S. Kuh, white; W. J. Whipper, P. E. Ezekiel, Robert Smalls, G. A. Bennett, W. C. Morrison, colored.

Charleston—Reuben Tomlinson, Joseph H. Jenks, John B. Dennis, F. J. Moses, Jr., B. F. Jackson, white; R. C. DeLarge, A. J. Ransier, W. H. W. Gray, B. A. Bosemon, George Lee, William McKinlay, W. J. Brodie, John B. Wright, William R. Jervay, Abraham Smith, Samuel Johnson, Stephen Brown, Edward Mickey, colored.

Chester—Barney Humphries, Sancho Sanders, Barney Burton, colored.

Chesterfield—H. L. Shrewsberry, D. I. J. Johnson, colored.

Clarendon—William Nelson, Powell Smyth, colored.

Colleton—George F. McIntyre, white; W. R. Hoyt, W. M. Thomas, Wm. Driffle, colored.

Darlington—G. Holliman, white; Jordan Lang, John Boston, Alfred Rush, colored.

Edgefield—T. Root, white; David Harris, Samuel J. Lee, John Wooley, Prince R. Rivers, John Gardner, Lawrence Cain, colored.

Fairfield—L. W. Duvall, white; Henry Jacob, Henry Johnson, colored.

Georgetown—Henry W. Webb, white; F. F. Miller, W. H. Jones, colored.

Greenville—Samuel Tinsley, John B. Hyde, white; Wilson Cook, W. A. Bishop, colored.

*Horry—Zadock Bullock, W. W. Waller, white.

Kershaw—S. G. W. Dill, white; John A. Chestnut, J. W. Nash, colored.

*Lancaster—T. Frank Clyburn, W. G. Stewart, white.

Laurens—Joseph Crews, white; Griffin Johnson, Wade Perrin, Harry McDaniels, colored.

Lexington—G. A. Lewie, white; H. W. Purvis, colored.

Marlboro—T. B. Stubbs, white; John G. Grant, colored.

Marion—W. S. Collins, white; Evan Hayes, B. A. Thompson, colored.

Newberry—Joseph Boston, James Hutson, James Henderson, colored.

*Oconee—O. M. Doyle, W. C. Keith, white.

Orangeburg—W. J. McKinlay, T. K. Sasportas, F. DeMars, E. J. Cain, James P. Mays, colored.

*Pickens—W. T. Field, white.

Richland—S. B. Thompson, William Simmons, C. M. Wilder, Aesop Goodson, colored.

*Spartanburg—Samuel Littlejohn, Robert M. Smith, Javan Bryant, C. C. Turner, white.

Sumter—John H. Feriter, white; W. E. Johnson, James Smiley, Burrell James, colored.

Union—Samuel Nuckles, June Mobley, Simon Farr, colored.

Williamsburg—C. H. Pettingill, white; R. F. Scott, Jeff Pendergrass, colored.

York—P. J. O'Connell, John L. Neagle, white; J. H. White, John W. Mead, colored.

The number of white representatives was forty-six, and of colored seventy-eight. The counties marked * were Democratic. On joint ballot there were sixty-seven whites and eighty-eight colored—135 Republicans and twenty Democrats.

The amount of taxes paid by the entire Legislature was $635.23, of which the twenty Democrats paid $203.84. The average tax of the Republican members was therefore $3.12; and of those members ninety-one paid no tax whatever. The senators and representatives from Charleston—twenty in all—paid a tax of $84.35, of which all but one dollar (paid by F. J. Moses, Jr.) was paid by William McKinlay, a colored man.

The Senate organized by the election of D. T. Corbin, president pro tem., and Josephus Woodruff, clerk. There were also a reading clerk and a sergeant-at-arms, together with a full corps of attaches, pages, etc.

The usual messages were sent to "Governor" Scott, and "Provisional Governor" Orr was informed that the Senate was ready to receive any communication which he might be pleased to make. Similar action was taken by the House.

The House organized by the election of F. J. Moses, Jr., speaker; and A. O. Jones (a Northern mulatto, who had come to Charleston) clerk. A full corps of attaches was provided.

There was something of a contest for the speakership between Moses and Elliott. The latter was nominated by Whipper, who took the ground that a colored man should be chosen as speaker of the first House organized under a "free government" in South Carolina. Moses won by a decisive majority.

The Governor-elect was inaugurated on July 9, 1868, and the new Lieutenant-Governor was sworn in on that day.

J. W. Denny, white Republican, was elected "printer to the State," though the figures of his bid were manifestly higher than those of Julian A. Selby, the proprietor of the *Columbia Phoenix*.

Both houses promptly ratified the Fourteenth Amendment to the United States Constitution—the Democratic members all voting in the negative. In the Senate, Cain, of Charleston, offered the following resolution, which, on the motion of Wright, of Beaufort, was tabled:

Resolved, That a committee of five be appointed, to inquire and report whether the senators who voted in the negative on the ratification of the amendment to the United States Constitution have or have not violated their oaths and committed perjury; and if so, to recommend what course should be adopted by the house to vindicate the purity of its organization.

"Daddy" Cain was a Northern negro preacher who got that soubriquet by his efforts to mimic the ways of the old-time Southern negro. For some time he edited in Charleston his paper, called the *Missionary Record*, the columns of which often contained matter of a most incendiary character—appeals to the passions of the negroes, coupled with outrageous abuse of the white people. For some of the bloodshed in this State during the Reconstruction period "Daddy" Cain and his *Missionary Record* were in part responsible. Though sometimes denouncing the corrupt practices of his party, his actual affiliation was generally with the thieves. He stumped the State in advocacy of the election of Frank Moses for Governor. The case of Cain is thus referred to in order to point out the influence, in some degree, once exerted by the African Methodist Episcopal Church on the side of dishonesty and discord in South Carolina.

Cain's performance in the Senate was not imitated in the House.

ELECTIONS IN JOINT ASSEMBLY.

Much interest among the Republican members centered in the election of the two Senators of the United States. The most prominent candidates were Dr. A. G. Mackey, lately the president of the Constitutional Convention; Mansfield French, a Northern man who had been for some time connected with the Freedmen's Bureau; Frederick A. Sawyer, of Charleston; and Thomas J. Robertson, of Columbia.

Robertson ran for the short term (two years) and was easily elected on the first ballot—the vote standing: Robertson, 130; B. F. Perry, 19; Mackey, 1; Sawyer, 1. The term for which Robertson was chosen was stated in the proceedings to be the term commencing March 4, 1865, and ending March 4, 1871. For the period between March 4, 1865, and the date of election, Robertson and some other Senators elected by the different negro Legislatures were, by an act of Congress, passed in 1862, declared entitled to pay as if they had actually served from the beginning of the term. For this imaginary service in the case of Robertson the allowance was something over $20,000. Mr. F. A. Sawyer, mentioned below, was of course included among the beneficiaries of the provision stated.

For the term commencing March 4, 1867, and ending March 3, 1873, the contest was much harder. There were eight ballots, and on the last the vote stood as follows: F. A. Sawyer, 76; A. G. Mackey, 68; James B. Campbell, 5. On the previous ballots Mr. Campbell had received a vote ranging from 13 to 15, and Mr. Mansfield French a vote ranging from 1 to 28. Ex-Governor Perry received one vote on the first ballot.

Thomas J. Robertson, as already stated, was a graduate of the South Carolina College, in the class of 1843. He was engaged in planting, and in that connection had been a slaveholder. After the war he was in business in Columbia, and was said to have operated extensively in the buying and selling of securities. He was without much experience in deliberative bodies and was accounted a poor speaker. He allied himself with the extremists of the Radical party in Washington. In 1869 he offered in the Senate "a bill to provide for the removal of political disabilities," which relieved the person under disability from taking the test oath prescribed in the act of 1862, and required one substantially similar to the oath of office as fixed in the South Carolina Constitution of 1868, adding this obligation to be taken by the affiant: "I will demean myself as a good citizen, supporting good order, tolerance of political opinions and freedom of the elective franchise." The bill contained a proviso "that no person shall be entitled to the benefit of the provisions of this law who was educated at the Military or Naval Academy of the United States, or who was twenty-one years of age or upwards on the 1st day of January, 1861." The extent of the disfranchisement thus proposed may be clearly seen from the very terms of the proviso. It was said by a contemporary critic that "neither Thaddeus Stevens nor Charles Sumner, nor even B. F. Butler, ever proposed a disfranchisement so cruel, so merciless, so sweeping." The bill did not become a law.

Among Mr. Robertson's earliest official acts was the recommendation of an incompetent colored man to be postmaster at Columbia. These two acts together sufficed of themselves to widen the breach already existing between Mr. Robertson and the white people of the State. His subsequent career in the Senate was inconspicuous.

Frederick A. Sawyer was a Massachusetts teacher who was engaged by the City School Board of Charleston a few years before the War of Secession to organize and superintend the Normal School, as a branch of the system of graded schools established previously. He was a man of considerable scholarship, of good address and of some ability as a speaker. In contrast with Robertson's measure of amnesty must be noted Sawyer's, previously introduced—substituting for the test oath of 1862 an oath simply obligating the affiant (if not disqualified by the Fourteenth Amendment) to support and defend the Constitution of the United States, bear true faith and allegiance to the same and faithfully discharge official duties. The bill was defeated. Sawyer had no part in corrupting the State Legislature, deported himself with dignity and courtesy, and seemed inclined throughout to be conservative. He was credited with having advised against the arming of the negro militia and with having denounced the corrupt practices of the State Government. He ardently opposed the nomination of Frank Moses for Governor, and after the nomination made some very strong speeches at different points in the State, denouncing Moses and urging the Republicans to repudiate him.

The new Supreme Court was organized by the election of Franklin J. Moses, Sr., chief justice; with A. J. Willard and Solomon L. Hoge, as associate justices.

Judge Moses had been elected to the circuit bench of the law court by the Legislature of 1865, and was recognized throughout South Carolina as a man of decided ability and of much learning in his profession. He had enjoyed a large practice before his election to the circuit bench. He was an excellent writer, his opinions taking rank among the best in the State reports—this in the estimate of lawyers of high standing and of no sympathy with Judge Moses in his affiliations at the time of his election to the bench of the Supreme Court. He served until his death in March, 1877.

Judge Willard was a New York lawyer who had in that State acquired considerable standing in the profession. He came to South Carolina as lieutenant-colonel of a negro regiment, served on the coast, and was honorably mentioned for gallant and efficient service in the battle of Honey Hill on November 30, 1864, one of the hottest and really most important battles of the war. Assigned to duty in Charleston he served as judge advocate, and was brought into public notice by his able though somewhat bitter prosecution of Keys and others (already mentioned) for the alleged killing of Federal soldiers in Anderson. Judge Willard was evidently a hard student—his opinions, especially in more important cases, showing wide and close study. His style was obscured by his tendency to metaphysical refinements and by unskilful sentential structure. These qualities gave rise to the generally unfavorable estimate in which many of his opinions were held by the profession. He served as Associate Justice till June, 1877, when he was elected by the Democratic Legislature to fill out the term of Chief Justice Moses.

Judge Hodge had come from Ohio as a captain of a Federal

company of infantry, and was practically without experience as a lawyer, except that he had acted as judge advocate in some courts-martial. He was evidently conscious of his utter incapacity—for in his eighteen months on the bench he never wrote a single opinion. "I concur" was the extent of his analysis of the legal questions on which he passed judgment. He resigned from the bench to go to Congress.

W. Hutson Wigg, of Columbia, was appointed reporter—a position he held for two years without doing any of its work.

For the First Circuit D. T. Corbin was elected, but he declined on the ground that the salary ($3,500) was insufficient. The Legislature then elected Richard B. Carpenter, who had come from Kentucky, and who was Register in Bankruptcy, resident in Charleston. He was a man of strong intellect, a lawyer of exceptional ability and a good writer, but of rather rough exterior. While on the bench he made such an impression that he was the choice of the people of Charleston for the nomination for Governor on the "Union Reform" ticket in 1870—which ticket, as will hereafter be related, was the result of an effort to bring together the people of the State, without regard to race or politics, in a movement for peace, order and honest government.

For the Second Circuit Zephaniah Platt, who had been appointed by General Canby when Judge Aldrich was removed, was elected.

For the Third Circuit the choice fell upon John T. Green, of Sumter, a lawyer of high standing and gentleman of unimpeachable character.

For the Fourth Circuit the judge elected was James M. Rutland, of Fairfield, a strong lawyer and an honest man.

The judge elected for the Fifth Circuit was Lemuel Boozer, of Lexington, a good lawyer and a man to whose integrity prominent citizens of all shades of political opinion united in bearing hearty testimony.

For the Sixth Circuit the choice first fell upon Mr. George W. Williams, of York—a gentleman of the highest character and a lawyer whose reputation, clientage and influence extended considerably beyond his own county. He declined the proffered distinction—saying that as his own people had not yet tendered it he could not accept it from novices and strangers. William M. Thomas, a native of Charleston, and for some years a resident of Greenville, was afterwards elected. Judge Thomas was a lawyer of fair ability and good character, and he conscientiously labored to discharge well the duties of his office. He very soon aroused the opposition of the Radicals.

The judge of the Seventh Circuit was Mr. T. O. P. Vernon, of Spartanburg, a good lawyer and an honest man, whose independent course so soon offended the Radical Legislature that he was impeached on trumped-up charges. Acting on the advice of friends he resigned—this in January, 1871.

Ex-Governor James L. Orr was, without solicitation on his part, elected for the Eighth Circuit.

The chief justice's salary was fixed at $4,000—the other justices and the circuit judges to receive $3,500 each.

NOTABLE LEGISLATION.

Some of the more important acts passed at the special session will serve to show somewhat the temper and the ideas of the new lawmakers.

By an act to establish a State police was organized what was popularly known as the State constabulary. The Chief Constable, appointed by the Governor, at a salary of $1,500 a year, was John B. Hubbard, who came last from New York, who was alleged to have helped to manufacture some of the evidence against Mrs. Surratt for alleged complicity in the assassination of Lincoln, and who was an unscrupulous hireling admirably suited for the dirty work for which he was employed—the endeavor to intimidate white people into quiet submission to negro domination. Deputies were appointed where the Republican managers wanted them, and received pay at the rate of $3.00 per day. In the election of 1870 the armed constabulary managed by Hubbard was flagrantly used to further the reelection of Governor Scott. A "deputy chief constable" was appointed in every county thought to be doubtful, and to each were assigned so many "deputy constables" as were deemed necessary to embolden the negroes and discourage the whites. The deputies were men of low type, suited to the work for which they were employed.

By "an act to suppress insurrection and rebellion" the Governor was authorized in his discretion to call out the militia, to "command the insurgents to disperse," to take possession of railroads and telegraphs and "to employ as many persons as he may deem necessary and proper for the suppression of insurrection, rebellion or resistance to the laws." In furtherance of the purposes of this act, a joint resolution was afterwards passed authorizing the Governor to employ an "armed force" of 100 men, to be armed, equipped, and, if necessary, mounted. This force, of whom twenty were mounted, was duly organized and was used to cooperate with the State constabulary for election purposes. Fraudulent statements were freely used to procure payment for fictitious services.

For the services of the constabulary for the fiscal year commencing October 1, 1868, the sum of $10,000 was appropriated, and for the fiscal year commencing November 1, 1869, the sum of $30,000 was allowed. The actual expenditures on the constabulary for the year last mentioned amounted to $55,056.60.

By an act entitled "an act to close the operations of the Bank of the State of South Carolina" it was sought to seize the assets of that institution and distribute them among certain holders of its bills (said to have been bought up at ten cents on the dollar), amounting to $486,823—the exact scheme being to fund the bills in six per cent. State bonds running twenty years. Attorney-General Chamberlain gave an opinion sustaining the validity of the act. The Supreme Court, upon a proper case made, held the act to be void because it impaired the obligation of the State's contracts with creditors other than the bill holders. The scheme thus blocked was manifestly a piece of jobbery. Whether corrupt means were used to "work" the Legislature to pass the act cannot be said—the parties objecting to it having sought and obtained relief in the court.

The "act to authorize a State loan to pay interest on the public debt," approved August 26, 1868, directed the borrowing of a sum not exceeding $1,000,000 on coupon bonds of the State, to be sold at the highest market price, and "for not less than a sum to be fixed by the Governor, the Attorney-General and the Treasurer, who are hereby authorized to appoint, under a commission signed by them, some responsible bank or banker in the city of New York, to act as financial agent of the State, to be subject to their direction and control."

By this act was inaugurated the series of irregular, unlawful and fraudulent acts committed in connection with the public debt of the State. The board thus created—Scott, Chamberlain and Parker—selected as the "financial agent" one Hiram H. Kimpton, of Boston, who was said to have been an intimate friend of the Attorney-General. Kimpton (apparently about forty) affected much style in dress and great elegance of manner—gold-rimmed spectacles being among the accessories used to give him a distinguished appearance. the *Charleston News* it was that first called him "cherubic"—so suave and calm and sleek did he always look. He was essentially what would now be called a "smooth article." From the time of his appointment to the end of his career he was the active agent, the constant helper of the Scott-Parker-Chamberlain ring that operated under the name and style of the "Financial Board."

In the first two years of his work Kimpton's "commissions" for services alleged to have been rendered under his contracts with the Board amounted to something over $75,000.

An "act to organize townships and to define their powers and privileges" was introduced in the Senate by D. T. Corbin, and duly became a law. It was but a copy of the statute of some Northern State—presumably Vermont, as Corbin had come thence to South Carolina. The act (of sixty-nine sections) embodied a most elaborate scheme of township government. Every township was made a body corporate, and provision was made for "town" meetings, each to be presided over by a "moderator." Every town was required to choose a town clerk, three selectmen, one or more surveyors of highways and one constable. The selectmen were made overseers of the poor, registers in town elections, general supervisors of the affairs of the town and auditors of its accounts. They were charged with the repair and maintenance of highways, and might levy taxes therefor. The surveyors, in addition to duties as such, were the "warners" to call out the road-working gangs, and to those officers the selectmen were to depute that work. The pay of the selectman was fixed at $1.50 per day, of the clerk the same, and of the surveyor fifteen cents per hour. This law was soon found to be so utterly inapplicable to conditions in South Carolina that it was summarily repealed—this by the act of January 19, 1870. The manifest object of the measure was to create a multitude of offices to be filled by negroes—for negroes would have controlled well-nigh every "town" (or township) meeting.

By the "act to authorize additional aid to the Blue Ridge Railroad Company" the Comptroller-General was authorized to pledge the "faith and funds" of the State to the payment of bonds of that corporation to the amount of $1,000,000, and also to pledge such "faith and funds" to "secure the punctual payment of any contracts which shall be made by said company to an additional amount not exceeding $3,000,000." Out of this act grew the issue of the famous "Revenue Bond Scrip"—the transactions under this act and in the circulation of the so-called scrip constituting one of the schemes of plunder instituted by the Republican ring in South Carolina.

A concurrent resolution was adopted which "requested the Governor to take such action as may be necessary to have the more important towns in the State garrisoned by United States troops, that peace and order may be preserved and the rights of the people may be protected"—an early acknowledgment of the inability of the negro government to sustain itself without the aid of Federal bayonets.

The salaries of State officers were fixed as follows: Governor, $3,500, with a private secretary at $2,000; Lieutenant-Governor, $10 a day during the session, with member's mileage; Secretary of State, $3,000—that sum to include clerk hire; Adjutant-General, $2,500; Comptroller-General, $3,000; Treasurer, $2,500, with a clerk at $1,800; Attorney-General, $3,000, with an allowance of $1,500 for clerical assistance; Superintendent of Education, $2,500.

The Senate passed a resolution fixing the pay of its president pro tem. at $6 a day, in addition to his allowance as a senator. The additional pay was drawn for the whole of every session until 1874. A question having in 1873 arisen as to the legality of this allowance, an investigation was ordered. Josephus Woodruff, the clerk of the Senate, swore that the additional pay had been regularly drawn under the resolution mentioned—which, however, is not to be found in the printed volume purporting to contain all the Senate resolutions of the session mentioned.

The Legislature omitted to fix the pay of its members—these contenting themselves with the constitutional allowance of $6 per day, with mileage at the rate of twenty cents per mile each way. The members always took pay for Sundays.

This first session consumed seventy-two working days, and the appropriation for the pay of members and for other legislative expenses was $130,000. There were passed seventy-one acts and nine joint resolutions.

The regular session commenced on November 24. The following acts are given as indicating the character of the legislation.

By an act to amend the criminal law the death penalty was removed from all crimes except wilful murder.

An "act to enforce the provisions of the civil rights bill of Congress" forbade any common carrier and any person doing business under a license to make any discrimination on account of race, color or previous condition of servitude—the violation punishable with a fine of not less than $200 and imprisonment not less than six months.

By "an act to confirm and declare valid the recent election of mayor and aldermen in the city of Charleston," the General Assembly "legislated into office" the first Radical council (mixed of whites and negroes) in that city, headed, as before stated, by Gilbert Pillsbury as mayor.

The county seat of Beaufort was changed from Gillisonville to Beaufort.

The county seat of Barnwell was directed to be changed from Barnwell to Blackville—the change to take effect upon the cession by the town of Blackville of a suitable site for a courthouse and a jail.

The Board of Trustees of the University was made to consist of seven members, elected by the General Assembly, with the Governor as chairman ex officio. The salary of each professor was raised from $1,000 to $2,000, without fees. The trustees were authorized to establish a preparatory school, and the institution was declared open to all students without regard to "race, color or creed."

The State orphan asylum was established, and was temporarily located in Charleston. As the institution was open to children of both races, on terms of actual social equality, the purpose of its founders to exclude white children was fully accomplished. The asylum afterwards fell into disrepute.

A commission of three members at an annual salary of $3,500 each was provided for "the revision and consolidation of the statute laws of the State." On this commission the Legislature afterwards elected D. T. Corbin, Charles W. Montgomery (of Newberry) and W. J. Whipper. The work was done almost entirely by Corbin, who had the use of a compilation previously made by James L. Petigru, and who copied almost literally the New York Code of Procedure. Governor Scott, in his message in 1871, charged that this work had already cost $50,000, whereas, in his opinion, and that of competent lawyers, it should have been done for $5,000.

An "act to reorganize and govern the militia" established an elaborate system of military forces, and forbade, on pain of fine and imprisonment, organizing, drilling or parading by any bodies other than the "national guard of South Carolina" thus provided. The organization of the negro militia cost in all certainly $200,000, besides a considerable sum fraudulently misapplied in procuring and altering certain arms given by the Federal Government.

An "act to provide for the enumeration of the inhabitants of this State," though ostensibly passed in obedience to a direction in the Constitution, was altogether useless in contemplation of the United States census to be taken in 1870. Many if not most of the persons employed for this business (chiefs at $5, assistants at $4 a day) were so grossly incompetent that the accuracy of their figures was never recognized—indeed was not much claimed by the Radicals themselves. The taking of the census cost the State $75,524. The cost of taking the United States census of 1870 in this State (the tables including much more than a mere enumeration of inhabitants) was $43,203.13, not counting tabulation, etc., in the office at Washington. It is fair to conclude that the work done here cost quite double what the same work cost under the management of Federal officials.

The salary of the State Auditor, an official provided for in the tax assessment law passed at the special session, was fixed at $2,500, with provision for a clerk at $1,000. Reuben Tomlinson got this easy job.

The sending or the acceptance of a challenge to fight "at sword, pistol, rapier, or any other dangerous weapon," was made punishable by imprisonment not exceeding two years, and the person so offending was to be incapable of voting or of holding office. The same penalties were denounced upon those who should carry any challenge to fight a duel or who should be present at such as second or aid.

At this session there was passed the act providing for the "land commission," consisting of a commissioner at an annual salary of $2,000, with fees and mileage in certain cases—the Governor, the Comptroller, the Treasurer, the Attorney-General, and the Secretary of State constituting the advisory board. The sum of $200,000—to be raised by the issue of six per cent. bonds of the State, running twenty years—was provided for the purchase of improved or unimproved lands, these to be divided into parcels of not less than twenty-five and not more than one hundred acres and sold to actual settlers who should pay therefor in five annual instalments, commencing at the end of the third year of possession, with annual interest at six per cent., reckoning from the date of purchase. Thus was inaugurated a scheme which throughout its workings constituted one of the great frauds that helped to fix the character of Republican rule in South Carolina.

By a joint resolution the Governor was authorized to purchase "2,000 stand of arms of the most improved pattern, with the usual complement of ammunition." Governor Scott selected Winchester rifles.

The Fifteenth Amendment to the Federal Constitution was duly ratified—the Democrats in each house, of course, voting in the negative.

The tax levy for the fiscal year commencing November 1, 1869, was five mills for State purposes, and the levy for the several counties ranged from three to seven mills.

In the House a resolution was adopted, January 15, 1869, expelling and excluding from the hall John T. Sloan, Jr., the Columbia correspondent of the *Charleston Courier*. The ground of this action was the correspondent's denunciation of the course of Whipper, one of the members from Beaufort, towards the State University—that black individual having shown a purpose to turn out the incumbent professors and put negroes in their places.

At this session the House voted the speaker a gratuity of $550.

The session of 1868-69 ended March 14 and included eighty-nine working days. The acts passed numbered 107 and the joint resolutions twenty-one.

Proceedings were purposely delayed in order to prolong the session. One device for killing time was the frequent demand for the ayes and noes—the rule (fixed in the Constitution) requiring but the demand of one member, seconded by one other. Another trick was the explaining of a member's vote by him when his name was called. On many occasions the yeas and nays were called on this matter. Sometimes, with a view to entangle matters, a member would ask to be excused from voting on the pending motion to excuse. These tactics were occasionally dignified with the name of "filibustering," and were more than once employed to postpone or to defeat investigation of fraudulent transactions. This vicious, expensive and dishonest procedure was common in all the negro Legislatures except that elected in 1874, which, though controlled by a debased and corrupt majority, affected to be better, and was in some things better, than any of its predecessors under negro rule.

At the session of 1868-69 Governor Scott instituted his custom of giving official receptions in the executive mansion—at which (according to general report) whites and blacks of both sexes intermingled on terms of actual social equality.

IGNORANCE IN OFFICIAL STATIONS.

Among the members of the new Legislature were necessarily a great number of men of very limited education, and a number also who could fairly be classed as ignorant. Of the colored members a very small portion only had more than the bare rudiments of an English education. Most of the native negro members had been slaves, to whom the opportunities for even elementary training had been of necessity very limited. Some of the newcomers claimed to have had academic or higher education in States where, as they alleged, negroes had the same entrance to schools and colleges as whites. There were instances of ignorance in stations where it should not have been tolerated. For example, one George W. Barber, the negro Senator from Fairfield (elected in November, 1868, to succeed Judge Rutland) could read but little, whilst his knowledge of writing was confined to his ability to write his signature, which he wrote mechanically. The device of learning to write the signature only seemed to be common among the negroes who aspired to office or to superiority over their fellows. A man who could read but poorly and could not write at all would learn to put his name down in ill-formed letters and would thus pass as educated—at least according to the standards set by the Republican party when it acquired control of the government in South Carolina.

There was much trouble in finding competent Republicans to fill the different county offices. For clerks of the circuit courts, probate judges and sheriffs white men of sufficient capacity were found to undertake the duties, but many of them needed to employ help in the persons of white Democrats, who did the required service largely at the request of good citizens, who realized the plight in which the new order of things placed those whose interests were involved in the proper conduct of the different offices.

The office of county commissioner was of especial importance, and in too many instances the new incumbents were clearly—in some cases confessedly—incompetent. By the employment of some capable white man—except in very rare cases a Democrat—as clerk, matters were kept straight, and there was some regard to correct standards in the conduct of a most important branch of the public business.

The school commissioners were, as a rule, grossly incompetent. In some counties capable white men were induced to accept the place on the urgent request of sensible colored Republicans who realized the situation. In others, white men were elected rather by default. But in many of the counties the school commissioner was without a single qualification for the office. In 1870 a colored man was elected commissioner in Richland County—this over a competent white man whose single disqualification, in the eyes of the negroes who controlled the county, was that he was not a Radical. The following paper emanating from the successful aspirant will serve to show the extent of his qualifications:

County School Commissioner's Office,
Richland County.
Columbia, S. C., Sept. the 27 1871

The foller ring name.person are Rickermended to the Boarde

[Here follows a list of names.]

for the Hower [Howard (?)] Schoole Haveing Given fool sat es fact Shon in thi tow Last years
the whit Shool

[Another list of names.]

The official heading was printed on the letter paper used.

Such was a document written by the official head of the common school system in one of the largest counties—an official who was required by statute to "have the general supervision of all the common and public schools in his county," to "counsel with and encourage trustees and teachers, see that the common school law is properly enforced, and do whatever may promote the cause of education in the county," and to "select two suitable and discreet persons who, together with himself, shall constitute a board of examiners, whose duty it shall be to examine all candidates for the profession of teacher."

The writer of the above-quoted paper was the Rev. N. E. Edwards, a regularly licensed preacher of the A. M. E. church.

In September, 1876, the following letter was written to a merchant in Columbia by a school trustee in Barnwell County:

Mr. ———— Pleas give to the Barrow for mee Dick Kenenedy one plug of to Baco and a Bar of soape i am Bussey my self trying to get a Bale of Cooton to you or i would acome.

One of the duties of school trustees was the employment of teachers and the approval of their pay certificates.

The new Board of Trustees of the State University was elected by the Legislature in February, 1869, and, besides the Governor, who was a member ex officio, was composed as follows: F. J. Moses, Jr., Thomas J. Robertson, John L. Neagle, Reuben Tomlinson, J. K. Jillson, white; B. A. Bosemon, Jr., F. L. Cardozo, colored. Of this board every man except Jillson was later on publicly charged with having been guilty of some corrupt act—with having taken or given a bribe, or having conspired to cheat the State, or having been otherwise guilty of corruption. It is safe to say that the destruction of the University would have occasioned no regret to any member of this governing body. That destruction, so far as the white people of the State were concerned, was effected a few years later by the enforcement of the policy to which this board was really committed—the conversion of the institution into a mixed school for whites and negroes.

In December, 1869, a new Board of Regents was elected for the Lunatic Asylum, as follows: Dr. A. G. Mackey, Henry Sparnick, Joseph Crews, white; W. B. Nash, B. A. Bosemon, Jr., Joseph Taylor, S. B. Thompson, R. C. DeLarge, R. B. Elliott, colored. Dr. Mackey had been the president of the Constitutional Convention, was then Collector of the Port of Charleston, and was a Mason of eminent degree; and as to his purposes touching the asylum the white people had no fears. There was a like feeling towards Mr. Sparnick, who had been connected with the *Charleston Courier,* who had been made Commissioner of Immigration by Governor Scott, and who had no ill-will towards the white people. Joseph Crews was among the most vicious incendiaries that the Radical party gave to South Carolina—hating the white people who opposed him and doing all he dared do to stir up strife between the races—a frequent participant in the schemes devised to rob the public treasury. Of the colored members of this board every one afterwards engaged in some corrupt transaction—every one sought so to adjust the relations of the two races as to humiliate the white man and keep South Carolina under the actual rule of the negro.

The transfer of the asylum to the care of this board caused infinite pain and positive alarm to those interested in the white patients, and the deepest concern to all the white people except the few who had affiliated with the Radical party—and some of these, it must in simple justice be said, deplored and criticised the manifest purpose of Joe Crews and the negro regents to mix the races or to negroize the management in this home for the afflicted.

Especial anxiety was felt about the superintendency of the asylum—it being feared that Governor Scott would yield to the demands of some of the new regents, seconded by prominent Republicans of both races, and, removing the capable and experienced incumbent (Dr. J. W. Parker), appoint some newcomer of doubtful character and manifest incapacity. The board demanded the appointment of one DeLamatta, a stranger to everybody in South Carolina, but the Governor insisted that he wished to retain the services of Dr. Parker—expressly stating that having inquired into DeLamatta's antecedents and qualifications, he was satisfied of that person's unfitness. The pressure continued, and in the summer of 1870 the Governor yielded to the extent of retiring the incumbent. Dr. J. F. Ensor, a Northern man who had served creditably in the Federal army, was appointed. Dr. Ensor continued in charge of the asylum until his resignation in 1877.

A further evidence of the policy of the new regents was given in their appointment of one Dr. J. D. Harris to a place on the staff of the institution. Harris was a colored man who had come from Virginia (where he had run for lieutenant-governor on the Republican ticket) and who had been recommended for the superintendency by many of the Radical members of the Legislature. The place assigned Dr. Harris was that of assistant physician—in which capacity he would come in constant contact with the patients. The outrage involved in this appointment is especially apparent from the fact that in the asylum at that time there were only about thirty colored patients, with about two hundred white.

Dr. Ensor represented to the board the conditions that would necessarily result from any attempt to force Harris upon the white patients, and plainly stated that the new official was distasteful to them. Thereupon Harris resigned, and the new board—evidently counseled by Dr. Ensor—made no further attempt like that of the appointment of the negro doctor.

The administration of Dr. Ensor was such as to allay the apprehensions caused by the dominance of negroes on the Board of Regents and, it must in simple justice be said, was throughout honorable to him.

The protection against incapacity or peculation, supposed to be afforded by requiring from public officials good and sufficient bonds for the performance of public duties, was wanting in the cases of numerous incumbents under the new government. In the cases of some of the most important officials—notably the clerks of the circuit courts—the bond was subject to the approval of the county commissioners only, many of whom, as already stated, were both incompetent and irresponsible.

MORE NEW LAWS.

Among the more important acts passed at the legislative session of 1869-70 may be noted those of which a statement is now given.

The census not being completed, the time for such completion was extended to December 31, 1869.

Claflin University, the institution for colored people, located at Orangeburg, was duly incorporated—the act requiring that students be received without regard to race or color.

An "act to prevent and punish bribery and corruption" made ample provision to punish all persons in any official relation who might be bribed.

An "act to secure equal civil rights and to provide for the enjoyment of all remedies in law by all persons, regardless of race or color," conferred upon persons of color the same legal rights and remedies theretofore allowed to any free white person.

The system of free common schools was regularly established—the previous legislation on this subject having been temporary only.

By "an act to regulate the publication of all legal and public notices" the Attorney-General, the Comptroller-General and the Secretary of State were authorized to designate one or more newspapers in which all public advertisements, whether for State or county, should be published. For some time the acts of the Legislature were published in full in designated papers—the usual price being ten cents per line. The Republican organ in Columbia received twenty-five cents per line (about $2.50 for an inch in the present type of *The State*) for publishing many columns of the acts. Among the statutes thus published was the code (hereafter noticed), which covered 109 pages in the printed book of acts. This publication was of no possible benefit to any citizen—the lawyers and magistrates having of necessity to buy the book itself.

The above-cited act gave rise to the use of "auxiliary sheets"—sheets partly printed elsewhere than in the office of publication. On this plan Republican organs were established in several of the counties, and to these, without reference to circulation, was given the public advertising.

By "an act to alter and amend the charter and extend the limits of the city of Columbia," those limits were so arranged as to take in the suburban population, composed entirely of negroes, and give that race a heavy majority in the municipal election. By this act the incumbent council were legislated out of office. The council elected under the act was composed of whites and negroes. Under the Radical administration the city debt was increased in four years from $360,000 to $850,000, whilst the value of all permanent improvements made during the period stated did not exceed $75,000.

The "act to grant certain persons therein named and their associates the right to dig and mine in the beds of the navigable streams and waters of the State of South Carolina for phosphate rocks and phosphatic deposits" gave the grantees the right for the term of twenty-one years to dig, mine and remove from the beds of the navigable streams of this State, for a royalty of one dollar per ton of rock or deposit so taken. This act was vetoed by Governor Scott, but was passed over his veto. To procure that passage one Timothy Hurley, a carpetbagger residing in Charleston, and a professional lobbyist not disguising his craft, spent $25,000 in bribing members of the House, Moses receiving $1,000 for his services as speaker, and each of several members getting $300 or more for his vote.

The salary of the Secretary of State was fixed at $3,000, with an allowance of $1,000 for clerk's salary—an increase to the extent of the latter salary.

The amount of bonds to be issued for the benefit of the Land Commission was increased by $500,000.

The per diem and mileage of members of the General Assembly were fixed at the maximum figures allowed by the Constitution.

The tax levy for State purposes for the fiscal year commencing November 1, 1869, was fixed at five mills, and the county tax at three—with extra levies in a few counties.

By the act entitled "an act to revise, simplify and abridge the rules, practice, pleadings and forms of courts of this State" the Legislature adopted the "code of procedure," generally called the "code." This code was almost a literal copy of that of the State of New York— the Code Commission and the Legislature even forgetting in some cases to alter the language to suit existing laws not affected. The adoption of this code gave well-nigh universal dissatisfaction to the lawyers. But after thirty-five years' use, with immaterial changes suggested by experience, it has come to be regarded an admirable system—the product of legal minds of extraordinary power, worthy of close study by every man aspiring to be an educated lawyer, and of great merit as a specimen of terse, technical and yet scholarly English.

By the adoption of the "code" and by accompanying legislation trial justices were provided in each county—officers having just the powers now exercised by magistrates. For the election, by the people, of justices of the peace, as required by the Constitution of 1868, the Legislature made no provision. In the selection of trial justices Governor Scott had little or no regard to qualifications of any kind. Many of these officers were grossly incompetent for lack of even elementary education, and some of them were vicious partisans who sought to stir up strife by encouraging colored people to controversies with the whites. Many of the constables were ignorant, some even illiterate, and there were frequent instances of misconduct on their part.

Among the appropriations at this session was one of $25,000 for the Governor's contingent fund for the year commencing November 1, 1869. The expenditures charged to this fund were $49,386.27. The expenditures on account of contingent funds of the other State officers was $41,987.12, against appropriations aggregating $9,300.

A gratuity of $500 was voted Speaker Moses.

Samuel W. Melton, of Columbia, was elected judge of the Fifth Circuit, to fill the vacancy caused by the death, in January, 1870, of Judge Lemuel Boozer. Judge Melton had but recently avowed his connection with the Republican party. He was a graduate of the South Carolina College, a man of far more than ordinary ability, a painstaking lawyer and one among the very best advocates that have ever appeared in any of the courts of South Carolina.

Associate Justice Hoge having resigned, the Legislature elected in his place Jonathan J. Wright, the negro senator from Beaufort.

Wright was a native of Pennsylvania, and thirty-three years old. He graduated from a high school in Lancaster, and then studied law for two years in Montrose. He was admitted to the bar in Susquehanna County—being the first negro licensed to practice in that State. He had practiced only four years before coming to South Carolina and when elected was practically without experience in any of her courts. No white man of his attainments and experience (except, of course, his immediate predecessor, Hoge) could have been elected to the bench of South Carolina. He was chosen because he was a negro—and most of the Democratic members of the Legislature thought it well to vote for him as against Whipper. It was generally believed that Wright frequently had the help of a capable lawyer in preparing his opinions. Some of those papers bear evidence of having been written entire by some good lawyer—being in their language, arrangement and citations manifestly beyond Wright's capacity. He remained on the bench till, in 1877, he resigned under impeachment for official misconduct.

Hoge having resigned about two months before Wright's election, the Legislature voted the latter the "undrawn salary" for that period —amounting to about $600.

The session of 1869-70 ended March 1, 1870—having consumed eighty-three working days. The appropriation for legislative expenses was $125,000. There were passed 110 acts and sixteen joint resolutions.

THE CIVIL RIGHTS BILL.

At this session the Legislature passed the "act to enforce the provisions of the civil rights bill of the United States Congress and to secure to the people the benefits of a republican government in this State." As indicating the temper and purposes of the lawmakers in their desire to enforce social equality between the races, the act is given in full:

Whereas, in this State the government is a democracy, the people ruling, and the government is also a republican one, in which all things pertaining to the government are in common among all the people; and whereas, it follows that no person is entitled to special privileges, or to be preferred before any other person in public matters, but all persons are equal before the law; and whereas, these propositions lie at the very foundation of our policy, and the American people have embodied the same, in the most emphatic manner possible, in their organic and statute laws, and the same do by their sovereign will and pleasure sustain; and whereas, notwithstanding all these great and glorious facts, there are found some brutal, ill-disposed and lawless persons in the State who persist in denying and trampling upon the sacred rights of certain of the people; therefore,

Section 1. Be it enacted by the Senate and House of Representatives of the State of South Carolina, now met and sitting in General Assembly, and by the authority of the same, It shall not be lawful for any common carrier, or any party or parties engaged in any business, calling or pursuit, for the carrying on of which a license or charter is required by any law, municipal, State or Federal, or by any public rule or regulations, to discriminate between persons on account of race, color or previous condition, who shall make lawful application for the benefit of such business, calling or pursuit.

Sec. 2. Whoever, being a common carrier, under any public license, charter, rule or regulation, shall, by himself or another, wilfully assign any special quarters or accommodations whatever to any passenger or person whom such common carrier may have undertaken to carry, or who shall, under any pretense, deny or refuse to any person lawfully applying for the same, accommodation equal in every respect to that furnished by him to any other person, for like compensation or reward, in a like case, having no regard to the persons *per se* who may be applicants therefor, shall, on conviction, be punished by a fine of one thousand dollars, and also by confinement at hard labor in the penitentiary for five years; and if such fine be not paid, the convict shall be confined in the penitentiary at hard labor, as aforesaid, for not less than six years.

Sec. 3. Whoever, conducting or managing any theater, or other place of amusement or recreation, by whatever name the same may be recognized, or however called or known, if such theater or place be licensed or chartered, or be under any public rule or regulation whatever, shall wilfully make any discrimination against any person lawfully applying for accommodation in, or admission to, any such theater or place, on account of the race, color, or previous condition of the applicant, or shall refuse or deny to any person lawfully applying therefor, accommodation equal in every respect to that furnished at such place for a like reward to any other person, on account of race, color, or previous condition of the applicant therefor, shall, on conviction, be punished by a fine of one thousand dollars, and also imprisonment at hard labor in the penitentiary for three years.

Sec. 4. Whoever, not being the principal offender under sections 2 and 3 of this act, shall aid or abet in or about the commission of any of the offenses therein mentioned, shall, on conviction, be punished by imprisonment at hard labor in the penitentiary for three years, and no such convict shall ever vote or hold any office under any law of this State.

Sec. 5. Any commander, conductor, manager or other person superintending or having charge of any vessel or vehicle, or any theater or other place mentioned in this act whatsoever, and as such having authority and power to order and manage affairs in or about the same, who shall suffer or permit to occur any violation of this act which such commander, conductor, manager or person so superintending, and having such charge as aforesaid, can possibly prevent, shall be considered an aider and abettor in the commission of any such offense, and, on conviction, shall be subject to the penalties provided in Section 4 of this act.

Sec. 6. Every corporation or party whatever, holding any charter or license under the authority of this State, who shall violate any of the provisions of this act, shall thereupon be deemed and held to have committed an abuse of the franchises conferred by or under every such charter or license, and, on conviction, shall forfeit every such charter or license; and any party or parties who, having so forfeited any such charter or license as aforesaid, shall nevertheless presume to use or operate under or by virtue of the same, as well as every person who shall be found aiding any such party or parties thereabout, shall, on conviction, be punished by a fine of one thousand dollars or imprisonment in the penitentiary for three years.

Sec. 7. In every trial for violating any provisions of this act, when it shall be charged that any person has been refused or denied admission to, or due accommodation in, any of the places in this act mentioned, on account of the race, color, or previous condition of the applicant, and such applicant is a colored or black person, the burden shall be on the defendant party, or parties, so having refused or denied such admission or accommodation, to show that the same was not done in violation of this act.

Sec. 8. Every case arising under the first section of this act, and not provided for specifically in some succeeding section, shall be prosecuted and decided in accordance with the general provisions of this act.

Sec. 9. The several solicitors of this State are hereby specially charged to take care that this act be promptly and rigorously enforced; and every such solicitor who shall fail in any respect in the performance of his duty under the requirement in this section contained, shall be deemed to have committed a misfeasance in office, and, on conviction, shall forfeit his office, and be incapable of holding office for five years, and shall also pay a fine of five hundred dollars; and, in every case in which any such solicitor shall fail in his duty, as herein prescribed, the Attorney-General shall make the most effective prosecution possible against him on behalf of the State; and neither any solicitor nor the Attorney-General shall settle or enter a *nol. pros.* in any case arising under this act, except by the consent of the court.

This act (section 7) undertook to lay upon the person charged with any offense thereunder the burden of establishing his own innocence—a provision which, whilst glaringly unconstitutional, seems to have been without precedent in any legislation ever attempted in this country.

Occasional attempts were made to enforce this act in the courts, but it seems that no case resulted in the conviction of the offender. The negroes, as a class, were little affected, and the few who undertook to assert their social rights in the courts were so plainly actuated by the desire for notoriety or political advantage that they gained nothing by their performances. The law soon became a dead letter. It was repealed in 1889.

A COSTLY INVESTIGATION.

On March 26, 1869, the Legislature passed a resolution to appoint a joint committee "to thoroughly investigate the disordered state of affairs in the Third Congressional District, and the causes of the intimidation, outrages and murders perpetrated preceding and at the late general election, whereby it is stated that a fair and unbiased expression of the people's choice could not be and was not given; and of the existence of organizations inimical to the peace and well-being of the State."

The committee was composed of five Republicans and two Democrats. It commenced work ($6 a day) on May 3, 1869, and held its last examination on October 2 following—there being many days of intermission. Witnesses were examined in Newberry, Abbeville, Anderson and Edgefield, and the printed testimony covered 830 pages. The majority of the committee reported intimidation, oppression and Kuklux outrages to have prevailed all over the district, evidencing a "party thoroughly organized for the sole purpose of defeating the real object of the Reconstruction acts of the United States Congress." They charged that the killing of Lee Nance and of B. F. Randolph was each the result of a preconcerted plan of the Democrats. The work of this committee had no relation to the contest of Hoge against Reed, already noticed—the congressional committee having made its own independent inquiry. The cost of the investigation here—for the pay of the members, the witnesses and the stenographer, printing and incidentals—was $68,000.

In February, 1871, the Senate appointed a special committee to "investigate the money transactions of the joint committee appointed to investigate the electoral affairs of the Third Congressional District." This senate committee, after taking testimony, reported that the sum of $7,500 appearing in the account of the joint committee to have been paid to "James Dunbar" had been "improperly and fraudulently drawn," and they recommended that legal proceedings be taken to recover the same. James A. Dunbar, a "carpetbag" lawyer living in Columbia, testified that he had been employed in a general way by Joseph Crews, chairman of the joint committee, but had received no pay whatever. Crews testified vaguely that he had employed James A. Dunbar, but declined to say whether the warrant drawn to the order of "Jas. Dunbar" was paid to him.

The prevailing opinion at the time of the exposure of this transaction was that Joseph Crews had pocketed the $7,500.

HE SOLD A CADETSHIP.

In the early part of 1870 a committee of the lower house of Congress found it necessary to investigate the alleged sale of West Point cadetships by members having appointments in their gift. As one result of this inquiry the Rev. B. F. Whittemore, representing the First Congressional District of South Carolina, was found guilty of having sold to a broker in New York, for the sum of $2,000 cash, the right to name a cadet from that district. Whittemore confessed that he had received money in connection with the appointment, but alleged that he had devoted the funds to "political and educational purposes." The house committee having reported that he had been guilty of conduct deserving of the penalty of expulsion, he sought to avoid the judgment of the body by vacating his seat. He sent his resignation to the Governor, who promptly answered with an acceptance. The House, however, refused to receive this paper, and, by a resolution unanimously adopted, expelled Whittemore— first declaring that he was guilty of "having dispensed an appointment to West Point and to the Naval Academy for valuable considerations, contrary to law," and further declaring that he was unworthy of his seat.

SCOTT'S FIRST TERM

Whittemore affected to be both aggrieved and mortified, and he forthwith asserted that he should with confidence appeal to his constituents for vindication. The vindication came soon enough. In the special election held very shortly after the expulsion he was returned to Congress by a large majority. When his credentials were presented, Gen. John A. Logan, of Illinois, moved that admission to the House be refused—this on the ground that the member-elect was "a man of infamous character." The motion was adopted by a vote of 131 to 24. Whittemore's principal champion in the entire affair was Benjamin F. Butler, of Massachusetts—in those days better known as "Beast Butler," a title which he had fairly earned by his conduct when in command over the city of New Orleans during the Civil War.

Whittemore bore a bad character before he came to South Carolina. It was publicly stated that he had swindled his associate in business (W. F. Shaw, of Boston,) out of about $5,000. He was a large man of good proportions, he had a striking face, to which his flowing beard added strength, and his voice was one of extraordinary power with no int of harshness. Speaking as if he were in ordinary conversation, he made every word plainly and pleasantly heard all over the Senate chamber. His enunciation was clear and accurate and his accent almost wholly free from that peculiarity which in its lower forms Southern folks have been accustomed to call the "Yankee twang." Some of his power over his negro constituency was explained by the fact that he sang well at his religious meetings and that his addresses—whether religious or political or both—could be easily heard by the many hundreds of people who were listening. He was a minister of the Northern branch of the Methodist Episcopal Church.

Whittemore's misconduct nowise impaired his standing among those whose votes he wanted. In the November election following his repudiation by the lower house of Congress he was elected to the State Senate from Darlington, and served in that body till 1877, when he left South Carolina to escape prosecution for some of the frauds in which as a Senator he had participated.

SOME FRUITS OF MISGOVERNMENT.

With the close of the legislative session of 1869-70 may be said to have ended the first two years of negro rule in South Carolina. In that short period the consequences were seriously hurtful to every interest of the people without regard to race or color.

The State debt was increased from $5,407,306.27 to $14,833,349.17, and in December, 1870, the amount as given in the official reports was $18,575,033.91.

At the close of the year 1870 all the counties except Anderson and Fairfield were in debt—the aggregate of these liabilities exceeding $250,000. At that time also there were outstanding pay certificates of teachers in the public schools amounting to $57,320.40.

The average annual tax levy for some years before the Civil War had been less than $550,000—which, however, did not include the interest on the State debt, amounting to about $350,000 annually, which was paid out of the net earnings of the Bank of the State of South Carolina. The taxes, State and county, for the fiscal year ending October 31, 1869, amounted to $1,764,357.41.

The public school system was grossly inefficient throughout, by reason not only of the incapacity of school commissioners and their consequent inability to organize any proper system of education, but because of the lack of funds. For the two fiscal years commencing November 1, 1868, the aggregate appropriations amounted to $100,000 and the revenues from the poll tax a little less than that sum—so that the average yearly fund was less than $100,000. Before the war the annual appropriation for free schools was $74,400, distributed among the several districts at the rate of $600 for each member to which the district was entitled in the House of Representatives. This fund went only to support free schools, to which none but the actually indigent could send their children—and, of course, no provision was made for the education of negro children. Under the Republican administration the public school system for the first two years at least was the merest pretense. Few schools were wholly free—the plan chiefly in vogue being the payment of money to a private school, thus reducing the tuition fees. The negro schools received considerable aid from churches or benevolent societies in the Northern States and thus managed to keep up a semblance of school work. The collection of the poll tax was so loosely conducted that only those who had some taxable property were required to pay. The negro population were thus almost wholly exempted from making the only contribution to the support of government to which under the Constitution and laws they were subject.

The land commission, to which the Legislature had allowed $700,000 for the purchase of "homes for the homeless, lands for the landless," had accomplished little but the acquisition of quantities of land, much of it at prices far beyond its real value, accompanied with many scandalous transactions. False entries in deeds of conveyance were made, so that the price paid for the property might appear more than the sum received by the seller. In one of these "deals" the land commission divided $90,000 as their profits. The doings of the commission were tainted throughout with fraud, and there were, besides, irregularities involving loss to the State.

The administration of the public business had been marked by reckless waste amounting to actual malfeasance. Members of the Legislature had sold their votes, and State officers had made money out of their positions at the expense of the taxpayers. The legislative and the executive department were tainted with corruption, and the entire administration was weak by reason of the incapacity of most of its agents. Among the white people the almost universal feeling towards the State Government was contempt for its weakness and disgust for its rottenness.

One cause of trouble—one obstacle to the due administration of the laws—was in the reckless use of the pardoning power. In his first year Governor Scott issued 332 pardons. For the first eighteen months of his term (1874-76) Governor Chamberlain issued seventy-three.

SCOTT'S CAMPAIGN PLANS.

The dissatisfaction among the white people was so plainly shown that it evidenced a purpose to make a fight to wrest the control of the government from the party in power and thus restore peace, order and the economical administration of public affairs. Governor Scott very soon disclosed his plans. In the early part of 1870 he made a speech in Washington, in which he pretended to depict the rebellious and bloodthirsty doings of the white people in South Carolina, and declared that the only law for those people was the Winchester rifle. Upon his return to the State he put his theory into practice by arming the negro militia and supplying them with an abundance of ball cartridges.

Of the evils and dangers of arming the negroes against the whites Governor Scott had had ample warnings.

In the summer of 1865 in Beaufort District a movement was started by a Federal officer to organize and arm companies of troops from among the negro population. The matter having been brought by Governor Perry to the notice of General Gillmore, the department commander, that officer promptly forbade the enrollment of any more negro troops.

When Governor Scott first appeared to contemplate the arming of his militia the *Charleston News* protested, and predicted that the course proposed would bring trouble. Thereupon Mr. George W Williams, of that city, a leading merchant and a conservative citizen, addressed a letter to the Governor, expressing surprise at the intimations of the *News,* and strongly presenting the troubles that would surely follow the arming of the negroes. Governor Scott answered by denouncing the suggestions of the *News* as sensational and as not warranted by his policy or purposes.

In York County, early in 1870, a company of negro militia was organized under the command of one John R. Faris, a white man, and duly supplied with rifles and ammunition. This company caused so much trouble in the neighborhood affected by the conduct of its members, that the grand jury, after making inquiry into the matter, presented the organization as dangerous to the peace of the county, wholly incompetent, in case of necessity, to enforce the laws, as a nuisance to the township in which it manoeuvered, and as "a violation of the Constitution of the United States, which guarantees to every State a republican form of government," in that "the lives, liberties and property of citizens are placed in the hands of a military organization not responsible to the law for their conduct." This remonstrance remaining unheeded and the conduct of the negro company afterwards becoming unendurable, a party of men proceeded to capture some of the guns and warn the soldiers that they must discontinue their operations. The company thereafter ceased to exist.

The number of guns issued to the negro militia between March and July, 1870, was over 7,000, whilst there was but one company of whites enrolled—that of Capt. Richard O'Neale, Jr., in Columbia. This company had been raised under the advice of some of the best men in the city—they thinking that the organization of white companies would help to preserve the peace. Applications were received from some companies in other parts of the State, but these were rejected on the ground, as alleged, that the quota of companies in the several regiments had already been enlisted, or that the supply of arms was exhausted.

Captain O'Neale's company never really formed a part of the militia. Assigned to a regiment commanded by a negro colonel, they promptly disbanded.

Col. Asbury Coward, principal of King's Mountain Military School, located at Yorkville, communicated with Governor Scott with reference to procuring guns and equipments for drill purposes. Governor Scott claimed to be unable to furnish what was desired, but at the same time called attention to that provision of the militia law which declared "that there shall be no military organizations or formations for the purpose of arming, drilling, exercising the manual of arms, or military manoeuvers, not authorized by this act and by the commander-in-chief, and any neglect or violation of the provisions of this section shall, upon conviction, be punished with imprisonment at hard labor in the State penitentiary for a term not less than one year, nor more than three years, at the discretion of a competent court."

At the session of the Legislature, 1870-71, a bill was introduced to exempt schools from the operation of the above-cited provision, but it was rejected on the unfavorable report of the military committee. A bill to exempt Colonel Coward's school suffered a like fate. A few years later the cadets used guns (furnished by Colonel Coward) without interference or objection.

The militia companies were located principally in Charleston, in Beaufort, and in upcountry counties where the Radical managers expected most trouble in electing their tickets. Preference seemed also to have been given to counties of the congressional districts represented by Hoge and Wallace respectively. In Laurens, where Joseph Crews, lieutenant-colonel of the "national guard," was the Radical leader, there were eight companies, and to that officer were issued 620 Remington rifles (changed to breech-loaders), fifty Winchesters and 11,000 rounds of ball cartridges. In York there were three companies, in Fairfield three, in Chester three, in Union three, in Spartanburg three, and in other counties in the upcountry two or three each.

In Union County the militia companies were directed by one June Mobley, a mulatto fellow whose incendiary talk caused much friction between the races, but who had no office in the "national guard." He received 10,000 rounds of ammunition.

The captains of the different companies were invariably negroes, all of them ignorant and some of them so poorly educated that they made their crossmarks in receipting for guns and cartridges. Each company operated in its own neighborhood, without any apparent recognition of superior authority.

The constabulary force, numbering about five hundred men, still commanded by John B. Hubbard, were armed with Winchester rifles, and most of them also carried a pistol, sometimes two pistols, apiece. This force was kept well in hand by Hubbard, under the direct orders of Governor Scott, for the purpose of overawing the whites in doubtful counties, and thus helping on the Governor's reelection.

The first term of R. K. Scott as Governor of South Carolina was marked by the inception of several of the schemes whereby the people were robbed and oppressed. It was during this term that what was then called the "Radical ring" was actually organized—a combination of men high in the councils of the Republican party, whose robberies, instituted very shortly after the inauguration of the negro government, continued without ceasing and without remorse for six years, and then stopped only because of the fear of opposition by the national Republican organization and repudiation by the National Government, whose bayonets were necessary to enable the State administration to maintain its authority.

Some of the schemes were completed in Governor Scott's first term, but their consequences extended into his second term and into the term of Governor Moses. Some of the later schemes were devised to cover up previous frauds. Some of the actors in these plans to defraud the State continued in their villainous work for the six years preceding the inauguration of Governor Chamberlain in 1874. The history of these frauds is the history of the Republican party in South Carolina—the continuous story of that party's abuse of opportunity, its infamous use of its power over the white race, its flagrant breach of every pledge contained in its platforms, its unvarying support of plunderers and corruptionists. For these reasons it is thought best that of the present history the account of the flagrant frauds and actual robberies perpetrated—whether by corrupt indi-

SCOTT'S FIRST TERM 139

viduals acting of themselves or by officials claiming to act under the forms of law—should constitute a separate chapter.

Of the different acts of the State government and its several officials enough will be written, as the main story proceeds, to show the character of the different administrations considered as governmental agencies and to show also the purposes of the men who corruptly used their powers or shamelessly abused their trusts.

THE CAMPAIGN OF 'SEVENTY.

There was much difference of opinion among the white people as to the best mode of seeking to drive Governor Scott and his party out of power. With a view to discussing the situation and settling on a policy a conference of editors was held in Columbia on March 16, 1870. The conclusions of the gentlemen thus assembled were expressed in the following resolutions unanimously adopted:

Resolved, That this conference recognizes the legal right of all citizens of this State, irrespective of color, to suffrage.

Resolved, That this conference recognizes the legal right of all the citizens of this State, irrespective of color or former condition, to office, subject alone to personal qualications and fitness.

Resolved, That in the judgment of this conference a convention of the people of the State, opposed to radicalism and in favor of good and honest government, should be held in the city of Columbia at some convenient time, for the purpose of nominating a State ticket, which, while assuring equal and exact justice to all, will afford some degree of security, prosperity and good government.

Resolved, That this conference respectfully suggest to the people of the State Wednesday, the 15th of June ensuing, as a suitable time for holding said convention.

In response to this call a convention duly assembled in Columbia on the day suggested. The delegates were as follows:

Abbeville—Not represented.

Anderson—White: James A. Hoyt, William Perry, M. B. Gaillard, B. F. Crayton, D. M. Watson, George Seaborne, Dr. W. C. Brown, J. H. Earle.

Barnwell—White: Bryan Weathersbee, Daniel Minor, R. B. Wilson, Robert Aldrich, B. W. Middleton, William Singleton, W. L. Ball.

Beaufort—Not represented.

Charleston—White: Robert Mure, George L. Buist, J. Francis Britton, John Campsen, Bernard O'Neill, R. Hunter, J. B. Steele,

A. Melchers, T. S. Browning, Thomas Y. Simons, F. W. Dawson, J. D. Parker, L. McLain, Alva Gage, J. J. Grace, W. E. Mikell, E. W. Marshall, A. O. Stone, E. G. Goodwyn. Colored: John Abbott, B. R. Kinloch, Charles Michael, W. E. Marshall, William Black, Rev. Jonas Bird, A. Harper, M. Cochrane, W. A. Sneed, W. G. Routt, Charles Miller, Theo. Mitchell, W. L. Shecutt, Cyrus Fenwick, Elias Johnson, William R. Fordham.

Chester—White: James Pagan, George W. Melton, John J. McLure, C. S. Brice, James G. Lowry, R. S. Hope, J. B. Atkinson, H. C. Brawley, D. R. Stevenson, W. A. Peden, C. H. Ragsdale, R. N. Hemphill, C. W. McFadden, W. P. Gill, J. H. Moffatt, H. J. Pride, John Sanders, John Simpson, J. W. Wilkes, John B. Cornwell. Colored: Henry Ware, Benjamin Blake, Philip Cloud, Daniel Witherspoon, Thomas Hardin, Green Johnson, Luke Debardelaben, Prince Young, Marbery DeGraffenreid, Robert Stratford, Elias Hopkins, Sancho Sanders, Philip Douglass, Jefferson Jordan, Gabriel Moore, Alexander Kelsey, Green Jackson, William DeGraffenreid, Thomas Brown, Alfred Walker.

Chesterfield—White: E. F. Malloy.

Clarendon—White: James M. Davis.

Colleton—Not represented.

Darlington—White: J. L. Coker, E. E. Evans, J. P. Chase, Dr. J. E. Bird, H. J. Lee. Colored: William Brearly, Rev. C. Jones, Rev. E. J. Snetter, H. Brown, Ben Dargan.

Edgefield—White: M. C. Butler, W. T. Gary, John E. Bacon, Lewis Jones, Dr. Thomas Jennings, Robert B. Watson. Colored: Dick Padgett, Harper Bostick, Henry Raford, Westley Jefferson, Clarke Simpkins, George Simpkins, Henry Barnes, Thomas Gregory.

Fairfield—White: James B. McCants, David Provence, Thomas Jordan, Abraham F. Lumpkin. Colored: Alfred Moore, Sandy Ford, Samuel Anderson, John O. Crosby.

Georgetown—Not represented.

Greenville—Not represented.

Horry—White: Joseph T. Walsh, Henry Buck.

Kershaw—White: James Chestnut, A. M. Boykin, J. B. Kershaw, John D. Kennedy, W. L. DePass, William M. Shannon, J. M. Davis, T. H. Clarke, W. A. Ancrum, T. F. McDow, W. Z. Leitner. Colored: Frank Anderson, Austin Loyd, Clayborne Hamilton, Henry Carlos, David Jenkins, John Miller.

Lancaster—White: Phin. B. Thompson, John B. Erwin, D. J. Carter, B. J. Witherspoon, J. R. McGill, K. G. Billings, R. E. Potts, Wesley Hilton, John Brown, R. Truesdale. Colored: C. L. Jones, Charles Walker, Robert Wilson, Nelson Crawford.

Laurens—White: G. W. Sullivan, T. J. Craig, B. W. Ball, R. P. Todd, B. F. Langford.

Lexington—White: F. S. Lewie, H. A. Meetze, H. W. Rice, D. T. Barre, Daniel Kinsler, J. H. Huffman.

Marion—White: Duncan E. McCormick. W. J. McKerall, Johnson B. Young. Colored: Rev. Erasmus Gourdin, George Murphy, Rev. Bruce Williams.

Marlboro—Not represented.

Newberry—White: J. J. Scott, J. M. Calmes, Y. J. Pope, E. S. Keitt, Jacob Singley, J. P. Kinard. Colored: Willis Sanders, Aaron Wilson, James N. Simms, James Washington, Allen Abernethy, Ben Harrington.

Oconee—White: J. L. Shanklin, Dr. A. E. Norman, Samuel Lovingood, Robt. A. Thomson, J. W. Livingstone.

Orangeburg—White: Paul S. Felder. Colored: M. Caldwell.

Pickens—White: J. H. Philpot, T. A. Rogers, W. E. Holcombe, F. B. McBee, L. M. Robbins.

Richland—White: William Wallace, John T. Sloan, Jr., E. W. Seibels, Alexander Smythe, John C. Seegers, J. C. Bell, Richard O'Neale, James Claffey, Charles P. Pelham, John P. Thomas, R. D. Senn, W. H. Stack, H. D. Hamiter, Jesse Lykes, William Weston, Warren Adams, S. G. Garner. Colored: Jackson Miller, James Mayrant, Louis Wallace, Washington Gibbes, Frank Faust, James Goodwin, Uriah Portee, Tip Brown, Henderson Burns, John Gilmore.

Spartanburg—White: W. K. Blake, John H. Montgomery, Isaac Morgan, Isaac Smith, H. H. Thomson, Cato Mooney, S. E. Means, A. B. Woodruff, William Choice, Rev. J. S. Ezell, H. H. Foster, Joseph Young, Sr.

Sumter—Not represented.

Union—White: William H. Wallace, J. E. Lindsey, D. H. Sheldon, T. A. Carlisle, G. D. Rake, W. T. Jeter, James Thomas, M. M. Montgomery. Colored: Daniel Clowney.

Williamsburg—White: Dr. J. A. James, N. M. Graham, S. T. Cooper, J. R. Lambson, Dr. S. D. M. Byrd, D. E. Gordon. Colored: Abraham Gibson, Robert Parsons.

York—Not represented.

The following officers were elected:

President—William M. Shannon.

Vice-Presidents—J. P. Kinard, S. E. Means, F. B. McBee, B. J. Witherspoon, J. E. Bird, A. Melchers, James Kennedy, Henry Barnes, Moses Benson, M. Cochran, M. Caldwell, J. Gibson.

Secretaries—Robert Aldrich, W. G. Routt.

Committees were appointed as the business of the Convention required, and to them were referred several papers declaring the policy and the purposes of the new movement thus inaugurated.

The committee on platform, through its chairman, Gen. M. C. Butler, submitted the following paper, which was unanimously adopted:

This convention, representing citizens of South Carolina, irrespective of party, assembled to organize the good people of the State in an effort to reform the present incompetent, extravagant, prejudiced and corrupt administration of the State government and to establish instead thereof just and equal laws, order and harmony, economy in public expenditures, a strict accountability of officeholders, and the election to office of men of known honesty and integrity, doth declare and pronounce the following principles upon which men of all parties may unite for the purposes aforesaid:

1. The Fifteenth Amendment of the Constitution of the United States having been by the proper authorities proclaimed ratified by the requisite number of States, and having been received and acquiesced in as law in all the States of the Union, ought to be fairly administered and faithfully obeyed as fundamental law.

2. The vast changes in our system of government, wrought by the internecine war between the two sections of the States, and following in its train, are so far incorporated into the constitutions and laws of the States and of the United States as to require that they be regarded accomplished facts, having the force and obligations of law.

3. This solemn and complete recognition of the existing laws brings the people of South Carolina into entire harmony upon all questions of civil and political rights and should unite all honest men in an earnest and determined effort to establish a just, equal and faithful administration of the government in the interest of no class or clique, but for the benefit of a united people.

The committee further recommended that the new political organization be known as the "Union Reform Party of South Carolina," and this suggestion was adopted.

After some discussion the Convention resolved to nominate candidates for the two State offices to be filled at the coming election—Governor and Lieutenant-Governor.

Judge R. B. Carpenter, of Charleston, was nominated for Governor—received 77½ votes against 4 for Judge George S. Bryan. Neither of these nominees had sought the position, and it was known that Judge Bryan would not accept.

Gen. M. C. Butler was unanimously nominated for Lieutenant-Governor. Two colored men were suggested for this place, but each declined in favor of General Butler.

The State Executive Committee was constituted as follows: J. B. Kershaw, of Kershaw, chairman; William Wallace, E. W. Seibels and John B. Palmer, of Richland; William T. Gary and Henry Barnes, of Edgefield; S. P. Hamilton, of Chester; Henry McIver, of Chesterfield; Y. J. Pope, of Newberry; James A. Hoyt, of Anderson; Henry Buist and Jonas Bird, of Charleston; William H. Wallace, of Union.

There was a "Union Reform" candidate in each of the Congressional districts, and a full ticket was nominated in each county. To the colored people was accorded representation by generally putting one of their race on the legislative ticket, and in most instances one on the list of nominess for the office of county commissioner.

The Republican State Convention met in Columbia on July 26. The session consumed two days, and there was so much apparent wrangling that an outside observer might have concluded that the party in South Carolina was about to be torn into hostile factions by internal dissensions. But such was not the case. The nominations were unanimous—R. K. Scott for Governor; Alonzo J. Ransier, colored, for Lieutenant-Governor.

The character of Scott's administration will have been gathered from what has already been given. Ransier was a man of little education—though he sometimes affected literary allusions in his speeches and writings, some of these latter evidently furnished by somebody else. He held extreme views on all matters then affecting the interests of the State, and was especially offensive, sometimes insolent, in his demands for "equal rights"—meaning social equality so far as penal statutes might effect the latter condition. While Lieutenant-Governor—his position then affording him his first opportunity—he became involved in some of the frauds done by the Radical ring.

The Republican platform (reported by B. F. Whittemore) contained the following "planks":

1. Approval of "the fidelity evinced by President Grant to the Republican party."

2. Endorsement of the administration of Governor Scott as "wise, economical and honest, and deserving, as it has received, the hearty approval of the loyal people of South Carolina."

3. Demand for "a continuance of strict and close economy in all departments of our government, in order to maintain the happy financial condition which our State has attained under Republican rule."

4. Gratitude for the adoption of the Fifteenth Amendment, as "the crowning act of American civil emancipation," and the pledge to elevate to public office only capable and honest Republicans, irrespective of race, color or previous condition.

5. The pledge of the Republican party in South Carolina to "a firm, fearless and unfaltering support of the civil rights bill."

6. An appeal to Congress to open to settlement and preemption the 48,000,000 acres of public lands in the Southern States—to be sold to the landless under the provisions of the homestead laws of the United States.

7. "Equality before the law, free speech, a free press, a free ballot and free schools."

The issue having been joined between the Union Reform party and the Republicans, both sides began preparations for an active canvass. Governor Scott had the State constabulary well in hand. The constables in the counties where they operated were regularly paid for their services and made regular reports to Chief Hubbard. These reports contained statements as to the progress of the campaign, gave assurances of Republican victory and in some instances expressed the purpose to overawe the white people in the neighborhood under surveillance. The constables were in most instances rough characters—it being impossible (even had it been desired) to get reputable citizens to undertake the work required. Negroes were put on the force about equally with whites—and the negroes selected were chiefly those whose own conduct was thought likely to bring on a disturbance. The efforts of the constabulary were directed towards the accomplishment of these objects—to embolden the negroes and inflame them against the whites, to exasperate the whites, and by a combination of the two results to bring about race conflicts which might be used to help the Republican party in South Carolina.

The negro militia were offensively active during the entire campaign. They drilled frequently—on nearly every occasion marching through some street or public road with bayonets fixed and drums beating. Frequently occupying the entire roadway, they thus needlessly incommoded and naturally irritated the white people for whose benefit their offensive movements were plainly intended. They were especially fond of moving about in independent squads, carrying their guns and firing them off—to the great annoyance of the white people and sometimes to the alarm of women and children.

Some of the Radical leaders were actually inflammatory in their harangues to the negroes. John L. Neagle, Comptroller-General, made a speech in Yorkville, in which, after exhorting his negro hearers to defend their rights and yield nothing to the white people, he significantly said: "Matches are cheap." June Mobley, a vicious and mouthy negro, a member of the House and a man of commanding influence with his race in Union, lost no opportunity to inflame the negroes against the whites, and, if he could do so with safety to himself, bring on a disturbance which should result in bloodshed. In one of his speeches he declared that for every negro who might be killed in Union County ten white men should die. Joseph Crews, lieutenant-colonel of the "National Guard," was always bitter in his denunciation of the white people, made constant appeals to the passions of his negro followers and openly advised them to use their guns and use the torch as well. Other Radical speakers of lesser prominence pursued similar methods, whilst the lower tier of negro leaders—notably the captains of militia companies—"added fuel to the flames" by their noisy boasts and their open threats to use their guns. This line of conduct appeared to meet the approval of the Radical leaders of both races. They made protestations of peace and in general terms exhorted their negro constituents not to resort to violence. But if any man of influence among those leaders (and teachers) of the black race disapproved the teachings of Crews or

Mobley or Neagle, or men of their type, such disapproval found no expression in words. On the contrary, the negroes were rather encouraged in their folly and made to understand that with them, as against the whites, was the State Government, backed by the army of the United States.

The white people were without organization except their political clubs, and were but poorly supplied with arms. The ugly conditions brought about by the arming of the negroes, by the incendiary teachings of many of the Radical leaders, and by the aggressive, frequently insolent, sometimes threatening, conduct of the negro militia induced the whites to prepare for the worst by having arms ready in the event of a conflict—a contingency which seemed reasonably certain and which appeared also to be desired by Scott and other Radical leaders.

The Union Reform party proceeded to an energetic canvass. Full tickets were nominated in all the counties—especial care being taken to select candidates whose high character, clean record and conservative course in life might commend them to the kindly consideration of the colored people. In the case of the Legislature and of the Board of County Commissioners the negroes were generally represented on the ticket. In some instances, where the Republican nominee was honest and capable, the opposition refrained from putting out a candidate. Every effort was made to promote peace and prevent misunderstanding between the races.

The burden of the campaign naturally fell upon the nominees for Governor and Lieutenant-Governor—Judge Carpenter and General Butler. They addressed meetings in every county—sometimes under circumstances requiring coolness, courage and consummate tact to prevent a breach of the peace, possibly attended with bloodshed, such as the Radical managers plainly desired. There were disturbances in some places, caused by the offensive behavior of some of the negroes, who were emboldened in their conduct by the readiness if not the actual presence of negro militia. Besides the two candidates named, the Union Reform nominees for Congress, together with leading men in different counties, took the stump and pleaded the cause of reform in the State government and peace between the races. Especial efforts were made to persuade the colored voters to break away from the control of their leaders and join with the whites in the effort to restore honest government. In this matter two difficulties especially were encountered throughout the campaign—the belief of the negroes that the oath taken in joining the Union League bound them to vote the Republican ticket, and the persecution visited upon colored men who declared the purpose to vote for Carpenter and Butler. That persecution took several forms—abuse, threats, personal violence, the severance of the marital relation, and in a few cases excommunication. There were some colored men killed during the canvass by men of their own race, and in the judgment of those best acquainted with the circumstances the sufferers were shot because of their avowed opposition to the Radical ticket.

The Radical managers evidently depended upon the power of the Union League, the influence of race prejudice and the demonstrations of the negro militia and the constabulary as the agencies by which the election was to be carried. Most of the speeches on their side were mere appeals to the negroes to stand by their new friends against their old masters who, some Radical orators vehemently declared, would not only deprive them of their political rights, but would, if such a thing were possible, put them back in slavery.

There was little opportunity for joint discussion—though at some town or neighborhood meetings spokesmen of the reformers were heard along with Republican speakers. The State committee of the Union Reform party urged that the nominees for Governor and Lieutenant-Governor have a joint discussion, and the Republican chairman (Ransier) affected willingness for such an arrangement. But the Reformers' demand that Scott and Carpenter, Butler and Ransier, should be the speakers being refused, no joint discussion ever came off.

In this campaign one incident which especially engaged the public attention was the letter of Judge James L. Orr, in which he declared his purpose to vote for Scott and Ransier, and gave his reasons for so doing. The letter was quite long, but it really contained only these reasons:

1. Because the objects which the Union Reform party proposed to accomplish were entirely impracticable and the results of the proposed canvass would be pernicious.

2. Because reform could be accomplished through the Republican party only—being impossible through the Union Reform movement.

3. Because, notwithstanding the existence of just cause for complaint in the conduct and condition of public affairs, "the Republican party had done much to ameliorate the condition of the white people"—in the adoption of the homestead exemption, in prohibiting the collection of debts incurred for the purchase of slaves, in the abolition of imprisonment for debt, and (notwithstanding the "extravagance and improvidence" of the dominant party) in raising the price of State bonds "from 26 in January, 1868, to 90 at the present time."

The statements of Judge Orr are deserving of especial notice because they constituted his reasons for separating himself from his own people—the reasons of a gentleman whose ability was everywhere recognized and of whose personal honesty there has never been a question. That Judge Orr's views were not shared by any considerable portion of the white people was plainly demonstrated in this election of 1870. The number of white men who followed him into the Republican party was inconsiderable, and these had been almost wholly without influence.

In the appointment of election commissioners (who selected the managers) Governor Scott ignored the Reformers' request for representation on the boards and put the election in the control of men who would do his bidding.

There were fears of trouble on election day—these due not only to the excited state into which the negroes had been worked during the campaign, but to the threats and demonstrations of the negroes themselves—particularly some of the negro soldiers. It was commonly reported, and naturally believed by the whites, that the negro militia intended to appear at the polls with their guns. In Yorkville it was stated that the negro company intended to stack their guns in front of the polling place for the day. In that instance the militia officers took advice and kept their guns in their armory—a course which undoubtedly prevented bloodshed. The white man who would have submitted to the indignity proposed would, in that day and time, have been accounted a craven of the lowest type. A like spirit pervading the white people all over the State, the miltia as such were not permitted to meddle in the election. But there were instances of misconduct on the negroes' part which showed the effects of their leaders' teachings. A few of these must suffice to indicate the spirit of the negroes as taught by their leaders, white and black.

In Charleston while Judge Carpenter was quietly going home he was hooted, jeered and insulted by a crowd of young negro vagabonds—this without protest from some grown negroes present and without interference by the city police.

A gentleman of Charleston who exercised the right to express his opinion and to use the street in walking from one point to another was set upon by negro policemen and severely clubbed about the head—the manifest purpose of this action being to assert the negro's power over the white man.

A gentleman having the care of the Union Reform ballots for one of the island precincts near Charleston was met by a crowd of five or six hundred negroes, insulted, maltreated and compelled by force to give up the tickets—the negroes actually threatening his life. Taking refuge in a house, he was after a few hours released by some friends. The lawless negroes immediately attacked the party and beat them all severely, using clubs or bludgeons. At the poll for which the ballots were intended a number of the more intelligent colored men voted the Union Reform ticket, and for this they were pursued by Radical negroes, some of these armed with guns, and in several cases were beaten almost to death.

Similar conduct marked the course of the negroes elsewhere on the coast—colored men being cruelly beaten for having voted with the Reformers.

At Laurens the tension was very great, but the knowledge by Joe Crews and the other Radical leaders that the whites were well prepared for any trouble that might come induced them to advise their followers to keep the peace, and the election passed off quietly. On the day following, however, there was a disturbance due to the riotous and seriously threatening behavior of the negro militia—the trouble growing out of a fight between a white citizen and a State constable. The negro militia repaired to their armory and fired a volley in the direction of the public square. The whites, with what pistols and guns they could get, with brickbats and walking canes, charged the building occupied by the negro troops. Three militiamen were hurt, one fatally. The guns of the company were captured, but were afterwards delivered up to the sheriff.

As a result of the excitement and irritation caused by this affray there were some lawless acts done, on the night of the riot, by unknown parties. One Powell, white, the Radical candidate for probate judge, was shot to death, as was also a negro accompanying him. Three other negroes were shot to death the same night—among them Wade Perrin, just elected to the House, whose incendiary talk and vicious conduct had caused much trouble in Laurens County.

There were incipient riots at several other polling places, but the coolness of the whites prevented serious results. In most instances the trouble was caused by the misconduct of State constables in interfering where they had no authority. Advised that in the event of bloodshed they would surely be among the sufferers, they very soon changed their procedure.

At several county seats there were United States troops, but their officers strictly obeyed orders—their instructions being not to interefere except to preserve the peace.

The Radical ticket was elected by a heavy majority—Scott receiving 85,071 votes and Carpenter 51,537.

The Radical nominee was declared elected in each congressional district, as follows:

First—Joseph H. Rainey (colored), of Georgetown, defeating C. W. Dudley, of Marlboro.

Second—Robert C. DeLarge (colored), defeating C. C. Bowen (Rep.) and R. S. Tharin (Dem.), all of Charleston.

Third—R. B. Elliott (colored) defeating John E. Bacon, both of Edgefield.

Fourth—A. S. Wallace, of York, defeating I. G. McKissick, of Union.

In the contest between DeLarge and Bowen the House decided that the election had been so tainted throughout with fraud that nobody was lawfully chosen. The contest of McKissick against Wallace was decided in favor of Wallace.

CITIZENS ARRESTED BY SOLDIERS.

Early in December of this year a body of United States soldiers proceeded to Laurens, accompanied by John B. Hubbard, as deputy marshal of the United States, to arrest certain gentlemen alleged to have participated in the disturbance above noted as having occurred on the day after the election. Warrants had been issued by a commissioner resident in Columbia, and the use of troops was ostensibly in aid of the marshal in executing process. Several citizens of the highest character were thus arrested—the charge being that they had engaged in a conspiracy against the rights of persons of color, contrary to the act of Congress, of March 30, 1870, known as the Enforcement act. There being a commissioner at Laurens, the accused waived a preliminary examination and desired to be admitted to bail. This was refused, and the prisoners were taken to Columbia and subjected to treatment that was extraordinary and oppressive throughout. They were duly charged in the United States court, but upon every indictment the grand jury returned "no bill." The accused were thereupon discharged.

A JUDGE IN TROUBLE.

Immediately upon the discharges above mentioned, the gentlemen were again arrested by Hubbard, now acting as chief constable of the State, upon a warrant issued upon his own affidavit, charging the parties with murder. Committed to the jail of Richland County, they promptly applied to Judge Vernon of the Seventh Circuit for a writ of habeas corpus. The writ was issued, and the Richland sheriff was in the act of obeying, when, waiting at the station with his prisoners, on his way to Laurens (where Judge Vernon had made the writ returnable), he was served with an order from Joseph Crews, requiring his instant attendance before the committee appointed to "investigate the official conduct" of Judge Vernon—Crews being its chairman. Resistance appearing to the sheriff useless, he found it necessary to return the prisoners to the Richland jail. A few days afterwards the judge himself was summoned to appear before the Crews committee.

Judge Vernon promptly went to Columbia, where the writ issued by his order was duly executed, and the prisoners were brought before him. The hearing was practically over when, sitting on the bench, he was served with the House resolution impeaching him of "high crimes and misdemeanors." Proceeding with the business in hand, the judge signed an order admitting the prisoners to bail. The bonds were promptly given and the accused set at liberty. They were never tried.

Judge Vernon was formally impeached—the board of managers appointed by the House consisting of W. J. Whipper, F. J. Moses, Jr., Warren D. Wilkes, of Anderson, Aaron Logan, of Charleston, and Joseph Crews. Mr. Wilkes was elected to the House as a "Conservative" or "Independent," was a man of some ability and of personal integrity. Every other member of the "board" was even then notoriously corrupt.

The charges had reference chiefly to Judge Vernon's personal habits, and were grossly unjust. So also was the charge of neglect of official duty. The charge that he had carelessly issued habeas corpus writs in blank was a mere fabrication. His real offense lay in according to the Laurens prisoners charged with murder the right of examination and the right of bail.

Mr. Joseph Daniel Pope and Col. A. C. Haskell appeared for Judge Vernon, and he pleaded not guilty. After further consideration, and on the advice of friends, he resigned. The resignation accepted, the impeachment was at an end.

One feature of the proceedings was the employment of one H. G. Worthington, a carpetbag lawyer and professional lobbyist, and R. B. Elliott, as counsel for the managers of the impeachment. Elliott received a fee of $1,000 and Worthington $500. A resolution (by Whipper) to make Worthington's fee $2,000 and Elliott's $1,500 was killed.

A GANG OF ROUGHS.

The personnel of the State constabulary, already referred to, was illustrated by the special employment of a gang of New York roughs, ostensibly to aid in making arrests in Laurens County—that being the object as stated by the Radical organ published in Charleston. The formal enrollment of the gang into the constabulary force was admitted, and there were statements as to the services to be performed, which tended to show that Scott and his fellows had in view the terrorizing of the white people in some parts of the State by a resort to assassinations. The chief of the New York detachment was one "Col." James E. Kerrigan, a genuinely tough personage, and he, along with six or seven of his squad, made oath that they were brought to South Carolina to defend Scott and his friends and kill off their enemies—among the latter being several prominent Democrats in Laurens and Union. For each Democratic leader thus disposed of the gang was to receive $10,000, coupled with the assurance of immunity from punishment in the event of exposure. The affiants further swore that the offers of money were expressly made to them by Joe Crews and W. F. Hague (a mouthy and insolent carpetbagger employed by Scott as private secretary) and confirmed

SCOTT'S FIRST TERM

by C. C. Puffer, C. C. Baker, and J. H. Runkle—all white carpet-baggers. Puffer attained notoriety chiefly as receiver of the Bank of the State, in which relation he "feathered his nest" satisfactorily and corruptly. Baker was working (or pretending to work) a gold mine in Union, and the New York gang were first told that they were to guard that property. Baker, by the way, was a lieutenant-colonel in the negro militia. Runkle was a pettifogger who then held some place in the revenue service of the Federal Government, and who afterwards disgraced the office of solicitor of the Fifth Circuit by ignorance so flagrant that it was more than once suspected that his alleged mistakes were induced by bribery or other corrupt means. The New York affiants swore that the trio mentioned furnished a list of about seventy citizens of Union County whom they were to "clean out."

Each of the five worthies accused swore that the statements of Kerrigan and his men were altogether false. Whilst the character of each of the five was such as to disentitle him to be believed on oath, yet it is probable that their talks to the Kerrigan party were but forms of "bluff" intended to impress the roughs with the bad character of the native citizens and with the importance of keeping the white people down. If, however, the New York fellows swore falsely, that fact but shows the sort of men whom Governor Scott, by his agent, Baker, selected to execute his orders in South Carolina. The episode made but little impression on the white people, except to confirm their estimate of Scott's character and purposes—though, really, nobody ever believed him bloodthirsty enough to contemplate the "cleaning out" of which some of his mouthy followers had undoubtedly talked.

The claim of the Kerrigan gang for their services, paid by the State, was over $6,000.

Not relying wholly upon his militia or his constabulary, Governor Scott, previous to the October election, applied to President Grant for Federal troops, and several additional companies were ordered into the State. After the election he made a further appeal, in response to which the President declared that the Governor should have all the troops he wanted. Senator Robertson urged that more troops be furnished and charged that the troubles in Laurens arose from the attempts of the Reformers to destroy the ballot boxes. Very soon the number of United States soldiers on duty in South Carolina was considerably increased.

CHAPTER IV.
SCOTT'S SECOND TERM.

The General Assembly elected along with Scott and Ransier (one-half of the Senators of course holding over) met November 22, 1870. C. W. Montgomery, of Newberry, was reelected president pro tem. of the Senate and Josephus Woodruff, clerk. F. J. Moses, Jr., was reelected Speaker of the House, and A. O. Jones, clerk.

Conspicuous among the members were some who, as was afterwards disclosed, were active in the several schemes of robbery that were initiated or consummated at this session—Senators W. Beverly Nash (colored), of Richland; S. A. Swails (colored), of Williamsburg; John Wimbush (colored), of Chester; George F. McIntyre, of Colleton; Robert Smalls (colored), of Beaufort; B. F. Whittemore, of Darlington; and C. P. Leslie, of Barnwell; Representatives C. D. Hayne (colored), of Barnwell; W. J. Whipper (colored), and N. B. Myers (colored), of Beaufort; William R. Jervay (colored), Timothy Hurley, John B. Dennis, H. H. Hunter (colored), B. A. Bosemon (colored), Aaron Logan (colored), of Charleston; William M. Thomas (colored), of Colleton; Samuel J. Lee (colored), Prince R. Rivers (colored), Lawrence Cain (colored), of Edgefield; William H. Jones (colored), James A. Bowley (colored), of Georgetown; Joseph Crews, of Laurens; Joseph D. Boston (colored), John T. Henderson (colored), of Newberry; Benjamin Byas (colored), of Orangeburg; Samuel B. Thompson (colored), William Simons (colored), of Richland; Franklin J. Moses, Jr., of Sumter; Junius H. Mobley (colored), of Union; J. Hannibal White (colored), John W. Mead (colored), of York.

In the Senate were one "independent," John Wilson of Anderson, and five Democrats—Diedrich Biemann, of Oconee; J. S. Burroughs, of Horry; G. W. Duvall, of Chesterfield; Joel Foster, of Spartanburg, and W. E. Holcombe, of Pickens.

In the House the opposition was maintained by three "independents" from Anderson—John Wilson, Warren D. Wilkes, William Perry—and by "Union Reformers" as follows:

Chesterfield—M. J. Hough, B. C. Evans. (These members were unseated by a resolution passed February 3, 1871, and two colored Republicans were declared to have been lawfully elected.)

Greenville—S. S. Crittenden, George W. Taylor, Hewlett Sullivan, Leonard Williams.
Horry—George T. Litchfield, James E. Dusenbury.
Lexington—F. W. Derrick, Daniel Kinsler.
Marion—Joel Allen, F. A. Miles, John C. Sellers, T. R. Bass.
Oconee—O. M. Doyle, J. S. Shanklin.
Pickens—James E. Hagood.
Spartanburg—Robert M. Smith, J. Banks Lyle, John L. Wofford, David R. Duncan.

Of the Senate eleven and of the House eighty-three were new men. Of the Senate eleven and of the House seventy-five were colored. On joint ballot the Republicans had a majority of 118, the blacks a majority of sixteen.

The Senate and the House each elected a chaplain, to draw the same pay as a member.

On Wednesday after the opening day both houses adjourned (for Thanksgiving) till the Monday following.

The vote for Governor was formally declared in joint session— Scott, 85,071; Carpenter, 51,537. The Governor and the Lieutenant-Governor were inaugurated November 28.

The Governor's message contained some items of note.

The entire debt of the State was put (Oct. 31, 1870) at $7,665,908, with assets held by the State on that date, $2,290,700—thus making it appear that the entire debt was actually $5,375,208.98.

"The land commission," declared the Governor, "was undoubtedly one of the wisest and most beneficent projects of the State, but from the odium which has been brought upon it by charges freely made of peculation and personal purposes in its administration the results have not been commensurate with the sagacity and philanthropy of its objects. About $600,000 has been expended and thousands of acres of land have been purchased, but up to this time only a comparatively small portion of the land has been sold to actual settlers, and the tardiness of the commission should be a subject of investigation thorough and searching by intelligent and honest men, who should examine fairly and fearlessly into alleged abuses which have excited widespread comment and denunciation."

Suggestions were made touching the different branches of the State government, with some references also to county matters, but all these were of the usual order—recommending, in general terms, economy, efficiency and fidelity.

Of alleged abuses in the trial justice system the Governor stated his ideas thus:

Owing to the existing prejudices and to the difficulties of obtaining impartial decisions in litigated cases, the Executive has unfortunately been thrown almost exclusively upon the members of one political party for his choice of trial justices, and in many cases persons without the requisite qualifications have been recommended. It is very important that this evil be corrected. . . . Complaints are prevalent that in many cases a spirit of litigation is promoted and stimulated with a view solely to personal acquisition, and it is asserted that not only individuals appearing before these magistrates are charged extravagant fees, but there is too much reason to believe that in many cases the costs have not only been charged to the parties, but in addition have been charged to and collected from the State. . . . I must necessarily depend very much upon the members of the Legislature for the character and fitness of trial justices, and I am disposed to consider education as an essential element among them. This would not only be proper in itself, but would afford an additional stimulus to its acquisition. By making a knowledge of the elementary branches an indispensable requisite to appointment for office a higher grade of service would be secured, as well as a more efficient performance of it.

The Governor's statements, thus given in his own words, confirmed the charge made by the white people that many of the trial justices then holding office were incompetent and venal. Governor Scott's own standard of qualification for this judicial office may be gathered from his acknowledgment that appointees should at least possess a "knowledge of the elementary branches." The efficiency and the influence of a judicial officer illiterate or, at the best, ignorant of the "elementary branches" may well be imagined. The respect for law and order, for the State government as its exponent, and for the judicial office in particular, was not much increased by the selections which the Governor or his advisers were pleased to make.

The Governor, whilst declaring that it was "highly important that the jury box should be placed beyond the reach of political influence or prostituted to the purposes of men who are themselves guilty of crime, and should be filled with our best and most reliable citizens," yet recommended the appointment of "commissioners of juries." The office of jury commissioner in each county was created and in more than one instance during the Republican regime it was plain that under the manipulation of that officer the jury lists had been corruptly tampered with.

Of this message the Senate ordered the printing of 2,000 extra copies, and the House 3,000.

ELECTIONS IN JOINT ASSEMBLY.

The term of Thomas J. Robertson as Senator of the United States expiring March 3, 1871, it became the duty of the General Assembly at this session to elect a successor.

The first apparent aspirant in opposition to Robertson was Niles G. Parker, the incumbent Treasurer of the State, who, according to the newspaper accounts, declared his readiness to put something like $50,000 into the contest. Whether Parker concluded that the sum named would not suffice or deemed the senatorship which should be bought at that price not worth the money cannot be said; but he did not enter the race.

The candidates voted for in joint assembly were, besides the incumbent, Gen. M. C. Butler, Franklin J. Moses, Sr., and F. L. Cardozo. Robertson was easily elected on the first ballot, the vote standing—Robertson, 87; Butler, 30; Moses, 23; Cardozo, 8. General Butler received the vote of all the "Reformers," and of one Republican—Frank Arnim, senator from Edgefield.

Mr. Robertson was nominated by Whittemore, who worked actively for his friend—the newspaper story being that Whittemore's devotion arose out of his gratitude for the assistance and support given him by Robertson at the time of the trouble growing out of the unlawful and corrupt sale of a West Point cadetship, for which, as already told, Whittemore was expelled from the House and was afterwards denied admittance, though reelected by the voters of his district.

Judge Moses, manifestly the superior of Mr. Robertson in intellect, experience and general equipment, was handicapped from the start by the circulation of the account of his action, in 1868, when it was reported that he had received some prominent negro at his house in a social way. Moses had promptly published a statement showing that he had received the negro in his study, really his office—which happened to be a room in the front part of his residence—and very flatly denied any imputation that he had intended to receive the negro either as a guest or as a visitor.

It was also stated that Moses had no money to spend in the contest. On the other hand the free use of money was, in more than one quarter, expressly attributed to Robertson. The Columbia correspondent of the *Charleston News* wrote, Deecmber 7:

"It is understood that $25,000 have been used by Robertson's friends since last night."

After the election the same correspondent wrote: "We hear, in the knowing circles, that $40,000 was used by Robertson in securing his election. The price of votes was $500 apiece for the rank and file, and for some of the more influential as high as $2,000 was paid. Every one is 'flush' today, and money can be borrowed easily. Mr. Robertson, with the aid of Governor Scott, has inaugurated this year the reign of bribery."

Some months later the *Washington Chronicle,* an organ of the extreme wing of the Republican party, having been called to account by the *Columbia Union* (the Radical paper edited by L. Cass Carpenter, a carpetbagger, who was afterwards convicted of forgery), for criticising certain things in the Scott administration, retorted thus: "But Governor Scott is not the sole pivot on which turn our comments on South Carolina. Defiant as it [the*Union*] is, we meet it in the same spirit. Will it explain the action of the South Carolina Legislature in electing T. J. Robertson United States Senator, when we know that he paid $40,000 for such election?"

To fill the vacancy in the judgeship of the First circuit, occasioned by the resignation of Judge Carpenter, the Legislature elected Robert F. Graham, of Marion. Judge Graham had been colonel of infantry in the Confederate army, had acted with coolness and gallantry in the defense of Battery Wagner, in Charleston harbor, had borne a good name among his own people, had been honorably dismissed from the South Carolina College in 1854, and had stood well at the bar of his own county. He was elected district judge by the Legislature in 1865. He had declared his adhesion to the Republican party in the summer of 1870—and to that declaration he owed his elevation to the bench. He died in 1874.

Montgomery Moses, of Sumter, a brother of the chief justice, was elected to succeed Judge Vernon in the Seventh circuit—the latter having previously resigned under the circumstances already related. Judge Moses had never declared himself a Republican. He had been for many years before the war engaged in law practice with his brother above mentioned.

NOTABLE LEGISLATION.

By an "act to provide a salary for the office of Lieutenant-Governor of this State" such salary was fixed at $2,500 per annum—the same to be exclusive of the pay ($10 a day) already provided for that officer while acting as President of the Senate. The actual sum received was thus about $3,500 a year.

The Clerk of the Senate and the Clerk of the House were authorized (subject to the approval of the two bodies) to provide by contract for the publication, in such newspapers of the State as might by them be deemed necessary, of the acts and joint resolutions of the General Assembly, and also to provide by contract for the permanent and the current printing of that body. Under this act was made the contract with the Republican Printing Company, hereafter mentioned, out of whose transactions grew the numerous and extensive frauds practiced in connection with the public printing.

An "act to promote consolidation of the Greenville and Columbia Railroad Company and the Blue Ridge Railroad Company" was a companion-piece to the act (already mentioned) to authorize additional aid to the Blue Ridge Railroad Company. Out of these two acts grew the schemes of robbery formulated by John J. Patterson and his associates—which will be duly noticed in the chapter on frauds. Both measures were passed by means of bribery—Speaker Moses, in the first instance, receiving a large sum for appointing certain men on the House Committee of Ways and Means and that on Railroads, and later for a like packing of committees and for working through the desired bill. State officials and members of the Legislature were likewise freely bought—bought with actual money.

By the act to create the "Sterling Funded Debt" to be used in retiring existing bonds the Governor was authorized to borrow a sum not exceeding £1,200,000, said debt to be represented by coupon bonds, bearing interest at 6 per cent. per annum, maturing in twenty years, the principal and interest payable in gold in the city of London. The execution of the scheme embodied in this act was placed in the hands of the financial board, composed of the Governor, the Attorney-General, the Treasurer, the Comptroller-General and the Secretary of State, who were required to place all bonds issued in pursuance of the act in the hands of a financial agent, to be appointed by the board, resident in London—the act further providing that the "financial agency" thereby created should not be placed in the hands of any one person, but should "be entrusted to the management of a responsible banking house of first-class reputation in the new and old world." This act, notable simply because it was one of the several schemes of the corrupt ring to make money by the manipulation of State securities, never became actually operative, and it was repealed March 13, 1872.

The tax levy for the fiscal year 1870 for State purposes was fixed at nine mills—an increase of four mills over the rate for the previous year—and the county tax was fixed at three mills, with extra levies in Beaufort, Georgetown, Barnwell, Newberry, Pickens, Edgefield and Laurens, in each of which the levy was four mills, and Clarendon, Darlington, Horry and Richland, in each of which the levy was five mills.

The State levy for 1871 was seven mills, with county levies about the same as those of the previous year.

The taxable property of the State amounting to $183,000, the State levy for 1870 was $1,647,000, and for 1871 $1,281,000. The county levies for 1870 aggregated $618,047, and for 1871 $549,000. The entire tax, due and payable during the year 1871 was $4,085,047 —this not including the poll tax amounting to $300,000. The rate of the property tax due and payable in a single year was, therefore, 2½ per cent. The taxes levied for the support of the State Government in 1860 (on a taxable basis of $489,000,000) was a little over $400,000.

The aggregate appropriations for the support of the Government, including interest on the State debt, was $1,180,544, but the expenditures exceeded that sum. The appropriation for the public schools, included in the sum above stated, was $150,000.

The session lasted 106 days, and there were passed 110 acts and sixteen joint resolutions. The legislative expenses were distributed as follows: Pay of members, $103,000; pay of 349 clerks, $80,665; 14 laborers, $1,075; 21 doorkeepers, $2,997.98; 3 firemen, $532; 3 chaplains, $1,182; 2 janitors, $386; 144 messengers, $22,340.50; 2 mail carriers, $456; 170 reporters, $13,995; 124 pages, $6,004; 17 sergeants-at-arms, $2,830; 22 solicitors, $9,515; 17 stenographers, $4,636; claims and accounts, $13,358; sundries (wines, cigars, liquors, groceries, dry goods, etc.), $157,800.03; fuel, $22; stationery, $20,199; newspapers, $3,895; postage stamps, $650.87;

telegrams, $332.45; furniture, $37,000; rent of committee rooms, $1,448; impeachment trial $1,187; joint committee to investigate finances, $41,000; printing, $152,565; total, $679,071.83. (The total of legislative expenses for the session of 1876-1877, under Democratic rule, was $75,019.)

A gratuity of $1,000 was voted to Speaker Moses.

A movement was started in the House for the appointment of a committee of one member from each county, to investigate the claims for fitting and furnishing the legislative halls and the committee rooms. While the resolution was under discussion a substitute was offered for the same purpose, differing from the original in unimportant particulars only.

When the resolution came up in the House there were preconcerted efforts to prevent its passage. The yeas and nays were repeatedly called—on some question made or on the application of some member to be excused from voting. On a motion to have the committee consist of one member from each congressional district the roll was called four times, and on the same day was called on a motion to adjourn. On the following day (January 28), on a motion to make the resolution a special order for February 6, the roll was called ten times. On January 30, on the same matter, the roll was called four times, and on the next day once. By the vote last taken the whole matter was laid on the table and the proposed investigation effectually gagged.

The claims thus disposed of consisted of the bills of certain dealers for furniture and fittings sold the State for use in the legislative halls and committee rooms. The articles bought were of the most expensive character, the prices paid for some being as follows: Chandeliers, from $1,500 to $2,500 each; window curtains, from $500 to $1,500; sofas, $150 to $175; Gothic chairs, $70 to $90; marble top washstands, $35; spittoons (billed as "cuspadores") $8 each.

The total of the bills actually presented for these articles was $40,189.87. The House committee reported the sum due to be $90,556.31, and that amount was actually paid out of the State treasury. The difference between the two amounts ($50,466.44) was divided among certain members, as their reward for putting the claim through the House.

By a concurrent resolution President Grant was requested to send into this State troops sufficient to protect the people from domestic violence. The House appointed a committee of three (Mr. Wilkes, of Anderson, Nuckles, of Union, and Whipper, of Beaufort) to visit the President and apprise him fully of the conditions which necessitated the presence of the troops. To this committee there was paid the sum of $800.

The contract for the public printing was awarded to the Republican Printing Company (composed of Josephus Woodruff, clerk of the Senate, and A. O. Jones, clerk of the House) at the following figures: Journals, calendars and other current work, at $2.75 per page; bills, $3.00 per page; permanent work (exclusive of acts), paper covers, $3.48 per page; permanent work (including acts) paper covers, $4.36 per page; rule and figure work double price. The figures thus allowed were more than double the highest paid between 1877 and 1898, and quite three times those allowed under the contract of 1905. There was, of course, no competition—the clerks as such making the contract with themselves as the Republican Printing Company.

A CONVENTION OF TAXPAYERS.

There was among the taxpaying citizens of South Carolina not only indignation but alarm at the reckless and corrupt conduct of those in control of the public interests. The press lost no opportunity to expose the misdoings of the Radical ring, and admonished the people of their duty to protest and within the limits of the law to resist. It was even suggested that the people should unite in a refusal to pay taxes, and thus not only leave the negro government without the means to run, but also expose to the country the actual extent of the burdens imposed upon those who in State affairs had little representation and no recognition.

The movement to unite the taxpayers in some sort of organization for their own protection originated in a meeting of the Charleston Chamber of Commerce, held in that city on March 24, 1871, at which the following preamble and resolutions were unanimously adopted:

Whereas, under the operation of the present State Government, the majority of the property holders and taxpayers of the State, from whom the public revenue is mainly derived, are excluded from any power in the legislation of the State, and from any practical influence in the imposition of taxes; and whereas, the moneys raised by taxation are improvidently and corruptly used and expended by persons who hold office under the State Government, and the sums appropriated for alleged public uses are excessive and extravagant; and whereas, the credit of the State has been pledged illegally and it is now proposed to pledge the credit of the State for further loans, by a new issue of bonds, to persons who may take them, in ignorance of the circumstances under which they are issued; therefore

Resolved, 1. That we, property holders and taxpayers of the State, residing in the city of Charleston, do hereby deem it our duty to declare that the bonds heretofore issued without legal sanction and the so-called sterling loan, or any other bonds or obligations, hereafter issued, purporting to be under and by virtue of the authority of the present State Government, will not be held binding on us, and that we shall, in every manner and at all times, resist the payment thereof, or the enforcement of any tax to pay the same, by all legitimate means within our power.

Resolved, 2. That we deem it our duty to warn all persons not to receive, by way of purchase, loan or otherwise, any bond or obligation hereafter issued, purporting to bind the property or pledge the credit of the State upon whom the public burdens are made to rest.

Resolved, 3. That the taxpayers of the State are hereby requested to meet in their respective counties for the consideration of this subject, and the enormous tax levies of the current year, and for the appointment of two delegates to represent each county in a State convention, to be held in Columbia on the second Tuesday in May next, for the same purpose.

Resolved, 4. That this State convention of taxpayers be requested to confer with his Excellency the Governor on the dangerous fiscal condition of the State, and request his official aid and cooperation in the investigation of the accounts of the Comptroller and the State agent in New York, so that the amount and character of the bonded debt and all other liabilities of the State can be clearly stated, with a view to such further action as may be necessary for the protection of the public creditors and of the taxpayers of the commonwealth.

A few days later resolutions of the same tenor were adopted by the Charleston Board of Trade.

Following the action of the Chamber of Commerce there were meetings in the different counties, at which delegates were elected to the convention. That body duly assembled in Columbia on May 9— the following counties being represented by the delegates named.

Abbeville—Armistead Burt, B. Z. Herndon.
Anderson—John B. Sitton, James A. Hoyt.
Barnwell—Johnson Hagood, T. J. Counts.
Beaufort—H. C. Smart, John H. Screven.
Charleston—G. A. Trenholm, T. Y. Simons, R. Lathers, George

Shrewsbury, W. D. Porter, W. B. Smith, Henry Gourdin, Myron H. Fox.

Chester—A. H. Davega, J. S. Wilson.
Chesterfield—E. B. C. Cash, A. M. Lowry.
Clarendon—John L. Manning, J. S. Richardson, J. E. Tindal.
Colleton—Not represented.
Darlington—F. F. Warley, Edward McIntosh.
Edgefield—O. Sheppard, A. P. Butler, M. C. Butler, M. W. Gary, James H. Giles, M. L. Bonham.
Fairfield—John Bratton, T. W. Woodward.
Georgetown—Benjamin H. Wilson.
Greenville—J. L. Westmoreland.
Horry—Not represented.
Kershaw—James Chesnut, William M. Shannon.
Lancaster—W. M. Connors, J. B. Erwin.
Laurens—B. W. Ball, G. W. Sullivan.
Lexington—J. M. Huffman, F. S. Lewie.
Marion—William Evans.
Marlboro—C. W. Dudley, T. C. Weatherly.
Newberry—Ellison S. Keitt, Robert L. McCaughrin.
Oconee—J. H. Doyle, William C. Keith.
Orangeburg—T. J. Goodwyn, D. J. Rumpf, A. D. Frederick.
Pickens—W. E. Holcombe, D. F. Bradley.
Richland—William Wallace, Edwin J. Scott, D. H. Chamberlain, R. D. Senn, W. K. Greenfield, C. H. Baldwin, Robert Adams, Dr. E. W. Wheeler, John H. Kinsler.
Spartanburg—Gabriel Cannon, A. B. Woodruff.
Sumter—John B. Moore, F. H. Kennedy.
Union—William H. Wallace.
Williamsburg—David Epps.
York—John R. London, Cadwallader Jones.

The following officers were elected:

President—William D. Porter.
Vice-Presidents—M. C. Butler, C. W. Dudley, D. H. Chamberlain, Gabriel Cannon.
Secretaries—W. M. Connors, Myron H. Fox.

On motion, the privileges of the floor were extended to Messrs. John P. Thomas, of Richland; A. P. Aldrich, of Barnwell; William

D. Simpson, of Laurens; C. H. Suber, of Newberry; William H. Trescott, of Greenville; and A. D. Goodwyn, of Orangeburg.

General Butler offered a resolution, which was agreed to, that a committee of eleven be appointed by the chair to confer with his Excellency, Governor Scott, in pursuance of the fourth resolution of the Chamber of Commerce and Board of Trade of the city of Charleston, and report to the convention in writing or otherwise.

The resolution was adopted, and the chair appointed as the committee Messrs. M. C. Butler, Cad. Jones, G. Cannon, B. W. Ball, W. H. Wallace, Richard Lathers, F. F. Warley, George A. Trenholm, E. J. Scott, C. W. Dudley, and T. C. Weatherly.

A number of resolutions were introduced, and, under the rule which had been previously adopted, referred without debate to the appropriate committee.

General Gary introduced a resolution to appoint a committee of seven to memorialize the Governor and the Legislature as to repealing or modifying the existing laws relating to elections, so as to incorporate therein the system of cumulative voting, with a view to protect the rights of minorities. The resolution was adopted.

The following named gentlemen were appointed on the executive committee: James Chesnut, Johnson Hagood, Thomas Y. Simons, C. W. Dudley, E. B. C. Cash, F. F. Warley, A. P. Aldrich, Henry Gourdin, H. C. Smart, William Wallace, R. L. McCaughrin, T. J. Goodwyn, J. L. Westmoreland, A. H. Davega, A. B. Woodruff, M. L. Bonham, Armistead Burt.

On motion of Mr. T. Y. Simons, it was

Resolved, That this convention of the property-holders and taxpayers of the State of South Carolina do hereby deem it our duty to declare that the bonds heretofore issued, without legal sanction, and the so-called sterling loan, or any other bonds or obligations hereafter issued purporting to be under and by virtue of the authority of the State as at present constituted, will not be held binding on us; and that we recommend to the people of the State, in every manner and at all times, to resist the payment thereof, or the enforcement of any tax to pay the same, by all legitimate means within their power.

Resolved, That we deem it our duty to warn all persons not to receive, by way of purchase, loan or otherwise, any bonds or obligations hereafter issued, purporting to bind the property or pledge the credit of the State; and that all such bonds or obligations will be held to be null and void as having been issued corruptly and improvidently.

The committee on suffrage and elections, through Col. John P. Thomas, submitted a report setting forth the operation of a system of cumulative voting, and urging that proper laws should be passed to incorporate such a scheme in the suffrage laws of this State.

The proposed plan contemplated a change in the manner of voting for members of the Legislature and the Board of County Commissioners—each voter being allowed as many votes as there should be places to be filled, and being allowed to cast the full number of votes for any one candidate or to distribute his votes among the different candidates, at his own will. It was estimated that in South Carolina the enforcement of this system would give the white people about forty members in the lower house of the General Assembly, and always one member of the Board of County Commissioners.

The scheme was favored in speeches by Messrs. John P. Thomas, George A. Trenholm, M. W. Gary and D. H. Chamberlain, and was strongly opposed by ex-Gov. John L. Manning.

The sense of the convention was expressed in the following resolution:

Resolved, That we recommend to the Legislature the passage of an election law, by which the 60,000 taxpaying voters will have a proportionate representation in the Legislature of the State, with the 90,000 voters who pay no taxes. A proposition so just, reasonable and conscientious cannot fail to commend itself favorably to every right-minded citizen.

Mr. James A. Hoyt offered the following resolution, which was adopted:

Resolved, That the report of the committee on election and suffrage laws, adopted by the convention, be placed in the hands of a special committee of seven members of the convention, whose duty it shall be to transmit the report as a memorial to the Legislature on the subject of proportional representation, accompanied with such suggestions as they deem advisable, in order to secure the passage of a law at the earliest practicable moment after the Legislature is convened, that the system of cumulative voting may be made applicable to the next general election, and that the principle may be engrafted in general upon our system of suffrage; and, further, that this special committee be instructed to use their best exertions in favor of the passage of this just, wholesome and equitable provision so as to bring about a complete and full representation of all the people.

The committee of seven was appointed as follows: James A. Hoyt, D. H. Chamberlain, M. W. Gary, Edwin J. Scott, William H. Wallace, B. H. Wilson, Henry Gourdin.

Upon the adoption of a resolution to communicate with the Governor as to postponing the collection of taxes, the President appointed the following committee: Thomas Y. Simons, William M. Shannon, M. L. Bonham, James H. Giles, John Peter Richardson.

On the report of the executive committee touching the sterling bond debt authorized by the Legislature, it was resolved: "That this convention, representing the propertyholders and taxpayers of the State of South Carolina, deem it their duty to declare that the so-called sterling loan or any other bonds or obligations hereafter issued, purporting to be by authority of this State, will not be held binding on us, and that we will resist the payment thereof, or the enforcement of any tax to pay the same, in every lawful way."

It was further resolved that the president appoint a committee, to consist of Messrs. A. P. Aldrich, Armistead Burt, John L. Manning, M. C. Butler and William D. Porter, to investigate and report a plan to restore the credit of the State, and also to report upon the present financial condition of the State as compared with that existing at the close of the War of Secession.

Mr. Edwin J. Scott offered a paper setting forth the fact that though the State's financial agent (H. H. Kimpton) was the custodian of State bonds to the amount of about $2,000,000 he had given no security but his personal bond, and presenting the following resolution, which was unanimously adopted:

Resolved, That the attention of the Governor and the Attorney-General be directed to the risk of loss by the death or default of said agent, and that they be requested to require of him a bond with such good and sufficient security as will protect the public interests in his charge.

The executive committee, reporting upon the resolution of Mr. W. K. Greenfield, looking to an investigation of the money transactions of the committee appointed to investigate the "electoral affairs" of the Third Congressional District, and upon his resolution relative to irregularities in drawing funds from the State treasury, recommended that these matters be referred to the Attorney-General. The report was adopted.

A resolution (Mr. Cannon) recommending the repeal of the law requiring legal notices to be published in certain newspapers was unanimously passed.

A resolution (Mr. Warley) expressing disapproval of all secret organizations and calling upon all good citizens to discountenance the same was also adopted.

Col. B. W. Ball, for the special committee appointed to inquire and report what reduction might be made in the number of offices and the pay of such as might properly be retained, submitted a statement showing that for the year 1871, for the pay of State officers and clerks, county auditors and county school commissioners, for legislative expenses and for contingent expenses the aggregate sum allowed was $549,250, whilst for similar purposes in 1866 the total expenditure was $106,300.

The committee further reported that in their conference with the Governor he suggested substantially the following reforms, which the committee approved:

1. The office of county auditor might be dispensed with, except in Charleston County, and the treasurer might discharge all the duties now performed by the auditor and treasurer.

2. The duties of State Auditor might with propriety be discharged by the Comptroller-General.

3. The duties of the commissioner of the bureau of agricultural statistics might be transferred to the Secretary of State, without additional compensation.

4. The place of Assistant Adjutant-General might be dispensed with, and the duties performed by the Adjutant-General.

5. The assistant librarian of the Supreme Court might be dispensed with.

The committee further reported that the following reforms were practicable:

The compensation of school commissioners should be reduced in all the counties to an equivalent for their services.

The compensation of county commissioners should be reduced, the number of days for duty fixed by law, and the per diem allowed only for days actually on duty; their accountability for moneys received for licenses, etc., should be regulated by law, requiring them to report to competent authority the amounts received, as heretofore such moneys have not been accounted for in many counties.

The fees of trial justices, solicitors and constables should be proper matters for legislation.

The Adjutant-General's salary should be reduced to an amount commensurate with his services.

In addition to the cases above particularized the committee expressed the opinion "that $10.00 per diem, during the sitting of the Senate, is ample compensation to the Lieutenant-Governor, whilst that officer now receives the further salary of $2,500 per annum."

In conclusion, the committee reported generally that "they are of opinion that the rate of compensation now paid to the various State and county officers might be very materially reduced, with great advantage to the people of the State, and without detriment to the public service."

Upon a resolution offered by Attorney-General Chamberlain, instructing the executive committee "to inquire into the alleged acts of public violence and report such plans as they may deem best for the enforcement of the laws and the protection of all the citizens of the State," that committee, through General Chesnut, reported as follows:

The committee have learned with regret that violence has prevailed in several counties, but in the greater portion of the State not a single instance of violence or outrage has occurred. Those that did occur were owing to bad government and corruption, which were followed by larcenies and incendiarism by deluded negroes. Corporal punishment and homicides resulted in cases where fraud and oppression existed.

These are lamentable truths, but the committee believe that the remedy can be found in the removal of bad officers and the appointment of competent and honest men in their places.

The convention adopted a resolution declaring that the taxpayers "meditate no resistance to the United States Government, that they accept the Reconstruction measures as finalities, that they look to peaceful agencies as a solution of the difficulties of administration and that the present exigencies demand more enlightened efforts than those intended to promote the success of party."

The committee to investigate the financial condition of the State reported the State debt to be $8,865,908.98—the report being founded upon official statements submitted to the committee by the Governor, the Treasurer and the Comptroller-General.

Thereupon the convention adopted a resolution declaring that the funded debt of South Carolina, as described in the report of the committee, "is a valid debt and that the honor and the funds of the State are lawfully pledged for the redemption thereof."

The committee appointed to confer with the Governor as to some measure of relief for the taxpayers, who were expected to pay the taxes of two years in one, reported that he expressed his purpose to extend the time for payment to March 1, 1872.

The president appointed Messrs. William Wallace, E. J. Scott and Richard Lathers a special committee to attend upon the Legislature and assist by their counsel and advice in the examining of accounts.

The convention adjourned after a session of four days.

GOVERNOR SCOTT'S LAST MESSAGE.

The General Assembly reassembled on Tuesday, November 28, 1871.

The annual message of Governor Scott contained several matters of note.

The State debt was reported at $11,994,908.98—thus showing an increase of $3,129,000 in the six months elapsed since the fiscal officers of the State made their statements to the committee of the Taxpayers' Convention.

The appropriations for the three years of Governor Scott's incumbency were reported as follows: 1868—$817,968.28; 1869 (including interest on the public debt)—$1,191,805.09; 1870 (including interest)—$1,604,053.54.

The total of the tax levies for the three years was reported at $3,502,933.77, and the total collections at $2,555,052.51—leaving uncollected $947,881.26, to which was added a penalty of 20 per cent.—making the amount actually owing by "delinquent" taxpayers $1,137,457.51.

Of the bonds, $700,000, issued for the Land Commission, the Governor declared that the State had "ample equivalent in the lands purchased, which will ultimately repay both principal and interest."

The Governor charged that the impairment of the State's credit, resulting in a depreciation of her bonds, was due entirely to the opposition and the declarations of those hostile to the existing administration.

The Governor stated that the total of legislative expenses for the previous session had been $583,651.44, and that the payment of $91,500 for furniture for the State House had been "without warrant of law."

On the line of retrenchment the Governor recommended that the members of the General Assembly should each receive an annual salary in lieu of their per diem; that the codifying commission—a "standing reproach to the State government"—be abolished and its work assigned to a competent jurist; that the office of land commissioner be abolished and his duties be devolved upon the Secretary of State; that the pay of the school commissioners be reduced from $31,500 in the aggregate to a sum not exceeding $10,000; that the salaries of all officers except the judges be reduced one-third; that the office of Assistant Adjutant-General be abolished; that the office of State Auditor be abolished and its duties be assigned to the Comptroller-General; that the office of county auditor be abolished and its duties devolved upon the county treasurer; that the pay of the clerk of the Senate and of the House be reduced; and that a change be made in the letting of the public printing, since the existing system had "involved an expenditure for the public printing so great as to have proved a real calamity to the State, and eventuated in a contract for the public printing which is a flagrant fraud upon the public treasury and should be instantly annulled."

The Governor called attention to the fact that the Republican Printing Company was "without legal existence" and that it neither owned nor controlled any journal or printing establishment.

A considerable portion of the message was devoted to a denunciation of the Kuklux Klan and to a presentation of the conditions which induced and justified the intervention of the Federal Government for its suppression and for the punishment of its members.

Touching the memorial of the Taxpayers' Convention on the subject of cumulative voting the Governor said: "I submit for your deliberate consideration whether the men who are now demanding the establishment by law of the system of minority representation are entitled to this act of magnanimity at your hands."

The Governor reported that the school funds of the State for the fiscal year ending October 31, 1871, was $240,000, to be derived from the following sources: regular legislative appropriation $150,000, poll tax collections (estimated) $50,000, deficiency appropriation $40,000.

The number of pupils attending the public schools was stated to be "about 67,098."

The lunatic asylum was reported in debt $21,271.48. It was only with the greatest difficulty that the institution was kept going.

LEGISLATIVE PROCEEDINGS.

The House elected a committee, composed of one member from each county, "on subordinate officers and attaches," a separate vote being taken for each county, and the performance consuming the greater part of each of two legislative days.

In the judicial elections Associate Justice Willard and Judges Graham of the First circuit, Green of the Third, Melton of the Fifth, Moses of the Seventh and Orr of the Eighth were reelected.

For the Second circuit the gentleman chosen was Mr. John J. Maher, of Barnwell, a citizen held in high esteem by his own people, an able and learned lawyer—one whose official conduct left upon the bar and the people of his circuit an impression than which none better or more lasting was ever made by any man who sat on the bench in South Carolina. The election of Judge Maher was wholly without solicitation on his part, and his displacement in 1876 occasioned widespread regret and disgust.

For the Third circuit Mr. C. P. Townsend, of Marlboro, was elected. Judge Townsend was a well-informed, industrious and painstaking lawyer, and his course on the bench was satisfactory to the people of the counties where he presided.

For the Sixth circuit Thomas J. Mackey, of Charleston, was elected. Judge Mackey had been distasteful to the white people of the State, by reason of his active and offensively partisan affiliation with the Republican party. He was without experience at the bar, and had but little knowledge of the law. By the adroit use of a mind of extraordinary quickness he managed to administer the judicial office without any betrayal of his want of knowledge.

C. C. Bowen, of Charleston, offered a resolution that "Robert K. Scott, Governor of South Carolina, be impeached of high crimes and misdemeanors," and a resolution, in the same terms, for the impeachment of Treasurer Niles G. Parker.

After a discussion at each daily session for four days the resolutions were severally rejected. The vote by which the Governor escaped was 65 to 32, and the vote in the Treasurer's favor was 63 to 27.

Thus Governor Scott escaped a trial for "high crimes and misdemeanors." To procure this result he resorted to the fund for the maintenance of the "armed force" already mentioned. Upon this fund he caused two warrants on the Treasurer to be drawn—one for

$25,545 in favor of "John Mooney," one for $10,600 in favor of "David Leggett" and one for $13,500 in favor of "David H. Wilson." The money ($48,645) procured from the State Treasury on these warrants drawn in favor of fictitious persons was used in bribing members of the House to vote against impeachment. The price of votes varied, according to statements current at the time, from $200 to $5,000, whilst the additional sum of $15,000 was paid to Speaker Moses for friendly rulings in the course of the proceedings upon the Bowen resolution.

It was stated also and generally believed that Bowen had an offer from Scott of $15,000 if the impeachment resolution should be withdrawn, but declined to stop unless he should receive $25,000.

Several acts particularly indicating the policy and purposes of the Legislature were passed at this session.

Divorces from the bonds of matrimony were provided for—the grounds recognized being adultery and desertion.

The act authorizing the Governor to employ an armed force was repealed.

The new county of Aiken was formed out of portions of Barnwell, Edgefield, Lexington and Orangeburg.

The office of State Auditor was abolished and its duties were devolved on the Comptroller-General.

By "an act for the relief of the widows and orphans of persons killed because of their political opinions," the county treasurers of Union, Spartanburg, York, Lancaster, Chester, Fairfield, Laurens, Newberry and Chesterfield were required to pay to each of such widows $10 per month, and to each of such orphans (between the ages of six and fifteen) $6.00 per month—the funds to be raised by the levy of a special tax not exceeding one-half of a mill on the dollar. This act had reference to the alleged killing of Republicans by the Kuklux Klan.

Instead of the per diem allowance the pay of the members was fixed at $600 per annum, with mileage at twenty cents per mile each way.

Two amendments to the State Constitution were directed to be submitted to the people at the next general election—(1) to fix the first Tuesday after the first Monday in November as the day for the election of all State and county officers to be chosen by the people;

(2) prohibiting the increase of the State debt, except by the vote of two-thirds of the qualified voters voting on the question.

The State tax for the fiscal year commencing November 1, 1871, was fixed at six mills, with a further tax of two mills for the support of the public schools, and a tax of three mills in each county, for county purposes, except Fairfield, where the tax was fixed at one and one-half mills. There were special levies in several counties.

The general appropriation bill contained simply the provisions for salaries and other regular expenses of the State government.

The session of 1871-72 ended March 13, having lasted 106 days. There were passed 216 acts and twenty-two joint resolutions.

The usual gratuity of $1,000 was voted to Speaker Moses.

The total expenses of the session amounted to $1,174,177.78, distributed as follows: Pay for members, $102,900; 475 clerks, $39,316; 16 laborers, $933; 16 doorkeepers, $3,863.50; 14 firemen, $2,186; 3 chaplains, $870; 5 janitors, $703; 212 messengers, $158,737.50; 2 mail carriers, $705.50; 23 porters, $98,639.75; 74 pages, $8,167; 7 sergeants-at-arms, $2,206; 27 solicitors, $10,449; 5 stenographers, $1,967; legislative accounts and claims, $73,127; sundries (wines, liquors, cigars, etc.), $282,514.50; stationery, $72,815.39; fuel, $11,708; newspapers, $5,238; postage stamps, $1,598.54; telegrams, $465.10; furniture, $116,578; rent of committee rooms, $3,778; impeachment trials, $3,026; printing, $173,000.

THE BLUE RIDGE SCRIP.

Mention has been made of the acts passed with the ostensible purpose of aiding in the construction of the Blue Ridge Railroad—the first of these (September 15, 1868) purporting to have "endorsed" a guaranty of the faith and credit of the State on $4,000,000 of bonds issued by the Blue Ridge Railroad Company. By the act of March 2, 1872, it was provided that upon the surrender of the said bonds to the State Treasurer that officer should "deliver to the president of the Blue Ridge Railroad Company, in South Carolina, treasury certificates of indebtedness (styled Revenue Bond Scrip) to the amount of $1,800,000"—said certificates to be issued in such form and in such denominations as might be determined on by the State Treasurer and the president of the said railroad company, and to "express that the sum mentioned therein is due by the State of South Carolina to the bearer thereof, and that the same will be received in payment of taxes and all other dues to the State, except the special tax levied to pay interest on the public debt." The "faith and funds" of the State were pledged for the ultimate redemption of the scrip, and the county treasurers were required to receive it in payment of the taxes mentioned. A tax of three mills, "in addition to all other taxes," was directed to be annually levied for the redemption of the scrip—one-fourth of the scrip to be retired annually. The State Treasurer was authorized to pay out, in satisfaction of any claims against the treasury, except for interest due on the public debt, so much of said Revenue Bond Scrip as might be received in the treasury for the payment of taxes. Provision was made for the cancellation of the bonds alleged to have been guaranteed, and for the release of the State's lien upon the property of the railroad company.

Governor Scott vetoed the bill on these grounds: 1. That the State's endorsement of the bonds of the company was a contingent liability merely, upon which the State could not be presently held. 2. That the "embarrassed condition of the finances of the State" forbade the incurring of the obligation entailed by the act. 3. That the act was unconstitutional because violative of those provisions of the State and Federal Constitution, respectively, prohibiting the State from issuing bills of credit.

The act was passed over the Governor's veto—in the Senate by a vote of 22 to 6, and in the House by a vote of 84 to 18.

The passage of the bill over the veto was procured by bribery—senators and representatives for their votes receiving sums ranging from $500 to $5,000 each.

John J. Patterson, as president of the Blue Ridge Railroad Company, gave to State Treasurer Parker a written order directing that official to deliver to H. H. Kimpton Revenue Bond Scrip due the Blue Ridge Railroad Company amounting to $114,250, upon the following conditions: "That $42,857 of said scrip, at par, is to be used for paying the expenses of passing through the House of Representatives bills styled 'a bill relating to the bonds of the State of South Carolina' and 'bill to authorize the Financial Board to settle the accounts of the Financial Agent.'" The letter further directed the delivery to Kimpton of $71,414 of the scrip, at par, if said bills should become laws and if he should "pay the sum of $50,000, the proceeds of said scrip at seventy cents on the dollar, in paying the expenses already incurred in passing through the Senate" the bond bill and the settlement bill already mentioned.

The bill referring to the Financial Agent authorized the Financial Board to "adjust and settle the claims and demands and accounts, and all or any matters of difference relating to the Financial Agent," to receive from him any balance due by him to the State, and thereupon to give him an acquittance of all demands against him, growing out of any of his transactions as the Financial Agent of the State of South Carolina. The bill "relating to the bonds of the State" provided in substance for the validation of all bonds issued between August 26, 1868, and March 26, 1869 (included in the Treasurer's report of October 31, 1871), with the pledge of the State's "faith, credit and funds" for the payment of the same, and reenacted the provision in each of the designated acts for the levy of a tax to meet the interest on the bonds validated. These two acts, with the act for the issuance of the Blue Ridge Scrip, constituted one scheme for the benefit of John J. Patterson, H. H. Kimpton and the members of the Financial Board—Governor Scott, Attorney-General Chamberlain, Treasurer Parker and Comptroller-General Neagle.

The Blue Ridge Scrip was declared void by the State Supreme Court in 1873, and a judgment to the same effect was rendered by the Supreme Court of the United States in 1904.

CHARGES OF A REPUBLICAN COMMITTEE.

On February 13, 1871, the House adopted a resolution directing that "a committee of three on the part of the House and two on the part of the Senate be appointed to make a complete and thorough examination of all the accounts of the State Treasurer, Comptroller-General, and Financial Agent since their induction into office, with power to send for persons and papers, said committee to have power to appoint a clerk and an expert if necessary; also to submit any part of the results of their examination to the Attorney-General for his official action."

The Senate having concurred, the joint committee was constituted as follows: Senators B. F. Whittemore, of Darlington, and S. A. Swails, of Williamsburg; Representatives John B. Dennis and Timothy Hurley, of Charleston, and W. H. Gardner, of Sumter—all Republicans.

This committee—styled the "Joint Special Financial Investigating Committee"—after taking much testimony, and after "having fulfilled the duties assigned them, as far as it was possible during the time allowed" for their investigation, made their report to the General Assembly at the session of 1871-72. The matters considered were presented under different heads.

The expenditures of the State Government for all purposes, from September, 1868, to October 31, 1870, were reported to have been $4,184,783.42.

The adoption of specific appropriations was recommended as necessary for the proper conduct of the Government and the maintenance of the State's credit.

Attention was called to the fact that none of the banks wherein State funds were deposited had been required to pay interest, as provided by the statute authorizing the Governor, the Comptroller-General and the Treasurer to select the depositories of such funds.

The cost of enrolling and arming the militia was reported at $374,696.59, and of the transactions involved the committee declared that "a glaring robbery of the treasury, for personal ambition and gain, had been perpetrated."

The committee considering that to the sum above stated should be added $5,000 "Adjutant-General's contingent," $8,000 salaries of that officer and his assistant, and $33,463.12, expenses of the State constabulary—reported the total expenditures for the militia, the purchase of arms, the "armed force" and the constabulary, $421,159.71; "nearly enough to pay the interest on the State debt for one year."

The Land Commission was characterized as a "gigantic folly" and "one of the most expensive experiments—productive of greater distress and dissatisfaction—that has been legalized or patronized by the State"—the committee further declaring that "a more outrageous and enormous swindle could not have been perpetrated and a more subtle manner of concealment perfected."

The aggregate of expenditures of the commission, "as far as known," was reported to be the sum of $746,724.07—being $326,723.07 in excess of the amount apparently realized from the sale of the bonds issued for the purchase of lands.

The "Advisory Board"—Governor Scott, Comptroller Neagle, Treasurer Parker, Attorney-General Chamberlain and Secretary

Cardozo—were explicitly charged with "neglect of duty and unwarrantable violation of law."

The land purchased—"the improved and unimproved, eligible or uneligible, the 104,078 acres, sandhill, swamp and otherwise"—was reported to have cost the State seven dollars an acre.

The committee represented that the State's relations to the Financial Agent were such that there was no real security against any malfeasance of which he might be guilty—special attention being called to the fact that the only security afforded was in the personal bond of H. H. Kimpton.

The board was charged with having made unwise appointments, given imprudent advice, recommended extravagant or ruinous financial operations, and thus made themselves responsible for any loss or damage to the State by reason of the acts of Kimpton.

The State debt, October, 1871, was reported at $22,371,306.27, besides $6,887,608.20 of contingent liabilities in the shape of endorsements of railroad bonds. The figures thus given, compared with those given the committee of the Taxpayers' Convention in May, 1871, led to the general belief that in the statements made by the State officials to that committee the figures were "doctored" so as to give out a false report of the debt.

Of the debt above stated the committee reported that bonds in the sum of $6,314,000 had been fraudulently and unlawfully issued.

No report was made of the transactions of the Financial Agent or of his indebtedness, if any, to the State—the committee recommending that these matters be further and fully investigated.

A special committee of the House (C. C. Bowen, Benjamin Byas, F. H. Frost, P. J. O'Connell, W. H. Jones, Jr.) reported that the above noted bonds, in the sum of $6,314,000 constituted an over-issue by which the State had been defrauded, and recommended that the House "take the necessary steps to hold accountable those persons who have violated the laws and ruined the credit of the State." The impeachment fiasco followed.

At this session the General Assembly formally discharged the "Joint Special Financial Investigating Committee."

CHAPTER V.

THE KUKLUX TROUBLES.

The condition of the white people of South Carolina, reference had to the protection which every citizen might rightfully expect from the Government, will have been learned from the account already given of the course of affairs in the three first years of Governor Scott's administration. The State Government was in fact hostile to the white race, and that government, without reference to its personnel—without reference to the character of its agents—was doggedly backed by the military power of the United States.

In view of the attitude of the negro government towards the unorganized white citizens, some of the latter joined the Kuklux Klan —more generally called by the shorter name, "Kuklux." The Klan was not active at this time. There never was a raid, the single complaint against the Kuklux being that at the election in the fall of 1868 some men—afterwards alleged to be Kuklux—crowded the polls at Rock Hill to prevent negroes from voting the Republican ticket. For this alleged conduct nobody was ever arrested or tried.

What the Klan was the Government officials undertook to show by a paper used in evidence in certain trials in the United States Circuit Court in 1871-72, alleged to embody the obligation, the constitution and the by-laws of the Kuklux Klan. The obligation was set out as follows:

I, [name] before the immaculate Judge of Heaven and Earth, and upon the holy evangelists of Almighty God, do of my own free will and accord subscribe to the following sacredly binding obligation:

1. We are on the side of justice, humanity and constitutional liberty, as bequeathed to us in its purity by our forefathers.
2. We oppose and reject the principles of the Radical party.
3. We pledge mutual aid to each other in sickness, distress, and especially pecuniary embarrassment.
4. Female friends, widows and their households shall ever be special objects of our regard and protection.

Any member divulging or causing to be divulged any of the foregoing obligation shall meet the fearful penalty and traitor's doom, which is death! death! death!

Constitution.

Article 1. This organization shall be known as the ———— Order, No. —, of the Kuklux Klan of the State of South Carolina.

Art. 2. The officers shall consist of a cyclops and scribe, both of whom shall be elected by a majority vote of the order and hold their office during good behavior.

Art. 3. It shall be the duty of the C. to preside in the order, enforce a due observance of the constitution and by-laws and an exact compliance with the rules and usages of the order—to see that all the members perform their respective duties, appoint all committees before the order, inspect the arms and dress of each member on special occasions, to call meetings when necessary, draw upon members for all sums needed to carry on the order.

Sec. 2. The S. shall keep a record of the proceedings of the order, write communications, notify other Klans when their assistance is needed, give notice when any member has to suffer the penalty for violating his oath, see that all books, papers or other property belonging to his office are placed beyond the reach of any one but members of the order. He shall perform such other duties as may be required of him by the C.

Article 4. Section 1. No person shall be initiated into this order under eighteen years of age.

Sec. 2. No person of color shall be admitted into this order.

Sec. 3. No person shall be admitted into the order who does not sustain a good moral character, or who is in any way incapacitated to discharge the duties of a Kuklux.

Sec. 4. The name of a person offered for membership must be proposed by the committee appointed by the chief verbally, stating age, residence and occupation; state if he was a soldier in the late war; his rank; whether he was in the Federal or Confederate service, and his command.

Article 5. Section 1. Any member who shall offend against these articles or the by-laws shall be subject to be fined and reprimanded by the C., as two-thirds of the members present at any regular meeting may determine.

Sec. 2. Every member shall be entitled to a fair trial for any offense involving reprimand or criminal punishment.

Aticle 6. Section 1. Any member who shall betray or divulge any of the matters of the order shall suffer death.

Article 7. Section 1. The following shall be the rules of order and any matters herein not provided for shall be managed in strict accordance with the Kuklux rules.

Sec. 2. When the chief takes his position on the right, the scribe, with the members shall form a half circle around them, and at the sound of the signal instrument, there shall be profound silence.

Sec. 3. Before proceeding to business the S. shall call the roll and note the absentees.

Sec. 4. Business shall be taken up in the following order: 1. Reading minutes; 2, excuses of members at preceding meetings; 3, report of committee of candidates for membership; 4, collection of dues; 5, are any of the order sick or suffering; 6, report of committees; 7, new business.

By-Laws.

Article 1. Section 1. The order shall meet at ———.

Sec. 2. Five (5) members shall constitute a quorum, provided the C. or S. be present.

Sec. 3. The C. shall have power to appoint such members of the order to attend the sick, the needy, and those distressed, and those suffering from Radical misrule, as the case may require.

Sec. 4. No person shall be appointed on a committee unless the person is present at the time of appointment. Members of committees neglecting to report shall be fined thirty cents.

Article 2. Section 1. Every member, on being admitted, shall sign the constitution and by-laws and pay the initiation fee.

Sec. 2. A brother of the Klan wishing to become a member of this order shall present his application with the proper papers of transfer from the order of which he was a member formerly; shall be admitted to the order by a unanimous vote of the members present.

Article 3. Section 1. The initiation fee shall be ———.

Article 4. Section 1. Every member who shall refuse or neglect to pay his fines or dues shall be dealt with as the chief thinks proper.

Sec. 3. Sickness or absence from the county, or being engaged in any important business, shall be valid excuse for any neglect of duty.

Article 5. Section 1. Each member must provide himself with a pistol, Kuklux gown and signal instrument.

Sec. 3. When charges have been preferred against a member in a proper manner, or any matters of grievance between brother Kuklux are brought before the order, they shall be referred to a special committee of three or more members, who shall examine the parties and determine the matter in question, reporting their decision to the order. If the parties interested desire, two-thirds of the members present voting in favor of the report, it shall be carried.

Article 6. Section 1. It is the duty of every member who has evidence that another has violated Article 2 to prefer the charge and specify the offense to the order.

Sec. 2. The charge for violating Article 2 shall be referred to a committee of five or more members, who shall, as soon as practicable, summon the parties and investigate the matter.

Sec. 3. If the committee agree that the charges are sustained, that the member on trial has intentionally violated his oath or Article 2, they shall report the facts to the order.

Sec. 4. If the committee agree that the charges are not sustained, that the member is not guilty of violating his oath or Article 2, they shall report to that effect to the order and charges shall be dismissed.

Sec. 5. When the committee report that the charges are sustained and the unanimous vote is given in favor thereof, the offending person shall be sentenced to death by the chief.

Sec. 6. The prisoner, through the cyclops of the order of which he is a member, can make application for pardon to the great grand cyclops of Nashville, Tenn., in which case the execution of the sentence can be stayed until the pardoning power is heard from.

(Of the origin of the word *kuklux* it is said that in the organization of the Klan the name "circle" was proposed. Then *kuklos,* the Greek equivalent, was taken. *Kuklos* became *kuklux.* For reasons suggested by the history of the word the author has preferred the from *kuklux* to *ku klux* and *ku-klux.*)

THE ARMING OF THE NEGROES.

Whatever the purposes of the organization, as indicated in its constitution and rules, the Klan was quiet until the latter part of 1870. Whatever the hostility of the whites to the negro government, whatever the acts which made that government at once a disgrace to its agents and a menace to the white race in South Carolina, it is safe to say that the Kuklux would have remained inactive but for the arming of the negroes and the conduct of the State militia into which they were enrolled. Of that conduct enough has been presented to give a fair idea of the conditions resulting—the lawless acts of the negroes in some portions of the State, and the feeling of the whites in the sections affected. Threats against the whites—against their persons and their property—were not infrequent, yet if matters had rested at talk, the bloody doings of the Kuklux might never have been enacted. But the negroes followed the counsels of their leaders with frequent acts of houseburning and, in one conspicuous case at least, with murder.

During the canvass preceding the State election of 1870 the negro militia constantly drilled and frequently moved about the country districts, to the disgust of the white citizens and the terror of their wives and children. There were as yet not many acts of actual violence by the negro militia, but their insolence was naturally a source of much irritation. For self-protection the whites armed themselves, but they were without actual organization. Just before election day at most of the county seats and at some points in the country some citizen was placed in charge, and the whites prepared to defend themselves. The conduct of the negro militia was offensive and at some places threatening. One favorite practice was in marching "company front" so as to occupy the entire street. On one occasion the captain of a negro company so marching sent a sergeant forward to order the driver of a carriage waiting at a store for its lady occupants to make way for the soldiers.

In Union County there were various acts of lawlessness accompanied with threats of violence against the whites. June Mobley, a mulatto member of the House of Representatives from that county, wielding great influence among the negroes, declared that for every Republican killed at the polls ten white men should die.

In Laurens County there were five or six companies of negro militia, and their conduct caused general concern for the safety of the white women and children in the section where the negro population predominated. In the town of Laurens the companies concentrated, and joined by other negroes armed with pistols and shotguns, riotously paraded the streets.

In Camden, on the occasion of a parade, several of the negroes got drunk and one of them for some misconduct was arrested by the town marshal, whereupon the negro militia became violent and threatened to "kill the damned white men." The marshal having gone into a house for safety, they assaulted the house, to the terror of the lady occupants.

These acts may be taken as specimens. Others of the same sort were very frequent.

The conduct of the negro militia became everywhere worse after the October election. Armed and equipped, they went about in groups or in regular formation, as if seeking a conflict. They incited their fellows to violence and incendiarism. They insulted ladies on the public highways. They moved about in the nighttime, firing their guns and in some instances shooting at dwelling houses. Behind these lawbreakers was the hostile local government sustained by the Federal authority. The apparent helplessness of the whites, far from inducing the consideration of the State Government or of the negroes' white leaders, seemed rather to give the idea that the power of the militia was sufficient to insure them immunity, whatever the extent of their crimes against peace and order.

The Kuklux made their "raids"—at first chiefly to quiet the negroes by letting them know that the whites had some sort of organization and were otherwise ready to defend their persons and their homes. Matters went from bad to worse until a trouble occurred which led to a raid that must be considered the climax of Kukluxism in South Carolina.

MURDER BY MILITIAMEN.

In January, 1871, Matt Stevens, an inoffensive white man who had lost an arm in the Confederate service, was going from Union Court House, driving his wagon in which were some barrels of whiskey which he was transporting in the pursuit of his business as a wagoner. On the public highway he met a company of Scott's negro militia, numbering about forty, some of whom demanded that he should give them whiskey. He complied to the extent of giving them all that he had in a bottle, but refused to let them interfere with the barrels. Thereupon he was seized, abused, beaten and finally shot to death.

Among the whites this murder by the militiamen naturally aroused indignation and alarm. It was assassination pure and simple—assassination by soldiers organized under the law and bearing arms supplied by the State Government. The demeanor of the negroes in Union County showed that as a body they were in sympathy with the slayers of Stevens and would do all in their power to shield them from arrest and punishment. It was natural that the whites should take some means to prevent a repetition of such a brutal murder—such an outrage against the whole white race. A "committee of safety" was formed, and after consultation it was determined to disarm the negro company at once. This accomplished without disturbance, the next step was to apprehend the murderers. Negro militiamen to the number of thirteen were arrested, though not without a conflict by them with the sheriff's posse, in which two or more of the latter were badly wounded. The prisoners were lodged in the county jail at Union.

RAIDS ON THE UNION JAIL.

On January 4, 1871, a party of Kuklux, all mounted and each disguised by means of a cap and mask that concealed the head and face, with some sort of gown or wrapper that enveloped the whole body, went to Union jail and seized five of the negro militiamen charged with participation in the murder of Stevens. Of these, two were shot to death and three escaped—the impression prevailing that the Kuklux allowed them to get away because they were thought not to have been actual participants in the crime.

The Kuklux appeared to contemplate no further interference with the orderly course of the law. But on Friday, February 10, there came from William M. Thomas, the judge of the circuit of which Union County formed a part, an order directing the removal of the eight prisoners aforesaid to Columbia. There had been no proceedings by habeas corpus, and there were suspicions that the order was not genuine. The sheriff seeking counsel, he was advised to communicate with Judge Thomas, but taking further advice he determined to carry the prisoners to Columbia on the following Monday. Somehow the purpose to remove the negroes got out. The general feeling among the whites was that such proposed removal was but a scheme to shield the prisoners from the just consequences of their crime, or at the best to obstruct the regular course of justice. However all this might have been, the order of Judge Thomas was not carried out. Its purpose, whatever it might have been, was balked by the Kuklux.

On Sunday night, January 12, 1871, the Kuklux visited Union again—this time in a body, all mounted and disguised, numbering, according to different estimates, from 1,000 to 1,500. They went to the jail, took out the eight militiamen above mentioned and shot them to death. This bloody work was done quietly. There was no uproar. Sentinels detailed from the ranks of the Kuklux body were posted, and these ordered back any of the town people who came out of their houses. The mounted men retired as quietly as they had come, their ranks well kept and their movements marked by a precision which was well-nigh military.

In explanation of their action the Kuklux, on the occasion of the second raid above mentioned, left the following paper:

TO THE PUBLIC.

K. K. K.

Taken by Habeas Corpus.

In silence and secrecy thought has been working, and the benignant efficacies of concealment speak for themselves. Once again we have been forced by force to use Force. Justice was lame, and she had to lean upon us. Information being obtained that a "doubting Thomas," the inferior of nothing, the superior of nothing, and of consequence the equal of nothing, who has neither eyes to see the scars of oppression, nor ears to hear the cause of humanity, even though he wears the judicial silk, had ordered some guilty prisoners from Union to the city of Columbia, and of Injustice and Prejudice, for an unfair trial of life; thus clutching at the wheel-spokes of Destiny—then this thing was created and projected; otherwise it would never have been. We yield to the inevitable and inexorable, and account this the best. "Let not thy right hand know what thy left hand doeth" is our motto.

We want peace, but this cannot be till Justice returns. We want and will have Justice, but this cannot be till a bleeding fight for freedom is fought. Until then the Moloch of Iniquity will have his victims, even if the Michael of Justice must have his martyrs.

This latter occurrence made a profound impression not only in South Carolina but in the National capital and in other parts of the country. The State Legislature was then in session, and the leading negro members, seconded by some white Republicans, were very violent in demanding strong measures of protection for the colored people and punishment for the Kuklux. Previous to the second raid on the Union jail, W. J. Whipper, a negro member of the House from Beaufort, had introduced a bill to authorize the Governor to enlist and arm a regiment to "preserve the peace and protect life and property" in any county where he might think such action necessary. Fortunately for the peace of the counties involved, fortunately for the negro race in South Carolina, the bill was defeated. Whipper was even more violent in his talk when the news came of the second raid, but the House contented itself with the resolution, adopted also by the Senate, calling on President Grant for protection. Very soon Federal troops were sent to the disturbed counties—a company to each of the county seats of York, Union and Spartanburg.

In the meantime two of the negroes who had escaped the raiders on their first visit to Union jail were recaptured and imprisoned. These two were tried in the civil court for murder, sentenced and executed.

The Kuklux continued their operations in Union County, though it does not appear that they killed anybody after the second raid on the jail. They seemed determined to get rid of certain officials whose course they had thought calculated to cause trouble between the races.

On the courthouse at Union there was posted a notice, "Special Order No. 3, K. K. K.," dated March 9, 1871, "by order of the grand chief," requiring the members of the Legislature, the school commissioner and the county commissioners to resign within fifteen days, with the declaration that in case of non-compliance "retributive justice will as surely be used as night follows day." In the same paper the clerk of the county commissioners and school commissioner was warned to "renounce and relinquish" his position forthwith.

The Kuklux in Union appear to have broadened the original scope of their purposes, as will be seen from the following notice found posted on the courthouse door on the morning of February 23, 1871:

Headquarters K. K. K.,
Department of S. C.,
General Order No. 49, from the G. G. C., S. S.

We delight not in speech, but there is language which, when meant in earnest, becomes desperate. We raise the voice of warning, "Beware!" "Beware!" Persons there are (and not unknown to us) who, to gratify some private grudge or selfish end, like Wheeler's men, so-called, are executing their low, paltry and pitiful designs at the expense not only of the noble creed we profess and act, but also to the great trouble and annoyance of their neighbors in various communities. We stay our hand for once; but if such conduct as frightening away laborers, robbery and connivance at the secrets of our organization is repeated, then the mockers must suffer and the traitors meet their merited doom. We dare not promise what we do not perform. We want no substitutes or conscripts in our ranks. We can be as generous as we are terrible; but stand back. We've said it, there shall be no interference.

By order of the grand chief.

A. O., Grand Secretary.

Whether there was any prompt cessation of the wrongs which this warning purported to expose does not appear. But there soon appared in the *Union Times* a card from the clerk of the board of county commissioners in which he announced that "in obedience to Special Order No. 3, K. K. K. (to which his attention had been called), he renounced and relinquished his position."

TROUBLES IN OTHER COUNTIES.

The Kuklux operated extensively in Spartanburg. The raid there which attracted most attention was made upon Dr. John Winsmith, a citizen of high standing, who had given offense by declaring his purpose to support the Scott ticket in the campaign of 1870. In March, 1871, his house was visited at night by a party in disguise, and on his learning their movements he went out into his yard and fired two shots with the purpose, as he himself afterwards avowed, to kill the invaders of his premises. His shots were promptly returned, and he received seven wounds. This act of the mob, whether of the Kuklux organization or of other parties, was very generally condemned. As Dr. Winsmith could not identify any of his assailants, none of them was ever punished.

There were a number of raids in Spartanburg, the victims being whipped and otherwise maltreated. Only one homicide was charged to the Kuklux, and for that nobody was ever arraigned in court. The charge was made by one A. W. Cummings, a preacher of the Northern Methodist Church, who degraded his calling by engaging in the work of a spy.

In York County the negro militia were especially aggressive and offensive. In Yorkville the local company had a fashion of parading the main street, "company front," so that they actually took possession of the roadway between the sidewalks. They went about at night in squads of five to ten, frequently carrying their guns and always wearing their bayonets and cartridge boxes. They would walk abreast so as to occupy the entire sidewalk, and more than once a lady and her escort had to take the "big road" rather than have a collision. One Sunday night, late in January, 1871, a gentleman was rudely jostled off the pavement by a squad of negro militiamen fully armed. A riot was narrowly averted, and there were fears of bloodshed. The white men of the town, reinforced by many from the country, prepared for what seemed an unavoidable collision. For a whole day and the following night there was constant danger of a conflict—the whites demanding that the negro company disarm, and the latter, crowded into a brick building occupied by one Rose, the county treasurer, refusing to do so. Major General Anderson (white), of the State militia, had been sent from Columbia to look into the trouble, and arriving in Yorkville when the danger of bloodshed was imminent, the General undertook to parley and there was some delay, but, on being informed that bloodshed could be averted by no action other than the disarming of the negro company, he gave the proper order. By noon the next day the guns and equipments had been turned in to him to be shipped to Columbia.

In York County there were many raids charged to the Kuklux. Numbers of negroes complained that they had been beaten or otherwise maltreated on account of their devotion to the Republican party. It was stated that five negroes had been at different times killed by the Kuklux. Some of these raids had so much part in bringing on the measures used by the United States Government to apprehend and punish the "conspirators" that they deserve particular mention.

In February, 1871, a raid was made upon the office of the county treasurer, one Rose, who had made himself obnoxious by his constant endeavors to stir up strife between whites and blacks and by his generally offensive bearing. The raiding party destroyed some books and papers of no value, among those unharmed being the tax duplicate in Rose's possession. Rose claimed that he had been robbed of public money, but the story was generally discredited. What the raiders particularly wanted they failed to get—Rose himself.

About the same time a party went into the probate judge's office, where, it had been rumored, was stored a quantity of ammunition for the negro militia. Not finding what they sought, the raiders left without doing any harm.

On December 3, 1870, a negro named Thomas Black (commonly called Tom Roundtree) was taken from his house by a party of men alleged to be Kuklux and shot to death. For this killing three white men were promptly tried in the Circuit Court of York County, and they proved an alibi by evidence so clear and conclusive that the jury were fully justified in promptly rendering a verdict of acquittal.

In the lower part of the county there was a negro militia company commanded by one Jim Williams, to whom the State authorities had issued ninety-six breech-loading rifles and a full supply of fixed ammunition. Williams was a bold and aggressive fellow, unquestionably a hater of the white race and evidently bent on mischief. His men behaved in a manner to cause alarm for the safety of the white women and children of the neighborhood. These negro soldiers paraded the roads as they pleased, and so recklessly fired off their guns that more than once their bullets struck the dwellings of white citizens. On one occasion a squad of Williams' soldiers, armed, equipped and uniformed, lawlessly seized a white citizen and took him a distance of several miles before a trial justice upon some charge so baseless that no warrant was issued by the officer. About this time there were several incendiary fires in the neighborhood and the state of affairs in general was actually alarming—so much so that some of the white people deemed it necessary to remove their wives and children for safety. Jim Williams himself heeded neither remonstrance nor counsel. He steadily refused to disband his company or give up their guns, declaring his purpose, in the event of trouble, to "kill from the cradle to the grave."

On March 7, 1871, in the nighttime, a party of mounted men, numbering about sixty, went to the house of Jim Williams, took him into the woods near by and hung him to a tree. Upon his body they left a paper on which was written: "Capt. Jim Williams on his big muster." They then departed as quietly as they had come. A short time afterwards the Williams company of negro militia turned in their arms and disbanded.

In the course of their operations, more particularly in York and Spartanburg, the Kuklux, or bodies of men alleged to be such, committed numerous acts against law and order. Irresponsible men, goaded by the infamies of the State Government, incensed and alarmed by the conduct of the negro militia, went far beyond the scope of the organization, considered either as a means of self-protection or as a counterpoise to the Union League. Raids were made with no apparent purpose but to punish the immediate victims for previous threats, sometimes for previous impertinence only. In many cases, according to the testimony of victims, the raiders exacted the promise that these should never again vote the Republican ticket. In some instances the conduct of raiders had no relation either to politics, to race troubles, or to the misconduct of the negro militia. A white man was visited and whipped because, against repeated remonstrances, he continued in the illicit sale of whiskey near a church, to the disgust of the community. A white lad was visited and whipped because of continued disobedience to his widowed mother, coupled with conduct otherwise distressing to her. A white man who had long refused or neglected to pay a bill due to a negro blacksmith was visited and informed that he must pay the debt or get a whipping.

QUIET RESTORED.

The doings of the Kuklux deeply impressed the white people in the counties affected. Public meetings were held in York, Union and Spartanburg, appealing to the people to abstain from all acts of violence and look to the law for redress of grievances. Governor Scott offered to cooperate with the white people in restoring quiet and preserving order. All the militia companies in the disturbed counties were finally disbanded. In several instances the Governor removed incompetent officials and appointed worthy white men in their places.

THE KUKLUX TROUBLES

The Kuklux ceased their operations, so that after the middle of May, 1871, there was nowhere any complaint of them. The great cause of trouble—the negro militia—no longer existing, the task of restoring peace and order was not difficult.

Later on the Federal Government used its power—principally the power of the bayonet—to "suppress" a "conspiracy" which no longer existed and to protect rights which were nowise threatened. The measures taken, though enforced under the forms of law, were little less subversive of the rights and liberties of the citizen than were the very worst acts ascribed to the Kuklux.

ACTION OF CONGRESS AND THE PRESIDENT.

On May 30, 1870, the President approved an act of Congress entitled "An act to enforce the right of citizens of the United States to vote in the several States of this Union, and for other purposes." This statute, generally styled the Enforcement Act, contained numerous provisions. The portions employed by the Federal Government in the day of its hostility to the white people of the Southern States to harry and oppress those people and to perpetuate negro rule in this section were as follows:

Section 1. That all citizens of the United States who are or shall be otherwise qualified by law to vote at any election by the people in any State, territory, district, county, city, parish, township, school district, municipality, or other territorial subdivision shall be entitled and allowed to vote at all such elections, without distinction of race, color, or previous condition of servitude; any constitution, law, custom, usage, or regulation of any State or territory, or by or under its authority, to the contrary notwithstanding. . . .

Sec. 4. That if any person by force, bribery, threats, intimidation, or other unlawful means, shall hinder, delay, prevent, or obstruct, or shall combine or confederate with others to hinder, delay, prevent or obstruct, any citizen from doing any act required to be done to qualify him to vote or from voting at any election as aforesaid, such person shall . . . for every such offense be guilty of a misdemeanor, and shall, on conviction thereof, be fined not less than $500, or be imprisoned not less than one month and not more than one year, or both, at the discretion of the court. . . .

Sec. 6. That if two or more persons shall band or conspire together, or go in disguise upon the public highway, or upon the premises of another with intent to violate any provision of this act, or to injure, oppress, threaten or intimidate any citizen with intent to prevent or hinder his free exercise and enjoyment of any right or privilege granted or secured to him by the Constitution or laws of the United States, or because of his having exercised the same, such persons shall be held guilty of felony, and, on conviction thereof, shall be fined or imprisoned, or both, at the discretion of the court— the fine not to exceed $5,000, and the imprisonment not to exceed ten years—and shall, moreover, be thereafter ineligible to and disabled from holding any office or place of honor, profit or trust created by the laws of the United States.

Sec. 7. That if in the act of violating any provision in the preceding sections, any other felony, crime or misdemeanor shall be committed, the offender, on conviction of such violation of said sections, shall be punished for the same with such punishments as are attached to the said felonies, crimes and misdemeanors by the laws of the State in which the offense may be committed.

On March 23, 1871, President Grant sent to Congress a message in which he said:

A condition of affairs now exists in some of the States of the Union, rendering life and property insecure, and the carrying of the mails and the collection of the revenue dangerous. The proof that such a condition exists is now before the Senate. That the power to correct these evils is beyond the control of State authorities I do not doubt. That the power of the Executive of the United States, acting within the limit of existing laws, is sufficient for present emergencies, is not clear.

On March 24, 1871, the President issued his proclamation setting forth that "combinations of armed men, unathorized by law, are now disturbing the peace and safety of the citizens of the State of South Carolina, and committing acts of violence in said State of a character and to an extent which render the power of the State and its officers unequal to the task of protecting life and property and securing public order therein"; that the Legislature of this State was not in session, and that "the executive of said State had made application to the President for such part of the military force of the United States as may be necessary and adequate to protect said State and the citizens thereof against the domestic violence hereinbefore mentioned." Thereupon the President did "command the persons composing the unlawful combinations aforesaid to disperse and retire peaceably to their respective abodes within twenty days from this date."

The President had recommended legislation to "secure life, liberty, property and the enforcement of the law in all parts of the United States." In pursuance of this suggestion Congress passed an act (approved April 20, 1871) entitled "An act to enforce the provisions of the Fourteenth Amendment to the Constitution of the United States, and for other purposes." Of this measure—popularly known as the "Kuklux Act"—a brief statement is necessary in order to a sufficient understanding of the course of events which followed.

The Kuklux Act imposed penalties upon "any two or more persons in any State or territory" who should "conspire or go in disguise on the highway or on the premises of another for the purpose of depriving, either directly or indirectly, any person or class of persons of the equal protection of the laws, or of equal privileges or immunities under the laws, or for the purpose of preventing or hindering the constituted authorities of any State or territory from giving or securing to all persons within such State or territory the equal protection of the laws." It declared unlawful any "combination" or "conspiracy" against the rights declared in the Fourteenth Amendment, and it contained the following provisions:

Sec. 4. That whenever in any State, or part of a State, the unlawful combinations named in this act shall be organized and armed, and so numerous and powerful as to be able by violence to either overthrow or set at defiance the constituted authorities of such State, and of the United States within such State, or when the constituted authorities are in complicity with or shall connive at the unlawful purposes of such powerful and armed combinations; and whenever, by reason of either or all of the causes aforesaid, the conviction of such offenders and the preservation of the public safety shall become in such district impracticable, in every such case such combinations shall be deemed a rebellion against the Government of the United States, and during the continuance of such rebellion, and within the limits of the district which shall be so under the sway thereof, such limits to be prescribed by proclamation, it shall be lawful for the President of the United States, when, in his judgment, the public safety shall require it, to suspend the priviliges of the writ of habeas corpus, to the end that such rebellion may be overthrown. . . . Provided, further, That the President shall first have made proclamation, as now provided by law, commanding such insurgents to disperse; and provided, also, That the provisions of this section shall not be in force after the end of the next regular session of Congress.

Sec. 5. That no person shall be a grand or petit juror in any court of the United States upon any inquiry, hearing or trial of any suit, proceeding or prosecution based upon or arising under the provisions of this act, who shall, in the judgment of the court, be in complicity with any such combination or conspiracy; and every such juror shall, before entering upon any such inquiry, hearing or trial, take and subscribe an oath in open court that he has never directly or indirectly counseled, advised or voluntarily aided any such combination or conspiracy; and each and every person who shall take this oath and shall therein swear falsely, shall be guilty of perjury, and shall be subject to the pains and penalties declared against that crime.

INVESTIGATIONS AND REPORTS.

Before the passage of the Kuklux Act Congress adopted a concurrent resolution appointing a joint select committee of seven senators and fourteen representatives "to inquire into the condition of the late insurrectionary States, so far as regards the execution of the laws and the safety of the lives and property of the citizens of the United States." This committee, consisting of thirteen Republicans and eight Democrats, organized on April 20, 1871—the very day of the approval of the Kuklux Act. The examination of witnesses, assigned to a sub-committee of eight, commenced in Washington on June 2 and continued until June 29, when a sub-committee of three visited South Carolina. That sub-committee consisted of Senator John Scott (Rep.) of Pennsylvania, chairman; Mr. Job E. Stevenson (Rep.) of Ohio, and Mr. Philadelph Van Trump (Dem.) of Ohio. The sub-committee sat in this State from July 10 to July 29—examining witnesses in Columbia, Union, Spartanburg and Yorkville.

The scope of this examination was apparently measured only by the desire of the committee to get all possible information, of whatever purport, upon the matters assigned for their inquiry—the Republican members seeking to establish the charges made by the President in his message, and the minority member educing testimony to explain conditions by reference to the conduct of the State Government in its various branches, including, of course, a presentation of the enrollment, the character and the misconduct of the negro militia.

Shortly after the return of the sub-committee to Washington the chairman addressed to President Grant a letter purporting to set forth conditions as disclosed by the testimony taken as to South Carolina, and urging prompt action by the executive. Thereupon the Attorney-General of the United States (Mr. Amos T. Ackerman, of Georgia) visited Yorkville for a conference with the military commander at that place. The Attorney-General confirmed the statements of Senator Scott and joined in the suggestion that the President should exercise to the utmost the executive power in the premises.

In the meantime at the September term of the Court of General Sessions the grand jury, under the instructions of Judge William M. Thomas, undertook an investigation of conditions in York County, with especial reference to the charges made in the letter of Senator Scott. The commandant at Yorkville (Maj. Lewis Merrill) was invited to appear before the grand jury and there was given him full opportunity to disclose the information which, as afterwards appeared, he then had, touching alleged outrages by the Kuklux in York County. That information withheld, the grand jury proceeded as best they could to examine and make presentment. They did present two men for riot, in firing their pistols and otherwise disturbing the peace on September 9. They further presented two citizens of York for participating in the Kuklux raid on the county treasurer's office. They declined to make presentment on the killing of Capt. Jim Williams and on the killing of Tom Roundtree—this for lack of sufficient evidence—and referred those cases to the law officers of the county.

The condition of the counties formerly the scene of Kuklux operations was at this time one of profound peace, there being better feeling and far less friction between the races than there had been at any time since the inauguration of the negro government in South Carolina. There had been no complaint of any act by the Kuklux since the middle of May. There was neither sign nor semblance of resistance to any law or to any process of any court. As to the conditions then prevailing in the counties indicated, the correspondent of the *New York Herald,* writing from Spartanburg November 1, 1871, after careful investigation, stated the following conclusions:

1. That for four months past no Kuklux outrages have been committed in Spartanburg County—which the Federal officials admit.
2. That the Kuklux organization was originally formed for the self-protection of its members, and not for any political purpose.
3. That men of infamous character entered the Kuklux organization and perpetrated a series of gross outrages upon individuals.
4. That in many instances white and black Republicans borrowed the disguises of the Kuklux and outraged their neighbors, knowing that the blame would not be laid upon them.
5. That if the State government had not been, as it still is, in the hands of corrupt and infamous political adventurers, and had the

laws of the State been fairly and impartially administered, public sentiment would have crushed the Kuklux organization in its incipiency.

6. That there was not any necessity for the suspension of the writ of habeas corpus, because there was not at any time any disposition on the part of the citizens to resist the warrants of arrest. Every man in Spartanburg County could have been arrested by a deputy marshal's posse.

7. That the Kuklux, while formidable in numbers perhaps, never entertained the idea of resisting the United States Government. If its designs were treasonable, it could, in a single night, have overpowered and annihilated the entire military force in this county.

The same correspondent writing from Union, November 3, stated that "the Kuklux troubles ended there seven months ago."

"REBELLION" IN NINE COUNTIES.

In this condition of actual peace, there being neither threat nor show of resistance, whether by individuals or combinations, to any law of the United States, or to any process of any court, the President of the nation, on October 12, 1871, issued his proclamation setting forth the existence of "unlawful combinations and conspiracies in the State of South Carolina" against "certain classes of the people" in the counties of Spartanburg, York, Marion, Chester, Laurens, Newberry, Fairfield, Lancaster and Chesterfield, and commanding "all persons composing the unlawful combinations and conspiracies to disperse and to retire peaceably to their homes within five days of the date hereof, and to deliver either to the marshal of the United States for the district of South Carolina, or to any of his deputies, or to any military officer of the United States within said counties, all arms, ammunition, uniform, disguises and other means and implements used, kept, possessed or controlled by them, for carrying out the unlawful purposes for which the said combinations and conspiracies are organized."

There having been, according to the official statement of the President himself, no response to the commands given in the above-cited proclamation, his Excellency, on October 17, 1871, issued another, in which, after declaring that "the public safety especially requires that the privileges of the writ of habeas corpus be suspended to the end that said rebellion may be overthrown," he proceeded to suspend such privileges within the counties named in the previous proclamation, "in respect to all persons arrested by the marshal of the United

States for the said district of South Carolina, or by any of his deputies, or by any military officer of the United States, or by any soldier or citizen acting under the orders of said marshal, deputy, or such military officer, within any one of said counties, charged with any violation of the act of Congress aforesaid [the Kuklux Act] during the continuance of such rebellion."

The inclusion of Marion County in the obnoxious list was manifestly the result of a clerical error. But by a subsequent proclamation (November 3, 1871) it was gravely declared that "whereas it has been ascertained that in said County of Marion said combinations and conspiracies do not exist to the extent recited in said proclamation," the suspension of the writ was revoked as to that county. By the same proclamation "all persons in the county of Union, composing the unlawful combinations and conspiracies aforesaid," were commanded "to disperse and to retire peaceably to their homes," etc., within five days. On November 10, 1871, the privileges of the writ were formally suspended in Union County.

ARRESTS BY SOLDIERS.

On March 26, 1871, Maj. Lewis Merrill, Seventh cavalry, U. S. A., had assumed command of the post of Yorkville—the force there stationed consisting of two companies of that regiment and two of the Eighteenth infantry. The career of Major Merrill before the war was inconspicuous. It was said that as a cadet at the United States Military Academy at West Point he was known as "dog Merrill." In the conflict between the Union and the Secession elements in Missouri he was actively and bitterly engaged on the Union side. First as colonel of "Merrill's Horse" and afterwards as brigadier-general of volunteer troops he did what he could to intensify the horrors of the conditions that made Missouri the scene of internecine strife to an extent not experienced in any other State. He was president of a "military commission" that "tried" men and sentenced them to death at the rate of two or three a day. He once tortured a prisoner by having the condemned taken to the execution ground, and there having read to him a commutation of the sentence —this in the presence of two Confederates then awaiting death. When advised by General Schofield that Colonel Poindexter, a captured Confederate officer, ought to be tried by military commisson, he flippantly replied: "I had intended to have him shot Friday, but you are probably right." He boasted that whilst "operating" in Missouri he had sent about 3,000 "rebels" into exile or prison—but not as prisoners of war.

In the interval between his arrival at Yorkville and the President's proclamation of "rebellion," Major Merrill was secretly engaged in getting the kind of information that he sought, by inducing and receiving the "confessions" of so-called Kuklux who "puked"—an ugly word, truly, yet the one generally employed by the white people to characterize the conduct of these informers. None of the facts thus procured did Major Merrill give to any public officer, or to the grand jury before which he appeared. "Two days after the telegraphic notification of the suspension of the writ of habeas corpus," the Major afterwards reported to his military superior, "by direction of the Attorney-General I began effecting the arrest of such persons as he had evidence to show were guilty of crimes, and whose arrest he directed." The form of these "directions" has never been disclosed.

These arrests were made by squads of cavalry, almost always in the nighttime. There were no warrants. The prisoners were taken to jail, there to remain at the pleasure of the Government, without the right to have inquiry made into the cause of their detention. Resistance in the modes prescribed by the Constitution and laws was impossible. It was, indeed, privately proposed by Judge Thomas that a test should be made by having him to issue a habeas corpus commanding Major Merrill to produce one or more of these prisoners before him, in order to determine the cause of detention. Such a procedure would have been fruitless.

The conduct of the officers and men in making these arrests was generally unobjectionable, but there were some exceptions. In some cases there was causeless disturbance of the peace of homes by unreasonable searches. There were instances of ruffianly conduct on the part of soldiers not restrained by the presence of a commissioned officer. In some cases the accused were needlessly hurried to jail, with no opportunity to arrange their affairs, to supply themselves with necessary clothing, or even to take leave of their families.

In some cases there was evident the deliberate purpose to humiliate or insult the party taken. A reputable citizen was arrested in a store in Yorkville by a soldier who required the negro with him to search the prisoner—the soldier standing by with cocked musket.

THE KUKLUX TROUBLES

The whole number of persons arrested by the military and confined in York jail was officially reported to be 195. Most of these were after a time taken to Columbia and there released on heavy bail. Some were thus released in Yorkville.

The effects of these extraordinary proceedings were very hurtful. Business was seriously affected—merchants in more than one instance returning goods purchased for the fall trade. No man considered himself safe—every white man (except, of course, the very few who called themselves Republicans) felt that he was at the mercy of any informer who might have chosen to give his name to Major Merrill as that of a Kuklux. The higher a man's standing, or the greater his influence in the community, the greater was the danger of arrest. Under these circumstances some white men left York County—returning, however, just as soon as bayonet rule gave place to civil order.

In these conditions there was necessarily much suffering entailed upon the people in the country districts where most of the arrests were made. The coming of a squad of cavalry in the nighttime was calculated to frighten women and children, and their fears were not allayed by the arrest of father or brother or both upon some charge of which the party taken was not advised. These troopers always went fully armed—carrying sabre, pistol and carbine. The anxiety resulting from the arrests may be said to have pervaded the whole county—no man feeling that his conduct or character or absolute innocence was sufficient to make him safe.

In Union County there were arrests in large numbers—probably 200. These were made by marshals of the United States, the troops apparently held in readiness for any resistance—of which, of course, there was never any danger. The prisoners were kept in Union jail and afterwards brought to Columbia. Some of them were confined fully five months before being tried or released on bail.

In Spartanburg the arrests numbered some hundreds. The county jail being unequal to the demand, the upper stories of two stores had to be used. These arrests were made by marshals—in some cases accompanied by troops—on warrants issued by a commissioner. Some of the prisoners were sentenced at the winter term of the Federal court, some were confined until the March term and others were admitted to bail when the Government got ready.

There were several arrests in Chester, the parties being brought before a commissioner. In some cases the accused were held to bail, whilst in others the proofs were so flimsy as to compel a discharge at the hands of a partisan official. None of those placed under bond were ever tried.

In Newberry there was a very sudden march of Federal soldiers into the county, and white citizens to the number of about thirty-five were arbitrarily arrested, taken to Columbia and there lodged in jail. After needless delay they were released on bail. None of these parties were ever indicted or tried.

There were no arrests in Fairfield, Lancaster or Chesterfield.

The Kuklux organization never operated in Laurens County. On October 20, 1870 (the day following the State election), there was a disturbance due to the riotous and seriously threatening behavior of the negro militia—the trouble growing out of a fight between a white citizen and a State constable. The negro militia repaired to their armory and fired a volley in the direction of the public square. The whites, until then without arms, with what pistols and guns they could get, with brickbats and walking canes, charged the building occupied by the negro troops. The occupants incontinently fled, most of them leaving their guns. Three militiamen were hurt—one fatally. For alleged participation in this riot about forty citizens were arrested on Sunday, March 31, 1872—the arrests being made by a marshal of the United States, accompanied by a squad of soldiers. The accused were taken to Columbia, there kept in jail for some days, under the commitment of a commissoner, and then transferred to Charleston. Indicted for "conspiracy and murder," they were promptly admitted to bail, but were never brought to trial.

A MILITARY MURDER.

In April, 1872, when it was supposed that the soldiers had captured all of the Kuklux wanted in York County, a squad was sent into the upper portion to execute a bench warrant issued by the United States Court. The squad halting on the bank of a stream, the officer in charge had ordered his men to shoot anybody that undertook to move the boat. Minor Paris and a companion, both white men, undertook to use the boat, when the squad, the sergeant first commanding them to halt, fired—one bullet taking effect in the body of Paris and causing his death. There was no warrant for the arrest of either of the men. Neither had resisted any process or any lawful officer. The killing was simple murder—for which nobody was ever called to account. If there was even any military inquiry into the action of the soldiers the fact was never made public.

A GENTLEMAN KIDNAPPED.

Among those in York County upon whom Merrill's suspicion rested, and who had incurred the ill-will of certain Radicals because of his insistance that Jim Williams' company should disband, was Dr. J. Rufus Bratton, a leading physician and a gentleman of the highest character. No man's liberty being safe under the rule of the bayonet, Dr. Bratton deemed it best to leave the country. While in the practice of his profession in London, Ontario, in the summer of 1872, he was seized in the nighttime by two hirelings of the United States Government, gagged, blindfolded and forcibly taken across the line to a point in this country and delivered into the custody of two deputy marshals who had expected and awaited his arrival. Brought to Yorkville, he was there admitted to bail in the sum of $10,000 for his appearance in the Federal Court in Columbia.

The Canadian authorities being informed of this kidnapping and of the unlawful detention of Dr. Bratton in this country, the proper demand was made upon the Government at Washington for his release. After the lapse of so much time only as was needed in the correspondence between the two governments, Dr. Bratton was formally released from his bond and restored to liberty. He resumed his residence in London, and there practiced his profession for some years. Upon the removal of the negro government by the revolution of 1876 he returned to Yorkville, and there spent the remainder of a useful and honorable life. Though ample opportunity was given his accusers, no case was ever brought against him in either State or Federal court.

The kidnappers were apprehended, tried in the Canadian court and sentenced to a term of penal servitude. The marshals who consummated the outrage on this side of the line were never disturbed.

The privileges of the writ of habeas corpus were never formally restored in any of the counties named in the President's proclamation. By the terms of the Kuklux Act the suspension of the writ ceased to be effective on the close of the second session of the Forty-Second Congress—June 10, 1872.

Of the persons arrested, the greater part by far were never called on by the Government to answer any charge. There were some trials in the Circuit Court of the United States—proceedings under the forms of law. These proceedings were marked throughout with acts and measures which were a blot upon the administration of the Federal laws in South Carolina.

THE KUKLUX TRIALS.

The winter term of the Circuit Court of the United States began in Columbia on November 28, 1871, the Hon. Hugh L. Bond, of Baltimore, circuit judge, and the Hon. George S. Bryan, of Charleston, district judge, sitting together. Public interest was centered on the cases against parties charged with violations of the Enforcement Act and the Kuklux Act, coming up at this term.

The Government was represented by District Attorney D. T. Corbin, a lawyer of decided ability, who came from Vermont, and was an official of the Freedmen's Bureau, on duty near Charleston at the close of the war. With him was Attorney-General D. H. Chamberlain, who had a commission from the Department of Justice. Mr. Solomon L. Hoge was also admitted as associate counsel. His connection with the Kuklux cases was merely nominal—he took no part in either the examinations or the arguments.

The course of the Kuklux trials in North Carolina, before Judge Bond and the district judge of that State, had attracted notice here, and steps were taken for a vigorous fight in behalf of the accused. A fund—said to have been $10,000—was raised to employ counsel to assist the local attorneys. Representing the defendants generally and especially charged with the handling of the legal and constitutional questions to be made on their behalf were the Hon. Reverdy Johnson, of Maryland, who had been attorney-general under President Taylor, and the Hon. Henry Stanbery, of Ohio, who had held the same place in the cabinet of Andrew Johnson—both eminent in the legal profession.

The grand jury was composed of six white men and twenty-one colored. Of the colored jurors five were not able to write their names. The foreman was one B. F. Jackson, a "carpetbagger," then or previously a minister of the Northern Methodist church. This fellow, notoriously bitter towards the white people, had been mixed up with some of the frauds of the Radical government in South

THE KUKLUX TROUBLES 203

Carolina, and had been himself guilty of the fraudulent misappropriation of other people's money. On the grand jury, however, were some white men of standing and character. Of this grand jury's presentments on the indictments submitted to them it is only fair to say that as they could hear one side only, it was necessary, under the instructions given by the court, to find a "true bill" in every case considered. The fault here lay in the character of the testimony and not with the conclusions of the grand jury.

Of the whole number of petit jurors summoned not enough attended to make the full panel required by law. The marshal was directed to summon the number necessary to make up the deficiency. Of the jurors thus summoned nine were white and twenty-six colored. Of the white men some were notorious as active Republicans and not one was recognized as a Democrat. Among the Republicans—to be taken as specimens—was C. Smith, a leader of the party in Marion; W. H. Jackson, a member of the staff of the *Daily Union,* the Radical organ in Columbia, and C. H. Bankhead, who during the trials turned up as a spy and a witness for the Government. The panel, as finally made up, had ten white men and thirty-nine colored. Of the white men only four were not in actual sympathy with the Radical party. Of the colored men several were active politicians, working with that party. It was evident that the panel of petit jurors had been corruptly manipulated in the interest of the Government.

All the jurors were required to swear that they had "never directly or indirectly aided any such combination or conspiracy as is set forth and described in the act of Congress . . . approved April 20, 1871"—meaning the Kuklux Act. Under the then existing law of Congress no person who had served in the Confederate army was qualified to sit as a juror in the Federal Court.

The first matter argued was a motion to quash the indictment in the case of Allen Crosby and others, charged with conspiracy (1) to violate the first section of the Enforcement Act (that section declaring that all citizens of the United States shall be entitled to vote without distinction of race, color or previous condition of servitude); and (2) "to injure Amzi Rainey, a citizen of the United States, on account of giving his support in a lawful manner in favor of the election of A. S. Wallace, a lawfully qualified person, as a member of the Congress of the United States." There were eleven counts, of which two (those substantially charging the offenses above stated) were held good and six were adjudged bad. Respecting the balance—those charging burglary—the judges were divided in opinion. It was generally believed that Judge Bond maintained the right of the court to try the question of burglary and Judge Bryan held otherwise.

Of the parties charged in this indictment eight afterwards pleaded guilty and were sentenced each to a fine of $100 and imprisonment for eighteen months. The others were never arrested.

There were other questions raised on behalf of the defendants generally—as to the measure of punishment, as to the right of challenge and as to the court's power to try the question of murder as presented in an indictment under the seventh section of the Enforcement Act. There was also argument on the question whether the right to keep and bear arms was a right secured by the Federal Constitution. On the question of trying for murder the court divided, and on that made as to the right to keep and bear arms forbore to render any decision. Judge Bond declared that the accused had no right to peremptory challenge, but yielded to the opinion of Judge Bryan, who held that the prisoner had ten challenges and the Government two.

These preliminary matters consumed so much time that it was on the eleventh day of the term that the first case came on for trial.

Robert Hayes Mitchell, a citizen of York, was arraigned upon an indictment containing two counts, the first charging, as in the Crosby case, a general conspiracy to violate the first section of the Enforcement Act, by preventing persons of color from voting at the election to take place in October, 1872, and the second charging (under the sixth section) a conspiracy to oppress, threaten and intimidate James Williams because he had exercised his right to vote in the election of October 19, 1870.

Of the twenty-one jurors presented to the prisoner three were white and eighteen colored—the others as they were drawn being required by the district attorney to stand aside. Under this proceeding—then and since held to be lawful—there was no chance for the accused to get on his jury any man whom the Government considered unacceptable. The jury in this case was made up of one white man and eleven colored—and the white man could not be suspected of sympathy with the Democratic party or with the people of his own race in South Carolina. The foreman of this jury was Joseph Taylor, colored, who some years later left Columbia under circumstances somewhat suspicious.

Messrs. Johnson and Stanbery, at the request of Maj. James F. Hart, the defendant's attorney, conducted his defense throughout—Major Hart advising as occasion required.

The Government undertook to prove the conspiracy by showing the origin, objects, constitution and acts of the Kuklux Klan. The constitution (as already given in full) had been delivered to Major Merrill on the order of Samuel G. Brown, of York, who afterwards admitted that he was a member of the order. Testimony was given by members who had joined in 1868, who stated that the Klan was inactive until the autumn of 1870. Other witnesses told of the grips, signs and secrets of the order and of several raids in which they themselves had taken part. These Kuklux witnesses had turned State's evidence on the promise of immunity—in some cases on the promise of pay. A principal witness for the Government—one Kirkland L. Gunn, of York—admitted (under the admirable cross-examination of Mr. Stanbery) that he received for his work $200 from the Department of Justice in Washington. Many victims of the Kuklux—all negroes—told of the visits of the raiders and of the beatings and other enormities suffered by themselves. The testimony took so wide a range that it was difficult to see where the rules of evidence were recognized or even tolerated. There were frequent protests by the prisoner's counsel—so many that Mr. Stanbery once wearily remarked, "We are tired of objecting."

For the defense it was contended that, at least so far as the prisoner was involved, the purpose of the raid on Jim Williams was simply to disarm and thus disable a man whose conduct had disturbed the peace of the neighborhood and was calculated to cause bloodshed. It was shown that the Klan in 1868 had no political character—one witness testifying to his membership while avowing that he had been an out-and-out Republican all his life. There was abundant proof of Jim Williams's inflammatory talk, of his dogged, insolent refusal to disband his company, and of his threat to "kill from the cradle to the grave." It was further shown that these threats, the aggressive conduct of Jim Williams's soldiers and the frequency of fires in the neighborhood caused much uneasiness, not to say alarm, among the white people. It was shown that Mitchell was on the Jim Williams raid, but was with the horses while others of the party went to do the lynching. It was further shown that he had joined the Klan.

The proof of the conspiracy to oppress and injure Jim Williams for having voted in the election of 1870, or to prevent him from voting in the election to be held in 1872, or to oppress and injure colored men generally on account of their race, color or previous condition of servitude, may fairly be said to have been altogether wanting. The only proofs along these lines were furnished in the statements of negroes, who swore that they were maltreated because they were Republicans—and such was one of the contentions of the Government's counsel in argument. Maltreatment for the cause stated constituted no offense against either of the laws under which the prisoner was tried.

The jury first found Mitchell "guilty of the general conspiracy," but Judge Bond held that the verdict in that form could not be entered. After further deliberation they found the defendant not guilty on the first count and guilty on the second count—in other words, Robert Hayes Mitchell was found guilty of having conspired to injure James Williams because he had exercised his right to vote in the election of October, 1870!

The trial had lasted six days. Motions in arrest of judgment and for a new trial having been overruled, Mitchell was sentenced to a fine of $100 and imprisonment for eighteen months.

The next case tried was that of the United States vs. John W. Mitchell and Thomas B. Whitesides. The indictment, containing four counts, charged the general conspiracy against the rights of citizens and a special conspiracy to injure and oppress one Charles Leach, by whipping him—this, in the language of the district attorney, "because he was a Radical and voted the Radical ticket heretofore, and to prevent his voting it hereafter."

The jury was composed of nine negroes and three white men—every one of the latter being of Republican proclivities.

The defendants, both gentlemen of high character and equally high standing in York County, were represented by local counsel—Mr. C. D. Melton, of Columbia, appearing for Captain Mitchell, and Col. W. B. Wilson, of Yorkville, for Dr. Whitesides.

As in the previous trial the evidence took a very wide range—the Government undertaking to show additional outrages by the Kuklux, including two murders. At one stage, as a witness was telling about some brutal conduct of raiders towards a white woman, the defendant's counsel objected on the ground of irrelevancy, when Judge Bond said: "They propose to connect it, and we might as well let the people hear and let the jury know what things exist about us." The purpose indicated by this ruling was well understood and properly appreciated by the Government's counsel. Their negro witnesses, naturally sensational and under the circumstances not much inclined to caution or accuracy, told all sorts of stories of all sorts of outrages by raiding Kuklux. Except in the case of the particular raid charged in the indictment no attempt was made to connect either of the accused with any of these outrages. Nor was there any evidence that the wrongs were done by the Klan—except, of course, the bare statement of each witness that he had been "visited by the Kuklux." None of the persons who were thus treated undertook to show that their persecutors were members of the order, except by the single statement that the raiders wore gowns. No sufferer testified that he was maltreated because of his race or color —the raiders' execrations being always against the Radical party.

John W. Mitchell offered no evidence to show that he had not joined the Klan, but, not permitted to testify, he could not explain his connection. He showed that he did not participate in the raid on Charles Leach by proving, beyond a reasonable doubt, that during the entire night of the raid he was at the home of his mother, who was ill.

Dr. Whitesides always denied having been a member of the Klan, and no witness stated that he had been. One of the Government's star witnesses—Kirkland L. Gunn—testified that he had given this defendant the Kuklux grip and there was no response. Gunn further stated that Dr. Whitesides had said to him that the Klan was "the most damnable affair in the country." Dr. Whitesides showed beyond any doubt that during the entire night of the Leach raid he was at the house of a patient.

One Foster, a confessed Kuklux, testified that Dr. Whitesides was on the Leach raid on the night of January 9, 1871, but he had previously stated that Whitesides was not present. To meet the difficulty thus arising and to destroy the effect of the alibi proven by the prisoners, the Government showed by witnesses other than Foster that the raid was on or about January 23. It thus became impossible for the defense to meet the Government's case as given in evidence, though they had met it as stated in the indictment. Whether this shifting of dates was a trick of the Government's witnesses or of its counsel, or of both, could never be determined.

Both defendants were found guilty on two counts—guilty of the conspiracy to injure Charles Leach because he had voted in the election of 1870, and guilty of the conspiracy to punish him because he had in that election voted for A. S. Wallace as member of Congress.

Captain Mitchell was sentenced to $1,000 fine and five years' imprisonment—Dr. Whitesides to $100 fine and twelve months' imprisonment.

The next party tried was John S. Millar—whose case was probably taken up because he had testified to the declaration of Charles W. Foster that Dr. Whitesides was not on the Leach raid. The jury was composed of eleven colored men and one C. H. Bankhead, white, who was a Radical and who afterwards showed up as a witness for the Government, spying on the private conversation of a defendant. The indictment charged simply a conspiracy to violate the first section of the Enforcement Act by unlawfully preventing "divers male citizens of the United States of African descent" from voting at the election to be held on the third Wednesday in October, 1872.

It was not shown that Millar had ever joined the Klan (though he attended one meeting) or that he ever went on a raid. It was actually shown that he was opposed to the Kuklux and that he was in sympathy with the Republican party. The jury promptly found him guilty, and he was sentenced to $20 fine and three months' imprisonment.

Dr. Edward T. Avery, of York, was arraigned upon an indictment charging a conspiracy to intimidate, injure and oppress Abram Brumfield, Samuel Sturges and Isaac A. Postle (otherwise called Isaac the Apostle) on account of their race, color and previous condition of servitude, because they had voted in the election in October, 1870, and in order to prevent them from voting in October, 1872.

The jury was composed of nine colored men and three white—these latter in active sympathy with the Radical party.

The defense was represented by Col. W. B. Wilson, of Yorkville and Col. F. W. McMaster, of Columbia.

THE KUKLUX TROUBLES

After the usual testimony as to the formation, constitution and some raids of the Kuklux Klan, the prosecution undertook to show that Dr. Avery had joined the order in 1868, and that on the night of March 25, 1871, he was one of a party that visited and maltreated Brumfield, Sturges and Postle.

For the defense it was shown that the Klan in 1868 was an organization simply for the protection against anticipated trouble with the negroes; that it was wholly inactive until the winter of 1870; that though Dr. Avery was present at the Rock Hill poll in the election of 1868, there was no interference by him or anybody else with any person's right or opportunity to vote; that his right arm was paralyzed in consequence of a wound received in the War of Secession; that it was physically impossible for him to have done with that arm the acts attributed to him by the negroes who told of the raid, and that during the entire night of the raid he was at home with his family. It was further shown that Postle had made a statement in writing that he was mistaken in charging that Dr. Avery was of the raiding party.

The evidence closed, Colonel McMaster began his argument for the defense. He had said but little when District Attorney Corbin interrupted, and addressed the court:

"If your Honors please, I don't notice the defendant in court. I have just asked the counsel where the defendant was, and the reply I received was—that was for me to find out."

Colonel Master—I repeat it now.

Judge Bond then inquired: "Where is your client?"

Colonel Wilson—I understood, may it please the court, when we adjourned on Saturday night [this being Monday] that Dr. Avery had gone to see his family and that he would return today.

Judge Bond—Do you expect him back?

Colonel Wilson—I had no interview with him. I expected him to return by the next train. I know nothing save from the information I have received from Mr. McMaster.

Judge Bond—Do you know where your client is, Mr. McMaster?

Colonel McMaster—I beg the court will excuse me from answering that question.

Judge Bond—Had you any knowledge from your client that he was going away?

Colonel McMaster—I hope the court will excuse me from answering.

Judge Bond—The clerk will lay a rule on Mr. McMaster to answer the question or show cause why he should not be thrown over the bar.

The bailiff, at the command of Judge Bond, called Edward T. Avery three times—and there was no answer. Thereupon the court made an order directing that the defendant's bond (in the sum of $3,000) be forfeited.

The trial proceeding, the jury promptly found the defendant guilty. Dr. Avery was never sentenced.

Colonel McMaster duly answered the rule—the arguments in his behalf being made by Mr. F. W. Fickling and Mr. John Waties. The respondent took the ground that Judge Bond had no right to ask the questions put to him and that he could not be required to disclose any communication made to him by his client. District Attorney Corbin and Attorney-General Chamberlain argued on the other side. Judge Bond took the matter "under advisement" and so kept it to the day of his death.

Dr. Avery had indeed fled. Some months later he received a pardon from the President and returned to his home. Major Merrill joined in the application for clemency, stating that he had doubts of Dr. Avery's guilt—doubts, it must be said, which existed at the trial, and which were suggested to Merrill while testifying for the prosecution. No part of the money paid by Dr. Avery in satisfaction of his bond was ever restored—the transaction furnishing a clear case of robbery under the forms of law.

When the negro preacher Postle reported to Major Merrill his own acknowledgment that his charge against Dr. Avery was untrue, that officer caused the arrest of Mrs. Avery, the Rev. R. E. Cooper (a Presbyterian clergyman) and two colored women employed in Dr. Avery's home on the charge of intimidating a government witness—meaning Postle. Mrs. Avery had sent for Postle, and, in the presence of Mr. Cooper, assured the negro that during all the night of the alleged raid Dr. Avery was at home—at the same time disclaiming any purpose to threaten or intimidate. The colored women joined in the statement that Dr. Avery had been at home on the night in question. In this matter the grand jury found a true bill, but the accused were never tried. While out on bond Mr. Cooper was arrested on a bench warrant issued on Corbin's motion and placed in the Richland jail—Corbin pretending that his action was taken under a misapprehension. The facts brought to the attention of the court, Mr. Cooper was promptly released.

During the trial of Mitchell and Whitesides Mr. Melton informed Judge Bond that Kirkland L. Gunn and Charles W. Foster, standing witnesses for the Government, had told a certain colored man that if he testified for Mitchell they would "make him smoke for it." Judge Bond ordered the names, with the evidence, to be sent before the grand jury. There the matter ended—the Government's course being in strong contrast with that taken against Mrs. Avery and others when a negro preacher-politician complained that he had been threatened and intimidated.

Samuel G. Brown, a highly respected citizen of York, well advanced in years, stated his purpose to plead guilty, submitting affidavits to explain his possession of the Kuklux constitution and to show what little actual connection he had had with the Klan. Judge Bond consented, but said to Mr. Brown: "We want to know not only your connection with the Klan, but that of every other person in your position in life in York County who belonged." When Brown came to be sentenced he made it manifest that he did not intend to meet Judge Bond's demand for testimony against the good people of York, and His Honor petulantly said: "You evidently don't propose to tell all you know, and I don't, therefore, propose to hear you. The judgment of the court in your case is that you be fined $1,000 and be imprisoned for five years."

The whole number of persons sentenced was fifty-five, of whom, as has been seen, only five were placed on trial. A large number of those pleading guilty were young men of little or no education, who gave no sign of any animosity to the negro on account of his race or color, and who surely had no consciousness of any purpose to conspire against the negro's rights as secured by the Fourteenth or Fifteenth Amendment. They had joined the Klan just to be joining it, and had done some raiding as a result of their indignation at the insolence of some of the negro politicians, the incendiary talk of others and the misconduct of the negro militia. The sentences of these parties ranged from three to eighteen months—a fine being nominally imposed in each instance.

In the broad range taken in the examination of witnesses much was brought out that had no bearing upon the conduct of the accused. Many acts were thus ascribed to men as Kuklux, though no attempt was made to show that they were of that organization. Many acts were alleged which were worse than cruel. The conduct ascribed to the raiders was contrary to the suggestions of common humanity, common decency. The lawyers for the defense in every case took occasion to denounce the acts described by some of the Government's witnesses. In the course of his argument in the case of Robert Hayes Mitchell, Mr. Reverdy Johnson used the following language:

I have listened with unmixed horror to some of the testimony which has been brought before you. The outrages proved are shocking to humanity. They admit of neither excuse nor justification. They violate every obligation which law and nature impose upon men. They show that the parties engaged were brutes, insensible to the obligations of humanity and religion. The day will come, however, if it has not already arrived, when they will deeply lament it. Even if justice shall not overtake them, there is one tribunal from which there is no escape. It is their own judgment—that tribunal which sits in the breast of every living man—that still voice that thrills through the heart, the soul, the mind, and as it speaks gives happiness or torture—the voice of conscience, the voice of God. If it has not already spoken to them in tones which have startled them to the enormity of their conduct, I trust, in the mercy of Heaven, that that voice will speak before they shall be called above to account for the transactions of this world; that it will so speak as to make them penitent, and that trusting in the dispensations of Heaven, whose justice is dispensed with mercy, when they shall be brought before that great tribunal, so to speak, that incomprehensible tribunal, there will be found in the fact of their penitence or in their previous lives some grounds upon which God may say—Pardon!

This extract was for some months printed daily at the head of the editorial column of the Radical organ in Columbia.

Allowance made for the somewhat rhetorical character of Mr. Johnson's protestations and for the zeal of the lawyer in trying to disconnect his client from acts which necessarily inflamed the jury against the accused, it must, nevertheless, be said that many acts were ascribed to the Kuklux which no good citizen could palliate or excuse. Allowance made for the negro's fondness for the dramatic or sensational and his manifest satisfaction in telling in public his stories against white men apparently at his mercy, it must, nevertheless, be admitted that there was truth enough in these stories to justify the strongest condemnation of the Kuklux doings described.

But it should also be stated that none of the parties indicted was shown to have had any part in such outrages.

Nor was any effort made, in the State courts or in the Federal, to bring to justice any of the men who committed those outrages. The Government undertook, in the Federal court, to show that five murders had been committed by the Kuklux in York County. Yet no official of the State Government, no officer of the United States, no man in sympathy with the Republican party, ever took steps to have the murderers brought to justice.

At the April term, 1872, of the Federal court in Charleston there were other trials—the accused being charged with having belonged to the Kuklux Klan, and with having joined in raids upon negroes. The Government's tactics in Columbia were repeated in Charleston—the petit jury panel bearing unmistakable evidences of having been fixed with a view to wholesale convictions. Conspicuous among these jurors was Gilbert Pillsbury, a Massachusetts carpetbagger, who had been the first Radical mayor of Charleston. The fixing was not quite so successful as it had been at Columbia—hence the failure, in some cases at least, to get the customary conviction.

A notable feature in some of these cases was the presentation of the charge of murder in the indictment—the understanding being that in the event of a conviction the division between Judge Bond and Judge Bryan, touching the court's jurisdiction to try the issue as to such a charge, should be certified to the Supreme Court, and sentence should be suspended till that tribunal should decide the question presented.

William Lowery, of York, was tried upon an indictment charging a conspiracy to injure and oppress one Dick Wilson, a person of color, because he had voted for A. S. Wallace in 1870 and in order to prevent him from voting as he might will in the election of 1872. Maj. James F. Hart, of York, and Maj. S. P. Hamilton, of Chester, appeared for the defense—the Government being represented by District Attorney Corbin. The accused was found guilty and was sentenced to a fine of $10 and imprisonment for two years.

Leander Spencer and William Smith, of York, were charged with conspiracy (in the usual form) and with the murder of Tom Roundtree—in pursuance of that conspiracy. The jury failing to agree, a mistrial was ordered. Major Hamilton represented the defendants. They were never tried again.

Elijah Ross Sepaugh, of York, was arraigned upon charges identical with those in the previous case—conspiracy and murder. The jury found him guilty upon both counts, but sentence was suspended upon a certificate of division on the question of the court's jurisdiction to try him for murder. Mr. John F. Ficken, of Charleston, by appointment of the court, represented the prisoner.

John Rogers, of Union, was arraigned upon the usual charges. Before the jury was drawn the defendant's counsel (Mr. G. Lamb Buist, of Charleston), submitted an affidavit of a colored man, alleging unfairness and partiality of the United States marshal in making up the jury list—the affiant declaring that having stated to that official a desire to serve on a Federal jury, the latter replied that if the deponent could refer to Mr. Corbin or to Mr. E. W. M. Mackey (the Radical sheriff of Charleston) it would be all right. Judge Bond overruled the objection.

The accusation in this case was conspiracy—the form of the oath alleged to have been taken by the defendant being somewhat different from that contained in the published constitution of the Kuklux Klan. In the course of the examination the circumstances of the second raid on the Union jail were recounted—the witness stating that he had helped in the hanging of the negro militiamen. The jury failing to agree, a mistrial was entered. The accused was never tried again.

Thomas Zimmerman, of Spartanburg, was next tried for conspiracy and murder—killing one Wallie Fowler, a negro of that county. On the close of the testimony for the prosecution the court, on the motion of the defendant, directed the jury to write a verdict of acquittal. Messrs. Carlisle & Duncan, of Spartanburg, appeared for the defense.

Robert Riggins, of York, was charged with conspiracy and murder—participation in the raid in which Capt. Jim Williams was hung. The defendant was acquitted of murder, found guilty of conspiracy and sentenced to $100 fine and imprisonment for three years. Major Hamilton appeared for the defense.

Several parties pleaded guilty at this term—their imprisonments ranging from three months to ten years and their fines from $10 to $1,000. There were twenty-eight sentences in all.

At the November term, 1872, other Kuklux cases were taken up in Columbia.

Robert Moore, of York, was accused of participation in the murder of Tom Roundtree. He was convicted of conspiracy only, and sentenced to a fine of $100 and imprisonment for five years. Col. Y. J. Pope appeared for the defense.

The case against John T. Craig and others, of Laurens, charged with conspiracy in the usual form, resulted in a mistrial. Mr. J. C. H. Jaeger, of Newberry, appeared for the defense. The accused were not tried a second time.

There were at this term several parties pleading guilty—among them two who stated that they had taken part in the second raid on the Union jail. The sentences ranged from two to five years' imprisonment and from $100 to $500 fine. There were nine sentences in all.

IN THE SUPREME COURT.

In the case entitled United States vs. Avery it was sought to have the decision of the highest court in the land upon the constitutionality of the Enforcement Act. The matter was carried up on the division between Judge Bond and Judge Bryan on the murder count of the indictment. The proceeding was dismissed by the Supreme Court on the ground that the prosecution on that count having in the court below been withdrawn by the Government there was no question upon which a certificate of division was proper or upon which the judgment of the Supreme Court could properly be invoked. Mr. Stanbery and Mr. Johnson appeared for the defendant in this proceeding.

Next an application was made by the same attorneys, in behalf of T. Jefferson Greer, for a writ of habeas corpus, to have inquiry into the cause of his arrest and detention and thus have a decision on the constitutionality of the statutes in question. On this matter the application failed because the court were equally divided. No opinion was filed.

In the case of Robert Hayes Mitchell, above noted, there were proceedings taken to have the constitutional questions heard in the Supreme Court. But as the same questions were presented, by the same process, in the Greer case, Mitchell's motion was withdrawn by his counsel—April 29, 1872.

The case of Elijah Ross Sepaugh was duly argued in the Supreme Court. Pending a decision the prosecution was withdrawn in the

Circuit Court, and that fact having been certified to the Supreme Court the case was there dismissed.

Thus it came about that every effort to have the judgment of the Supreme Court upon the constitutionality of the Enforcement Act and the Kuklux Act came to nought.

In the summer of 1873 President Grant declared a purpose to pardon all convicted Kuklux whose neighbors and fellow citizens might ask clemency for them. Applications were made accordingly, and one by one the parties involved were set free. Except in the cases where the term of imprisonment was one year or less none of them served out his term.

JUST A LITTLE JOBBERY.

The Republican organ in Columbia printed daily stenographic reports of the Kuklux trials in that city—an undertaking then too expensive for any other newspaper in South Carolina. It was afterwards discovered that the cost of this enterprising act of the organ had been paid out of the public funds.

The Legislature ordered the printing of 5,000 copies of the court proceedings in book form. For this work the Republican Printing Company charged $45,788. Their man Woodruff afterwards swore that the real value of the work was $22,894, and that the bill had been raised because his company had had to take their pay in Blue Ridge Scrip, which they thought worth only half its face. The actual value of the work was about $10,000.

On July 28, 1871, Governor Scott issued a proclamation offering a reward of $200 for each person arrested, with proof to convict, under the Enforcement Act. During the session of 1872-73 the Legislature appropriated $35,000 to pay these rewards. The Governor appointed a commission of five lawyers to pass upon the claims presented under the act. This commission (first awarding themselves $500 apiece for their services) reported the following persons entitled to pay as follows:

Maj. Lewis Merrill, U. S. A., $15,700; Thos. M. Wilkes, U. S. Commissioner, $7,000; F. B. Lloyd (assignee of Merrill), $5,000; H. H. D. Byron, U. S. Commissioner, $1,200; Capt. W. H. Brown, U. S. A., $200; James Canton, U. S. Marshal, $1,200.

Lloyd was the brother-in-law of Judge Thos. J. Mackey, and they both claimed to have helped to lobby the bill through the Legislature.

THE KUKLUX TROUBLES

The Federal officials—civil and military—had, of course, received their regular pay from the Government.

There was considerable comment upon the course of Major Merrill in demanding money for military services performed in obedience to the orders of his superiors, and he evidently lost caste with the army officers. In 1886 the bill to retire him with the rank of lieutenant-colonel was defeated in the Senate—the Southern senators having exposed his conduct in taking pay from South Carolina for services already paid for by the National Government. A second effort on the part of Merrill's friends, in 1890, was successful.

CHAPTER VI.

MOSES' ADMINISTRATION.

During the second term of Governor Scott the Republican party was so fully in control in South Carolina that it had nothing to fear from any act or protest of the opposition—that opposition represented by the white population owning well-nigh all the property in the State and paying well-nigh all the taxes. The exposures and remonstrances of the press counted nothing. The appeals of the taxpayers were equally unavailing. No man was accounted worthy of any opinion on public affairs unless he should first have called himself a Republican and should next have acquiesced in every act of that party. Moral standards usually deemed applicable to public trusts were deliberately set aside and men of notoriously bad character were deliberately elected or appointed to public office.

The policy of the negro party—fixed by such leaders as Scott, Cardozo, Chamberlain, Elliott, Parker, Whittemore, Swails, Smalls, Moses (Jr.) and Whipper—was one of stolid enmity to the white race, and that policy was enforced by the Legislature, by the Executive and, with one or two honorable exceptions, by every governing board in the State administration.

The ruling majority in the Legislature was utterly dishonest—the Republican members, with few exceptions, flagrantly holding themselves out as so many puppets or hirelings to be bought with money.

A seat in the United States Senate had been bought—corruptly bought with money actually put into the hands of men who by thus taking it became guilty of wilful and corrupt perjury.

One notable scheme, the issue of Revenue Bond Scrip, in aid of the coterie of corruptionists of whom John J. Patterson was the acknowledged head, had been carried through the Legislature by bribery so flagrant that few of the guilty members undertook to conceal their acts. As already shown, Patterson, in a paper signed by himself, declared in effect that the votes of members of the General Assembly had been bought by him with money.

The extravagance, the incapacity and the corruption of the negro government in each of its various departments were manifest to all who cared to see or read or listen or learn. The charges made, the warnings uttered, the protests entered in the campaign of 1870 were more than justified by the actual history of Governor Scott's second term. No regard was had in any department of the State Government to party pledge, to official responsibility or to the personal obligation which every honest officer recognizes.

The finances of the State and the counties alike were in bad plight. The State debt, principal and accrued interest, was admitted to be $18,350,000, exclusive of the "contingent liabilities" already mentioned. State bonds were scarcely marketable, and then only at low figures—the maximum price offered being 60. The State was without credit in any of the exchanges of the world, and the moral character of her agents was such as to render them incapable of reestablishing confidence or of restoring the good name of the commonwealth. The "floating debt" was more than $700,000.

The condition of most of the counties was little better—the aggregate of county indebtedness, November 1, 1872, being over $250,000. County paper was hawked about by its holders—sold to speculators at exorbitant discounts. Defalcations among county treasurers amounted to more than $450,000—and the defaulters still maintained their standing in the Republican party. Pretensive efforts were made to bring these criminals to justice, but no one of them was ever punished. The so-called prosecutions lacked the real sympathy of the prosecutors and thus naturally came to nought.

The free-school system was worse than a failure. Of the $300,000 appropriated at the session of 1871-72 not a dollar was available for the pay of teachers; this entire fund having been applied to other claims, on the principle, "first come, first served"—and the agents or the favorites of the "ring" always came first. Teachers' pay certificates were sold at ruinous discounts—usually 50 per cent.—and in some counties were absolutely valueless. The school commissioners, with occasional exceptions (chiefly in the counties controlled by whites) were incompetent to do even the routine work of the office—much less were they able to organize, maintain or expand a school system. The school sessions were irregular, the teachers became discouraged, the white taxpayers were naturally disgusted, and the entire system had sunk into a state of disrepute and worthlessness.

The condition of the lunatic asylum was not only a disgrace to the State, but an outrage upon the inmates. The superintendent in his official report, November, 1872, stated that the institution had had "no assistance from the State from July, 1871, to January, 1872." Upon asking of the State Treasurer the money appropriated, Superintendent Ensor was informed that there was none in the treasury. On April 30 the Treasurer, in response to an urgent appeal of the superintendent, again declared that there were no funds, nor was any assurance given of any relief. It seemed as if the asylum must be closed. That calamity was averted through the credit extended by certain merchants and by a loan procured on the endorsement of Dr. Ensor, Governor Scott and Mr. Chamberlain. The money thus obtained being exhausted the superintendent had actually to beg help of merchants in Columbia. Those who extended accommodations and thus averted the necessity to turn the patients out into the streets were Mr. John Agnew and Mr. Edward Hope of that city. Mr. Bernard O'Neill, a Charleston merchant, aided the good work by extending unusual accommodations to Messrs. Hope & Giles, of which firm Mr. Hope was the senior member.

In November, 1872, the asylum was in debt, for expenses of maintenance, $62,015—of which the sum of $15,496 was due to employees, including the superintendent and the physicion.

The personnel of the Radical government was generally so disreputable that there was little confidence in the character or the motives of those holding office. There were, of course, honorable exceptions. But in some cases the character of the Radical incumbent (whether white or black) was such that he would not have been permitted to enter a gentleman's premises by the front gate—would scarcely have been permitted to interview his negro cook without a certificate of character.

There was a heyday of enjoyment among the plunderers assembled in Columbia. At the expense of the State, with money taken in bribes or actually stolen from the public treasury, they had their fine garments, their wines, liquors and cigars, their blooded horses and their spic-and-span turnouts—and plenty of money to spare. These things were impudently flaunted in the faces of the white people powerless to protect themselves against the insolence of thieves, the arrogance of officeholders or even the swagger of loose women who shared the benefits of the money stolen from the people.

The position of the negro party seemed impregnable. They controlled the State Government, and they were backed by the civil and the military power of the United States. Flattered by politicians, weakened by the gifts of corruptionists, carried away by the receipt of more money than he had ever dreamed of making, with little conception of the dignity of his station, ignored by well-nigh all the self-respecting white people of the South, distrusted by large numbers of Northern men without regard to party affiliation, President Grant cast the weight of his influence and actively used the powers of his office in aid of the negro government, known by him to be corrupt.

The active sympathy of the President threw the whole weight of the Federal power on the side of the negro Government in South Carolina. The organs and the dependents of that Government had been assured of the sympathy and the backing of the President—the commander-in-chief of the Federal army. Troops were ready at the call of the Governor just whenever that official should see fit to demand them. These soldiers were employed for the double purpose of emboldening the negro population and of notifying the white taxpayers that the State Government, by which they were being plundered, was actually sustained by the armed forces of the United States. The pretense that these troops were sent to keep the peace and protect the polls was so palpably hollow that numbers of people in the "loyal" States heartily disapproved the President's policy and deplored its enforcement. Nevertheless the Republican managers in South Carolina, assured of the President's sympathy, held their ground against every appeal, from whatever quarter it came.

The courts of the United States had so used the extraordinary powers given by the Enforcement acts of Congress, and the machinery of these tribunals was so far controlled by Republicans, actively associated in the prevalent schemes of plunder, that in no issue between a supporter and an opponent of the State Administration could the latter expect even meagre justice. Juries were flagrantly and corruptly packed in the interest of the political party dominating the State. Perjury was invited, then condoned, then rewarded. No white man's life or character was a safeguard against accusation—and suspicion sufficed for the incarceration of any reputable citizen whose opposition to the negro regime or its agents had gotten him the ill-will of the Radical leaders. The right of personal liberty, thought always to be protected by the writ of habeas corpus, was destroyed by the acts of the President—proclamations whose statements were absurdly untrue. The vicious and cowardly libels thus uttered against a large body of white citizens were justified on the ground that the President had acted upon official statements made to him. Could the President have risen above his own low conception of the duties of his office he could easily have ascertained that his informants were unworthy of belief.

The civil courts of the United States, pretensively exercising civil powers, cooperated with the military in the purpose to crush the spirit of the white people so that they might never rise against the robbers.

Thus, after four years of Republican rule, the white people of South Carolina were in a state of actual subjugation. The rule of the negro was absolute. The will of the negro party was the law of the situation. It remains to be seen how the Republican leaders used their opportunity—what measure of justice they meted out to the white people who by sheer brute force had been placed at their mercy.

REPUBLICAN NOMINATIONS.

There were protestations from many Republicans of both races that there must be reform—that corrupt men must be driven from power, and that the party must itself expect to go down to defeat unless there should be a change.

For some time before the meeting of the Republican State Convention it seemed that the nomination for Governor would go to F. J. Moses, Jr. There were many in the party who expressed the opinion that such a nomination was not to be tolerated. The action of the party through its authorized representatives is now to be stated.

The Republican State Convention met in Columbia on August 21, 1872. The membership contained few new men, the leaders in the different counties—most of these being officeholders—controlling the convention. The first day's session was consumed in preliminaries and in speech-making while waiting for the report of the committee on credentials. The roll of delegates, as finally fixed, contained the names of thirty-three white men and 115 colored. Four counties—Chesterfield, Lexington, Newberry and Union—were without representation. The following officers were elected:

President—R. B. Elliott (colored).

MOSES' ADMINISTRATION

Vice-Presidents—B. F. Whittemore, Robert Smalls (colored), F. L. Cardozo (colored), Thomas J. Mackey.

Secretaries—T. J. Minton (colored), C. Smith.

Sergeant-at-Arms—J. E. Green (colored); assistant—C. D. Lowndes (colored).

Doorkeeper—M. D. Long (colored).

For the office of Governor Samuel W. Melton was nominated by Robert Smalls (colored); M. R. Delany (colored) by J. L. Jamison (colored) of Orangeburg; Franklin J. Moses, Jr., by H. J. Maxwell (colored), of Marlboro, and Daniel H. Chamberlain by John L. Neagle, of York.

Judge Mackey urged the nomination of Chamberlain—warning the convention that the choice of Moses would disrupt the party and bring defeat.

R. B. Elliott bitterly opposed the nomination of Chamberlain.

S. A. Swails suggested Reuben Tomlinson as "a pioneer in education, a man whose skirts are clean of any soil or stain."

Judge James L. Orr (who was a delegate from Anderson) warmly seconded the nomination of Tomlinson.

Elliott declared that Neagle had offered money to a delegate from Edgefield and to one from Abbeville—sums ranging from $300 to $500. Neagle retorted that a delegate from York (one M. L. Owens, white) had had an offer of $1,000 if he would vote for Moses.

Elliott denied Neagle's statement, but admitted that he had said that if he could get the roll of delegates the night before the nomination he could with money make things all right. He further said that he could produce a dozen persons who had been approached with money in Chamberlain's interest, and that some of these had actually received money.

Judge Mackey denounced Tomlinson as utterly corrupt, and charged that he had distributed bribes in carrying through the phosphate bill at the session of 1869-70. He further denounced Whittemore for having corruptly sold a West Point cadetship, and charged that he had been guilty of other rascalities.

Judge Orr stated that a colored delegate from Barnwell (one Mayer) had had from Moses an offer of $2,000 for his support in the convention.

Elliott, speaking for Moses, said that Moses had approached Mayer with an offer of $2,000—or, rather, had asked Mayer what his price was, and whether $2,000 would be sufficient. Mayer assenting, the conversation ended.

Amid great confusion the vote was then taken—Moses, 69; Melton, 18; Chamberlain, 16; Tomlinson, 15. Moses was declared the nominee.

Upon this announcement Judge Orr stated that he could not support the nominee, and must withdraw from the convention.

R. H. Gleaves, colored, of Beaufort, was nominated for Lieutenant-Governor—defeating R. H. Cain, of Charleston, and E. J. Adams, of Columbia, also colored.

Henry E. Hayne, colored, of Marion, was named for Secretary of State—defeating F. H. Frost, of Williamsburg, also colored.

For the office of Attorney-General Samuel W. Melton, of Columbia, received 100 votes (six being cast for D. H. Chamberlain), and the nomination was made unanimous. A committee consisting of Messrs. Smalls, Hedges and Jones (all colored) was appointed to inform Judge Melton of his nomination and conduct him to the president's stand. In a few minutes the committee returned with the judge upon their shoulders, and were greeted with great applause—the band playing a national air. The president, on behalf of the Republican party of the State, congratulated him upon his nomination. Judge Melton responded in a few remarks.

Pending the nomination of a candidate for the office of Treasurer a row occurred among some of the members, causing such an uproar that the convention had to adjourn.

On the next day F. L. Cardozo was put in nomination. He was bitterly denounced by a few delegates, but received the nomination by a vote of seventy-seven against thirty-five for his five competitors.

Solomon L. Hoge was nominated for Comptroller-General, J. K. Jillson for Superintendent of Education, and H. W. Purvis (colored) for Adjutant and Inspector General—each without opposition.

The platform adopted contained the following planks: 1. Fidelity to the national Republican party, and support of its nominees. 2. Financial reform in the State, including a scrutiny of the outstanding bonds. 3. Reduction of public expenditures. 4. Repeal of the State license law. 5. Specific appropriations as conditions precedent to the disbursement of public moneys from the State treasury. 6. Enforcement of all the laws by peaceful and constitutional agencies.

The convention was in session four days.

Pursuant to a call issued by Judge James L. Orr a number of the delegates lately in the Republican State Convention assembled in the Richland courthouse on August 22.

Among the prominent white Republicans present, besides Judge Orr, were William E. Earle, of Greenville, Senator F. A. Sawyer, B. F. Whittemore, C. C. Bowen, D. T. Corbin and Timothy Hurley; with the following colored men: Samuel Lee, of Sumter, B. A. Bosemon, of Charleston, W. J. Whipper, of Beaufort, S. A. Swails, of Williamsburg, J. Hannibal White, of York, Benjamin Byas, of Orangeburg.

Speeches were made by several delegates, denouncing Frank Moses and declaring that his nomination would disgrace and destroy the Republican party in South Carolina. Particular stress was laid upon the issuance by Moses of fraudulent pay certificates—the amount being stated at $1,200,000.

The following ticket was nominated:

Governor—Reuben Tomlinson, of Charleston.
Lieutenant-Governor—James N. Hayne (colored), of Barnwell.
Secretary of State—Macon B. Allen (colored), of Charleston.
Comptroller-General—J. Scott Murray, of Anderson.
Attorney-General—John T. Green, of Sumter.
Treasurer—Edwin F. Gary, of Richland.
Superintendent of Education—B. L. Roberts (colored), of Greenville.
Adjutant and Inspector General—Philip E. Ezekiel (colored), of Beaufort.

The platform denounced the Republican administration in general and Frank Moses in particular, and declared for retrenchment and reform in every department.

The campaign was without special incident—presenting only a wrangle between two contending factions of the dominant party, in which the white people took little interest. The bolters' ticket was weak—the only two nominees at all acceptable to the white people being Judge Green and Mr. Murray. The character of each of these was above reproach.

The election resulted in an overwhelming victory for the Moses ticket, the vote standing—Moses, 69,838; Tomlinson, 36,533. Tomlinson carried only ten counties—Anderson, Charleston, Greenville,

Horry, Lancaster, Lexington, Oconee, Spartanburg, Union and York.

Congressmen were elected as follows:

At Large—R. H. Cain (colored), defeating L. E. Johnson.

First District—Joseph H. Rainey (colored), without opposition.

Second District—A. J. Ransier (colored), defeating William Gurney, bolter.

Third District—R. B. Elliott (colored)—William H. McCaw and Samuel McGowan, Democrats, receiving each a small vote.

Fourth District—A. S. Wallace, of York, defeating Benjamin F. Perry, of Greenville.

Solicitors were elected as follows:

First Circuit—Charles W. Buttz (Republican).

Second Circuit—P. L. Wiggin (Republican).

Third Circuit—S. T. Atkinson (Democrat).

Fourth Circuit—D. D. McColl (Republican).

Fifth Circuit—J. H. Runkle (Republican).

Sixth Circuit—William H. Brawley (Democrat).

Seventh Circuit—W. Magill Fleming (Republican).

Eighth Circuit—Absolom Blythe (Republican).

The Legislature was overwhelmingly Republican—that party carrying all the counties except Lexington, Oconee, Pickens, Spartanburg and Union.

The Anderson delegation (House) was composed of one Democrat and two bolting Republicans. The bolting Republicans carried Charleston and York. In many counties the Democrats made no nominations. On joint ballot the General Assembly stood—130 Republicans, 27 Democrats; 51 white, 106 colored.

The national Republican ticket carried the State by a majority of nearly 50,000.

The returns showed that a large portion of the white people took no part in the election—at least 40,000 not going to the polls.

The constitutional amendments were both adopted.

MOSES INAUGURATED.

The new Legislature assembled November 26.

S. A. Swails was elected president pro tem. of the Senate, and Josephus Woodruff, clerk.

The House organized by the election of Samuel J. Lee (colored), of Aiken, speaker; and A. O. Jones, clerk.

MOSES' ADMINISTRATION

The usual complement of attaches were appointed in each branch. The House elected a chaplain, but the Senate engaged the services of different clergymen to open its proceedings with prayer.

The message of Governor Scott contained nothing striking—except the charge that the increase in the public debt had been caused by the taxpayers' enmity to the State Government and the denial of the charge that "the people have been burdened with grievous taxation and have been sorely oppressed by misgovernment in the State and counties."

"I frankly admit," wrote the Governor, "as I now clearly perceive, that I have committed many errors in the administration of the State during the past four years, but they have been errors that any man would have committed unless he approached nearer to infallibility of judgment than usually falls to mortal lot."

The newly elected Governor and Lieutenant-Governor were inaugurated on December 3. The addresses of these officials contained little new and nothing striking. Of the Governor's address the Senate ordered the printing of 2,000 extra copies, and a like order was made by the House.

Governor Moses sent his first message a few days after his inauguration. In that paper he stated that the deficiencies on October 31, 1872, amounted to $1,266,395—distributed as follows: Schools, $300,000 (being the entire appropriation); printing claims, $325,000; Treasurer's bills payable, $230,000; pay certificates, $20,000; "other purposes under general appropriation act," $391,395.

ELECTION OF JOHN J. PATTERSON.

On December 10, 1872, the Senate and the House voted separately for a Senator of the United States for the full term to commence March 4, 1873. There were three prominent candidates—John J. Patterson, already mentioned as president of the Blue Ridge Railroad, and a prominent member of the Greenville railroad syndicate; R. B. Elliott, the black Congressman from the Third District; and Robert K. Scott, lately Governor.

Patterson's campaign was managed by H. G. Worthington, the carpetbagger already mentioned, who was for hire to anybody having money to pay for his services. He seemed to have money—though whence it came honest people could only conjecture. He was a smart fellow, without any affectation of character, and was evidently the very man whom "Honest John" wanted. Over a barroom near the State House Worthington opened up "Patterson's Headquarters," and here it was that he, with his subordinates, did his work in buying up a sufficient number of Senators and Representatives to secure Patterson's election. The prices of votes ranged from $50 to $2,500 each. One Senator favorable to Elliott stated that John B. Dennis, speaking for Patterson, asked him whether $5,000 would change him from Elliott to Patterson. It was afterwards testified that Patterson himself had asserted that his election had cost him more than $40,000.

The result of the election was a great victory for Patterson—the vote standing: Patterson, 90; Elliott, 33; Scott, 7; scattering, 27.

The conduct of the Patterson men was so flagrant that there was a prosecution instituted by a Republican member of the House against another, alleging bribery. Patterson himself was also charged. When the cases came on for hearing the witnesses had "changed their tune," and the trial justice (a Republican, of course) promptly dismissed the proceedings as to the members, though he bound Patterson over for trial.

In this emergency Moses appointed John B. Dennis jury commissioner for Richland County, and the appointee promptly proceeded (according to his own sworn statement) to "manage the jury box in such a way as to insure Patterson's protection. That is," (Dennis went on to say) "I would not, when listing the jury for the year, have or allow any names to go in the box that I thought would in any way be inimical to Patterson." The case against Patterson never came on for trial.

A written protest was submitted to the Senate of the United States against the admission of Patterson—the signers, it seems, alleging that he had procured his seat by bribery. The Senate held that the paper was irregular, and Patterson was promptly sworn in.

The career of John J. Patterson before he came from Pennsylvania to South Carolina was said to have been very disreputable. In an interview with the Columbia correspondent of the *Charleston News*, after Patterson's election to the Senate of the United States, Dr. T. J. Moore, Patterson's brother-in-law, declared him to be a "swindler and cheat of the first water"—further stating that in the winter of 1861-62, at Wheeling, Va., he had defrauded the soldiers of an Ohio regiment out of $3,500, and that, continuing to swindle

MOSES' ADMINISTRATION 229

them, his appointment as paymaster was finally rejected by the Senate. Moore further charged that Patterson had tried to induce him to forge the name of Comptroller-General Leaphart to certain bonds of the Greenville and Columbia Railroad Company, alleged by Patterson to have been guaranteed by the State of South Carolina. Moore emphatically declared that Patterson had bought the votes of Senators and Representatives, in order to secure his election to the Senate—the bribes ranging in amount from $150 to $1,000 each.

Patterson was called—or he called himself—"Honest John." A political associate explained this nickname by saying: "Patterson will do what he says. If he promises to pay you he'll do it; if he promises to vote for you he'll do it; if he promises to work for you he'll do it; and if he promises to steal for you he'll do it."

When, in the midst of the rottenness of the Moses administration, it was suggested to Patterson that there must be reform, he replied—"Why, there are still five years of good stealing in South Carolina." The phrase "five years of good stealing," and more especially the shorter form, "good stealing," stuck to the Republican party of South Carolina long after the publication of this story.

OTHER ELECTIONS.

Thompson H. Cooke, of Orangeburg, was elected judge of the Eighth Circuit, to succeed Judge Orr, who had accepted the Russian mission tendered him by President Grant. Judge Cooke was a lawyer of some experience, a graduate of the State Military Academy and a well-meaning, good-natured man. He eschewed politics when he went on the bench, until the nomination of the Radical ticket in 1876, when he promptly declared for Hampton. He effectively stumped the State for the Democratic ticket.

In the Fifth Circuit, to succeed Judge Melton, the Legislature elected Richard B. Carpenter—that astute individual having been taken back into full fellowship with the same party whose leaders and whose misdoings he had vigorously denounced in the Union Reform campaign in 1870.

Trustees of the University were elected as follows: J. K. Jillson, D. H. Chamberlain, L. C. Northrop (white); Samuel J. Lee, J. A. Bowley, S. A. Swails, W. R. Jervay (colored)—the Governor continuing a member ex officio.

Macon B. Allen, colored, was elected judge of the Inferior Court of Charleston. Allen had been the nominee of the bolting Republicans for Secretary of State—his election to the judgeship showing that the apparent factions in the party had pleasantly come together.

NOTABLE LEGISLATION.

There were few acts passed at this session to indicate the policy and purposes of the General Assembly.

The tax levy for State purposes was for the support of the Government, including interest on the State debt, five mills; for deficiencies, five mills; for public schools, two mills; making a total of twelve mills. The ordinary county tax was fixed at three mills, with additional levies in several counties, ranging from one and one-half to three mills.

The act requiring a State license to do business was repealed.

An act to enforce the collection of the poll tax imposed a penalty of one dollar for non-payment, and upon failure then to pay, the delinquent was required to labor on some public road for three days.

An act to establish the State Normal School prescribed the government and curriculum of that institution, and provided that students should be admitted without regard to race, color or previous condition of servitude. The professors of the State University were required to do duty in this school as its board of regents might direct. The board of regents was authorized to use for the school such of the buildings and grounds of the University as should be necessary. The library of the University was required to be open to the students of the Normal School. There was provided an annual appropriation of $15,000 for its support.

The sum of $250,000 was specifically appropriated for claims of the Republican Printing Company for work done during the sessions 1870-71 and 1871-72.

The constitutional amendments adopted at the election of 1872 were duly ratified.

The two houses adopted a concurrent resolution instructing the State's representatives in Congress "to use their influence against the withdrawal of the United States troops from this State and to represent to the President of the United States that the withdrawal of the same would be at the present time detrimental to the permanent establishment and maintenance of law and order in this State."

A gratuity of $1,000 was voted to the speaker of the House, and one of $500 to its reading clerk.

The Assembly adjourned February 26—the session having lasted seventy-six days, including Sundays and excluding the Christmas recess of sixteen days—and there were passed 171 acts and thirty joint resolutions.

The legislative expenses were as follows: Pay of members, $103,-600; pay of 176 clerks, $50,857; 17 laborers, $5,680; 15 doorkeepers, $2,870; 10 firemen, $1,054; 3 chaplains, $445; 2 janitors, $104; 32 messengers, $4,075; 3 mail carriers, $486; 4 porters, $539; 30 pages, $1,497; 8 sergeants-at-arms, $3,900; legislative accounts and claims passed, $72,803; sundries (wines, liquors, cigars, groceries, dry goods, etc.), $50,412; stationery, $30,876; newspapers, $3,649; postage stamps, $1,132; telegrams, $267; furniture, $17,286; rent of committee rooms, $3,312; printing, $450,000; total, $817,017.

NEGROES IN CONTROL OF THE UNIVERSITY.

The composition of the board of trustees of the State University, elected in 1869, had caused the gravest apprehensions as to the policy of the dominant party towards that institution. There was naturally the fear that an effort would be made to mix the races in the student body—a condition which plainly involved the destruction of the University as a school for white students. The new Constitution declared that all schools and colleges supported by public funds should be "free and open to all the children and youths of the State, without regard to race or color." The act of 1869 reorganizing the University contained a like provision. Whether the negroes would avail themselves of the privilege thus conferred seemed at first doubtful. Some of their counselors had strongly advised against any attempt to mix the races in school or college. Governor Orr in his message to the Legislature in 1868 and on other occasions had urged the separation of the races—suggesting that the University be reserved for whites and that the Citadel Academy in Charleston be used as a college for colored students. Governor Orr's views were then shared by some native white Republicans and also by many of the more intelligent and conservative negroes.

At the close of the session in June, 1868, the faculty consisted of the following professors: Robert W. Barnwell, History; William J. Rivers, Ancient Languages; A. Sachtleben, Modern Languages; M.

LaBorde, Belles-Lettres; J. L. Reynolds, Mental and Moral Philosophy; John LeConte, Physics; Joseph LeConte, Chemistry; E. P. Alexander, Mathematics; John T. Darby, Surgery; A. N. Talley, Practice of Medicine; A. C. Haskell, Law. Professors LaBorde, John LeConte and Joseph LeConte also lectured in the medical department.

In the summer of 1868 Professor Haskell resigned, and his place was filled, in 1869, by the election of Mr. C. D. Melton, of the Columbia bar—a prominent lawyer peculiarly well fitted for this professorship.

In 1869 Professors John and Joseph LeConte accepted calls to the University of California, and their places were respectively filled by Prof. T. E. Hart, of Darlington, and Dr. James Woodrow, of Columbia—each eminently qualified for his chair. Professor Hart also served in the department of mathematics—Professor Alexander having later on resigned. Professor Sachtleben next resigned, his successor being Prof. John C. Faber, of Charleston, a gentleman of high character and broad scholarship. The chair of physiology and anatomy was assigned to Dr. John Lynch, of Columbia, a gentleman enjoying the respect of the people, and a physician in good standing. Then Dr. Darby resigned to engage in practice in New York, and his place was filled by the election of Dr. Robert W. Gibbes, of Columbia, a prominent physician in every respect fitted for the chair to which he was thus assigned.

The faculty was still such as to command the respect of the white people, and these would have sent their sons to the University but for the widespread belief that its continued existence was doubtful and the general apprehension that negroes would sooner or later be induced to enter.

Other changes in the faculty followed. Professors Woodrow and Hart having resigned, their places had been filled respectively by T. N. Roberts and the Rev. A. W. Cummings; and the Rev. B. B. Babbitt was elected to the chair of physics. To fill the vacancy caused by the resignation of Professor Rivers (1873) Fisk K. Brewer, a Northern man of small repute, was elected to the chair of ancient languages.

The election of Mr. Babbitt was distasteful to the white people, and that of Cummings was offensive.

Mr. Babbitt came from New York to Columbia ostensibly to establish a mission of the Protestant Episcopal Church, of which he was an accredited clergyman. He was of unattractive appearance and small abilities, and was generally accounted a carpetbagger on the lookout for a job.

Cummings owed his election to the fact that he had been an informer against alleged Kuklux in Spartanburg, had been a hanger-on of the congressional committee sent to "investigate" matters in this State in 1871, and had actively affiliated with the negro party. He was a man of ordinary intelligence and small scholarship, and was otherwise unfit for a professorship in any reputable college.

Roberts was unknown to the people and was generally accounted an adventurer whom the trustees thought they could use in their scheme to convert the University into a mixed school for whites and blacks.

The introduction of these new men increased the distrust of the white people. Then followed a distinct blow to the institution—the passage of the act to organize the State Normal School, to locate it in a building in the University campus, to require the University professors to lecture to its students, and to admit these to the University library. The Normal School was, of necessity, to be composed largely if not exclusively of negro students.

The policy and purposes of the trustees were finally disclosed in the summer of 1873 by the removal of Professors Barnwell, Reynolds and Faber—against none of whom was there any suggestion of inefficiency. It was about this time that Professor Rivers resigned. The others of the old faculty retained their places at the manifest wish of the white people, who vaguely hoped that the institution might be saved to their sons. But the Radical leaders (the trustees evidently included) had determined upon a mixed school.

On October 7, 1873, Henry E. Hayne, a person of color, then Secretary of State, matriculated as a student in the school of medicine. Hayne was almost white, and his quiet demeanor had given many white people the impression that he was neither vindictive nor aggressive. In 1871, however, he had caused trouble in Mr. Babbitt's mission church by going to the communion table along with the white members of the congregation—a proceeding which made quite a stir at the time and before long caused a suspension of the mission services. Hayne was afterwards shown to have been corrupt and to have actively participated in some of the schemes by which the State was robbed.

Immediately upon Hayne's matriculation Professors LaBorde, Gibbes and Talley resigned. In accepting these resignations the board of trustees made the following declaration:

Resolved, That this board accepts the resignations of M. LaBorde, M. D., A. N. Talley, M. D., and R. W. Gibbes, M. D., in the University of South Carolina; and in accepting the same this board deem it due to the public to place upon record their conviction that the resignations of these gentlemen were caused by the admission, as a student of the medical department of the University, of the Hon. Henry E. Hayne, a gentleman of irreproachable character, against whom said professors can suggest no objection except, in their opinion, his race; and recognizing this as the cause of these resignations this board cannot regret that a spirit so hostile to the welfare of our State, as well as to the dictates of justice and the claims of our common humanity, will no longer be represented in the University, which is the common property of all our citizens without distinction of race.

The board thus formally declared their design to convert the University into a mixed school for whites and blacks—where the students of both races should intermingle on terms of actual social equality. That purpose was afterwards explicitly avowed in the report of Samuel J. Lee, president of the board, to the Legislature, in which paper occurred these words: "In the chapel, recitation room, on the ball ground and in study the lessons of equality and mutual self-respect have been inculcated."

Governor D. H. Chamberlain is on record as approving this scheme to mix the races on terms of actual social equality in the State University. In his message to the Legislature, November, 1875, he wrote: "I do not hesitate to say that I think the University is now doing a good work, and deserves the support of the State."

Immediately after the admission of Hayne other students matriculated—among them the following grown men: Niles G. Parker, State Treasurer; H. C. Corwin, senator from Newberry; George F. McIntyre, senator from Colleton, white; C. M. Wilder, postmaster at Columbia; Joseph D. Boston, representative from Newberry; Lawrence Cain and Paris Simkins, representatives from Edgefield; colored. Each of these seven entered the law department. N. T. Spencer (colored), representative from Charleston, entered the school of medicine. It was plain that each of these matriculations was at the time pretensive only—the purpose being to show the white people of South Carolina that the negroes intended to dominate in the State University and there enforce the social equality of the black with the white race. Some of these new students, it may be stated, did afterwards receive certificates of graduation.

Negroes now entered in large numbers—apparently admitted with little regard to previous preparation. The student body was composed almost entirely of boys and men of the black race.

A notable matriculation was that of F. L. Cardozo, the colored Treasurer of the State, who in October, 1874, entered the law school. Cardozo, it may be noted again, was a few years later convicted of having conspired to cheat the State. Indeed, every one of the colored matriculates above named (except Wilder) had taken part in some scheme to defraud.

All questions of race aside, it ought not to have been expected that the white people would send their sons into such very bad company.

The trustees promptly proceeded to fill the vacancies in the faculty, so that when the work of the session of 1873-1874 actually began there were the following professors: Rev. B. B. Babbitt, Rev. A. W. Cummings, T. N. Roberts, M. D., Rev. Henry J. Fox, William Main, Fisk J. Brewer, R. T. Greener (colored), R. Vampill, C. D. Melton, John Lynch, M. D.

Except Dr. Lynch and Mr. Melton these professors were strangers to the people of South Carolina. Mr. Vampill was a Northern man who had lived in Marion County for a few years and had there served as county treasurer.

Of the action of the men who thus dragged the University down from the place it had held in the affections of the people a distinguished son of the State shortly after the outrage wrote as follows:

The faculty had entered upon the work of building up a university which, as the literary institution of the State, should equal if not surpass the fame and usefulness of the old college; and this work would have been accomplished but for the egregious folly and wickedness of those who held the control of the State. The old trustees who had the confidence of the people of the State were rudely set aside to make place for adventurers who were unknown or known unfavorably. In the mere wantonness of power, or for the satisfaction which a rude nature takes in the humiliation of his superiors, negroes were placed upon the board of trustees. This act, although less cruel than that which needlessly outraged the sentiments of our people by thrusting negroes among the regents of the lunatic asylum, was more pernicious in its results. It excited suspicion of what ultimately followed—the attempt to mix the races in public education—and kept students away. But the professors, with the advice of friends of the University, stood at their posts, hoping to save the institution by averting a change which would prove its degradation and ruin. In short, they wished to save the University for the white sons of the State. A mixed school was impracticable. The colored people neither needed nor desired it. Claflin University, at Orangeburg, established expressly for the education of their children, offered them the facilities—the means of varied culture—obtainable at the University of the State. But the trustees were bent on a mixed school, and there were needy adventurers at hand to aid them in their attempt. Supposing, correctly, that the old professors would not lend themselves to the perpetration of such an act of wanton injustice, they removed them and conferred their places upon strangers who, even if unknown, or known only to be despised, as incompetent or immoral, were yet more subservient to their views. The University thus became, both in its officers and its matriculates, a mixed school; and a policy which a Republican Congress has since refused to adopt, and thus virtually repudiated, was allowed to effect the ruin of that seat of learning.

It now remains to give (though already given) the names of the men—the board of trustees—who by their influence and their actions thus deliberately proceeded to defile, degrade and destroy an institution always dear to the people of South Carolina. Here is the list:

Franklin J. Moses, Jr., native white.
Justus K. Jillson, white, lately of Massachusetts.
Daniel H. Chamberlain, white, lately of Massachusetts.
L. C. Northrop, native white.
Samuel J. Lee, native negro.
James A. Bowley, negro, lately of Maryland.
S. A. Swails, negro, lately of New York.
William R. Jervay, native negro.

To this defilement of the University, this new outrage upon the white people of South Carolina, none of the few of its alumni affiliated with the Republican party was ever known to object.

The Legislature provided liberally for the so-called University—the appropriation for the year 1873-74 being $31,750, and that allowance being somewhat increased in later years. Beneficiary scholarships to the number of 124, yielding $200 each per annum, were established and all tuition fees were abolished. The number of students greatly increased, so that it soon exceeded 200—more than nine-tenths being negroes. The requirements for admission were so lax—the regulations in this matter were so flagrantly disregarded—that the so-called University soon became little more than a high school, whose chief aim was to inculcate and illustrate the social equality of the black race with the white. The establishment, taken as a whole, was a fraud upon the taxpayers—a fraud deliberately perpetrated in the name of progress and enlightenment! In this degraded condition the institution continued until it was closed by the white Legislature of 1877.

The purpose of the Republican party in South Carolina to enforce the social equality of negroes with white men was further illustrated by the action of the governing board of the State institution for the education of the deaf and the blind, located at Cedar Spring, in Spartanburg County. In the school year 1872-73, by direction of the board a building on the grounds of the institution was suitably fitted up for the opening of a separate department for colored pupils. But on September 17, 1873, Mr. Jillson, the State Superintendent of Education, wrote the superintendent of this asylum in these words:

The following points relative to the admission of colored pupils into this institution will be strictly and rigidly insisted upon: 1. Colored pupils must not only be admitted into the institution on application, but an earnest and faithful effort must be made to induce such pupils to apply for admission. 2. Such pupils when admitted must be domiciled in the same building, must eat at the same table, must be taught in the same classrooms and by the same teachers, and must receive the same attention, care and consideration as white pupils.

Besides Jillson, the board issuing this order was composed of Solomon L. Hoge and F. J. Moses, Jr.

The officers of the asylum having promptly resigned, it was closed, and it so continued for three years—the efforts to get a new faculty proving fruitless. The unfortunate boys and girls who had been in the institution were thus barbarously turned adrift—this act done with the purpose to maintain the ascendency of the Republican party in South Carolina by enforcing the domination of the negro over the white man. Jillson's act was the act of the Republican party. The leaders of that party manifestly approved the act, and if, indeed, any white man affiliated therewith ever objected the fact is not ascertainable by reference to the records of the time. Governor Chamberlain, in his message to the Legislature in 1875, simply urged the reopening of the institution, making no suggestion as to the status of white and of black inmates. This suggestion, coupled with the Governor's explicit commendation of the University after it became a mixed school controlled by negroes, makes it uncertain whether he approved the endeavor to force white children into personal contact with colored upon terms of actual social equality.

In September, 1876, the institution was reopened, there being separate departments for white and for colored pupils. The former superintendent and most of his corps of teachers were reappointed.

AN EXTRA SESSION.

In obedience to the call of Governor Moses the Legislature met in extra session on October 21, 1873. In presenting the "extraordinary occasion" which had induced him to convene the body the Governor stated that "certain bond-creditors of the State, holding or representing bonds of several classes, having in the last resort appealed to the Supreme Court to pass upon the validity of the State securities held by them, and to afford them the relief to which they deem themselves entitled, the Court decided that the bonds in question are valid, and that the Comptroller-General shall, 'in obedience to the Constitution and the laws,' levy a tax to pay the interest on the said several classes of bonds, such levy to be made on or before the 15th day of November next, the rate per centum of the tax to be thus levied to be adequate to liquidate the interest past due and also that for the present year."

The Governor stated that the judgment of the Court covered "five classes of bonds amounting in the aggregate to $3,549,000—$545,000 of which have been exchanged for Conversion bonds, and are now outstanding in that form." He reported that the bonded debt of the State was $15,027,503.35—this amount including $5,965,000 of Conversion bonds, of which mention has been made in a previous chapter.

The floating debt was given as follows: Interest upon bonded debt to October 1, 1873, $2,342,293.18; debt fundable under acts of 1866 (ante-Reconstruction), $116,751.63; pay certificates and bills payable, sessions of 1870-71, 1871-72, $500,000; pay certificates of session of 1872-73, $100,000; debt due Blue Ridge Railroad Company (Blue Ridge Scrip), $1,797,352.94; miscellaneous floating debt, $450,000; total floating debt, $5,306,397.75. Added the bonded debt the entire indebtedness of the State was thus declared to be $20,333,-901.10—an increase of about $14,000,000 in the six years of so-called Republican rule.

The Governor stated that South Carolina bonds were quoted at figures ranging from fifteen cents to forty cents on the dollar.

The message contained the recommendation that the whole debt be funded—the bondholders to receive in new bonds such percentage of the face of the outstanding bonds as might be fixed by the Legislature, and that body to levy an annual tax sufficient to pay interest and ultimately retire the principal.

The chief business of the session consisted in the discussion of a measure to adjust the State debt—an act entitled "An act to reduce the volume of the public debt and provide for the payment of the same." This bill (passed by the House at the special session and by the Senate at the regular meeting immediately following) "scaled" the acknowledged bonded debt at fifty cents on the dollar, and formally repudiated the entire issue of Conversion bonds as given in the Governor's message. The interest on the new debt thus to be substituted was to be paid from the proceeds of an annual levy of two mills—the enactment of the levy to be endorsed on each bond and to form a part of the contract thus made between the State and the bondholder. The faith and credit of the State were pledged for the payment of principal and interest, and safeguards (somewhat elaborate) were provided for the creditor's protection. How far the State's creditors accepted this adjustment, so long as the Government continued in the control of negroes and irresponsible whites, remains to be related. It is enough to say here that this measure—popularly styled the "Consolidation Act"—had not effected its purpose when the white people recovered possession of the State Government. The personnel of the Radical administration continuing to be disreputable, the State's credit was still bad.

The act providing for an annual tax to redeem the Revenue Bond Scrip was repealed.

The sum of $125,000 was appropriated to the Republican Printing Company for special work (immigration literature, Supreme Court reports and county tax duplicates) and the State Treasurer was authorized to issue "certificates of indebtedness" to cover that amount.

The sum of $125,000 was appropriated to pay the claims of the "South Carolina Bank and Trust Company"—a private bank run by one Hardy Solomon, a white man who seemed wholly devoid of character and whose business as a broker was chiefly the cashing of State paper held by officials of high or low degree, by members of the Legislature, and by different fellows who, calling themselves "attaches," received money for fictitious services. Solomon had also a grocery, and from him were bought in large quantities the "supplies" (including liquors) with which the Radical members of the General Assembly regaled themselves and their friends. As will be seen later on this so-called bank of Solomon was one of the several schemes by which the people of South Carolina were robbed in the time when negro domination was enforced by Federal bayonets.

For the pay of members during the extra session (at $6 per day) and "for the pay of subordinates and employees and incidental expenses at the usual rates proportioned to the extra session," the sum of $75,000 was appropriated. For the printing of the extra session there was an allowance of $50,000.

The House voted a gratuity of $600 to the speaker.

The extra session ended November 24, and the work done included twenty-four acts and six joint resolutions.

THE REGULAR SESSION.

When this session began, not only was the public debt in a condition such as to demand some action by the legislative department, but the finances of the State were in such shape as to have discredited the State and county governments and to have entailed actual loss upon honest and innocent creditors.

For the fiscal year ending October 31, 1873, the State Treasurer reported that the total collections had been $1,719,728.37, and the expenditures, $1,717,318.60, distributed as follows: Salaries, $290,797.39; printing, $331,945.66; free schools, $361,101.37; repairs and furnishings, $57,975.57; contingent funds, $71,033.75; militia, $25,719.42; penitentiary, $75,415.36; lunatic asylum, $117,253.11; orphanage, $14,973.62; deaf and dumb institute, $11,179; refunded taxes, $29,272.75; election of 1872, $32,471.63; sundries, $62,840.50.

The deficiencies—sums of money still due creditors or institutions of the State—amounted, October 31, 1873, to $540,328, that sum not including accrued interest on the public debt. This condition was officially explained in the statement that whilst the appropriations for the fiscal year mentioned (not including interest on the State debt) aggregated $2,260,056, the Treasurer had received from all sources only $1,719,728.

The message of the Governor purported to be a presentation of all the matters which should engage the attention of the General Assembly.

The State debt was reported as it had been to the Legislature at the extra session, and the deficiencies were stated as they were given in the Treasurer's report. The Governor took occasion to say that Treasurer Cardozo had discharged his duties "with fidelity and integrity."

The Governor urged the continued maintenance of the negro militia and particularly endorsed the Adjutant-General's suggestion that the regiments in Charleston, Columbia and Beaufort be not only armed and equipped but also uniformed at the public expense.

The Governor deplored the resignation of certain of the University professors because of the admission of "the Hon. Henry E. Hayne, our colored Secretary of State, whom all who know him acknowledge to be a true gentleman of the highest character and sternest integrity." The Governor felt proud to look upon the University as "the healthy child of the present administration," and felt also that "the narrow spirit of bigotry and prejudice has been banished from its portals." He took especial pleasure in the fact that one of the professorships was filled by a colored man—congratulating the State upon "this onward stride in the march of civilization" and hailing it as "the harbinger of the happy day which is coming when all class distinctions shall be forever laid in the dust of the past."

Commenting on the order requiring that negro children should be invited and admitted to the asylum for the deaf and the blind upon terms of actual social equality with white, and the resignations which followed, the Governor said:

It was hoped that even political malice would have felt some touch of pity in contemplating the victims of the most awful bereavement that Providence has visited upon humanity, and that no discrimination would have been made as to those whom God himself had reduced to the same common level of helpless calamity. . . . You will see by the action above referred to of the board of directors of the asylum for the deaf and dumb and the blind, as well as by the action of the board of trustees of the State University, that at least in South Carolina "the chaff is being rapidly winnowed from the wheat" and that we are fast getting rid of influences prejudicial in our State institutions.

The penitentiary was reported in debt $77,338.40 and the lunatic asylum in debt $60,160.66.

The Governor declared that the conduct of the State Government under Republican rule had been "characterized by the equal administration of just and impartial laws," that it had "endeavored vigilantly to protect all the rights of persons and to maintain all the safeguards of property"—had "signalized its authority by the enactment of wise and beneficent statutes, in happy contrast to the legislation which distinguished the former Government of the State."

The customary resolution directing the printing of 2,000 copies of the message for the Senate and an equal number for the House was promptly passed.

The reports of the Comptroller-General, referred to by the Governor, showed the past indebtedness of different counties to be more than $350,000.

The sum of $209,189.75 was due, October 31, 1873, to teachers for services in the public schools.

The aggregate shortages of county treasurers was officially reported, November 1, 1872, to be $445,000.

The number of acts of general purpose passed at the session of 1873-74 was strikingly small. Of public acts—those affecting general laws or general rights—there were only forty-one. The remaining 195 were private acts—incorporating societies, conferring special rights upon individuals or amending the law in relation to certain localities.

The tax for State purposes was fixed at twelve mills—a distinct levy being made for each item of expense—salaries, schools, printing, etc. The levy for schools was fixed at two mills. The ordinary county tax was three mills, but there were extra levies in several counties.

The total levy for State purposes amounted to $2,654,347, against $2,512,215 for the previous fiscal year. The previous levy had been fifteen mills, but the property assessed for taxation had increased as indicated.

By "an act to repeal an act to provide for the issue of bills receivable in payment of indebtedness to the State, to the amount of $500,000," approved December 21, 1875, the "loyal" General Assembly recognized the authority of the Legislature assembled as a part of the Government organized under the Reconstruction scheme of Andrew Johnson—which Government the Congress of the United States had declared to be "provisional only" and without lawful authority.

The State was divided into five congressional districts, as follows: First—Georgetown, Williamsburg, Darlington, Marlboro, Marion, Horry, Chesterfield, Sumter.

Second—Charleston, Orangeburg, Clarendon, Lexington.

Third—Richland, Newberry, Laurens, Anderson, Oconee, Pickens.

Fourth—Greenville, Spartanburg, Union, York, Chester, Fairfield, Kershaw, Lancaster.

Fifth—Colleton, Beaufort, Barnwell, Aiken, Edgefield.

The State was thus gerrymandered in the interest of the Republican party—every district having a negro majority.

The general appropriation bill contained the usual provisions for the support of the Government—a special sum being given for each designated purpose.

An act to relieve the sureties on the bond of James M. Allen, the defaulting treasurer of Greenville County, discharged those sureties —this on the ground that said Allen, "now a fugitive, expended the moneys collected by him for State and county purposes for the purchase of the following claims against the State and the county of Greenville, to wit: [Here were given in detail the claims in question, consisting of legislative pay certificates issued to different senators, representatives and attaches of the General Assembly, school claims and claims against Greenville County], all of which above recited claims are now in possession of the State under attachment made by the Attorney-General and by the county commissioners of Greenville County."

These claims amounted to more than $35,000, and as most of them were afterwards "scaled" or repudiated by the State the discharge of these sureties was to the extent of such repudiation a fraud upon the State. Many of the claims were themselves flagrantly fraudulent. No part of Allen's indebtedness was ever made good.

By an act to regulate the number and pay of attaches, clerks and laborers of the General Assembly the number of such employees was limited and their per diem fixed.

By "an act to regulate the public printing" it was required that the work should be let by contract to the lowest responsible bidder.

A joint resolution, duly passed and approved, required the submission to the people of an amendment to the Constitution, providing that the term of all State officers should be two years.

An amendment was also proposed to limit county or municipality subscription to the stock of any corporation in excess of 5 per cent. of the taxable property thereof, and in every case to require the approval of a majority of the legal voters of such county or municipality.

A joint resolution to appoint a committee to assist in the prosecution of Niles G. Parker, late Treasurer of the State, for his conduct in connection with the over-issue of Conversion bonds, was duly passed, and it was formally ratified in the Senate chamber. Between that chamber and the Governor's office the paper was "lost," and thus it never became effective. The "loss" was never satisfactorily explained. It was evident that the paper had been destroyed by somebody in the pay of Parker—this, in the general opinion at the time, with the connivance of Governor Moses. There were afterwards some proceedings in the courts against Parker, but they amounted to little and he went unpunished.

A concurrent resolution, regularly passed, expressed the opinion that the standing army should not be reduced and urged "the necessity of the retention of United States troops in South Carolina, to the end that harmony and good order may prevail throughout the State during the coming political campaign and the rights of the elective franchise may be guaranteed to all her citizens in the election that is to follow."

The House voted a gratuity of $500 to the speaker and one of $300 to its reading clerk.

The Senate adopted a resolution excluding from its chamber Mr. William H. McCaw, the Columbia correspondent of the *Charleston News and Courier.* Mr. McCaw was a gentleman of the highest character and of extraordinary gifts as a journalist. His letters to this paper, written over the signature "Qui Vive," were always full of interest, and he lost no opportunity to expose the schemes of plunder which were then the chief work of the Legislature of South Carolina. It was for a denunciation of one of those schemes that he was excluded from the Senate chamber.

Mr. McCaw was accidentally burnt to death in February, 1874—the young life thus ended having been full of usefulness to the State and full of promise of a career that should have added still further to the distinction which, at the early age of 29, he had already attained. The death of Mr. McCaw was universally deplored—

his political enemies joining with his friends in paying tribute to his extraordinary talents, his unflinching courage and his invariable honesty of purpose.

The session ended March 17, 1874—having lasted eighty-five days, including Sundays and excluding the Christmas recess of twenty-eight days. The legislative expenses were as follows: Pay of members, $103,000; pay of 126 clerks, $60,328; 159 laborers, $32,030; 13 doorkeepers, $4,143; 8 firemen, $1,095; 3 chaplains, $2,082; 2 janitors, $823; 28 messengers, $4,253; 4 mail carriers, $407; 9 porters, $1,054; 41 pages, $3,053; 12 sergeants-at-arms, $2,325; 16 solicitors, $7,528; legislative accounts and claims passed, $47,261; sundries (wines, liquors, cigars, dry goods, etc.), $53,508; stationery, $4,975; newspapers, $6,967; telegrams, $378; furniture, $5,780; printing, $385,000; total, $926,101.

TAXPAYERS IN CONVENTION.

Pursuant to a call of the Hon. William D. Porter, of Charleston, president, the Taxpayers' Convention assembled in Columbia a second time—February 17, 1874—the following named delegates being present:

Abbeville—Armistead Burt, B. Z. Herndon, W. J. Smith, F. A. Connor.

Aiken—J. H. Giles, A. P. Butler, D. S. Henderson, E. H. Wood, Isaac A. Givens (colored), T. C. Morgan, J. M. Miller, B. P. Chatfield (Republican), Samuel Lark (colored), Nathan Salley.

Anderson—James A. Hoyt.

Barnwell—A. P. Aldrich, Johnson Hagood, H. H. Easterling, B. Weathersbee, J. C. Allen, H. Hartzog, James M. Williams.

Beaufort—John H. Screven, William Elliott, John Conant, William M. Lawton, James G. Thompson (Republican), S. C. Millett, J. M. Williams.

Charleston—William D. Porter, George A. Trenholm, Richard Lathers, Thomas Y. Simons, B. H. Rutledge, C. I. Walker, C. R. Miles, W. G. Hinson, C. W. Stiles, C. H. Simonton, F. W. Dawson, W. St. Julien Jervey, E. E. Sill, Robert Hunter, L. D. DeSaussure, A. B. Rose.

Chester—James Hemphill, S. P. Hamilton, A. H. Davega, J. S. Wilson, C. S. Brice, Giles J. Patterson, Julius Mills, J. J. McLure, O. Barber.

Chesterfield—E. B. C. Cash, A. McQueen, G. W. Duvall.

Clarendon—Joseph Galluchat, W. L. Reynolds, John L. Manning, J. E. Tindal.

Colleton—Robert Fishburne, Harry E. West, J. J. Fox, C. J. Henderson.

Darlington—J. J. Lucas, B. F. Williamson, D. Strother (colored), J. A. Law, E. R. McIver.

Edgefield—M. L. Bonham, M. W. Gary, Lewis Jones, A. D. Bates, John C. Sheppard, R. G. M. Dunovant, W. H. Timmerman, William Lott, M. C. Butler, J. Y. Culbreath, J. H. Bouknight.

Fairfield—John Bratton, T. W. Woodward, B. E. Elkin, H. A. Gaillard, John Wallace, Thomas McKinstry, James R. Aiken.

Georgetown—B. H. Wilson, W. W. Walker, L. P. Miller.

Greenville—W. A. Mooney.

Kershaw—James Chesnut, J. B. Kershaw, T. H. Clarke, M. Baum, John D. Kennedy, E. M. Boykin, L. J. Patterson.

Lancaster—John D. Wylie, John M. Beaty.

Laurens—C. M. Miller, J. C. Davis, R. S. Griffin.

Lexington—Gerhard Muller, J. N. Huffman, J. J. Knotts, A. D. Haltiwanger.

Marion—William Evans, William R. Johnson, David Leggett, William D. Johnson.

Marlboro—C. W. Dudley.

Newberry—W. G. Mayes, E. S. Keitt, J. K. Nance, George Johnstone, J. R. Spearman, Sr.

Orangeburg—T. J. Goodwyn, T. J. Odom, W. T. Rives, A. D. Frederick, O. N. Bowman, R. W. Bates.

Pickens—W. E. Holcolmbe, D. F. Bradley.

Richland—William H. Stack, J. C. Seegers, F. W. McMaster, L. F. Hopkins, W. P. Spigner, William Wallace, E. J. Scott.

Spartanburg—W. M. Foster, A. B. Woodruff.

Sumter—John S. Richardson, John B. Moore, C. H. Moise, C. R. F. Baker, F. H. Kennedy, E. H. Hollman, W. J. Pringle.

Union—B. H. Rice, T. B. Jeter, D. P. Duncan, W. H. Wallace, W. H. Gist.

Williamsburg—James McCutchen, S. W. Maurice, N. M. Graham, W. D. Knox, Thomas M. Gilland.

York—Cad. Jones, A. B. Springs, R. M. Sims, D. Harrison, Iredell Jones, B. H. Massey.

MOSES' ADMINISTRATION

There were only two counties not represented—Horry and Oconee. The following named gentlemen were appointed secretaries: George Johnstone, Giles J. Patterson, W. St. Julien Jervey, D. S. Henderson.

With the view to expediting the business of the convention there were appointed an executive committee, with committees on memorial and address to Congress, on State and municipal taxation, on address to the people of the State, on expense and printing and on immigration.

A number of resolutions were introduced, and, under the rule, properly referred. The suggestions contained in these papers having, so far as they were approved by the convention, been incorporated in resolutions adopted, they need not be set out.

Mr. J. G. Thompson, of Beaufort, introduced the following:

Whereas, the Hon. F. L. Cardozo has truly defined the duties of the State Treasurer, in his communication sent to the General Assembly on the 10th inst., in regard to claims passed and appropriations made, in which he holds that it is his duty to stand between the State and the claimant, even though an appropriation has been made to pay the claim, and to see that the vouchers representing the claim are correct; and, whereas, we believe this view of his duties is a correct one:

Resolved, That we respectfully request the Hon. F. L. Cardozo to furnish the executive committee of this body with a copy of the vouchers upon which he paid $331,000 for the printing of the year 1873, it having been asserted by the contractor that he could have done the whole of the work for which this sum was paid for less than one-third of the amount.

On the recommendation of the appropriate committee the convention adopted the following substitute:

Resolved, That we respectfully request the Hon. F. L. Cardozo, the State Treasurer, to furnish the convention with a copy of the vouchers upon which he paid $331,000 for the printing for the year 1873.

Resolved, That the President of the convention appoint a committee of three who shall be charged with the execution of the resolution and who shall report to this convention.

On motion of Gen. M. C. Butler the following resolution, favorably reported by the proper committee, was adopted:

Resolved, That a committee of fifteen be appointed by the chair to proceed to Washington and present to the President the address prepared on behalf of the people of this State to the people of the United States, and request him to lay the same before Congress.

The committee on State and municipal taxation, through Col. Charles H. Simonton, submitted a paper on the cause of the increase of taxes, together with the following resolutions, which were adopted:

Resolved, That in this State taxation has reached the last point of endurance, and that the taxpayers cannot continue to bear the excessive burdens imposed upon them.

Resolved, That the most efficient steps be taken for organizing in every county, township and precinct in the State a Taxpayers' Union, to membership in which each taxpayer shall be eligible; the object of which shall be the reduction of taxation to the legitimate amount necessary for the administration of the government and the honest expenditure of the money raised thereby.

Resolved, That among its duties the Taxpayers' Union shall keep watch upon the acts of the State and county officials, and shall promote all proper legal measures for repressing and punishing fraud, extravagance and malpractice in any of them.

Resolved, That this convention hereby request the General Assembly that they will so amend, simplify and abridge the tax laws of the State, especially that they will so amend the law as to secure a fair and equal assessment of property, and to enable any citizen who has been over-assessed to apply to the courts for redress before he is forced to pay the tax.

The committee on the organization of Tax Unions submitted the following resolutions, where were adopted:

Resolved, That the executive committee be empowered to prepare a system of organization of Tax Unions throughout the State, with authority to take all necessary steps for carrying the same into effect.

Resolved, That the delegations from the several counties represented in this convention be constituted committees for their respective counties and charged with the duty of organizing Tax Unions therein.

On the subject of the registration of voters and the introduction of the cumulative system of voting it was

Resolved, That a committee of five be appointed to represent the Taxpayers' Convention in presenting to the General Assembly such grievances arising from the operation of laws heretofore passed by that body, or growing out of an inadequate protection for the minority by legislation not adapted to our real wants, and, among other things, to urge the accomplishment of the objects named below, to wit:

1. To direct the attention of the General Assembly to the requirement of Section 3, Article VIII, of the Constitution of this State, which declares that "it shall be the duty of the General Assembly

to provide, from time to time, for the registration of all electors," which provision has been totally disregarded in the past.

2. That proportional representation would tend to remove much of the dissatisfaction now existing, whereby complaint is most reasonably urged that a large proportion of property holders and taxpayers of the State are practically debarred from representation in the General Assembly, and that the adoption of the cumulative system of voting would tend to secure a fair representation of the minority; and to this end we ask the General Assembly to give an early and earnest consideration to this subject, with the view of applying this system in the conduct of the State election next fall.

3. That the provision of the Constitution, Section 21, Article IV, in relation to the election of justices of the peace and constables by the people should be complied with by the General Assembly, and that it should be urged to give the election of these officers to the qualified electors at the earliest day practicable, instead of the appointment of trial justices by the executive.

The committee appointed to prepare an address to the people of the State submitted through Gen. J. B. Kershaw a paper setting forth existing conditions in the State, advising the taxpayers to unite for the protection of their rights and particularly urging the immediate organization of Tax Unions all over the State.

Mr. J. G. Thompson, chairman, submitted the following report of the committee appointed to wait upon Treasurer Cardozo:

The committee appointed under a resolution to request the Hon. F. L. Cardozo for the vouchers under which he paid $331,000 for public printing in 1873 waited upon Mr. Cardozo, who had already prepared a reply to the request of the convention. The main portion of the reply consists of a personal attack upon the character of the chairman of the committee, in which the convention is not interested and which has no bearing upon the information which it desires. The attacked party is entirely able to take care of himself in this matter, and will doubtless do it.

Your committee, therefore, reports that the only material matter of the reply is embraced in the following closing paragraph: "I have no right to permit any one to inspect my vouchers except those who are legally authorized to do so."

By a series of resolutions the convention suggested the formation of a State bureau of immigration, which should be charged with disseminating information as to the resources of South Carolina and the opportunities here awaiting actual settlers.

Resolutions were adopted which looked to an investigation into the disposition made of the assets of the Bank of the State of South

Carolina and to a conference with the committee already appointed by the Legislature for a similar purpose.

Resolutions expressing the regret of the delegates on the death of the late William H. McCaw (which had occurred during the session) and paying a hearty tribute to his worth, talents and services were unanimously adopted.

The executive committee was constituted as follows: James Chesnut, Johnson Hagood, John L. Manning, A. P. Aldrich, Thomas Y. Simons, John D. Wylie, John H. Screven, James A. Hoyt, William Elliott, M. L. Bonham, M. C. Butler, John Bratton, William Wallace, Charles S. Brice, J. J. Lucas, B. H. Wilson, R. M. Sims, W. E. Holcombe, F. W. Dawson, A. D. Frederick, T. B. Jeter.

This committee was charged with the duty of keeping in view the objects of the convention and was authorized to reconvene the convention whenever such action should become necessary.

The convention was in session four days.

THE APPEAL TO CONGRESS.

Mr. Armistead Burt submitted the following draft of a memorial to the Congress of the United States, which was adopted:

To the Senate and House of Representatives of the Congress of the United States:

The memorial of the taxpayers and other citizens of South Carolina respectfully showeth:

That upon the reconstruction of the State Government and the admission of the Senators and Representatives into the Congress of the United States it was doubtless intended by Congress, as it was expected by them, that they would become partakers of the rights enjoyed by citizens of the United States and of other States. The history of the country teaches that taxation without representation is tyranny. Our Revolutionary fathers combined to resist such tyranny, and we feel assured that it was never the intention of the sons of those men to allow this very system to be fastened upon any of their fellow citizens. It has, nevertheless, come to pass that the government established in South Carolina, under the legislation of Congress, has been made the instrument of effecting this monstrous oppression. That department of the State Government which exercises the taxing power is administered by those who own a mere fraction of the property of the State. Seven years have elapsed since the reconstruction of the State Government, and during that period, of the property taxed a majority of the members of the Legislature owned no part whatsoever, and the remaining members owned so little that their pay as members counterbalanced their entire interest as property holders. The result is that those owning the property have no voice in the government, and those imposing the taxes no share in the burden thereof.

The taxes have advanced yearly, until in many cases they consume more than one-half of the income from the property taxed. The annual expenses of the Government have advanced from $400,000 before the war to $2,500,000 at the present time. The following comparison of leading items of expenditures will best exhibit the change:

	1865-66.	1873.
Salaries	$76,481.61	$230,797.39
Public printing	17,446.66	331,945.66
Legislative expenses	51,337.00	291,339.47
Public asylums	25,897.00	128,432.11
Contingent fund	6,092.99	75,033.75
Sundries	83,413.31	298,668.35
	$260,668.59	$1,356,216.73
Deficiencies		540,328.00
	$260,668.59	$1,896,544.73

These facts exhibit the unprecedented spectacle of a State in which the government is arrayed against property. It has been openly avowed by prominent members of the Legislature that the taxes should be increased to a point which will compel the sale of the great body of the land and take it away from the former owners. The fruit of this policy is shown in the fact, stated by the Comptroller-General in his official report, that for default in the payment of taxes for the year 1872 alone 268,523 acres of land were forfeited to the State. And this result proves the fallacy of the belief that the policy pursued promotes the elevation of the black population and the acquisition by them of the lands thus virtually confiscated. The reverse is the necessary result. Lands are unavailable as security; mortgages on default of payment cannot sell; wages have declined; the cost of living is made greater by the addition of the taxes to the price of the commodities; the poor are made poorer and rendered every day more incapable of purchasing lands and more hopeless of rising above the condition of mere laborers. It would have ameliorated the condition of your petitioners if the effect of this policy had been to create an active demand for lands on the part of our population. But while the owners are by oppressive taxation driven to sell, others are for the same reason disqualified from buying.

The abuses in the legislative department, that have been described, are not confined to the mere raising and expenditure of revenues, but they pervade the entire conduct of the departments. Schemes have been devised for issuing State bonds and for contracting other loans, by which the public debt has in six years been raised from $5,000,000 to $16,000,000, and that without advancing any public work and without adding one dollar to the public property or to the payment of the public debt. Large as the sum of the public debt is admitted to be, there is reason to believe it goes beyond that amount. It is found impossible to ascertain the actual sum of the obligations that have been issued.

Schemes of public plunder have been openly advanced by corrupt measures of which one single example will suffice. The clerks of the Legislature, in their official capacity, made contracts with themselves as private persons for the public printing. The appropriations made in one year for the work done and to be done by these two officials amounted to $475,000, exclusive of $100,000 for publishing the laws. And in the fiscal year 1873 there was actually paid to them for printing, $331,000, leaving a large sum still due them by the State—and this notwithstanding the avowal of the two officials themselves that the work done was worth no more than $100,000, and the testimony of others that its value was only $50,000. The stupendous fraud involved in this and similar modes of making the legitimate objects of public expenditure the medium of plundering the treasury cannot be better illustrated than by the following facts: The total appropriations for public printing, made by the Legislature of South Carolina during a peiod of sixty years from 1800 to 1859 is $271,180. During the last year the amount actually expended for public printing by the present Legislature was $331,945—that is, $60,765 more than it cost the State for sixty years before the war. .

Committees have received large sums as compensation for reporting favorably on private bills. Strong reasons exist for believing that a large amount of State Bank bills, funded by the State to discharge her liability, have been reissued by those entrusted by the Legislature with the cancellation thereof.

In the judiciary department evils equally grievous have been produced under the present State Government. The judges hold their offices for short terms. Their continuance in office depends upon the caprice of the Legislature. The result is that the duties of their high office are discharged under influences and responsibilities necessarily adverse to the independent administration of justice. The jurors, moreover, are selected by three officials, of whom two are the appointees of the Governor. The consequence is that the defeat of an obnoxious litigant may be made certain by the selection of the jury—or if no special object be contemplated by the officials the choice is frequently made, simply for the small pay, of men who are unable to either read or write. In either case the ends of justice are defeated.

In the executive department all these evils culminate. It is openly asserted and believed that offices are the subject of barter, and the manner in which such offices are administered proves that qualification has little influence in the appointments. In the matters under the control of a single individual it is difficult to prove corruption, but there is one state of facts that always stands for proof. A large expenditure of money by an official who is without any estate and receives but a moderate salary establishes beyond a doubt that the money must come from some irregular source. On this principle the two Governors elected under the present Constitution stand condemned in public opinion.

To detect and punish these crimes is impossible; the Governor controls the avenues of justice. Indeed, the entire system is one of self-sustaining and self-protecting corruption. In most of the States there might be some chance of redress through the ballot box. But here, again, the State Government interposes an insuperable barrier. The elections are conducted by persons appointed in the interest of the officials, and the returns are under the absolute control of the parties in power. Under such circumstances voting is a form and election a mockery.

Suffering under such grievances and despairing of relief from this Government your memorialists come respectfully to your honorable body for redress. The Government which thus oppresses us was virtually established by Congress, and while we believe they did not foresee the evils to which it has given rise we cannot doubt that they will assist in removing them so soon as they are satisfied of their existence. All that we have asserted is capable of proof; but knowing as we do that the evils of which we complain are certain in their existence and are more likely to increase than to diminish, your memorialists most earnestly ask your aid in providing the proper remedy.

The committee appointed by the convention to submit by way of memorials certain matters to the Legislature duly presented them to that body. These several memorials were by the Senate and the House simply "laid on the table."

REPLY OF THE REPUBLICAN PARTY.

The taxpayers' appeal to Congress called forth from the "State Central Committee of the Union Republican party of South Carolina" a paper which has such bearing upon then existing conditions that it must be given in full:

To the Honorable the Senate and House of Representatives of the
    United States:

    Certain citizens of South Carolina, styling themselves "The Taxpayers' Convention," having memorialized your honorable bodies to grant them relief from unjust burdens and oppressions, alleged by them to have been imposed by the Republican State Government, we, the undersigned, members of the State Central Committee of the Union Republican party of South Carolina, beg leave most respectfully to submit to your honorable bodies the following counter statement and reply thereto:

The memorialists of the Taxpayers' Convention state "that upon the reconstruction of the State Government . . . it was intended by Congress . . . that they would become partakers of the rights enjoyed by citizens of the United States and other State Governments."

The memorialists have only themselves to blame that the intention of Congress in this respect was not carried out. The Republicans of this State earnestly invited them at that time to aid by their intelligence and experience in the work of reconstruction, but they contemptuously declined, assigning the same reasons that were afterwards given by Gen. Wade Hampton in the Democratic National Convention of 1868—that the Reconstruction Acts were unconstitutional, null and void. They then relied upon the promise of General Blair, the Democratic candidate for Vice-President, that he would overturn them with the sword.

The statement that "the annual expenses of the Government have advanced from $400,000 before the war to $2,500,000 at the present time," is entirely incorrect, and the items of expenditures given to illustrate and prove this statement are wholly inaccurate and untrue, and skilfully selected to deceive.

The year 1865-66 is given in such a manner as to convey the impression that the expenditures under its head are for two years, especially when 1873 only is given at the head of the other column, so as to show that it is unquestionably for one year. Why was not 1872-73 given to correspond with 1865-66?

In the next place, the appropriations and expenditures of 1865-66, under the provisional government established by ex-President Johnson, are no criterion whatever of the regular annual expenses of this State Government before the war. That was the year immediately after the war, when there was an unsettled and chaotic condition of things, and the expenses of the State Government were, therefore, exceedingly light. The presence and supervision of the military also relieved the State of a large portion of her usual regular expenses.

The items of expenditures given for 1873 are totally and wholly incorrect. The period alluded to is evidently the fiscal year beginning November 1, 1872, and ending October 31, 1873. At the beginning of that fiscal year the present administration came into power. The previous administration left debts of two or three previous years, amounting to one million, two hundred and thirty-three thousand nine hundred and ninety-six dollars ($1,233,966), which the present administration had to provide for, in addition to their own regular annual expenses. These annual expenses during the fiscal year

MOSES' ADMINISTRATION

above referred to were, as shown by the appropriations, one million, one hundred and eighty-four thousand, three hundred and seventy-six dollars ($1,184, 376), which, with the deficiencies of $1,233,996, made a sum of $2,418,872, which the present administration was called upon to pay during the fiscal year 1872-73. Of this amount, $1,719,728.37 was paid, leaving a balance of $689,143.63 unpaid.

We present a true statement of the appropriations of the fiscal year before the war, beginning October 1, 1859, and ending September 30, 1860, and the fiscal year beginning November 1, 1872, and ending October 31, 1873, that are properly chargeable to those respective fiscal years:

	1859-60.	1872-73
Salaries	$81,100	$194,989
Contingents	73,000	47,600
Free schools	75,000	300,000
State normal school	8,704	25,000
Deaf, dumb and blind	8,000	15,000
Military academies	30,000	....
Military contingencies	100,000	20,000
Roper hospital	3,000	....
State lunatic asylum	......	77,500
State Normal and High School	5,000	....
Jurors and constables	50,000	....
State orphan house (colored)	......	20,000
State penitentiary	......	40,000
Sundries	184,427	444,787
	$618,231	$1,184,876

Remember that the appropriation of 1859-60 represents gold value.

By the census of 1860 there were in South Carolina at that time 301,214 free population and 402,406 slaves. By the census of 1870 there were 705,606 free population. Now, "remember," in the eloquent language of another, "that in 1860, 402,406 souls, now a part of our body politic, voters amenable to our laws, the cost of governing whom is now chargeable to the Government of our State, were in 1860 chattels, merchandise, with not one civil or natural right which white men were bound to respect. In 1860 the slave was no charge on the State Government, save when he was hung for some petty misdemeanor, and the State compelled to pay his loss."

It would be, therefore, but just and fair to divide the amount appropriated in 1859-60, viz., $618,231, by the then free population, 301,214, and it will be found that the cost of governing each citizen was $2.05; and then divide the amount appropriated in 1872-73 by the free population now, viz.: 705,606, and it will be found that the cost of governing each citizen is $1.67—$2.05 in 1859-60, during the boasted Democratic period, and $1.67 in 1872-73, under the so-called corrupt Radical rule—a difference of 38 cents per capita in favor of the latter. So that if the Democrats had the same number of free citizens to govern in 1859-60 that the Republicans had in 1872-73 it would have cost them $261,616.30 more than it cost us.

The State having been organized upon a free basis necessarily created a larger number of offices, and, therefore, a larger amount of salaries. We are not ashamed of the fact that our appropriation for schools in 1872-73 is four times greater than in 1859-60. Ignorance was the cornerstone of slavery and essential to its perpetuity, but knowledge prevents the existence of that "sum of all villainies." Now in every hamlet and village of our State "the schoolmaster is abroad." In 1857 the number of scholars attending the free schools was only 19,356, while in 1873 the number of scholars attending the schools was 85,753 (of which 37,218 were white, 46,535 colored).

It will also be observed that there were no appropriations for the State lunatic asylum and penitentiary in 1859-60. The lunatic asylum was then supported by the friends of its wealthy inmates and the counties. But in 1872-73 this was found to impair the efficiency of the institution, and the State assumed its support and made liberal appropriations for its unfortunate patients.

The erection of the penitentiary was not begun until after the war, and there was, therefore, no appropriation for it in 1859-60.

The appropriation in 1872-73 for military purposes was but $20,000. We had no occasion to appropriate $130,000 for military academies and contingencies, in order to furnish nurseries to train the young to strike at the nation's life, and to purchase material for the War of Secession.

There was no appropriation in 1859-60 for a colored State orphan house. The colored orphans that were then uncared for were free, but their parents, when living, were heavily taxed to support white orphans, while their own children, after their death, were neglected.

To show the unjust and adroit manner in which the statement of expenditures has been manipulated by the memorialists of the Taxpayers' Convention for their purposes of deception we furnish a statement carefully compiled from the official records of the expenses of the State Government before the war and the first three years after:

1851-1852	$463,021.73
1852-1853	482,974.67
1853-1854	533,123.20
1854-1855	484,883.29
1855-1856	591,145.98
1856-1857	608,294.85
1857-1858	1,036,924.39
1858-1859	908,698.02

MOSES' ADMINISTRATION 257

1859-1860............................. 967,968.57
1865-1866............................. 266,248.04
1866-1867............................. 474,453.57

October 1, 1867, to April 30, 1868.......$340,415.00
Balance........................ 265,727.96—$606,142.96

These figures do not include interest on the public debt or the heavy expenses incurred by the military of the United States.

The statement that "it has been openly avowed by prominent members of the Legislature that the taxes should be increased to a point which will compel the sale of the great body of the land and take it away from the former owners" is not correct.

It is, however, a fact that the present system of taxation, like that of almost all civilized countries, is based chiefly upon real estate. In the days of slavery before the war it was not so. Taxes were levied by the large planters, who absolutely controlled the State, upon trades, professions, free colored persons, a mere nominal per capita tax upon slaves, and upon the lands assessed at one-tenth their true value.

This method of taxing lands enabled the planters to acquire and retain large and uncultivated tracts of land, and thus form that most dangerous of all oligarchies—a landed aristocracy.

It was from this class that secession and the war sprung. Our present method of taxation very naturally and properly prevents the perpetuation of this system which is so repugnant to our republican institutions.

It is stated "that the fruit of this policy is shown in the fact, stated by the Comptroller-General in his official report, that for default in payment of taxes for the year 1872 alone, 268,523 acres of land were forfeited to the State, and this result proves the fallacy of the belief that the policy pursued promotes the elevation of the black population and the acquisition by them of the lands thus virtually confiscated."

We admit with regret that it is a fact that there seems to be a combined determination on the part of the owners of the land to permit their uncultivated and unproductive lands to be forfeited to the State for non-payment of taxes rather than sell them to the colored people. They seem resolved to prevent the colored people from becoming land owners unless they can control their labor and political opinions. The colored men have labored long and faithfully, and with but little remuneration, and have produced as large crops since the war as in any year previous, as shown in the statistics and admitted by all; and yet the land holders of the State are not satisfied unless they can reduce them to a condition of serfdom or virtual slavery and control their labor.

The assessment of property in some counties of the State has given rise to complaints and been considered excessive. There is a prompt and complete remedy for all unjust assessments that may have been made by subordinate officers. The Comptroller-General and the Legislature have politely and patiently listened to the representations made by those who consider themselves aggrieved thereby, and immediately corrected the wrong where it was shown to be such, as is seen in the case of the county of Marion, that has petitioned the Legislature and Comptroller-General for relief.

The debt of the State under the Republican administration that controlled the State from 1868 to 1872 has been increased from $5,000,000 to $16,000,000, but $6,000,000 of that amount has been declared by the present Legislature to have been issued by the officer who had the matter in charge without authority of law, and has, therefore, been pronounced illegal. This leaves the unquestionably valid debt at $10,000,000. Of this amount $5,000,000 were issued by the Democrats and $5,000,000 by the Republicans who were in power from 1868 to 1872. But of the amount issued by the Republicans, they are only really responsible for $1,700,000, issued for the "relief of the treasury" and the "Land Commission." The remaining $3,300,000 were issued to pay the past due interest on the debt that had accrued previous to their accession to power, and to redeem the bills of the Bank of the State that had been issued before the war, and also to redeem the "bills receivable" that had been issued during the Democratic administration of Governor Orr, previous to Reconstruction. The Republicans, therefore, found on their accession to power in 1868 a funded debt of $5,000,000 and a floating debt of $3,300,000, which they funded and increased $1,700,000, for which alone they are responsible—making a total of $10,000,000.

A constitutional amendment was proposed by the General Assembly at its session of 1871-72, to prohibit the increase of the State debt, unless with the consent of two-thirds of the qualified voters, which amendment has been adopted and is now a part of our organic law.

The State has issued bonds amounting to $700,000 for the Land Commission, as above referred to, to purchase lands for sale in small farms to the poor. This beneficent object has accomplished much good.

The statement that "the appropriations made in one year for the work (i. e., printing) done, or to be done, by these two officials (i. e., the clerks) amounted to $475,000, exclusive of $100,000 for publishing the laws," is wholly incorrect.

The present Legislature, during the session of 1872-73, made appropriations for $450,000 for printing and advertising the laws as follows:

For publishing the following works, ordered by the General Assembly of 1870-71 and 1871-72:

Five volumes of the Statutes of the State (embracing a period of thirty years); 3,500 copies of Revised Statutes; 5,000 copies Kuklux trials; 5,000 extra reports Joint Special Investigating Committee; 2 volumes Supreme Court decisions; 1,000 extra copies of Reports and Resolutions of the General Assembly, and sundry books and documents ordered by the executive departments.. ..$250,000
Advertising the laws in almost all the newspapers of the State, ordered by the General Assembly of 1870-71 and 1871-72.. 75,000
For the regular printing of the fiscal year 1872-73.. 100,000
For advertising the laws passed at the session of 1872-73.. 25,000

Total.. .. ..$450,000

It will be seen that these appropriations, though made in one year, are for work ordered and performed during a period of three years.

The works for which the appropriation of $250,000 was made were extraordinary and will not probably occur again for twenty years. Thus it will be seen that the appropriations that are properly chargeable for work done during the fiscal year are $125,000, instead of $575,000.

It is stated that the total appropriations for public printing made by the Legislature of South Carolina during a period of sixty years, from 1800 to 1859, is $271,180. This statement is not correct; but, even if it were, is it a cause for boastfulness that but that amount was expended for printing during the sixty years that the people were kept in ignorance, and no public information disseminated amongst them for their enlightenment and elevation? We think not.

It is stated that "the committees have received large sums as compensation for reporting favorably on private bills." Whatever corruption may exist in the Legislature is to be attributed to the Democrats as well as the Republicans. They never hesitate to offer bribes when they have a private bill to pass. But corruption existed long before the advent of the Republican party of this State into power, only it was carried on then with the artistic skill of more experienced operators, and not easily seen.

The reference to the judicial department calls for a special notice. The judges of the supreme and circuit courts of this State number eleven, eight of whom are natives. These gentlemen held positions of trust and honor during the days of the Confederacy, but have shown the patriotic wisdom since the war to accept the situation and lend their learning and influence to aid the work of reconstruction.

For this course they have been pursued with unrelenting hate and vigor, and every possible insult offered them by those who do not desire to see the work of reconstruction successful.

Of the remaining three, one was selected as the candidate for Governor in 1870 by the party which the taxpayers represent, and the learning and ability of the other two have never been questioned.

The allusion to the executive department, being general, calls for no specific answer from us. It simply amounts to this, when divested of its spleen and misrepresentations—that the Republicans are in power and control the State, and they do not. Their complaints remind us most forcibly of the reply of that profound and astute statesman, Prince Bismarck, to the Papal hierarchy, who complained of the oppressive nature of the Prussian laws: "Unfortunately," says he, "you are accustomed to complain of oppression when not permitted to lord it over others."

The gentlemen who have assembled in this convention, constituting themselves the peculiar representatives of the so-called taxpayers, are not what they would have the country believe. They are the prominent politicians of the old regime—the former ruling element of the State—who simply desire to regain the power they lost by their folly of secession. They are not endorsed by the masses of the sober, thinking white Democrats of the State, who look upon their actions as unwise and ill-timed. We will state a well-known fact in proof of this:

The Democratic members of the Legislature, numbering thirty-one, held a caucus and unanimously resolved not to participate in the proceedings of the convention, and addressed a letter to the president, advising against the calling of the convention as unwise and injudicious. The letter was received and the president replied, regretting that they had not informed him of their intention previous to the meeting of the executive commmittee that had already called the convention together.

The Republicans admit the existence of evils amongst them. They acknowledge they have committed mistakes and errors in the past, which they deeply regret. But those mistakes and errors are being daily corrected, and they see no necessity whatever to resort to the desperate remedies asked for by the convention of the so-called taxpayers. There are enough able and good men among those who have the present charge of the Government in their hands to right every existing wrong. They are determined to do so.

In this work the difficulties under which they have labored have been naturally great, and have been increased tenfold by the determined hostility and opposition of the Democratic party ever since Reconstruction. This is their third effort to regain power. First, they expected it through the election of Seymour and Blair; second, through the midnight murders and assassinations of Kukluxism; and now, thirdly, by the distortion and misrepresentation of facts, in order to create a public sentiment in their favor and obtain relief from Congress.

MOSES' ADMINISTRATION

Relying upon the justice of our cause, we submit these facts to your impartial judgment.

Samuel J. Lee, chairman pro tem.; S. A. Swails, W. M. Thomas, Joseph Crews, H. H. Ellison, P. R. Rivers, John R. Cochran, Robert Smalls, E. W. M. Mackey, John Lee, H. L. Shrewsbury, George P. McIntyre, Wilson Cook, John H. McDevitt, A. W. Hough, Y. J. P. Owens, C. Smith, H. J. Maxwell, Thad. C. Andrews, P. C. Fludd, J. S. Mobley, M. L. Owens, E. S. J. Hayes, C. M. Wilder.

The Democratic members of the General Assembly promptly published a statement flatly denying the committee's charge that they had opposed or deprecated the calling or the assembling of the convention of taxpayers.

REPRESENTATIVE REPUBLICANS.

As to the personnel of this committee bearing the "reply" of the Republican party of South Carolina to the complaints made by the Taxpayers' Convention, some statement is proper in order to show the class of men who represented that party at a time when it undertook to answer charges affecting its character and its moral right to control the Government of South Carolina.

Samuel J. Lee, colored, was active in the Republican schemes of plunder—having admitted under oath that when a member of the House he had taken bribes.

S. A. Swails (colored) had received bribes, he had been active among the corruptionists, and his conduct afterwards became so outrageous that (as already told) he was actually driven out of Williamsburg County.

Joseph Crews, white, started early to rob the people—having corruptly taken money for fictitious services, and having otherwise defrauded the State. On the occasion of the death of Judge Orr (April, 1873,) he put in a claim for draping the hall of the House, in the sum of $954, which the Legislature cut down to $454—the extra $500 being plainly fictitious. He had taken bribes from the Republican Printing Company.

Prince R. Rivers (colored), according to his own sworn statement, had sold for money his votes as a member of the House.

John R. Cochran (white) was a man of good standing, who took no part in the frauds or robberies of his party. Yet in 1875, as a Representative from Anderson, he voted to place on the circuit bench W. J. Whipper, a negro, who all through the Reconstruction period was notoriously corrupt.

Robert Smalls (colored) was, in 1877, convicted of having, in 1873, taken a bribe of $5,000 for having as Senator from Beaufort voted for a bill in the interest of the Republican Printing Company. He was always affiliated with the corrupt leaders of his party.

E. W. M. Mackey (white) was a vicious partisan, the fomenter of strife between the races, totally unscrupulous, and a frequent slanderer of the white people. In 1876 he claimed to be speaker of the House of Representatives, and acted as such, after the Supreme Court had declared that his so-called house had "no legal status whatever" and that he was "a private citizen subject to arrest and punishment." He also had taken a bribe from the Republican Printing Company.

George F. McIntyre (white) was recognized as one of the leading corruptionists in the Legislature. He had received bribes from the Republican Printing Company.

John H. McDevitt (white) had been responsible for much trouble in Edgefield and, being treasurer of the county, had been a defaulter in a large amount—about $30,000.

Thad. C. Andrews (white), Senator from Orangeburg, was a close friend and staunch ally of Governor Moses, whom he had procured to appoint one Humbert treasurer of the county—Andrews stipulating that he should control the county funds. By that control he had committed various frauds upon the State and the county. He had also taken bribes from the Republican Printing Company.

John Lee (colored), Senator from Chester; M. L. Owens (white), Representative from York; Y. J. P. Owens (white), Senator from Laurens; C. Smith (white), Senator from Marion; and H. J. Maxwell (colored), Senator from Marlboro, had each taken bribes from the Republican Printing Company.

Of this committee of twenty-four representative Republicans at least fourteen had been guilty of bribery and therefore of perjury. Of the others it must be said that they were all in active association with the robbers, and that few of them were ever known to have protested against the misdoings of their party.

Touching the truth and fairness of this "reply" a just opinion may be formed from a view of the administration of public affairs under Governor Scott, Governor Moses and the Legislatures with which the members of this committee were in active sympathy.

In order to raise funds for the expenses of this committee in presenting their case to the President some of the members executed a note to one of the banks in Columbia, which was duly discounted. When, a few months later, the paper matured, the makers being either unable or unwilling to respond, a pay certificate for $2,500 for "services" to the Legislature was issued to L. F. Christopher (a fictitious personage), the money was drawn from the State treasury and the note was paid.

THE COMMITTEES IN WASHINGTON.

The committee to present the taxpayers' appeal to the President and to Congress assembled in Washington on March 30, the following named gentlemen being present:

From the Taxpayers' Convention—William D. Porter, Henry Gourdin, John L. Manning, M. L. Bonham, J. B. Kershaw, John H. Screven, M. C. Butler, C. W. Dudley, W. A. Holcombe, T. W. Woodward, B. H. Rutledge, C. H. Simonton, William Elliott, James A. Hoyt, James G. Thompson (Republican), Thomas Y. Simons.

From the Charleston Chamber of Commerce—President Samuel Y. Tupper, Richard Lathers, James Simons, William Aiken, L. D. DeSaussure, E. H. Frost.

The taxpayers' appeal was presented in an appropriate speech by the Hon. William D. Porter, of Charleston—a gentleman whose life had been distinguished for its purity as well as for its usefulness to South Carolina.

President Grant listened with apparently close attention, and when Mr. Porter had concluded spoke as follows:

Gentlemen: After listening to your remarks I do not see that there is anything that can be done either by the executive or by the legislative branch of the National Government to better the condition of things which you have described. The State of South Carolina has a complete sovereign existence, and must make its own laws. If its citizens are suffering from those laws it is a matter very much to be deplored. Where the fault lies may be a question worth looking into. Whether a part of the cause is not due to yourselves—whether it is not owing to the extreme views which you have held—whether your action has not consolidated the non-taxpaying portion of the community against you—are questions which I leave to your own consideration. Allow me to say, however, that I always feel great sympathy with any people who are badly governed and overtaxed, as is the case in Louisiana, and seems also to be the condition of South Carolina.

I would say to you candidly that while I have watched the proceedings of your Taxpayers' Convention with no little interest, a portion of my sympathy has been abstracted by the perusal of a speech delivered during its deliberations, and which contained a viler and more villainous slander than I have ever experienced before, even among my bitterest enemies in the North. It was far worse in its personality and falsehood than anything I have ever seen in the *New York Sun.*

(The *New York Sun,* it may be well to note, had been constant and unrelenting in its criticisms of General Grant—losing no opportunity of showing him up before the country as totally unfit in intellect or in any of the attributes of a great man to be the President of the nation.)

There was some little talk between the President and different members of the committee as to the alleged attack which had so excited him—in the course of which he hotly remarked:

"I have never seen a speech equal to it in malignity, vileness, falsity and slander. When I think of it I can scarcely restrain myself."

The committee shortly retired—their visit to the President evidently a failure. The disgust at the indecency of the President's behavior was very general.

General Grant's excuse for his extraordinary treatment of a body of gentlemen who had called upon him as the head of the nation, and whose conduct was throughout dignified and respectful, lay in certain statements alleged to have been made by Gen. M. W. Gary, of Edgefield, in a speech before the Taxpayers' Convention. General Gary had very plainly denounced the President's course towards the South, and had declared that neither help nor sympathy was to be expected from him. The views thus expressed well-nigh all the white people of South Carolina heartily shared. The charge that General Gary had unduly assailed the President personally was a fabrication of the Radical organ in Columbia.

The President's rudeness to the committee was also explained by the fact that just before the interview Honest John Patterson had had a conversation with him.

The taxpayers' committee next appeared before the judiciary committee of the Senate and of the House.

In due time the committee of Republicans presented to the President the "reply" to the taxpayers' appeal. The committee was chaperoned and introduced by L. Cass Carpenter, a carpetbagger who had participated in several schemes to rob the State treasury, and who, as already stated, was afterwards convicted of forgery in connection with an alleged claim for advertising.

The President stated to this committee that his remarks to the taxpayers' committee had been incorrectly reported—disclaiming the apparent criticism of the Government of South Carolina. He further declared that the "reply" of the Republican committee seemed conclusive.

The Senate and the House committee each reported that the matters presented in the taxpayers' memorial were beyond the jurisdiction of Congress.

The minority of the House committee on the judiciary reported that Congress should act in the premises, and presented at some length their reasons for that conclusion—stating that the duty of Congress arose out of the constitutional guaranty to each State of a republican form of government; that Congress having the power to propose amendments to the Constitution, and no amendment being possible without such proposal, it was the duty of Congress to propose in proper cases and, in order to ascertain conditions which should justify such action, to investigate conditions in the different States. Such investigation the minority urged should be ordered by Congress and should be effectively prosecuted. Concluding, the minority said:

In view of the whole case, we cannot hesitate to recommend the appointment of a committee of both houses of Congress, with power and authority to go into the State of South Carolina and fully inquire and investigate into the condition of the State and the charges and complaints of the memorialists. To do less, we feel, we should violate or neglect a most solemn and imperative duty. The cry of that outraged, helpless and suffering people has reached our hearts as well as our understanding. That once prosperous and beautiful State is on the verge of ruin. She is indeed already prostrate. A horde of thieves and robbers, worse than any that ever infested any civilized community on earth, have her by the throat and are fast sucking her life-blood. Three hundred thousand of her citizens, descendants of those who fought and won with our fathers the battles of American liberty, are crying to Congress for redress—for help. They have exhausted every resource and are of themselves utterly helpless. To refuse their request is to drive them to despair and ruin.

THE ROBBER GOVERNOR.

It will have been seen from what has been written of the administration of Franklin J. Moses, Jr., Governor of South Carolina, that the helpless condition of the white people continued unrelieved during the two years of his tenure.

Moses soon made himself notorious, not only in this State, but in the other States of the Union. The opinions expressed of him by the Republican minority that sought the election of Tomlinson were more than justified by his course in the executive office—the white people's estimate of his character was shown to have been more than fair to him. That Moses, as a member of the House of Representatives, and more especially as speaker of that body, had been frequently bribed, nobody but the blindest partisans or the active participants in his corrupt transactions ever affected to deny. In the executive office he justified every charge which before his accession had been made against him—this by pursuing a course which from first to last was flagrantly dishonest and which was in other respects a disgrace to him and an outrage upon the whole people—a course which made him infamous in the eyes of every fair-minded man in the country.

Moses entered the Governor's office without money—all that he had previously gotten having been spent in his fast life, some features of which were grossly immoral.

He very soon indicated his determination to live in most expensive style. He bought for $40,000 the residence then known as the Preston mansion—having for a long time been the home of John S. Preston, a wealthy and prominent citizen. This building with its grounds and with others erected on them has in recent years been used as the Presbyterian College for Women.

Moses had this mansion elegantly furnished and the building and grounds he always kept in first-class condition. His style of living was most extravagant. He had a handsome carriage drawn by a pair of beautiful horses—the whole turnout calculated to give the impression that it belonged to some rich man fond of making a display of his wealth. Away from home—on the frequent trips which he made to Washington and New York—he spent money even more lavishly (and more disreputably) than he did at home. He had the reputation of spending thirty to forty thousand dollars on his salary of $3,500. These estimates might have been excessive because made by people who were unaccustomed to such a display of wealth as Moses gave them. The general opinion was that in his two years in the Governor's office he must have spent not less than $50,000 for his living expenses. He expended large sums otherwise. In May, 1874, it was publicly stated that his debts amounted to more than $225,000 and his assets to $67,000. These figures were afterwards verified when he filed his petition as a voluntary bankrupt. The corrupt means which he employed to get money made him famous as "the Robber Governor."

The frauds by which Moses procured the money that he spent chiefly in "riotous living" have been stated by himself or by those who joined him in his schemes. He received a large share of the money paid by Josephus Woodruff and A. O. Jones to have their printing bills passed. For the approval of one printing appropriation (December 21, 1872,) Moses received $20,000. For a like service in relation to the act of December 19, 1873, he received $10,500, and on different days in that month several sums aggregating about $5,000. Moses himself admitted under oath that on a single occasion he had received from Woodruff $15,000, which was used to make the first payment in the purchase of the Preston mansion.

It was commonly reported that Moses exacted money of numbers of his appointees among the county officials, and that he sold many pardons for actual money. Certain it is that whenever his official station gave him opportunity he used it corruptly in his own interest. His conduct became so brazen, his villainies were so much advertised the country over, that it was plain to the Republican leaders in South Carolina that unless they should really "turn over a new leaf" they must not expect the countenance of the national party or the help of the National Government. The fears of those leaders had ample foundation in the actual condition of the State's finances, of her different institutions, of the State credit, of the public schools, of the different counties, and indeed of every institution or interest which the State Government had been expected to foster.

Of these matters Governor D. H. Chamberlain made some statements in his inaugural address to the General Assembly on December 1, 1874. Of the expenses of previous legislatures he said:

Since 1868 six regular and two special sessions of the General Assembly have been held. The total cost of those sessions has been $2,147,430.97. The average cost of each regular session has been $320,405.16. The lowest cost of any regular session was that of the regular session of 1868-69, amounting to $160,005.79; and the highest cost was that of the regular session of 1871-72, amounting to about $617,234.10. Besides these amounts now specified there are outstanding of bills payable on account of legislative expenses during the same period, $192,275.15.

The Governor stated that the average expenditure at each regular session since 1868, for attaches and contingent or incidental expenses, had been about $258,424.65, and that of this amount not less than $190,000 had been expended for contingent legislative expenses at each regular session. And there remained "still a vast amount of unpaid claims in the form of legislative pay certificates, estimated at not less than $500,000." He further said:

The cost of the permanent and current printing from 1868 to the present time was $848,073.59. The cost of advertising the statutes, that is, of printing them in the newspapers, for the same period was $261,496.32; making a total cost of $1,104,569.91. During the past three years the cost to the State of permanent and current printing was $743,943.20, and the cost of printing the laws in newspapers for the same period was $174,696.66; making a total cost to the State of $918,629.86. Deducting from this last amount such items of printing as may be called extraordinary, including the republication of certain volumes of the statutes at large, the printing of the Kuklux trials, immigration reports, tax duplicates and Supreme Court decisions, amounting to $375,000, there remains as the cost of printing for three years the sum of $543,629.86, or an average annual cost of $181,209.95. . . .

The existing deficiencies running back to 1868 are simply enormous. The deficiencies for the fiscal year ending October 31, 1874, were $472,619.54. The deficiencies for the fiscal year ending October 31, 1873, were $540,328, of which about $440,000 have been paid during the last fiscal year, leaving about $100,000 still unpaid. The levy of taxes made the present year for payment of deficiencies for the last fiscal year will not be sufficient to pay more than one-half the amount of such deficiencies.

Governor Chamberlain further declared that in the past six years there had been appropriated and paid for contingent funds "the astounding sum of $376,832.74."

These statements of a leading Republican, always loyal to his party in South Carolina, are especially noteworthy in connection with the "reply" of its State central committee to the taxpayers' appeal to Congress—a paper which the President of the nation was pleased to consider conclusive. The Governor's figures show just how much of wilful misstatement the "reply" contained.

MOSES' ADMINISTRATION 269

The State debt remained at its former figures—only about $2,000,000 of bonds having been funded under the Consolidation Act.

The aggregate of county indebtedness was over $400,000.

The amount of outstanding claims against the State, for legislative expenses—the bills of employees, newspapers and sellers of "sundries"—was reported by the clerks of the two houses to be $883,762.

The amount due by defaulting county treasurers was over $500,000.

The Sinking Fund Commission had used over $100,000 of State assets, without reducing the State debt by a single dollar.

The lunatic asylum was in debt $56,295, and the penitentiary in debt $102,238.

The unpaid balances of appropriations for the free schools amounted to $350,962—which amount (and much more) was due to teachers for services.

The land forfeited to the State for nonpayment of taxes in the fiscal year 1873 was 268,523 acres, and in the fiscal year 1874 was 507,759 acres—a total of 776,282 acres. The taxes charged against this land amounted to $86,548. Few pieces were sold for taxes—this because it was considered well-nigh impossible for the selling officer to make a title that was not palpably worthless.

There was some show of prosecution of defaulting or otherwise delinquent officials.

J. L. Humbert, county treasurer of Orangeburg, was charged with fraudulent breach of trust—the embezzlement of $16,200 of the public funds. Governor Moses was indicted with Humbert—the charge being that he had combined with Humbert to rob the State and had actually received a part of the stolen money.

Judge Graham, presiding in Orangeburg, issued a bench warrant for the arrest of Humbert, and the sheriff of that county proceeded to Columbia for the purpose of apprehending the accused. Moses flatly refused to be arrested, and that fact was communicated to the sheriff by John B. Dennis. The Governor immediately called out the three companies of negro militia in Columbia, and by these the executive residence and office were guarded for two days. The sheriff made return to Judge Graham that his effort to execute the process had been fruitless, but no further step was taken to arrest the defendant.

A day was set for the trial of Moses and Humbert, and on the call of the case the Governor was represented by counsel in the persons of

D. H. Chamberlain and R. B. Elliott. After some preliminary squabbling these lawyers moved to quash the indictment on the ground that the Governor was not liable to indictment and could be reached only by impeachment. After some delay (the court in the meantime having adjourned) Judge Graham granted the motion as to the Governor. Neither Moses nor Humbert was ever again troubled about the embezzlement case. Humbert was afterwards convicted of neglecting to make monthly reports to the State Treasurer and was sentenced to imprisonment for one year. Before the expiration of that term he was pardoned by Governor Chamberlain.

Henry A. Smith, county treasurer of Fairfield, was indicted in March, 1874, for embezzling over $20,000 of the public money, and for failing to make his monthly reports. He pleaded guilty of the latter charge and was sentenced to one year's imprisonment. He was very soon pardoned by Governor Moses. Later on he was tried for the embezzlement and was acquitted—the general opinion being that the jury list had been "fixed" in his interest.

The three county commissioners of Barnwell were convicted of malfeasance in office, and were forthwith pardoned by Governor Moses.

It was during Moses' term (and with his official approval) that the Financial Board "settled" the accounts of H. H. Kimpton, as Financial Agent. That individual presented his so-called accounts, wherein he claimed $735,969.13 for commissions, and he was formally discharged of all debts or other obligations to the State of South Carolina.

TROOPS FOR THE CAMPAIGN.

Early in September, in evident anticipation of the election in South Carolina, Senator John J. Patterson went to Washington, and there made a statement of conditions in South Carolina, which was given in the newspapers as follows:

Senator Patterson, of South Carolina, arrived here today, with accounts of fresh outrages, and depicts with great earnestness the terrorism that exists in his State among the negroes and the white Republicans. He says he has never seen such a condition of affairs in the State before; that murders and murderous outrages are of almost daily occurrence, and he fears an armed outbreak is inevitable. He says that the ones who led in the Kuklux outrages are organizing and drilling rifle clubs all over the State, and that no Republican is admitted. He says that the leader of the organization, whoever he is, can call into the field 25,000 drilled men fully armed and equipped.

The Senator said he had a militia composed mostly of negroes, but if they were called out they would be attacked and a war of races would ensue. The Senator said the only hope for South Carolina is in the Federal army, and his present mission to Washington is to have the army distributed through the State and held there till after the election. He says there are already troops enough in the State to preserve order, but he wants them scattered throughout the State.

The Columbia Board of Trade having passed resolutions exposing the falsity and absurdity of Patterson's charges, he replied with a statement reiterating and emphasizing them.

By a good many people it was thought that whilst Patterson was desirous to have more troops in the State, for the double purpose of emboldening the negroes and of exciting the feeling of Northern people against the whites of South Carolina, yet he had been scared by an occurrence near Columbia just before he gave the papers his first statement. It seems that one night late in August, while Governor Moses was entertaining Patterson, Neagle, Dennis and some other leading Republicans at the executive mansion, a report came to the party that seventy mounted men from Georgia had arrived at Granby (two miles from Columbia) and were going to "clean out" the State officials. The only apparent foundation for the story was in the fact that four or five citizens were fox-hunting in Lexington (just across the Congaree), and the sound of their horns inciting their hounds had given the Governor's informants the idea that there was coming a company of cavalry whose buglers thus made known the threatened onslaught.

The Federal commandant of the post was summoned to Neagle's house and was there begged to put his men under arms—a request promptly refused. About this time came Charles Minort, the mulatto colonel of the regiment to which the Columbia companies belonged. He reported that he had had his skirmishers out, but had not found the enemy. The Federal captain left in disgust, and the affrighted officials stealthily sought shelter in different parts of the city.

The impressions made on the President by Patterson's statements, supplemented with others of like import from leading Republicans in the South, were evidenced by the directions which he promptly gave to Attorney-General George H. Williams, who at once issued orders to the department commanders in the South for such a disposition of troops as would meet the situation as it had been presented to the Executive.

On September 25 Governor Moses officially telegraphed to President Grant that a reign of terror existed in Edgefield County, and concluded with this request: "I ask that you will send immediate orders to Col. H. M. Black, commanding the United States forces in Columbia, to report to me with such of his command as it may be found necessary to employ, as speedily as possible."

To this appeal Attorney-General Williams replied that, in the opinion of the President, the company of United States troops then stationed at Edgefield would afford adequate protection for the lives and property of citizens.

There had been some trouble in Edgefield, growing out of the conduct of a negro captain of State militia and the men under his command. It being reported from a section of Edgefield (Reese's Store) that the negroes were in arms, threatening to burn and kill, Gen. M. C. Butler, gathering such force as was obtainable in the neighborhood, sent to Augusta for assistance. On Sunday, September 23, General Butler had discovered a force of about seventy-five negroes, all armed, going in the direction of Reese's Store. Suspecting an evil design on the negroes' part, he gave the alarm, and very soon a large force of whites had assembled. It was ascertained that negroes to the number of 300, all armed, had gathered near Reese's Store, under the command of one Ned Tennant, a captain of militia. A committee of whites being sent to parley with Tennant, he declared that some parties unknown had fired into his house on the night previous and he had called out the militia for protection. He was defiant in the extreme. Holding out one hand full of cartridges he declared his intention to kill and to burn. Later in the afternoon Tennant, after further talk, surrendered at discretion. He was put under arrest on the charge of riot, and his negro soldiers soon dispersed.

A few days later Tennant went with his company to Edgefield and delivered up their guns to the officer in command of the United States troops. Another company soon followed the example set by Tennant and turned in their guns. There was no further trouble.

THE STATE TAX UNION.

Pursuant to the call of Gen. James Chesnut, of Kershaw, (by authority of the executive committee of the Taxpayers' Convention) the delegates chosen by the several County Tax Unions assembled in Columbia on September 10, 1874—all the counties being represented except Abbeville, Greenville, Horry, Lancaster, Oconee, Pickens and Spartanburg.

General Chesnut was elected chairman and Mr. W. Gilmore Simms, of Barnwell, secretary.

The executive committee was elected as follows:

First Congressional District—C. W. Dudley, of Marlboro, S. W. Maurice, of Williamsburg.

Second—Charles Richardson Miles, of Charleston, Gerhard Muller, of Lexington.

Third—William Wallace, of Richland, James N. Lipscomb, of Newberry.

Fourth—Thomas W. Woodward, of Fairfield, Robert W. Shand, of Union.

Fifth—M. L. Bonham, of Edgefield, William Elliott, of Beaufort.

A number of resolutions were offered and were, under the rules, referred to the executive committee.

The following report was adopted:

The executive committee, to whom were referred the resolutions on the subject of the authority of the State Union to make nominations and the expediency of its exercise, respectfully report that they have carefully weighed and considered all the different opinions on the subject which have been expressed, and have agreed upon a recommendation which they hope and believe will harmonize and unite our actions. The committee recommend the adoption of the following resolutions in substitution of all others:

Resolved, That the executive committee of the State Tax Union be authorized and empowered, in the exercise of their discretion, to recommend to the citizens of the State in favor of honest and good government to send delegates to a convention to assemble in Columbia on such day as shall be fixed by the executive committee, to consider the necessity of making nominations for State officers to be elected at the approaching election.

Resolved, That for carrying out this purpose the executive committee request the presidents of the several County Tax Unions, or such other persons as they shall select, to call primary conventions of their counties to elect as many delegates to said convention as their respective counties are entitled to in the House of Representatives.

The executive committee, after considering various resolutions on the subject of President Grant's statements as to conditions in South Carolina, submitted the following, which was unanimously adopted:

Whereas, to our great surprise, a communication of President

Grant to the Attorney-General, of date September 2 instant, contains the following declaration: "The recent atrocities in Alabama, Louisiana and South Carolina show a disregard for law, civil rights and personal protection that ought not to be tolerated in any civilized government"; and whereas, we are confident that the information conveyed to the President regarding these alleged atrocities in South Carolina is not true,

Resolved, That one delegate from each county be selected by the President of this Union to inquire what atrocities of the above nature, if any, have been recently committed in this State, and, if any, in what section, and by what class of persons; and that said delegates report, without delay, the result of their investigations to the executive committee of the State Union.

Under this resolution the president appointed the following named gentlemen:

From Aiken, E. S. Hammond; Abbeville, F. A. Connor; Anderson, J. S. Murray; Barnwell, William Gilmore Simms; Beaufort, William Elliott; Charleston, C. R. Miles; Chester, W. A. Walker; Chesterfield, A. McQueen; Clarendon, J. E. Tindall; Fairfield, James H. Rion; Kershaw, E. M. Boykin; Laurens, J. W. Watts; Lexington, G. Muller; Marlboro, C. W. Dudley; Newberry, J. N. Lipscomb; Orangeburg, J. H. Kellar; Richland, E. W. Wheeler; Sumter, J. B. Moore; Union, J. W. Finch; Williamsburg, S. W. Maurice; York, J. F. Hart.

The several members of the committee were requested to investigate thoroughly and report promptly to Col. James H. Rion, at Winnsboro, Fairfield county, who was authorized to act as chairman, consolidate the several reports and transmit the whole to the chairman of the executive committee of the State Tax Union.

The committee appointed as above stated took time for investigation and then submitted their report. This paper (besides a recital of the resolution under which the committee had been appointed) was as follows:

We have failed to ascertain a single case in the State of an injury, outrage or wrong committed during the present year by a white man upon a negro in the slightest degree attributable to the race, color or previous condition of servitude of the negro, or upon any Republican on account of his political opinions.

There have been too many instances of outrages committed upon whites by negroes because the sufferers were white; but these are not within the scope of the matter submitted to us.

There have been instances, of late, of flagrant breaches of the peace, but these have been between negroes, or caused by armed bands of negroes assembling on Sunday and on other days and threatening violence to the whites; or by negroes endeavoring to resist arrest of those of their color. These cases are also outside of the matter submitted to us.

We deem it, however, not irrelevant to report that a conflict of races has only been avoided by the uniform forbearance of the whites; which forbearance is especially commendable, as the whites under grievous provocation, with their males for the greater part veteran and disciplined soldiers, and thus having it in their power to crush at a blow the undisciplined negroes whose numerical superiority (only four to three) is of no consideration, have, from a regard for peace and good order and a desire to avoid conflict with the Federal authorities, hitherto borne and forborne.

The tendency to a conflict exists entirely on the side of the negroes, and arises from the existence of the following condition of affairs:

The negro is generally too apt to regard the administration of justice in which any white man has any instrumentality as an invasion of his rights.

The negro is taught to consider that the whites (except Republicans) have not the right to form volunteer military organizations, and hence regard the rifle clubs lately formed, for martial, social and defensive purposes, the evidence of incipient rebellion. The fact that almost the entire militia of the State are negroes, and that white companies have not been accepted by the State authorities where tendered, may have caused this opinion.

The negro militia are commanded by turbulent officers, are armed with fine arms, and abundantly supplied with ball cartridges, as if their services in actual conflict might any day be required.

The negro is taught to believe that the whites design not only to deprive him of the right of suffrage, but even to reduce him to his original condition of slavery.

The negro is taught to regard the United States troops as only intended to keep down the whites, and not for the common protection of all citizens.

The carpetbaggers (by which term we do not mean those from other States who remove here, but the dishonest political adventurers who now infest this State) do everything in their power by incendiary speeches, slanders and otherwise to inflame the blacks against any of their own color who might dare to vote as they call it "against their race." Thus, there is no political freedom in South Carolina for either race, and little civil liberty for the whites.

It is true, and it could not be otherwise, that there exists a feeling of deep indignation on the part of the whites, but it is not against the negro, nor against the honest Republicans of either color, but against those who have organized a system of election frauds, invent and publish abroad shameful slanders for political purposes; crush us with taxes; steal the money raised by taxation; teach the negro the infamous doctrines above mentioned, and in general teach the negroes to regard all white men not of the Republican party as their natural enemies.

In conclusion, we repeat that we have failed to ascertain a single case in the State of an injury, outrage or wrong committed during the present year by a white man upon a negro in the slightest degree attributable to the race, color or previous condition of servitude of the negro, or upon any Republican on account of his political opinions.

This paper making an absolutely dispassionate presentation of conditions in South Carolina was but one of many evidences of the wish of the white people to present to the country the actual truth in relation to matters in this State.

REPUBLICAN NOMINATIONS.

Among the Republican leaders, whether white or colored, there was a feeling that something had to be done to save their party from defeat or from a loss of that active support of the national administration which was thought essential to the party's life. Every man calling himself a Republican was crying out for reform—reform coupled with Republican ascendency.

The State Convention met in Columbia on September 8. There being some wrangling, caused by contesting delegations, it was only on the fourth day that a permanent organization was effected by the election of the following officers:

President—C. M. Wilder (colored) of Richland.

Vice-Presidents—Joseph H. Rainey, of Georgetown; W. R. Jervey, of Charleston; Robert Smalls, of Beaufort, colored; John R. Tolbert, of Abbeville; John C. Winsmith, of Spartanburg, white.

Secretary—Josephus Woodruff (white), of Charleston; assistant—James R. Kennedy (white), of Richland.

Sergeant-at-Arms—M. Williams (colored), of Barnwell.

For Governor the name of D. H. Chamberlain was presented by F. L. Cardozo, seconded by W. J. Whipper and T. J. Mackey.

Other delegates nominated respectively Dr. John Winsmith, of Spartanburg, and Judge John T. Green, of Sumter.

The ballot resulted as follows: Chamberlain, 73; Green, 40; Winsmith, 10.

For Lieutenant-Governor R. H. Gleaves, the incumbent, received 92 votes, M. R. Delany, 11; A. J. Ransier, 3.

Mr. Chamberlain, on being introduced to the convention, made a polished speech, in which he pledged himself and the Republican party of South Carolina to retrenchment, reform and good government.

The following resolution was unanimously adopted:

Resolved, That in the distinguished soldier and statesman now at the head of our nation we recognize one who in peace as well as war possesses that fidelity of purpose and integrity of character so necessary to insure tranquility at home, respect abroad, and the permanency of the grand and glorious principles which have become the cornerstone of the great Republican party to which we belong, and, for this reason, we pledge ourselves to the support of President Grant for a third term, assured that by so doing we shall preserve that peace and unity throughout the whole country, so necessary for its prosperity.

The following platform of the Republican party of South Carolina was enthusiastically adopted:

I. We reaffirm our earnest adhesion to the platform and principles adopted by the National Republican Convention at Philadelphia, on the 6th day of June, 1872, as embodying the true ideas of American progress.

II. We maintain the authority of the General Government to interfere for the preservation of domestic tranquility in the several States, and we acknowledge with gratitude such interposition in this State.

III. We deprecate lawlessness in any form, condemn turbulent agitations in any place, deplore violence, intimidation, or obstruction of personal or political rights by any party, demand an universal respect and consideration of the elective franchise in the hands of the weakest, and shall hold all men as enemies to equality of rights who interfere with or deny the full and lawful exercise of its use to any citizen, whatever may be his party creed.

IV. We pledge ourselves to continue, scrupulously, to enact and enforce the financial reforms promised two years ago, and in large measure fulfilled, in proof of which we point to the following laws, viz.: The law to levy a special tax; the law to reduce the volume of the public debt; the law to regulate the public printing; the law to regulate the number of attaches; the law to regulate the disbursement of public funds; the law to regulate assessments.

V. We pledge ourselves to reduce the public expenses within the public revenue, and to secure the enactment of a law requiring all public officers who disburse moneys to give to the public a detailed monthly statement of all receipts and expenditures derivable from a moderate assessment and tax rate, and by proper enactments shorten the annual sessions of the General Assembly, and a reduction of appropriations for contingent and incidental expenses of the legislative and executive departments of the Government.

VI. We earnestly entreat the Congress of the United States to pass the Civil Rights Bill, which is absolutely essential to enforce the constitutional guaranty of equal rights for all American citizens.

VII. We especially pledge ourselves to maintain the settlement of the public debt made last winter, and to reject all claims against which there is a shadow of suspicion.

VIII. We hold that all franchises granted by the State should be subservient to the public good, that charges for travel and freight should be equitable and uniform, and no unjust discriminations be made between through and local travel and freights.

IX. We shall advocate such a modification of our present system of taxation as will prove of the largest advantage to our agricultural interests, and shall lend our earnest endeavors to the enactment of such laws and to the encouragement of such means as will the most speedily develop the resources and build up the manufacturing and industrial prosperity of South Carolina, and the construction of such new railroads as will give the largest and cheapest facilities to all our citizens.

X. We will not only protect, in the truest sense, the property of the State, but we pledge ourselves to such wise, just and humane laws as will perfect the education and elevation of our laboring classes.

XI. With full faith in the justice of these principles, acknowledging our errors in the past, but feeling confident of our ability and determination to correct them, we appeal to all true Republicans to unite in bearing our candidates to victory, and pledge ourselves to carry out in the practical administration of the Government every principle inscribed upon our standard in the interest of the whole people of the State.

The convention passed a resolution of thanks to Senator Patterson for his "efforts in behalf of peace," and to President Grant and the Department of Justice for the prompt response to Honest John's request for troops.

The conservative white people of South Carolina were almost unanimously opposed to Chamberlain—regarding him as partly responsible, along with Scott, Moses, Patterson, Parker, Neagle and others with whom he had been closely associated, for the misgovernment and the corruption under which the State had suffered for six years. Many Republicans of both races felt that Chamberlain was unworthy and that his nomination was the work of men who had brought the party to disgrace.

On October 2 there was a State convention of the "independent" Republicans. The body met in Charleston, nineteen counties being represented.

This convention, after adopting the Republican platform, made the following nominations:

For Governor—John T. Green, of Sumter.

For Lieutenant-Governor—Martin R. Delany, of Charleston.

Judge Green's career has been sufficiently stated in another connection.

Major Delany was a genuine negro. He was born in Charlestown, Va., in 1812. He had received no college education, but had been a reader and student. He had edited a newspaper in Pittsburg, Pa., and later on graduated from the Harvard Medical School—practicing his profession in Canada. He had traveled in Europe and explored parts of Africa. He had been active in the anti-slavery movement. He had served as surgeon in the Union army, and had finally risen to the rank of major of infantry. After the war he was connected with the Freedmen's Bureau on the South Carolina coast, and in that relation had made a good impression on the white people. He lived in Charleston, where he practiced medicine. He was a man of unusual intelligence and a very good speaker.

The convention adopted the following resolution:

Resolved, That, while maintaining the integrity of the Republican party in South Carolina, we cordially invite the whole people of the State to support the nominees of this convention as the only means of preserving their common interests—especially requesting the Conservatives that, having persistently declared that their desire was only for good government, without regard to partisan politics, they will now attest the sincerity of their declarations by marching with us, shoulder to shoulder, for the triumphant election of Green and Delany and the certain redemption of the State from the corrupt "rings" which have disgraced the Republican party and trampled upon the interests of the Republicans and Conservatives alike.

CONSERVATIVES IN CONVENTION.

Acting under the authority contained in a resolution of the State Tax Union, Gen. James Chesnut, chairman of the executive committee of that body, issued, September 15, the following call:

The citizens of South Carolina in favor of honest and good government are requested to send delegates to a convention to assemble in Columbia on Thursday, the 8th day of October next, to consider the necessity of making nominations for State officers at the approaching election.

In response to this call (which, it should be noted, involved the institution of a political organization distinct from the Democratic party) the following named delegates from the several counties met in Columbia on October 8:

Abbeville—R. C. Sharp, J. H. Morrow, R. S. Beckman.

Aiken—A. P. Butler, E. S. Hammond, D. S. Henderson, John Stevens.

Anderson—J. Scott Murray.

Barnwell—R. Weathersby, James C. Brown, J. C. Miller.

Beaufort—John Conant, J. H. Ruddle, John Lawton.

Charleston—C. R. Miles, G. L. Buist, F. W. Dawson, J. P. Lesesne, J. F. Ficken, M. H. Nathan, James Cosgrove, Rudolph Seigling, R. T. Morrison, J. S. Browning, W. B. Smith, A. G. Magrath, Jr.

Chester—John J. Hemphill, Grandison Williams.

Chesterfield—S. W. Evans, J. W. Harrington.

Clarendon—John L. Manning, James E. Tindal, Joseph Rhame, W. J. McFadden.

Colleton—J. Otey Reed, Robert Black, C. P. Fishburne, Newman K. Perry.

Darlington—L. R. Ragsdale, Jerome P. Chase.

Edgefield—L. Cheatham, R. B. Hughes, O. Sheppard, John E. Bacon, W. H. Timmerman.

Fairfield—R. Means Davis, R. S. DesPortes, James H. Rion.

Georgetown—Benjamin H. Wilson.

Greenville—T. Q. Donaldson, William Beattie.

Kershaw—W. Z. Leitner, William M. Shannon.

Laurens—C. M. Miller, J. C. Davis, Dr. E. B. Martin.

Lexington—Gerhard Muller, Drury Nunamaker.

Marion—William D. Johnson, David W. Bethea.

Marlboro—C. W. Dudley.

Newberry—John S. Hare, William Ray, Joseph Caldwell.

Oconee—Robert A. Thompson.

Orangeburg—W. T. Rives, W. A. Easterling, Charles P. Inabinet, Ned Edwards (colored).

Richland—John H. Kinsler, Charles F. Janney, Nathaniel Barnwell.

Spartanburg—Simpson Bobo, John H. Evins.
Sumter—John B. Moore, John S. Richardson, J. S. Bradley, W. E. Miles.
Williamsburg—S. W. Maurice, W. J. Nettles, R. D. Rollins.
York—John S. Bratton, A. E. Hutchison.
Horry, Lancaster, Pickens and Union were not represented.

The convention adopted without a dissenting voice the following preamble and resolutions:

Whereas, The Republican party, being in the majority in this State, is responsible for its government, and the Conservatives of the State having declared that if the Republican party would nominate for Governor and Lieutenant-Governor men of their own party, of honesty and character, entitled to confidence, the Conservatives would refrain from opposition to them; and, whereas, the regular nominating convention of the Republican party has nominated for Governor and Lieutenant-Governor men whose antecedents show them to be unworthy of confidence and whose success would insure the continuance of the corruption, dishonesty and party tyranny which have prostrated the State; and whereas, the independent wing of the Republican party has declared its intention to reform the government of the State, and in pursuance of this intention have made nominations of men whose antecedents entitle them to confidence in their integrity and honesty, for which nominations they have asked the support of the Conservative voters of the State; and whereas, the necessity of checking corruption and procuring honest officials is paramount to all questions of party politics or affiliation; and believing that the only opportunity afforded of securing such reform will be in the success of the nominees of the Independent Republican party:

Resolved, That it is the sense of this convention, called to "consider the necessity of making nominations for State officers in the approaching election," that no nomination for Governor or Lieutenant-Governor in the approaching election be made by the Conservative citizens of the State.

Resolved, That in the opinion of this convention the Conservative citizens will best promote the interest and welfare of the State by giving their support to the candidates for Governor and Lieutenant-Governor nominated by the Independent Republican party.

Resolved, That we adopt as the platform of the Conservative party of South Carolina—honesty and economy in the administration of the State Government.

A permanent executive committee of the Conservative party of South Carolina was appointed as follows:

First Congressional District—J. W. Harrington, of Chesterfield, B. H. Wilson, of Georgetown.

Second District—John L. Manning, of Clarendon, James Conner, of Charleston.

Third District—William Wallace, of Richland, James N. Lipscomb, of Newberry.

Fourth District—Simpson Bobo, of Spartanburg, James H. Rion, of Fairfield.

Fifth District—William F. Colcock, of Beaufort, M. L. Bonham, of Edgefield.

Colonel Bobo was elected chairman.

An executive committee was appointed for each county.

It was resolved that the delegates to the convention attend to having supervisors appointed for each election precinct in their respective counties by the judge of the United States Circuit Court.

The work of the convention having been concluded, Gen. J. B. Kershaw was (on motion of Col. John H. Evins) invited to address the convention.

"General Kershaw," reported the *Columbia Phoenix,* "responded in a masterly speech full of those wise, pacific and just counsels which have distinguished his utterances. He alluded in pathetic terms to his belief that Divine Providence had inspired the action of the convention and directed it to the only mode of escape from the evils which surround the State. He dwelt with effect upon the duty of a full recognition of the rights of the colored race and upon the duty and the necessity of seeking their cooperation in all measures tending to the rehabilitation of the State, the restoration of its prosperity, and the recovery of its good name. Should he be elected to the House of Representatives, for which position he had been nominated, he would address himself with all his powers and all his zeal to the grateful tasks which would then devolve upon him. He discerned already a change in the feeling of the people of this great country towards the Southern States, and it would be the ambition of his life to throw himself upon the wave of its returning justice. He felt a conviction that he would live through these dark times and yet see such representatives as he now looked upon meet in these very halls to rejoice over a ransomed people."

The convention then adjourned.

The Conservatives had candidates in but two congressional districts—Samuel McGowan in the Third, and J. B. Kershaw in the Fourth.

In most of the counties the only candidates offering were those of the Republican factions.

The candidates of the "Regulars" and the "Independents" made a canvass of the State—meetings being held in nearly all the counties. There were but few disturbances—these in every instance growing out of quarrels between persons of the two factions of the Republican party.

There were Federal troops stationed in many towns, but there was no occasion for them to leave their quarters.

The "Independents" were defeated. The total vote cast was 149,221, of which Mr. Chamberlain received 80,403 and Judge Green 68,818—a majority of 11,585 for the "Regular" Republican candidate. This vote was the largest cast since 1868. In 1870 the total vote was 136,608, and Scott's majority 33,534. In 1872 the total vote was 106,471, and Moses' majority 33,305. In none of these elections was the full white vote polled.

The "Independents" carried twelve counties, as follows: Anderson, Charleston, Chesterfield, Clarendon, Greenville, Horry, Lexington, Marion, Oconee, Pickens, Sumter and Union. They charged that fraudulent votes in great numbers were counted for the Chamberlain ticket.

The Conservatives elected to the House of Representatives were as follows:

Anderson—H. R. Vandiver, James L. Orr, Richard W. Simpson.

Charleston—George A. Trenholm, Joseph W. Barnwell, Alexander Melchers, James Cosgrove, John G. Gaillard.

Chesterfield—J. C. Coit, D. T. Redfearn.

Colleton—R. A. Willis.

Greenville—Thomas B. Ferguson, Stanley S. Crittenden, J. Thomas Austin, Samuel Tinsley.

Horry—Daniel Lewis, Francis J. Sessions.

Lexington—Gerhard Muller, Henry A. Meetze.

Marion—William D. Johnson, R. G. Howard.

Marlboro—T. C. Weatherly.

Oconee—J. W. Livingston, A. B. Grant.

Pickens—D. F. Bradley, John L. Hornsley.

Richland—John T. Sloan, Jr.

Spartanburg—John E. Bomar, Gabriel Cannon, A. B. Woodruff, Robert M. Smith.

Union—William H. Wallace, B. H. Rice.

The election of Conservatives in Charleston resulted from a "fusion" of their party with the Independent Republicans.

The election of a Conservative in Richland resulted from a contest between two Republican factions led respectively by W. Beverly Nash and Charles Minort, the colored candidates for the Senate—both, by the way, equally steeped in corruption, and each grossly incompetent. The Nash faction gave the Conservatives one place on the legislative ticket and the probate judgeship; Nash further agreeing to have a Conservative appointed to one of the two trial justiceships in Columbia. The Nash ticket carried the county by 602 votes, though Mr. Chamberlain defeated Judge Green by 2,483 votes in a total of 5,465. Among the candidates defeated on the Minort ticket was F. J. Moses, Jr., who ran for a seat in the House of Representatives.

In York there was a "straightout" Democratic ticket for the House. The Republicans had previously placed on their ticket Col. William C. Beatty, an independent in politics and a gentlemen of the highest character. His course in the House was throughout moderate and honorable.

Of the new senators, three were Conservatives—W. Augustus Evans, of Chesterfield, R. E. Bowen, of Pickens, and Thomas B. Jeter, of Union. The Conservative senators holding over were T. Q. Donaldson, of Greenville, J. C. Hope, of Lexington, W. C. Keith, of Oconee, and D. R. Duncan, of Spartanburg.

The House contained ninety-one Republicans and thirty-three Conservatives—the Senate twenty-six Republicans and seven Conservatives. Of the representatives sixty-one and of the senators sixteen were colored. On joint ballot the Republicans had a majority of seventy-three, and the whites a majority of three.

Congressmen were elected as follows:

First District—Joseph H. Rainey, defeating Samuel Lee, both colored Republicans.

Second—E. W. M. Mackey, defeating C. W. Buttz, both Republicans.

Third—Solomon L. Hoge, Republican, defeating Samuel McGowan, Conservative.

Fourth—A. S. Wallace, Republican, defeating J. B. Kershaw, Conservative.

Fifth—Robert Smalls, colored, defeating J. P. M. Epping, both Republicans.

The Independent Republicans carried only the Second District.

The constitutional amendments were adopted—reducing the term of all State officers to two years, and restricting the powers of counties and municipalities in creating bonded debts.

CHAPTER VII.

CHAMBERLAIN'S ADMINISTRATION.

The General Assembly met November 24.

S. A. Swails, of Williamsburg, was reelected president pro tem. of the Senate and Josephus Woodruff clerk.

In the House the contest for the speakership was between R. B. Elliott, of Aiken, and N. B. Myers, of Beaufort, both colored. The ballot stood—Elliott 64, Myers 49. The Conservatives, with the exception of Mr. Beatty, of York, voted for Myers.

Elliott had been a conspicuous figure in South Carolina politics ever since the meeting of the Constitutional Convention called under the Reconstruction acts. He was violent, sometimes almost incendiary, in his appeals to the negroes to stand by their race, and held extreme views on all questions of civil rights—meaning social equality. He soon became a leader among the negroes and was courted by most of the white men who called themselves Republicans. He was the first chairman of the House Committee on Railroads, and in that capacity was believed to have received large bribes from John J. Patterson for helping on the schemes for the acquisition of the Blue Ridge Railroad and the Greenville and Columbia Railroad. On the occasion of the attempt to impeach Governor Scott, Elliott received one bribe of more than $10,000 and, according to common report at the time, considerable sums besides. He was generally considered utterly corrupt, and his influence, in whatever sphere he had opportunity, was always on the side of the robbers. He was directly responsible for some of the race troubles in South Carolina. His personal character, aside from his conduct in office or in politics, was of a low order—immoral to an extent difficult to understand in a man of his education and his prominence in the Republican party. Though very mouthy, he was generally accounted a coward. As a product of Reconstruction in South Carolina Robert B. Elliott must be classed among the very lowest and the very worst.

Bowen, of Charleston, managed Elliott's campaign—which was said to have cost over $5,000.

It will be noticed that Elliott forbore to run for Congress in order to reenter the State Legislature and become speaker of its lower house.

A. O. Jones was reelected clerk without opposition.

Governor Moses omitted to send the usual message to the General Assembly.

THE GOVERNOR'S INAUGURAL.

Daniel H. Chamberlain was inaugurated as Governor on December 1. In his address on that occasion he departed from the custom observed by his two predecessors, in that he undertook to present the conditions which the General Assembly must meet, and suggested important reforms in various departments of the State Government. His introductory statement was as follows:

Fellow citizens of the Senate and House of Representatives: I have appeared before you today to assume the office of Governor, and to state my views of the action and policy on the part of our State Government which will best promote the public welfare.

Our recent political canvass presents one or two aspects which are significant of the will of the people. The two parties which sought supremacy were equally emphatic in their demand for the correction of existing abuses in the administration of our Government, and both presented to the public the same platform of principles and policy for the future conduct of public affairs. The remarkable spectacle was thus presented, among a people hitherto considered most widely divided in their political sympathies and aims, of an absolute identity of sentiment upon all the questions which were presented to the public in either party. It is true that a large minority of our citizens did not take part in either of the political conventions which presented the respective candidates for State officers, yet in the election wherein the total number of votes cast was more than 12,000 greater than in any previous election since 1868, only two parties appeared, both of which professed to seek similar ends by similar means. The result is that we who have been elected to office are united in the general objects which we seek and the general methods by which those objects are to be reached.

Without intending to overstate the extent to which our recent party combinations have bound us in respect to our future action, I congratulate all our people upon the substantial harmony of purpose which now prevails. I take strength and hope from that fact. If we are honest in our professions, I cannot find myself in antagonism to any member of the executive or legislative department of our Government, except upon matters of detail in our common pursuit of the same ends. I feel bound to say that, until experience shall correct me, I shall rely for support in the course which I intend to pursue upon members of the General Assembly who were opposed to me in the recent political contest as confidently as upon those who favored my election.

The paramount duty before us may be stated to be the practice and enforcement of economy and honesty in the administration of the Government. Fortunately our evils are chiefly evils of administration. Our State Constitution commands the undivided approval of our people. The body of our statute law is believed to be, in general, just and wise. The present demand is for a faithful application and enforcement of the existing Constitution and laws; in a word, good administration.

Wise statesmanship aims at practical results, and concentrates its strength upon those measures which are of prime importance. I must be pardoned if I omit to catalogue all the matters of public interest to which consideration must be given by the General Assembly and confine my attention to those topics which appear to be most pressing.

The Governor then proceeded with suggestions of reform in the various departments of the State Government.

He recommended changes in the tax system, with the view to greater simplicity, fairness and efficiency.

He urged a reduction of expenses and the limiting of the amount of taxes to the actual requirements of the Government—especially commending the plan of making a specific levy for each authorized object.

As the "specific measures" which would bring the State Government "nearer to a correct rule of public expenditure," he suggested: That the payments from contingent funds be regulated in the same manner as other disbursements of public money and that these funds be reduced to the lowest figures consistent with efficient service; that the expenditures of the General Assembly, already constituting an "intolerable abuse," be reduced by shortening the session to a term not exceeding thirty days, by passing a general law for the granting of charters, by cutting off useless employees and attaches, by stopping the excessive appropriations of money for contingent or incidental expenses, and by prescribing proper rules for auditing and paying all legislative expenses; that the system prevailing in the matter of public printing, being "utterly incapable of defense or excuse," be abolished, the printing to be let to a responsible bidder in a fair competition, and the cost be reduced to reasonable figures; that the amount needed to pay accumulated deficiencies be ascertained and a tax levy made adequate to pay the amount; that the issuance of "certificates of indebtedness" be discontinued; that all unnecessary offices, whether in State or in county government, be at once abolished; that the provisions of the Consolidation Act, to reduce the volume of the public debt, be faithfully and carefully carried out and the interest on the recognized bonds be promptly and regularly paid; that some effective measure be taken to retire the outstanding bills of the Bank of the State of South Carolina; that justices of the peace and constables be elected by the people, in accordance with the requirement of the State Constitution; that the powers of the State Board of Canvassers be so extended as to increase their means of determining questions arising out of contested elections; that the requirement of the Constitution as to the registration of electors be no longer disregarded, and that the existing scheme of public education be carefully fostered, liberally supported and generally improved.

The Governor presented in their proper places the statements showing the gross extravagance of former administrations. The figures have been given in a previous chapter. He concluded as follows:

The work which lies before us is serious beyond that which falls to the lot of most generations of men. It is nothing less than the reestablishment of society in this State upon the foundation of absolute equality of civil and political rights. The evils attending our first steps in this work have drawn upon us the frowns of the whole world. Those who opposed the policy upon which our State was restored to her practical relations with the Union have already visited us with the verdict of absolute condemnation. Those who framed and enforced that policy are filled with anxiety for the result, in which fear often predominates over hope. The result, under Divine Providence, rests with us.

For myself, I here avow the same confidence in the final result which I have hitherto felt. The evils which surround us are such as might well have been predicted by a sagacious mind before they appeared. They are deplorable, but they will be transitory. The great permanent influences which rule in civilized society are constantly at work and will slowly lift us into a better life. Our foundations are strong and sure. Already we have seen the day when no party or no man in our State was bold enough to seek the favor of the people except upon the most explicit pledges to remove our present abuses. If we who are here today shall fail in our duty, others more honest and capable will be called to our places. Through us or through others freedom and justice will bear sway in South Carolina.

I enter upon my duties as Governor with a just sense, as I hope, of my own want of such wisdom and experience as the position demands. I shall need the friendly aid not only of my political associates but of all men who love our State. We must move forward and upward to better things.

The address was noticed by the press of the State and by some leading papers in other parts of the country—all the comments being highly complimentary. The State papers took pains to say that in any efforts to effect the reforms suggested in the inaugural the Governor would have the active and hearty support of all good citizens—more particularly of those opposed to him politically.

The Governor later sent a message to the General Assembly, in which he amplified some of the suggestions contained in his inaugural—referring particularly to the finances of the lunatic asylum, the condition of the penitentiary, the progress of the free schools, the past indebtedness of the counties, the floating debt of the State, minority representation (which he unreservedly recommended), the election of justices of the peace and constables, the registration of electors and the reduction of expenses.

In a message (December 22) approving the act appropriating funds for the payment of legislative expenses the Governor called attention to the fact that whilst the amount required by the act was $150,000, the sum to be received from the tax levy (one mill) would not exceed $115,000—and took occasion to warn against the making of deficiencies.

In his message of March 12, 1875, the Governor stated his reasons for not approving the "act relative to the deposit of moneys of the State, and other provisions in relation thereto," requiring all State funds to be deposited in two banks in Columbia—the Carolina National and the private bank of Hardy Solomon, styled "The South Carolina Bank and Trust Company." The Governor took the position that any such designation was unwise and that the selection of depositories should remain with the board consisting of the Governor, the Comptroller-General and the Treasurer. The veto was sustained.

The Governor next vetoed "an act to provide for the settlement and redemption of certain claims against the State"—a measure intended to effect the payment of the floating debt. The Governor stated, as his principal objection to the measure, that it did not afford proper means for discriminating between valid and fraudulent claims. The veto was sustained.

The bill to amend the act in relation to the public debt—the Consolidation Act—was vetoed on the ground that the proposed measure involved material changes in the settlement contemplated by the act and was therefore in violation of the contract made with the bondholders, and contrary also to the pledges contained in the Republican platform and the pledges made by the Governor himself. This veto was also sustained.

The bill in relation to the past indebtedness of Edgefield County was vetoed on the principal ground that the interests of the county were not therein sufficiently safeguarded, and for the further reason that that indebtedness was soon to undergo investigation in pursuance of certain proceedings already had in the Circuit Court. This veto was also sustained.

These messages of the Governor are here mentioned, rather out of their proper places, because they show how he sought to carry out the views stated in his inaugural and in his message supplementary thereto.

NOTABLE LEGISLATION.

The "act for the relief of the widows and orphans of persons killed because of their political opinions" was so amended as to exempt Fairfield County from the tax thereby imposed—the proceeds payable to the families of persons alleged to have been killed by the Kuklux. There was never a pretense of any such killing in Fairfield.

The inferior court for the trial of criminal cases in the county of Charleston was abolished. That court had long been a source of needless expense and constant vexation to the people of Charleston.

The State Treasurer was required to publish in one Charleston and one Columbia paper monthly statements of his receipts and disbursements.

The statute requiring the Attorney-General, the Comptroller-General and the Secretary of State to designate certain papers in which all legal notices should be published was repealed.

The "civil rights" act was amended so as to prohibit parties keeping an inn, restaurant or other place of accommodation or refreshment from discriminating between persons on account of race, color or previous condition—such discrimination punishable by fine and imprisonment.

The taking of the census of 1875 was committed to the Secretary of State.

County treasurers were authorized to pay claims only when the same should have been approved by the county commissioners, and then only upon checks issued by such commissioners.

The pay of the members of the General Assembly was fixed at "such per diem compensation as will amount to and not exceed $600" for each regular session, with mileage at twenty cents—the per diem compensation of extra sessions to be determined by the per diem compensation of the regular session next preceding the extra session.

The "act to provide for the settlement and redemption of certain claims against the State" appointed W. B. Gulick, Thomas S. Cavender and J. P. Southern (all of Columbia) as a "commission on claims," whose duty it was to audit, as liquidated debts of the State, all outstanding bills payable, certificates of indebtedness and pay certificates—the commission being vested with the right to determine the validity of each claim presented. On claims adjudged valid the act provided that fifty per cent. should be paid in discharge thereof, payment to be made in four parts—out of the taxes of the years 1875, 1876, 1877 and 1878, respectively. The total of claims to be allowed was fixed at $500,000, and the amount of the warrants to be issued under the act was limited to $250,000. An annual tax levy of one-half of one mill was provided for the payment of the claims that should be audited. This scheme was known as the "Bonanza."

The tax levy for the year commencing November 1, 1874, as already given, was ten and one-quarter mills for State purposes, and three mills for county purposes, with extra levies in several counties, ranging from one mill to three. Most of these special levies were continued by acts passed at the session of 1874-75.

After the appropriation bill had been passed by the House and sent to the Senate the Governor addressed to the chairman of its finance committee an official letter in which he called attention to the fact that the appropriations made involved a deficiency of $148,555, which, added to the deficiency arising under the legislative appropriation bill, made the aggregate of deficiencies $178,555. The Governor suggested reductions aggregating $76,530—being a reduction of the deficiencies to $72,024. He further recommended the application of the proceeds of the phosphate royalty (estimated at $40,000) to general expenses—thus reducing the deficiency to $32,024.

There was little regard paid to these suggestions, the act as passed (and approved by the Governor) showing only two changes—the Governor's contingent fund being fixed at $3,000 and the Attorney-General's at $8,000.

The appropriations were as follows: Executive department, $38,200; judicial department, $59,400; superintendent of lunatic asylum, $2,500; superintendent of penitentiary, $2,500; county auditors, $45,530; school commissioners, $32,200; health officers, $5,500; contingent funds, $19,000; election expenses (1874), $15,000; penitentiary, $40,000; lunatic asylum, $75,000; orphan ayslum, $15,000; Catawba Indians, $800; university, $43,250; normal school, $10,000; agricultural college, $10,000; public printing, $50,000; free schools, $330,000; portraits of Abraham Lincoln and Charles Sumner, $5,000; interest on State debt (estimated), $203,000. Added legislative expenses and the payment of "Bonanza" claims, the appropriations aggregated over $1,250,000.

A gratuity of $1,000 was voted to the speaker and $300 to the reading clerk of the House. The colored clergyman who had "gratuitously" opened the House proceedings with prayer received a "gratuity" of $300.

In the Senate an effort was made to award a "gratuity" of $500 to the colored clergyman who had performed the like service for that body, but after a considerable fight the resolution was defeated by a very close vote—13 to 12.

The contract for the public printing for two years, commencing November 28, 1874, was awarded to the Republican Printing Company at $50,000 per annum—that concern being the only bidder.

At this session the Legislature passed the usual supply act levying taxes for the support of the Government. This act made a levy of ten and one-half mills. Governor Chamberlain, on the reassembling of the Legislature in November, 1875, returned the act without his approval, showing by a careful statement of all conditions that a levy of nine and five-sixths mills was sufficient for all legitimate purposes.

During this session the Governor sent to the Senate a message in which he urged an improvement of the trial justice system by the appointment of competent and worthy men, and declared: "My determination is not to consent to the appointment of any man as trial justice whom I do not upon my conscience believe to be honest and capable." The Governor made several appointments from among the Conservatives. In some cases these appointments were rejected by the Senate.

A few weeks after sending this message Governor Chamberlain declared to H. V. Redfield, the well-known correspondent of the *Cincinnati Commercial,* that when at the end of Moses' administration he entered upon the duties of the executive office there were quite 200 trial justices who could neither read nor write the English language.

The following preamble and resolution offered by William E. Johnston, the negro Senator from Sumter, were adopted by both houses:

Whereas, by a so-called Republican gazette of this city, known as the *Union-Herald,* owned and controlled by certain State officials and edited by one James G. Thompson, a well-known enemy to Republicanism, an erroneous impression may go abroad that it is the desire of the majority of the people of the State that the Federal troops now stationed here should be removed; and

Whereas, the peaceful and law-abiding citizens of this State desire that no opportunity be given for domestic violence or bloodshed, and the presence of the Federal troops is a restraint to organized and disciplined conspirators and disturbers of the public peace; therefore be it

Resolved by the Senate, the House of Representatives concurring, That it is the sense of this General Assembly that the majority of the people of the State desire the presence of the Federal troops now here, and that they shall remain and continue to serve as conservators of the peace and the rights and liberties of peaceful citizens.

Mr. Thompson was an ardent supporter of Governor Chamberlain. Later in the session he incurred the displeasure of the House by declaring that the Governor by his veto of the original "Bonanza" bill had incurred the wrath of "the plunderers led by C. P. Leslie." By a resolution offered by Thomas Hamilton (colored) of Beaufort, the sergeant-at-arms was instructed to arrest Mr. Thompson and bring him before the bar of the House, there to be dealt with as the House might see proper. The speaker issued his warrant in due form and the offender was brought before the bar of the House.

C. P. Leslie moved that the accused be discharged.

A substitute (by Thomas A. Davis, colored, of Charleston) requiring that Thompson be committed to the Richland jail and there remain until he should have made a sufficient apology to the House was promptly rejected.

The Leslie resolution was then adopted and the editor was discharged from custody.

ELECTIONS IN JOINT ASSEMBLY.

In anticipation of the election of a judge to fill the vacancy caused by the death of Judge Graham in the first circuit there was a caucus of the Republican members of the Legislature, at which speeches were made by the candidates—Col. Jacob P. Reed, W. J. Whipper, and Elihu C. Baker, a lawyer from Massachusetts, who had lately settled in Darlington.

Governor Chamberlain, in his speech in the caucus, said: "There are three qualifications to be considered—first, the candidate must be a Republican; second, he must be a man of ability, qualified to fill the position; and, third, his character and integrity must be above suspicion." He urged the election of Colonel Reed, and declared that in point of ability and legal learning Whipper was not equal to the position. He further declared that there were some things in the transactions of the Sinking Fund Commission which Whipper (he being its chairman) should explain.

Whipper replied in a speech abusing the Governor, challenging him to prove his imputations as to the sinking fund transactions, and calling on the Republicans to disregard his dictation.

The caucus adjourned without declaring a choice.

The vote in joint assembly was as follows: Reed 105, Whipper 39, Baker 10, scattering 3. One white man voted for Whipper—Representative Lemuel L. Guffin, of Abbeville.

Judge Reed was a prominent lawyer of Anderson—a gentleman of high character and high standing. He had served for some years before Reconstruction as circuit solicitor, and in 1868 was the Democratic candidate for Congress from the third district against S. L. Hoge. He owed his election to the bench to the fact that in the campaign of 1874 he had declared his purpose to vote for Mr. Chamberlain against Judge Green.

There was a considerable contest over the judgeship of the third circuit, made vacant by the death of the Hon. John T. Green. The candidates presented were F. J. Moses, Jr., L. C. Northrop, W. J. Whipper, C. D. Melton and A. J. Shaw. On the first ballot the vote stood—Northrop 42, Shaw 42, Moses 36, Melton 9, Whipper 7, scattering 5. There were changes on the subsequent ballots, the vote on the sixth standing—Shaw 76, Northrop 58, Melton 2, scattering 1.

Mr. Archibald J. Shaw, thus elected to the circuit bench, was a native of Georgetown, where he practiced his profession for some years, afterwards removing to Marion. He had served one term as solicitor. He was a man of good mind, excellent judgment and studious habits. His course on the bench—ended by his death in 1878—was throughout creditable to him, satisfactory to all parties and honorable to the profession whose highest principles had been illustrated in the career of this capable lawyer and upright judge. He never affiliated with the Republican party.

To fill the vacancy caused by the resignation of Comptroller S. L. Hoge (elected to Congress) Senator T. C. Dunn, of Marlboro, was chosen on the first ballot—receiving 127 votes out of a total of 143. The election of Dunn was noteworthy because of the fact that in the campaign of 1874 he had been one of the leaders in the opposition to Mr. Chamberlain.

AFTER THE STATE TREASURER.

A special joint committee of the two houses, appointed to ascertain (1) what bonds and coupons had been funded under the Consolidation Act, and (2) whether the funds for the payment of the interest on such bonds had been kept separate and apart from all other funds, as required by that act, reported that certain coupons had been funded contrary to law and that the funds indicated had not been kept separate as provided by law.

The House, concurring in the report of the joint committee, further resolved that "a committee of five on the part of the House and three on the part of the Senate be appointed by the respective presiding officers to prepare an address to his Excellency the Governor, in accordance with Section 4, Article VII of the Constitution, demanding the removal of F. L. Cardozo from the office of State Treasurer, said address, when prepared, to be submitted to the two houses for final action."

The Senate having concurred, the joint committee was duly appointed.

The constitutional provision above mentioned is in these words: "For any wilful neglect of duty, or for any other reasonable cause which shall not be sufficient ground for impeachment, the Governor shall remove any executive or judicial officer on the address of two-thirds of each house of the General Assembly."

On March 10 the joint committee submitted in due form the address demanding the removal of the Treasurer. The charges and specifications were in substance as follows:

Charge I. Irregularity and misconduct in office.

Specification 1. In funding $978,500 of the hypothecated bonds, which were in the possession of persons not the actual owners thereof, which bonds were not lawfully issued and were, therefore, not legal obligations of the State.

Specification 2. That the Treasurer did, between June, 1874, and February, 1875, fund $241,071 of detached coupons which matured before July 1, 1871, when he had the means of knowing, and should have known, that the whole of the interest due on the bonds of the State up to that date had been paid, and that said coupons were not entitled to be funded.

Specification 3. That the Treasurer funded $196,485 of coupons which matured between April, 1869, and October, 1871, and which were detached from bonds of the State before and during the period of the hypothecation of the said bonds, and that he should have known that said coupons were the property of the State.

Specification 4. That the Treasurer funded $6,950 of coupons detached from bonds and which matured before the bonds themselves were issued from the State treasury.

Specification 5. That the Treasurer funded $69,205 of detached coupons which matured between January, 1870, and July, 1871, and the bonds from which they were detached having always been the property of the State, and still being in the possession of the State Treasurer, marked cancelled and unused.

Specification 6. Diversion of the interest fund, thereby defeating the intent of the funding act and endangering the security guaranteed to the creditors of the State.

Charge II. Wilful neglect of duty in failing to make monthly reports to the Comptroller-General of the cash transactions of his office, which neglect of duty dates from October 31, 1874.

The address concluded with a formal demand upon the Governor for the removal of the Treasurer.

The case was heard at length in joint assembly. The Treasurer was represented by prominent lawyers—William D. Porter, LeRoy F. Youmans and C. D. Melton—and all the points involved were exhaustively argued. The matter was also debated in House and Senate.

The Senate rejected the resolution by a vote of 19 to 11 and the House did the same by a vote of 63 to 45.

In the Senate all the Conservatives and in the House all but Messrs. R. G. Howard, Meetze and Muller voted against the resolution of removal.

Governor Chamberlain was heartily opposed to the effort to remove the Treasurer, saying that he had found nothing to shake his confidence in that officer's honesty, and declaring the movement the manifestation of a "conspiracy to knock down one of the strongest pillars of the present reform administration." He further expressed his belief, previously formed, that "any man that did his duty as Treasurer, who lent himself to no jobbery and had no private ends to serve, would make himself the most unpopular man in South Carolina."

After the Treasurer's acquittal the *Columbia Union-Herald*, the Governor's accredited organ, said:

The result is a distinct triumph for Governor Chamberlain. . . . The struggle has been really and distinctly a struggle between honesty and corruption, between an effort to restore good government on the one hand and an effort to perpetuate the disgraceful records of the Scott and Moses administrations on the other. It is now perfectly apparent that a large section of the Republican party regarded the platform and professions of the last campaign as mere baits to catch votes. All they wanted of Mr. Chamberlain was a respectable name to cover disreputable practices. They really wanted Frank Moses, minus his personal profligacy and debauchery. Official integrity, public duty, economy in expenditures, competency in officers, low taxes—all these things they neither desired nor intended to permit. . . . The plot was well laid and enticing. Under the guise of punishing official misconduct they sought really to introduce unbounded official profligacy. The cloak for a time concealed the assassin. The Conservatives were led to array themselves against the Treasurer and alongside the corruptionists, but the alliance was accidental and short-lived; and we say now, what we have not said in times before, that the Conservatives in the final vote have vindicated the purity of their motives and deserve the unqualified approval of all who uphold public morality. The blow aimed at Governor Chamberlain was parried by a combination of the true friends of reform.

SENATOR ANDREWS "VINDICATED."

The Senate having adopted a resolution appointing a committee to "investigate charges made against the Hon. T. C. Andrews, senator from the county of Orangeburg, in regard to his connection with the county treasurer, John L. Humbert, and the transactions in said county treasurer's office," the President appointed Robert Smalls, B. F. Whittemore, James M. Smith (of Barnwell), D. R. Duncan (Con.) and Thomas B. Jeter (Con.).

The evidence taken by this committee established a corrupt bargain between Andrews and the Republican county committee of Orangeburg for the appointment of Humbert, and a corrupt agreement between Humbert and Andrews that the latter should control the public moneys coming to the county treasurer. Humbert's willing subserviency to Andrews and their conspiracy to defraud the public were abundantly proven. It was shown that Andrews had said to Humbert's clerk, who had a key to the treasurer's safe, that Andrews had procured Humbert to pay different claims which were fraudulent; that Andrews had frequently taken money out of Humbert's cash drawer; that Andrews had advised Humbert to report to the State Treasurer—"Nothing received, nothing paid out"; that Humbert had, at the request of Andrews, marked certain taxes paid and charged the amount to Andrews; that Humbert had sent different sums, aggregating about $1,200, to Andrews while the latter was sitting in the Senate; and that Andrews had procured Humbert to cash a warrant for $6,000 given to Andrews by Frank Moses in part payment of the sum of $12,000 which Moses had agreed to pay Andrews for a controlling interest in the *Columbia Union-Herald*—the warrant afterwards proving worthless.

A majority of the committee (Senators Smalls, Duncan and Jeter) reported that the conduct of Andrews had been "highly improper and unbecoming a senator" and recommended that he be expelled. The minority (Senators Whittemore and James M. Smith) concurred in the judgment of the majority, but recommended that instead of expulsion a resolution of censure be passed by the Senate.

The committee having reported, Senator Duncan, of Spartanburg, offered a resolution that Andrews be expelled from his seat in the Senate—which was defeated by a vote of 19 to 12. No further action was taken and Andrews retained his seat.

The Legislature was in session from November 24, 1874, till March 26, 1875—having taken twenty days for the Christmas recess. There were passed 155 acts and forty-eight joint resolutions.

THE GOVERNOR COMMENDED.

The course of Governor Chamberlain in his relations to the Legislature just adjourned was heartily commended by numbers of the Conservative papers in South Carolina and by leading journals, without regard to politics, in other parts of the country. These papers united in the declaration that the Governor had sought to perform every promise and redeem every pledge that he had made in his campaign speeches, his inaugural and his messages. From the white people of South Carolina, whose sentiments the State press undoubtedly expressed, there was the assurance that the Governor's efforts towards the restoration of good government and honest administration would always command the hearty and active support of those people.

The Governor was the recipient of several invitations indicating the impressions he had made among the real citizenship—the representative people—of South Carolina. He was invited to attend the anniversary dinner of the New England Society of Charleston—an ancient organization of the highest standing. A like invitation (coupled, as in the former case, with the request to respond to the toast, "The State of South Carolina") was extended by the German Fusiliers of that city—one of the oldest military companies of the State and having on its roll the names of worthy citizens, among them several who had distinguished themselves in the State's service in war as well as in peace. The next call was from the literary societies of Erskine College—an invitation to deliver the address at the approaching commencement. In response to the request of the Barnwell County Agricultural Society the Governor delivered an address before that body. On the occasion of his visit to Charleston in November he was serenaded by the Republican clubs of the city and in response made to the large crowd assembled a speech which was warmly commended by the press. On the following day he was the guest of honor at a reception given by the Charleston Chamber of Commerce, whose membership embraced many of the business men of the city, including its prominent merchants and bankers. The Burns Club, a social and fraternal organization composed of worthy citizens of Columbia, invited the Governor to be present at its anniversary banquet and represent the State by responding to a toast. In December, 1875, he was invited by Dr. William H. Whitsitt, a professor in the Baptist Theological Seminary in Greenville, to visit that city and present the prizes to the successful contestants in an examination on the Greek language—in compliance with which request Governor Chamberlain delivered an address which was widely commended as the production of a finished scholar.

The Governor also delivered addresses at places without the State—before the law school of Yale College; at the centennial celebration of the battle of Lexington, and of the Mecklenburg declaration of independence—his utterances on such occasions being commended for their literary merit and for the sentiments of broad patriotism to which this Northern man representing a Southern State gave expression.

TROUBLE IN EDGEFIELD.

Early in January, 1875, there was a very serious disturbance in Edgefield County. Some weeks prior to the outbreak of the trouble Ned Tennant, the negro captain who, as already told, had surrendered his guns and disbanded his company, went with his men to the county seat and there received the same arms from Senator Lawrence Cain, who was then colonel in the "National Guard of South Carolina." The company returned home and at once resumed their nightly drills, accompanied with conduct well calculated to disturb and irritate the white population—to whom it was plain that the negroes, misled and influenced by bad leaders, meant mischief.

At a meeting of citizens held to consider the situation a committee was appointed to visit Governor Chamberlain, make known to him the trouble and ask that he require the negroes to return their guns to the State authorities. The Governor, after hearing the committee, stated his purpose to call in the guns, disband the militia companies in Edgefield and do all in his power not only to restore peace in the county but also remove the grievances which were said to have aggravated the situation in that county.

The committee visited the Governor on January 5, and his purposes were at once made known to the public.

On the night of the 13th the dwelling on the plantation of Gen. M. C. Butler was destroyed by fire—the inmates barely escaping. Suspicion pointing to a negro as the man who had applied the torch, he was after some trouble arrested by an officer, and he then confessed that he had set fire to the house, but declared that Ned Tennant had hired him to do the deed. A warrant was now issued by a trial justice for Tennant's arrest, and placed in the hands of a negro constable, who called to his aid a posse of his own race. This posse having been defied by Tennant, the constable asked help of General Butler, who, taking with him a few of his neighbors, proceeded in quest of Tennant. On their way the posse were fired on from ambush, and returned the fire—the negroes then retiring in disorder, their leader still defying the law. Gathering at another point, the negroes (bearing the guns that had been lately issued) patrolled the road and challenged travelers as they passed. The whites, determined that the trial justice's process should be executed and that Tennant's resistance thereto must cease, gathered quite a company, but in the meantime the negro captain and his followers had left the scene of trouble and, according to common report, had taken to the swamp. Tennant was soon after (about January 20) apprehended and committed to jail, and the disturbance was at an end.

On January 28 Governor Chamberlain issued his proclamation commanding all the militia companies in Edgefield County to disband and to deliver their arms, ammunition and equipments to Lawrence Cain, the regimental commander. The Governor further commanded "all military organizations now existing in said county, not forming a part of the State militia, nor sanctioned by the commander-in-chief, forthwith to disband and henceforth to cease from assembling, arming, drilling, parading or otherwise engaging in any military exercises." The Governor's commands obeyed, quiet was restored in Edgefield.

In his response to the statements of the committee of Edgefield citizens Governor Chamberlain had announced his purpose to "send a capable and responsible man to examine into this whole matter and into other matters of interest in the county." Upon this mission the Governor dispatched Judge Thomas J. Mackey.

Judge Mackey's report was submitted January 25. After reporting that Tennant, according to his own voluntary confession, had with an armed force resisted an officer acting under a lawful warrant issued for his arrest on the charge of arson and had fired on the posse duly summoned to aid that officer, and that Tennant had been duly committed to jail, the Judge asserted: "The sheriff of the county appears to be a worthy and inoffensive man; but his whole intelligence and sense of duty seem to have lapsed into a strong instinct of self-preservation—he being afraid to enter Meriwether township [the scene of the trouble] because the black people there didn't know him and the white people did know him."

Touching conditions in Edgefield County, Judge Mackey reported:

It is impracticable for me at present to present a full exhibit of the facts in regard to the condition of Edgefield County, which facts are of the gravest concern to the State and should be made known to your Excellency. They will be set forth in a future report when the pending examinations shall have terminated. Suffice it now to say that, in my deliberate judgment, no such iniquity as the county government of Edgefield has been inflicted upon any portion of the English-speaking race since the Saxon wore the iron collar of the Norman. In that case, however, the harsh domination was that of a superior civilization which elevated while it chastened. In this it is the reverse.

The condition of Edgefield presents a problem that demands an instant solution in the interest of the public peace and the due preservation of life and property. To this end, I earnestly recommend that your Excellency will forthwith issue and enforce an order withdrawing the State arms from the eight or ten militia companies now organized and equipped, and supplied with ammunition, in the county of Edgefield, with the view to have the said arms deposited in the State armory at the capital. During the past year the officials commanding several of the companies, to wit, Captains Edward Tennant, Bullock and others, have ordered the assembly to beat, and have called their companies to arms, to redress the real or fancied grievances of an individual member of a company in a personal quarrel with a white man. In the vicinity of Pine House, at a point about sixty-two miles from Columbia, in Edgefield County, Captain Bullock is located with some forty armed men of his company and their families, on a tract of land leased by Senator Lawrence Cain of that county, embracing only about sixty acres, and I am informed by a gentleman living in the vicinity that on last Friday and Saturday nights that company alarmed the neighborhood by beat of drums and the rapid and long-continued discharge of their firearms.

There are also several white rifle clubs in Edgefield County, which have been armed and equipped by their individual members as counter organizations to the militia. I therefore recommend that your Excellency will assume the attitude to require them to disband.

In addition to his formal report Judge Mackey made some public statements as to conditions in Edgefield—saying that the schemes of the county officials to plunder the taxpayers constituted "a vast system of larceny—a huge grand larceny"; that the board of county commissioners was composed of three negroes who were barely able to write their own names—Ned Tennant being a member; that the probate judge was a negro who was grossly incompetent; that the clerk of the circuit court, the school commissioner and the coroner—all negroes—were almost illiterate and disgracefully incompetent; that the sheriff (white) was an "honest and trustworthy man, with a disagreeable habit of appropriating the funds of judgment creditors to his own use, on the ground that the county has not paid him for dieting the prisoners under his charge;" that "any citizen who has done wrong to person or property, even the most violent and ultra Democrat, can obtain justice, provided he first makes satisfactory arrangements with the jury commissioner."

In a later statement Judge Mackey said:

The government of Edgefield has been for eight years a festering ulcer upon our body politic, and a diligent attempt is now being made to hide with the "bloody shirt" the appalling wrongs committed by the Republican party on the white population of that section. For example, there have been three county treasurers, all Republicans, appointed in Edgefield since 1868. The first, John Wooley, proved a defaulter to the amount of $25,000; the second, Eichelberger, in the sum of about $30,000, and the third, McDevitt, estimated at $40,000 or $50,000.

The government is wholly composed of negroes elected on the race issue, asserted even against white Republicans.

In the Senate resolutions (introduced by Lawrence Cain) were adopted which besought public sympathy for the "starving unfortunates of Edgefield" and directed that affairs in that county be investigated by a joint committee of the two branches of the General Assembly—the preamble setting forth that "a large number of people in the County of Edgefield are suffering for employment, and are without the necessary means of subsistence"; that "the condition of these people appeals to every instinct of humanity for relief"; that "the suffering and want is not the result of their indolence or improvidence, but the consequence of their adhesion to, and support of, Republican principles and their advocates"; that "their political belief and action has called down upon them 'the proscriptive policies' of the enemies of universal liberty, which have culminated in the driving of these people from their former homes, and refusing them employment, as well as in the formation of leagues against their further continuance as residents of the County of Edgefield."

In the House these resolutions were adopted and the joint committee was appointed. The committee having reported that the information sought had been furnished in official reports to the Governor, the "investigation" was not undertaken.

Paris Simkins, a representative from Edgefield, introduced a bill to "provide for the protection of certain laborers lately employed on farms in said county, and who have been discharged from such employment because of having exercised their political rights and privileges"—the author of the measure stating that in consequence of the recent troubles negroes in Edgefield had been discharged from employment and driven off the farms. The bill contemplated a tax of two mills on all the property of the county—the proceeds (about $8,000) to be distributed among the alleged victims of persecution. The measure was rejected.

It may be well to mention, in passing, that at the session of 1874-75 Simkins presented a claim for $628 for services on a committee appointed to examine the books of the Treasurer and the Comptroller-General, which claim was cut down to $375—the House evidently seeing that the excess over that amount was fraudulent.

FAILURE OF SOLOMON'S BANK.

In July, 1875, it was announced that Hardy Solomon's bank, called the "South Carolina Bank and Trust Company," had suspended payment and ceased to do business. This failure might well have been apprehended from the character of the bank's president, from his connection with numerous schemes to defraud the State, and from the notorious fact that the bank was sustained by the Republican ring simply as a means of furthering their peculations. The very statement of the so-called bank, published January 9, was calculated to warn prudent men that its solvency was at the best very questionable. The figures were as follows:

Resources—Charter, $25,000.00; furniture and fixtures, $2,659.23; bonds, $11,035.31; State claims, $23,664.17; coin, $265.69; expense, $1,265.07; due from banks and bankers, $24,789.70; loans and discounts, $203,027.95; cash, $82,100.43; total, $373,807.55.

Liabilities—Profit and loss, $13,764.22; capital stock, $105,963.00; bills payable, $60,000.00; individual deposits, $133,590.77; State treasury deposits, $11,220.19; certificates of deposits, $42,017.19; savings account, $1,553.63; interest, $243.36; due banks and bankers, $5,455.19; total, $373,807.55.

The asset item of $25,000 as the value of the bank's charter was never explained by Solomon. It was said, however, that John J. Patterson procured the charter at a cost of $5,000, this modest sum having been spent by him in getting through the Legislature the act of incorporation. The balance Honest John claimed as his reward for his services in the matter. The State claims were chiefly of most uncertain value—for Solomon had dealt largely in paper fraudulently issued by public officials.

When the so-called bank suspended, the State had on deposit $205,753.79. There were also deposits of county funds. The liabilities were stated at $368,455.06 and the assets at $314,960.24—an apparent deficit of $53,494.82. Between January 9 and July 2, the date of suspension, the State deposits had increased from $11,000 to the sum above stated, and the cash had entirely disappeared.

The affairs of the bank were settled in the courts. The State's loss by the "failure" was the entire amount of its deposit.

The action of the board of State officers in continuing to deposit public funds in Solomon's bank after it was reputed to be insolvent caused the Legislature to ask of Governor Chamberlain an explanation of the board's course. The Governor, after reviewing the case fully, stated that at their meeting on April 12 the board had directed the State Treasurer to make certain dispositions of the public moneys—to deposit $200,000 in the Solomon bank and allow the same to remain there until July 1. The Governor and the Comptroller-General voted for this resolution and the Treasurer against it. Of his action on this occasion the Governor made the following statement to the Legislature:

Nothing had occurred since January, 1875, which had diminished my confidence in the soundness of the South Carolina Bank and Trust Company. I am forced now to say that I find it impossible to understand from the statement of the condition of the bank, January 9, 1875, how the failure of the bank could have occurred July 3, 1875, except from positive fraud or mismanagement so gross as to be equivalent to fraud. Against such causes I know of no protection in the case of any bank, except in the moral character of those who manage it. Of course I do not hesitate to say that if I had known what is now known to the public I should without doubt have joined with Mr. Cardozo in regarding the South Carolina Bank and Trust Company as entirely unsafe as a depository of State funds. Mr. Cardozo's longer and more intimate acquaintance with the affairs of that bank seems now to have given him a knowledge of its condition and to have enabled him to form a judgment respecting its soundness, which was superior in correctness to the judgment of any other member of that board.

In his report to the Legislature Treasurer Cardozo, after stating that he had previously lost all confidence in the capacity or integrity of President Solomon (he being the sole owner of all the stock of the bank and therefore the sole manager of its affairs) and had communicated his opinion to the General Assembly, said:

The president of the bank had himself furnished the information upon which I based my opinion of the unsoundness of the bank. From a list of the "assets and liabilities" of the bank thus furnished I saw that the "liabilities," exclusive of the capital stock, exceeded the market value of the "assets" by about $50,000.

The amount of deposit of State funds at this time, January, 1875, was about $11,000. The board of deposit, consisting of the Governor, Comptroller-General and Treasurer, which has the designation of depositories and the regulation of the amount therein, authorized the deposits to be increased to $200,000 in April, and when the bank failed, July 2, 1875, there was $205,753.79 on deposit —$5,000 having been made as a special deposit for the payment of interest on the public debt in New York.

As soon as I was furnished with a statement of the "changes in assets and liabilities between January 9 and July 2, 1875," I saw that the "liabilities" had been paid to the extent of $181,585.48, and the "assets" had been increased only to the extent of $10,260.90. These sums could not account for the disposal of $347,951.72—the amount of the increase of the State Treasurer's deposit during the period referred to, the amount of "cash on hand" January 9, 1875, and the receipts from other sources. The difference was attempted to be accounted for, partially, by charging for the retirement of a large amount of the stock of the bank and a large amount of money alleged to have been expended in bribing the Legislature, under the head of "legislative expenses."

The subsequent developments, however, proved that these expenditures, which would be criminal, if true, could not possibly account for the expenditure of the money received since January 9, 1875, as they took place, according to the books of the bank themselves, prior to that period.

A statement of some of the bank's transactions showed that the "legislative expenses," from November 21, 1873, to March 6, 1874, were $81,105. The capital stock retired between January 13, 1872, and June 25, 1875, was $75,000—of which $40,000 was withdrawn within five months before the suspension. The "capital stock retired" represented $75,000 in money taken out of the bank's vault by Hardy Solomon himself.

There were some proceedings in court to have Solomon account, but they accomplished nothing.

EX-TREASURER PARKER IN COURT.

The constant charges brought by the opposition press against Republican officials had not been ignored by the Legislature. There were resolutions requiring investigation and some directing prosecution. Some county officials had been arraigned—with results as already related. At last, in July, 1875, one of the leaders in the schemes of peculation and robbery was brought into court—this proceeding being taken in accordance with a resolution of the Legislature.

At the special term of the Circuit Court for Richland (Judge R. B. Carpenter presiding) was tried the case of the State of South Carolina against Niles G. Parker—being a civil action to recover the sum of $250,000. The complaint alleged, and the State undertook to prove, that during the years 1869, 1870 and 1871 Parker, having paid coupons of valid bonds, left uncanceled such coupons to the amount of $450,000—preserving them in order to have them again presented and paid at the treasury. To conceal the non-cancellation of these valid coupons he cut from Conversion bonds in his possession coupons to the amount of $450,000, which, according to their dates, had already matured, which bore his engraved signature and which, under the law, required no further authentication. Of these latter coupons he substituted $450,000 for the genuine articles and then canceled according to law. The valid coupons which should have been canceled were afterwards presented at the State treasury and were duly funded in bonds under the provisions of the Consolidation Act—thus entailing a loss on the State of $225,000.

The trial of the case consumed ten days. The State was represented by Attorney-General Samuel W. Melton, assisted by James H. Rion, of Winnsboro, and the defendant's attorneys were C. D. Melton, LeRoy F. Youmans and Solomon L. Hoge, all of Columbia.

The jury found for the plaintiff $75,000—apparently a "compromise" verdict, intended to indicate that the coupons in question only $150,000 had been traced to Parker's possession.

In the report of the committee to investigate the transactions of the Sinking Fund Commission, it appeared that the sum of $28,100, funds arising from the sales of property of the State, had been turned over to Parker, as State Treasurer, by order of the Commission, and applied to other uses than those prescribed by law; and the Attorney-General was directed by the General Assembly to institute proceedings against the ex-Treasurer to recover this fund. Action was brought accordingly and Parker held to bail in $56,200.

By another concurrent resolution the Attorney-General was directed to bring suit against Parker for $25,000 for the embezzlement and fraudulent appropriation to his own use of certain certificates of indebtedness. By joint resolution of March 12, 1872, the Treasurer had been required to pay certain certificates of members and subordinate officers of the General Assembly, and had been authorized to borrow a sufficient amount for this purpose. The sum of $25,000 was thereupon borrowed from Hardy Solomon, the note of the Treasurer given therefor, and the fund thus procured applied in payment of certificates as required by the joint resolution. Instead of cancelling the certificates so paid, and filing them as vouchers, Parker had appropriated them to his own use, and, leaving the note unpaid and without entering a corresponding charge against himself, had taken credit for the whole amount upon the books of the treasury.

Parker had been committed to jail in the suit first started—that for $28,100—and there remained for some weeks. He got out of prison, but was recaptured and recommitted after an absence of about two weeks.

Three weeks after the trial of Parker he was brought before Judge T. J. Mackey, of the Sixth circuit, sitting in Columbia (Judge Carpenter being absent from the State), and released from custody—this on the ground that the order of arrest was "without authority of law and repugnant to the Constitution of this State." Immediately upon his release, Parker was served with the papers (including a warrant of arrest) in the case arising out of the misappropriation of $25,000 worth of certificates of indebtedness. Judge Mackey forthwith prohibited the sheriff from executing the order of arrest—and Parker went free. These orders of Judge Mackey were afterwards reviewed by the State Supreme Court—that tribunal holding them to have been without authority, null and void.

Parker was again arrested—this time on the criminal charge of breach of trust and larceny of the coupons involved in the verdict for $75,000. Taken before a trial justice (an incompetent white man), he was released on a bond of $2,000—the sureties being irresponsible and worthless.

Parker soon fled the State, and no further action was taken against him. The State took from him property worth at the time of the transaction about $15,000.

OTHER PROSECUTIONS.

In the campaign of 1874 the *Union-Herald* charged that James A. Bowley, of Georgetown, the black chairman of the House committee of ways and means, had been bribed by John B. Dennis, superintendent of the State penitentiary, to include in the appropriation bill an allowance of $80,000 for that institution—the specification being that Dennis had stipulated to pay Bowley one-sixteenth of whatever sum should be passed. The matter was first published in the *Union-Herald* in the campaign of 1874—Bowley being a supporter of Judge Green against Mr. Chamberlain. Judge Carpenter brought the matter to the attention of the Richland grand jury—of which it happened that L. Cass Carpenter, editor of the paper mentioned, was foreman. There was no presentment by that jury, and the matter went over to the February term, 1876.

On the trial, Dennis testified to his agreement to pay Bowley for reporting the appropriation, as above stated, and there was evidence of a written contract between the parties. The State Treasurer testified that Dennis had directed a certain portion of his salary to be paid to Bowley.

On the motion of the defendant, Judge Carpenter directed the jury to acquit—this on the ground that whereas the indictment charged that Bowley had been elected and had duly qualified as chairman of the committee and that the penitentiary appropriation had been referred to the same, the evidence showed (1) that Bowley had been appointed and had become chairman because his name was first on the list and (2) that the appropriation had been reported by the committee without previous reference. Thereupon the defendant was discharged.

Bowley was a native of Maryland, and went to Georgetown in March, 1867, as a showman in charge of a traveling panorama. Apparently liking the place, he concluded to stay. First engaged in teaching, he soon went into politics and easily rose to prominence among the negroes. He figured considerably in the frauds—having been more than once bribed by the Republican Printing Company.

At the previous term of this court Robert Smalls (senator from Beaufort) was tried on the charge of having counseled Josephus Woodruff, clerk of the Senate, and A. O. Jones, clerk of the House of Representatives, to commit a breach of trust with fraudulent intention—this by advising and procuring them to certify that a claim of Smalls for $2,250 had been passed and approved by the Senate and the House, by falsely representing to them that such claim had been provided for in the appropriation bill.

On the close of the evidence for the prosecution, Judge Carpenter directed a verdict of acquittal on the ground that the State had failed to make out any case against the accused.

JOSEPH CREWS SHOT.

On September 7, 1875, Joseph Crews, of Laurens, while riding in his buggy on the public highway leading to the county seat, was shot by parties in ambush, and so seriously wounded that he died a few days later. The Radical organs endeavored to give to this homicide a political coloring, but without any success. It was next sought to show that Crews had been killed by men who thus meant to avenge the death of Dr. E. E. Shell, who had in 1868 been killed by unknown parties.

One Thomas Canton, a white carpetbagger and a hanger-on at Republican headquarters in Columbia, was sent to Laurens to work up the case. After awhile he caused the arrest of Mr. G. Wash. Shell and his son—both citizens of the highest character and standing. These gentlemen were committed to jail, but were shortly released on bail. Other arrests followed. On the trial the State's evidence was so flimsy that upon it alone all the accused were promptly acquitted. The excuse for the corrupt endeavor to make a case against them was in the alleged statement of Joseph Crews, shortly before his death, that he believed that Mr. Shell the older had caused his death, in revenge for his supposed incitement of negroes to assassinate Dr. Shell.

Governor Chamberlain had offered a reward of $1,000 for the apprehension of the slayers of Crews. The Legislature by resolution approved that act and also authorized and requested the Governor forthwith to offer an additional reward of $3,000. A proclamation was issued accordingly.

Of the qualities which Crews exhibited in public and in private life the following statement (an editorial of Mr. Charles P. Pelham in the *Columbia Register*) is just, clear and strong:

Lying back of the chronic quarrels and embittered memories which might have broken out any time in bloodshed or instigated revenge, between Mr. Joseph Crews and his personal and political enemies in Laurens, was a deeper cause of trouble, danger and embarrassment to him as a public man. His position as such was anomalous. He was entirely out of place in having its powers and responsibilities to bear.

Joseph Crews was shrewd, but not of the kind of shrewdness which benefits one's fellow men. He had the milk of human kindness flowing in his veins, but it curdled at the slightest touch. He was generous to his friends and dependents, but his nature was essentially piratical. He created consternation on whatever sea he sailed his craft. The purposes, the objects, the inspiration of his life, were such as to bring him into conflict with the best and most stable interests of society. The men who sought to serve it, who if in public positions would place duty and obligation of trust above personal emoluments and advantage, he instinctively shrank from, disliked and, if need be, persecuted. Such a man was not fitted to take any conspicuous, honorable or just part in public affairs. He could only enter into combinations for mere gain. He had necessarily, as a matter of course, his sympathies and his antipathies, his spites and his ring proclivities to indulge in, all turning mainly upon their relations to his personal advantage. We are ready to believe, however, that even with such peculiar susceptibility to selfish influences and constitutional exemption from such as would qualify him for public usefulness, he was to a considerable extent the victim or football of circumstances. Had he not lived in an era of gross corruption, in such times as brought obscurity into notice, exalted chicanery and trickery into virtues and made public men out of the commonest and coarsest clay, he would have escaped undeserved notoriety, perhaps lived a better life and died a more peaceful death. Lifted into prominence only by party and to serve mere party and personal ends, he could never feel easy in any respectable society or enjoy the confidence of any respectable community. He was not in his place as a leader of men, and necessarily gravitated towards

CHAMBERLAIN'S ADMINISTRATION

acquiring ascendency by any means over the lowest and most ignorant classes, in order to secure a lever of control over the higher who repudiated him. He was consequently always in hot water. He had victims to immolate, enemies to punish, friends to raise up and reward at the expense of better men and at the cost of the public interests.

It is claimed for him that he was affectionate to his family, and ready and willing to lavish favors and kindnesses upon his friends. We can well believe it to be true. It is a great and redeeming virtue.

A FAMOUS LIBEL CASE.

Capt. F. W. Dawson, as editor of the *Charleston News* and afterwards as editor of the *News and Courier,* had been constant in his pursuit of Christopher C. Bowen, one of the organizers of the negroes upon the initiation of the Reconstruction measures in South Carolina. Bowen was a mischievous fellow who would stop at nothing in trying to accomplish his purposes—the chief of these being to get office and keep it under the new order of things. He was a member of the Constitutional Convention of 1868, and was afterwards sheriff of Charleston County. In this position, which gave him leadership in his party, his conduct and influence were always hostile to every interest of the people and tended frequently to incite the negroes to acts of violence upon the whites. The *News and Courier* fought him bitterly at every stage of his public life—denouncing him as personally depraved and politically infamous—charging him with bigamy, forgery, larceny and murder. Its attacks were constant, vigorous, effective—effective because their single motive was evidently the purpose to rid the community of a very bad man. In its pursuit of Bowen the *News and Courier* clearly had the sympathy of every reputable white citizen in South Carolina.

Bowen sought redress in court—causing the indictment of Captain Dawson and Mr. B. R. Riordan, the proprietors of the *News and Courier,* for libel. The particular libel alleged in the indictment was the publication of a story with the display heading—"The Murderer Bowen. True History of the Assassination of Colonel White." The story as published was a detailed account of the murder of Col. William Parker White in Georgetown, S. C., on March 7, 1864, by one Eli Grimes, at the instigation and by the procurement of C. C. Bowen. There had been other articles holding up Bowen as the coward who had, of his own malice, incited and procured another to commit a murder, to satisfy a private grudge. Captain Dawson was among the best editorial writers in the journalism of this country—and never did his pen do stronger work than in his presentations of Bowen as an assassin by nature and instinct, yet too much of a coward to execute his own bloody purposes. Incidental to the charge of murder there were frequent presentations of Bowen's other misdeeds—his bigamous marriage, his conviction therefor, his forgery of a furlough during the war, his doings as a faro dealer and, ever and anon, his conduct as a leader of a faction of the Republican party in the city of Charleston.

The prosecution was represented by Solicitor Buttz, assisted by D. T. Corbin, United States Attorney for South Carolina, and the counsel for the defense were James Conner, J. Barrett Cohen, H. A. M. Smith and William H. Brawley. The case, commencing April 19 and ending April 28, was by the fine tactics of the defense converted into a trial of Bowen for murder, forgery, bigamy and general rascality. The evidence was carefully brought out and the arguments for the defense so far surpassed the presentations of Bowen's lawyers as to make the latter show to decided disadvantage. Corbin was a rough fellow, having and caring to have few of the qualities or aspirations of a gentleman, whilst Buttz was an ill-trained pettifogger who had gotten into office by the choice of the negroes.

There was a mistrial—the jury (composed of seven white and five colored men) standing eleven for acquittal. The twelfth juror was one W. H. Ahrens, white, who was reputed to be a henchman of Bowen.

The *News and Courier* did not waver in its fight against Bowen. It continued its pursuit of him till his death in 1880 rid South Carolina of one of the very worst of the men whom negro rule made prominent or powerful.

THE LAST SESSION UNDER NEGRO RULE.

In his first message to the General Assembly when it reassembled on November 23, 1875, Governor Chamberlain congratulated that body on several facts—that out of a tax levy of $1,555,201.68 for the past fiscal year all had been paid except $12,519.47, being less than four-fifths of one per cent.; that legislative expenses and contingent funds had been greatly reduced; and that in other departments "great advances have been made during the past year towards a proper scale and measure."

The Governor informed the Legislature that the amount of bonds issued under the Consolidation Act was $3,618,290, leaving of the recognized debt $2,121,726 still unfunded; that the statement of the State census bureau that the population of the State was 923,447 (an increase of 216,841 over the United States census of 1870), presented "a result which will not bear examination," though the industrial statistics given "may be regarded as reasonably accurate"; that the duties of the Attorney-General "appear to have been performed with vigor and ability and with the best possible results to the State"; that the State Agricultural College and Mechanical Institute was "in a condition far from flourishing," owing to the want of funds—the Governor evidently referring to the fact that the bonds representing the sum donated by Congress for the maintenance of the school had been misappropriated by Parker or Kimpton or both; that the condition of the State University had been improved during the past year; that the lunatic asylum was still $34,514 in debt; that the past indebtedness of the penitentiary was $87,918.

The Governor recommended: That the legislative session be so curtailed that the appropriation for its expenses be brought within $120,000; that all payments to be made on account of legislative expenses, or claims passed by the General Assembly, be made by the State Treasurer upon warrants drawn by the Comptroller-General, for which the vouchers should be filed with the Comptroller-General; that for all necessary expenditures there should be adequate appropriations in order to avoid deficiencies—these having in the past fiscal year amounted to $308,872.15, including losses by the failure of Solomon's bank; that the matter of selecting depositories for State moneys be referred to a joint committee of the two houses to suggest the safest plan; that some scheme should be adopted whereby to settle the floating indebtedness of the State and also of the several counties; that the county commissioners be required to apportion the tax levy to the several objects of public expenditure.

The Governor further recommended that proper provision be made for the registration of electors, for the election of justices of the peace, and for minority representation; and that the powers of the State Board of Canvassers be more clearly defined.

The Governor summed up his suggestions as follows:

The measures which I deem most essential to the present welfare of the State are: First, the prompt passage of a supply act which shall impose the lightest possible burden of taxation; second, the enactment of a law which shall require all disbursements of public funds, except the interest on the public debt, to be made upon warrants of the Comptroller-General, issued upon vouchers approved by that officer and permanently recorded in his office; third, the keeping of all appropriations within the limits of the funds actually provided for by taxation; fourth, the immediate and large reduction of the scale of all public expenditures; fifth, the equitable adjustment of the floating indebtedness of the State upon a plan embracing the rigid scrutiny, by impartial agencies, of all claims, and the gradual payment by taxation of the valid claims; sixth, the inflexible observance of exact good faith respecting the public debt.

The Governor returned to the House, without his approval, the supply bill passed at the session of 1874-75 fixing the levy for State purposes at thirteen mills—pointing out that a smaller levy would suffice for all purposes. The veto was sustained.

The act to make appropriations for the payment of the per diem and mileage of the General Assembly appropriated $140,000, being $10,000 less than the sum allowed by the act passed at the previous session.

The general appropriation bill covered the following sums: Executive department, $57,500; judicial department, $57,300; auditors, $40,000; school commissioners, $32,200; health department, $7,500; penitentiary, $42,000; lunatic asylum, $67,500; orphan asylum, $10,000; institution for deaf and dumb and blind, $5,000; Catawba Indians, $800; university, $43,400; normal school, $15,000; agricultural college, $10,000; schools, $250,000; printing, $50,000; interest on public debt, $200,000 (estimated); sundries, $21,000; total, $893,200—that sum not including deficiencies or past indebtedness of any class.

The Governor had proposed changes which if effected would have reduced the aggregate appropriations by $240,000. His suggestions were almost wholly unheeded. At this session also he urged reductions which would bring the State tax, for all purposes, to eight or eight and one-half mills.

The act to raise supplies for the fiscal year commencing November 1, 1875 (taking the place of the act vetoed by the Governor) made the following levies: Salaries and contingents, one mill; penal and charitable institutions, one mill; schools, two mills; legislative expenses, one and one-tenth mills; printing, one-half mill; interest, two mills; deficiencies, one and nine-tenths mills; total, nine and one-half mills. Added the levies for deficiencies provided for in special acts, the total levy for State purposes was eleven mills.

This supply act conformed very nearly to the estimates and suggestions of Governor Chamberlain in his message disapproving the previous act.

The county levies ranged from two to five mills.

Doubts having arisen as to the validity of the act (noted in a previous chapter) "to provide for the settlement and redemption of certain claims against the State," the General Assembly at this session passed two measures intended to provide for the floating indebtedness.

By an "act to provide for the payment of certain indebtedness of the State" (December 24, 1875) there was levied an annual tax of one mill for three years, commencing November 1, 1875, from the proceeds of which was to be paid certain past indebtedness of the State, amounting to about $500,000. This measure was known as the "Big Bonanza."

By the new "act to provide for the settlement and payment of certain claims against the State" (approved December 24, 1875), the Governor was required to appoint three commissioners to constitute a commission on claims, who were authorized to audit as adjusted claims against the State all demands founded upon legislative pay certificates or State Treasurer's due bills. To the holders of claims so audited the act authorized the payment of one-half of their face, in four equal annual instalments, the first payable out of the taxes for the fiscal year commencing November 1, 1875. The aggregate sum to be certified and liquidated under this act was limited to $500,000, and for effecting its purposes there was levied an annual tax of one-half of one mill. The measure was known as the "Little Bonanza."

By these two acts the State undertook to pay in full a debt approximately $500,000 and to pay one-half of a debt approximately the same amount—so that the Legislature apparently acknowledged that the valid floating debt of the State was at least $1,000,000.

The act (March 13, 1872) levying a special tax to provide for the families of persons alleged to have been killed "because of their political opinions" was repealed so far as it included Chesterfield

County—but no provision was made for refunding the amounts that had been wrongfully exacted.

By an "act to fix the salaries of certain public officers" the pay of certain officers in the executive department was reduced about 30 per cent., and that of certain county officers about 10 per cent.

A slight change was made in the composition of the Congressional districts—Lexington being transferred from the second to the third.

The Constitutional amendment reducing the term of all State officers to two years was ratified.

The Legislature proposed an amendment requiring the commissioners of each county to levy an annual tax of two mills, of which the proceeds should be applicable solely to the support of public schools in the county.

A concurrent resolution provided for an investigation into the affairs of the Solomon bank and the causes of its failure.

The committee appointed under this resolution made a lengthy report, which was but a detailed presentation of the main facts already given in this chapter. The report alleged the falsification of the bank's books, the appropriation of its cash by Solomon, the publication of false statements and the fraudulent retirement of capital stock. The committee charged Treasurer Cardozo with "acts not only officially irregular but criminally dishonest and corrupt"—specifying his wrongful application of public funds to the payment of Solomon's claims.

A special committee of the House reported that there had been numerous irregularities and some frauds in the transactions of the land commission under the management of C. P. Leslie.

The House voted a "gratuity" of $1,200 to the speaker, $350 to the reading clerk and $200 to the colored clergyman who opened its proceedings with prayer. The speaker, of course, received his salary of $600 as a member, and the reading clerk his $6 per diem.

In the early part of the session Mr. J. K. Blackman, the correspondent of the *News and Courier,* was by resolution (offered by Paris Simkins) excluded from the privileges of the House—this because, in the words of the preamble, he "fails to treat the members of the House with the respect which is due them as representatives of the people, and abuses the privileges extended him by sending to the said paper misstatements and groundless insinuations unworthy of an honest chronicler of events."

Mr. Blackman's offense lay in his course in sending to his paper truthful and therefore scathing accounts of the conduct of certain members of the Legislature in resisting reforms and promoting schemes of plunder.

The Legislature was in session till April 14—having passed 203 bills and thirty-three joint resolutions.

The House committee on privileges and elections was charged with investigating certain published statements reflecting upon the action of the text-book commission in relation to the selection of books for the common schools, and more especially the charges of corrupt conduct publicly made against J. Douglass Robertson, a member of the commission and also a representative from Beaufort County.

The committee, after taking much testimony and hearing Robertson in his defense, reported that he had while a member of the House and of the text-book commission made to certain book publishers propositions discreditable and corrupt, and that his conduct could "only be regarded as a betrayal of a high and sacred trust."

The committee recommended that Robertson be expelled from the House and be displaced as a member of the text-book commission. He was expelled by a vote of 56 to 25.

Robertson had proposed, in behalf of the State, to make a contract with such houses as would join him, by which the State would be bound for ten years to the adoption of such of their books as the commission should select. The consideration for this was that these houses should appoint his brother-in-law as the sole distributing agent for their publications, and that a central depot should be established, say at Columbia, in charge of this brother-in-law, where the books would be sent on commission, and that the brother-in-law should get a percentage on all the books distributed from this depository. Robertson himself said he would be chosen State Superintendent of Education at the next election, and that he would then use the influence of his office to force the books into the schools. He further stated that he would need some money to procure the cooperation of the other members of the board.

The publishers to whom these corrupt proposals were made rejected them promptly and took steps to expose Robertson's conduct.

CHARGES AGAINST JUDGES.

The House having charged Judge Montgomery Moses of the Seventh circuit with official misconduct, he was formally impeached for "high crimes and misdemeanors"—the trial before the Senate commencing March 8 and continuing through March 14, the Senate meantime transacting its regular business.

On the close of the case for the prosecution the counsel for the accused asked that further proceedings be postponed till March 20—this on the ground that the testimony for the defense could not be procured in shorter time.

This request being refused, the lawyers representing Judge Moses withdrew from the case and presented a communication setting forth the reasons for their action. They stated that the charges were vague and indefinite, that witnesses were allowed to testify to matters not sufficiently stated in the articles of impeachment, that counsel's ideas of law and practice were deemed erroneous, that the ordinary rules of evidence were disregarded, and that there were "other unfavorable manifestations." The statement continued:

We are therefore compelled to leave the case with your honorable body as it now is—the respondent, though protesting his innocence and his ability to prove it were sufficient opportunity allowed, yet undefended.

And we do this because the various rulings of the court thus far in this trial have forced upon us the painful conclusion that we have been mistaken in supposing that we were before a court constituted to "do impartial justice according to the Constitution and the laws," and restricted to judicial functions as distinguished from a legislative or political body. The several oaths of each membei, the words of which we have repeated, warranted us in this belief and inspired us in the hope that the respondent would have on his trial the application and protection of well-settled rules of law and established modes of procedure. We feel, and we say upon our professional knowledge, that in our opinion he has been deprived of them, and if he shall be the victim and suffer, the law will not, as we understand it, be administered, but will be, however unintentionally, subverted in the manner of his conviction.

The lawyers who were thus impelled to withdraw from the defense of their client were Messrs. Y. J. Pope, Silas Johnstone and James M. Baxter, of Newberry; James B. Campbell, of Charleston; LeRoy F. Youmans, of Columbia, and James H. Rion, of Winnsboro.

Judge Moses was found guilty and was removed accordingly. It was claimed by his friends that he had incurred the displeasure of some of the Republican leaders by refusing to order the deposit of litigants' funds in Hardy Solomon's bank. Whatever the merits of the case, it must be said that some of the men who pursued him were themselves so manifestly corrupt that they might fairly have been suspected of ulterior motives.

In Judge Moses' place the Governor appointed Mr. L. C. Northrop, of Charleston, lately resident in Columbia—a man of small abilities and little legal knowledge. His chief claim to preferment lay in the fact that he was a member of the governing board of the State University when that body formally declared their approval of mixing whites and negroes in the student body upon terms of actual social equality.

Mr. Northrop had been elected to succeed Judge Moses upon the expiration of the latter's term in August, 1876.

Complaints were made to the Legislature of the conduct of Judge Thomas J. Mackey, of the Sixth circuit, but no action was taken. It was clear that Judge Mackey's conduct on the bench had been often arbitrary and sometimes grossly improper, but it happened that some of his accusers were men of his own party in Chester, whom he had pursued because of their dishonest transactions in public office. It was thought by many who had no feeling for Judge Mackey himself that to arraign him might have the appearance of sympathy with bad men, and he thus escaped inquiry into the matters charged against him. One of these deserves mention—a complaint made by a committee of the grand jury of Lancaster.

The grand jury at the spring term, 1876, having returned "no bill" in a certain case, the Judge "became intensely enraged and assailed the grand jury with rude, indecent and opprobrious language and, in contempt of the laws of the land and of their rights and privileges as jurors and in an angry and peremptory manner, ordered their discharge before they had completed or had time to complete the performance of the duties devolving upon them—thus arbitrarily obstructing the free course of the law, to the manifest injury and oppression of all the citizens of the county of Lancaster." It was further shown that Judge Mackey had brought before him two witnesses who had testified before the grand jury and had them tell in open court what they had told in the jury room.

At the succeeding term of court Judge Mackey made a complete apology to the grand jury, saying that in his unpardonable haste he had used language and taken action which neither his heart nor his judgment could now approve.

A House committee appointed to "inquire into and make full examination of all matters pertaining to the official conduct of the Hon. J. P. Reed, judge of the first circuit," reported that they had taken evidence accordingly and that there was no ground for the charges made. The report was unanimously adopted.

WHIPPER AND MOSES FOR THE BENCH.

On December 16, 1875, the two houses met in joint assembly to elect circuit judges. Those chosen were: First circuit, W. J. Whipper; Second, Pierce L. Wiggin; Third, Franklin J. Moses, Jr.—the incumbents (except Montgomery Moses) being reelected in the other circuits.

Whipper received 83 votes out of 142 and Moses 70 out of 139.

The white men who voted for Whipper were—Senators Thad. C. Andrews, of Orangeburg; John R. Cochran, of Anderson; Jerry Hollinshead, of Abbeville; Y. J. P. Owens, of Laurens; James M. Smith, of Barnwell; Representatives Joel Copes, of Fairfield; Lemuel Guffin, of Abbeville; C. P. Leslie, of Barnwell; J. D. Robertson, of Beaufort.

The white men who voted for Moses were—Senators Thad. C. Andrews, of Orangeburg; H. C. Corwin, of Newberry; Jerry Hollinshead, of Abbeville; Y. J. P. Owens, of Laurens; James M. Smith, of Barnwell; B. F. Whittemore, of Darlington.

Whipper was at this time a member of the House.

The election of Whipper and Moses caused widespread indignation and disgust. Governor Chamberlain declared it "a horrible disaster—a disaster equally great to the State and to the Republican party—a calamity infinitely greater than any which has yet fallen on this State or upon any part of the South." He further said: "Neither Whipper nor Moses has any qualities which approach to a qualification for judicial positions. The reputation of Moses is covered deep with charges, which are believed by all who are familiar with the facts, of corruption, bribery and the utter prostitution of all his official powers to the worst possible purposes."

A few days after the election the Governor, having to decline an invitation of the New England Society of Charleston, wrote: "I cannot attend your supper tonight; but if there ever was an hour when the spirit of the Puritans, the spirit of undying, unconquerable enmity and defiance to wrong ought to animate their sons, it is this hour, here in South Carolina. The civilization of the Puritan and the Cavalier, of the Roundhead and the Huguenot, is in peril."

In a letter to President Grant the Governor said: "Unless the universal opinion of all who are familiar with his career is mistaken, he [Moses] is as infamous a character as ever in any age disgraced and prostituted public position. The character of W. J. Whipper, according to my belief and the belief of all good men in the State, so far as I am informed, differs from that of Moses only in the extent to which opportunity has allowed him to exhibit it. The election of these two men to judicial office sends a thrill of horror through the State. It compels men of all parties who respect decency, virtue or civilization to utter their loudest protests against the outrage of their election."

Writing to Senator Oliver P. Morton, of Indiana, who had characterized Governor Chamberlain's attitude as "in practical identification with the Democrats" and as having already given up the State to the opposition, the Governor said: "Unless the universal belief among all classses of people in this State is mistaken he [Moses] is as infamous a character as ever in any age disgraced and prostituted public position. . . . Of Whipper it can be said that he seems to have lacked only opportunity to prove himself the equal of Moses in infamy. Ignorant of law, ignorant of morals, a gambler by open practice, an embezzler of public funds, he is as unfit for judicial position as any man whom by any possibility you could name. . . . Their election has sent a thrill of horror through the whole State."

Of Wiggin the universal opinion was that though incompetent he could not be classed with Whipper or Moses. As already stated, he was in 1872 elected solicitor of the Second circuit. He has been a lawyer of little note and, as his career on the bench plainly showed, was but poorly qualified for the judgeship. He was never thought to be corrupt.

Governor Chamberlain declined to sign the commissions of Whipper and Moses—taking the ground that the election of Judges Reed and Shaw, at the preceding session of the Legislature, was in law an election for the full term of four years. He formally commissioned those two judges for full terms. His position was afterwards sustained by the Supreme Court in a case brought by Whipper against Judge Reed for the possession of the office.

The election of Whipper and Moses was widely noticed and universally condemned. The press of the State, seconded by leading papers all over the country, denounced the act as outrageous and infamous. Public meetings were held in many counties of the State to give expression to the feelings and purposes of the people. Resolutions were adopted condemning the corrupt majority in the Legislature, thanking Governor Chamberlain for the stand he had taken and assuring him of unvarying support.

In Charleston, where Whipper was first to hold court, there was a meeting attended by citizens representing every interest. Several speeches were made. Resolutions were adopted, protesting against the election of Whipper and Moses and declaring the purpose to resist their accession to the end. Governor Chamberlain was assured of support in his action in refusing to commission.

Among the speeches made was one by Mr. B. C. Pressley, a prominent lawyer well advanced in years (afterwards a distinguished judge of the Circuit Court), the conclusion of which was in these words:

I tell you that we have drunk the last drop of the bitter cup that we intend to drink, unless the United States army says so. I thought we had taken enough already before Whipper and Moses were elected to be our judges. So, fellow citizens, Governor Chamberlain may go to sleep and sleep soundly—for they don't dare to touch a hair of his head, because the people are awake and they are not going to sleep again. The time has come for action! There must be no mental reservation when we say we will stand by Governor Chamberlain. We mean it as our fathers meant it when they pledged their lives, their fortunes and their sacred honor; and I see by your responses and in your faces that this is what you all mean by it. Stand up for your civilization, your property, your lives and your honor!

The applause which followed this speech showed that the audience—and the white people of Charleston—intended that, come what might, the black judge Whipper should not hold court in that county.

It was resolved that to carry into effect the resolutions previously passed the chairman should appoint a committee of fifteen citizens, who should thoroughly organize Charleston County for the attainment of the ends proposed.

In Sumter (one of the counties in the circuit for which Moses was elected) a large body of representative citizens assembled in the courthouse. Col. Thomas B. Fraser, a lawyer of high standing and a gentleman who was noted as well for his moderation as for his exemplary life, upon being called to preside, said:

It is one of the purposes of this meeting to announce that F. J. Moses, Jr., shall never take a seat as a judge in our courthouse, unless placed there by Federal bayonets.

Resolutions denouncing the election of Whipper and Moses, approving the action of the Governor and declaring the purpose to resist by all lawful means the accession of Moses to the bench, were enthusiastically adopted.

Speeches were made by several representative citizens. The concluding sentence of that of Mr. Charles H. Moise was as follows:

Should F. J. Moses, Jr., by any legal trickery attempt to ascend the steps of the courthouse to take his seat as judge, I, Charles H. Moise, forty-six years of age, with a wife and ten children to support, am ready to unite with a band of determined men and with muskets on our shoulders defend that temple of justice from such a desecration.

The temper and purposes of the meeting were evidenced by the heartiness of the applause with which this declaration was received.

In Barnwell the mass meeting was presided over by Gen. Johnson Hagood. The principal speech was made by Judge A. P. Aldrich, who said:

I say to you, as I have said to Governor Chamberlain, that I cannot withhold the expression of my thanks for the patriotism and manhood he has displayed in the rebuke administered to the Legislature for their outrage against virtue, decency and justice in the election of these judges. You all know Maher; he was born here in this village of virtuous parents, raised in our midst, accepted this office at the solicitation of the Republican party who elected him, has been true to his education and instincts, has made a judge of whom we and they are proud, and because he has administered the law without fear or favor or partiality his place has been supplied by Wiggin! You all know Wiggin so well that I need not increase your disgust by dwelling on his incompetency. I say this reluctantly, for the creature has the good quality of amiability; but he proves, as every lawyer in this circuit knows, his utter unfitness for the office. . . .

I cannot contemplate this stupendous outrage without horror and dismay. . . . The Governor has disposed of Moses and Whipper—let us see that Wiggin makes a graceful retreat. . . . I am perfectly satisfied that if these men attempt to preside in these three circuits it will be a deliberate act of suicide.

Mr. Alfred Aldrich offered resolutions (which were adopted) warmly commending the course of Governor Chamberlain "from his inaugural address to his last veto," particularly his action in refusing to commission Whipper and Moses, and assuring him of "cordial support in his efforts to redeem his pledges and effect reforms."

A resolution was also adopted urging Wiggin to decline the judgeship in order that the Legislature might at the present session elect some person fit for the place. It was further

Resolved, That we heartily endorse Governor Chamberlain in his efforts to redeem the State from plunder and degradation, and while he has been faithful to his own party he has also been faithful to ours, and we hereby pledge ourselves to stand by and support him promptly, faithfully, fearlessly and defiantly.

As the beginning of the term for which Whipper claimed to have been elected approached there were rumors that he intended to enter by force upon the duties of the judgeship. On August 21 Governor Chamberlain issued his proclamation warning Whipper against such attempt, also warning all citizens against abetting his alleged design and calling upon the officers of the law in the First circuit to sustain the authority and execute the orders of Judge Reed.

For any use of force to which Whipper might have resorted the white citizens of Charleston had made due preparation; and any such attempt by him, or by a mob acting in his behalf, would have been promptly thwarted and severely punished by those citizens acting of themselves.

Wiggin qualified upon the expiration of Judge Maher's term.

THE EXTENT OF REPUBLICAN REFORM.

The administration of Governor Chamberlain may be said to have ended with the close of the legislative session of 1875-76. His actions thereafter had little relation to the reforms which, demanded on all sides, had been promised by him and his party. The political campaign of 1876 had in a sense begun before the adjournment, and most of the issues between the Republican party and its opponents in the struggle for supremacy had already been made up. It is proper, therefore, to judge that party's work commencing with the Governor's inauguration by what had been accomplished when the session of 1875-76 ended.

Perhaps the strongest presentation ever made of Governor Chamberlain's efforts and their fruits was contained in a series of editorials in the *News and Courier* (July, 1876) in which that paper gave some of its reasons for its judgment that the Democratic party of South Carolina should make no nomination for Governor if he should be the Republican candidate. Summing up, the *News and Courier* undertook to show that despite the opposition of the extreme Radicals in the Legislature Governor Chamberlain had accomplished results creditable to him and of great advantage to all public interests—the specifications being as follows:

The character of the officers of the Government, appointed by the Executive, has been improved and the sureties upon the bonds of public officers have been required to make affidavit of their ability to meet the liability they assume.

The settlement of the public debt has been maintained unchallenged, and faith with the public creditor, so far as dependent on executive and legislative action, has been fully kept.

The effort to place the whole of the public funds in two banks of small capital was frustrated, and the State so saved from the danger of far greater loss than was sustained by the failure of the Solomon bank.

The floating indebtedness of the State has been provided for in such a way that the recognized and valid claims are scaled to one half the amount, and their payment is distributed over a term of four years, resulting in a saving to the State of at least $400,000.

The tax laws have been amended so as to secure substantial uniformity and equality in the assessment of property for taxation.

The contingent funds of the executive department have been so reduced in amount that the savings in two years, upon the basis of the average of six previous years, is $101,260.

Legislative expenses, in like manner and upon a similar basis, have been so reduced as to save the people in two years $350,810.

Legislative contingent expenses in the same way have been so reduced as to save to the State $355,000.

In the expenditure of contingent funds accountability and publicity have been secured.

The cost of public printing has been reduced from an annual average of $306,209 to $50,000, saving in two years $512,418.

The salaries of public officers have been reduced $30,000 a year.

The tax levy for the current year for State purposes has been reduced from 13½ mills to 11 mills, a saving to the people of $300,000.

The deficiencies (including the losses by the Solomon bank) are for the year 1874-75 $308,872, which is $291,024 less than the deficiencies of 1872-73 and $233,315 less than the deficiencies of 1873-74.

Under the several heads the savings that have actually been made are:

In the bonanza bills	$400,000
In the executive contingent fund	101,260
In legislative expenses	350,810
In contingent expenses	355,000
In public printing	512,418
Total	$1,719,488

The *News and Courier* went on to say: "To realize this amount would require a tax of nearly one and a half per cent. Had the appropriations of the past two years been so inordinate as the average of the appropriations and expenditures of the preceding years, the State taxes of the past two years would have been three-fourths per cent. per year more than the outrageous rate already levied."

Attention was also called to Governor Chamberlain's careful exercise of the pardoning power—the records showing that whilst Scott had issued 579 pardons in four years and Moses 457 in two years, the incumbent had in eighteen months issued only seventy-three.

Against this showing, the very strongest that could be made for Governor Chamberlain, it must be noted that in several matters of gravest importance no attention had been paid to his recommendations, though seconded by the press of the State, by the Taxpayers' Convention and by several prominent citizens of moderate views on all public questions. Among these may be mentioned the proposed system of minority representation, the election of justices of the peace and constables by the people, and the registration of electors.

The Legislature had been controlled, whenever control was really in question, by the worst elements in the Republican party—by the men who united to elect Whipper and Moses to the bench. The legislative sessions had been drawn out to great length and legislative expenses, though greatly reduced, continued at figures that were extravagant in the extreme. The trial justice system, though somewhat improved, was still seriously infected with the incapacity and

CHAMBERLAIN'S ADMINISTRATION

dishonesty which were its distinctive characteristics under the Scott and Moses administrations.

The school system was still grossly inefficient. There was yet due to teachers over $185,000 for services already rendered, whilst the number of fraudulent pay certificates issued by irresponsible school boards was unknown. The University was still a mixed school for whites and blacks, upon which large sums were annually spent in paying professors for giving college education which in the cases of a majority of the students was pretensive only. The Agricultural College was still suffering from the fraudulent diversion of the bonds given by Congress for its support.

The funding of the State debt under the Consolidation Act had progressed but unsatisfactorily, and there was general complaint that under its operation the honest holder of an ante-bellum bond must take his chances with the holder of bonds evidently tainted with fraud.

The floating debt of the State continued unpaid and largely unadjusted. The total of this debt was found in 1877 to be $1,046,929, including about $400,000 which had been funded under the "Big Bonanza" and "Little Bonanza." For the outstanding bills of the Bank of the State of South Carolina, amounting to $739,179, no provision had been made.

The amount due the State by defaulting treasurers in different counties was over $500,000.

Most of the counties were still seriously in debt.

The efforts to punish the men who had engaged in the schemes by which the people had been robbed had come to nought.

The tax levy had not been reduced—as will be seen from the following statement of the levies made for the different fiscal years since the State Government passed under the control of the negro:

Year commencing November 1, 1869, 5 mills.
Year commencing November 1, 1870, 9 mills.
Year commencing November 1, 1871, 7 mills.
Year commencing November 1, 1872, 12 mills.
Year commencing November 1, 1873, 12 mills.
Year commencing November 1, 1874, 10 3-8 mills.
Year commencing November 1, 1875, 11 mills.

The levy for the year commencing November 1, 1876, made by the Democratic Legislature in 1877, was seven mills.

The domination of the negro continued—disguised though it was as the rule of the Republican party. Confidence in that party as organized and influenced had been totally destroyed—this by the manifest disinclination of the majority in the Legislature to reduce expenses and their evident purpose to set their schemes above the rights of the minority. The election of Whipper and Moses was but the outburst of a feeling that really controlled every Republican member of that body.

The white race in South Carolina, their property, their liberties, their opportunities in life, lay at the mercy of an ignorant majority under the leadership of corrupt men.

THE LEGISLATURE AND ITS WORK.

From the accounts already given of the doings of the General Assembly of South Carolina some idea may have been gathered of the general character and the significant methods of the body. A brief account of their manner of transacting their part of the public business may be interesting.

Each house met at 12, noon, and the session rarely lasted more than three hours. Any suggestion that the hour of meeting should be advanced or that the session should be prolonged was met by the statement that to do either would interfere so much with the work of the standing committees that there would be no economy of time, whilst the efficiency of the committees would be seriously impaired. The time consumed in debating this matter (which was brought up at every session for six years) tended, of course, to increase the number of days for which the legislators were paid.

One device of the members was the making of various questions—of privilege, of order, of information, of every kind which these mimic parliamentarians had learned to employ. The members who thus sought to consume time and also advertise themselves really knew enough only of the rules to enable them to make these different points. In numerous instances the ayes and noes were demanded on the vote upon these non-legislative matters—this, of course, consuming time in order to prolong the session.

The demand of the ayes and noes was carried to flagrant excess in both Senate and House—the facility for using this device being shown in the fact that the demand of one member needed to be seconded by one other only. The vicious and actually corrupt excess to which this proceeding was carried was shown in the House debate on the resolution ostensibly looking to the investigation of the bills presented for furnishing the legislative halls. Upon the first question made the roll call was demanded, and it was repeated so that for two hours or more the House voted by ayes and noes upon matters nowise germane to that question. On this occasion the dilatory tactics appeared to be in the hands of W. J. Whipper and Benjamin Byas, a mulatto member from Orangeburg. On every question announced Byas would say: "Mr. Speaker, I call the ayes and noes." "Second the call," said Whipper, keeping his seat and occasionally turning his eyes to right or left to get the approving glance of some member. For days this procedure continued until, as already related, the resolution was defeated.

In minor matters—an immaterial amendment—the change of names in the list of corporators in a bill to form some company— some local measure manifestly foredoomed to defeat—the motion to adjourn or to take a recess—the various parliamentary devices to sidetrack a bill or smother a resolution—the call of the roll in both Senate and House was carried to an excess which, corrupt purposes not imputed, involved criminal waste of the public money.

Discussions were prolonged to absurd lengths—sometimes with the actual purpose to kill time, but frequently because of the maudlin incapacity of some of the speakers. Ben Byas, for example, was more than once known to talk an hour upon a single matter—indeed, one of his speeches against the impeachment of Governor Scott consumed quite two hours. Having the floor he could keep it unless he should yield—and yield he would not. This particular speech was a mixture of ignorance and insolence, without even the appearance of thought or the semblance of argument. Byas was a burly fellow with a hard face, ignorant, insolent, vindictive and corrupt—whose presence in the Legislature was a continuing outrage upon the white race in South Carolina and equally a disgrace to the Republican party everywhere.

There were some good speakers among the negroes—their imitative faculty enabling them, even though lacking the knowledge to read well or to write anything but their own names, to make speeches that really sounded well and, truth to tell, were marked by few faults of grammar and fewer still of style. One striking case, under the writer's personal notice, will serve to illustrate conditions in this particular obtaining in every county—an illustration also of the quasi-oratorical powers of the well-developed negro. Andrew B. Stewart was a leader in his neighborhood in Fairfield County. Of a height a little above medium, a fine figure, with a complexion almost jet black, a well-formed head which was kept nicely cropped, a set of teeth that might well have excited the envy of some Adonis of the white race, a rather shapely hand, and a foot a little unlike the ordinary negro's, Andy had also a voice of unusual power with no harshness, which he had always under excellent control. His language was homely but rarely ungrammatical, his expression at every stage most admirable, his gestures natural, graceful, timely—though the ideas given out betrayed both his want of education (he was well-nigh illiterate) and his totally untrained mind. He had little sense of right, rose to local prominence only, and never went to the Legislature—though, truth to tell, he was in all things the equal of most of the colored men who represented his county in either branch of that body.

The Rev. H. H. Hunter, a member from Charleston, at the session of 1870-71 made a most excellent speech against Whipper's proposition to send State troops (meaning negroes) to restore peace in Union County—a speech full of good counsel to his race and of the desire for peace and justice, coupled with a respectful demand upon the white people to do their part. The speaker's English was really excellent, his sentences well constructed and very rarely broken in the haste of utterance, his cadences well done and his pauses so well distributed that the emphasis given to his main propositions was very striking, whilst his approach to the climax of his appeal was as smooth as the appeal itself was actually powerful. Yet this good speaker at another time exposed his want of culture in a poorly written, ill-constructed letter sent by him to Josephus Woodruff, complaining that a certain pay certificate given by the latter for Hunter's "services" in connection with a claim of the Republican Printing Company had proven so unmarketable as to subject the reverend member to serious loss.

This man Hunter, though a regular preacher of the gospel, had quite a share of the plunder while a member of the Legislature. He received a good sum as his part of the spoils in the passage of the claims for furnishing the halls, and shared also in other dishonest schemes.

W. J. Whipper was said by some of his party to be easily among the very ablest colored men in public life in this State. He showed considerable shrewdness, but was not generally thought to be either capable or well informed. A paper drawn by him in court in 1869 indicated a degree of ignorance of everyday English, not at all justifying the claim of some of his white and colored associates that he was a highly educated man. As a member of the commission to codify the laws (1869-71) he showed gross incapacity. He was but a fairly good speaker—though it is possible that had he not so often used his powers to stir up strife and promote villainous schemes there might have been a different estimate of his ability. Corrupt to the core, always insolent, fond of flaunting his stolen money in the faces of white men, a mouthy incendiary in great part responsible for every race trouble in South Carolina, a coward, a blackleg and a perjurer, he was a good specimen of the leaders whom the Republican party raised up for the negroes in South Carolina.

R. B. Elliott, already noticed, illustrated the somewhat rare combination presented by the knave in the person of an educated man apparently having every incentive to lead an honest life. Elliott was unquestionably the ablest negro that figured in the Reconstruction period in South Carolina—an excellent speaker and a fine presiding officer. Yet he was officially corrupt and personally without any regard for decency or morality.

June Mobley—Junius S. he put it—was ignorant, without the accompaniment of any of the gifts which belonged to the negroes already mentioned. He was a bright mulatto, of poor figure, no presence, and a repelling countenance. His specialty was the making of incendiary speeches to the more ignorant among his race—thus leading them into trouble while he dodged the consequences. He accomplished nothing but to cause bloodshed in which men of his own race almost exclusively suffered. In the Legislature he but exposed his dense ignorance, his vicious purposes, his cowardly hatred of every white man as such, and his total lack of moral character. Yet he maintained to the end his standing in the Republican party.

Dr. B. A. Bosemon, a mulatto carpetbagger, who was one of the Charleston delegation in the House in 1868-70 and later, was a man of unusual intelligence, considerable information and inordinate vanity. He passed as one of the few honest men of his party, but he fell by the wayside—having taken a bribe from the Republican Printing Company. The writer's opinion of Bosemon's alleged purity of character was formed when the Doctor came from a committee room, thick-tongued from drinking champagne paid for with the money stolen from the State treasury—the drinking acknowledged by him in declining some request (possibly to take some more champagne?) made of him by a fellow member.

Such were some of the types among the leading negroes. The white men were chiefly inconspicuous, their principal performances being in the secret making of schemes of robbery.

The Senate and the House were alike controlled and "run" by a few leaders. The greater number of the members had little to say and nothing to do. They simply voted—very frequently voting for man or measure because they had been bought with money to do so.

Much time was consumed in the passage of unimportant matters—the number of acts incorporating societies running up into the dozens at every session. The negroes were fond of having their societies and these wanted charters from the Legislature. Many of the charters were never used. Some of the societies had peculiar names—such as the Young Men's Africanus Debating Club of Charleston, the Young Men's Free Enterprise Council of Georgetown, the American Union Literary Club of Gadsden, Richland County, the Refulgent Society of Columbia, the Reform Apollo Society of Charleston, the Rising Sons of Benevolence of Edgefield, the Elliott Republican Club of Barnwell, the Union Republican Wide Awake Association of Charleston, the Young Sons of Honor, the True Blue Union Republican Society and the Planters' Republican Society of St. Helena Island, the Sons' and Daughters' Cain Manuel Society of Charleston, the Grant and Wilson National Guards of Charleston, the Ladies and Gentlemen of Charity Society of Lady Island, the Christian Hope Society of Paris Island. Numbers of charters were needlessly granted to companies of the negro militia.

Citizens desiring to form a company had, of course, to go to the Legislature for their charter; and to the names in the original bill the committee of the House or the Senate would add the names of leading Republicans, taking care to include several negroes—this with the purpose to enforce quasi-social recognition and intercourse. In some instances the men thus made corporators would attend the meeting for organization—this for the purpose of mingling with the gentlemen whose names were in the original bill.

Useless lawmaking and the constant waste of time continued through the Chamberlain administration, notwithstanding that the members each drew a salary and not a per diem allowance. The session of 1875-76 consumed 109 days, not counting the Christmas recess and also excluding Sundays.

The handsome and also comfortable furnishings of the legislative halls served possibly to lengthen the sessions. To a man accustomed to a house of the plainest sort and to furniture of the roughest kind the opportunity to sit on a cushioned chair or a sofa of velvet surface—meantime having a page to buy his pinders or bring him water in a cut-glass goblet—presented a very strong temptation to linger amid his new surroundings.

The ignorance of the legislators never appeared in the bills or resolutions as seen by the public—care being taken to have these framed or rewritten by a competent draughtsman. An example of this procedure is shown in the following paper introduced in February, 1874, by one Tarleton, a colored representative from Colleton:

Resolved by the House of Representatives the Senate concurren, that whereas the leageslatures of South Carolina had conveane by his Excellency the governor F. J. Moses, Jr., the 21 of Oct. 1873 for the purpose of the Reduction of the Bounding dept of the State.

and whereas the Leageslators are failed to imbracing the Bounding which is Required as a Servant to the People interest but from day after day introduce Bill and Resolution which is know servance to the people; therefor Be it Resolved that the House now adjourn sine die.

In the official journal of the House the paper appeared as follows:

Whereas, the Legislature of South Carolina was convened by his Excellency the Governor, Franklin J. Moses, Jr., on the 21st of October, 1873, for the purpose of reducing the bonded debt of the State; and whereas the Legislature has failed to take any measures tending to effect such reduction, which was a duty demanded of them as faithful servants of the people; and whereas bills and resolutions of no public interest are introduced day after day; therefore be it

Resolved by the House of Representatives, the Senate concurring, that the General Assembly adjourn this day *sine die.*

The resolution was tabled.

The following letter written by a colored man in the summer of 1876 to the Republican county chairman of Marion well illustrates the attainments of many who, after eight years of opportunity, aspired to hold high place in the Government of South Carolina:

Marion County S C August The 27 Mr. Chair man dear Sir Therse Lins will Inform you That I am well At This Time and Hoping That You The same Mr C Smith dear Sir I have Ben offort for a Representatives Please write Me Some Information I have ben Put to the House and Reserve 706 when Ben deas reserve 7 Please write to me whot you Think of my run writ soon. E. G. Gregg.

CHAPTER VIII.

THE CAMPAIGN OF 'SEVENTY-SIX.

On December 23, 1875, Thomas Y. Simons, of Charleston, the South Carolina member of the National Democratic Executive Committee, summoned each member of the Democratic State Central Committee (which had been constituted in 1872) to attend a meeting in Columbia on January 6, 1876. The State Committee assembled accordingly, the following named gentlemen being present: M. C. Butler (chairman), of Edgefield; Samuel McGowan, of Abbeville; John S. Richardson, of Sumter; Thomas Y. Simons, of Charleston; William D. Simpson, of Laurens; W. W. Sellers, of Marion; William Wallace, of Richland; S. P. Hamilton, of Chester; Johnson Hagood, of Barnwell, M. P. O'Connor, of Charleston; F. W. Dawson, of Charleston.

After a free and earnest interchange of views the committee embodied their conclusions and suggestions in the following address:

To the People of South Carolina:

The State Central Executive Committee of the Democratic party do not deem it necessary to publish any lengthy statement of the reasons which induced them to meet at this time. It is sufficient to say that events with which the people of the State are painfully familiar made it indispensable that the organization of the Democratic party in South Carolina should be revived, as the speediest and most practicable means of bringing together our hitherto scattered forces, and of concentrating them in the struggle into which we are forced for the maintenance of liberty and law in the State. Thus it has become the duty of the State Committee to take such steps as will enable the people of the State to begin the work of party organization at once, and make it thorough and complete.

In the contest in which we are about to engage we must win. Success cannot be expected to crown our labors unless there be absolutely unity in the Democratic party, together with such discipline as will insure the prompt and efficient execution of its policy when declared. From our adversaries we must learn, at last, the lesson of organization and activity. When the agencies on which society relies for the conservation of its varied interests menace those interests with destruction, and threaten a whole people with ruin, politics is no longer a matter of sentiment in which the citizen is free to engage or not according to his tastes. Upon the management of our political affairs depends the security of property, as well as the safety of person. By political movements alone can the purification of the State Government be accomplished. Only through political instrumentalities can honesty, fidelity and capability regain a preponderating influence in the councils of the State. To politics, then, for their own salvation, must the people of South Carolina now address themselves with the vigor, the persistency and the systematic endeavor which mark their conduct in business life. It would not be wise to declare a policy before the party which shall give effect to it is ready for both deliberation and action. The officers must not be chosen until the rank and file of the political army shall have been mustered in and trained. There should be, in fine, such organization in each ward, township and county that when the State Convention shall assemble, it shall represent, by its delegates, the known wishes, opinions and purposes of the organized Democracy of the State. Then will its voice be the purpose of the people; its determination theirs; its fight their battle. To such organization, searching and far-reaching, should the people of the State, without delay, address themselves. Without it the State cannot be saved!

The State Convention, when it shall assemble, will determine authoritatively the policy of the party; and by the decision of that convention shall we all be bound. As, however, the Democratic party, as such, has had no active existence in South Carolina for some years, the State Committee desire to say emphatically that, in recommending its instant and comprehensive organization, their sole purpose is to obtain an honest and economical government in South Carolina, which shall maintain, without abridgment or change, the public rights and liberties of the whole people, and guarantee to all classes of citizens the blessings of freedom, justice and peace. And in this crisis in the constitutional life of the State, when civilization itself is in peril, we look for and confidently expect to receive the sympathy and aid of every citizen whose aims and desires are like unto our own.

In common with their fellow citizens, the State Democratic Committee have watched with anxious solicitude and growing confidence the course of the present Governor of the State. They recognize and appreciate the value of what he has done, promoting reform and retrenchment during the past year. They applaud his wise and patriotic conduct in exerting his whole official power and personal influence for the undoing of the infamous judicial election, and they declare their belief that the Democracy of the State, rising above party, as he has done, will give an unfaltering support to his efforts as Governor for the redress of wrongs, for the reduction of taxation, to obtain a just administration of the law, and make the State Government a faithful guardian of the public and private interests of the people.

Therefore the State Executive Committee earnestly advise the people of the State to reorganize thoroughly the Democratic party, in preparation for the State Democratic Convention, which will meet at a time and place to be hereafter designated by this committee. The following gentlemen are charged with this organization of the party in every precinct, ward and township in their respective counties:

Abbeville, J. S. Cothran; Aiken, George W. Croft; Anderson, James A. Hoyt; Barnwell, T. J. Counts; Beaufort, William Elliott; Clarendon, B. P. Barron; Chester, W. A. Walker; Colleton, J. J. Fox; Darlington, F. F. Warley; Edgefield, J. Scott Allen; Fairfield, John Bratton; Georgetown, B. H. Wilson; Greenville, T. B. Ferguson; Horry, J. T. Walsh; Kershaw, E. M. Boykin; Lexington, Gerhard Muller; Lancaster, John D. Wylie; Laurens, B. W. Ball; Marion, A. Q. McDuffie; Marlboro, J. H. Hudson; Newberry, Y. J. Pope; Oconee, Robert A. Thompson; Orangeburg, James F. Izlar; Pickens, R. E. Bowen; Richland, John McKenzie; Spartanburg, John H. Evins; Sumter, Thomas B. Fraser; Union, Robert W. Shand; Williamsburg, S. W. Maurice; York, James F. Hart.

The organization of Charleston County is entrusted to the Committee of Fifteen, of which Col. Charles H. Simonton is chairman.

In conclusion, the State Committee earnestly say to their fellow citizens that we are not as those who are without hope. The magnitude of the task before us can hardly be overrated. Every step is beset with difficulty, if not danger. But, knowing this people, the Committee are confident that the future can be made as bright as the present is dark. Now is the accepted time! By organization, labor, patience, boldness and liberality can peace and plenty and political security be restored to the State.

The gentlemen thus detailed went at once to work in their different counties. A Democratic club was formed in every township, ward or voting precinct, as conditions required. The club had its officers and its standing committees, and it constituted in each county the unit of organization. The county convention was composed of delegates from the several clubs in proportion to their membership. Every member signed the roll—and thus signed a pledge to abide by and support all nominations of the Democratic party, whether for national, State, county or municipal offices. Municipal officers were usually nominated by a local club organized for the occasion—in some cases by a mass meeting of citizens.

The white people promptly joined the clubs in very large numbers and the enrollment constantly increased, so that on the day before the election those not enrolled (and not acknowledging themselves Republicans) were so few that it might fairly be stated that these organizations embraced the entire Democracy of South Carolina.

At a meeting held February 22 the State Committee called a convention of the Democratic party of South Carolina to be held in Columbia on May 4, "for the purpose of appointing delegates to the National Democratic Convention, to be held in St. Louis on the 27th of June next, and to take such further action as the convention shall deem proper and necessary."

The call for a State convention imparted new energy to the work of organization, and the club rolls were greatly increased. County conventions were held and delegates duly elected.

THE MAY CONVENTION.

The Democratic State Convention met in Columbia on May 4. On motion of Gen. M. C. Butler, Col. D. Wyatt Aiken, of Abbeville, was made temporary chairman, and Mr. T. C. Gaston, of Chester, temporary secretary. The following delegates were enrolled:

Abbeville—J. S. Cothran, F. A. Connor, J. W. Perrin, J. C. Maxwell, G. M. Mattison, A. M. Aiken, J. C. Bradley, D. W. Aiken, J. H. Morrow.

Aiken—James Aldrich, Paul F. Hammond, J. M. Miller, R. Elmwood Lyler.

Anderson—J. A. Hoyt, E. B. Murray, John B. Moore, C. W. Brown, C. S. Mattison, John M. Glenn.

Barnwell—Johnson Hagood, T. J. Counts, J. S. Stoney, G. B. Lartigue, W. T. Blanton, J. W. Holmes, I. S. Bamberg.

Beaufort—James W. Moore, C. J. C. Hutson, James E. DeLoach.

Charleston—E. McCrady, Jr., H. A. M. Smith, R. Seigling, James Conner, C. R. Miles, C. H. Simonton, M. P. O'Connor, James Cosgrove, W. L. Daggett, J. F. Ficken, J. B. Campbell, George L. Buist, J. D. Aiken, J. W. Hutto, J. G. Gaillard, W. G. Hinson, E. L. Rivers, W. J. Gayer, T. Y. Simons, L. Sherfesee.

Chester—W. A. Walker, Julius Mills, T. C. Gaston, John W. Wilkes.

Chesterfield—W. A. Evans, A. McQueen, J. L. M. Irby, D. S. Miller.

Clarendon—John L. Manning.

Colleton—J. J. Fox, John F. Townsend, Allen Izard, N. K. Perry, F. E. Bissell, J. Otey Reed, T. J. Harley, H. D. Elliott, Charles Boyle.

Darlington—J. A. Law, S. A. Gregg, J. E. Keith, E. R. McIver.

Edgefield—M. W. Gary, M. C. Butler, G. D. Tillman, James Callison, M. L. Bonham, J. C. Sheppard, J. H. Brooks, T. G. Bacon, John R. Abney, W. H. Timmerman.

Fairfield—T. W. Woodward, John S. Reynolds, James Pagan, B. E. Elkin, Henry Heins.

Georgetown—B. H. Wilson.

Greenville—James McCullough, B. F. Perry, W. L. Mauldin, T. J. Austin, C. A. Perkins.

Horry—L. D. Bryan, Daniel Lewis, T. J. Sessions, B. W. Ward.

Kershaw—J. B. Kershaw, John D. Kennedy, W. D. Trantham, Lewis C. Thompson, W. L. DePass.

Laurens—B. W. Ball, J. W. Ferguson, W. Watts, W. A. Shands, F. M. Setzler.

Lexington—H. A. Meetze, T. S. Fox, J. N. Huffman, W. T. Brooker.

Marion—W. W. Harllee, E. J. Moody, W. S. Mullins.

Newberry—James N. Lipscomb, E. S. Keitt, J. S. Hair, Y. J. Pope, J. F. J. Caldwell.

Oconee—J. M. Keith, J. T. Reid, John W. Zimmerman.

Orangeburg—A. D. Goodwyn, Ira T. Shumaker, Dr. B. H. Knotts, F. W. Fairey, N. E. W. Sistrunk, W. C. Hane, H. G. Sheridan.

Pickens—R. E. Bowen, D. F. Bradley.

Richland—W. B. Stanley, A. C. Haskell, J. C. Seegers, R. O'Neale, Jr., W. H. Stack, J. H. Kinsler, J. A. Kaminer, E. S. Percival.

Spartanburg—John H. Evins, W. K. Blake, H. L. Farley, G. Cannon, W. P. Compton, John A. Leland, T. Stobo Farrow.

Sumter—T. B. Fraser, E. W. Moise, John S. Richardson, Samuel Earle, Matt. Brooks, London Sumter, Robert Ross; the three last named being colored.

Union—I. G. McKissick, John P. Thomas, Asa Smith, Thomas A. Carlisle.

Williamsburg—T. M. Gilland, James McCutchen, W. J. Nettles, Thos. R. Greer.

York—John S. Bratton, B. H. Massey, A. Baxter Springs, J. L. Adams, Richard Gillespie.

The counties of Lancaster and Marlboro were not represented.

The following officers were unanimously elected by acclamation:

President—J. B. Kershaw.

Vice-President—M. L. Bonham, Thos. Y. Simons, James A. Hoyt, A. McQueen, B. F. Perry, Johnson Hagood.

Secretaries—T. C. Gaston, J. J. Fox.

On motion, the President appointed a committee composed of one member from each county, to which were referred without debate all resolutions offered in the convention. A number of resolutions were referred accordingly.

In deference to the wish of General Kershaw the rule making the President of the Convention chairman ex officio of the State Executive Committee was rescinded, and it was provided that such committee should choose its own chairman.

The following named gentlemen were elected to represent the State in the National Democratic Convention:

At Large—John Bratton, W. D. Porter, D. Wyatt Aiken, John D. Kennedy. Alternates—M. C. Butler, B. F. Perry, Jas. A. Hoyt, M. L. Bonham.

First District—John S. Richardson, J. D. McLucas. Alternates—E. R. McIver, J. B. McLaurin.

Second—M. P. O'Connor, John F. Ficken. Alternates—John L. Manning, James F. Izlar.

Third—Samuel McGowan, W. B. Stanley. Alternates—B. W. Ball, Sampson Pope.

Fourth—John H. Evins, B. F. Perry. Alternates—W. H. Wallace, Gabriel Cannon.

Fifth—J. C. Sheppard, William Elliott. Alternates—J. J. Fox, Paul F. Hammond.

Governor Perry having declined to serve as alternate at large, Col. William Wallace was elected in his place.

The Convention then proceeded to the election of three members of the State Executive Committee from each Congressional District, with the following results:

First—W. W. Harllee, J. A. Law, T. B. Fraser.

Second—T. Y. Simons, J. F. Izlar, James Conner.

Third—A. C. Haskell, J. N. Lipscomb, John B. Moore.

Fourth—W. L. DePass, T. Stobo Farrow, B. H. Massey.

Fifth—A. C. Izard, Geo. D. Tillman, T. J. Counts.

At intervals during the counting of the ballots and while awaiting the report of the committee on resolutions the Convention went into caucus. There was a full interchange of views on the situation in the different counties and on the policy to be declared by the Convention.

The committee on resolutions submitted the following report on the various papers referred to them:

The committee of one from each county, to whom was referred the resolutions of the gentleman from Charleston, Mr. O'Connor; of the gentlemen from Newberry, Messrs. Lipscomb and Keitt; of the gentleman from Edgefield, Mr. Sheppard; of the gentleman from Barnwell, Mr. Lartigue; of the gentleman from Charleston, Mr. McCrady—beg leave to make the following report:

That the committee deem it inexpedient to take any action upon the resolutions submitted to them for consideration, but recommend that this Convention urge on the respective counties the utmost vigor and zeal in perfecting a thorough and compact organization of the Democratic party, with the view of consolidating every possible strength until the time comes for the nomination of a State ticket.

We further recommend that the State Executive Committee take such action at once as will promote the purpose indicated in the foregoing.

Gen. M. W. Gary offered the following resolutions as a substitute for the report of the committee:

Resolved, That the platform of the National Democratic party be adopted as the platform of the Democratic party of South Carolina.

Resolved, That the Democratic party of South Carolina, when they make nominations for State officers, put a straightout ticket in the field.

Resolved, That the county conventions where the Democrats are in a minority make such nominations as they deem expedient, and be governed by the circumstances surrounding them.

After considerable debate the yeas and nays were called, when the report of the committee on resolutions was adopted by a vote of 70 to 42.

Col. James A. Hoyt introduced the following resolution, which was adopted:

Resolved, That the State Executive Committee is hereby authorized and empowered, whenever in their judgment it may be deemed proper, to call a convention of the Democratic party to nominate State officers and announce a platform of principles, to be composed of delegates from the several counties in proportion to the number of members to which each county may be entitled in both houses of the General Assembly under the new apportionment of the various counties.

The Convention then adjourned, after a session of two days.

One of the purposes of the May Convention in postponing a declaration of policy was that there might be further enrollment of the white voters in the Democratic clubs and further opportunity for discussing, among the white people, the policy to be pursued by the party in South Carolina.

There were among the white people two distinct views of what should be done. Some thought that the Democratic party should make no nomination for Governor if Chamberlain should be the Republican candidate—the latter contingency being regarded certain. This wing of the Democracy considered that by such a policy there would be stronger chances of electing the rest of the State ticket and of getting control of the Legislature—the latter object being on all hands admitted to be of first importance. The otner wing of the party—known as the "straightouts"—urged the nomination of Democrats for all offices "from governor to coroner" and a fight for supremacy on that line. There was full discussion in the papers —by contributors and editors—of the questions thus presented. Each side had its advocates among the best and truest and ablest men of South Carolina—men who had distinguished themselves in peace and war alike and of whose disinterested purpose to serve and save the State no doubt was ever suggested.

BLOODSHED IN HAMBURG.

The town of Hamburg, in Aiken County, on the Savannah river separating it from the city of Augusta, once a place of great commercial importance in South Carolina, was in 1876 the abode of negroes chiefly. These controlled the town, men of their race, to the exclusion of whites, filling all the offices—those of intendant, wardens, policemen, trial justice and constable.

There was here a company of negro militia commanded by one Doc Adams, whose hostility to the white race had been frequently manifested and who did about all he dared to aggravate such of that race as necessity compelled to visit or to traverse the negro-ridden town of Hamburg. This company, it was officially stated, had been organized during Scott's first term, with Prince Rivers as captain, and had then been supplied with arms and ammunition. The company was inactive for a time, but in May, 1876, it had an enrollment of eighty men, with Doc Adams as captain. The men had a supply of ammunition said by Adams to have been issued in 1870—a statement bearing little semblance of truth.

On July 4, 1876, two citizens of Edgefield were driving through a street of Hamburg, and thus met Doc Adams' company. Seeing the approach of the buggy, the negro soldiers intentionally extended their company front across the street so that the vehicle bearing the gentlemen could not pass—there being a ditch on one side of them, a fence on the other and a well in their rear. They were forced to stop; and while they stood still the negroes cursed and vilified them in the grossest manner and beat their drums around their horse's head. They were finally permitted to go on their way.

The father of one of the men thus treated made complaint against certain of the negro soldiers (including their captain) for obstructing a highway, and a warrant for their arrest was issued by Prince Rivers, the trial justice resident in Hamburg. Upon this the negro militiamen became indignant and threatened to lynch the citizens whose lawful use of a public highway had been insultingly interrupted. In view of these threats some white men gathered at Hamburg on the day finally fixed for the trial.

Gen. M. C. Butler had been retained for the prosecution, and, after some fruitless endeavors to have Doc Adams and the other offenders end the trouble by making a proper apology for their misconduct, repaired to the justice's office where the trial was to take place. On the suggestion of a colored man proceedings were again postponed in the expectation of an adjustment. There was further delay—long enough for General Butler to visit Augusta, dispatch some personal business there, and return to Hamburg. In a conference with Rivers and others General Butler proposed that all further trouble could be prevented if the negro company—whose very existence was by many believed to be unlawful—would deliver up their guns to some responsible person who should ship them to the Adjutant-General in Columbia. Very soon there came a report that the negroes refused to disarm and intended to fight. Quite a number of whites had by this time gathered in anticipation of trouble—some having come from Augusta. The fighting soon began. The negroes, fortified in their drill room in a brick building, defied the whites, raised a yell and fired from the windows—to which act the whites promptly responded with a volley. Soon after the firing began McKie Meriwether, a worthy young citizen of Edgefield, was shot through the head and killed—this before any negroes had been hurt. In the meantime a small cannon had been brought from Augusta, and from it four or five charges of canister had been successively fired on the building occupied by the negroes. These commenced to retire and as they did so they were intercepted by the whites.

As the negroes were escaping from the building they were fired on and one of their number was killed. The rest were captured and later five of these—regarded as the ringleaders in bringing on the difficulty—were singly shot to death by their infuriated captors.

This shocking affair was the culmination of troubles which had long been brewing in and around the negro-ridden town of Hamburg—in the language of General Butler, "the culmination of the system of insulting and outraging white people which the negroes had adopted there for several years."

"Many things," General Butler went on to say, "were done on this terrible night which cannot be justified, but the negroes 'sowed the wind and reaped the whirlwind.'"

This affair was the subject of widespread comment. Governor Chamberlain, styling it "the Hamburg massacre," denouncing it as an act of "atrocity and barbarism," evidencing a "murderous and inhuman spirit" and presenting a "darker picture of human cruelty than the slaughter of Custer and his soldiers."

The extreme Republican press took up the cry and denounced in fiercest language the bloody doings of "Sitting Bull Butler and his Edgefield Sioux." General Butler contented himself with dignified denials of the charges preferred against him and the repeated declaration that he was ready to meet his accusers face to face in the courts.

Governor Chamberlain awaited an official statement of the "massacre" before he made public his own conclusions. He sent the Attorney-General (William Stone, his recent appointee in the place of Mr. Melton, resigned) and that official proceeded to the headquarters of Prince Rivers, whom Governor Chamberlain had appointed to judicial office. Rivers was corrupt, incapable, vicious and insolent. According to his own sworn confession in 1877, he had, before Governor Chamberlain selected him to be a judge, been guilty of thievery and perjury—having on more than one occasion taken a bribe from the Republican Printing Company. It was upon the statements of Rivers and of negroes whom he procured to testify that Governor Chamberlain formed his judgment and framed his indictment of the white people of South Carolina.

It is worthy of notice that Governor Chamberlain never intimated regret for the killing of Meriwether.

No proceedings were ever taken to punish any of the parties alleged to have participated in "the Hamburg massacre." A jury (twelve negroes, ten of whom could not write) empaneled by Rivers, acting as coroner, imputed the killing to certain citizens, but the matter ended there. The parties thus accused were bound over to appear at Edgefield court, and they were duly present at the appointed time. The case was then postponed by the State's attorney, and it was never again brought up.

Governor Chamberlain appealed to the President for help, and of course received from General Grant the assurance that soldiers were at his disposal.

The course of Governor Chamberlain in connection with this Hamburg affair—his intemperate utterances, his appeal to the President and his subsequent attempts at evasion when charged with having called for troops—had a decided effect in settling the policy of the white people in the contest then in contemplation.

THE AUGUST CONVENTION.

On July 12, 1876, the State Executive Committee called a convention of the Democratic party of South Carolina to be held in Columbia on August 15, at 8 p. m., "to announce a platform of principles, nominate State officers and electors for President and Vice-President, and to consider such other business as may be brought before it."

The Convention assembled in response to this call—the roll of delegates being as follows:

Abbeville—J. S. Cothran, Dr. J. C. Maxwell, Dr. J. A. Robertson, D. Wyatt Aiken, W. K. Bradley, F. A. Connor.

Aiken—G. W. Croft, D. S. Henderson, J. H. Giles, Paul F. Hammond, T. J. Davis.

Anderson—J. A. Hoyt, W. C. Brown, C. S. Mattison, R. W. Simpson, John B. Moore.

Barnwell—Johnson Hagood, Dr. G. B. Lartigue, Robert Aldrich, I. S. Bamberg, J. M. Williams, L. W. Youmans.

Beaufort—William Elliott, J. W. Moore, C. J. C. Hutson, J. E. DeLoach, Abram Martin, G. H. Hoover, J. B. Morrison.

Charleston—James Conner, T. D. Jervey, J. Adger Smyth, George H. Walter, C. H. Simonton, L. D. Mowry, Zimmerman Davis, T. G. Barker, J. Bennett Bissell, R. Seigling, J. Ralph Smith, W. S. Adams, S. S. Solomon, S. D. Hutson, C. Irvine Walker, T. S. Browning, W. G. Hinson, C. Kerrison, Jr., A. Melchers.

Chester—Julius Mills, T. C. Gaston, R. S. Hope, J. H. McDaniel.

Chesterfield—J. W. Harrington, W. W. Spencer, J. S. Miller.

Clarendon—John L. Manning, Wm. R. Coskrey, Wm. D. McFaddin.

Colleton—M. C. Conner, T. J. Harley, Robert Fishburne, H. E. Bissell, Dr. J. C. Dick, W. C. Fishburne.

Darlington—J. A. Law, L. R. Ragsdale, A. F. Edwards, E. W. Cannon, E. Gregg.

Edgefield—M. C. Butler, M. W. Gary, G. D. Tillman, J. R. Abney, O. Sheppard, P. Blackwell.

Fairfield—James H. Rion, John Bratton, T. W. Woodward, James Pagan.

Georgetown—L. P. Miller, J. J. Pringle, A. W. Cordes.

Greenville—J. W. Gray, W. H. Perry, Wm. Beattie, A. C. Steppe, Alex. McBee, Sr.

Horry—B. L. Beaty, Danl. Lewis, E. D. Richardson.

Kershaw—W. L. DePass, J. Duncan Shaw, L. B. Stephenson.

Lancaster—John B. Erwin, J. D. Wylie, Dr. J. C. Blakeney.

Laurens—B. W. Ball, A. W. Shands, R. R. Blakely, Dr. J. R. Smith.

Lexington—H. A. Meetze, Gerhard Muller, Godfrey Leaphart.

Marion—J. G. Blue, W. W. Harllee, H. H. McClenaghan, J. G. Haselden, R. H. Rogers.

Marlboro—C. W. Dudley, H. H. Newton, Knox Livingston,

Newberry—J. N. Lipscomb, T. W. Holloway, W. D. Hardy, R. L. McCaughrin.

Oconee—James A. Doyle, John W. Shelor, W. C. Keith.

Orangeburg—J. F. Izlar, Dr. B. H. Knotts, W. A. Easterlin, I. T. Shumaker, A. D. Goodwyn, O. B. Riley.

Pickens—R. E. Bowen, John R. Gossett, A. B. Tolley.

Richland—Wade Hampton, John T. Rhett, A. C. Haskell, J. H. Kinsler, William Wallace, R. O'Neale, Jr.

Spartanburg—G. Cannon, H. L. Farley, A. B. Woodruff, H. F. Scaife, John W. Wofford.

THE CAMPAIGN OF 'SEVENTY-SIX 349

Sumter—E. W. Moise, T. B. Fraser, J. S. Richardson, J. W. Stuckey, E. D. Shiver (colored).

Union—W. H. Wallace, T. B. Jeter, J. C. Richards, Dr. J. P. Thomas.

Williamsburg—W. H. Kennedy, S. T. Cooper, J. A. May.

York—B. H. Massey, Cad. Jones, J. F. Hart, Andrew Jackson, Robert Plexico.

James A. Hoyt was unanimously elected temporary chairman.

For the presidency of the Convention, two gentlemen were presented—Gen. W. W. Harllee and Col. C. H. Simonton. It was understood that Gen. Harllee represented the immediate-nomination party, and Colonel Simonton the "watch-and-wait" party—those who favored postponement until the Republican Convention should act.

The vote resulted as follows: Harllee, 80; Simonton, 66. By counties the vote was as follows: For Simonton—Charleston, 19; Chester, 4; Darlington, 4; Fairfield, 4; Georgetown, 3; Abbeville, 4; Barnwell, 2; Beaufort, 5; Clarendon, 2; Lancaster, 1; Lexington, 1; Orangeburg, 6; Spartanburg, 2; Sumter, 4; Union, 3; York, 2. For Harllee—Aiken, 4; Anderson, 5; Colleton, 6; Edgefield, 6; Abbeville, 9; Barnwell, 4; Greenville, 5; Horry, 2; Kershaw, 4; Lancaster, 2; Laurens, 4; Lexington, 1; Marion, 4; Marlboro, 2; Newberry, 4; Oconee, 3; Pickens, 3; Richland, 5; Spartanburg, 3; Sumter, 1; Union, 1; Williamsburg, 1; York, 1.

The announcement of the result was received with cheers from the floor of the hall.

Messrs. John R. Abney and Zimmerman Davis were elected secretaries.

Vice-presidents were elected as follows: Johnson Hagood, J. S. Cothran, John L. Manning, Cad. Jones, J. W. Harrington.

Colonel Cothran introduced the following resolution:

Resolved, That the sense of this Convention be ascertained as to whether in the approaching campaign the nominations for State officers, when made, shall be of straightout Democrats.

Colonel Rion offered the following:

Resolved, That it is inexpedient at this time to make a nomination for State officers, or to adopt a platform by which we are to be governed as far as the same relates to State officers.

The Convention then went into secret session. That session lasted from 11:30 in the morning till 6:30 in the evening, with a recess of about an hour for dinner.

At the close of the discussion the doors were thrown open and it was announced that the following had been adopted by a vote of 82 to 65:

Resolved, That this Convention do now proceed to nominate candidates for Governor and other State officers.

General Butler nominated Gen. Wade Hampton for Governor. Mr. Robert Aldrich seconded the nomination.

General Hampton ascended the speaker's stand and said:

Mr. President and Gentlemen: I need not tell you that the words of kindly allusion to myself which I have heard spoken have deeply touched my heart. But I desire to say a few words in personal explanation. I have all along refrained from expressing my opinion in one way or another, except when called upon to do so as a delegate. I have not tried to influence this convention in word or deed. I came here only to pour oil on the troubled waters, if necessary, and to promote unity and harmony if I could.

In the card I published in the *Columbia Register* the other day I expressed my opinions fully and earnestly. When the war was raging I was asked to come here and allow my name to be used as a candidate for Governor, but I preferred to stay where I thought I could do the most good for my State and my country; and since the war I have never offered one word of advice unless it was asked of me. I felt that my day was past, and that in returning to my native State I was like him who said: "An old man whose heart is broken is come to lay his weary bones among you. Give me a little earth for charity."

I have claimed nothing from South Carolina but a grave in yonder churchyard. But I have always said that if I could ever serve her by word or deed, her men had only to call me and I would devote all my time, my energy and my life to her service.

I will now be perfectly unreserved with you on another point. Men whose patriotism is beyond question, and in whose wisdom I have great confidence, think that my nomination would injure the Democratic party of the United States. If it were left with me to decide between that party and the interests of South Carolina, I would not hesitate in my choice. But I believe the success of the Democratic party of the United States will bring success to South Carolina, and that if Tilden is elected we can call South Carolina our own. Now, I do not wish to embarrass the gentlemen of the convention, nor to jeopardize the general Democratic party. I would, indeed, gladly decline the nomination. Besides this, there are men in South Carolina who think I possess a disqualification of which I cannot divest myself, and would not if I could. I mean what they call my war record. That is the record of fifty thousand South Carolina soldiers, and if I am to forfeit that, and say that I am ashamed

THE CAMPAIGN OF 'SEVENTY-SIX 351

to have been one of them, all the offices in the world might perish before I would accept them.

These are grave topics, gentlemen, and I implore you to look over the whole field and not let any kindness for me lead you astray. I will now retire, so that you may discuss them freely. If you decide to nominate some other as true and as sincere as I, and I know there are thousands of them, I will devote myself to secure his election. Come weal or come woe, I am with you to the last.

General Hampton then withdrew from the hall.

Colonel Rion nominated General Bratton, saying that he did so with great pleasure in obedience to his instructions. Major Woodward seconded the nomination.

General Bratton declined in favor of General Hampton.

Mr. Stuckey nominated ex-Governor Manning, who also declined in favor of General Hampton.

General Hampton was then unanimously nominated by acclamation.

On motion of Colonel Simonton the Convention proceeded to select a candidate for Lieutenant-Governor.

Colonel Lipscomb nominated W. D. Simpson of Laurens, who was chosen by acclamation—the names of J. B. Kershaw and Wm. H. Wallace being withdrawn.

The following were then chosen by acclamation:

For Secretary of State—R. M. Sims, of York.

For Attorney-General—James Conner, of Charleston.

For Superintendent of Education—Hugh S. Thompson, of Richland.

For Comptroller-General—Johnson Hagood, of Barnwell.

For Treasurer—S. L. Leaphart, of Richland.

For Adjutant-General—E. W. Moise, of Sumter.

When Gen. Conner was nominated by Colonel Haskell the wildest enthusiasm prevailed, and cheer upon cheer greeted the latter's little speech. When the nomination was made unanimous, the Convention with almost one voice cheered and called upon the nominee to speak.

General Conner was not in the hall. He entered shortly afterwards and being again loudly called for spoke as follows:

Mr. President and Gentlemen of the Convention—I can hardly express how grateful to me is this mark of the confidence and regard of those who are here as representatives of the people of South Carolina, devoted to her and hoping to bring back to her by the effort of every true son of the State those days when to be a South Carolinian was a pride and distinction. I feel that in this compliment you have paid a tribute to something higher than any individual—a tribute to freedom of thought and freedom of discussion.

On the issue which divided the Convention, I was in the minority. You have taken me as a candidate on your ticket and thus heralded it abroad that the Democrats of South Carolina are united as one man.

I have only to return you my heartfelt thanks for the honor you have done me, and to pledge you that every effort in my power, every thought and feeling of my nature, will be devoted to advance the cause which we have so much at heart.

The selection of a State Executive Committee of seven was assigned to the candidates on the State ticket.

John A. Wagener and Samuel McGowan were the nominees for electors from the State at large.

The following were nominated by the conventions for their respective congressional districts:

First—Congress, J. S. Richardson; Elector, J. W. Harrington.

Second—Congress, T. G. Barker; Elector, J. A. Ingram. (Colonel Barker afterwards withdrew and Mr. M. P. O'Connor was substituted.)

Third—Congress, D. Wyatt Aiken; Elector, William Wallace.

Fourth—Congress, John H. Evins; Elector, J. B. Erwin.

Fifth—Congress, G. D. Tillman; Elector, Robert Aldrich.

The following nominations were made by the judicial conventions:

First Circuit, W. St. Julien Jervey; Second, F. Hay Gantt; Third, J. J. Dargan; Fourth, W. W. Sellers; Fifth, J. R. Abney, Sixth, T. C. Gaston; Seventh, B. W. Ball; Eighth, J. S. Cothran.

The committee appointed to wait on General Hampton then came in and conducted him to the president's desk, and reported to the Convention that he was now present.

General Hampton was greeted with prolonged applause. As soon as it subsided he said:

Mr. President and Gentlemen of the Convention—In accepting the honorable post to which you have called me, that of your standard-bearer in the great struggle for reform which you have begun, I do so with the most grateful appreciation of your kindness and the most profound sense of the high duties, the grave responsibilities, pertaining to the position. In the better days of our country, when the surest passports to official station were found in the ability, the honesty and the integrity of her public servants, the most distinguished sons of South Carolina looked upon the chief magistracy of the State as the goal of their highest ambition and the best reward of their public services. If men of whom Carolina is justly proud held in such deserved estimation the distinction of being thought worthy by their fellow citizens of the highest office in the gift of the State in the days of her prosperity and peace, how much more highly should I esteem the honor you have done me by calling me unanimously to lead you in this hour of gloom and peril.

You are struggling for the highest stake for which a people ever contended, for you are striving to bring back to your prostrate State the inestimable blessings which can only follow orderly and regulated liberty under free and good government. We believe that these blessings can only be secured by a complete change in the administration of our public affairs, National and State, and believing this, our sympathies and our interests lead us naturally and inevitably into alliance with that great party upon whose banners are inscribed the watchwords of Democracy—"Reform, good government, hard money and home rule." You have endorsed and ratified the platform of the Democratic party adopted at St. Louis, and planting yourselves firmly on that, you look forward hopefully and confidently to a victory in which you will not only share, but to which you will have contributed. The platform which you have adopted here is so catholic in its spirit, so strong in its foundations, so broad in its construction, that every man in South Carolina who honestly desires reform can find room to stand upon it. With such a platform, where our citizens of all parties and all races can stand assured of equal rights and full protection, you can surely bring back to our distracted State the great blessings of good government. For myself, should I be elevated to the high position for which you have nominated me, my sole effort shall be to restore our State government to decency, to honesty, to economy and to integrity. I shall be the Governor of the whole people, knowing no party, making no vindictive discriminations, holding the scales of justice with firm and impartial hand, seeing, as far as in me lies, that the laws are enforced in justice tempered with mercy, protecting all classes alike, and devoting every effort to the restoration of prosperity and the reestablishment of honest government.

Thanking you, gentlemen, for the honor you have conferred upon me, and invoking the blessing of God on your praiseworthy effort to redeem our State, I here pledge myself to work with you in that sacred cause with all the zeal, all the energy, all the ability and all the constancy of which I am capable.

Prolonged applause followed General Hampton's remarks.

The Convention adjourned in the afternoon of August 17.

The State Executive Committee was constituted as follows: A. C. Haskell (chairman), John Bratton, John D. Kennedy, T. B. Fraser, James A. Hoyt, J. Adger Smyth, R. O'Neale, Jr.

THE DEMOCRATIC PLATFORM.

The committee on platform submitted a report through Colonel Simonton, which was unanimously adopted, as follows:

The Democratic party of South Carolina, in convention assembled, announces the following as its platform of principles:

We declare our acceptance, in perfect good faith, of the Thirteenth, Fourteenth and Fifteenth Amendments to the Federal Constitution. Accepting and standing upon them, we turn from the settled and final past to the great living and momentous issues of the present and the future. We adopt the platform of principles announced by the National Democratic party recently assembled at St. Louis, and pledge ourselves to a full and hearty cooperation in securing the election of its distinguished nominees, Samuel J. Tilden, of New York, and Thomas J. Hendricks, of Indiana, and believe that under the wise and just administration of its distinguished reform leader, assisted by the eminently patriotic and able counselors by whom he will be surrounded, peace and prosperity will again bless our country, and the dissensions, confusion and maladministration of the past eight years will give place to concord, good government and a thorough restoration of the Union.

In accordance with the declarations of that platform and the utterances and acts of our distinguished leader, we demand a genuine and thorough reform in the State of South Carolina, and call upon all its citizens, irrespective of race, color or previous condition, to rally with us to its redemption, for it is evident that substantial and lasting reform is impossible within the ranks of the Republican party of this State.

We charge that party with arraying race against race, creating disturbances and fomenting difficulties; with prostituting the elective franchise, tampering with the ballot box and holding unfair and fraudulent elections; with having accumulated an enormous debt, mismanaged the finances and injured the credit of the State; with levying exorbitant taxes and squandering them when collected, thus wringing from the toil and livelihood of the honest poor man of the State a large per centum of his hard earnings without giving in return any compensation therefor, and having hopelessly involved in debt a majority of the counties of the State; its management of our penal and charitable institutions is a shame and a disgrace.

We charge its legislation as demoralizing, partisan and disgraceful, and the venality and corruption which have characterized every branch of the Government, executive, legislative and judicial, have no parallel in the history of nations. It has created a multiplicity of unnecessary and useless offices complicated in their systems and unnecessarily expensive. And to crown its disgraceful rule it has attempted to elevate to the bench two most corrupt and degraded men. It can never purify itself, give good and impartial government, or by its moral force and character exercise in its full sovereignty the law of the land. We do not charge this condition of things, which every patriot must deeply deplore, upon the masses of the party, but upon their leaders, who have made such false use of their confidence and trust; for it is our firm conviction that all the people of the State, of both races, desire peace and prosperity. We, therefore, call upon our fellow citizens, irrespective of race or past party affiliation, to join with us in restoring the good name of our State, and in elevating it to a place of dignity and character among the commonwealths of this great country.

We discountenance all disturbances of the peace of the State, and denounce all instigators and promoters thereof; and earnestly call upon all of our fellow citizens, irrespective of party lines, to exercise forbearance and cultivate good will; and if the government of the State is committed to our control, we pledge ourselves to protect the person, rights and property of all its people, and to speedily bring to summary justice any who dare violate them. We desire a fair, peaceful election, appealing to the reason, and not the passions, of the people, and demand of the Republican party a fair showing in the appointment of commissioners of election. We demand a fair election and a fair count. We call upon all the patriotic sons of Carolina to join us. We ask but a trial of committing the State to our keeping; and if good government, security, protection and prosperity do not dawn on our overtaxed, despoiled and disheartened people, then drive us from power with scorn and indignation. Our object is reform, retrenchment and relief, that by honesty and economy we may reduce the taxes and lighten the burthens of the people, giving at the same time absolute security and protection to the rights and property of all.

Upon this paramount issue we cordially invite the cooperation of every Democrat and every Republican who is earnest and willing, in this crisis of our State, to unite with us in this great work.

DEMOCRATS MARCH TO VICTORY.

The nomination of the Hampton ticket settled all differences among the white people of South Carolina. Discussion as to the policy of the Democratic party was at an end. There was actual unanimity, among the white people and among their papers, in the determination to elect their nominees and thus restore peace, order and honest government. The small number of white men who had not yet joined a Democratic club promptly had their names enrolled. The club organizations were disciplined and strengthened. Proper steps were taken for the enrollment of colored voters into Democratic clubs officered by colored men—the assurance being given in the plainest language that any attempt by Republicans, black or white, to intimidate, injure or oppress any colored man because he should join a Democratic club or should declare his purpose to vote for Hampton would lead to bloodshed in which the intimidators would surely be the sufferers. The colored Democrats, whenever they appeared in a procession or at a meeting, wore the Democratic uniform—the red shirt—and sometimes a single negro was detailed to appear in public in that garb, the purpose being to impress the fact that a colored man could thus show himself to others of his race and yet go unharmed.

Preliminary to the actual opening of the campaign at the first public meeting addressed by General Hampton and others of the State ticket, ample preparations were made to preserve the peace. It was understood by the white people, and it was plain to all impartial observers, that for the prevention of trouble nothing could be expected of the State Government or any of its agents. Indeed, the desire of most of the Republican leaders, white and black, was seemingly for such breaches of the peace as would give them excuses for charging the whites with intimidation of colored men, and thence for invoking the further help of the National Government and the sympathy of the Northern press. The "Hamburg massacre" had served the Republican managers well, but they sought further opportunity to win their fight by means of Federal troops and by giving false impressions of the course of the campaign. The Republican leaders in South Carolina—from D. H. Chamberlain down—apparently desired bloodshed. If the negroes should be the sufferers, opportunity would come for "waving the bloody shirt." If white men should be killed, there was hope that the spirit of that race might be cooled and the colored people emboldened or even inflamed.

Every Democratic club constituted an organization available in case of trouble. The men were sufficiently provided with arms, and especial care was taken that in the event of any disturbance the members—especially in thinly settled neighborhoods—should be promptly notified.

There were also some military organizations among the whites—rifle clubs and sabre clubs. These clubs had a full complement of officers designated by unmilitary names—president (captain), vice-presidents (lieutenants), wardens (sergeants), and directors (corporals). There were no battalions or regiments, but in sections where two clubs or more could act together some person had been selected to command. The club was also to serve, when necessary, as the nucleus around which white citizens might gather in the event of trouble. The clubs were at all times the peace conservators to whom the white population looked for that protection which the State was incapable of affording.

The Democratic canvass opened at Anderson on September 2, and a meeting was held in every county—the final "rally" being at Columbia on November 4.

Every meeting was attended by all the white men of the county, except the very few that it was thought necessary to leave at home— these, in many of the counties, patrolling the roads to look out for any misconduct of the negroes and visiting the houses to let the women and children know of their movements.

The Democratic clubs (every man in a red shirt) came to the county seat in military order, each commanded by its president. The column was formed by marshals or aides under the orders of the county chairman and he commanded the procession—riding with his staff at the head of the column as it escorted the canvassers to the place of speaking.

The red shirt procession was a feature of every campaign meeting—the number of mounted men in uniform varying, according to the white population of the county, from 500 to 5,000. The use of mounted men had the effect to exaggerate in the estimate of onlookers the number of men actually present. The city fellow who saw a red shirt procession for the first time might honestly misrepresent its numbers. A thousand men on horseback, riding in easy order, every man yelling as long as his throat could stand the effort—the marshals meantime riding up and down the column, carrying orders or "closing up" the men—the route to the speaking ground lined with men (the "non-combatants"), women and children, waving flags or hats or handkerchiefs to the riders and doing their part to increase the volume of lusty yells and defiant hurrahs—such a body of men might well be taken for one double their number in fact.

On arriving at the speaking ground (usually a grove on the outskirts) the ranks were opened, and General Hampton, escorted by committeemen and others in red shirts, walked to the stand. Usually he was greeted with the songs of young women, who strewed his path with flowers. Music was an invariable feature.

The mounted men formed a semi-circle in front, except that a place near the stand was reserved for the colored voters—who were always urged to attend.

A novel and suggestive feature of these meetings where General Hampton and his campaigners made their speeches to the people was the presence of ladies in such large numbers that the town was well-nigh deserted, whilst as many came from the country as could be brought—most if not all of the animals on the farms being used by the men in the red shirt procession. The interest of the women was particularly shown in dressing the speakers' stand with bunting, evergreens and flowers. What was a platform of ordinary lumber was converted into a veritable bower of roses, fit for the throne of some fair woman whose obeisant knight, in the flush of victory, was to crown her Queen of Love and Beauty.

The presence of the good women and their hearty interest in the campaign helped to show that it was not a mere effort to get office or to oust officeholders, but a movement of the people against unworthy men in control of the State. Of the many thousands of red shirts worn by South Carolinians in 1876, scarcely one was made except by wife or mother or sister or sweetheart.

General Hampton spoke in every county, and there were speeches by the other nominees and by gentlemen detailed for this service in different parts of the State.

There was little reference to National politics—though it was understood that the Democrats of South Carolina were loyal to the party and would do their best to carry the electoral vote to Tilden and Hendricks, against Hayes and Wheeler. Appeals were made to all good citizens, without regard to party, to give their votes for honesty, reform and good government. The colored people were especially urged to break away from their bondage to the Republican party and vote for Hampton and his ticket. The white people were pledged by their leaders and spokesmen to give the negro justice in the administration of the government and protect all his rights under the Constitution and laws. The men of the white race were exhorted to work unceasingly for the election of the Democratic ticket, and they were especially urged to see that no colored man should ever suffer because of his joining a Democratic club or for otherwise showing his purpose to vote the Hampton ticket.

Besides these campaign meetings at the county seats there was a canvass of every county by the Democratic nominees for the Legislature and for the different county offices. Impromptu meetings were also held on the plantations, these addressed by citizens who were not candidates at all. Using the steps of a ginhouse or a cottonbale or a wagon for a platform, there would be a regular little meeting. A colored man (always a Republican) would be called to the chair, and he would introduce the Democratic speakers—some of whom, just from office or store or school or farm-house, had never made and could not make a political speech.

Individual work among the negroes was unceasing. Whatever the occasion, whenever a white man had a chance to talk to a negro there was an effort to win a vote for Hampton. Little attention was paid to the so-called leaders among the negroes—except to let them understand that they must not trouble negro Democrats, that they must not stir up strife, and that in case of disturbance they must expect to suffer. White Republicans becoming both rare and unobtrusive, they were not regarded as of any particular consequence.

Much work was done by youths and in many cases by mere boys. These could not vote, but they could swell the red-shirt column, they could do a deal of work and (within certain ages) could join the ranks of a fighting force.

Every means was taken to maintain the peace. Coolness, forbearance, prudence, were incessantly urged upon the white people. Yet they were ordered to be prepared for trouble—prepared to defend their persons and their homes. The negroes' knowledge of the perfect readiness of the white race for self-defense was undoubtedly the principal factor in the maintenance of the peace. The Republican white leaders evidently wanted disturbances, and many of the black leaders would have made trouble had they not known that upon themselves would fall the worst consequences.

A distinct feature of the campaign was the plan to "divide time" at negro meetings whenever these were known to be contemplated. Sometimes the negro leaders refused the joint discussion, but it was insisted on by the whites. The purpose of this peculiar proceeding was to get the ears of the colored people, to show them the villainous character of their leaders and representatives, and to let them understand that the white race would endure no longer. One effective feature of the joint discussion was the "taking down" of some unworthy negro leader whose misdoings a Democrat present would take pains to expose.

On the subject of dividing time the State Democratic Committee published the following:

The Executive Committee, in view of the requests made of the Republican party at recent meetings for a division of time in discussing the questions at issue between the parties, announce that we deem it due to the voters to have a full, fair and free discussion on all such occasions, and we express our willingness and readiness to extend the same right to Republican speakers whenever they desire a respectful hearing at our meetings. And to this end we urge the Democratic party to observe decorum and propriety in attending the meetings of the opposite party.

The object of the Democratic party is peaceful and untrammeled discussion, that the people may become enlightened on the issues of the day.

Efforts were made by the Democratic State Committee to have joint discussions at the campaign meetings—these to be addressed by General Hampton, Governor Chamberlain and such other speakers from each party as might be present. Colonel Haskell, in the letter written by him as chairman of the Democratic Committee (September 28) informed Governor Chamberlain of the committee's desire and urged that some plan be adopted to carry it out. He then stated at some length the purposes of the Democratic party in the campaign and their desire to accomplish these by peaceful and lawful means only.

Governor Chamberlain answered at great length, reviewing the course of events since his inauguration. He gave his experiences at certain meetings addressed by him in the course of his individual canvass of a number of counties during the months of July and August—particularly charging that at Edgefield, Newberry, Abbeville and Midway (Barnwell County) the course of the Democrats in demanding and enforcing a division of time had been unseemly, offensive, riotous and threatening.

The Edgefield meeting had come off on the 12th of August. Generals Butler and Gary insisted on dividing time with the Republican speakers, Chamberlain, Mackey and Smalls. There were several hundred mounted Democrats present. Governor Chamberlain having spoken, General Butler replied to him—that reply constituting a vigorous denunciation of the Governor in his public career, of his conduct in relation to the Hamburg riot, of his charges against Gen-

THE CAMPAIGN OF 'SEVENTY-SIX

eral Butler and of his appeal to the President for troops. Judge Mackey followed General Butler and General Gary spoke next. He denounced the Governor in plainest language, and held him up to the negroes as unworthy in all things. The platform having fallen, the meeting came to an end. Nobody was hurt.

At Newberry there were like experiences—the Democratic spokesmen being Col. James N. Lipscomb and Col. D. Wyatt Aiken.

Next at Abbeville, and then at Midway, the Republicans were compelled to divide time. Colonel Aiken spoke at Abbeville and Col. George D. Tillman at Midway.

There was neither bloodshed nor any breach of the peace at any of these joint meetings.

There was some correspondence between the Democratic and the Republican committee, wherein the former proposed and the latter conditionally agreed that there should be ten joint discussions between General Hampton and Governor Chamberlain—the Democratic committee plainly desiring to make the arrangement and the Republican committee evidently seeking to dodge it. The negotiations accomplished nothing.

"HURRAH FOR HAMPTON."

As the election approached, the activity of the Democrats increased—so that for some little time before the day fixed by law the white people of South Carolina did practically nothing but work for Hampton and his ticket. Stores were actually closed, farms were left almost to take care of themselves, and everybody went to work for the redemption of the State. "Hurrah for Hampton" went out all over South Carolina, and in that slogan there was a ring of resolution that made it veritably the death-knell of negro rule in this commonwealth. "Hurrah for Hampton," cried the red shirt from his horse or mule taken from the plough that he might join the procession. "Hurrah for Hampton," said the peace-making citizen who had just used his efforts to prevent a difficulty. "Hurrah for Hampton," was the jeer of a spirited man, when some arrogant negro Republican would pompously pass by. "Hurrah for Hampton" would (unconsciously) say a good Democrat as some white Republican happened to come along. "Hurrah for Hampton," laughed the schoolboy as he scampered along street or road. "Hurrah for Hampton," would say the swain as he bade his lady-love good night and joined some fellows in a search for a negro meeting where they might divide time.

"Hurrah for Hampton," was the battle-cry of the white people of South Carolina in the fight to rid the State of negro rule!

THE REPUBLICAN CONVENTIONS.

The Republican State Convention, to elect delegates to the National Convention in Cincinnati, met in Columbia on April 12, and remained in session till the morning of the 14th. The advocates and organs of Governor Chamberlain had stated that in this body the opposition to him would find its exponents in the persons of disaffected Republicans—among them Senator John J. Patterson (said to be the agent and emissary of Senator O. P. Morton), H. G. Worthington, then collector of the port of Charleston, R. B. Elliott and C. C. Bowen. Associated with these was Judge R. B. Carpenter, who, though a citizen of Columbia, had been elected a delegate from Edgefield County. Governor Chamberlain was present as a delegate from Horry County.

The first test of Governor Chamberlain's strength came in the contest for the temporary chairmanship—S. A. Swails (the senator from Williamsburg) receiving eighty votes, whilst the Governor received forty. Swails was afterwards elected president.

Among the prominent Republicans present as delegates were: R. B. Elliott, S. J. Lee, C. C. Bowen (white), Robert Smalls, J. H. McDevitt, H. G. Worthington (white), Beverly Nash, R. H. Gleaves, B. F. Whittemore (white), F. L. Cardozo, J. S. (June) Mobley, S. A. Swails, John J. Patterson (white), J. Hannibal White, Lawrence Cain—every one of whom had been guilty of bribery or of some act involving wilful and corrupt perjury.

The proceedings of this body were sometimes marked by disgraceful conduct on the part of the delegates. There were noisy (and apparently angry) discussions among some of the members—the line of division indicating the contest between the supporters and the opponents of Governor Chamberlain. At one time there was danger of bloodshed. Confusion reigned for a while, and the disturbance was only stopped by a motion to take a recess—an expedient accepted by all parties with evident satisfaction. In the height of the trouble —aggravated by one member's throwing an inkstand at another's head—a chair was raised over the person of the Governor, as if to strike him down.

Owing to the squabbles over contesting delegations and lengthy debates on insignificant matters the Convention sat two whole days and one entire night. It was during this night session that the contest between the friends and the enemies of the Governor was really waged.

The opposition was led by Judge Carpenter, who charged that the Governor had not kept faith with the Republican party—that "from the day he entered the office of chief magistrate of this State he turned his back upon the men who fought for him and with him, and has sought only to advance himself at the cost of his allegiance to his party"—that the Governor "had refused to counsel with his party friends, but had acted dictatorially and arbitrarily in all matters, and this was the reason why they had revolted from his leadership."

"The Legislature and not the Governor," declared Judge Carpenter, "are the judges of the judges they elect. It is neither his business nor mine; and when they attempt to say that because the Governor says that a man is not moral or learned enough for a judge he can withhold his commission and enforce his arbitrary and imperial power to a tyrannical extent, they take a ground that I cannot indorse. . . . There is an irrepressible conflict between the Governor's policy and the principles of Republicanism."

It was towards daylight when Governor Chamberlain began his speech in answer to Judge Carpenter. In meeting the issue of party fealty he twitted the Judge with his candidacy for Governor on the Union Reform ticket in 1870 and with his having been a witness for the defense in the first of the Kuklux trials in 1871—referring to the campaign of 1870 as a time "when the Republican party's life was assailed and a strong and vigorous hand clutched at the throat of the Republican party," and to the Kuklux cases in which "when we were in one of the most critical of those trials, the first, that was to determine the question whether we could proceed far enough to bring these red-handed assassins to justice, among witnesses brought from afar and brought here to give testimony that should shield the Kuklux was the Hon. R. B. Carpenter."

Of his own devotion to his party the Governor said: "I scorn, I put the foot of my uttermost contempt upon any charge from mortal lips that I have swerved from my allegiance to the Republican party or that the thought has ever lodged in my breast that did not breathe fidelity, honor and allegiance forever to the principles and organization of the Republican party."

The Governor then went over the principal phases of his official course, and undertook to show that he had been "immovable in the efforts to lift up the Republican party above the crimes of the campaign of 1870 [referring to alleged outrages by Kuklux] and above the crimes of 1874 [apparently meaning the misdoings of Governor Moses]."

Concluding, the Governor said: "Thank God, I have one or two friends who have stood by me. Let me tell you that if I knew that your suffrages would sink me so deep that no bubble would rise to tell where I went down, I would stand by F. L. Cardozo. If you think that I am to be bought by going to Cincinnati to go back on a man who to my knowledge has never done a dishonest act, and who has always stood by me, you are mistaken—that's all. Do with me as you please. If you dismiss me to the shades of private life, be it so. You called me. I am your servant always, and I bow to your commands."

Governor Chamberlain was elected a delegate-at-large to the National Convention (over John J. Patterson) by a vote of 89 to 32. The delegation was as follows:

At Large—R. B. Elliott (colored), D. H. Chamberlain, R. H. Gleaves (colored), John J. Patterson.

First District—S. A. Swails, Joseph H. Rainey (both colored).

Second District—H. G. Worthington, W. J. McKinley (colored)

Third District—H. C. Corwin, W. Beverly Nash (colored).

Fourth—A. S. Wallace, John Winsmith.

Fifth—Robert Smalls, Lawrence Cain (both colored).

By a resolution of the Convention these delegates went uninstructed.

In the interval between the April and the September convention of the Republicans there was some activity among the two factions into which they seemed to be divided—the supporters and the opponents of Governor Chamberlain.

The Governor made a personal canvass of several counties. It was in the course of this canvass that he visited those places at which, according to his complaint in his letter to the chairman of the State

Democratic Committee, there had been serious misconduct on the part of Democrats present. There had been a general inclination among the white people to let the Governor have a quiet hearing, but his course in the Hamburg trouble had irritated them, and there were fears that by intemperate allusions to that affair he might excite the negroes to offensive demonstrations. Besides, the Governor was unfortunate in the selection of his companions.

At Edgefield he had Lawrence Cain and Robert Smalls, who were offensive to the white people because of their swagger and their bad character.

At Newberry he had J. K. Jillson, superintendent of education, who was obnoxious because of the utter failure of the school system of which he was the official head, because he had tolerated ignorance and incapacity among teachers and school officials, and, most of all, because of his part in the order intended to enforce actual social equality among white and black children in the school for the deaf and the blind. There was also present Solomon L. Hoge, who had joined Jillson in the order just mentioned, who had been a close friend of Frank Moses, who had defrauded the State by drawing his salary as a Supreme Court justice, though too ignorant to write a single opinion, who had shared in the frauds connected with the public printing, and who had given offense by his insolent bearing towards gentlemen who had been forced into controversy with him as an official.

At Lancaster Governor Chamberlain had as a companion Congressman A. S. Wallace, of York, who had been largely responsible for the Kuklux troubles in the upper counties, whose vindictiveness had had frequent expression in his language and his conduct towards the white people, and who was especially obnoxious in Lancaster, because he had caused that county to be included in the list of counties in which President Grant had in 1871 virtually declared martial law. At the Chamberlain meeting in Lancaster Wallace was not permitted to speak.

At the Midway meeting Governor Chamberlain had carried Hoge along, and at Abbeville he was accompanied by both Hoge and Jillson.

At every one of these meetings there were present men who had for eight years actively aided in the schemes of the Republican managers to "feather their nests" at the expense of the taxpayers.

As the time for the Republican nominating convention drew near it was evident that the opposition to Governor Chamberlain would amount to nothing. The body met in Columbia on September 13.

Robert Smalls was elected temporary chairman—defeating S. A. Swails by a vote of 65 to 56—and was afterwards made president.

The personnel of the body differed little from that of the April convention. Among the delegates was W. J. Whipper. The leaders of the opposition to Governor Chamberlain were Elliott and Dunn.

There was no contest over the electoral ticket, which was as follows:

At Large—John Winsmith, C. C. Bowen.
First District—T. B. Johnston.
Second—Timothy Hurley.
Third—W. B. Nash, colored.
Fourth—Wilson Cooke, colored.
Fifth—N. B. Myers, colored.

On the third day the platform was adopted and the body proceeded to nominations.

For the office of Governor the names suggested were D. H. Chamberlain and T. C. Dunn. On the first ballot the vote stood: Chamberlain, 88; Dunn, 32; D. T. Corbin, 2; Elliott, 1. The Governor delivered a speech in which he reviewed the reforms accomplished during his administration, declared the Republican party bound to further improvement, and pledged himself to stand by its platform.

The State ticket was completed as follows:

Lieutenant-Governor—R. H. Gleaves.
Attorney-General—R. B. Elliott.
Treasurer—F. L. Cardozo.
Secretary of State—H. E. Hayne.
Comptroller-General—T. C. Dunn.
Adjutant-General—James Kennedy.
Superintendent of Education—John R. Tolbert.

Most of these nominees have been sufficiently introduced to the reader.

Tolbert was a white man living in Abbeville. He was without any apparent qualifications for the office for which he was named. Kennedy (also white) was the clerk of Purvis, the mulatto incumbent.

This ticket evidenced the restoration of absolute harmony between the two factions into which the Republican party had apparently been divided. Dunn and Elliott especially had been outspoken in their opposition to Governor Chamberlain and his policy.

Elliott had denounced the Governor because in 1871 he had said that he would be willing to run for the United States senatorship if such course were necessary to save the party from "negroism," and had been especially severe in his comments on the refusal to commission Whipper and Moses. On another occasion Elliott had declared that he had in his possession a paper that would consign Chamberlain to infamy.

There was some comment upon the Governor's acceptance of a nomination which committed him to the active support of Elliott, who had opposed him bitterly. Governor Chamberlain, first in an editorial in the *Union-Herald*, written by himself, and next in the course of his letter to Colonel Haskell, about the conduct of the campaign, justified his action—maintaining that Elliott was pledged and bound as a man and as a politician to stand by the Republican platform and by him. "The causes of his nomination," said the Governor, "were not his opposition to me or to reform, but his admitted ability for the position, his long record of political service to his party, and a desire to conciliate an element of the party which had been defeated in my renomination; and I am in no sense compromised or dishonored in my character as a reformer by my association upon the same ticket with Mr. Elliott."

When Governor Chamberlain wrote thus, Elliott had become notorious as a leader among the corruptionists in the Legislature and as a leader also of the negroes who sought actually to dominate and humiliate the white race. He had had little experience as a lawyer.

Governor Chamberlain, in a letter to William Lloyd Garrison (June 11, 1877), explained thus his course in running on the same ticket with Elliott:

I made a grave mistake in that I did not refuse to run on a ticket with R. B. Elliott. I saw it then, but not so clearly as now. I do not mean that this excuses, or tends to excuse, the conduct of those who have overthrown us. What I mean is that Elliott's bare presence on the ticket justly gave offense to some honest men of both races. He had opposed me brutally, especially in the nominating convention. Unable to defeat me, he determined to foist himself on the ticket with me to cover his defeat. I saw at once the bearing in part of this and I took the resolution, unknown to any friends, to walk into the convention and throw up my nomination and avow that I did it because I would not run on a ticket with Elliott. I knew it would result in putting him off the ticket. I had actually risen in my office to go into the hall for this purpose when I was met at the door by a dozen or more of my most devoted colored supporters who came to congratulate me on the surrender of Elliott in seeking to stand on a ticket with me! I was disarmed of my purpose and relinquished it. It was a mistake. Whether it affected the result which has now come I do not know. But I ought to have made Elliott's withdrawal the condition of my acceptance.

THE REPUBLICAN PLATFORM.

The Convention adopted the following platform:

I. The Republican party of the State of South Carolina, in convention assembled, believing that the principles of equal civil and political rights are vital to the interests of good government, and that they can only be enforced by the party which has engrafted them upon the State and national Constitutions, hereby reaffirms its confidence in the National Republican party by pledging firm adherence to the platform adopted by the Cincinnati Convention in this the one hundredth year of American independence.

II. We hereby pledge our undivided support to the standard-bearers of that party, Rutherford B. Hayes and William A. Wheeler, whose unblemished and statesmanlike record in the past is sufficient assurance that all reforms lying within the province of their respective offices will be earnestly prosecuted, and the National Government wisely and economically administered, with due regard to the rights and interests of the whole American people.

III. We heartily endorse the administration of President Grant, so honestly and economically conducted as to exalt the nation in the estimation of the world and advance its faith and credit. We recognize in the soldier statesman and President a firm, devoted lover of American liberty, a stern, unflinching champion and protector of the rights of American citizens at home and abroad, and we will ever hold in grateful remembrance his deeds in war, in peace, in all that makes our country great—though the youngest of the nations, yet the equal of all.

IV. That in presenting to the people of South Carolina our nominees for the high offices of the State for the coming two years, we believe we should make plain and unmistakable the aims and principles to which we stand pledged, in the event of their election, not in glittering generalities of reform, but in specific and substantial articles.

V. We declare our abhorrence and repudiation of all forms of violence, intimidation or fraud in the conduct of elections, or for political purposes, and denounce the same as crimes against the liberty of American citizens as well as the common rights of humanity; and while we insist upon and will jealously guard the right of every citizen freely to choose his political party, and deny the unfounded charge that the Republican party countenances any interference with colored voters who may choose to vote the Democratic ticket, yet we protest against and denounce the practice now inaugurated by the Democratic party in this State of attending Republican meetings and by show of force and other forms of intimidation disturbing such meetings or taking part therein without the consent or invitation of the party calling them.

VI. We pledge ourselves to thorough reform in all departments of the State Government where abuses shall be found to exist, and, as an earnest of the same, declare our purpose of submitting to the qualified voters of the State the following specific reforms as amendments to the State Constitution:

1. That the present adjustment of the bonded debt of the State shall be inviolable.

2. That the General Assembly shall meet only once in every two years, and that the length of no session thereof shall exceed seventy days.

3. That the number of sessions of courts of general sessions and common pleas shall be reduced to two annually in each county, with power reserved to the judges to call special sessions when necessary.

4. That the veto power of the Governor shall be so modified as to allow of the disapproval of a part without effect upon the rest of an act.

5. That agricultural interests shall be relieved from burdensome taxation by a more equitable distribution of taxes and by the inauguration of a system of licenses fixed upon fair principles.

6. That no public funds shall ever be used for the support of sectarian institutions.

7. That the enormous evil of local and special legislation shall be prohibited whenever private interests can be protected under general laws.

8. And inasmuch as the system of free schools was created in the State by the Republican party, and should be especially fostered and protected by it, we pledge ourselves to the support of the amendment to the State Constitution, now before the people, establishing a permanent tax for the support of free schools, and preventing the removal of school funds from the counties where raised.

VII. We pledge ourselves and the nominees of the Republican party of this State to the securing of the following purposes by legislative enactment:

1. The further and lowest reduction of salaries of all public servants, consistent with the necessities of government.

2. The reduction of fees and costs, especially of attorneys in civil cases, and the amendment of the laws governing the settlement of estates in such manner as to secure a more economical administration and settlement of small estates.

3. The immediate repeal of the agricultural lien law.

4. Public printing to be reduced at least one-third of the present appropriation.

5. Convict labor to be utilized under such laws as shall secure humane treatment and the support of convicts without needless expense to the State.

6. The annual appropriations for public institutions to be economically made and properly expended.

7. The number of trial justices to be reduced throughout the State, and each justice to be assigned to specific territory; with moderate salaries to cover costs of criminal business, adjusted in proportion to populations.

VIII. Recognizing the enormous expense of fencing farms and the scarcity of timber in some sections of the State, we feel it to be necessary that practical relief be afforded to the people of the State, and we pledge ourselves to secure such legislation upon the subject as will give to the electors of each county the right to regulate this question for themselves.

IX. That, whereas, in some of the upper counties of the State certain evil-disposed persons have induced many citizens to disregard and violate the revenue laws of the United States by representing them to be oppressive and in violation of the rights of the citizen, and it is apparent from the action of the National Democratic House of Representatives that the revenue tax will be continued, we therefore earnestly recommend that his Excellency the President of the United States do grant a general amnesty and pardon for all violations previous to this time. And the senators are hereby instructed, and the representatives in Congress are requested, to urge this action without delay.

X. We charge the Democratic party with perversion of all truth and history; with opposition to all the interests of the masses; with fostering class preferences and discriminations; with a denial of rights to those who do not accept their political dogmas; with constant and persistent antagonism to the principles of justice and humanity; with a resistance to the manifest will of the people and the spirit of the age; with a determination to make slavery national and liberty sectional; with a purpose to rend the Union in twain to perpetuate human bondage; with plunging the nation into a fratricidal war; with deluging the land in blood and filling it with sorrow and distress; with burdening the people with a debt that makes a higher taxation necessary and continuous; with opposition to the reconstruction of the States they had violently forced into a confederacy; with resistance to the passage and ratification of the amendments to the Constitution of the United States, made necessary by the results of the war, which clothed the humblest in the nation with citizenship and placed in his hands the power of protecting it; with a purpose to reopen sectional prejudices and animosities, to make "the war a failure," "reconstruction void," and the amendments to the Constitution nullities; with deception, misrepresentation, extravagance in the conduct of government, dishonesty in the disbursement of the public funds, and an abuse of the public confidence; with fraud in the management of elections; with intimidation of electors; with atrocities during political campaigns, unheard of in civilized communities; with assassinations and murders of those whose only offending was a steadfast adherence to the principles of the Republican party; with threatenings of violence and death against those who advocate the perpetuity of the Republican party; with armed preparation and hostile intent in the States of the South, intending by such a formidable array to frighten or force Republicans into a support of their party and partisans, or to remain away from the polls; with dissembling to the North, by assurances of an acceptance of the results of the war, a desire for reconciliation and brotherly relations, when they are only thirsting for the opportunity to secure what they have lost by the ascendency of the National Democratic party to power, and thus inflict upon the nation further evils and embarrassments; with nominating National and State officers known for their antagonism to all the Republican party has accomplished.

XI. Reiterating our reliance in the justice of our cause and the truth of the principles underlying our national platform, and of the Thirteenth, Fourteenth and Fifteenth Amendments to the Constitution of the United States, pointing with gratification to the many important reforms established by the Republican party of our State during the last few years, we invoke the guidance and blessing of Divine Providence upon our standard-bearers and upon the whole people of South Carolina. And we, the members of the Republican party, in convention assembled, do hereby earnestly pledge ourselves to an uncompromising support of its nominees, with the firm hope and the solemn determination to guard our rights, protect our friends and elect our candidates.

Some of the planks in this declaration were entirely new—the proposal of biennial sessions of the Legislature, the repeal of the agricultural lien law, the submission of the question of fence or no fence to the voters in the several counties, and the promise of amnesty for offenders against the internal revenue laws of the United States.

Biennial sessions were advocated as a means of abating the nuisance thus far inhering in every session under Republican rule.

The repeal of the lien law was promised in the hope of winning votes from among those of the whites who opposed the law and from among a certain class of negroes who had complained that the law afforded white men opportunities to commit extortion in business.

The fence law had been a source of much discussion among the white people, because of the growing expense of fencing lands against the incursions of cattle. One of the earliest changes made by the State Government after its restoration to the hands of the white people was in this fence law—the statute now requiring the fencing in of cattle.

The promise of amnesty to violators of the revenue laws was intended to catch votes in the upper counties, where the whites largely predominated and where the administration of those laws, disgraceful to the Government, had outraged and disgusted the white people —including many who had always obeyed the laws and who had no sympathy with "moonshiners."

REPUBLICAN WEAKNESS MANIFEST.

There was much dissatisfaction among a large class of Republicans of both races, these claiming that the State ticket as a whole was unworthy, that Elliott's nomination was especially disgraceful, and that Governor Chamberlain had surrendered to the worst men in his party—the very men who had promoted the election of Whipper and Moses, who had opposed his reforms and who had denounced him in most violent language.

Immediately upon the adjournment of the Republican Convention Judge Thompson H. Cooke, of the Eighth circuit, declared for Hampton, and offered his services to the Democratic committee. A few days afterwards Judge Mackey made a like declaration. Both of these converts did active and effective work for the Hampton ticket.

There were numerous defections among the white Republicans and some of the best colored men in every county joined in the Democratic movement. The number of colored men in the clubs grew apace—this notwithstanding the persecution visited upon them by others of their race. Colored Democrats were pursued, insulted, beaten, wounded, threatened with death, expelled from church and subjected to numerous indignities and annoyances, and would have suffered much more but for the constant watchfulness of the white people. Against these outrages no organ or spokesman or leader of the Republican party in South Carolina was ever known to protest.

One remarkable feature of the behavior of the negroes was seen in the treatment of negro Democrats by the women of their race. Wives deserted their husbands—or, rather, forbade their lords to come about home. Abuse of the worst sort issued from the lips of some negro women—though, to the credit of the race, it must be said that many of these were of bad character. The red shirt was actually torn from negro Democrats by their wives—and sometimes the act was accompanied with beating.

Among the Democrats the Republican ticket was received with considerable satisfaction, the general opinion being that it was weak in its personnel, and that it especially showed Governor Chamberlain's surrender to the worst elements in his party—to the very men who had fought him and resisted his recommendations of reform. Among the Governor's present supporters were Whittemore, Swails, Gleaves, Bowen, Smalls, Elliott, Whipper, Nash, Bowley, Jones, of Georgetown, Ransier, S. J. Lee—each of whom, it must be noted, took rank as a chief among the corruptionists.

It was generally felt that Governor Chamberlain had surrendered to the very men who had perpetrated the wrongs against which the taxpayers had long protested—who were indeed notoriously corrupt—whose bad character, in each instance, was actually known to him.

The fight for Hampton was very much aided in the State ticket selected by the Republicans. The character of the Republican county tickets was, as a rule, no better, and in some instances decidedly worse. The domination of the negro was more marked than ever, and the servility of the few white men who stood by Chamberlain was abject in the extreme. In some counties white Republican nominees refused to run—assigning as their reason the bad character of the other candidates.

The canvass of the Republican nominees on the State ticket was so irregular—so lacking in the "dash" which characterized every movement of the opposition—that it seemed almost pretensive. Indeed, the *Union-Herald,* Governor Chamberlain's own organ, admitted that the Republicans attached little value to public discussions or any of the recognized methods of a political campaign—that paper declaring: "Public meetings are not necessary to arouse the Republicans, nor to inform them. On the day of election nine-tenths of them could be directed to cast their ballots at one poll, if necessary, and they would be there in spite of all the clubs in the country."

There were, however, several Republican campaign meetings in the interest of the State ticket. At some of these the negroes were mounted, and there was a poor imitation of the red shirt procession—the red shirt lacking—but the pretense was so plain that it rather detracted from the effect naturally expected of the gathering of a few thousand negroes apparently beyond the reach of any influence that might be employed to break their allegiance to the Republican party.

There was constant danger of disturbance. It was evident that many of the negroes were armed—armed with guns furnished by the State. The number thus supplied was reported to be 40,000, but it was certainly not so large. The arms had been distributed secretly.

In some sections of the lower counties, where the blacks largely outnumbered the whites, the conduct of the negro soldiers and of negro mobs carrying guns was well calculated to cause race conflicts. They paraded the roads, they went about in squads, they made a display of their guns, they threatened the white people with violence and swore vengeance upon any colored men who should vote the Democratic ticket. Many negro women increased the trouble by loud-mouthed harangues to the men in arms, with insolent remarks about the white people and with violent abuse of all colored Democrats. All the self-control that the whites could exercise, all their resolution to follow their leaders' advice to keep the peace at all hazards, was needed to prevent bloodshed.

The arming of the negroes and their hostile demonstrations served to swell the enrollment and improve the equipment of the rifle clubs.

Despite the determination of the whites to keep the peace and to strike in self-defense only there were serious disturbances—each resulting in loss of life.

THE CHARLESTON RIOT.

On the evening of September 6 there was a meeting of one of the colored Democratic clubs of Charleston, at which speeches were made by two colored men who were prominent in their advocacy of the Hampton ticket. Certain Republican negroes had evidently planned to break up the meeting, but were prevented by the presence of a number of white men. When the meeting closed, the white men, fearing trouble, formed a hollow square and placed the two negroes within. The white escort was soon swarmed by a dense crowd of rampant Republican negroes, armed with clubs and crying aloud for vengeance upon the colored men being protected. Presently a negro in the rear of the escort struck a white man with a club and the blow was returned. Immediately the negroes began shooting on the whites, and the latter instantly returned the fire. The firing lasted about twenty minutes, during which clubs and bludgeons were used by those negroes who were without arms.

The white men persistently defended the two negro Democrats until these were carried to a place of safety.

For an hour a portion of the street was in the possession of the negro mob—crying for vengeance, striking right and left, firing their pistols and breaking the windows of stores on the street. A squad of thirty policemen arrived after much delay, but they were defied by the negro mob. After much trouble the mob were somewhat quieted and the police took charge of the street—first escorting to a place at some distance a small party of white men who, largely outnumbered, had been at the mercy of the rioters.

In this affair, one white man, J. M. Buckner, was mortally shot and died the day following, and seven were wounded—two severely. Five colored men—three of them being of the police force—were wounded, but not seriously.

The riot was followed with turbulent demonstrations by negroes in different parts of the city, but the assembling of the rifle clubs prevented the bloodshed which many of that race seemed resolved to bring on.

It was manifest that the mayor of the city—George I. Cunningham—was powerless, whether by influence or by action, to preserve the peace or to protect the lives of citizens. Cunningham was, of course, a Republican.

THE ELLENTON RIOT.

On September 15 the residence of a citizen of Aiken county, living some distance from the railroad, was entered by two negroes with burglarious intent. The owner was absent and his wife was sick in bed—the only other person in the house being a boy of ten. Upon the lady's protesting against the robbery, the negroes beat her severely, and also beat the little boy because he tried to go for help. The lady managed to get her husband's gun—which happened to be unloaded—and frightened off the plunderers by pointing the weapon at them.

When this outrage became known, some citizens, including the lady's husband, went in pursuit of a negro—one Peter Williams—who was suspected of the crime. He was positively identified by the lady. During her statement he suddenly fled and was shot down by his captors and severely wounded. He confessed to having committed the robbery and to have been privy to the assault upon the lady and her little son. He implicated another negro—one Fred Pope—and steps were at once taken to have that man arrested by legal process.

A warrant was issued by a negro justice, who, fearing that Pope would resist, empowered Mr. Angus P. Brown, a citizen of recognized prudence and courage, to make the arrest. Collecting a posse of fourteen men, the constable thus appointed proceeded on his lawful errand. Pope had stationed himself at Rouse's Bridge, attended by a considerable number of armed negroes. Scouts sent out to ascertain the situation reported that the negroes had assembled at the bridge and were armed, excited and defiant. The posse moving towards the bridge, they were fired on by the negroes aligned on the edge of a swamp, and returned the fire. The only casualty was the slight wounding of one negro. The negroes then massed in the swamp, to the number of about forty.

The posse sent a white flag by a negro woman and proposed a parley. She returned with the answer that the negroes refused. She was sent again, and did not return, but in her place came a negro who stated that his men would confer with six of the posse (whose names he gave) if they would go to the place indicated. This was carried out, and when the whites showed the warrant of arrest the blacks stated that Pope was not of their party. The posse then agreed to disperse if the negroes would do so. The agreement was carried out on both sides.

As some of the posse were returning to their homes they were fired upon by negroes in ambush, and one of them was slightly wounded as he rode off. The whites who were riding near followed him after the shooting, and they, too, were fired on. About an hour later, near Silverton, about five miles distant, two white men quietly riding along the public road were fired on by negroes who were lying down under a large tree. One of the white men—John Williams—fell dead, and the other's horse being killed, he sprang into the woods and made his escape.

About this time the mill, barn and ginhouse of a citizen of Ellenton were destroyed by a fire which had been started by negroes. The killing of Williams and the fire occurred on Sunday, in the nighttime.

The whites believing that there was an uprising of negroes with murderous intent, couriers were dispatched in different directions, and by 2 o'clock in the morning about two hundred men gathered at Silverton, with Col. A. P. Butler and Capt. George W. Croft in charge. At daylight the whites moved towards Ellenton and to a point where the negroes, having first gathered in force, had torn up a part of the railroad and wrecked a train. The whites charged the negroes who had gathered about the wreck—killing one. The negroes weakly returned the fire and then scattered.

The wreckers now retired to Ellenton, where they were reinforced by a negro company from Barnwell, under Simon Coker, and were in actual possession of the town, threatening bloodshed. When the whites reached Ellenton they found that the negroes had just left—one party going towards Rouse's Bridge and the other towards a swamp where they expected to ambush white reinforcements coming from Barnwell under Gen. Johnson Hagood. The whites pushed on to Rouse's Bridge—it then being about 4 o'clock of Monday afternoon. They had not proceeded far when their scouts were fired on by negroes in ambush. The main body rushing up, the negroes fled. Three negroes were killed.

On the earnest request of the whites at Ellenton the party returned to that place and remained during the night. Up to this time there had been one white man killed and four wounded, whilst the negroes had lost five killed and two wounded. Three other negroes were killed during Monday night.

The force under General Hagood was a posse of the sheriff. Simon Coker's company, armed with Winchester rifles, had left Ellenton for Penn Branch swamp, where they intended to ambush the white reinforcements. Before reaching the swamp the Barnwell whites were fired on from ambush and the white sheriff, James

Patterson, was severely wounded. The advance guard of white men were suddenly confronted by about seventy negroes, who fired upon them. Robert Williams was killed and three other whites were wounded. The whites instantly returned the fire, killing three negroes and wounding several. The negroes then plunged into the swamp, leaving their captain, Coker, in the hands of the whites—and he, it was alleged, was afterwards killed, with two other negroes, at Ellenton. The Barnwell men killed seven negroes on the march to Ellenton. Three white men were wounded.

The whites were preparing to charge the negroes in the swamp, when a company of United States infantry (sent on the demand of Governor Chamberlain) appeared on the scene. It was agreed that the whites and negroes at once disperse. The whites retired first, and the colored men promptly followed their example.

This Ellenton trouble had lasted three days. The total of casualties was as follows: Whites, two killed, eight wounded; negroes—fifteen killed, two wounded.

THE CAINHOY MASSACRE.

On October 16 a meeting was arranged to be held near Cainhoy, in the parish of St. Thomas and St. Dennis, in Charleston County. Having to go by water, the Democratic committee chartered a steamer for the exclusive use of Democrats who as speakers or listeners should attend the meeting. Before the steamer left the Charleston wharf a number of negroes had gathered, and these noisily demanded that they be permitted to take passage, and threateningly declared that they intended to go anyhow, and that they wanted a chance to "clean out the Democrats." There had been an agreement that no guns should be taken to the meeting by either party, and arrangements were made for a joint discussion in which the two parties were to be equally represented by speakers. The Democrats had taken along a band, in order that their music might supplement the other agencies for peace.

There had been a speech by one Democrat, and a colored Republican (McKinlay) was speaking when trouble commenced. The negroes evidently intended to create a riot as soon as Martin R. Delany should start to speak, and they evidently mistook McKinlay for him. There were conflicting accounts of the origin of the riot. One story was that some negro women raised a cry that the whites had taken the negroes' guns concealed in a building not far away. Another statement was that in the course of a difficulty between a white man and a negro a pistol had been drawn by the former in self-defense. In violation of the agreement that neither party should carry guns or rifles to the place of meeting the negroes had brought their muskets and secreted them in a near-by swamp and in an old house near a church not far from the speaking-ground, and had left a guard over them. Very soon after McKinlay began speaking a company of the negroes marched out of the swamp with their arms and opened fire upon the whites, who were unarmed. Some white men made a rush for the house where the negroes had concealed about forty of their muskets. The rest of the negroes retreated to the swamp, where their guns were concealed, and seizing them, opened a brisk and indiscriminate fire upon the whites. C. C. Bowen interfered, or affected to interfere, but his principal henchman (one Cyrus Gaillard, colored,) ordered him to stand out of the way—saying that the negroes intended to get the white men anyhow. Bowen, first saying that he was powerless to keep the peace, fled to a place of safety. McKinlay, whose violent talk had no doubt inflamed the negroes, did likewise.

In the meantime Delany, Mr. William E. Simmons and several other aged white men had taken refuge in a brick house adjoining the church. Under the rapid fire poured into them the whites had retreated to the graveyard west of the church—such of them as had pistols returning the fire. The negro militia charged out of the swamp, surrounded the brick house and tried to batter down the door. Failing in this, they broke open the windows and pointed their muskets at the helpless occupants. These started to retreat, and they all escaped except Mr. Simmons, who upon emerging from the door was knocked down and beaten to death—the assailants then firing a load of buckshot into his prostrate body.

After the fight commenced the whites retreated to the village of Cainhoy. A stand had been made among the tombstones, and another was made about half way to the village, among piles of cut wood.

By the fire of the negroes six white men were killed—William E. Simmons, Alexander McNeill, William Daly, Thomas Whitaker, J. King and Walter Graddick. Sixteen whites were wounded—some of them severely.

There was but a single negro killed, and he and all the whites who were slain or wounded were shot after the negroes opened fire. The actions of the negroes evidenced a treacherous ambuscade, with every appearance of careful preparation, having for its purpose the slaughter of the white and colored Democrats at the meeting.

As soon as the news of the outrage reached Charleston a force of men, fully armed, went to Cainhoy for the protection of the white people there—the negroes outnumbering these more than ten to one. There was so much danger of bloodshed that a committee of citizens waited upon Governor Chamberlain and requested that United States troops be sent to the locality of the recent trouble. A company was ordered there accordingly—and remained for some days after the election.

TROUBLE IN OTHER COUNTIES.

After the Democratic campaign meeting in Edgefield, October 17, a party of six white men were riding along the main road, about a mile and a half from the town, when two of them were fired upon by a party of negro militia in ambush. One of them—John Gilmore—was instantly killed, and the other badly wounded. The others of the party were armed with pocket pistols, and, seeing a negro running through the bushes with a gun in his hand, they fired upon him, without doing any harm.

One of the party went at once for the coroner, and as that official was riding towards the place of the murder he was shot from ambush—one ball shattering his leg and wounding his horse.

There was intense excitement and there were threats of retaliation upon the black militia, but the counsels of prudent leaders prevented further trouble. The members of the militia company were settled upon a piece of State land within a mile of the spot where the murder was done.

On the night of October 23, at Mount Pleasant, a village near Charleston, a mob of several negroes, armed with guns, behaved in a manner to cause fears for the lives of the inhabitants. They took complete possession of the streets, firing their weapons, and, with whoops and yells, threatening to kill every man, woman and child in the place. They were loud in their denunciations of colored Democrats. So much alarmed were the villagers that the white families were hastily moved into a single house and the white men of the place, aided by some of the colored Democrats, kept guard around

THE CAMPAIGN OF 'SEVENTY-SIX

the building during the entire night. The ferry steamer running between the village and Charleston kept steam all night to be ready, in case of necessity, to transport the women and children to the city. The town authorities were powerless to disperse the mob, and the residents continued in apprehension until the next morning, when the invading negroes retired, at the same time swearing that they would soon return and execute their threats.

At many places in the State bloodshed was narrowly prevented by the self-restraint of the whites, who refrained from using force to check the lawless interference of negroes with the orderly proceedings of Democratic meetings.

The Democratic campaign meetings were sometimes seriously interrupted by the conduct of negroes, acting under the incitement of Republican leaders.

In Charleston there were violent threats against colored Democrats riding in the red shirt procession, and also endeavors to cause a disturbance. A club of colored Democrats, mounted, were assailed with brickbats, and a number of them were badly hurt. Bloodshed was prevented only by the coolness and forbearance of the whites.

At Beaufort the Democratic meeting had to be adjourned when General Hampton had spoken and one other speaker had said but little—this because of the riotous interference and angry threats of a negro mob led by prominent colored Republicans.

WHITES COMMANDED TO "DISPERSE."

Governor Chamberlain on October 7 (three days after his letter to the Democratic State chairman, already noted) issued the following proclamation:

Whereas, it has been made known to me by written and sworn evidence that there exist such unlawful obstructions, combinations and assemblages of persons in the counties of Aiken and Barnwell that it has become impracticable, in my judgment as Governor of the State, to enforce, by the usual course of judicial proceedings, the laws of the State within said counties, by reason whereof it has become necessary, in my judgment as Governor, to call forth and employ the military force of the State to enforce the faithful execution of the law; and whereas, it has been made known to me as Governor that certain organizations and combinations of men exist in all the counties of the State, commonly known as "rifle clubs"; and whereas, such organizations and combinations of men are illegal and strictly forbidden by the laws of this State; and whereas, such organizations and combinations of men are engaged in promoting illegal objects and in committing open acts of lawlessness and violence;

Now, therefore, I, Daniel H. Chamberlain, Governor of said State, do issue this my proclamation, as required by the 13th section of chapter 132 of the General Statutes of the State, commanding the said unlawful combinations and assemblages of persons in the counties of Aiken and Barnwell to disperse and return peaceably to their homes within three days from the date of this proclamation, and henceforth to abstain from all unlawful interference with the rights of citizens, and from all violations of the public peace. And I do further, by this proclamation, forbid the existence of all said organizations or combinations of men commonly known as "rifle clubs," and all other organizations or combinations of men, or formations not forming a part of the organized militia of the State, which are armed with firearms or other weapons of war, or which engage, or are formed for the purpose of engaging, in drilling or exercising the manual of arms or military manoeuvres, or which appear, or are formed for the purpose of appearing, under arms, or under the command of officers bearing titles or assuming the functions of ordinary military officers, or in any manner acting or proposing to act as organized and armed bodies of men; and I do command all such organizations, combinations, formations, or bodies of men forthwith to disband and cease to exist in any place and under any circumstances in the State.

And I do further declare and make known by this proclamation to all the people of this State that in case this proclamation shall be disregarded for the space of three days from the date thereof, I shall proceed to put into active use all the powers with which, as Governor, I am invested by the Constitution and laws of the State for the enforcement of the laws and the protection of the rights of the citizens, and particularly the powers conferred on me by Chapter 132 of the General Statutes of the State, as well as by the Constitution of the United States.

The rifle clubs have already been mentioned. Their existence, their public drills and parades, their open possession of arms, had for many months been actually sanctioned by the State Government—some of them having been supplied with State arms. A number of these clubs, uniformed, armed and equipped, had paraded in Charleston on June 28—celebrating the centennial of the battle of Fort Moultrie—and had been complimented by the Governor as a part of the "citizen soldiery" of South Carolina.

THE ANSWER OF THE DEMOCRACY.

In answer to the proclamation of the Governor, the Democratic State Executive Committee on October 7 issued the following paper:
To the People of the United States:
In a period of profound peace, with the laws unrestrained and the process of the courts unopposed, the Governor of South Carolina has, by proclamation, declared that in the counties of Aiken and Barnwell it has become impracticable to enforce by the ordinary course of judicial proceeding the laws of the State, and that it has become necessary for him, the Governor, "to call forth and employ the military force of the State to enforce the faithful execution of the law." He has also alleged that certain organizations and combinations exist, contrary to law, in all the counties of the State, which are engaged in promoting illegal objects and in committing open acts of lawlessness and violence, and he has threatened to declare martial law and to suspend the writ of habeas corpus.

The charges preferred by Governor Chamberlain against the citizens of the State are as false and libelous as his threatened usurpation of power is tyrannical and unwarranted; and his extraordinary proclamation can be explained only upon the assumption that Governor Chamberlain, with a similar disregard of law and fact, is determined to resort to the most extreme measures to prevent the otherwise certain defeat of himself and his corrupt party.

There have been disturbances in Aiken County, non-political in their character. They have long since ceased. All the parties for whom warrants were issued have promptly surrendered themselves to the law. Perfect peace and the profoundest quiet prevail. No armed combinations hinder the processes of the courts, and the Republican county convention last week held a continuous session of two days without molestation. The disturbances in Barnwell were Republican in their origin, beginning in the resistance, by an armed band of negroes, of the arrest of a robber for whom a warrant had been duly issued. This band tore up a railroad, wrecked the train, fired upon and wounded the sheriff of the county, and were dispersed by a so-called armed band of whites who had been duly summoned by the sheriff as a posse, with the sanction of the judge of the court then in session. This posse, after performing their duties, quietly dispersed. So far from opposing the law, the whole people desire the prompt dispatch of business in the courts and the enforcement of the law by the civil arm.

The white people throughout the State have volunteered their services to the Governor to maintain the law, and he has refused them in a libelous communication, intended solely to furnish a pretext for the introduction of Federal troops to be placed under the control of irresponsible and unscrupulous officials, to overawe the people and control the election.

The Democratic nominees in nineteen of the thirty-two counties in the State have held meetings, attended by thousands of citizens of both races and parties. The Republicans have held meetings when and where they pleased, and not a single act of violence has yet occurred.

On the 18th ultimo the Democratic Executive Committee invited the Republican canvassers to a joint discussion at their meetings. This invitation was renewed on the 28th ultimo and accepted by the Republican Executive Committee on the 5th instant on the usual terms.

The proclamation of the Governor is utterly at variance with the acts of the executive committee of his own party. The latter acquiesces in free discussion. The former in effect suppresses debate and substitutes armed force for free speech.

We assert earnestly, with a full sense of our responsibility, that no condition of things exists in this State which justifies so extraordinary a proceeding on the part of Governor Chamberlain. Its sole object is to irritate and provoke collisions which may be the excuse for an appeal to the administration of the United States to garrison the State. We shall counsel our people to preserve the peace, observe the laws and calmly await the day of their deliverance from this wanton despotism.

To the people of the United States we submit our wrongs, confidently relying on their wisdom and justice to rebuke this daring attempt to regulate the ballot by the bayonet and crush the liberties of a people.

Telegrams were submitted from Chief Justice Moses, Associate Justice Willard, Judge Mackey and Judge Cooke, each of whom explicitly declared that there was no organized or general resistance to the laws and that they could readily be enforced through the ordinary channels.

On October 9 the Democratic committee issued a second address to the people of the nation, as follows:

To the People of the United States:

In further answer to the charges against this State, made by Governor Chamberlain, we ask leave to submit the following:

The judiciary of South Carolina consists of three justices of the Supreme Court and eight circuit judges, all elected by the Republican Legislatures. One of the Supreme Court justices is absent, and has been for some months; two of the circuit judges are out of reach of communication, and we have failed as yet to get the views of the third, but the testimony of Governor Scott and Justices Moses and Willard apply to most of the circuits under this judge's jurisdiction.

We sent yesterday the testimony of Chief Justice Moses, Associate Justice Willard and Judges Mackey and Cooke. We attach today the evidence of Judge Northrop, Judge Wiggin (Aiken and Barnwell are in his circuit) and Judge Shaw. Thus we have the conclusive answer from the Supreme Court, five-eighths of the Circuit Court, whose jurisdiction covers three-fourths of the territory of the State. All our inquiries have failed to elicit a single instance of resistance to officers of the law, except by Republican negroes. The answer from Judge Wiggin explains these. They were at Ellenton and in the rice field region, where the white population is sparse. In the latter armed bodies of negroes, bearing State arms and ammunition, marched about for days whipping negroes—men and women—most cruelly to compel them to join in a labor strike. Some were whipped almost to death.

In this instance there was resistance; arrests were made, the prisoners were rescued, the posse of the sheriff driven across the country, and the law defied. These facts were officially represented to the Governor, and he received appeals from the suffering negroes. But under all these circumstances no proclamation of insurrection was issued, because no political capital could be made out of it.

As to the riot in Charleston, the judge is absent, but we cite Governor Chamberlain's own statement in his letter of the 4th instant: "The most trustworthy information seems to fix the chief responsibility for causing the riot upon the Republicans."

Judges Shaw, Northrop and Wiggin united in saying that they knew of no lawlessness or violence which the law could not remedy, and that there was no sign of resistance to process in their respective circuits. Judge Carpenter afterwards gave similar testimony.

The sheriff of Aiken and the sheriff of Barnwell each declared his ability to execute process and further declared that there was no evidence of any purpose to resist officials in the discharge of any duty.

On October 9 Governor Chamberlain published an address to the people of the United States, in which he stated that "the lawlessness, terrorism and violence" to which he had referred in his proclamation "far exceeded in extent and atrocity any statements yet made public," and further said:

All the evidence in my hands and in the hands of the United States district attorney will be made public so soon as the interests of public justice will permit it. I pledge myself to the country to prove a condition of affairs in this State, produced by the Democratic party, more disgraceful than any statement yet made by me, and I shall not stay my hand until punishment overtakes its guilty authors.

My only offense is too great caution in obtaining evidence, and too great delay in exercising my utmost powers to protect our citizens.

"INSURRECTION AND DOMESTIC VIOLENCE."

In the early part of October Governor Chamberlain had applied to President Grant "for aid in suppressing domestic violence in the State." On the 17th day of that month the President issued his proclamation, in which, after setting forth his ideas of his duties and powers under the Federal Constitution in relation to the suppression of insurrection or domestic violence in any State, he declared:

Whereas, It has been satisfactorily shown to me that insurrection and domestic violence exist in several counties of the State of South Carolina, and that certain combinations of men, against law, exist in many counties of said State, known as "rifle clubs," who ride up and down by day and night in arms, murdering some peaceable citizens and intimidating others, which combinations, though forbidden by the laws of the State, cannot be controlled or suppressed by the ordinary course of justice; and

Whereas, The Legislature of said State is not now in session, and cannot be convened in time to meet the present emergency, and the Executive of the State, under Section 4 of Article IV of the Constitution of the United States, and the laws passed in pursuance thereof, has therefore made due application to me in the premises for such part of the military force of the United States as may be necessary and adequate to protect said State and the citizens thereof against domestic violence, and to enforce the due execution of the laws; and

Whereas, It is required that whenever it may be necessary, in the judgment of the President, to use the military force for the purpose aforesaid, he shall forthwith, by proclamation, command such insurgents to disperse and retire peaceably to their respective homes within a limited time:

Now, therefore, I, Ulysses S. Grant, President of the United States, do hereby make proclamation and command all persons engaged in said unlawful and insurrectionary proceedings to disperse and retire peaceably to their respective abodes within three days from this date, and hereafter abandon said combinations and submit themselves to the laws and the constituted authorities of said State.

On the same day the Secretary of War issued the following order to Gen. W. T. Sherman, commanding the United States army:

Sir: In view of the existing condition of affairs in South Carolina there is a possibility that the President's proclamation of this date may be disregarded. To provide against such a contingency you will immediately order all the available force in the military division of the Atlantic to report to General Ruger, commanding at

Columbia, S. C., and instruct that officer to station his troops in such localities that they may be most speedily and effectually used, in case of resistance to the authority of the United States. It is hoped that a collision may thus be avoided; but you will instruct General Ruger to let it be known that it is the fixed purpose of the Government to carry out fully the spirit of the proclamation, and to sustain it by the military force of the General Government, supplemented, if necessary, by the militia of the various States.

Upon the publication of these papers, General Hampton sent the following telegram to Gen. Johnson Hagood, Barnwell, and to Capt. George W. Croft, Aiken:

"Urge our people to submit peaceably to martial law. I will see and consult with them."

To Gen. M. C. Butler he telegraphed: "Use your influence to keep our people in Aiken from resisting martial law."

There was no resistance—and none was ever thought of. The rifle clubs all disbanded—at least they ceased their drills, parades and other appearances in public.

There was universal disgust among the white people at the action of the Governor, and their poor opinion of the President was not at all improved. By this action General Grant only strengthened the opinion of the people of South Carolina that, great soldier and magnanimous victor as he had been, he was the smallest character that ever got into the White House.

The action of the President and the Governor served but to strengthen the determination of the white people to carry the State. It served also to bring over the doubtful and some in actual affiliation with the Republican party. It is safe to say that not more than 1,000 white men voted for Chamberlain.

Federal troops in large numbers moved into South Carolina—the whole force concentrated here being estimated at 5,000 men. Before the day of election there were a company or more at almost every county seat in the State.

The Federal officials were called into requisition. In Aiken and Barnwell there were upwards of two hundred arrests—the parties being charged with violations of the Enforcement Act, as evidenced by their participation in the efforts of certain white men to execute process and preserve the peace in those counties. There were some arrests in Edgefield, Pickens and Marion—the offense of the accused consisting in "dividing time" at Republican meetings. The parties promptly gave bail. A few only of those arrested were ever tried and these—citizens of Aiken County—were not convicted. The jury failed to agree. The trial came off in Charleston in April, 1877.

AN APPEAL TO THE PEOPLE.

On October 18 the Democratic State Executive Committee published the following address:

To the people of the State of South Carolina who desire honest government, without regard to political party or race:

His Excellency, the President of the United States, did, on the 17th day of this month, issue a proclamation whereby he commanded "all persons engaged in unlawful and insurrectionary proceedings to disperse and retire peaceably to their respective abodes within three days from this date, and hereafter abandon said combinations, and submit themselves to the laws and constituted authorities of said State."

This proclamation is based upon the statements made by Daniel H. Chamberlain, the Governor of this State; which statements are aimed exclusively against his political opponents and are proven to be untrue by the testimony of every judge in the State, every trial justice or other officer of the law from whom response has been obtained. Every resident of the State knows them to be untrue. Every Republican of character or intelligence, or who is not in office or seeking office, and many who are in office in the State, have expressed horror and disgust at the course which the Governor has pursued.

We say this much for our vindication: Never has a people suffered more by dishonor of office and dishonesty of officers. Never has such bald untruth been used for the support of a movement which shakes the pillars upon which rests the constitutional temple of a mighty people. Our State is but a petty portion of the Union, but we call upon our sister States of the North to remember that the experiment now being made for "the domination of our elections by the bayonet and by soldiers as the irresistible instruments of a revolutionary local despotism," if successful, will become the precedent before which the whole fabric of American liberty will fall, and will be applied to other States just as soon as party exigencies require it.

We make this declaration of our innocence not in disrespect of the President of the United States, but as an act of justice to ourselves as American citizens, and to put our case upon the record for an impartial trial before the great national tribunal. We bow in perfect submission to the proclamation of his Excellency the President, and exhort our fellow citizens whom we represent in the present canvass to yield full and entire obedience to every command of the said proclamation.

We know that the clubs called "rifle clubs" are associations formed for home protection; that they are not combinations as charged by the Governor of this State; that there are but few that have arms or ammunition; that those which have been equipped were so done with the sanction and sometimes with the aid of the Governor, and have been recognized by him as useful and appropriate bodies, and not one of them has been accused of disorder.

We know that their necessity was occasioned by the reckless distribution of arms and ammunition among the colored people by the State officials; and we further know that our white fellow citizens were, on the 16th day of this month, massacred at a peaceful political assemblage, where (by agreement with C. C. Bowen, Republican chairman for Charleston County, and sheriff of said county, and present at the meeting, and first presidential elector for the State at large on the Republican ticket) they went without arms to meet the colored race—the voters of the so-called Republican party in this State—who were likewise, by Mr. Bowen's agreement, bound to be without arms; and we know that the politicians who are the authors of all our evils are teaching among the colored race the use of the rifle and the torch; we know that our homes are in peril, and that our women and children are exposed to the horrors of ruthless butchery and barbarity; but, nevertheless, we advise and command, so far as our authority goes, that every such "rifle club" against which the misrepresentations of the Governor of the State are aimed be forthwith disbanded, and that the members thereof be held in future only by those ties of humanity which bind all good men together; that the name of the club be abandoned, and the officers cease to exercise their powers. This is said with the express declaration that these clubs are not associated with or subject to our political control.

We repeat that we speak without disrespect to the President of the United States. He acts upon the statements made by the Governor of this State. But we say it that we may show our unwillingness to obey without committing an untruth against ourselves by seeming to acknowledge that of which we are not guilty.

We are not engaged in "unlawful and insurrectionary proceedings." We cannot "disperse" because we are not gathered together. We cannot "retire peaceably to our abodes," because we are in our homes in peace, disturbed alone by the political agitations created by the Governor and his minions.

But we resignedly—and cheerfully in the performance of our duty—suspend the exercise of our individual and private rights in order to prevent evil to the whole people.

Relying upon the universal sense of right, and appealing to the Almighty to sustain us, we exhort our people to the continuance of submission to the authorities of the Government, feeling sure that time and patience will work our deliverance.

Remember that the campaign is now a short one and that all signs are hopeful that the seventh day of November next will witness the full and complete vindication of our cause through the peaceful instrumentality of the ballot box.

The counsel of the committee was faithfully followed. There was no relaxation of effort, no wavering in the determination to drive Governor Chamberlain and his party from power. But there was a degree of self-control which whilst it helped to keep the peace yet increased the strain to which the white people were subjected.

On October 26 religious services were held in churches all over the State—this in response to the suggestion of the Democratic State Executive Committee that on that day the people assemble at their several places of divine worship; and the ministers of the gospel were "solicited to open the churches for service and lead us in the prayer unto Almighty God that justice, peace and prosperity, mercy and truth, with fellowship and good feeling to all men, may come back and prevail among our long suffering and much disturbed people."

The last meeting of the State canvass was held in Columbia on November 4. And the campaign of 'seventy-six was over.

NO BLOODSHED ON ELECTION DAY.

The election on November 7 passed off without bloodshed and without serious breaches of the peace. The election machinery was practically in the control of the Republicans—two of the three managers at each polling-place being of their party. At each poll there were two Federal supervisors—one from each political party. At many county seats and at some other points there were United States troops, but as their officers strictly obeyed the orders given them not to act except to preserve the peace there was no occasion for any of them to leave camp. The men apparently had orders to remain in camp during the entire day; for none of them was seen elsewhere.

The white Democrats worked with great activity during the entire day—their energies directed to having all their colored recruits vote without molestation from any source and to making votes among negroes who had hitherto persisted in calling themselves Republicans. Efforts among the colored men were centered on the State and county tickets. Many colored Republicans voted for Hayes and Hampton—this accounting for the fact that whilst Hampton won the

THE CAMPAIGN OF 'SEVENTY-SIX 391

Republicans got in their electoral ticket. In some of the lower counties negro Democrats were subjected to threats and even assaults, and in Charleston County there were numerous acts of intimidation and fraud.

RIOTOUS NEGROES IN CHARLESTON.

In the city of Charleston on the afternoon of November 9 there was a riot resulting in the death of one white man—E. H. Walter, a peaceable, worthy and well-known citizen—and in the wounding, more or less severely, of many others. Broad street for four blocks was crowded with people of both races, all excited, and the blacks evidently enraged by the reports that Hampton was elected. An altercation arose between a Democrat and a Republican, in the course of which a white man not connected with the trouble accidentally fired his pistol, when a negro raised the cry that E. W. M. Mackey had been shot because he had boasted of the election of Hayes and Wheeler. The negroes immediately raised a yell and crowded down Broad street, armed with pistols and bludgeons. The whites stood their ground and received the attack firmly. Another pistol shot was fired and then came a dozen more in rapid succession. The black mob stampeded and retreated toward Church street—between the starting point of the riot and the police station. A squad of police arrived and did some shooting, but without effect on the negroes, some of whom rushed for their guns concealed not far off, others using fence-palings and tree-boxes with which to beat the unarmed whites whom they could reach. At one stage of the row a negro deliberately fired down the street at a white man, and a negro policeman asked by another white man to arrest the assailant clubbed the former unmercifully. The shot of the negro just mentioned caused further firing by white men, near the station, and from the building came volleys which did the most harm—killing Walter and wounding most of those who so suffered. A negro policeman was seen to aim at Walter, killing him almost instantly.

The casualties in this dreadful affair were as follows: Of whites —one killed and twelve wounded; of negroes—one mortally and eleven otherwise wounded.

About the time of the killing of Walter the whites had gathered for self-defense, and these to the number of 500, with rifles, volunteered to act as special police. In the meantime two companies of

United States soldiers appeared on the scene, to find that the riot had about exhausted itself.

In another part of the city a mob of about two hundred negroes assembled, with their muskets, and, no white faces being in sight, they proceeded to fire in the air and to smash store windows in their reach. Some white men passing in another street were brutally clubbed by negroes. A Federal soldier walking on the street was fired on by negroes, and narrowly escaped with his life. Several other white men, in different parts of the city, quietly using the streets, were beaten or shot—some of them being badly wounded.

In all this trouble the city authorities—the mayor and the police—were powerless to preserve the peace or prevent bloodshed. In this state of affairs it was decided by a committee of leading white citizens (in a conference at which the mayor was present) to put the policing of the city in the hands of the officer commanding the United States troops. At this conference the mayor—George I. Cunningham—was made to acknowledge his total inability to protect life or property. He was also made to promise that in case of further trouble he would call on Gen. James Conner, then in command of the white forces, to quell the riot and maintain the peace. The Federal commander continued in control for several days—until all signs of trouble had disappeared.

The white citizens of Charleston were amply prepared to protect themselves and also to punish any lawbreakers of either race who might undertake to repeat the performances of the afternoon of November 8. These good and true men consented to give their city over to the military simply because they were urged to that course by their recognized leaders—including Wade Hampton himself.

There were disturbances with more or less bloodshed in other parts of the State. In Beaufort, after the close of the polls, a negro was brutally beaten, by men of his own race, simply because he had voted the Democratic ticket. On the next day he made complaint to a trial justice, who first sent a constable and, that officer failing to make the arrest, then a posse composed of white citizens of known coolness, to arrest the offender. The posse were resisted by a mob of armed negroes and a fight ensued in which one of the posse— J. H. Shuman—was killed and some other white men were wounded.

In several other localities bloodshed was averted only by the readiness and the determination of the whites.

THE CAMPAIGN OF 'SEVENTY-SIX 393

THE ELECTION AND THE COUNT.

The returns came in but slowly. On Wednesday morning it seemed that Tilden and Chamberlain had carried the State. On Thursday it appeared that Hampton had won, and that there was a good chance for the Hayes electors. Incomplete returns—or figures changed by the later reports—made it certain that the race was as close as the fight had been hard. On the morning of the 9th the returns showed a majority for Hampton of 2,974. On the 17th Hampton's majority was reported to be 1,323, and this figure stood until the official count which changed it slightly.

The following table shows the Hampton and the Chamberlain majorities in this election, together with the white and the colored majorities given in the State census of 1875:

	Hampton.	Chamberlain.	White.	Colored.
Abbeville	187			2,023
Aiken	742			979
Anderson	3,031		1,114	
Barnwell	1,233			2,151
Beaufort		5,330		6,481
Charleston		6,233		10,289
Chester		390		1,686
Chesterfield	650		344	
Clarendon		445		1,031
Colleton		1,179		1,739
Darlington		758		1,385
Edgefield	3,225			1,678
Fairfield		623		1,919
Georgetown		1,729		2,476
Greenville	2,443		2,019	
Horry	1,352		984	
Kershaw		299		1,136
Lancaster	305			34
Laurens	1,112			585
Lexington	873		653	
Marion	657		198	
Marlboro	337			342
Newberry		565		1,529
Oconee	1,559		1,343	

	Hampton	Chamberlain	White	Colored
Orangeburg		1,599		2,203
Pickens	1,596		1,270	
Richland		1,422		2,874
Spartanburg	3,210		2,352	
Sumter		1,479		2,535
Union	755			377
Williamsburg		686		1,164
York	786			206
Totals	24,053	22,730	10,277	46,722

On the face of the returns as tabulated by the Board of State Canvassers it appeared that the Democrats elected the Secretary of State, the Attorney-General and the Comptroller-General, whilst the Republicans elected the Treasurer, the Superintendent of Education and the Adjutant-General.

The Democrats elected five solicitors—W. W. Sellers in the Fourth circuit, John R. Abney in the Fifth, T. C. Gaston in the Sixth, B. W. Ball in the Seventh, and James S. Cothran in the Eighth; the Republicans electing C. W. Buttz in the First, S. J. Lee (colored) in the Second, and M. J. Hirsch in the Third.

The Democrats elected two Congressmen—D. Wyatt Aiken in the Third district and John H. Evins in the Fourth; the Republicans electing J. H. Rainey (colored) in the First, C. W. Buttz (unexpired term) in the Second, R. H. Cain (colored) in the Second (full term), and Robert Smalls (colored) in the Fifth.

The Republican electors were elected by a majority of over 1,100—the vote varying a little among the different candidates.

Senators and representatives in the General Assembly were elected as follows:

*Abbeville—Senator, J. C. Maxwell; Representatives, W. K. Bradley, R. R. Hemphill, F. A. Connor, Wm. Hood, J. L. Moore.

*Aiken—Senator, A. P. Butler; Representatives, C. E. Sawyer, J. J. Woodward, L. M. Asbill, J. G. Guignard.

*Anderson—Representatives, H. R. Vandiver, R. W. Simpson, W. C. Brown, James L. Orr.

*Barnwell—Senator, J. M. Williams; Representatives, I. S. Bamberg, John W. Holmes, L. W. Youmans, W. A. Rountree, Robert Aldrich.

THE CAMPAIGN OF 'SEVENTY-SIX 395

Beaufort—Senator, Samuel Green; Representatives, Thomas Hamilton, Hastings Gantt, Joseph Robinson, George Reed, N. B. Myers, Thomas E. Miller.

Charleston—Senator, W. M. Taft (white); Representatives, E. W. M. Mackey (white), J. J. Lesesne, B. F. Smalls, Robert Simmons, W. C. Glover, F. S. Edwards, Isaac Prioleau, John Vanderpool, William J. Brodie, J. S. Lazarus, S. C. Brown, Benjamin F. Capers, A. P. Ford, Richard Bryan, Julius C. Tingman, Abram Smith, W. G. Pinckney.

Chester—Representatives, John Lee, Samuel Coleman, Purvis Alexander.

*Chesterfield—Representatives, J. C. Coit, D. T. Redfearn.

Clarendon—Representatives, S. Melton, H. Boston.

*Colleton—Representatives, H. E. Bissell, J. M. Cummins, S. E. Parler, William Maree (colored), R. Jones.

Darlington—Representatives, R. H. Humbert, S. J. Keith, Z. Wines, J. A. Smith.

*Edgefield—Senator, M. W. Gary; Representatives, W. S. Allen, J. C. Sheppard, James Callison, T. E. Jennings, H. A. Shaw.

Fairfield—Senator, Israel Byrd; Representatives, John Gibson, Daniel Bird, Prince Martin.

Georgetown—Senator, B. H. Williams; Representatives, C. S. Green, P. R. Kinloch.

*Greenville—Senator, S. S. Crittenden; Representatives, J. W. Gray, J. F. Donald, J. T. Austin, J. S. Westmoreland.

*Horry—Senator, William L. Buck; Representatives, L. D. Bryan, J. K. Cooper.

Kershaw—Representatives, R. D. Gaither, A. W. Kough, E. H. Dibble.

*Laurens—Senator, R. P. Todd; Representatives, J. B. Humbert, J. W. Watts, W. D. Anderson.

*Lancaster—Representatives, J. B. Erwin, J. C. Blakeney.

*Lexington—Senator, H. A. Meetze; Representatives, G. Leaphart, G. Muller.

*Marion—Senator, R. G. Howard; Representatives, J. G. Blue, J. McRae, R. H. Rogers, J. P. Davis.

*Marlboro—Representatives, Philip M. Hamer, Thomas N. Edens.

Newberry—Senator, H. C. Corwin (white); Representatives, William Keitt, J. S. Bridges, W. H. Thomas.

*Oconee—Senator, J. W. Livingston; Representatives, B. F. Sloan, J. S. Verner.

Orangeburg—Senator, J. L. Duncan; Representatives, D. A. Straker, S. Morgans, W. H. Reedish, C. M. Caldwell, E. Forrest.

*Pickens—Representatives, D. F. Bradley, E. S. Bates.

Richland—Representatives, A. W. Curtis, Charles Minort, R. J. Palmer, J. W. Lowman, James Wells.

*Spartanburg—Senator, Gabriel Cannon; Representatives, W. P. Compton, J. W. Wofford, E. S. Allen, Charles Petty.

Sumter—Representatives, J. Westberry, Thomas B. Johnston (white), J. H. Ferriter (white), T. Andrews.

*Union—Representatives, W. H. Wallace, G. D. Peake, William Jefferies.

Williamsburg—Representatives, W. Scott, J. F. Peterson, John Evans.

*York—Senator, I. D. Witherspoon; Representatives, A. E. Hutchison, J. A. Deal, W. E. Byers, B. H. Massey.

One-half of the senators held over from the last election.

The new House contained sixty-four Democrats and sixty Republicans, the Senate fifteen Democrats and eighteen Republicans—giving the Democrats a majority of one vote on joint ballot.

There was, of course, great rejoicing among the white people, and the colored men who had helped to elect Hampton were no less joyous. The Republicans managers, including Governor Chamberlain, denied that the Democrats had won, and vehemently declared that there had been monstrous frauds and general intimidation. These claims and charges having been expected, they had no effect upon the white people, except to strengthen their determination to see that they were not cheated of the fruits of their hard-earned victory.

When the returns showed the election of the Democratic State ticket, General Hampton issued the following address:

To the People of the State:

In offering to our people my heartfelt congratulations and gratitude for the grand victory they have won, I venture to beg them to prove themselves worthy of it by a continued observance of good order and a rigid preservation of peace. Let us show that we seek

---

*Democratic counties. Except as otherwise noted, all the Democrats were white and all the Republicans colored.

only the restoration of good government, the return of prosperity and the establishment of harmony to the whole people of our State.

In the hour of victory we should be magnanimous, and we should strive to forget the animosities of the contest by recalling the grand results of our success. Proscribing none for difference of opinion, regarding none as enemies, save such as are inimical to law and order, let us all unite in the patriotic work of redeeming the State. By such conduct we can not only bring about good feeling among all classes, but can most surely reap the best fruits of victory.

THE REPUBLICAN RETURNING BOARD.

To understand the action of the Board of State Canvassers and the court proceedings had in connection with the acts of that body, some statement of their powers is necessary.

The commissioners of election (three in number, appointed by the Governor) were required to meet at the county seat on the Tuesday next following the election and organize as a board of county canvassers, and within ten days of the time of their first meeting such board were to make such statement of the votes "as the nature of the election required" and transmit to the Board of State Canvassers any protests and all papers relating to the election. Duplicate statements were required to be made out and filed in the office of the clerk of the Circuit Court, and if there should be no clerk, then in the office of the Secretary of State. Besides these, statements of the votes, each containing the names of the persons voted for and the number of votes cast for each were to be made out and transmitted by mail to the Governor, the Comptroller-General and the Secretary of State.

At the time of the election of 1876 the Board of State Canvassers consisted of H. E. Hayne, Secretary of State; F. L. Cardozo, Treasurer; T. C. Dunn, Comptroller-General; William Stone, Attorney-General; and H. W. Purvis, Adjutant and Inspector General. All of these persons were active partisans of Governor Chamberlain, and three of them, Hayne, Cardozo and Dunn, constituting a majority of the board, were candidates for reelection.

By the statute this board was required to meet on or before the 10th of November, "for the purpose of canvassing the votes for all officers voted for" at the election preceding.

The law required that the board when formed should, "upon the certified copies of the statements made by the boards of county canvassers, proceed to make a statement of the whole number of votes given at such election for the various officers and for each of them voted for, distinguishing the several counties in which they are given." They were required to certify such statements to be correct and subscribe the same with their proper names. They were further required to "make and subscribe on the proper statement a certificate of their determination and deliver the same to the Secretary of State." The law further provided:

Upon such statements they shall then proceed to determine and declare what persons have been by the greatest number of votes duly elected to such offices or either of them. They shall have power, and it is made their duty, to decide all cases under protest or contest that may arise when the power to do so does not by the Constitution reside in some other body. In case of a contest of the election for Governor (if the General Assembly by concurrent resolution shall entertain the same) the Senate and House of Representatives shall, each separately, proceed to hear and determine the facts in the case so far as they deem necessary, and decide thereon who, according to the tenth section of article 8 of the Constitution, is entitled to be declared elected.

The board had power to adjourn from day to day "for a term not exceeding ten days."

Section 10 of article 8, above referred to, read: "In all elections held by the people under this Constitution the person or persons who shall receive the highest number of votes shall be declared elected." This was a general provision embracing not only the election for Governor, but also the election for other State officers, for members of the General Assembly and for Presidential electors.

The Constitution (Article III, Section 4) provided: "The person having the highest number of votes shall be Governor."

Section 14 of Article II provided: "Each house shall judge of the election returns and qualifications of its own members."

The elections in the respective counties of Edgefield, Laurens and Barnwell, in which the Democratic candidates had the majorities, were contested, and it was generally feared and believed by the white people that the members of the Board of State Canvassers would assume judicial powers and give the certificates of election for those counties to the Republican candidates, and thus give to that party the control of the organization of the House. It was also believed that that board would set aside, disregard or ignore the returns or statements of the canvassers in the disputed counties, of the election for Governor and Lieutenant-Governor and the State ticket generally, and thus give a majority to D. H. Chamberlain and the other Republican candidates. These fears and beliefs grew out of the fact that all of the members of the State board were Republican politicians, and the further fact that three out of the five composing that board were candidates for reelection. It was therefore manifest that if they assumed judicial powers and undertook to decide which of the candidates for the Legislature from the contested counties were entitled *prima facie* to certificates of election, and also to decide on the returns or statements of the local boards of canvassers of those counties as to the validity of the election for State officers, they would be acting as judges in their own cause.

These objections having been brought to the notice of the board, in a protest against their exercising any other than ministerial powers, they passed resolutions declaring that they did not purpose to canvass the returns for Governor and Lieutenant-Governor; that as the Board of State Canvassers they had the right to hear protests as to the election of electors for President and Vice-President and of members of Congress, and to give their certificates to such persons as had the highest number of votes; and that "it is the opinion of the Board of State Canvassers that the Secretary of State, State Treasurer and Comptroller-General have the right to sit as members of this board, to hear and determine all questions coming before them, except that neither of the said officers shall vote upon his own election."

The objections above mentioned were taken before the board, on behalf of the Democratic candidates for State offices, in proceedings regularly brought. The conclusions of the board, as far as indicated, being unsatisfactory to the protestants they applied to the State Supreme Court, then in session, for the relief which they had demanded.

The board held its first meeting on November 13, and on November 14 the protestants appeared before the Supreme Court. The proceedings before that tribunal, so far as they had relation to the Board of Canvassers, lasted till November 25, with occasional intermissions made necessary by the nature of the litigation.

IN THE SUPREME COURT.

The object of the proceedings brought by the Democrats claiming to have been elected to the several State offices (except, of course, that of Governor and of Lieutenant-Governor) was to confine the

Board of State Canvassers to the exercise of such powers as the statutes conferred—to compel them to do the ministerial acts therein commanded and to restrain them from exercising any judicial function whatever.

The complainants applied to the court for an order requiring the board to show cause why they should not be compelled and restrained according to the prayers of the complainants, and prayed that, pending action upon such application, the board should be restrained from proceeding. The court granted the order to show cause, but refused the restraining order—this on the ground that for the board to proceed under the circumstances would be a high contempt of court, and such action on their part was not to be contemplated.

Upon being served with the court's order the Board of Canvassers resolved that they would not act upon any proposition until the question of their powers and duties should be decided by the Supreme Court.

On November 21 the board, in obedience to an order of the Supreme Court, filed therein a certified statement of the persons who at the general election on the 7th had received the greatest number of votes for the offices for which they were respectively candidates, according to the statements of the boards of county canvassers, at the same time informing the court that there were clerical errors in regard to T. C. Dunn and J. R. Tolbert, and that there were contests and protests from the counties of Barnwell, Edgefield and Laurens, on account of alleged irregularities, frauds and intimidation in said counties. In their statement the canvassers disclaimed authority to correct clerical errors or to adjudicate the protests and contests—their duty and authority in those respects being then under consideration by the court.

On November 22 the court commanded the Board of Canvassers forthwith to declare duly elected as senators and representatives the persons who, according to the board's certified statement to the court, had received the greatest number of votes, and to deliver immediately a certified statement and declaration thereof to the Secretary of State, and also commanded that officer forthwith to make the proper record in his office and transmit a copy thereof, under the seal of his office, to each person declared thereby to be elected, and a like copy to the Governor, and to cause a copy to be printed in one or more newspapers of the State.

The board immediately, and without adjournment, took up the matter of canvassing and tabulating the votes for electors for President and Vice-President—wherein it was claimed by the Democratic candidates that there were many errors and irregularities. Those candidates (claiming of course to have been elected) had applied to the Supreme Court for an order requiring the board to take the proper steps to ascertain the actual vote lawfully given for each person for the office of elector, and report to the court. To this order the board responded with a request for further time—this on the ground that the performance of the duties enjoined upon them by the previous commands of the court would prevent their answer in the time fixed. Additional time was accordingly granted.

While these proceedings were being had in court and the board were asking the court's indulgence the board on November 22 assembled, without the knowledge of any of the parties interested, corrected the alleged clerical errors in favor of Dunn and Tolbert, thereby reversing the certified aggregation of votes which they had submitted to the court, and further failed to certify as elected the persons who in Edgefield and Laurens had received the greatest number of votes for seats in the General Assembly. H. E. Hayne, the Secretary of State, voted against this action, on the ground that the testimony before the board came from one side only. The board next proceeded to declare elected all the Republican candidates for State offices (except Governor and Lieutenant-Governor) and then, between the hours of 12, noon, and 1, afternoon, adjourned *sine die*.

When on November 24 the final act of the Board of Canvassers was brought by the complainants to the notice of the Supreme Court that tribunal made an order requiring the board to show cause, at 4 p. m., why they should not be attached for contempt in that they had desregarded the order requiring them to tabulate the votes according to law and certify a statement thereof to the Secretary of State. The board appeared by counsel at the hour fixed, and asked for further time. Their application was refused, and they were adjudged to be in contempt of the court. On the morning of November 25, they were each sentenced to pay a fine of $1,500, and to be taken by the sheriff of Richland into his custody and committed to the county jail, there to remain until the further order of the court.

The five members of the Board of State Canvassers were accordingly arrested and placed in the Richland jail.

The case involving the duties of the board in relation to the votes for Presidential electors, and also intended to determine whether the Democratic or the Republican candidates had been lawfully chosen, was duly argued. On January 26, 1877, the Supreme Court filed its decision—which was throughout adverse to the contentions of the Democrats.

In the several phases of the litigation in the Supreme Court the Democratic complainants were represented by James Conner, James H. Rion, Theo. G. Barker, E. W. Moise, John T. Rhett, Louis Le-Conte, LeRoy F. Youmans, Joseph Daniel Pope and John B. Gordon.

The lawyers for the Republican officials were D. T. Corbin, R. B. Elliott, Thomas Settle, of North Carolina, J. R. Denny, of Indiana, and A. T. Ackerman, of Georgia. Judge Settle was a prominent Republican in North Carolina—having there served with credit on the circuit bench. He was beaten by Zeb. Vance for Governor in 1876. Judge Denny was a lawyer of some note in his own State. Mr. Ackerman was Grant's Attorney-General when the President suspended the writ of habeas corpus in some counties, and was active in pushing the prosecution of so-called Kuklux in the Carolinas. It was Ackerman who paid the "star witness" Kirkland L. Gunn $200 for "services."

In the course of the proceedings in the Supreme Court both Corbin and Ackerman were attached for unprofessional conduct in contempt of court. The hearings were postponed and, the Hampton Government having been finally established, the proceedings were abandoned.

There was much indignation at the conduct of the Board of State Canvassers in defying the mandates of the Supreme Court—many of the leading papers of the North joining in the declaration that the course of these officials was in contempt of the law, subversive of the rights of the citizen and dangerous to the liberties of the people.

General Hampton immediately declared his views as follows:
To the People of South Carolina:
The Board of State Canvassers have by their unprecedented action today shown not only their contempt and defiance of the Supreme Court of the State, but their utter disregard of their own

office and integrity. While the grave questions determining the results of the recent election were pending before the Supreme Court, composed of three judges belonging to the Republican party, and in direct violation of the orders of this tribunal, the board have issued certificates of election to the Republican Presidential electors, and to Republican State officers, and have refused to give certificates to Democratic members of the Legislature, shown by the returns of this same board to have been elected in the counties of Edgefield and Laurens.

This high-handed outrage is well calculated to arouse the indignation of our long-suffering people, but I assure them that this daring and revolutionary act of the board can have no force whatever. I appeal to you, therefore, in the fullest confidence that the appeal will not be unheeded, that you will maintain, even under these provocations, your character of an orderly and law-abiding people. During the late exciting political canvass you have studiously avoided even the semblance of a purpose to disturb the public peace or to transgress the law.

Your cause, and it is the cause of constitutional government in this country, has been carried to the highest court of the State, and we are willing to abide by its decision, feeling assured that this tribunal will see that the laws shall be enforced and justice succeed.

Governor Chamberlain took occasion immediately upon the adjournment of the Board of Canvassers to express his approval of the action of that body. He declared that the board had simply done its plain duty in certifying the election of the Republican electors and in throwing out the votes of Edgefield and Laurens; that the board's term of service was by law limited to ten days, and that upon the expiration of that period adjournment was imperatively required by law; that the Supreme Court had no power to control its action or extend its term; and that the board had not been guilty of contempt—this for the reason that the Supreme Court had never made any order restraining the board from acting. He expressed the opinion that the jurisdiction of the Federal court would be invoked to determine the board's powers in relation to the canvassing and declaring of the vote for Presidential electors—contending that in those matters the board was in the discharge of Federal duties and that, having performed them according to law, it could not be punished by the State court as for contempt of process. He further declared that the Federal court might interfere and stop the proceedings of a State court with respect to State matters if such matters affected the action of any Federal official.

When asked what he thought would happen if two bodies, each claiming to be the State Legislature or one of its component branches, should assemble in Columbia, the Governor said: "I don't know, but I suppose, if it comes to that, the Federal Government will interfere, as it has done in similar cases, and settle the matter one way or the other."

THE COURT'S ORDER NULLIFIED.

The fall term of the Circuit Court of the United States began at Columbia on Monday, November 27. Judge Bond had come to the city a few days previous, and this fact gave rise to considerable surmise and some comment among the Democrats—by whom, of course, the Judge was regarded as a warm (and rather unscrupulous) partisan of the Republican administration.

Referring to some newspaper statements Judge Bond declared: "The canvassing board have never been advised by me. No one has applied to the Federal Circuit Court of this district. If any person does so apply, and there is a statute for it, he shall have relief; if there be no statute he must seek his remedy elsewhere."

Judge Bond further said that he had no idea of interfering, that he was in Columbia one week before the meeting of his court solely for the purpose of examining into the business to come before him and without any other object whatever.

On the opening of the Federal Court, Hayne and others, constituting the Board of State Canvassers, petitioned Judge Bond for a writ of habeas corpus, commanding the Richland sheriff to bring the prisoners before him on that day, to the end that inquiry be made into the cause of their detention, etc.

The petition set forth the transactions of the Board of Canvassers and the action of the State Supreme Court. It further declared:

That in the lawful discharge of their duties as a board of State canvassers the petitioners duly canvassed according to law the returns of the election of electors of President and Vice-President of the United States and members of the House of Representatives of the United States, and determined and certified that certain persons [naming the Republican electors] were duly elected by the greatest number of votes, and that certain persons [naming them] were duly elected members of the House of Representatives of the United States.

That in canvassing the returns of said election for President and Vice-President, and determining, declaring and certifying the result thereof, the petitioners were compelled to canvass and declare the election for all the State and other officers voted for at said election, except the Governor and Lieutenant-Governor, not only by reason of their duties as defined by the laws of said State in respect to such State officers, but also by reason of the fact that the returns of all the votes of the persons voted for, and all other papers and evidences pertaining to said election and within the custody and jurisdiction of the Board of State Canvassers, covered and embraced the entire election and were therefore necessarily blended and commingled as one general whole.

That if the petitioners had failed to discharge their duties in full on or before the said 22d day of November, 1876, the said election for electors for President and Vice-President and members of Congress would have failed, inasmuch as by the laws of said State no power is given to the Board of State Canvassers or to any other person or persons to canvass and determine said elections after said day. That all the orders of the Supreme Court of South Carolina, including the order committing the petitioners to jail, were an attempt by unlawful means to induce the petitioners as a board of State canvassers to violate and refuse to comply with their duty and the laws regulating the same, and for this reason said proceedings and said order committing the petitioners to jail were and are in violation of Section 5111 of the Revised Statutes of the United States.

That the petitioners are in custody and confinement, and are restrained of their liberty, for acts done in pursuance of laws of the United States, and that they are in custody in violation of the Constitution and laws of the United States.

Section 5111 of the Revised Statutes, referred to in the petition, imposed penalties upon any person who "interferes in any manner with any officer of such Federal election in the discharge of his duties, or by any unlawful means induces any officer of an election or officer whose duty it is to ascertain, announce or declare the result of any such election or give or make any certificate, document or evidence in relation thereto, to violate or refuse to comply with his duty or any law regulating the same."

Jurisdiction was claimed for the Federal court, under a Federal statute which extended the privileges of the writ to persons "in custody for an act done or omitted in pursuance of a law of the United States." On behalf of the prisoners it was contended that a "Federal question" arose out of the fact that the canvassers, in the course of the acts for which they were held to have been in contempt, had determined the rights of certain persons to be electors of President and Vice-President of the United States.

The Richland sheriff promptly produced the prisoners, informing the court that he held them in obedience to the order of the Supreme Court of South Carolina. They were then placed in the custody of the United States marshal.

The matter was fully argued before Judge Bond—Messrs. Bradley T. Johnson, of Maryland, W. A. Clark and James Conner appearing for the sheriff, whilst Messrs. Corbin, Settle and Denny represented the prisoners.

After due consideration Judge Bond discharged the prisoners from custody—holding that "it is competent for a Federal court to issue the writ of habeas corpus, in favor of prisoners imprisoned for contempt by a State court, where the acts of alleged contempt were committed in the performance of duties created by the Constitution and laws of the United States, and the petitioners were acting under the protection of the laws and the courts of the United States," and that "where it clearly appears from the record that the State court exceeded its powers in committing such petitioners it is competent for a Federal court to release and discharge them from imprisonment."

In the course of his opinion Judge Bond said:

While it gives me great concern to hear and determine a cause where parties are charged with disobedience of the orders of a State court, yet where the liberty of men is concerned, who have a right to appeal, under the act of Congress, to the Federal courts, I am sure my brother judges of the State courts will not think me wanting in courtesy if I hear them, as I am bound to do by law, and will believe me when I say there is no one who regrets more than myself this conflict of jurisdiction.

I think this proceeding in the Supreme Court was beyond the jurisdiction of that court; that the State Board of Canvassers were clothed under the law with discretionary powers which required them to discriminate the votes, to determine and certify the candidates elected after scrutiny; that they were a part of the executive department of the Government and were in nowise subject to the control, as to what they should do after they had commenced to perform that duty, of the judicial department; and that as this was a general election at which members of Congress were to be elected and electors of President and Vice-President of the United States were to be chosen they were acting in a Federal capacity or, in other words, in pursuance of a law of the United States, and therefore if any one disturbs them in the exercise of their functions they are entitled to the protection of the courts of the United States.

There was nothing further done in this matter. Some months after Judge Bond's decision there were in the State Supreme Court proceedings looking to an enforcement of the orders passed in relation to the conduct of the canvassers, but these were never pressed to a judgment. President Hayes was peaceably in office, the Hampton government was regularly performing all its functions, and there was no need of further litigation of any of the questions which had so much occupied the attention of courts and people alike.

CHAPTER IX.

THE DUAL GOVERNMENT.

Tuesday, November 28, was the day fixed by the State Constitution for the meeting of the General Assembly. The action of the Board of State Canvassers in withholding certificates from the Democrats claiming to have been elected from Edgefield and Laurens had induced among the white people the belief that the Republican managers, backed, of course, by Governor Chamberlain, intended to attempt to organize the lower house without the presence of the members from those two counties, and thus initiate a scheme to declare him elected and acquire a new control of the entire State Government.

The Democrats remained firm in their purpose to yield none of their rights, to stand by the men of their choice and to use every lawful means to prevent the accomplishment of Governor Chamberlain's designs. The white people were in a condition of nervous expectation—their feeling could scarcely be called apprehension—as the day for the meeting of the Legislature drew near. Their doubts as to what might happen were soon set at rest.

The press dispatches from Washington, dated November 27, brought the news that Governor Chamberlain had on the day previous applied to the President for troops to be used in the State House on the day appointed for that meeting, and that the President, after consultation with the Cabinet, had concluded to comply with the Governor's demand. News of the President's purpose having reached Columbia there was an instant protest from a large number of well-known citizens, who published on November 28 a statement setting forth that profound peace prevailed in Columbia and the entire State, that no resistance to the laws was to be feared, and that the use of troops would be unwarrantable.

SOLDIERS SEIZE THE STATE HOUSE.

The President's attitude was indicated in the following orders:

Washington, November 26, 1876.

Gen. Thomas H. Ruger, or Col. H. M. Black, Columbia, S. C.

The following has been received from the President:

Executive Mansion, November 26, 1876.

"Hon. J. D. Cameron, Secretary of War.

"Sir—D. H. Chamberlain is now Governor of the State of South Carolina beyond any controversy, and remains so until a new Governor shall be duly and legally inaugurated under the Constitution. The Government has been called upon to aid with the military and naval forces of the United States to maintain republican government in the State against resistance too formidable to be overcome by the State authorities. You are directed, therefore, to sustain Governor Chamberlain in his authority against domestic violence until otherwise directed.
U. S. Grant."

In obeying these instructions you will advise with the Governor, and dispose of your troops in such a manner as may be deemed best in order to carry out the spirit of the above order of the President. Acknowledge receipt.

J. D. Cameron, Secretary of War.

On the demand of Governor Chamberlain, General Ruger, at midnight before the day for the meeting of the Legislature, placed a company of United States infantry in the State House. Most of these troops were stationed on the upper floor, about midway between the door of the Senate chamber and that of the hall of the House. A sentinel was posted at each of the doors opening into the first floor of the building—north, east, south, west. The alleged purpose of this disposition of the soldiers was to prevent the unauthorized entrance of persons not connected with the Legislature, and thus insure the peaceful organization of that body according to the Constitution and laws. Whatever the purpose of the President or of General Ruger, the military possession of the State House went far beyond. For several days after the meeting of the Legislature the sentinels downstairs undertook to halt and examine persons entering at any of the doors. The judges of the Supreme Court, having to use the eastern door in going to their consultation room, were halted and asked whether they had a pass or were otherwise authorized to enter. At the door of the hall of the House were posted two sentinels—one on each side of the entrance—and the entrance to the gallery was similarly guarded.

Before noon of November 28 (the hour at which the House should by law assemble) A. O. Jones, who had been clerk of the former House, but whose term had expired, furnished to John B. Dennis a list of those members whose election had been declared by the Board of State Canvassers—that list not containing the names of any persons claiming to represent Edgefield or Laurens. Dennis had been selected by Governor Chamberlain to stand at the House door, examine the credentials of members and say who should pass the armed sentinels and enter the hall.

The Republican members-elect, numbering fifty-nine, assembled in the hall and proceeded to organize themselves as the House of Representatives. They elected E. W. M. Mackey speaker; A. O. Jones, clerk; Warren R. Marshall (white), of Fairfield, reading clerk; and Henry Daniels (colored), of Richland, sergeant-at-arms.

The Democratic members-elect, numbering sixty-four, proceeded in a body to the hall of the House, the Edgefield delegation in front and the Laurens men coming next. When the head of the column reached the door the Edgefield members demanded admittance, at the same time presenting the certified copy (made by the clerk of the Supreme Court) of the State Canvassers' report of the vote in that county for members of the House, showing that the bearers had each received a majority of the votes cast. Dennis, supported on each side by an armed soldier in the uniform of the United States army, refused to recognize these certificats as lawful credentials and forbade the holders to enter. Thereupon the Democratic members retired, leaving one of their number (Gen. W. H. Wallace, of Union) to observe for a time the doings of the Mackey body.

Shortly after this General Hampton and Col. A. C. Haskell approached the House door and demanded to be admitted as spectators. The demand was refused, but the white assistant of the negro calling himself the sergeant-at-arms offered to get these gentlemen a permit to enter. The offer was promptly declined, and the gentlemen at once retired.

It was at this juncture that a new disposition was made of the soldiers in the upper hall. They were marched to the hall door, made to open ranks and face inward—so that any one going in must pass between the two single-rank platoons of soldiers carrying loaded rifles with bayonets fixed. The troops had thus taken actual possession of the hall of the House.

Before leaving the upper hall the following protest, signed by all the Democratic members of the House, was read by Mr. John C. Sheppard:

We, a majority of the House of Representatives elect, protest against the refusal to admit us to the hall of representatives. We protest against the military power of the United States barring the passage into the State House of members-elect of the Legislature. We protest against the legality of the proceedings, and especially against the army of the United States being placed for the purpose of this exclusion under the command of John B. Dennis, a partisan of Governor Chamberlain. We protest against the said Dennis' instructions to the guard to admit no one to the State House except upon his own pass or a pass of A. O. Jones, the former clerk of the House, who may thus exclude all except his own partisans, and who, by the Republican program, is to organize the said House.

We have presented ourselves with the judgment of the highest court of South Carolina, certified to by its clerk, with the great seal of the court attached, as to our right to participate in the organization of the said House. We are refused, by the orders of the said Dennis, admission into said hall except upon his pass, the pass of said Jones, or the certificate of H. E. Hayne, Secretary of State, who is now under condemnation of said court for refusal to issue certificates in accordance with its judgment and mandate.

In protesting against this barefaced usurpation, this trampling on the laws and Constitution of the State, this defiance of the highest tribunal of the State, it is our purpose to offer no resistance to this armed intervention, but to make our solemn appeal to the American people, without distinction of party. Our veneration of law and our respect for the Supreme Court and the usages of all legislative assemblages forbid our participation in such unprecedented and revolutionary proceedings.

During the excitement an immense crowd had assembled in front of the State House, when the Federal officer in charge approached General Hampton, who was in the building, with a request to prevent the crowd from pushing in. General Hampton immediately appeared upon the front steps and addressed the crowd as follows:

My friends: I am truly doing what I have done earnestly during this whole exciting contest, pouring oil on the troubled waters. It is of the greatest importance to us all, as citizens of South Carolina, that peace should be preserved. I appeal to you all, white men and colored, as Carolinians, to use every effort to keep down violence or turbulence. One act of violence may precipitate bloodshed and desolation. I implore you, then, to preserve the peace. I beg all of my friends to disperse, to leave the grounds of the State House, and I advise all the colored men to do the same. Keep perfectly quiet, leave the streets, and do nothing to provoke a riot. We trust to the law and the Constitution, and we have perfect faith in the justness of our cause.

The crowd promptly and quietly dispersed.

The Democratic members repaired to Carolina Hall—a building diagonally in rear of the Richland courthouse. The House then proceeded to organize. The members having been duly sworn in, William H. Wallace was elected speaker, John T. Sloan, Sr., of Richland clerk, W. B. Williams, of York, reading clerk, and John D. Browne, of Barnwell, sergeant-at-arms. Immediately after these elections two colored Republicans left the Mackey body, joined the lawful House and were duly sworn in—J. W. Westberry, of Sumter, and W. H. Reedish, of Orangeburg. Two days later Thomas Hamilton and N. B. Myers, of Beaufort, and J. S. Bridges, of Newberry, were sworn in. Immediately afterwards John Gibson and Daniel Bird, of Fairfield, were received, but these two very soon rejoined the Mackey body. The number of members sworn into the lawful House, excluding those from Edgefield and Laurens, was a majority of the number holding certificates of the Secretary of State, issued in accordance with the action of the Board of State Canvassers.

In the so-called House of which Mackey claimed to be speaker resolutions were soon adopted which purported to unseat the Democratic members elected from Abbeville, Aiken and Barnwell and seat the Republican claimants. These latter were duly sworn in—including a negro personating Silas Cave, of Barnwell. A few days later Cave himself turned up, and he, too, was solemnly sworn in.

THE SENATE ORGANIZED.

The Senate met promptly at 12, noon. The names of the senators from Edgefield and Laurens were omitted from the roll as called by Josephus Woodruff, who claimed to act as clerk, and their credentials were referred to the committee on privileges and elections. The other new senators were duly sworn in.

S. A. Swails (colored) was elected president pro tem., Josephus Woodruff, clerk; R. A. Sisson, reading clerk; and J. E. Green (colored), sergeant-at-arms.

The usual message was sent to the House—the Democratic senators objecting and afterwards entering upon the journal the following protest:

In accordance with notice given, we, the undersigned senators of the State of South Carolina, beg leave to place upon record this our solemn protest against all proceedings by this body which in any degree recognize the legality of a body calling itself the House of Representatives of South Carolina, over which E. W. M. Mackey claims to preside as speaker, and which met on the 28th instant and claimed to organize in the hall of the House of Representatives. The Constitution of South Carolina makes each house the judge of the "election returns and qualifications of its own members." The Supreme Court of this State has by formal judgment decided that the members from the counties of Edgefield and Laurens who received the highest number of votes were entitled to seats. These members have been refused admission to the hall and all participation in its organization by the armed soldiers of the United States, who barred with bayonets the door of the hall of the House of Representatives, and acted as judges of the "election returns and qualifications of its members."

We have seen armed forces of the United States overriding the plain declaration of the Constitution of this State. We have witnessed the solemn mockery of the corporal of the guard reviewing and revising the judgment of the highest court. We have seen the spectacle, humiliating in the last degree to every right-minded American, of the halls of the Legislature occupied at the hour of midnight and held against the ingress of the law-making power—and this at a time of profoundest peace, and when not a single act of violence furnished the slightest pretext for the usurpation. We have seen the still more humiliating spectacle of the United States troops having been placed under the immediate control, and receiving orders from, a citizen without authority and a partisan of the present administration. We have seen this citizen assuming absolute control over the capitol of a commonwealth, and admitting through the lines of armed sentinels his own partisans, upon his own edict or the written pass from another citizen who was selected by his partisans to organize a House of Representatives. We have seen this body of partisans, thus admitted, claiming to organize the house, but without a quorum, in violation of law, in defiance of the Supreme Court and under the protection of the United States troops.

We therefore enter this our protest against any recognition of said body pretending to be the House of Representatives of South Carolina, and for the following reasons:

1. The said body having organized without a constitutional quorum, there being but fifty-nine members present, as shown by its own journal, whereas a majority of the entire representation is requisite to a quorum, to wit: sixty-three members, as set forth in the journals of the House during the past eight years, and as confirmed by the immemorial practice of legislative bodies in every American State; and we do further allege, on our responsibility as senators,

that the said body is still without a constitutional quorum, and therefore wanting in the organic character of the House of Representatives of South Carolina, and ought not to be recognized as such.

2. That said resolution was adopted by the Senate before any announcement was made of any organization by any House of Representatives.

3. That in fact and in truth no legal and effectual organization of a House of Representatives was at that time made.

4. That the body of men claiming to be a House of Representatives, and from which the announcement of said organization came, has not organized and cannot organize by reason of the non-existence of a quorum.

5. We further and finally protest against the adoption of the said resolution [communicating with the Mackey body] for this reason—that we have since received official notification of the organization of the House of Representatives, now sitting in Carolina Hall, where a quorum of legally constituted members does exist, and of which body the Hon. William H. Wallace has been elected speaker and John T. Sloan clerk.

Mr. Cochran, of Anderson, submitted the following protest, to be entered on the journal:

As senator, I do solemnly protest against any further communication with the House of Representatives sitting in the further end of this building until it be ascertained whether or not the said body is composed of a lawful quorum, as well as the causes preventing the same.

At the close of the day Governor Chamberlain made the following report to the President of the United States:

The House and Senate organized today. The Democrats on the refusal to admit the members from Edgefield and Laurens Counties withdrew, leaving sixty members in the House, a quorum of all the members chosen. The Senate organized without delay. General Ruger has preserved the peace and acted with perfect impartiality and great good judgment.

THE LAWFUL HOUSE IN THEIR HALL.

On the morning of November 30 the members of the lawful House left Carolina Hall and proceeded in close column to the State House. On reaching the lower entrance they passed the sentinels—who, it seemed, had received new instructions. Ascending to the Representatives' hall the head of the column was soon at its very door guarded by a United States marshal and a man claiming to be an official of the Mackey body. The members bore their certificates of election. Those in front entered before the official seemed to realize what was going on. The doors were then pressed back and all the members entered without difficulty—these taking seats, the speaker and the clerks occupying the stand and the sergeants-at-arms stationing themselves at the door.

About this time General Hampton reached the door and proposed to enter, when Mackey's sergeant-at-arms objected, and bloodshed was narrowly averted—this by General Hampton's declining to press his demand and going away.

In a few moments Mackey, followed by most of those who recognized him as speaker, entered the hall.

Mackey ascended the stand and demanded that Speaker Wallace should vacate the chair. The latter refused and made a brief statement of his claims as the presiding officer of the lawful House.

Mackey: "I claim that I was elected speaker of this House by a legal quorum of members legally sworn in. We do not recognize that any others than those sworn in here on Tuesday last are members of this House, and these men who are visiting this hall without our consent must keep order. I must again demand that you, General Wallace, leave this chair."

Speaker Wallace: "I have already declared that I am the lawfully elected speaker of this House, and must ask you to retire."

Mackey: "The sergeant-at-arms will please step forward and enforce my order."

Speaker Wallace: "The sergeant-at-arms will please step forward and enforce my order."

The two sergeants-at-arms came forward and ascended to the stand. At the same time a number of men, Democrats and Republicans, crowded around the speaker on one side and Mackey on the other. The excitement was intense and bloodshed seemed imminent. Both parties stood firm.

A Democratic member moved the appointment of a committee of six to adjust matters. The committee (all members of the lawful House) was appointed—Mackey ordering his men to take no notice of the speaker or of his acts.

The danger of bloodshed was over for a time.

There were various motions, suggestions, protests and questions, but they were heeded only by the side from which they came.

GENERAL RUGER BREAKS FAITH.

A new phase was now put on the situation by the course of General Ruger, which was made known to the public by means of the following letter:

Columbia, S. C., November 30, 1876.

Gen. T. H. Ruger, Commanding United States Troops in South Carolina:

Dear Sir—We have just heard through Major McGinnis, of your staff, of your order communicated to William H. Wallace, speaker of the House of Representatives, that at 12 o'clock tomorrow the members-elect from Edgefield and Laurens would not be allowed upon the floor of the House.

To say that we are surprised at such an order, after the explanations and pledges made by you to each one of us, is to use very mild language. When the outrage of Tuesday last was committed by the placing of armed sentinels at the door of the House of Representatives, who decided upon the admission of members to their seats, and when the provisions of the Constitution and the decision of the Supreme Court were brought to your attention, you distinctly and warmly asserted, again and again, that your orders were misunderstood; that your did not intend to have sentinels at the door of the hall, and that you had not and did not intend to assume to decide upon the legality of any man's seat, or upon his right to enter the hall. You were then reminded by us that your guard received instructions from one Dennis, a citizen and a partisan of Governor Chamberlain, to admit parties upon his own pass or that of one Jones, and had, through armed forces, excluded all Democrats from the hall until the Republican organization was completed.

You assured us again that such were not your orders, and were told by us that, notwithstanding the perpetration of this inexpressible shame upon free institutions and the rights of the people, the evils could still be remedied without violence or bloodshed by a simple withdrawal of your guard from the doors of the hall, and letting a majority of votes decide all questions in accordance with law and the usages of legislative bodies. You stated that no troops should be at the door, and that under no circumstances would you interfere, except there should occur a serious disturbance of the peace. You affirmed your determination to exercise no supervisory control whatever over the body or bodies claiming to be the House of Representatives. All this occurred on yesterday. Last night, in a later interview with Senator Gordon, you made the same assurances, and this morning after both bodies were assembled in the hall, you assured General Hampton that under no circumstances would you interfere, except to keep the peace.

What can now justly measure our astonishment at the issuance of such an order as the one just sent by you? There is no breach of the peace and no prospect of its disturbance. You had it officially brought to your notice that absolute good humor prevails in that hall. We cannot refrain from expressing the apprehension that the fact that a number of leading Republicans are taking issue with the legality of the proceedings of the Republican House has changed your views as to your line of duty. It is proper that we should say, in conclusion, that we relied upon your honor as a man and your character as a soldier to maintain your pledged position of non-intervention.

The Democratic members from Edgefield and Laurens are entitled to their seats by the judgment of the Supreme Court of this State, and we have advised them to remain in that hall until removed by your troops, that the issue may be made in this centennial year of American independence whether we have a government of law as construed by courts or a centralized despotism whose only law is force.

Let the American people behold the spectacle of a brigadier-general of the army, seated by the side of Governor Chamberlain in a room in the State House, issuing his orders to a legislative body peacefully assembled in one of the original thirteen commonwealths of this Union.

Respectfully yours,
J. B. Gordon,
Wade Hampton,
A. C. Haskell.

General Ruger explained his action in the following dispatch:

Columbia, December 1, 1876.

Gen. W. T. Sherman, or the Secretary of War, Washington, D. C.:

I have carefully abstained from interference with the organization of the House from the first. On the application of the Governor, and my own belief for the necessity therefor for the preservation of the peace, I placed troops in the State House (but not in the rooms of assembly of either of the houses) on the day of meeting. It came about that for a time soldiers were placed on either side of the door of entrance to the hall of representatives under the following circumstances: A person at the door of the House, and who claimed authority to examine the certificates of those claiming to be members prior to their admission to the hall, but who, I think, had no legal authority for so doing, applied to the officer in command of the troops placed in the corridor for the preservation of the peace for assistance, on the ground that he was being pressed upon and could not perform his duty. The soldiers were placed as stated. As soon as I was fully informed of the circumstances I ordered the soldiers withdrawn, as I had previously informed Governor Chamberlain that I should confine my action to the preservation of the peace, and should do nothing with reference to keeping the doors of the rooms of meeting of the houses, or the rooms themselves, unless it became necessary because of a breach of the peace which the civil officers of the houses should be unable to quell. No act was done by the soldiers except that of their presence, as stated, but while they were so present persons claiming the right of entrance under certificate of the clerk of the Supreme Court were refused admission.

Thos. H. Ruger, Commanding Department.

General Ruger did not execute the purpose stated in the order of which he had given Speaker Wallace formal notice. What induced his change of purpose was never stated, but after occurrences indicated that the President concluded that the use of troops in the manner threatend by General Ruger would not be wise or politic.

A BLOODY PLOT DISCOVERED.

The proceedings of the House on December 1, 2 and 3 were inconsequential. Both bodies remained in the hall day and night, but there was neither excitement nor any sign of disturbance.

On Sunday, December 3, it was made known to the Democratic leaders in Columbia that the Republicans had laid their plans to eject from the House the members from Edgefield and Laurens—selecting for that purpose a body of about one hundred negroes who had come or were to come from Charleston. These constituted in part the "Hunkidori Club," composed of negro roughs and bullies organized by certain Republican leaders in that city to intimidate and insult the white people and to embolden and solidify the blacks. These roughs, always armed and commonly displaying heavy bludgeons, had caused much trouble in Charleston. These "Hunkidoris" had incited the trouble which ended in the riot in which Buckner was killed, and they had participated in the riot on the day after the election. Their conduct had long been a menace to the peace of Charleston and to the safety of the women and children there. Such were the men whom Governor Chamberlain selected to effect the ejection of certain of the members of the House of Representatives.

The plan, as arranged by Governor Chamberlain, was to appoint these negro roughs to be sergeants-at-arms of the House, each wearing a badge which should be concealed till the time should come to consummate the bloody scheme. Members of the Mackey body were to retire and their places to be filled by the roughs—the badges of the latter still concealed—and others of these were to be admitted to the floor of the House. When arrangements should be completed the roughs were to expose their badges and Mackey was to demand the retirement of the Edgefield and Laurens members. Refusal to retire was to be met by force, and resistance was to be overcome by the immediate intervention of the Federal troops waiting just outside the hall.

When this "Hunkidori" plot was made known, telegrams were sent to different parts of the State, requesting the presence in Columbia of armed white men in numbers sufficient to protect the lawful House from the intrusions or other misconduct of the mob. By Monday morning quite two thousand white men had come to Columbia, and there were additions by every train—so that by Monday night the number asssembled had reached five thousand. They were all well armed and were in most instances organized by counties into companies each commanded by a head officer. A commander was also appointed over the whole body. Constant efforts were made to keep the men together and to keep them quiet. The discipline and the behavior of the men was remarked as excellent throughout.

In the House chamber ample arrangements were made for effective resistance to any efforts to remove the Edgefield and Laurens members. A certain citizen of known courage and exceptional coolness was to take charge of any fight which circumstances might necessitate on the part of the lawful House, and the dispositions of its members and of men recruited from outside were arranged with a view to the most effective resistance possible. Especial care was taken that on the first act of violence in the hall, Mackey, the pretended speaker, should be instantly shot to death. It may be regarded as certain that had bloodshed ensued Governor Chamberlain would have paid with his life the penalty of his own conduct.

THE LAWFUL MEMBERS RETIRE.

On the morning of December 4, after roll call, Mr. Orr moved that the House adjourn, when Speaker Wallace rose and spoke as follows:

Gentlemen of the House of Representatives:

I have just been officially informed that there are now in readiness upwards of one hundred armed men who are about to enter the hall for the purpose of ejecting certain members upon this floor. The members to whom it is intended that the force shall be applied have been recognized by this House as members, and we dispute the authority of the State Government to eject from this floor any member of this House upon the ground that he is not a legal member of the House of Representatives of the State of South Carolina. We insist that this House is the only competent authority to pass upon the qualifications and election returns of its own members. The force to which I have alluded is acting directly under the authority of Governor Chamberlain and under his commission. The chair is given distinctly to understand that if that force is resisted by the members of this House the military force of the United States will be invoked to its assistance; that that assistance will be rendered, not for the purpose of upholding another body claiming to be the House of Representatives in South Carolina, but upon the ground that that force is under the Governor, and that the action of the military is in support of the executive authority of the State.

With a view of preventing a collision upon this floor in which lives may be lost and blood shed; with a view of submitting to proper and legal arbitrament of all the rights we claim on this floor, the chair is of the opinion that this House should withdraw from this hall. It is not essential to the legality of the House of Representatives that it should sit in this hall. The Constitution requires that the General Assembly should meet in the city of Columbia, and with a view to giving emphasis to the reasons for our withdrawal, I desire to repeat that while we claim and insist upon all our legal rights, for the purpose of keeping the peace, preventing violence and preventing bloodshed, we will repair to another hall and exercise the proper functions that appertain to this body.

I may as well state that the only legal House that can exist in South Carolina is a body consisting of sixty-three members. That number constitutes a quorum of that body under the Constitution, the membership of that body being fixed at 124; the Constitution also providing that a majority of those members is alone competent to do business.

Therefore, gentlemen, upon the grounds stated and for the reasons given, while insisting that we are the only constitutional House of Representatives in South Carolina, and for the purpose of preventing bloodshed, I recommend that we do adjourn to another hall in this city.

At the conclusion of Speaker Wallace's remarks Mackey handed a paper to his reading clerk and requested him to read it—prefacing this action with the remark that he had intended that the preamble and resolution be read immediately after the roll call, but that he had, through courtesy to General Wallace, withheld it until the latter finished his remarks.

The preamble set forth Mackey's version of the acts of his body and the entry of the Wallace House, and imputed to the latter the purpose to "resist by force of arms any attempt on the part of the officers of the [Mackey] House to enforce its orders and authority." Then followed this resolution, which Mackey claimed had been adopted by his men:

Resolved, That the Governor of the State be, and he is hereby, requested to take such measures as will protect the House of Representatives against the unlawful intrusion, interruption and violence caused and done by the said body of men who have unlawfully intruded themselves in the hall of the House of Representatives, as hereinbefore set forth, and who now are engaged in unlawfully interrupting the proceedings thereof, and who are also by their unlawful conduct and presence in the House of Representatives preventing the assembling of the General Assembly in joint convention as is provided by the Constitution of the State of South Carolina.

Governor Chamberlain's action in assembling the "Hunkidori" mob was in response to this resolution.

The members and the officers of the lawful House of Representatives withdrew and repaired again to Carolina Hall, where they resumed the day's session.

The armed men who had been summoned to Columbia to protect the members of the lawful House from assault promptly returned to their homes.

THE WALLACE HOUSE ADJUDGED LAWFUL.

Proceedings were taken in the Supreme Court to have that tribunal decide which of the two bodies, each claiming to be the House of Representatives, was the lawful House. The specific object of the proceedings, brought against H. E. Hayne, as Secretary of State, and E. W. M. Mackey, was to compel the delivery to Speaker Wallace of the returns of the vote for Governor and Lieutenant-Governor—this in order that the lawful House and the Senate might ascertain and declare the result of the election for those two offices.

Hayne answered that he had already delivered the returns to Mackey, whilst the latter answered that he lawfully held them as speaker of the lawfully elected and organized House of Representatives.

On December 6, after full argument, the Supreme Court decided that "William H. Wallace is the legal speaker of the lawfully-constituted House of Representatives of the State of South Carolina, and as such officer was and is entitled to the possession of the returns of the election for Governor and Lieutenant-Governor, held on the 7th day of November, A. D. 1876, and which were transmitted to H. E. Hayne, Secretary of State."

The court reserved for further argument the question whether, Hayne having unlawfully delivered the papers to Mackey, the writ of mandamus could issue to compel a delivery to Speaker Wallace.

The petition was dismissed as to Mackey, on the ground that he was not a public officer, but a private citizen.

Immediately upon this decision of the Supreme Court the House of Representatives by resolution appointed a committee to ascertain from General Ruger his attitude and purposes towards that body. To the committee's inquiries that officer replied as follows:

I have the honor to say, in reply to your inquiries based upon the resolutions of which you handed me a copy, that the United States troops now in the State House were placed there by my order for the purpose of executing such orders as might be given; and in this connection I would say that if your body should appear at the State House for the purpose of entering the hall of the House of Representatives and should be refused admission by those having charge of the doors, and such persons should apply to the officer in command of the troops at the State House for assistance necessary to prevent you from entering, the present orders to the officer would require him to render such assistance.

There was great rejoicing among the Democrats and their sympathizers over the decision of the Supreme Court—so great, indeed, that there was comparatively little feeling over General Ruger's declaration that his orders required him to ignore the judgment of the highest court of South Carolina and, in upholding the Mackey body, exclude the lawful House at the point of the bayonet.

CHAMBERLAIN'S SHAM INSTALLATION.

On December 5 the Republican members of the Senate (except Mr. Cochran, of Anderson,) repaired to the hall of the House, where they and the Mackey body went through the form of aggregating and declaring the vote for Governor and Lieutenant-Governor. The votes of Edgefield and Laurens having been thrown out, the results were declared as follows:

For D. H. Chamberlain...................................86,216
For Wade Hampton 83,071
For Richard H. Gleaves................................86,620
For William D. Simpson................................82,251

Chamberlain and Gleaves were declared elected.

On December 7 the Republican senators (except Mr. Cochran, of Anderson), against the protest of the Democratic senators, joined the Mackey body for the purpose of inaugurating Daniel H. Chamberlain as Governor of South Carolina.

Mr. Chamberlain delivered the following address:

Gentlemen of the Senate and House of Representatives:

I accept the office to which by the voice of a majority of the people of this State I have a second time been called, with a full knowledge of the grave responsibilities and difficulties by which it is now attended. No considerations except the clearest convictions of duty would be sufficient to induce me to accept this great trust under the circumstances which now surround us. I regard the present hour in South Carolina as a crisis at which no patriotic citizen should shrink from any post to which public duty may call him. In my sober judgment our present struggle is in defense of the foundations of our Government and institutions. If we fail now our Government —the Government of South Carolina—will no longer rest on the consent of the governed, expressed by a free vote of a majority of our people. If our opponents triumph—I care not under what guise of legal forms—we shall witness the overthrow of free government in our State.

My chief personal anxiety is that I may have the firmness and wisdom to act in a manner worthy of the great interests so largely committed to my keeping. My chief public care shall be to contribute my utmost efforts to defend the rights, to guard the peace, and to promote the welfare of the people of our State.

The constant occupation of my time with other duties which I could not postpone has prevented me from preparing the usual statements and recommendations respecting our public affairs. At the earliest practicable day I will discharge this duty. Our greatest interest, our most commanding duty, now is to stand firmly, each in his appointed place, against the aggressions and allurements of our political opponents. Our position up to the present time has been within the clear limits of our Constitution and laws. Nothing but the cowardice or weakness or treachery of our own friends can rob us of the victory.

I state what facts show, what overwhelming evidence proves, when I say that if we yield now we shall witness the consummation of a deliberate and cruel conspiracy on the part of the Democratic party of this State to overcome by brute force the political will of a majority of 30,000 of the lawful voters of this State. I have mourned over public abuses which have heretofore arisen here. I have, according to the measure of my ability, labored to make the conduct of our public affairs honest and honorable. But I stand appalled at the crimes against freedom, against public order, against good government, nay, against government itself, which our recent political experience here has presented. And I am the more appalled when I see the North, that portion of our country which is secure in its freedom and civil order, and the great political party which has controlled the republic for sixteen years, divided in its sympathies and judgment upon such questions. It is written in blood on the pages of our recent National history that no government can rest with safety upon the enforced slavery or degradation of a race. In the full blaze of that great example of retributive justice which swept away a half million of the best lives of our country, we see the American people divided by party lines upon the question of the disfranchisement and degradation of the same race whose physical freedom was purchased at such a cost. And what is more astonishing still, there are Republicans who permit the errors which have attended the first efforts of this race in self-government to chill their sympathies to such an extent that they stand coldly by and practically say that the peace of political servitude is better than the abuses and disquiet which newly acquired freedom has brought.

I denounce the conduct of the recent election on the part of our political opponents in this State as a vast brutal outrage. . Fraud, proscription, intimidation in all forms, violence—ranging through all its degrees up to wanton murder—were its effective methods. The circumstances under which we have assembled today show us how nearly successful has been this great conspiracy. It is for us, in the face of open enemies, to show that we understand the cause in which we are engaged, and that no earthly sacrifice is too great to secure its triumph.

The gentleman who was my opponent for this office in the late election has recently declared, as I am credibly informed, that he held not only the peace of this city and State, but my life, in his hands. I do not doubt the truth of his statement. Neither the public peace nor the life of any man who now opposes the consummation of this policy of fraud and violence is safe from the assaults of those who have enforced that policy.

My life can easily be taken. I have held it, in the judgment of all my friends here, by a frail tenure for the last three months. But there is one thing no man in South Carolina can do, however powerful or desperate he may be, and that is to cause me to abate my hatred or cease my most vigorous resistance of this attempted overthrow and enslavement of a majority of the people of South Carolina. "Here I stand; I can do no otherwise: God be my helper." Wife and children—dearer to me than "are the ruddy drops that visit my sad heart"—all other considerations must give way before the solemn duty to resist the final success of that monstrous outrage under whose black shadow we are assembled today.

Mr. Chamberlain was then "sworn in" by the probate judge of Richland County, and the oath was administered also to Gleaves, claiming to have been elected Lieutenant-Governor.

The Republican candidates for State offices on the same day went through the form of taking the oath prescribed by law.

One passage in Mr. Chamberlain's address called forth the following statement from General Hampton:

To the Public: The following paragraph appears in an address of D. H. Chamberlain, delivered in the capitol today:

"The gentleman who was my opponent for this office in the late election declared, as I am credibly informed, that he held not only the peace of this city and State, but my life, in his hands. I do not doubt the truth of his statement. Neither the public peace nor the life of any man who now opposes the consummation of this policy of fraud and violence is safe from the assaults of those who have opposed that policy."

I pronounce this statement infamously false. I, by my unwearied exertions, have endeavored to preserve the peace of this State, and I have thus contributed to shield from popular indignation one who has proved himself a disgrace to his rank and a traitor to his trust. His conscience may make him tremble, but neither I nor the men with whom I act countenance the hand of the assassin.

To contradict General Hampton Mr. Chamberlain used the statement of R. B. Elliott, confirmed by that of Beverly Nash—each of whom had been guilty of bribery and perjury in connection with some scheme to defraud the State.

Mr. Chamberlain also had a note from Judge Settle, the counsel of the Board of State Canvassers, but that gentleman's statement did not sustain the ex-Governor's charge.

The pretended inauguration of Mr. Chamberlain caused much excitement in Columbia—the white people considering it a bold usurpation, an insolent defiance of the law and the courts. On the night of the performance General Hampton, in response to calls, made a speech counseling self-control, patience and the strictest preservation of the peace.

It was in this speech that Wade Hampton said: "The people have elected me Governor, and, by the Eternal God, I will be Governor or we shall have a military governor."

Early in December committees of both houses of Congress came to Columbia to investigate the circumstances of the November election. Some members of these committees sent out reports of conditions—the Democratic members taking especial care to inform the country of the legal aspect of things, as shown by the decisions of the courts.

GOVERNOR HAMPTON INAUGURATED.

In the House of Representatives on December 10 a concurrent resolution was adopted (and sent to the Senate) fixing December 14 as the day for tabulating the returns of the vote for Governor and Lieutenant-Governor, declaring the election and inaugurating the two officers-elect.

The House passed a resolution that as, in view of pending cases in the Supreme Court, it might embarrass any one of its justices to be asked to administer the oath, the committee of arrangements request one of the circuit judges to perform that duty. Judge Mackey was invited accordingly.

Upon a certified statement of the Secretary of State, made up of the returns of the commissioners of election in the several counties (including Edgefield and Laurens) the vote for Governor and Lieutenant-Governor was ascertained and declared as follows:

Wade Hampton 92,261
D. H. Chamberlain....................................91,127
    Hampton's majority, 1,134.
Wm. D. Simpson.......................................91,689
R. Howell Gleaves....................................91,150
    Simpson's majority, 539.

The Democratic senators were present at the count and the declaration.

The returns showed the total vote for Governor to have been 183,388. According to the State census of 1875 the whole number of voters was 184,943—indicating that only 555 persons had not voted.

The inauguration ceremonies took place in front of Carolina Hall. The members of the House and the Democratic senators attended, and there was an immense crowd of citizens present. The address was made and the oath administered on a platform in the open air—the House having promptly voted down a motion to have the proceedings indoors.

The platform was beautifully decorated with wreaths and garlands of flowers and evergreens, among which was plainly seen the national as well as the State flag.

As General Hampton came upon the platform he was received with a volume of cheers that indicated both the extent and the enthusiasm of the welcome.

The Governor-elect then spoke as follows:
Gentlemen of the Senate and House of Representatives:
It is with feelings of the profoundest solicitude that I assume the arduous duties and grave responsibilities of the high position to which the people of South Carolina have called me. It is amid events unprecedented in this republic that I take the chair as Chief Magistrate of this State. After years of misrule, corruption and anarchy, brought upon us by venal and unprincipled political adventurers, the honest people of the State, without regard to party or race, with one voice demanded reform and with one purpose devoted themselves earnestly and solemnly to this end. With a lofty patriotism never surpassed, with a patience never equalled, with a courage never excelled; and with a sublime sense of duty which finds scarcely a parallel in the history of the world, they subordinated every personal feeling to the public weal and consecrated themselves to the sacred work of redeeming their prostrate State. To the accomplishment of this task they dedicated themselves with unfaltering confidence and with unshaken faith, trusting alone to the justice of their cause and commending that cause reverently to the protection of the Almighty.

When the corrupt party which for eight years had held sway in this State, bringing its civilization into disgrace and making its government a public scandal, saw that the demand for reform found a responsive echo in the popular heart, and that the verdict of the people would be pronounced against those who had degraded the State, they appealed for Federal intervention, and by a libel on our whole people, as base as it was false, called in the soldiery of the United States army to act as supervisors of our election. In a time of profound peace, when no legal officer had been resisted in the proper discharge of his functions, we have witnessed a spectacle abhorrent to every patriotic heart and fatal to republican institutions—Federal troops used to promote the success of a political party. Undismayed though shocked by this gross violation of the Constitution of the country, our people with a determination that no force could subdue, no fraud could defeat, kept steadily and peacefully in the path of duty, resolved to assert their rights as American freemen at the ballot box—that great court of final resort before which must be tried the grave questions of the supremacy of the Constitution and the stability of our institutions. What the verdict of the people of South Carolina has been you need not be told. It has reverberated throughout the State, and its echoes come back to us from every land where liberty is venerated, declaring in tones that cannot be mistaken that, standing on the Constitution of our country, we propose to obey its laws, to preserve, as far as in us lies, its peace and honor, and to carry out in good faith every pledge made by us for reform and honest government. We intend to prove to the world the sincerity of our declaration that the sole motive which inspired the grand contest we have so successfully made was not the paltry ambition for party supremacy, but the sacred hope of redeeming our State. It was this hope which led our people to a victory which was grander in its proportions, greater in its success, nobler in its achievement and brighter in its promise of prosperity than any other ever waged on this continent.

But it was sought to wrest the fruits of this magnificent victory from the hands that won it, by a gigantic fraud and a base conspiracy. When the members-elect of the General Assembly repaired to the capitol to take the seats to which the people of South Carolina had assigned them, armed soldiers of the Federal Government confronted them, and their certificates of election were examined and passed upon by a corporal of the guard. A spectacle so humiliating to a free people, and so fatal to republican institutions, had never been presented in America. It could not have been witnessed even here, where civil liberty has for years been but a mockery, had not the ruthless hand of military power struck down the most sacred guaranties of the Constitution, for the tread of the armed soldier, as he made his rounds through the halls of legislation, was over the prostrate form of Liberty herself. It was amid these ominous, these appalling scenes that the members of the General Assembly were called on to assume their duties as the representatives of a free State, and that State one of the original thirteen that won our independence and framed our Constitution. That the natural, patriotic indignation of our people did not find expression in violence is creditable in the highest degree to them, and this was due in a large measure to the statesmanlike and dignified conduct of those members of the General Assembly who had been made the victims of this gross outrage on their persons and this daring conspiracy against their constitutional rights.

Debarred the free exercise of their rights by the presence of an armed force, a legal quorum of the lower house, after placing on record a noble protest, quietly withdrew from the capitol and proceeded to organize that branch of the General Assembly. Not one form of our law, not one requirement of the Constitution, was wanting to give force and legality to this organization; and that its authority has not been fully recognized is due solely to the same armed usurpation which has subordinated the civil to the military power throughout this whole contest.

Of the disgraceful, dangerous and revolutionary proceedings resorted to by the defeated party after the organization of the lower house it is needless for me to speak. You have been the witnesses and the victims of these, and the civilized world has looked on with amazement, disgust and horror; you have seen a minority of that house usurp the powers of the whole body; you have seen the majority expelled from their hall by threats of force; you have seen persons having no shadow of a claim as members admitted to seats as representatives by the votes of men who themselves were acting in direct violation of the Constitution; and you have seen the last crowning act of infamy by which a candidate for Governor, defeated by the popular vote, had himself declared elected by his co-conspirators.

I make no comment on these flagrant outrages and wrongs; it pertains to the General Assembly to take such action in regard to them as that honorable body may deem proper. But it is due to my position as the chief magistrate of this commonwealth to place on record my solemn and indignant protest against acts which I consider subversive of civil liberty and destructive of our form of government. These are questions which concern not us alone, but the people of the United States; for if acts so unauthorized and so unconstitutional are allowed to pass without rebuke, popular government as established by the Constitution will give place to military despotism. Our duty, the duty of every patriot, is to demand a strict construction of the Constitution and a rigid adherence to its provisions. We can only thus preserve our liberties and our government.

A great task is before the conservative party of this State. They entered on this contest with a platform so broad, so strong, so liberal, that every honest citizen could stand upon it. They recognized and accepted the amendments of the Constitution in good faith; they pledged themselves to work reform and to establish good government; they promised to keep up an efficient system of public education; and they declared solemnly that all citizens of South Carolina, of both races and of both parties, should be regarded as equals in the eye of the law; all to be protected in the enjoyment of every political right now possessed by them.

To the faithful observance of these pledges we stand committed, and I, as the representative of the conservative party, hold myself bound by every dictate of honor and of good faith to use every effort to have these pledges redeemed fully and honestly. It is due not only to ourselves but to the colored people of the State that wise, just and liberal measures should prevail in our legislation. We owe much of our late success to these colored voters who were brave enough to rise above the prejudice of race and honest enough to throw off the shackles of party in their determination to save the State. To those who, misled by their fears, their ignorance, or by evil counseling, turned a deaf ear to our appeals, we should not be vindictive but magnanimous. Let us show to all of them that the true interests of both races can best be secured by cultivating peace and promoting prosperity among all classes of our fellow citizens. I rely confidently on the support of the members of the General Assembly in my efforts to attain these laudable ends, and I trust that all branches of the Government will unite cordially in this patriotic work. If so united and working with resolute will and earnest determination, we may hope soon to see the dawn of a brighter day for our State. God in His infinite mercy grant that it may come speedily, and may He shower the richest blessings of peace and happiness on our whole people.

General Hampton then announced that he was ready to take the oath prescribed by the Constitution.

The oath was administered by Judge Mackey—the Governor repeating after him the entire obligation ending with the words, "So help me God."

As Governor Hampton raised the Bible to his lips, Trial Justice J. Q. Marshall, who had held the book while the Governor's right hand rested upon it, said: "You swear to that."

This proceeding had been thought proper because there had been a question whether the circuit judges, elected by a *viva-voce* vote and not by ballot, as the Constitution required, had been legally chosen; and the Democratic managers desired to withhold from Chamberlain and his followers every chance of objection or subterfuge.

Just as the Governor released the Bible the "Hampton Saluting Club" (successor to the Columbia Flying Artillery, "dispersed" by President Grant's proclamation) fired a national salute, and the assembled multitude sent up a volume of cheers long and loud.

Lieutenant-Governor Simpson was next sworn in according to the constitutional requirement.

As Governor Hampton was about to retire he was taken by four young men, placed in a chair and by them borne to his hotel—the people following in a rush and cheering as they went.

The cry "Hurrah for Hampton" was stronger and more significant than ever.

THE CAMPAIGN FORMALLY CLOSED.

On December 15 the Democratic State Executive Committee issued the following paper:

The inauguration of Governor Hampton and Lieutenant-Governor Simpson concluded the labors which the recent campaign devolved upon the State Executive Committee of the Democratic party, and we take occasion to express our gratitude to the Democracy of South Carolina for their unwavering support of every measure proposed, and our admiration of that spirit of forbearance, subordination and fortitude which has secured universal praise amid the exciting and aggravating incidents of a most momentous struggle. Enthusiasm has been tempered with prudence, zeal with calm judgment; and we are confident that the sublime patience, so sorely tried by the events of the last eight years, will still be exercised unto the end.

The fruits of our victory are sought to be wrested from our grasp, and an usurping body, whose only prop is the Federal bayonet, seeks to control the State. We feel assured that our government, which represents the will of the people and is based upon the consent of the governed, will speedily become the recognized government in the State, as we firmly believe that the indignant protest of the entire people of these United States, who are not slaves to party prejudice, will sustain our action and vindicate our cause.

Our campaign has been conducted upon the basis laid down by our honored chieftain at the outset, and through peaceful and lawful agencies we won the victory, acknowledging the legal and political rights of all classes and pledging ourselves to maintain them inviolate. We know that every pledge of the party will be redeemed. With kind feelings for the masses of the opposition, we must exercise magnanimity towards them.

Generosity demands that proscription shall not be visited upon the rank and file of the opposite party, and we earnestly recommend that steps be taken at once to guarantee protection to laborers in every county of the State. Governor Hampton heartily concurs in this recommendation, and we have his authority to make it known to the public.

Under the severe trials of the present hour let fortitude mark the conduct of our party, and we urge every Carolinian, without regard to past political affiliations, sternly to refuse allegiance to the monstrous usurpation claiming to exercise the functions of the State Government, firmly resolving never to contribute one dollar of taxation for its sustenance, and steadily maintaining the verdict of the people at the ballot box. Every interest of the present and every hope of the future—aye, the peace, prosperity and happiness of the State for generations—demand a firm, unwavering and persistent determination never under any circumstances to recognize the pretended authority of a degraded and disgraced man, whose slanders and vituperations of our people will always be remembered as the emanations of a vindictive and baffled politician and adventurer thwarted in an unholy ambition. The issue must be made, and to yield is to seal the political fate of a brave people.

In conclusion, we urge every one to resume the ordinary routine of business, and seek to widen the avenues of material prosperity, confiding their cause to the wisdom of our beloved chief magistrate whose course has won the confidence and excited the admiration of the civilized world. Under his guidance and protection the issue will eventuate in the complete fruition of our hopes and aspirations, unless constitutional liberty has perished in America.

THE STRUGGLE FOR POSSESSION.

The following correspondence took place very soon after the inauguration of Governor Hampton:

         State of South Carolina,
           Executive Chamber.
       Columbia, December 18, 1876.

Sir: As Governor of South Carolina, chosen by the people thereof, I have qualified in accordance with the Constitution, and I hereby call upon you as my predecessor in office to deliver up to me the great seal of the State, together with the possession of the State House, the public records, and all other matters and things appertaining to said office.

      Respectfully, your obedient servant,
         Wade Hampton, Governor.

D. H. Chamberlain, Esq.

         State of South Carolina,
          Executive Chamber.
      Columbia, S. C., December 18, 1876.

Sir: I have received the communication in which you call upon me to deliver up to you the great seal, etc., etc.,

I do not recognize in you any right to make the foregoing demand, and I hereby refuse compliance therewith.

I am, sir, your obedient servant,

         D. H. Chamberlain,
        Governor of South Carolina.

Wade Hampton, Esq.

Lieutenant-Governor Simpson had sent to the Senate an official communication, as follows:

       Columbia, S. C., December 15, 1876.
To the Honorable the Senators of South Carolina:

I have the honor of informing the senators that yesterday, 14th of December, instant, the election returns for Governor and Lieutenant-Governor were opened and published by the Hon. W. H. Wallace, speaker of the House of Representatives, in the presence of the members of the House and senators, that Wade Hampton having received a majority of the votes cast for Governor and W. D. Simpson having received a majority of the votes cast for Lieutenant-Governor, we were declared duly elected to those offices respectively; that thereupon his Excellency Wade Hampton was inaugurated as Governor and the oath of office was administered to him, and I was inaugurated as Lieutenant-Governor—then and there taking the oath prescribed in the Constitution.

Under the provision of the Constitution I am ex-officio president of the Senate and am entitled to the privilege of presiding over that body when present. The law-making power of the State is, by virtue of the Constitution, vested in the General Assembly, to be composed of the Senate and the House of Representatives, organized according to its provisions. The two houses together compose the General Assembly and each is an integral part thereof.

The Supreme Court of this State—the court of last resort—has decided that the body over which the Hon. W. H. Wallace presides as speaker is the constitutional House of Representatives and consequently it must be a portion of the General Assembly. Such being the case, I respectfully submit that it is the duty of the senators composing the Senate to unite with the House and thus organize the General Assembly. Should this union take place and the Senate thus form a part of the General Assembly, the legislative power of the State will be in full action.

I respectfully announce to you that as Lieutenant-Governor I am present in the city of Columbia and am prepared to discharge the duties of your presiding officer, which devolve upon me under the provisions of the Constitution, and I hereby claim the right of taking my seat as president of the Senate.

With great respect, your obedient servant,

W. D. Simpson,
Lieutenant-Governor, ex-officio President of the Senate.

This communication was referred by the Senate to its judiciary committee—which never reported. The Democratic senators formally protested that after the qualification of Lieutenant-Governor Simpson, his predecessor, Gleaves, was without authority of any sort.

The House of Representatives fixed a day for the election of a senator of the United States for the term commencing March 4, 1877, and informed the Senate of such action. The House voted on two separate days without result. On December 20 the Democratic senators repaired to Carolina Hall, and a joint vote was taken—resulting in the election of Gen. M. C. Butler by a vote of 64 out of a total of 79.

The House did not pass an appropriation bill or a supply bill—this for the reason that the majority in control of the Senate continued to act in combination with Mr. Chamberlain and the so-called House over which Mackey pretended to preside.

Funds being required for certain expenses of the State Government the House of Representatives authorized Governor Hampton to call upon the taxpayers to contribute each a sum not exceeding one-fourth of the tax last paid—the amount so contributed to be deducted from the contributor's tax as fixed by the levy to be made by the Legislature when the Senate should recognize the authority of the lawful House and the lawful Governor.

It was necessary to have some printing done for the lawful House of Representatives and for the Governor. Dr. James Woodrow, then at the head of the Presbyterian Publishing House in Columbia, when that body organized offered to do the desired printing and wait for his compensation till the lawful Legislature should make provision for payment. The offer was thankfully accepted.

The Mackey body undertook to elect a senator of the United States. In "joint assembly," held after the Senate and the so-called House had each failed to elect, the individuals recognizing Mackey as speaker, together with the Republican members of the Senate, went through the form of voting and declared D. T. Corbin elected to succeed Senator Thomas J. Robertson.

The Mackey body and the Senate pretended to pass several acts—including one levying a tax of thirteen mills for the support of the Government. Under the pretended act—"ratified" in the Senate chamber and actually signed by Mr. Chamberlain, calling himself Governor—instructions were sent to the several county auditors to enter on the books and to the treasurers to collect the so-called tax. The entries were made, the treasurers announced themselves ready to receive, but they got less than a thousand dollars.

Among the pretended acts was one repealing the agricultural lien law.

An amusing effort of the Mackey body was seen in the passage of "a bill to prevent and punish any person or persons for setting up, or attempting to set up, or maintaining a government of the State in opposition to the legitimate and lawful government of the State." Offenders against this proposed law were punishable with a fine not less than $20,000 or more than $100,000, and imprisonment for a term not less than ten or more than forty years. To enforce this measure the Governor was to be authorized to use the militia and the constabulary and to call on the President for troops. The pretended passage of this measure afforded some amusement to the supporters of the lawful State Government.

The so-called House voted the usual gratuities—$1,000 to their speaker, $300 to their reading clerk and $200 to the colored preacher who had opened their proceedings with prayer.

The Republican members of the Senate and the members of the so-called House under Mackey received each $200 for their services. This money was procured by F. L. Cardozo, claiming to be State

Treasurer, from D. T. Corbin, who really used it in bribing certain members to vote for him to be senator of the United States. Several Republicans (including E. W. M. Mackey) testified that many men had voted for Corbin on his promise that should he be elected to the Senate he would pay over to Cardozo $20,000 to be distributed among the members.

Corbin and his partner, William Stone, had collected royalties due the State by a company engaged in mining phosphate rock. It was of the money thus held in trust for the State that Corbin used a portion for paying the Republican members of the Legislature. The State Supreme Court afterwards decided that Corbin and Stone had fraudulently converted this money to their own use, and affirmed a judgment against them for nearly $24,000. They had previously fled the State.

Cardozo, in a proceeding instituted by authority of Governor Hampton, had been enjoined from paying out any State funds; and he afterwards declared that the $20,000 was "an individual loan" by Corbin and had not been entered on the books in the Treasurer's office.

The Senate and the House adjourned *sine die* on December 22, and the Mackey body dispersed on that day.

CONTRIBUTIONS TO THE STATE GOVERNMENT.

After the inauguration of the Governor there were meetings in most of the counties, at which the assembled citizens declared their purpose to sustain the lawful government by obedience to its officers and more especially by paying such contributions as should be asked for its support.

Governor Hampton's authority was soon recognized, respected and obeyed by the circuit judges and the county officials. Some of the latter refused to recognize Mr. Chamberlain's order of removal, held possession and, where the nature of their powers permitted, acted under the directions of Governor Hampton.

The executive authority of the new State Government was administered by Governor Hampton, aided by General Johnson Hagood, elected Comptroller-General, but excluded from his office by his Republican competitor (T. C. Dunn) holding under the decision of the Board of State Canvassers. These two officials, with a private secretary and a clerk, had rooms above a store and there conducted the business of the State.

Governor Hampton found it necessary to call for only ten per cent. of the contribution contemplated in the House resolutions. He appointed in each county a "special agent" who notified the people of his readiness to receive what they should choose to pay. Before there could be returns from these agents the Governor, in a letter to a friend in Charleston, incidentally referred to the immediate need of some money for the public institutions. The gentleman addressed having mentioned the letter, there came at once contributions in advance by taxpayers of that city, in sufficient amount to enable the Governor to relieve the pressing wants of the penitentiary and the lunatic asylum. Conditions in the latter institution had become so distressful that Dr. Ensor, the superintendent, wrote an appeal to the board of regents and to Speaker Wallace of the House of Representatives, setting forth the danger of actual starvation among the patients and the necessity for instant help. Superintendent Parmele had made to Governor Hampton a similar statement about the penitentiary.

On March 1, 1877, General Hagood, "acting Comptroller and Treasurer," published a statement showing that of the contribution called for he had received $119,432.41, the amounts from the several counties being as follows: Abbeville, $6,840; Aiken, $3,662.50; Anderson, $4,042.90; Barnwell, $4,042.90; Beaufort, $2,300; Charleston, $28,663.31; Chester, $3,561.50; Chesterfield, $1,450; Clarendon, $1,179.64; Colleton, $1,908.90; Darlington, $3,150; Edgefield, $3,400; Fairfield, $3,580.45; Georgetown, $1,278.39; Greenville, $3,700; Horry, $620; Kershaw, $1,921.71; Lancaster, $1,706.19; Laurens, $2,819.60; Lexington, $2,272.40; Marion, $2,835.77; Marlboro, $2,015; Newberry, $5,841.37; Oconee, $1,279.70; Orangeburg, $3,000; Pickens, $968.40; Richland, $4,482.93; Spartanburg, $2,700; Sumter, $2,970; Union, $3,173.55; Williamsburg, $1,900; York, $4,767.25. The total of office fees received was $706.30.

The disbursements amounted to $37,794.64—covering payments to the Legislature, to the judicial and the executive department, to the different State institutions, and for contingent expenses.

In his first message to the General Assembly (April 27) the Governor reported the total of contributions and office fees to have been $135,839.48, and the disbursements $76,661.09—leaving a cash balance of $59,178.39. The receipts from taxpayers had been considerably more than ten per cent. of the previous year's tax.

HAMPTON ADJUDGED TO BE GOVERNOR.

On February 9 Governor Hampton issued a pardon to one Tilda Norris, a convict undergoing sentence within the walls of the State penitentiary. The superintendent of the prison refusing to recognize that pardon, the prisoner applied to the Supreme Court for a writ of habeas corpus, to the end that the cause of her detention might be inquired into and that she might be discharged from custody.

The case was duly brought before the court and testimony was taken in relation to the count and declaration of the vote for Governor, and the inauguration of Governor Hampton.

Chief Justice Moses being disabled by illness, the court hearing the case consisted of Associate Justices Willard and Wright.

On March 2 the following order was filed with the clerk of the Supreme Court:

It is ordered that the relator be discharged from the custody of the superintendent of the penitentiary.

A. J. Willard, A. J., Presiding.

I concur in the above.

J. J. Wright.

This order had been signed on February 27. On March 1, before it was filed, Justice Wright filed with the clerk a long opinion in which he held that Wade Hampton, "having never been declared to have received the highest number of votes at the last election by the only power competent to ascertain and declare that fact, cannot, under the Constitution, be Governor," and further held that as the State Constitution prescribed that the Governor's term of office should continue "until his successor shall be chosen and qualified," and as Mr. Chamberlain had been elected Governor in 1874, "he must be held entitled to the office of Governor at this time."

To this opinion Justice Wright annexed the following statement over his official signature:

Having attached my name to an order discharging the petitioner in this case on the 27th day of February, 1877, after mature deliberation, believing that the order should not have been made, I now hereby revoke, recall and cancel said order so far as my signature may have given it sanction, and substitute the foregoing opinion in its stead.

On March 7 Justice Willard filed a statement setting forth the fact of Justice Wright's signing of the order of discharge, relating the circumstances of the attempted cancellation of the same and concluding as follows:

Without receiving any subsequent communication from Judge Wright I attended the court on Friday, the 2d day of March, pursuant to adjournment.

It was my intention to express orally at that time the results to which I had arrived as to the questions involved in the case, but in consequence of the absence of Judge Wright the court was necessarily adjourned and no opportunity afforded for such statement. I deem it important, in view of the important questions involved, deeply affecting the feelings and interests of the people of the State, and in view of the anomalous and unprecedented character of the recent proceedings taking place before a court of last resort, to put on record a brief statement of the results arrived at by myself, intending to place them in the form of a formal opinion at the earliest practicable moment.

Judge Willard held: 1. That under that provision of the State Constitution which declares that "the person having the highest number of votes shall be Governor" the candidate who, according to the returns of the managers of election, has received the highest number of votes is entitled, where there is no contest, to the possession of the office, and if he takes possession of it without going through the regular form of installation he is at least *de facto* Governor. 2. That an incumbent of the office of Governor who, being a candidate for reelection, is defeated, but who nevertheless claims the office, gets himself inaugurated as if he had been reelected and takes possession in part of the office, is not entitled to be recognized as Governor holding over or as Governor *de facto* against the person who received the highest number of votes and who also has entered upon the discharge of the duties of the office.

The prisoner, Tilda Norris, was promptly set free.

The conduct of Justice Wright was attributed to the coercion of his late political associates of both races. On all the questions previously raised in the Supreme Court he had unswervingly followed the law and the precedents. For this he had been assailed by Republican papers and denounced by men of his own race. When the case involving the Governorship came on he was beset with appeals and threats. Resisting these, he signed the order which in effect adjudged that Wade Hampton was Governor. Having, it seemed, disclosed his action, he was set upon by the Republican leaders and really coerced into signing the pretended withdrawal of his signature from the order previously made and into filing an opinion embodying a contrary conclusion. That opinion had evidently been written for him by some lawyer—probably by Mr. Chamberlain or by one in the latter's employ.

Mr. Chamberlain on December 20, 1876, issued a paper purporting to be the pardon of Peter Smith, a convict confined in the State penitentiary. The superintendent refusing to recognize the alleged pardon, the prisoner applied to Judge Carpenter for an order of discharge. Judge Carpenter held that neither Hampton nor Chamberlain had been legally installed in right of the election of 1876, and that Chamberlain held over in right of his election in 1874. Holding the pardon granted to Smith valid, the Judge ordered his discharge from the penitentiary. On appeal the Supreme Court (Chief Justice Willard and Associate Justice McIver) held: 1. That a candidate for Governor who receives the highest number of votes, whose election has not been contested and who qualifies in the presence of the House of Representatives and of such of the senators as choose to attend, after notice to the Senate, is the duly elected and qualified Governor of the State and entitled to discharge the functions of the office. 2. That where one holding the office of Governor is a candidate for reelection and, being defeated, goes through the form of inauguration as if he had been reelected, he is estopped by such conduct from afterwards admitting his defeat and claiming the office under a provision of the Constitution giving him the right to hold over until his successor is qualified. 3. That Chamberlain's pardon was invalid.

By these two decisions all conflicting claims to the office of Governor were settled. In the Norris case it was decided that Hampton was Governor—in the Smith case it was decided that Chamberlain was not Governor.

Mention has been made of the illness of Chief Justice Moses. That illness terminated fatally on March 6. The following tribute to the dead jurist is taken from an editorial in the *Columbia Register*:

He was a man of much learning, whose resources were at easy command. He was well read in general literature, for which he had contracted a strong taste from his college days. He was deeply versed in the science and the practice of the law. His judgment was keen, clear, discriminating. His power of expression was ready and ample. Language waited as a nimble servant upon his thoughts, and his discourse flowed in a fresh and copious stream to convey the deductions and decisions of his acute and active mind.

Chief Justice Moses was an amiable man, esteemed by his friends and deeply loved by his family. We have heard it remarked of him that he was singularly devoid of resentment.

South Carolina today bends over his bier, choosing not to recall his foibles and defects, but gratefully to remember only his faithful services when her "need was the sorest."

PRESIDENT GRANT'S PARTING BLOW.

In Charleston and Columbia it had been arranged to have a parade of the rifle clubs in honor of Washington's birthday. There was no such parade—this in consequence of the action of the President of the United States, as indicated in the following paper:

Post of Columbia,
Columbia, S. C., February 20, 1877.

Capt. Hugh S. Thompson, Columbia, S. C.

Dear Sir: I have the honor to notify you that I have this day been directed by the honorable Secretary of War to inform you that his Excellency the President of the United States directs me to notify you that the members of the so-called rifle clubs, who under his proclamation of the 17th of October last were instructed to disband, will not be permitted to make any public demonstration or parade on the 22d instant, as is said to be contemplated; and it is hoped that you will give a cheerful obedience to this order and notify the members of your club or company thereof, in order to prevent a parade taking place.

My orders require me to see that no such parade takes place.

I am, sir, very respectfully, your obedient servant,

H. M. Black,
Lieutenant-Colonel Eighteenth Infantry, Commanding Post.

Upon receiving information of the President's order Governor Hampton issued the following proclamation:

State of South Carolina,
Executive Chamber.
Columbia, S. C., February 20, 1877.

His Excellency the President of the United States having ordered that the white militia companies of this State should not parade on the 22d instant to celebrate Washington's birthday, in deference to the office he holds I hereby call upon these organizations to postpone to some future day this manifestation of their respect to the memory of that illustrious President whose highest ambition it was, as it was his chief glory, to observe the Constitution and to obey the laws of his country.

THE DUAL GOVERNMENT

If the arbitrary commands of a Chief Executive who has not sought to emulate the virtues of Washington deprive the citizens of this State of the privilege of joining publicly in paying reverence to that day so sacred to every American patriot we can at least show by our obedience to constituted authority, however arbitrarily exercised, that we are not unworthy to be the countrymen of Washington.

We must, therefore, remit to some more auspicious period, which I trust is not far distant, the exercise of our right to commemorate the civic virtues of that unsullied character who wielded his sword only to found and perpetuate that American constitutional liberty which is now denied to the citizens of South Carolina.

Wade Hampton, Governor.

To this proclamation there was obedience prompt and uncomplaining—this notwithstanding the course of the President was ranked among the smallest acts of the smallest man that had ever sat in the chair of Washington.

THE CONTEST CARRIED TO WASHINGTON.

Notwithstanding the adjournment of the Senate and the voluntary dispersion of the Mackey body, the company of Federal troops which Governor Chamberlain had demanded as a protection to the Legislature against unlawful intrusion continued to occupy the State House. The Republican nominees claiming to have been elected as State officers held the different rooms in the building. There was no sign of other unlawful intrusion or of a breach of the peace.

The State Government as administered by Governor Hampton and his assistants continued to perform its functions, sustained by the courts—and not resisted anywhere in South Carolina, except by Mr. Chamberlain and by those holding on to the different State offices.

The actual contest for possession was transferred to Washington. There Senator John J. Patterson represented the Chamberlain usurpation, and bitterly opposed both the removal of troops and any recognition of the lawful House of Representatives or the Governor of South Carolina.

Senator Robertson took the opposite position. He first notified the Mackey body that he did not recognize their right to any part in the election of his successor. He informed the President that there was no disposition to break the peace and no ground for Federal interference in the settlement of matters in South Carolina. He publicly declared that Hampton had a fair majority of more than eleven hundred votes over Chamberlain, and that many colored men voted for Hampton while voting for Hayes. He stated to President Grant that Hampton and Hayes had carried the State, and emphasized the fact that there had been quite as much intimidation and fraud in Beaufort as there could have been in Edgefield or Laurens. He further stated to the President his conviction that under no circumstances could the people of South Carolina be compelled to yield any obedience to the Chamberlain government or contribute anything to its support. He urged in the Senate the adoption of Senator Gordon's resolution declaring that the State Government represented by Wade Hampton was the lawful Government of South Carolina, and took occasion to declare that under Republican rule in this State the administration of local affairs had been so bad that it must be better if transferred to Democratic hands. He protested against the use of troops to uphold the Chamberlain usurpation, and declared that Governor Hampton was able to protect all classes, all interests, and could safely be trusted to do so. Senator Robertson's statements had very wide circulation, and they were regarded as contributing largely towards setting before the country a fair presentation of actual conditions in South Carolina—including, of course, the fact that the State Supreme Court had formally adjudged that the so-called House recognized by Mr. Chamberlain was without authority, without legal existence.

Senator Gordon was constant in his efforts to have the truth told in the Senate, to the President and to the country at large, and he had the active assistance of several Southern members.

MEMORIALS TO CONGRESS.

On December 29, 1876, General Gordon presented to the Senate of the United States the memorial of Governor Hampton, Lieutenant-Governor Simpson, Speaker Wallace and sixty-eight senators and representatives in the General Assembly. The paper contained a full statement in relation to the election, the action of the Board of Canvassers, the decisions of the Supreme Court and the Federal Court, and the interference of the Federal troops. The paper concluded with the following prayer:

Wherefore your petitioners, unable to assert their rights in the premises by peaceable means, recognizing the supremacy of the Constitution and laws of the United States, and relying upon the right and duty of Congress to guarantee to this State a republican form of government wherein the constituted civil authorities of the State shall not be suppressed by the military, respectfully apply to your honorable bodies to cause a cessation of the unwarranted interference of the military authorities and the United States troops in the affairs of this State, and for such action as will relieve them from the unwarranted conduct of the United States authorities, hereinbefore set forth, and as will enable the Governor, the Lieutenant-Governor and the House of Representatives peacefully to exercise the rights and perform the duties of the offices to which they have been elected.

Senator Gordon offered the following resolution:

Resolved by the Senate, That the State government now existing in the State of South Carolina and represented by Wade Hampton as Governor is the lawful government of said State, that it is republican in form, and that every assistance necessary to sustain its proper and lawful authority in said State should be given by the United States when properly called upon for that purpose, to the end that the laws may be faithfully and promptly executed, life and property protected and defended, and all violators of law, State or National, brought to a speedy punishment for their crimes.

On January 17 Senator John J. Patterson submitted the petition of Mr. Chamberlain and the other Republican candidates claiming to have been elected to the several State offices in South Carolina, and claiming also to have duly qualified and to have entered upon the discharge of their functions in accordance with the State Constitution and laws—the memorial being signed also by E. W. M. Mackey, as speaker. This paper purported to be an exhaustive review of events in this State, including the election on November 7 and the campaign preceding—charging that the Republicans had been abused, intimidated and defrauded. The memorialists undertook especially to review the decision of the Supreme Court, whereby the Wallace House had been declared lawful and the Mackey body unlawful, and to repudiate the authority of that judgment of the tribunal of last resort. They alleged that no lawfully elected representatives had been excluded from the House, and that the troops had been used only to prevent the intrusion of persons unlawfully claiming to have been elected in Edgefield and Laurens.

In conclusion, the memorialists prayed that Congress "will by all lawful and Constitutional means continue to uphold the authority of the lawful and Constitutional Executive and Legislative Departments of the Government of South Carolina, as represented by D. H. Chamberlain as Governor and the State officers and Senate and House of Representatives of said State, by protecting the said State

Government against domestic violence now threatened by Wade Hampton and others falsely styling themselves officials of said State."

Senator Patterson submitted a resolution declaring that the State Government existing in South Carolina, represented by D. H. Chamberlain, was the lawful Government of the State, and republican in form, and that every assistance should be given to it by the United States, to the end that the laws might be faithfully executed.

To the above-mentioned memorial Governor Hampton and those claiming to have been elected with him to the several State offices made a reply in which, after combating the positions taken, they went on to say:

As long ago as October 4, 1876, Mr. Chamberlain, in a widely circulated document over his own signature, in which he confessed his utter inability to administer the government of the State and his reliance on military aid, threatened "action which would inflict great temporary injury upon the material interests of the State;" and right faithfully has he acted as he threatened, shielded and supported in the ruin he has wrought by the army of the United States. The material interests of the State have been greatly injured, commerce languishes, trade scarcely exists, capital is repelled, industry is paralyzed.

The corridors of the Capitol still resound with the measured tread of the sentinel, and bristling bayonets proclaim to the favored few who are permitted without molestation to enter its portals, in language not to be misunderstood—*Inter arma silent leges.*

In defiance of the Constitution and of the will of the people lawfully expressed at the ballot box the Governor, the Lieutenant-Governor and the House of Representatives are still excluded from the State House by armed troops of the Federal Government. Mr. Chamberlain and his pretended government are supported and upheld by them and by them alone.

These papers were all referred to proper committees—which never reported.

HAMPTON TO TILDEN AND HAYES.

Immediately after the adjournment of the Legislature Governor Hampton sent the following letter to Mr. Hayes:

Executive Chamber,
Columbia, S. C., Dec. 23, 1876.

My Dear Sir—I have the honor to enclose a copy of my inaugural as the duly elected Governor of South Carolina. In view of the present events and the official sanction given to gross misrepresentation of the acts and purposes of the majority of the good people of this commonwealth, I deem it proper to declare that profound peace prevails throughout the State, that the course of judicial proceedings is obstructed by no combination of citizens thereof, and that the laws for the protection of the inhabitants in all their rights of person, property and citizenship are being enforced in our courts.

While the people of this State are not wanting either in the spirit or means to maintain their rights of citizenship against the usurper's power, which now defies the supreme judicial authority of the State, they have such faith in the justice of their cause that they propose to leave its vindication to the proper legal tribunals, appealing at the same time to the patriotism and public sentiment of the whole country. The inflammatory utterances of a portion of the public press render it, perhaps, not inopportune for me to state that, although the people in South Carolina view with grave concern the present critical juncture in the affairs of our country, which threatens to subject to an extreme test the republican system of government itself, it is their firm and deliberate purpose to condemn any solution of the existing political problem that involves the exhibition of armed force, or that moves through any other channel than the prescribed forms of the Constitution, or the peaceful agencies of law.

Trusting that a solution may be had which, while maintaining the peace of the country, shall do no violence to the constitutional safeguards of popular rights, and will tend still further to unite the people of all the States in an earnest effort to preserve the peace and sustain the laws and the Constitution, I am, very respectfully, your obedient servant, Wade Hampton,
Governor of South Carolina.

His Excellency R. B. Hayes, Governor of Ohio.

P. S.—As the settlement of the vexed political questions which now agitate the public mind must ultimately depend upon yourself or upon your distinguished competitor for the Presidency, I have addressed a letter similar to this to his Excellency Governor Tilden.
Yours, Wade Hampton.

The fact that Governor Hampton had addressed a communication to Mr. Hayes was very widely noticed, and it gave rise to some comment calculated to create the impression that the Governor was in some way negotiating with the Republican candidate whose followers were then claiming that he had been elected to the Presidency. This impression had no place whatever with the people of South Carolina, and Hampton's friends elsewhere were equally sure that any reflections upon him in this connection were altogether groundless.

Among those friends was Gen. William Preston, of Kentucky, who resolved to get the truth from the Governor himself—whereupon the following correspondence by telegraph took place:

Cincinnati, Dec. 29, 1876.

Gov. Wade Hampton, Columbia, S. C.:

A telegram from Columbus, Ohio, announces that Judge Mackey, in your behalf, has made propositions to Governor Hayes, to support him for President against Governor Tilden, recognizing Hayes as legally elected, and offering to support him against the Northern Democracy. This I do not believe, but it is injuring the Democracy here. Your wise and noble course has strengthened my long friendship for you. In my judgment there should be a prompt denial, and this I submit to your decision.
William Preston.

Columbia, S. C., Dec. 29, 1876.

To Gen. William Preston, Cincinnati, Ohio:

No one is authorized to make declarations for me or for our party here. We abide the decisions of legitimate authority and hope for a peaceful solution.
Wade Hampton.

There was really no need of any denial or explanation from Governor Hampton. There was a general feeling among the Democrats of South Carolina that neither Mr. Hayes nor Mr. Tilden nor, indeed, any considerable number of the people of the sections where these gentlemen lived had any realization of actual conditions in South Carolina—the actual issues between the people who acknowledged Hampton as Governor and those who asserted that Chamberlain had been fairly elected and lawfully inaugurated. It was generally considered that Governor Hampton's letters would at least induce inquiry as to the truth and thus remove much misapprehension.

Whatever the apparent tendency of some Southern Democrats to favor concessions in the struggle over the electoral vote, in order to assure peace in the South, it was plain that neither Governor Hampton nor the people who had made him their standard-bearer had any part in any movement of which those concessions were or would be the principal agencies. Governor Hampton's position—the position of the Democratic party of South Carolina—was at this time made perfectly clear in connection also with statements to the effect that in the recent campaign there had been lukewarmness towards the National ticket or at least a willingness to subordinate the effort for the electoral ticket to the fight for Hampton and home rule.

There was considerable newspaper talk. But the matter was set at rest by the published statement of Col. A. C. Haskell, who, as chairman of the State Democratic Executive Committee, had been personally familiar with the purposes and policies of the party in South Carolina. Colonel Haskell carefully reviewed the action of the

Democratic leaders in relation to the electoral ticket and showed conclusively that there never had been any movement, any inclination, towards the subordination of the claims of the National Democratic party to those of the nominees on the State ticket—whose election, indeed, might have been rendered comparatively easy by conceding South Carolina to Hayes and Wheeler. When Judges Mackey and Cooke declared their purpose to support the Hampton ticket, they urged the abandonment of the National contest. The proposition was discussed by the State committee, but no action was taken, except the unanimous passage of a resolution that nothing should be done without consultation with the National committee. There was some correspondence with Mr. Tilden through his chief advisers, Mr. Manton Marble and Mr. Abram S. Hewitt. Before any answers came it was unanimously determined by the State committee and candidates that the electoral ticket should stand and the fight continue as it had begun—for all the Democratic nominees, National, State and local.

In due time answers came from Mr. Tilden and from Mr. Hewitt as the chairman of the National Democratic committee. They both declared that the fears expressed by some, that the fight for Hampton might embarrass the party in other parts of the country, were groundless and that, on the contrary, that fight was of actual help to the National cause. Neither the question of withdrawing the electoral ticket nor the policy of subordinating it to the State ticket was again broached in South Carolina.

Some little attempt was made to give significance to the fact that Governor Hampton's letter to Mr. Hayes was carried by Judge Mackey. The Judge—who, by the way, invariably expressed the opinion that Hayes would be seated—having stated his purpose to visit the President-elect and interest him in the peaceful settlement of matters in South Carolina by constitutional means, asked of Governor Hampton the privilege of bearing his letter already written to Mr. Hayes. The request was granted—the Governor simply using the Judge as a messenger instead of using the mail. Judge Mackey took occasion to declare that in his visit to Mr. Hayes he was neither the emissary nor the spokesman of Governor Hampton, but had gone and had spoken upon his individual responsibility alone.

COUNTING THE ELECTORAL VOTE.

For a few weeks before the inauguration of Mr. Hayes the public attention was centered chiefly on the counting of the electoral vote—

the contest arising on the vote of Florida, Louisiana and South Carolina. Before the Electoral Commission created by Congress the following grounds were taken against the counting of the vote of South Carolina:

1. That no legal election was held in South Carolina for Presidential electors, the General Assembly of that State not having provided, as required by article 8, section 3, of the Constitution thereof, for the registration of the people entitled to vote, without which registration no valid or legal election could be held.

2. That there was not existing in the State of South Carolina on the 1st of January, 1876, nor at any time thereafter up to and including the 10th of December, 1876, a republican form of government, such as is guaranteed by the Constitution to every State in the Union.

3. That the Federal Government, prior to and during the election on November 7, 1876, without authority of law, stationed in various parts of said State, at or near the polling precincts, detachments of the United States army, by whose presence the full exercise of the right of suffrage was prevented, and by reason whereof no legal or free election was or could be held.

4. That at the several polling places in said State were stationed United States deputy marshals, appointed under the provisions of sections 2021 and 2022 of the United States Revised Statutes, which provisions were unconstitutional and void; that said deputy marshals, exceeding over 1,000 in number, by their unlawful and arbitrary action, in obedience to the improper and illegal instructions received by them from the Department of Justice, so interfered with the full and free exercise of the right of suffrage by the duly qualified voters of said State that a fair election could not be and was not held in said State on November 7, 1876.

5. That there was not, from the 1st of January, 1876, up to and including the 10th of December, 1876, at any time, a State government in the State of South Carolina, except a pretended government set up in violation of law and of the Constitution of the United States, by Federal authority and sustained by Federal troops.

THE NEW PRESIDENT'S POLICY.

The action of the Electoral Commission in "counting in" Mr. Hayes was viewed in South Carolina with about as much disgust as it aroused all over the South and also among conservative people in other parts of the country. But the feeling uppermost was one of anxiety about the course to be pursued by the incoming President in relation to affairs in South Carolina. The general belief was that Mr. Hayes, unless thwarted by some action of Congress, would carry out a policy which would permit the lawful government in this State to perform all its functions without interference or obstruction by the Federal courts or the Federal army. In some quarters it was stated that he would formally recognize the Hampton government—in others that he would simply withdraw the troops and leave that government to stand which could stand by itself.

In his inaugural address the new President had very dispassionately discussed matters in the South, and had said:

Let me assure my countrymen of the Southern States that it is my earnest desire to regard and promote their truest interests—the interests of the white and the colored people both and equally—and to put forth my best efforts in behalf of a civil policy which will forever wipe out in our public affairs the color line and the distinction between North and South, to the end that we may have not merely a united North or a united South, but a united country.

The President's policy towards the South had been foretold in a letter (February 26) from Senator Stanley Matthews and Congressman Charles Foster (both of Ohio) to Senator John B. Gordon, of Georgia, and Congressman John Young Brown, of Kentucky, in which the writers declared:

We can assure you in the strongest possible manner of our great desire to have him adopt such a policy as will give to the people of the States of South Carolina and Louisiana the right to control their own affairs in their own way, subject only to the Constitution of the United States and the laws made in pursuance thereof, and we say further that from an acquaintance with and knowledge of Governor Hayes and his views, we have the most complete confidence that such will be the policy of his administration.

PROPOSITIONS TO THE PRESIDENT.

Shortly after the inauguration of Mr. Hayes, Governor Hampton sent to the President a letter in which he briefly stated the condition of affairs in South Carolina and formally requested the immediate withdrawal of the Federal troops from the State House. The committee selected to present this letter consisted of Gen. J. B. Kershaw, Col. James H. Rion, ex-Gov. R. K. Scott, Senator Robertson and Judge Mackey. After performing the duty with which they had been specifically charged the committee submitted in writing a statement more fully treating the subject-matter. After a careful presentation of the course of events starting with the initial action of the State Board of Canvassers, the committee declared "the unalterable resolution of the Governor and the majority of the people not to permit the subversion of their liberties and civilization and never to submit to the domination of usurped authority"—the paper concluding as follows:

They will resist it everywhere and continually to their utmost power, yet always within the limits that prescribe their paramount duty as American citizens to bear true faith and allegiance to the Constitution and the Union, and yield true obedience to the laws.

Such resistance cannot be deemed inconsistent with a law-abiding citizenship, for the Hampton government has received the recognition directly or indirectly of all the circuit judges save one [Judge Carpenter] and even he has decided that Governor Hampton received the highest number of votes, although holding that the election was not legally declared, the Senate having failed or refused to attend at the publication of the vote by the speaker of the House of Representatives. The Circuit Courts are now virtually our courts of last resort, owing to the death of the Chief Justice, the absence or non-concurrence of one of the two Associate Justices who now constitute the Supreme Court, and the fact that the General Assembly, which is alone empowered to fill the vacancy, has the same dual character as the governorship.

The government of Governor Hampton has also the active support of almost the entire intelligence and respectability of both races and parties in the State, while that of Chamberlain is upheld chiefly by bayonets and the mercenary hands of unworthy office-holders and office-seekers.

The President received also a paper purporting to represent the views of the Republicans of South Carolina—signed by John J. Patterson, D. H. Chamberlain and D. T. Corbin. With a view to "adjust all political differences as to the lawful government in South Carolina," the authors of the paper proposed:

1. That all the election returns for Governor and Lieutenant-Governor be submitted to a commission of five persons, who, after full investigation, should find and declare the results of the election for those offices; or—

2. That such commission should in like manner inquire and determine what persons had been duly elected members of the House of Representatives, and that such members should organize as such House and with the Senate proceed to tabulate the returns of the

election of Governor and Lieutenant-Governor—the results thus ascertained to be declared in accordance with the provisions of the State Constitution.

It was proposed that the commission be appointed by the President, or that two be selected by each of the contending parties, with the Chief Justice of the United States Supreme Court as the fifth member, or that each party choose two members and the fifth member be drawn by lot or otherwise chosen as the four might determine.

The paper concluded thus:

The foregoing propositions are presented solely with a view to a practical adjustment of the present difficulties, and the undersigned, on behalf of the Republicans of South Carolina, while submitting them, affirm that their course heretofore in relation to the election of Governor and Lieutenant-Governor and the organization of the House of Representatives has been strictly just and legal, and that the State government which the undersigned represent is in all respects the lawful and only lawful government of South Carolina.

THE PRESIDENT TAKES ACTION.

On March 4 Mr. Stanley Matthews sent to Mr. Chamberlain by the hands of Col. A. C. Haskell a letter in relation to public affairs in South Carolina, in the course of which the writer used this language:

It has occurred to me to suggest whether by your own concurrence and cooperation an arrangement could not be arrived at which would obviate the necessity for the use of Federal arms to support either government and leave that to stand which is able to stand by itself. Such a course would relieve the administration from the necessity, so far as the Executive is concerned, of making any decision between the conflicting governments, and would place you in a position of making the sacrifice of what you deemed your abstract rights for the sake of the peace of the community, which would entitle you not only to the gratitude of your own party, but to the respect and esteem of the entire country.

To this letter there was a postscript by Wm. M. Evarts (already selected for the position of Secretary of State) in which he expressed a wish "to aid in a solution of the difficulties of the situation and especially to hear from you [Mr. Chamberlain] speedily."

To the letter of Mr. Matthews Mr. Chamberlain sent the following answer:

I feel grateful for the interest you manifest in the public welfare here, as well as in my personal good. To give you my views of the situation here, and my duty in connection therewith, with anything approaching fullness, would require a conversation. I can only say here, in substance, that I am wholly unable to see any line of conduct on my part, consistent with personal honor or personal duty, which would permit me to yield my claims to the Governorship. I am equally unable to see any course which can be pursued by the National administration toward the Government here which I represent, consistent with political or constitutional duty, which will not require it to support, against violence or overthrow, the lawul Republican government.

I certainly wish most devoutly that I could relieve myself of this duty. I have been exposed to personal danger by day and night constantly for five full months, and I am wearied nearly to death; but there are one or two things dearer to me than comfort or life— one is my honor as a public man and another is my duty to the Republicans of this State. Neither of these, in my judgment, would permit me to accept any accommodation or compromise which was not forced upon me by a power which it would be idle to resist. I desire to aid and relieve President Hayes, but this is a life or death struggle, and I know that I should consign myself to infamy in the eyes of all Republicans here, who know the situation by fearful experience, if I were to accept any terms or do any act which could result in the success of the monstrous conspiracy against law and humanity which the Democracy of this State embody and represent.

There are better ways than this to conciliate and pacify the South. Let the present administration, while firmly standing by the law and the right for Republicans, manifest a spirit of charity and sympathy for our opponents here, as countrymen and citizens, in the thousand ways open to an administration, and peace will come and will abide —the peace of justice and law, the only peace worth fighting for. To permit Hampton to reap the fruits of a campaign of murder and fraud, so long as there remains power to prevent it, is to sanction such methods.

All this I say, my dear sir, with feelings of profound respect for you, but as in duty bound to declare the truth as I understand it. Of one thing I am sure—neither you nor any man moved by a sense of justice can understand the situation here and be willing, for any political advantage or freedom from embarrassment, to abandon the Republicans to the fate that awaits them whenever Hampton becomes the undisputed Governor of this State.

I despair of being able to set our case in its true light before those who have had no such experience, but I do feel that if I had the privilege of personal conversation I could do much more toward it.

The situation in South Carolina continued the subject of more or less discussion by the President and his Cabinet until March 23, on

THE DUAL GOVERNMENT 453

which day there was sent to Governor Hampton and to Mr. Chamberlain the following letter of Mr. Hayes' secretary:

Sir—I am instructed by the President to bring to your attention his purpose to take into immediate consideration the position of affairs in South Carolina, with a view of determining the course which, under the Constitution and laws of the United States, it may be his duty to take in reference to the situation in that State as he finds it upon succeeding to the Presidency. It will give the President great pleasure to confer with you in person, if you shall find it convenient to visit Washington and shall concur with him in thinking such a conference the readiest and best mode of placing your views as to the political situation in your State before him. He would greatly prefer this direct communication of opinion and information to any other method of ascertaining your views upon the present condition and immediate prospect of public interests in South Carolina. If reasons of weight with you should discourage this course, the President will be glad to receive any communication from you in writing, or through any delegate possessing your confidence, that will convey to him your views of the impediments to the peaceful and orderly organization of a single and undisputed State government in South Carolina, and of the best methods of removing them.

It is the earnest desire of the President to be able to put an end as speedily as possible to all appearance of intervention of the military authority of the United States in the political derangements which affect the government and afflict the people of South Carolina. In this desire the President cannot doubt he truly represents the patriotic feeling of the great body of the people of the United States. It is impossible that protracted disorder in the domestic government of any State can or should ever fail to be a matter of lively interest and solicitude to the people of the whole country. In furtherance of the prompt and safe execution of this general purpose, he invites a full communication of your opinions on the whole subject in such one of the proposed forms as may seem to you most useful.

Mr. Chamberlain at once proceeded to Washington—Governor Hampton going a few days later.

On his journey the Governor was the recipient of frequent manifestations of the people's confidence and of their faith in the permanence of the State administration of which he was the recognized head. In acknowledging these, Governor Hampton took occasion to state explicitly his motives and purposes in accepting the invitation of the President. In the course of a short speech to the citizens assembled at the railway station to see him off he said:

I go to Washington simply to state before the President the fact that the people of South Carolina have elected me Governor of that State. I go there to say to him that we ask no recognition from any

President. We claim the recognition from the votes of the people of the State. I go there to assure him that we are not fighting for party, but that we are fighting for the good of the whole country. I am going there to demand our rights—nothing more—and, so help me God, to take nothing less.

At different places on his journey Governor Hampton stated his position in similar language—so that when he reached Washington the purpose and spirit of his acceptance of the President's invitation were very generally understood.

On arriving in Washington the Governor addressed to the President the following letter:

To the President—Sir: In compliance with your invitation I am here for the purpose of uniting my efforts with yours to the end of composing the political differences which now unhappily distract the people of South Carolina. I beg you to believe that my anxiety to bring about the permanent pacification of that State—a pacification in which the rights of all shall be protected—is as sincere as I feel assured is your own for the accomplishment of the same ends.

My position for years past in reference to the political rights of colored citizens, with my solemn pledges given during the late canvass in South Carolina, that under my administration all their rights should be absolutely secure, should furnish a sufficient guaranty of my sincerity on these points, which appear to be the subject of special anxiety.

I have the honor to ask at what hour it will be your pleasure to receive me.

The President through his private secretary promptly replied, and there was at once an interview with his Excellency—there being present, the Governor, Senator Gordon and Attorney-General Conner. There was a full presentation of the situation in South Carolina—followed with further discussion in later interviews.

Mr. Chamberlain was also received by Mr. Hayes and was requested to state his position freely and fully. Following his conferences with the President, Mr. Chamberlain (on March 31) addressed a letter in which after giving his own version of the course of events which had in his opinion necessitated the placing of soldiers in the State House, he presented the following as his reasons for opposing the withdrawal of those troops:

1. Because such withdrawal would be a withdrawal of that support and aid against domestic violence by the Government of the United States, to which the State and "the State government" repre-

sented by Mr. Chamberlain were entitled under the Constitution and laws of the United States.

2. Because "such withdrawal at the present time, pending the decision of the question of the validity of one or the other of the two governments, would be a practical decision in favor of my opponent—by which I mean that my opponent is at this moment fully prepared, in point of physical strength, to overthrow the Government which I represent."

The letter contained these further statements:

My opponent demands the withdrawal of the United States forces from the State House. It will be of service, in judging what results will follow compliance with this demand, to ask why the demand is made. I suppose neither courtesy nor charity will warrant the suggestion that it arises from a zealous regard for constitutional limitations on the part of my opponent. On the other hand, the demand is plainly made for the purposes of political advantage in the present struggle. What is this advantage? It has been suggested that it is to enable my opponent to pursue his legal remedies in the premises. It is a sufficient answer to this to say that no hindrance of any kind now exists to the peaceful and complete enforcement of all legal remedies whatever. Every legal right and remedy which belongs to my opponent under any circumstances is within his unobstructed reach today, and has been on all days. This fact points at once to the conclusion that in demanding the withdrawal of the troops from the State House my opponent does not desire thereby to secure his own right by lawful means or peaceful agencies, but to rob me and my associates and constituents of our rights by unlawful means and violent agencies.

If reference be made to the profession of those who demand the withdrawal of the troops, that they seek only to secure their rights by lawful means, I respectfully answer that I am familiar with such professions. They have been made with endless iteration during a campaign of unprecedented length, marked from the opening to the close by every degree and form of physical violence. To one not familiar with the condition of South Carolina, the statements I have now made may seem extravagant. I refer for confirmation of all I have stated to the testimony taken by the Congressional committees during the past winter, and I affirm that my present acquaintance with the facts compels me to say that this testimony falls short of the truth. The Republicans of South Carolina have carried on a struggle up to the present time for the preservation of their rights; their hope has been that they might continue to live under a free government. The withdrawal of the troops from the State House will close the struggle—will close it in defeat to a large majority of the people of the State, in the sacrifice of their rights, in the complete success of violence and fraud as agents in reaching political results.

To restate the results which will follow the withdrawal of the troops from the State House I say:

1. It will remove the protection absolutely necessary to enable the Republicans to assert and enforce their claim to the government of the State.

2. It will enable the Democrats to remove all effective opposition to the illegal military forces under the control of my opponent.

3. It will place all the agencies for maintaining the present lawful government of the State in the practical possession of the Democrats, through the admission it will require.

4. It will lead to the quick consummation of a political outrage against which I have felt and now feel it to be my solemn duty to struggle and protest so long as the faintest hope of success can be seen.

Mr. Chamberlain's letter was read in a meeting of the Cabinet on April 2—at which also there was a full discussion of the situation as presented by both sides to the controversy in South Carolina. On the following day it was determined in a Cabinet meeting that the troops should be withdrawn from the State House on April 10.

Governor Hampton at once returned to Columbia, his journey homeward being marked by constant manifestations of the people's regard and of their actual joy over the assurance of peace and good government in South Carolina. In Columbia there was a turnout of the military, the fire companies, civic societies and citizens generally—the number of these last having been swelled by the coming of many from different parts of the State. The Governor made a brief speech in which he congratulated the people upon their final triumph, and pledged himself and them to perform every promise made and to restore harmony and honest government.

The good news was received with expressions of satisfaction all over the State. There were several public meetings, at which the speeches were interrupted with the wildest cheering and sometimes with the booming of cannon.

"Hurrah for Hampton" was now the people's cry of triumph.

THE ORDER TO REMOVE THE TROOPS.

The following was the President's order for the removal of the Federal troops from the State House:

Washington, April 3.

Sir: Prior to my entering upon the duties of the Presidency there had been stationed, by order of my predecessor, in the State House at Columbia, S. C., a detachment of United States infantry. Finding them in that place, I have thought proper to delay a decision of the question of their removal until I could consider and determine whether the condition of affairs in that State is now such as to either require or justify the continued military occupation of the State House.

In my opinion, there does not now exist in that State such domestic violence as is contemplated by the Constitution as the ground upon which the military power of the National Government may be invoked for the defense of the State. There are, it is true, grave and serious disputes as to the rights of certain claimants to the chief executive office of that State, but these are to be settled and determined not by the Executive of the United States, but by such orderly and peaceable means as may be provided by the Constitution and laws of the State.

I feel assured that no resort to violence is contemplated in any quarter, but that, on the contrary, the disputes in question are to be settled solely by such peaceful remedies as the Constitution and the laws of the State provide. Under these circumstances, in this confidence, I deem it proper to take action in accordance with the principles announced when I entered upon the duties of the Presidency.

You are, therefore, directed to see that the proper orders are issued for the removal of said troops from the State House to their previous place of encampment. R. B. Hayes.

To Hon. Geo. W. McCrary, Secretary of War.

On the same day the Secretary of War directed Gen. W. T. Sherman, commanding the United States army, to carry out the President's order, and to cause the withdrawal of the troops from the State House on Tuesday, April 10, 1877, at 12 o'clock, noon.

CHAMBERLAIN'S FAREWELL.

On his return to Columbia Mr. Chamberlain held a conference with those who had been candidates with him on the Republican ticket, and was by them advised to "discontinue the struggle for the occupancy of the gubernatorial chair." Thereupon—on the very day of the departure of the soldiers from the State House—Mr. Chamberlain issued the following paper:

To the Republicans of South Carolina:

By your choice I was made Governor of this State in 1874. At the election on the 7th of November last, I was again by your votes elected to the same office. My title to the office, upon every legal and moral ground, is today clear and perfect. By the recent decision and action of the President of the United States I find myself unable longer to maintain my official rights, and I hereby announce to you that I am unwilling to prolong a struggle which can only bring further suffering upon those who engage in it.

In announcing this conclusion it is my duty to say for you that the Republicans of South Carolina entered upon their recent political struggle for the maintenance of their political and civil rights. Constituting beyond question a large majority of the lawful voters of the State, you allied yourselves with that political party whose central and inspiring principle has hitherto been the civil and political freedom of all men under the Constitution and laws of our country. By heroic efforts and sacrifices which the just verdict of history will rescue from the cowardly scorn now cast upon them by political placemen and traders, you secured the electoral vote of South Carolina for Hayes and Wheeler. In accomplishing this result you became the victims of every form of persecution and injury. From authentic evidence it is shown that not less than one hundred of your number were murdered because they were faithful to their principles and exercised rights solemnly guaranteed to them by the nation. You were denied employment, driven from your homes, robbed of the earnings of years of honest industry, hunted for your lives like wild beasts, your families outraged and scattered—for no offense except your peaceful and firm determination to exercise your political rights. You trusted, as you had a right to trust, that if by such efforts you established the lawful supremacy of your political party in the nation the Government of the United States, in the discharge of its constitutional duty, would protect the lawful Government of the State from overthrow at the hands of your political enemies. From causes patent to all men and questioned by none who regard truth you have been unable to overcome the unlawful combinations and obstacles which have opposed the practical supremacy of the government which your votes have established. For many weary months you have waited for your deliverance. While the long struggle for the Presidency was in progress you were exhorted by every representative and organ of the National Republican party to keep your allegiance true to that party, in order that your deliverance might be certain and complete.

Not the faintest whisper of the possibility of disappointment in these hopes and promises ever reached you while the struggle was pending. Today—April 10, 1877—by the order of the President whom your votes alone rescued from overwhelming defeat, the Government of the United States abandons you, deliberately withdraws from you its support, with the full knowledge that the lawful Government of the State will be speedily overthrown. By a new interpretation of the Constitution of the United States, at variance alike with the previous practice of the Government and with the decisions of the Supreme Court, the Executive of the United States evades the duty of ascertaining which of two rival State governments is the lawful one, and by the withdrawal of troops now protecting the State from domestic violence abandons the lawful State Government to a struggle with insurrectionary forces too powerful to be resisted. The grounds of policy upon which such action is defended are startling.

It is said that the North is weary of the long Southern troubles. It was weary, too, of the long troubles which sprang from the stupendous crime of chattel slavery, and longed for repose. It sought to cover them from sight by wicked compromises with the wrong which disturbed its peace, but God held it to its duty until, through a conflict which rocked and agonized the Nation, the great crime was put away and freedom was ordained for all.

It is said that if a majority of a State are unable by physical force to maintain their rights, they must be left to political servitude. Is this a doctrine ever before heard in our history? If it shall prevail, its consequences will not long be confined to South Carolina and Louisiana. It is said that a Democratic House of Representatives will refuse an appropriation for the army of the United States if the lawful government of South Carolina be maintained by the military forces. Submission to such coercion marks the degeneracy of the political party or people which endures it. A government worthy the name, a political party fit to wield power, never before blanched at such a threat. But the edict has gone forth. No arguments or considerations which your friends could present have sufficed to avert the disaster.

No effective means of resistance to the consummation of the wrong are left. The struggle can be prolonged. My strict legal rights are, of course, wholly unaffected by the action of the President. No court of the State has jurisdiction to pass upon the title of my office. No lawful Legislature can be convened except at my call. If the use of these powers promised ultimate success to our cause, I should not shrink from any sacrifices which might confront me. It is a cause in which by the light of reason and conscience a man might well lay down his life.

But, to my mind, my present responsibility involves the consideration of the effect of my action upon those whose representative I am. I have hitherto been willing to ask you, Republicans, to risk all dangers and endure all hardships until relief should come from the Government of the United States. That relief will never come. I cannot ask you to follow me further. In my best judgment I can no longer serve you by further resistance to the impending calamity.

With gratitude to God for the measure of endurance with which He has hitherto inspired me, with gratitude to you for your boundless confidence in me, with profound admiration for your matchless fidelity to the cause in which we have struggled, I now announce to you and to the people of the State that I shall no longer actively assert my right to the office of Governor of South Carolina.

The motives and purposes of the President of the United States in the policy which compels me to my present course are unquestionably honorable and patriotic. I devoutly pray that events may vindicate the wisdom of his action, and that peace, justice, freedom and

prosperity may hereafter be the portion of every citizen of South Carolina.
D. H. Chamberlain,
Governor of South Carolina.

THE LAWFUL GOVERNMENT IN POSSESSION.

At noon on April 10, 1877, the company of United States soldiers, about thirty men commanded by a captain, marched out of the State House of South Carolina and returned to their quarters in Columbia. There were a number of people gathered to witness the evacuation, but there was no demonstration.

On the same day, in response to a communication from Governor Hampton, Mr. Chamberlain informed him of his readiness to turn over to him the executive chamber, with the records and property appertaining to the executive office, at noon of the following day.

Accordingly, on April 11, 1877, at 12 o'clock precisely, the transfer was made to Governor Hampton's private secretary by the gentleman who had served Mr. Chamberlain by that designation.

The Republican claimants for the several State offices soon surrendered—so that by May 1 all the lawfully elected officers were in full possession.

Governor Hampton called the General Assembly to meet in special session on April 24.

In the Senate Gleaves yielded the place of Lieutenant-Governor—affecting, however, to believe that he was the victim of a "great wrong." Swails taking the chair, there was an attempt by the Republicans to have Lieutenant-Governor Simpson take the oath of office—which, of course, he declined to do. After some noisy demonstrations by some of the negro senators he took the chair vacated by Swails, and there was no further trouble.

In the House those who had been of the Mackey body were simply ignored. It was resolved that before being sworn each must apologize to the House and "purge himself of his contempt." Two or three refused and were never admitted. The case of the delegation from Charleston was referred to a committee which afterwards reported that owing to the prevalence of fraud and violence in that county there had been no lawful election there—whereupon Mackey and his fellows were excluded.

At this session Judge Willard was elected Chief Justice of the Supreme Court and Mr. Henry McIver, of Chesterfield, Associate

Justice. At the following session Col. A. C. Haskell was elected in the place of Associate Justice Wright, who had resigned under charges of official misconduct.

At this session Gen. J. B. Kershaw was elected judge of the Fifth circuit—it appearing that the last election of Judge Carpenter had been contrary to law. At the following session the Hon. Wm. H. Wallace was elected judge of the Seventh circuit, in the place of Judge Northrop, resigned.

In January, 1878, the Supreme Court decided that the election of each of the circuit judges (except Kershaw and Wallace) had been illegal because the vote had been taken *viva voce* and not by ballot. The vacancies resulting from this decision were filled as follows:

First Circuit—B. C. Pressley, of Charleston.
Second—A. P. Aldrich, of Barnwell.
Third—A. J. Shaw, of Sumter, reelected.
Fourth—J. H. Hudson, of Marlboro.
Sixth—Thomas J. Mackey, of Chester, reelected.
Eighth—Thomas Thomson, of Abbeville.

In the meantime the Supreme Court had decided that C. W Buttz, elected solicitor of the First circuit, had surrendered his office by taking a seat in Congress. Mr. W. St. Julien Jervey of Charleston (the Democratic nominee in 1876) was appointed to the vacancy.

Samuel J. Lee, the colored lawyer elected solicitor in the Second circuit, resigned under charges of bribery and of conspiracy to cheat, and was succeeded by Col. F. Hay Gantt, of Barnwell—also the Democratic nominee in 1876.

Josephus Woodruff having resigned the clerkship of the Senate, he was succeeded by Col. T. Stobo Farrow of Spartanburg. In like manner the Republican reading clerk was succeeded by Col. Artemas D. Goodwyn, of Orangeburg.

There were several resignations among the Republican senators and representatives—Democratic successors being elected as a matter of course. Charleston sent a solid Democratic delegation to the House.

The credentials of Gen. M. C. Butler and of D. T. Corbin were submitted to the United States Senate in January, 1877, and were laid over till the regular session following. General Butler was seated.

Many of the leading Republicans of both races quitted South Carolina almost immediately after the departure of the troops from the State House. Mr. Chamberlain engaged in the practice of law in New York. Cardozo and Elliott became department clerks in Washington. Whipper nominally practiced law in Beaufort. Purvis at last accounts held a Government position in Charleston—being a hanger-on in the United States marshal's office. Corbin spent some time in Washington—his after career being unknown to the writer. Ransier became a day laborer under the city government in Charleston. Whittemore, Hoge and Neagle promptly left the State, and were no more heard of. Gleaves remained a while in Beaufort, but soon fled the State to escape prosecution. Nash gave up some of his property to the State, to escape the penitentiary, and was generally despised for the remainder of his days. Smalls remained in Beaufort—having first been pardoned of his criminal offense. F. J. Moses, Jr., left the State, wandered about Northern cities and became both a vagrant and a criminal. Swails, as has already been mentioned, was driven out of Williamsburg by the white people of that county. All the Republican politicians who remained in South Carolina soon sank into actual obscurity or harmless inactivity.

CHAPTER X.

THE STORY OF THE FRAUDS.

The principal charge brought by the white people of South Carolina against the negro government under which they lived and suffered for eight years was that it was corrupt—corrupt in its objects, its methods and its agents. Whilst the country at large became in some degree informed about prevailing conditions, and whilst the Republican leaders themselves admitted the general charge of misgovernment and even that of venality, yet the extent to which corruption permeated every branch of the public service and affected every agency of government was never realized until, after the robbers had been driven from power, there was an investigation by committees who made it their business to probe to the bottom—who aggressively undertook to justify the charges made at intervals for eight years that the Government of South Carolina was steeped in rottenness and that its agents were with very few exceptions actual thieves and perjurers. From the reports of these committees, founded in every instance upon sworn testimony which every accused party was invited to answer, and which has been constantly accessible in the public records, the printed documents of the State, is made up the presentation now to be given of the most significant chapter in the history of Reconstruction in South Carolina—the chapter which contains the proofs of the charges made against the State Government by the white people in every remonstrance, every appeal, every effort to shake off the rule of the plunderers.

THE STATE DEBT.

The figures of the public debt of South Carolina have already been given and they need not be repeated. Naturally the manipulation of the different series of bonds gave great opportunity for peculation—and these were well employed by the Financial Board. Under the act of 1868, authorizing the issue of bonds to pay the accrued interest on the public debt, bonds to the amount of $1,000,000 were issued in excess of the sum authorized by law. Under the act for the relief of the treasury, passed in 1869, there was an unauthorized and therefore fraudulent issue of another million. Under the act authorizing the issue of what have already been noted as Conversion bonds, there was an over-issue of $5,965,000, which was so palpably fraudulent and contrary to law that the bonds were formally repudiated by the negro Legislature. These Conversion bonds were for a long time carried on the lists of the New York Stock Exchange at one cent on the dollar—a fact which so affected the State's credit that it interfered for a time with the funding of a portion of the public debt in 1892.

The manipulation of the State debt was in the hands of the Financial Board already mentioned and their trusted agent, H. H. Kimpton. The recklessness and dishonesty of their performances may be inferred from what has been stated, but may be particularly illustrated by reference to a comparatively small matter. The proceeds of the "land scrip" issued by Congress in aid of the State Agricultural College was invested, as required by the statute, in State bonds. These bonds were hypothecated by Kimpton, under alleged instructions of the Financial Board, to secure a loan to the State. The debt maturing and not being paid, the bonds were forfeited and sold. The Agricultural College was thus for about seven years deprived of the benefit of the fund provided by Congress—the bonds being restored and set apart for the use of the College as soon as possible after the return of the State Government to the control of the white people.

Under the act (March 7, 1871,) to create the Sterling Funded Debt, bonds in the sum of £1,200,000 were to be issued for the purpose of funding and retiring bonds outstanding. Of these Sterling bonds, about £600,000 had been printed, signed by the State officers designated in the act, and stamped with the great seal of the State—Cardozo, the Secretary of State, having taken the seal to New York to expedite the performance. The purpose to put these bonds on the market and thus further increase the State debt was told to the "Joint Special Financial Investigating Committee" by C. C. Bowen, who claimed great credit for his discovery of what he declared to be a new scheme to defraud the State by an over-issue of bonds. The scheme was never carried out, and the bonds were afterwards canceled in pursuance of a joint resolution of the Legislature. Bowen claiming a fee for his disclosure, he received a pay certificate for $2,500, which, it seems, he had great difficulty in collecting.

After four years of Republican administration the bonded debt was found to be $18,515,033.91, including past-due interest. The debt on July 9, 1868, when the negro government was inaugurated, was $5,407,306.27. By the repudiation of the Conversion bonds the debt in 1873 was reduced to $11,480,033, and this the Legislature undertook to reduce one-half by means of the Consolidation act of that year—leaving the recognized debt at $5,740,016.

For the increase of the State debt there was no showing by way of public works or of funding any outstanding liability. The entire increase represented the waste of public funds or their misappropriation by the trusted agents of the State.

As before stated, the Financial Board consisted of Gov. R. K. Scott, Treasurer Niles G. Parker and Attorney-General D. H. Chamberlain. These selected the financial agent and to him committed the custody of immense amounts of State funds and State securities whilst having required him to give only his personal bond without surety of any sort. Kimpton was evidently on terms of intimate friendship with at least two of the board—Chamberlain and Parker. The former called him "Dear Kimpton" and he always addressed the Treasurer as "Friend Parker."

Of the floating debt enough has been stated to show that by far the greater part resulted from transactions conceived and consummated in fraud, and that the other portion was founded upon expenditures wholly unnecessary for the proper administration of the Government. In 1877 this floating indebtedness was found to be $1,046,926.

THE GREENVILLE AND COLUMBIA RAILROAD.

One of the schemes of the Republican ring was that to control certain railroads in which the State was a stockholder—a scheme set forth in the following letter:

Office of the Attorney-General,
Columbia, S. C., Jan. 5, 1870.

My Dear Kimpton—Parker arrived last evening, and spoke of the G. & C. matter, etc. I told him that I had just written you fully on that matter, and also about the old Bk. Bills.

Do you understand fully the plan of the G. & C. enterprise? It is proposed to buy $350,000 worth of the G. &. C. stock. This with the $433,000 of stock held by the State will give entire control to us. The Laurens branch will be sold in February by decree of court, and will cost not more than $50,000, and probably not more than $40,000. The Spartanburg and Union can also be got without difficulty.

We shall then have in G. & C. 168 miles, in Laurens 31, and S. & U. 70 miles—in all 269 miles—equipped and running. Put a first mortgage of $20,000 a mile on this—sell the bonds at 85 or 90, and the balance, after paying all outlays for cost and repairs, is immense, over $2,000,000. There is a mint of money in this or I am a fool.

Then we will soon compel the South Carolina Railroad to fall into our hands and complete the connection to Asheville, N. C.

There is an indefinite verge for expansion of power before us.

Write me fully and tell me of anything you want done. My last letter was very full.

Harrison shall be attended to at once. I don't think Neagle will make any trouble. Parker hates Neagle, and magnifies his intentions,   Yours truly,

D. H. Chamberlain.

The means taken to obtain possession of the State's holdings of stock was to have it offered for sale. To this end the Legislature passed an act organizing the Sinking Fund Commission (composed of Governor Scott, Attorney-General Chamberlain, Comptroller Neagle, the chairman of the finance committee of the Senate and the chairman of the House committee of ways and means) who were authorized to sell all unproductive property of the State—the real purpose of the act being to effect the sale of 21,698 shares of stock in the Greenville and Columbia Railroad. This purpose was carried out—the stock which cost the State $20 per share, aggregating $433,960, being sold to the syndicate at $2.75 per share, the State thus realizing only $59,969.50. Other railroad stocks of the State were sold to the syndicate in like manner.

The ring having secured a majority of the stock of the company (some shares being bought from individuals) the Legislature was induced to pass an act releasing the railroad property from the State's lien securing its guaranty of the company's bonds to the amount of $1,500,000—thus giving the syndicate their opportunity to place a second mortgage on the property for their own benefit. The passage of these acts was procured by bribing different members of the Legislature—the sums paid ranging from $25,000 paid to Speaker Moses, for friendly rulings and for arranging the House committees to suit the purposes of the syndicate, to $500 paid each of several members for his vote.

The stock held by the syndicate amounted to $240,000, divided into twelve shares, distributed as follows; J. J. Patterson, 1; N. G. Parker, 1; C. P. Leslie, 1; Joseph Crews, 1; Tim Hurley, 1; Reuben Tom-

THE STORY OF THE FRAUDS 467

linson, 1; G. W. Waterman (of New York), 2; H. H. Kimpton, 2; J. L. Neagle, 1½; D. H. Chamberlain, ½; F. L. Cardozo, ½. The holdings of Kimpton, Neagle, Crews, Cardozo, Waterman (for R. K. Scott), Chamberlain and Leslie were paid for by Kimpton out of the sale of State bonds held by him in trust. It was understood by Kimpton and the Financial Board that the sums used in such payment should be realized from the sale of State bonds and covered by the difference between the actual amounts for which the bonds were sold by Kimpton and the amounts which he should report as having been received therefor.

John J. Patterson was president of the Greenville and Columbia Railroad and the manager of the different schemes above mentioned. Not content with robbing the State, he afterwards proceeded to rob his confederates. The treasurer of his railroad having absconded with $25,000 of its funds, Patterson had John B. Hubbard to capture the runaway and make him disgorge that sum. Of the money thus recovered, Patterson paid Hubbard one half and kept the other himself.

THE BLUE RIDGE SCRIP, ETC.

Another of the schemes of "Honest John" Patterson was the act to relieve the State of its guaranty of the bonds of the Blue Ridge Railroad Company. On its face this act purported to relieve the State of a contingent liability of $4,000,000 by enabling the company to discharge its debts. It contemplated the issuance of $1,800,000 of Revenue Bond Scrip, receivable for taxes and constituting a contract between the holder and the State.

There was abundant evidence in the sworn statements of members of the Legislature that the passage of this measure had been secured by bribery—the sums paid ranging from $200 to $3,000.

The act was passed (over the Governor's veto) on March 2, 1872, and on March 4 Patterson as president of the Blue Ridge Railroad Company addressed to the State Treasurer a letter directing him to deliver to H. H. Kimpton Revenue Bond Scrip in the sum of $114,250, of which Patterson explicitly stated that scrip of the par value of $42,857 was to be used "for paying the expenses of passing through the House of Representatives bills styled 'A bill relating to the bonds of South Carolina' and 'Bill to authorize the Financial Board to settle the accounts of the financial agent,'" and that scrip of the par value of $71,414 should be delivered to Kimpton, "provided that he shall pay the sum of $50,000, the proceeds of said scrip at 70 cents on the dollar, in paying the expenses already incurred in passing through the Senate" the bill for the issuance of the Blue Ridge Scrip.

In the effort to procure the passage of the two acts above mentioned numerous bribes were paid to members of the Legislature—the sums ranging from $200 to $2,000. In some instances members received each a lump sum for supporting the three bills mentioned. The money was furnished by Kimpton, having been borrowed by him on pledges of the Blue Ridge Scrip as collateral.

The act in relation to the financial agent authorized and required the Financial Board to "adjust and settle the claims, demands and accounts and all or any matters of difference relating to the financial agent and to receive any balance which on such adjustment may be found to be owing to this State by him or for which he may be or become liable to this State," to receive all property in his hands belonging to the State, and upon such settlement to give him a full release and discharge from all liability to the State.

Of the settlement made in pursuance of this act Niles G. Parker testified as follows:

At the time the settlement was made with the Financial Board and Kimpton he received a due bill from the Financial Board for about $130,000 as the balance of the commissions due him. This, according to our agreement, would be equally divided between Chamberlain, Kimpton and myself, and just before Chamberlain addressed his communication to the public in the summer of 1874, concerning the charges made against him with reference to the public debt and other matters connected with Governor Scott's administration, he promised me by the side of his sick bed in his own house that if I would permit that letter which he had prepared to go before the public without contradiction and he should be nominated and elected as Governor, I should be paid my share of the $130,000, as expressed in said due bill, and that, too, at an early day.

In the communication referred to by Parker, written August 1, 1874, Mr. Chamberlain, after reviewing all the charges against himself, said: "To every specific and general charge involving moral delinquency or conscious wrong in my official action in this State I give my absolute and solemn denial." In this letter Mr. Chamberlain did not include among the charges which he undertook to meet the statement afterwards given by Parker in his sworn testimony as above. Immediately upon its publication Mr. Chamberlain, in an interview with a newspaper reporter in New York, emphatically denied all of the charges of Parker and called attention to the fact that the ex-Treasurer had been practically convicted of stealing coupons and afterwards converting them into State bonds.

Everidge Cain, a member of the House from Abbeville from 1870 to 1874, testified that when the two bills in question were under consideration Kimpton protested against his opposition to these measures and offered him $500 to support them—whereupon he consulted Mr. Chamberlain and Governor Scott, each of whom advised him to vote for the financial settlement bill, saying that the friends of the bill would be taken care of. Cain confessed that Patterson had paid him $200 for voting for the Blue Ridge Scrip bill.

The Validating bill—the name given to the above noted measure relating to State bonds—undertook to validate all State bonds (about $6,000,000) mentioned in the Treasurer's report for the year ending October 31, 1871, and to provide for the regular payment of interest—the real purpose of the measure being to facilitate the corrupt manipulation of State bonds by the financial agent with the corrupt connivance of the Financial Board.

In moving the passage of the three measures above mentioned Kimpton was very active, one of his main objects being to have Speaker F. J. Moses, Jr., arrange the House committees to suit the syndicate. Kimpton agreed to pay Moses his price—$25,000—and performed his agreement by lifting a mortgage of $13,000 on Moses' property and paying him $12,000 in money. While the Greenville and Columbia Railroad bill was on its passage there were signs of trouble—whereupon Patterson sent Dennis to the speaker's stand with an offer of $10,000 to Moses if he would "push the bill through." The bill went through accordingly, and Moses received from Patterson $10,000—this in addition to the $25,000 previously paid.

Patterson continued his efforts in behalf of his Blue Ridge Scrip after the passage of the act authorizing its issue. When the case involving its validity was before the Supreme Court he attempted to bribe F. J. Moses, Jr., to procure a favorable decision. When the act to repeal the act authorizing the levy of a tax to redeem the scrip had been passed, he succeeded in bribing H. J. Maxwell, of Marlboro, the colored chairman of the Senate committee on enrolled acts, to withhold or destroy the document, so that the measure failed of passage at the session of 1872-73. Maxwell afterwards swore that for his support of the three measures in question Patterson paid him between $3,000 and $5,000.

When the Consolidation act was under discussion in 1873 Patterson sought to have the Blue Ridge Scrip recognized as a valid obligation and funded accordingly—offering large bribes to have it included at its face value.

IMPEACHMENT OF SCOTT AND PARKER.

In the report of the "Joint Special Financial Investigating Committee," made to the General Assembly at the session of 1871-72, the fraudulent over-issue of Conversion bonds to the extent of about $6,000,000 was brought to the attention of that body. On December 18, 1871, C. C. Bowen, then a representative from Charleston, introduced a resolution to impeach Governor Scott and Treasurer Parker of high crimes and misdemeanors. John J. Patterson, assisted by H. G. Worthington, encouraged the movement so that it might take such shape as to impress Scott with its reality and its consequent danger. The Governor was thus induced to engage their services to defeat the pending resolution, through the purchase of votes in the House. Money was necessary—and Scott was ready with an expedient for raising it.

In 1869 the Legislature had by joint resolution authorized the Governor to organize and employ an armed force "for the preservation of the peace"—the expenses of which should be paid "out of any funds in the treasury, not otherwise appropriated." Upon this fund the Governor issued and delivered to Patterson three warrants, one payable to John Mooney for $25,545, another payable to John Leggett for $10,600, and a third payable to David H. Wilson for $12,500 —making a total of $48,645. The names as given, though fictitious, were severally endorsed on the warrants. These were collected, one by Hardy Solomon and the other two by Jacobs, the cashier of his bank. Thus amply supplied with funds, Patterson and Worthington proceeded to the task of buying votes enough to save Scott, and therefore Parker, from the trouble threatened.

It became important to Scott to have the impeachment resolution acted upon before December 22, on which day the Legislature had resolved to take a recess for the Christmas holidays. The Governor therefore issued his proclamation reconvening the body on the 23d— taking the ground that it was "neither decent nor proper, but injurious to the State, for the General Assembly to adjourn from the 22d of December, 1871, to the 5th of January, 1872, while the Governor and the Treasurer are charged with 'high crimes and misdemeanors.'" In the meantime the Bowen resolution was being pressed in the House and there appeared some danger of its passage. Patterson, with the aid of Worthington, proceeded to use the money paid on the warrants fradulently issued and bearing fictitious endorsements. A committee room was selected as headquarters, and there was abundance of wines, liquors, cigars and viands—furnished from Hardy Solomon's grocery store. Here most of the negotiations with the members took place—though another room was used for the disbursement of money. The sums paid aggregated about $20,000—the bribes ranging from $200 to $500. The balance remaining of the proceeds of the three warrants was divided between Patterson and Worthington—"Honest John" taking the lion's share.

The needed number of votes having been secured, there yet remained a difficulty that had to be overcome in order to save the accused officials. Whipper, then violently opposed to Scott, had obtained the floor, would hold it till the adjournment on one day and thus have it on the day following—being the day on which the House had agreed to take its Christmas recess. On the night before, Speaker Moses was called in consultation and it was arranged that he should recognize Samuel J. Lee, and by prearranged rulings on questions which Lee was instructed in writing to make, force Whipper to yield the floor. The plan was executed as made, Whipper was silenced and the House, without further discussion, rejected the resolution of impeachment by a vote of 63 to 27. The resolution as to Parker was killed by about the same vote.

For his services Lee received $500, whilst the sum paid to Moses for his rulings was $15,000. Elliott (then in Congress) was active in his efforts to save Scott, and for his good offices received $10,500 out of the "armed force" fund.

On the day when the Legislature took its recess—December 22—Governor Scott revoked his proclamation calling the extra session.

Bowen affected to be both chagrined and outraged by the failure of his scheme to punish Scott and Parker. He openly declared that the result had been procured by bribery. On the other hand, it was reported that Bowen had rejected an offer of $15,000 for a withdrawal of his resolution—his price being $25,000.

PATTERSON'S ELECTION TO THE SENATE.

In the winter of 1872 there were three principal candidates for the Senate of the United States to succeed Frederick A. Sawyer, whose term would expire on March 3, 1873—R. B. Elliott, then member of Congress from the Third District, ex-Gov. R. K. Scott and John J. Patterson. Elliott's principal claims were that he was a negro and that the time had come for a negro to represent South Carolina in the Senate.

Scott sought promotion on the ground that in his four years of service he had borne the brunt of the fight for the Republican party against the Democrats, the Union Reform movement and the Kuklux Klan.

Patterson evidently relied upon the use of money—upon actually buying votes enough to overcome whatever strength his opponents might develop. He soon took in the situation and proceeded to meet it. He established headquarters over a barroom near the State House and placed in command H. G. Worthington, upon whose judicious use of money, whiskey and "refreshments" he could safely rely, and of whose character as an arrant knave he could have no possible doubt. Money flowed freely—distributed by Worthington and his helpers, whom he had selected with the same good judgment which had been shown by Patterson in choosing him as the agent to debauch the Legislature and induce its members to commit wilful and corrupt perjury. Patterson declared that he was prepared to spend $75,000 —and after his election he stated that it had cost him $40,000. Sixty members testified that offers of money had been made to them to induce them to vote for Patterson, and in nearly all cases the offer had been accepted. The bribes ranged from $200 to $2,000—the average price of votes being $300. In some cases part only of the money was paid down and the balance made good later. In other instances there were complaints that Patterson never paid all that he promised.

Worthington was rewarded with the post of collector of customs at the port of Charleston.

Patterson was arrested on the charge of bribery, but was promptly released and he was never tried. In view of a possible trial, he had Governor Moses to appoint John B. Dennis jury commissioner for Richland County, and that personage afterwards said under oath:

I consented to act in the manner desired. Moses turned out the jury commissioner and appointed me in his place; and I managed the jury box in such way as to insure his [Patterson's] protection—that is, I would not when listing the jury for the year have or allow any names to go into the jury box that I thought would in any way be inimical to Patterson, so in this way there could not be any possibility of an enemy of his getting drawn either on the grand or the petit jury, and those that were drawn would act in Patterson's interest, and such jurors were drawn.

A statement was promptly addressed to the United States Senate, charging that Patterson had procured his election by flagrant bribery, but that body declined to consider it—this on the ground that it was unofficial and irregular—and Patterson retained his seat until March 4, 1879, when he was succeeded by Wade Hampton.

THE PUBLIC PRINTING.

There was no department of the State Government under negro rule in which greater or bolder frauds were committed than those which marked the manipulation of the public printing from 1868 to 1874. It was manifest from the first that the printing was to be awarded to some organ or partisan of the Republican administration. At the special session of the Legislature in the summer of 1868 the contract was given to a party whose figures were considerably higher than those offered by a responsible competitor. The contractor not meeting the desires of certain members of the Legislature in the division of the spoils, a company was formed with the purpose of controlling the State printing in all its branches. Hence in 1870 arose the Carolina Printing Company, consisting of Governor Scott, Attorney-General Chamberlain, Comptroller-General Neagle, Treasurer Parker, J. W. Denny, J. W. Morris and L. Cass Carpenter. Denny and Morris were in charge of the *Charleston Republican* and Carpenter of the *Columbia Union*—both papers owned by the company. Some months later Josephus Woodruff and A. O. Jones associated themselves as the Republican Printing Company, and by that name did all the State printing—all contracts and all payments being made on their approval as the clerks of the Senate and the House, respectively.

The volume of printing was very great in consequence of the long sessions of the Legislature, and it was increased by the printing of much matter in addition. The appropriations for given years were as follows:

Session 1868-69 ....$ 21,124
Session 1869-70 45,000
Session 1870-71 152,465
Session 1871-72 173,000
Session 1872-73 450,000
Session 1873-74 385,000
Session 1874-75 50,000
Session 1875-76 50,000

The aggregate in the eight years was $1,326,589—being $717,589 in excess of the total expenditures for the same purpose in the seventy-eight years previous to 1868. In the period between 1877 and the present time the cost of the public printing has never in any year exceeded $35,000—the amount usually being far less.

Allowance duly made for differences in the volume of work and in prices fairly chargeable at the different periods indicated, it is plain that under the manipulations of the Republican ring enormous sums were paid without even the pretense of work done for the State. Indeed, the organization of the Carolina Printing Company was the inception of that systematic bribery which marked the public printing for at least six years. Shortly after the formation of that company Senator C. P. Leslie of Barnwell declared that "the friends" in the Senate thought that as the printing was a matter of Senate patronage they should have a percentage of the profits—suggesting that pay certificates ranging from $3,000 to $5,000 for current printing be drawn, and that one-third or one-fourth of the whole amount realized be given to the chairman of the committee on printing for division among "the friends"—meaning certain of the senators whose votes and influence should be found useful. Under this arrangement—before Woodruff and Jones formed themselves into the Republican Printing Company—there was divided among nineteen senators and eight representatives more than $15,000 in sums ranging from $50 to $5,000. About the time of this transaction, by a combination between Scott, Parker and Neagle, printing accounts to the amount of $45,000 were sold to Neagle, were afterwards raised to $90,000 and were receipted for on the Treasurer's books at that sum—the State being thus defrauded of at least $45,000.

On the passage of the act of January 31, 1871, authorizing the two clerks to make contracts for the current and permanent printing of the General Assembly, those two officials awarded the contract to

themselves under the style of the Republican Printing Company—
and they soon succeeded in first controlling and then liquidating the
Carolina Printing Company, their only competitor. Neagle was at
first a silent partner in the new concern, but he soon retired.

At the session of 1870-71 (after the formation of the Republican
Printing Company) there was distributed by Woodruff and Jones
among the senators and representatives over $21,000. About the
same amount was distributed at the session of 1871-72.

At the session of 1872-73 the rapacity of the legislators had so
much increased that much larger sums were needed to procure the
payment of printing bills. In reference to the appropriation of
$250,000, approved December 21, 1872, Woodruff and Jones swore
that they paid to Governor Moses $20,000, to Treasurer Cardozo
$12,500, and to senators and representatives $21,000—all of these
being Republicans save one, and the charge against him being
inconsistent with a previous life altogether honorable. To procure
the appropriation of $231,000, December 19, 1873, the sum of
$94,469 was distributed among Republican legislators whilst Lieu-
tenant-Governor Gleaves received $2,500, Governor Moses $10,500,
Secretary Cardozo $12,500, and Comptroller Hoge $5,000—making
the total disbursement among Republican officeholders $124,969. The
Democratic senator above referred to was accredited with $1,000,
but the accusation was never thought to be true. In procuring the
passage of the appropriation of $250,000, December 21, 1872, Wood-
ruff and Jones spent $36,590 in the House of Representatives—the
sums paid varying from $20 to $4,400, which last was paid to James
A. Bowley, colored, chairman of the committee of ways and means.
The cost of getting through the act of December 19, 1873, was
$41,269—the largest payments being to Tim Hurley $6,300, Samuel
J. Lee $5,000, and James A. Bowley $7,500.

The prices charged for work done by the Republican Printing
Company were always excessive and in many instances fictitious. Yet
Woodruff complained that the legislators were bleeding him to such
an extent that the actual profits to his company were by no means
large.

One of the frauds committed by the Republican Printing Company was the collection of a bill, December 8, 1873 (officially approved by Woodruff and Jones), for $75,000 "for the compilation and

printing of the report on immigration, ordered by the General Assembly at the session of 1872-73"—no part of the work having ever been done.

There were many frauds also committed under the guise of publishing the laws in pursuance of the statute, really intended to establish and subsidize Republican newspapers in different counties. The *Charleston Republican* received for such publishing $60,982.14, whereas, according to the sworn testimony of practical printers of high character, the sum lawfully chargeable under the act was only $24,583.20.

For like work L. Cass Carpenter, proprietor of the *Columbia Union,* received from November, 1870, to May, 1873, the sum of $59,987.64—being $33,527.59 in excess of what the statute allowed. Carpenter further defrauded the State by raising the figures of his accounts—turning $181.28 into $1,181.28, $486.40 into $1,486.40, $720 into $1,720, $878.33 into $1,878.33, $784.60 into $1,784.60, $540 into $1,540, $195 into $695, $155 into $655, $676 into $1,676 and $1,500 into $2,500. It was for one of these forgeries that he was tried in 1877.

SUPPLIES.

In stating the expenses of certain sessions of the Legislature the following figures, under the head of "sundries, wines, liquors, cigars, groceries, dry goods, etc.," have been given:

Session of 1870-71.. .. ..$157,800.03
Session of 1871-72.. .. .. 281,514.50
Session of 1872-73.. .. .. 50,412.00
Session of 1873-74.. .. .. 53,508.00

Under the head of "supplies" there were purchased various articles for the use of senators and representatives, the orders being given generally through the clerk, the bills referred to the committee on accounts, duly reported and finally ordered to be paid. Certificates were accordingly drawn and these were paid (so long as there was money in the treasury) out of the appropriation for legislative expenses. In the category of "supplies" was included everything that a member might wish—as appears from the lists of articles furnished. In the first stages of these transactions the members would buy what they wanted and give the seller orders on the clerk for their pay, but very soon the orders exceeded the pay. Then came the practice of including these expenditures in the report of the committee on contingent accounts and thus having them paid out of the public funds. "Gratification certificates," for the use of senators, founded upon no service or other consideration, were issued in large numbers and were either paid by the Treasurer or sold to speculators who held them as claims against the State—these constituting a part of the floating indebtedness outstanding at the close of Chamberlain's administration.

In reporting on claims the committee would give the names of some bona-fide creditors, adding the words, "and others"—that phrase covering accounts either wholly fictitious or made up of items for which the State was not lawfully or honestly responsible.

A room in the State House was fitted up wherein to serve "wines, liquors, eatables and cigars." The largest bills rendered were for refreshments served in this room—which was so popular a resort that it was kept open daily from eight in the morning until long after midnight, a porter (paid by the State) being kept constantly busy in attending to the wants of State officials, senators, representatives and their guests. The liquors and cigars used were always of the best quality—articles not coming fully up to the standard being rejected. Liquors and cigars were sent to the houses of members and their friends and also to the committee rooms. Bowley, the chairman of the House committee of ways and means, on one occasion ordered and received one box of champagne, one of port wine, one of sherry, one of brandy, one of whiskey and three boxes of cigars. There were various bills for furnishing eatables, wines, liquors and cigars to different legislative committees—one dealer testifying that he presented a single bill for $1,800 and received therefor a pay certificate. Hardy Solomon did an immense business in furnishing "supplies," in one series of transactions receiving certificates for $24,380.50, whilst the actual amount of his bills was only $11,203.48. In three days in March, 1872, Solomon furnished the Senate wines and liquors which were billed at $3,483.75, and in the same period other large purchases were made for both houses. In two months of the same session Solomon sold the House wines and liquors to the amount of $5,877.15. From March 1 to March 7, 1871, there were bought from one dealer, for the use of the Senate, wines and liquors to the amount of $3,157.80. In a single day there were delivered for the use of the Senate fine groceries, including wines and liquors, to the amount of $1,680, and for the use of the House similar goods to the amount of $2,088. The prices charged were most extravagant—$20 per gallon for brandy, $10 per gallon for sherry, $8 per gallon for whiskey, $10 per hundred for cigars, $4.50 per dozen for lager beer. The average daily consumption of liquor (not including ale or beer) was more than a gallon for every member of the Legislature.

For furniture alone there was expended in four years, 1870-73, more than $200,000, and of the articles thus bought there remained in 1877 enough only to be valued at $17,715. Many of the bills were "padded" with fictitious figures and most of the articles were appropriated by legislators, officials or employees. Many rooms outside of the State House were handsomely furnished, the articles removed at the close of one session and new ones supplied at the next.

The extent to which the tastes of the legislators in the matter of furnishings were educated in the course of a very short time may be seen from a comparison of the following statements of actual purchases:

1868-1870.	1871-72.
$5 clocks.	$600 clocks.
40-cents spittoons.	$8 cuspadores.
$4 benches.	$200 crimson plush sofas.
Straw beds.	Sponge mattresses.
$1 chairs.	$60 crimson plush Gothic chairs.
$4 pine tables.	$80 library tables.
25-cents hat-pegs.	$30 hat-racks.
$8 desks.	$50 to $175 desks.
50-cents coat-hooks.	$100 wardrobes.
Cheap matting.	Body Brussels carpeting.
Clay pipes.	Finest Habana cigars.
Cheap whiskey.	Champagne.
$4 looking-glasses.	$600 mirrors.
$2 window curtains.	$600 brocatel curtains.
$5 cornices.	$80 walnut and gilt cornices.

In furnishing the assembly halls and the committee rooms in July, 1870, John B. Dennis, authorized by Speaker Moses, made the purchases—the bills aggregating $40,189.87. The claims were referred to a committee (with Ben Byas as chairman) which, after due consideration, reported the amount due to be $90,556.31. The report was adopted and certificates were issued accordingly. The difference between that sum and the amount of the bills rendered was divided among fifty members of the House in sums ranging from $50 to $3,000—Byas, however, receiving a certificate for $12,319.50. The sum of $12,000 was divided among Speaker Moses, Clerk Jones, Treasurer Parker, John B. Dennis and Tim Hurley.

The bills for stationery—aggregating $128,865 in the four years, 1870-73—were almost wholly fictitious, being made to cover purchases of dry goods, groceries, carpets and furniture, and the hire of horses and carriages. During one session each senator received a copy of Webster's unabridged dictionary and a calendar inkstand, the latter costing $25. Gold pens at $10 each were freely supplied.

Watches and jewelry of various kinds, including diamonds in different settings, were among the "supplies" bought with money stolen from the public treasury. A handsome gold watch was included in the "pickings" of B. F. Whittemore at a single session—these said by Woodruff to have exceeded $10,000.

At one session the State was charged with 1,320 tons of coal and with more than 1,000 cords of wood—though there was not a wood-burning stove or a fireplace in the State House. Coal and wood were freely furnished to members at their private quarters.

State officials, senators, representatives, clerks and attaches were supplied with newspapers at the public expense—the sums thus spent, 1870-73, aggregating $19,749.

Not content with actual expenditures, which amounted to actual robberies, the leaders among the corruptionists presented claims under fictitious names and these were reported by the committee under the category "and others." At one session there were eleven of these false claims approved, aggregating $21,061—these forming but a small part of the whole number passed.

The wide range of the members' desires in the matter of "supplies" may be seen from the following list of articles actually furnished by different dealers on the order of Woodruff or Jones or of different members of the General Assembly:

Refreshments, Wines and Liquors.—Heidsick champagne, green seal do., vin imperial do., Verzenay do., Moet and Chandon do., scuppernong, sparkling Moselle, Catawba, Chateau la Rose claret, Chateau La Fitte claret, imperial pale sherry, best Madeira, port and malaga wines, blackberry wine, finest Otard-du-Puy brandy, finest French cognac do., Baker, cabinet rye, Bourbon, nectar and corn whiskeys, Holland gin, Jamaica rum, cases of Hostetter's, Indian,

Kerr's Russian, San Domingo and wine bitters, congress water, best bottled ale, lager and porter, sarsaparilla, curacoa, maraschino, ale by the cask.

Cigars and Tobacco.—Imported Brevas, Portugas, Espanolas, Espanola Londres, Conchas, Live Indian, Pantillo, Espanola Conchas, finest plug chewing tobacco, finest cut chewing tobacco, Durham and other best smoking tobaccos.

Refreshments, Groceries and Delicacies.—Best Westphalia hams, Bologna sausages, bacon strips, diamond hams, Java and Rio coffee, pineapple, Edam, Switzer and English cheese, gilt edge butter, sardines, smoked and canned salmon, smoked beef and buffalo tongues, canned oysters and lobsters, fresh Norfolk oysters, deviled ham, black and green teas, French chocolate, olive, oil, catsups, Worcester and pepper sauces, imported mushrooms, preserved ginger, Guava jelly, pickles, brandy cherries and peaches, lemon syrup, assorted extracts, sea foam, citron, assorted nuts, lemons, oranges, wax and adamantine candles, Colgate, fancy and toilet soaps, starch, table and Liverpool salt, kerosene oil, bacon sides and shoulders, English mustard, vinegar, mackerel, concentrated lye, Orleans and fancy syrups and molasses, assorted English crackers and biscuits, condensed milk, parlor matches, Irish potatoes, leaf lard, assorted pepper, sugar, flour and pearl grist.

Furniture.—Finest walnut office chairs, office desks, continental chairs, washstands, hat racks, marble-top washstands, wardrobes, library tables, marble-top sideboards, book cases, hair seat rocking chairs, large and small easy chairs, marble-top bureaus, saloon tables, bedsteads, opera chairs, leather seat chairs, cane seat chairs, stuffed back chairs, stuffed back arm chairs and rockers, umbrella stands, large library book cases, small library book cases, oval library tables with carved legs, red rep lounges, green rep lounges, finest plush velvet tete-a-tetes, finest walnut fancy rep tete-a-tetes, large and small Gothic chairs, Prescott arm chairs, extra large striped rep Prescott arm chairs, green rep French lounges, large shelf-back marble-top washstands, counter desks, hat stands, marble-top tables, crimson plush sofas, large looking-glasses, superior refrigerators, large willow chairs, towel racks, folding chairs, fine coffin, fine cradle, bed lounges, fancy fire screens, extra large and heavy feather beds, extra large and heavy cotton mattresses, extra large and heavy feather beds, extra large and heavy feather bolsters, extra large and heavy feather pillows, double spring mattresses, cots and mattresses, sponge pillows, sponge bolsters, sponge mattresses, gilt mantel mirrors.

Furnishings.—Finest English tapestry, Brussels carpeting, English body Brussels carpeting, three-ply ingrain carpeting, English velvet rugs, English velvet door mats, English thread door mats, English oilcloths, English velvet hassocks, cocoa mats, cocoa matting, rich heavy cornices, satin delaine curtains, lambrequins, window shades and fixtures, large cords and tassels, gimps, brocaded curtains and trimmings, gold bound shades and spring rollers, white and checked mattings, dry goods, finest French velvets, extra fine large gray hair cloth, silk damask, linen damask tablecloth, linen damask wire cloth, Irish linens, billiard table cloths, linen towels, woolen blankets, linen doylies, linen napkins, imported flannels, imported insertions, imported edgings, finest dress goods—all kinds—honeycomb quilts, Marseilles quilts, shawls, linen sheeting, linen pillow casing, linen shirting, cotton shirting, sheeting, cotton pillow casing, imported kid gloves, ladies' satchels, men's white and brown hosiery, linen cambric handkerchiefs, ladies' hoods, cambrics, ribbons of all qualities, fine plaid goods, extra long bath towels, pieces of crepe, scissors, skirt braids and pins, baize, spool cotton, prints, tooth brushes, hair brushes, heavy combs, flax, buttons, whalebone, ginghams, hooks and eyes, boulevard skirts, bustles, extra long stockings, chignons, palpitators, garters, chemises, undervests, parasols, sun umbrellas.

Clothing in general assortment and variety.

Jewelry and Fancy Goods.—Gold watches and charms, rich sets gold jewelry, diamond rings, diamond pins, gold lockets, gold charms, gold finger rings, gold necklaces, gold pencil cases, gold pens, gold breastpins, ivory-handle knives and forks, pocket knives, teaspoons, tablespoons, table forks, call bells, extra fine table castors, rich toilet sets, pocket pistols, japanned tea trays, cuckoo clocks, extra fine Belgian marble mantel clocks, French china vases, French artificial flowers, ladies' fine work boxes, finest colognes, French extracts, bottles Florida water, gold and rubber pens and holders, pocket books, stereoscopes and views, writing desks, ladies' portemonnaies, French mantel clocks, key rings, tape measures, feather dusting brushes, plated spoons, baskets, Webster's unabridged dictionary, latest and most expensive library works, drop lights, sixty-four-light chandeliers, twenty-seven-light chandeliers, six-light chandeliers, five-light chandeliers, four-light bracket chandeliers, fine cornices with gilt eagles, fine shields with coat-of-arms.

Crockery and Glassware.—Champagne glasses, salt cellars, cup plates, decanters, tumblers, ornamental cuspadores, extra fine punch mugs, fancy granite chamber sets, fancy lamps, wash basins, soap boxes and trays, French china coffee cups, French china dinner sets, French china cups and saucers, French china candlesticks, fine glass globes, all sizes, decorated spittoons, decorated tulip toilet sets, decorated tulip oval pitchers, rich cut-glass goblets with monograms.

Printing Matter, Etc.—Warrants of arrest, recognizances, summonses, election tickets, contracts, articles of agreement, lodge circulars, visiting cards, diaries, morocco memorandum books, perpetual calendars, packages finest initial note paper, reams Juniata paper, scrap books, envelopes, ink, mucilage, wall paper, bordering, lead pencils, ruling pens, paper weights, letter clips, bill files, rubber bands, paper cutters, sponge cups, envelope openers, inkstands, ink vents, slate pencils, rulers, magic ivory, leather and black pencils.

Live Stock, Etc.—Fine horses, mules, carriages, buggies and harness.

Sundries.—Eggs, coal, cords oak wood, cords lightwood, andirons, fenders, shovels and tongs, grate baskets, stoves and pipes, coffee biggins, teapots, saucepans, cooking stoves and utensils, tin buckets, wooden baskets, tin cases, blacking, blacking brushes, jugs, bags, demijohns, lead pipes, lanterns, brooms, fruit jars and elastics, kegs, wash tubs, wash boards, cork screws, slop pails, dusters and dust pans, foot tubs, hand saws, files, axes, water coolers, coffee mills, axe helves, stove polish.

Not content with the actual purchases which were unlawful, some of the officials rendered and collected fraudulent accounts. In one case the printed bill-head was taken from a small account honestly rendered and was skilfully pasted to a false claim against the House: "To account rendered, $5,127.28." This account was duly approved by the House and was afterwards collected.

A bill of James M. Allen of Greenville for certain repairs, originally $500, was fraudulently raised to $2,000 by changing three items—$40 to $340, $50 to $650 and $50 to $650. On another occasion Allen raised a claim for $188 to $6,880, and collected the latter sum.

PAY CERTIFICATES.

The total of legislative expenses in each of certain years during the Republican regime has already been given.

The different heads under which these so-called expenses were incurred have been given in the statements following the account of legislative proceedings. One of the most effective means of defrauding the State and of supplying money to legislators, public officials and political helpers was in the issue of legislative pay certificates—papers purporting to evidence the performance of services to some branch or some official of the General Assembly. The pay certificate, in order to constitute a claim against the State, needed but the approval of the presiding officer and the clerk of the Senate or of the House, according to the sphere of the alleged service. Whether the simplicity of the procedure served to swell the volume of pay certificates might be a question were it not that the officials who issued them, like the parties who took them, showed great aptitude in devising other methods, not so simple yet quite as effective, for robbing the public treasury. Nevertheless, the number of frauds separately committed and the variety of the beneficiaries were such as to show that in the issuance and manipulation of these pay certificates the corrupt purposes of officials and legislators found their greatest opportunity and had their most striking illustration. By the use of pay certificates it became comparatively easy to continue the fraudulent practices in connection with "supplies" and the public printing. "Indeed," declared the legislative committee of 1877, "this, like the famous hydra, threw out its hundred heads, encircling and poisoning every department of the Government, and giving comfort and support to local leaders. In its trail followed the low, despicable forgeries and perjuries necessary to effect the end proposed. It is not surprising that the poor and ignorant members of the General Assembly fell into these practices when they were conceived and brought forth by such adroit swindlers as those who led. This immense fund produced and nurtured a bond ring, a printing ring and this legislative ring—the most popular and at the same time most unscrupulous."

At the session of 1871-72 there were issued pay certificates (not including printing certificates) to the amount of $1,168,255, all of which were fraudulent except those lawfully issued to members or employees—and these footed up about $200,000. The number of clerks alleged to have been employed was in 1870-71 349, and at the following session 475. At the former session pages to the number of 124 were on the rolls, and at the next 74—certificates being issued for the imaginary boys as well as to those actually employed. Doorkeepers, laborers, chaplains, clerks, stenographers, messengers, janitors, mail carriers, firemen, porters, pages, sergeants-at-arms, solicitors—these constituted the array of employees, actual and fictitious, in whose names pay certificates were issued. Other people also came in for a share—friends of the presiding officers, leading politicians, alleged victims of the Kuklux Klan or of persecution on account of their devotion to the Republican party, and visiting strangers whom the party leaders wished to compliment. "Gratification" certificates were issued in sums ranging from $500 to $5,000—the amount of these having at one session been at least $250,000. Reluctance being shown in the issuance of this class of papers, the objector was informed that "these are small matters and the State does not suffer from them—it is only a fight between the representatives of the people and the vultures of the bond ring."

At the session of 1871-72 the certificates issued in the names of fictitious persons called for more than $250,000.

In February, 1873, a "gratification" certificate for $5,000 was given to one senator (name not stated) for services in the interest of the Republican Printing Company.

A certificate for $1,000 was issued to pay the rent of Senator Patterson's house.

A certificate for $1,321 went to pay for furniture for Senator C. P. Leslie's residence.

A certificate in the sum of $5,000 was issued to B. F. Whittemore, for purchasing the portraits of Abraham Lincoln and Charles Sumner, as authorized by joint resolution. Whittemore collected most of the sum named, but neither portrait was ever bought.

Certificates aggregating $7,102.75 were issued to Hardy Solomon in March, 1872, for furnishing certain senators (on their individual orders) with groceries, liquors and cigars.

One batch of certificates, aggregating $68,000, were issued in the names of fictitious persons purporting to have performed some service for the State.

During the session of 1871-72 Speaker Moses delivered to John J. Patterson blank certificates in the sum of $30,000 and received from him $10,000. Patterson filled out the certificates with fictitious names and different amounts (odd sums ranging from $843.19 to $2,234.76) and collected the entire amount. Moses constantly issued certificates to various persons—actually including women of loose character.

The expenses of the "Joint Special Financial Investigating Committee" (appointed at the session of 1870-71) were paid, in various sums, by various certificates. The first month's pay came from the "armed force fund" on the order of Governor Scott. Attorney-General Chamberlain then advised that the committee arrange with Kimpton for their money. On arriving in New York the committee concluded to take a month's rest—drawing pay, however, for the whole time, amounting to $10,285, besides $2,016 for clerks and other help. Speaker Moses thought he ought to have a part in this scheme, so he caused himself to be summoned to New York as a witness. For this service he claimed $2,500, but as the certificate needed the signature of Lieutenant-Governor Ransier, a like sum was paid that dignitary for his part in the transaction—the certificate ($5,000) being issued to "John Gershon for room rent, fees, etc., for the joint special investigating committee in New York." The total amount drawn by the committee from the public treasury was more than $41,000.

In January, 1874, Cardozo, finding in the treasury an unexpended balance of $4,000 of an appropriation for legislative expenses, procured the issuance of five pay certificates, each for $800, payable respectively to Lieutenant-Governor Gleaves, Speaker Samuel J. Lee, Clerk Woodruff, Clerk Jones and "C. L. Frankfort"—the last named representing the Treasurer's share. These certificates, having been approved by the two clerks, the speaker and the Lieutenant-Governor, were cashed by the State Treasurer. It was for his part in this particular transaction that Cardozo was afterwards tried and convicted.

Of the many fictitious certificates there were two traced to the possession of Associate Justice Wright—one payable to J. N. Dobson for $642 and another to C. N. Smith for the same amount, as committee clerks. Wright claimed to have discounted these papers.

In the four years, 1871-73, the legislative expenses were as follows:

1,126 Clerks ....$	236,811 00
206 Laborers	49,718 00
63 Doorkeepers	14,074 48

35 Firemen	$ 4,867 00
12 Chaplains	4,279 00
11 Janitors	2,016 00
416 Messengers	189,406 00
11 Mail carriers	2,054 50
206 Porters	114,277 75
269 Pages	18,721 00
44 Sergeants-at-arms	11,122 00
78 Solicitors	31,288 00
24 Stenographers	7,398 00
Accounts and claims	206,549 00
Sundries	543,234 53
Stationery	108,865 39
Fuel	13,572 00
Newspapers	19,749 00
Postage stamps	1,381 41
Telegrams	1,442 55
Furniture	176,644 00
Rent of committee rooms	8,038 00
Impeachment trials	4,213 00
Joint special committee	41,000 00
Per diem and mileage	309,500 00
Printing	$1,160,565 00
Total legislative expenses	$3,280,786 61
Yearly average	$ 820,196 65

The legislative expenses for the year 1905 were as follows:

Per diem and mileage	$28,999 35
Employees	7,180 00
Contingent funds	1,713 40
Public printing	14,500 00
Total	$52,392 75

MISCELLANEOUS FRAUDS.

The assets of the Bank of the State of South Carolina and the railroad shares owned by the State in 1867, amounting to $7,069,674, disappeared under Republican financiering. The State found it necessary, in consequence of the dissipation of the bank's assets, to issue bonds in the sum of $1,259,100 to redeem the bills—that issue not including the considerable amount of bills used in the payment of State taxes.

The organization of the militia in preparation for the campaign of 1870 cost the State in round numbers $400,000. One scheme was the alteration of muskets received from the Federal Government into breechloaders—the business being entrusted to F. J. Moses, Jr., as Adjutant and Inspector General. He first arranged that for each gun altered he should get from the contractor a royalty of one dollar—thus pocketing $10,000. This claim Moses sold to Kimpton for $7,000. The total amount agreed by the State to be paid for altering arms and for buying arms, accoutrements and ammunition was $180,750, yet the payments on these accounts from the public treasury came within a fraction of $250,000—the difference having been divided between Frank Moses and John B. Dennis.

Under the provision for the employment of the "armed force" already mentioned, a "State guard" was organized in some counties, receiving pay and rations at the expense of the State, while really doing no actual service—captains at $90 each per month, and privates at $26.33 each per month. The "armed force," like the constabulary, was used for political purposes, and the expenditures in both cases were in many instances fraudulent.

In connection with the passage of the "phosphate bill," March, 1870—being a bill to grant to certain persons the right to dig and mine phosphate rock in the rivers of the State—bribes aggregating $20,000 were distributed among senators and representatives. Samuel J. Lee testified that he received $250 from D. H. Chamberlain for voting to pass the bill over Governor Scott's veto.

The passage (1873) of the claims of Hardy Solomon's bank, amounting to $125,000, was procured by bribery—the actual sum claimed being $103,865.71, and there being therein included several items manifestly fraudulent. Solomon evidently believed that he had given himself ample margin for the effective use of money among the members, but he was mistaken—the passage of the bill having cost him $80,000. Solomon discovering that he could get $20,000 of his claim by some scheme independent of the bill, it was arranged that the measure go through in its original shape and that of the $125,000 the sum of $20,000 should be divided among Speaker

S. J. Lee, Lieutenant-Governor Gleaves, Governor Moses, Comptroller-General Hoge and Treasurer Cardozo.

The transactions of the Sinking Fund Commission afforded opportunities for defrauding the State. Mention has been made of its sale of railroad stocks to the syndicate seeking control of certain lines. The commission pretended to handle other assets of the State, applicable to the retirement of State bonds, but no bonds were ever retired. Whipper was secretary of the commission and claimed to be its attorney—though Neagle testified that there had been no such engagement. Whipper presented a statement (1872), in which he made out that he had collected for the State $6,517.99 and had credits amounting to $8,156.62—thus making the State debtor to him in the sum of $1,638.63. In this matter Whipper took credit for $7,033.33 for his services as attorney, and converted that sum to his own use. In this connection it may be mentioned that Whipper charged and collected $50 per day for forty-three days' services as legal adviser to the committee appointed at the session of 1872 to investigate the affairs of the Bank of the State of South Carolina—the assets of which, as already stated, had been dissipated under receiverships provided for in different orders of the circuit court.

Among the loans made (1873) from the assets of the Bank of the State of South Carolina (in the hands of the receiver) was one of $7,000 to F. J. Moses, Jr., secured by the pledge of three warrants on the fund for the support of the penitentiary, each in the sum of $5,000. These warrants had been presented at the treasury by Hardy Solomon, and, payment being refused, were by him returned to Governor Moses, who thereupon issued other warrants in their stead, which latter Solomon received and used. The original warrants were then pledged to secure the loan to Moses—the application having been filed and the warrants delivered to the receiver by Mr. Chamberlain, to whom Moses swore that he paid a fee of $1,000 for this service.

The Governor's contingent fund was the means of supplying the Executive with ready money and of buying for him certain men's influence which he thought useful. James A. Bowley, the chairman of the House committee of ways and means, received $2,500 for making a favorable report on the bill providing for the contingent fund. R. B. Elliott received $3,500—apparently an outright gift from Governor Moses. Worthington received $1,000 on his statement that he was short in his accounts as collector of the port of Charleston. John A. Barker, a member of the House committee on claims, received $1,500, which he had agreed to divide with the committee, but which he invested in a coach and pair. Dennis received frequent orders on the fund. Numerous other payments were made to officials or legislators, ranging from $500 to $5,000—this last payable to Hardy Solomon's bank for Moses' benefit. When, on September 19, 1873, Moses bought of Thad. C. Andrews a half interest in the *Columbia Union,* payment was to be made in an order for $6,000 on the contingent fund next to be appropriated, and $6,000 on February 1 following. The warrant mentioned was cashed by Humbert, the negro treasurer of Orangeburg—whose misappropriation of public money has already been mentioned.

Under the act of March 4, 1872, authorizing the State Treasurer to borrow money for legislative expenses, that officer issued his notes or due bills in large numbers. In one transaction Hardy Solomon received from Treasurer Parker $95,100 for certain "bills payable," though there were vouchers for only two-thirds of that sum—the balance having evidently been divided between those two individuals.

The State penitentiary afforded many opportunities for peculation. During the superintendency of Carlos J. Stolbrand, Scott's first appointee, the Governor lent Stolbrand $15,000, taking as collateral treasury warrants in the sum of $30,000, ignored the loan and sold the warrants for his own benefit. Stolbrand purchased machinery for $2,903.35 and charged it to the penitentiary at $6.480—thus making a profit of $3,576.65. During Stolbrand's term Hardy Solomon furnished supplies to the amount of $42,049.55 and collected therefor $75,170.75. On April 1, 1873, John B. Dennis was appointed superintendent, and the board to which he was accountable included Comptroller-General Neagle, Senator Beverly Nash and H. E. Hayne, the Secretary of State. "Nash had a brickyard and his bills for bricks furnished would go far to throw a Chinese wall around the whole of Columbia; while Hayne, with no woodyard at all, furnished fuel enough to burn all of Nash's bricks." The bricks were sold by Neagle and Nash at $8 per thousand and charged at $12 —the difference of $4 per thousand being divided among Dennis and the three directors named. In one transaction Neagle received for himself and Nash $10,000 for 500,000 bricks; on the same account Nash received $4,962, while Hardy Solomon paid in addition (and charged to the State) $1,627.76—making the total cost of the bricks $33.38 per thousand, being quite four times their market value. For four months Nash received (in addition to the lawful per diem) $300 per month in orders on Solomon, who charged these amounts to the institution. Hayne desiring that he should receive a like allowance, an imaginary contract for wood was made with one "Wm. Seidner," and upon this Hayne received about $1,800. Of a lot of uniforms bought for the guard (costing $2,020.85) Nash used the greater portion for the militia regiment of which he was colonel. Dennis was succeeded in May, 1875, by T. W. Parmele—whose administration was free from the frauds and misdoings that had previously marked the management. The expenses of the penitentiary from 1868 to 1877 amounted to more than $750,000. The institution is now (1905) and has been for some years self-sustaining.

The State orphan asylum established in 1869 was located first in Charleston and thence removed to Columbia. The affairs of the institution appear to have been honestly managed until March, 1873, when Governor Moses appointed a new board of trustees—among them S. E. Gaillard, one of the senators from Charleston, and Beverly Nash, the former being chairman. The expenses to May 13, 1875 (when the asylum was removed to Columbia), were $51,565.91, of which sum vouchers for $8,381.75 were reported to have been "lost." From May 13, 1875, to August 1, 1877, the funds received by Nash amounted to $55,791.57, and he accounted for $49,915.74—showing a misappropriation of $5,875.93. The evidence taken in relation to this institution showed that in the four years of the management of Gaillard and Nash there was lost by wilful waste or by fraud and embezzlement the sum of $40,700. The asylum was closed in 1877—not before it had become "an offense to decency and an eyesore to the community."

Fraudulent transactions were by no means confined to the State Government. In many of the counties there were fictitious charges for services or supplies—the officials combining with outsiders to defraud the public in this way and by other means also.

THE LAND COMMISSION.

Mention has been made of the Land Commission created by different acts of the Legislature, passed in pursuance of the ordinance of

THE STORY OF THE FRAUDS 491

the Constitutional Convention. The first land commissioner was C. P. Leslie, he was succeeded by R. C. DeLarge (colored) and the management was later turned over to the Secretary of State.

The "Joint Special Investigating Committee" appointed at the legislative session of 1870-71 pronounced the commission a "gigantic folly," and charged that its powers had been employed "to subserve a certain organized result, viz.: the primary benefit of the members of the advisory board and the land commissioner and their subservient allies." The advisory board here referred to was composed of Governor Scott, Comptroller-General Neagle, Treasurer Parker, Secretary Cardozo and Attorney-General Chamberlain.

The commission purchased for the State 103,546 acres of land at a cost of $568,192—the total amount expended being $888,335. The land was divided up into parcels—much money being spent for surveying and incidental expenses.

Of the land acquired there had been, on November 1, 1877, 56,277 acres settled by parties to whom the State had issued certificates of purchase—leaving 47,269 acres unsold and unoccupied. The entire amount paid in by such parties had been $45,588.74. This sum included, the entire amount realized by the State was about $250,000. The Land Commission scheme therefore entailed a loss of about $600,000.

In the purchase of lands there was flagrant and criminal carelessness, coupled in many instances with actual fraud on the part of the State's trusted agent. Deeds from sellers were filled in with sums far larger than the actual amounts paid—the officials pocketing the difference. Lands so poor as to be practically worthless were bought at high prices from friends or partners of the commission.

One purchase was of several tracts, aggregating 17,533 acres, in Charleston and Colleton counties for $120,754—showing an average cost of $6.87 per acre. This property—known as "Hell Hole Swamp"—remained unproductive in the State's possession for many years and was sold at a great sacrifice—15,000 acres fetching thirty-five cents an acre and the rest one dollar an acre.

In numerous other instances the State paid extravagant prices for lands of indifferent quality—much of it unfit for cultivation.

The scheme underlying the creation of the Land Commission had been exploited among the negroes even before the inauguration of the State Government under the Reconstruction acts. Many of the colored people believed that it was the mission of the Freedmen's Bureau to furnish them each with "forty acres and a mule." The loose talk of some of the members of the Constitutional Convention of 1868 really strengthened the notion that this was somehow to be done. Though the Land Commission nominally sold, yet the purchasers were made to understand that they might pay at their own pleasure. Some paid in full—in many cases getting land not worth the price paid. Some paid in part and, not further complying, lost the money thus laid out. Some sold to speculators their "certificates of purchase," and thus suffered loss. As a scheme to encourage and enable colored people to become landowners, the Land Commission was a failure. It did harm to many of the negroes, by making them indolent and also indifferent to obligation.

CORRUPTING A JUDGE.

In the case of Whaley vs. Bank of Charleston, the Supreme Court on April 7, 1874, rendered a decision affirming a circuit judgment for more than $30,000 in favor of the plaintiff—Chief Justice Moses delivering the opinion, Justice Wright concurring and Justice Willard filing a dissenting opinion.

F. J. Moses, Jr., testified that before the decision was filed, it being known that there was disagreement between Justices Moses and Willard, he was requested by D. H. Chamberlain, one of the plaintiff's attorneys, "to see Judge Wright and ascertain how much would be demanded for his concurrence with the Chief Justice." Moses swore that having neglected this request for a time he received from Mr. Chamberlain a note which was put in evidence in the following form:

Columbia, S. C., Feb. 5, 1876.

I hereby certify that I have this night, in the presence of General Dennis and Mr. Thomas S. Cavender, received from Governor Moses a paper in the handwriting of Governor Chamberlain, of which paper the following is a copy:

"S. W. Melton.   D. H. Chamberlain.
"Melton & Chamberlain.
"Law Office,
"Columbia, S. C., April 6, 1874.

"Dear Governor: Please arrange that matter at 2,000 or 3,000 as may be necessary. Let me know exactly what is needed after your interview, and I will be on hand. I will call at your office 11:30 a. m. Don't delay the matter. Yours,   Chamberlain."

THE STORY OF THE FRAUDS 493

I pledge my word that I will not use the said paper publicly (without the consent of Governor Moses) to the prejudice of Governor Moses. Thomas C. Dunn.
Witness: John B. Dennis, Thomas S. Cavender.

Moses further testified that Wright, after some hesitation, finally agreed to concur with the Chief Justice on payment of $2,500; that Chamberlain delivered to him two notes for $1,000 and $1,500, respectively, which were discounted by different individuals named, the proceeds being paid to Wright and from him borrowed by Moses.

John B. Dennis corroborated Moses' statements as to the letter alleged to have been written to Moses by Chamberlain and as to the receipt and pledge given by Dunn.

On hearing of Moses' testimony, Wright addressed to the investigating committee a letter denying the charge made and requesting judicial investigation.

Upon the testimony taken, the committee concluded:

That Chamberlain paid $2,500 to Moses for the purpose of securing a favorable decision your committee have no doubt. Whether Judge Wright was to receive any part of it, or whether he did receive any part of it, your committee are unable to determine. In either case the guilt of Mr. Chamberlain is the same.

There were several indictments against parties concerned in one or more of the schemes to defraud the State—F. L. Cardozo, Niles G. Parker, Y. J. P. Owens, S. L. Hoge, Thomas C. Dunn, R. H. Gleaves, Samuel J. Lee, Josephus Woodruff, A. O. Jones, F. J. Moses, Jr., C. W. Montgomery, John J. Patterson, F. S. Jacobs, R. K. Scott, H. H. Kimpton, L. Cass Carpenter, Robert Smalls, B. F. Whittemore and D. H. Chamberlain.

Efforts were made to bring Patterson and Kimpton into the State to answer indictments, but without effect. The courts—that of Massachusetts and that of the District of Columbia—each held that the accused was not extraditable for the offense with which he was charged.

As already stated, Smalls was duly convicted of bribery, Carpenter of forgery and Cardozo of conspiracy to defraud the State by means of a fraudulent legislative certificate issued by the two clerks and paid by him as Treasurer. They were pardoned by Governor Hampton.

The other prosecutions were all dropped in 1879—this under an arrangement by which certain cases against white citizens charged with violations of the Federal election laws were also discontinued. The jury lists in the Federal courts were still manipulated, the white people had little expectation of justice in those tribunals, and trials therein were attended with great expense and much vexation.

CHAPTER XI.
REVIEW AND REFLECTIONS.

President Johnson's scheme for the restoration of the Southern States to their places in the Union (which he claimed to be just that contemplated by Abraham Lincoln) imposed but two conditions—the renewal of allegiance to the Federal Government and the abolition of slavery. Disqualification resulting from past conduct was to be removed by the act of the Executive—by his use of the pardoning power vested in him by the Constitution. The two conditions performed, the lately rebellious State was to be restored to the Union, with all rights, including representation in each branch of Congress, reestablished as fully as they had existed before the suspension of its relations by the act of secession. The repeal of the ordinance of secession was from the President's standpoint perfunctory merely, because in his view that ordinance was originally and always void.

The President's scheme of restoration not only recognized the white citizens of the State as vested exclusively with the sovereignty prerequisite to the performance of the acts necessary as conditions precedent, but it left to them the power to fix the civil and political status of the freedmen. In the solution of the problem thus presented—more fraught with difficulty than any that had ever confronted any people—it was plain that no aid could come from that Federal power which, in the President's view, had exhausted itself in the process of restoration.

The people of South Carolina, first in convention and then in legislature, attempted a solution of the problem which they plainly saw would not solve itself—they attempted to establish by law the civil status of the freedmen and the relations of these not, as might have seemed, to the white race, but to the new body politic of which each race should be a recognized component. Realizing that the negro could not take care of himself they undertook, after their own fashion and guided by the best lights then available, to take care of him. The "Black Code" embodied the results of that undertaking. To the negro was accorded the right to contract, to acquire, hold and alien property, to sue and be sued, to testify in the courts—to have or to do all these things as fully as they could be had or done by white citizens. Other rights were withheld—the right to vote, to hold office and to sit in the jury box. It seemed plain to the whites that the negro just emerged from a state of slavery—in which, according to the view of most abolitionists, he had been so treated that he had become almost brutalized and altogether incapable of intelligent choice—could not safely be entrusted with the power of the ballot or of sitting in judgment upon the liberty or the property rights of others.

The "Black Code" further undertook to establish between the white man and his negro employee the relation of master and servant, but the relation could not exist except by contract between the parties. As already stated, it never actually existed. The negroes on the farms generally worked on shares—the relation thus arising being in fact and in law a partnership founded upon the agreement of parties whose several rights thereunder were amply protected by equal laws. Where the negro worked for wages he was an employee, but he was never a servant within the meaning of the "Black Code."

How far the conditions wrought by the legislation under the Constitution of 1865 could have been maintained is matter of conjecture, for the intervention of Congress—nay, the previous interference of the military authority—arrested the experiment before it had been fairly tried. Already the Southern people, their views being expressed by recognized leaders, had come to think that the right to vote and the right to sit on the jury, each judiciously circumscribed, were necessarily incident to freedom—that enfranchisement must follow emancipation. After what time and to what extent, without compulsion or suggestion from the Federal power, these rights, separately or concurrently, would have been given to the negro, is matter of conjecture. The opportunity to try fairly the experiment which inhered in every legislative act enlarging the negro's rights was not allowed to the white people. Congress intervened to prevent this and more particularly to assert its right to fix the terms upon which the States "lately in rebellion" should be received back into the Union.

THE COURSE OF CONGRESS.

When the thirty-ninth Congress met, December 4, 1865, it was evident that, so far as the will of that body might be enforced, the Johnson plan of restoration would be neither recognized nor tolerated. Thaddeus Stevens put the attitude of Congress plainly when he declared that it should "take no account of the aggregation oi white-washed rebels who without any legal authority have assembled in the capitals of the late rebel States and simulated legislative bodies."

The purposes of Mr. Stevens, who was the accredited leader of the Republican majority in Congress, were principally two—to perpetuate his party's control of the country and to punish the Southern people whom he called rebels and whose leaders he denounced as traitors. He said that under the Presidential plan, without any changes in the basis of representation, the Southern States, with Democrats likely to be elected in other sections, would control the country, and further declared that the "insurrectionary" States should not be recognized as States until the Federal Constitution should have been amended "so as to secure perpetual ascendency to the party of the Union." To attain this end Mr. Stevens had two plans—(1) to reduce the representation of the seceded States, and (2) to enfranchise the negroes and disfranchise certain classes of whites in those States. These controlling purposes were approved by other representative men of the Republican party.

Of the alternatives contemplated by Mr. Stevens the Republican majority in Congress chose that of enfranchising the negroes and putting them in power over the white race. The Reconstruction acts in terms accomplished the one condition and the other necessarily followed. The general spirit and purpose of these measures were plainly stated by accredited spokesmen of the Republican party.

James A. Garfield, not usually given to violent speech, said in discussing the first of the Reconstruction acts: "This bill sets out by laying its hands on the rebel governments and taking the very breath of life out of them—it puts the bayonet at the breast of every rebel in the South—it leaves in the hands of Congress utterly and absolutely the work of reconstruction."

A few days later Henry Wilson said on the floor of the Senate: "With the exercise of practical judgment, with good organization, scattering the great truth and facts before the people, a majority of these rebel States will within a twelvemonth send here senators and representatives who think as we think, speak as we speak and vote as we vote, and will give their electoral votes for whomever we nominate for President in 1868."

"Pass this bill," said Henry Wilson on another occasion, "and you make the South Republican for all time."

Thus out of the mouths of accredited representatives of the Republican party were expressed the purposes always uppermost in its plans respecting the South—the purpose to punish the Southern whites and the purpose to perpetuate the power of that party. These were the leading objects in the policy of the National Government towards the Southern whites from the passage of the Reconstruction measures to the removal of the Federal soldiers from the State House in Columbia.

What Congress did—the subversion of certain State governments —the destruction of certain States themselves—the establishment of a military autocracy in every Southern State—the enfranchisement of the negro—the disfranchisement of a large class of white men— the admission into the Union of new bodies politic, called States—all this has been sufficiently told. The Reconstruction scheme of Congress, it may fairly be said, was actually consummated at the point of the bayonet. By the very terms of the acts every official in the several States affected held his place and used his powers in actual subordination to the military authority of the United States.

In the two plans of Reconstruction—the Presidential and the Congressional—there were presented two extremes. Mr. Johnson proceeded summarily to restore the States to full relations in the Union. This policy was resented by the extremists in the "loyal" States and, truth to tell, was doubted by numbers of conservative people who thought there should be time to consider the new conditions and adopt those means which should be best for all interests. Some allowance may fairly be made for the unreadiness of Northern people to have Southern leaders yesterday in active war against the National Government received today in full relations to it, with the right to influence, possibly to control, its Congress and thus shape its policy—the single condition of restoration being that they, with the people whom they represented, should disavow their recognition of a confederacy no longer in existence and declare (in some cases renew) their allegiance to the Government with which they had so lately been at war. The transition was sudden, to say the least.

The process of Reconstruction under the acts of Congress was slower, but it effected at once the actual subjection of the white people to the negroes. Without reference to the unfitness of the black race to dominate the white, it had been not only conceded but actually contended by the Republican leaders that the negroes in the Southern States were, in consequence of the alleged barbarities of slavery, so debased as to be incapable of self-government—and all the more were they incapable of organizing a government under circumstances actually without precedent in the history of the world.

The Congressional idea was simple in the extreme. The one act including and yet underlying all others was the clothing of the negro with the right to vote. "Manhood suffrage" was instituted in the South when the different commanders ordered registration preliminary to the vote upon the question of calling a convention to frame a new Constitution which should meet the requirements of Congress. The negro thus enfranchised by Congress—and the will of Congress enforced at the point of the bayonet—it necessarily followed that negro domination would be instituted and perpetuated as far as these results could be wrought by express provisions in the new Constitutions. These conditions, considered right and proper for the South, were unacceptable to some of the States in other sections. Negro suffrage was rejected by the people of Connecticut in 1865 by a majority of 6,272; by those of Ohio in 1867 by a majority of 50,629; by those of Kansas in that year by a majority of 8,938, and by those of Minnesota in the same year by a majority of 1,298.

The compromise measures proposed in the conference of Southern Governors in the early part of 1867 presented a middle ground. The constitutional amendment then suggested embodied all the provisions of the Fourteenth Amendment, with the disqualifying clauses omitted and with the additional inhibition that no State should require as a property qualification for voters more than $250 of taxable property, or as an educational qualification more education than enough to enable the voter to read the Constitution of the United States in the English language and write his own name.

It was further proposed that there should be qualified suffrage impartially allowed to all male citizens, with the reservation to the effect that persons entitled in 1865 to vote should not be disfranchised—which meant that all white men should vote, that negroes must be qualified under the new provisions and that the restrictions thereby fixed should apply to all persons of either race who should reach maturity after the adoption of the provisions embodied in the amendments.

The compromises thus proposed were ignored by Congress—that body plainly manifesting its purpose to institute and perpetuate negro rule in the Southern States.

What might have followed the adoption of these compromise measures is, of course, matter of conjecture. Certainly it would have had some advantages over the Congressional plan—in that it would have appeased instead of outraging the feelings of the Southern whites, that it would have put to a test their good faith and their professions of fairness toward the negroes, and that it would have averted the disastrous consequences necessarily following the attempt to place the white race under the rule of the black. However all this may be, it is now clear that the course of the Republican majority in Congress in sullenly, insolently, nay, almost brutishly rejecting every proposition which was counter to their purpose to put the Southern States under negro governments and sustain those governments with Federal bayonets, was fixed beyond the reach of appeal or remonstrance from any quarter. The folly of this determination would be inconceivable but that it marked the conduct of men who were mad with power.

One weakness of the course of Congress was in its dishonesty—in the pretension of its authors that they intended to restore and perpetuate free government when in truth their purposes were to humiliate the Southern whites and to perpetuate party ascendancy. Thus originally dishonest their scheme of reconstruction naturally evolved governments whose agents and representatives were always corrupt.

THE COURSE OF THE WHITES.

The white people of South Carolina have been criticised for their attitude taken when the Reconstruction acts were put in operation by the appointment of a military commander over the State. The consideration which chiefly moved them to reject the terms contained in those acts arose out of the fact that the Radical scheme of restoration enfranchised the negroes and by so doing placed the whites at the mercy of an ignorant and irresponsible majority. It was not to be expected that the superior race should thus surrender—and in truth the Republican authors of the Reconstruction acts had no such expectation. Another consideration, secondary but powerful, was in the fact that by those measures many of the best white men—men whom the Southern people had deliberately chosen as leaders—were disfranchised and left to beg Congress for their rights of citizenship. The negro, however ignorant, however debased, however incompetent to understand his rights or appreciate his responsibilities, was vested with every power of citizenship. It was neither fair nor brave to expect the white people to accept a measure which made some of their very best citizens actually inferior to the lowest type of negro. It was no more reasonable to expect them to acquiesce in the punishment and contribute to the humiliation of men who if chiefly guilty of "rebellion" or "treason" were so because their own people had raised them to places of leadership.

But, could the white people have overcome their feelings to the extent of cooperating with the negroes in accepting and enforcing the Reconstruction policy of Congress, it is certain that the latter, turning their backs upon their former masters, would have obeyed the commands of the few whites who called themselves Republicans —the "scalawags" and the "carpetbaggers." The whites, even if they had joined the Republican party, could not have accepted the notions of equality demanded by the leading negroes and cringingly accepted by "scalawags" and "carpetbaggers." A principal doctrine of that party in South Carolina was the doctrine of civil rights— meaning social equality so far as it might be enforced by penal statutes. To this the Republican party here was positively committed.

Most of the white Republicans ate and drank, walked and rode, went to public places and ostensibly affiliated with negroes. During the session of the Convention of 1868 Thomas J. Robertson, in company with two colored members of that body, went into a billiard-room—the colored men declaring their purpose to have a game. The proprietor saying that negroes could not play in his place, the colored members became noisily indignant, threatened the man with the law, and walked out—Mr. Robertson meanwhile expressing his feelings by saying that he thought this was a free country. Niles G. Parker was particularly given to walking on Main street in Columbia arm-in-arm with some colored man. B. F. Whittemore in his home in Darlington practiced social equality to such an extent as to disgust the white people, demoralize some of the negroes and humiliate his own family. John L. Neagle's home in York was the scene of performances which involved his recognition of negro visitors as his social equals. He, too, used to walk arm-in-arm with negroes on the public streets. A prominent white Republican, rather priding himself on his education and refinement, once selected a negro clergyman to perform the funeral service over the body of his own child.

In certain State institutions—the University and the school for deaf-mutes and the blind—the effort of the ruling element, as already related, was to enforce actual social equality.

It could not fairly be expected that the men of the white race would acquiesce in these conditions. Indeed, it was never expected. One underlying motive of all the civil-rights legislation and regulation in South Carolina was to band the negroes in a political organization which should be so offensive to the whites that these would have nothing to do with it.

One principal reason for the white people's opposition to the Reconstruction legislation lay in the fact that they believed it unconstitutional and therefore not entitled to either obedience or respect. This belief was shared by distinguished men of whose devotion to the Union, of whose fidelity to the Constitution, there was never a question.

In the Egan case, already noticed, Mr. Justice Nelson had held that upon the adoption of the Constitution of 1865 and the reorganization of the State Government thereunder South Carolina was "in the full enjoyment, or was entitled to the full enjoyment, of all her Constitutional rights and privileges." It was that State Government which Congress had subverted by the use of military power. If Justice Nelson was right, the contention of the Southern people that the Reconstruction acts were void was necessarily correct. Of that distinguished jurist's fidelity to the Union and the Constitution no doubt was ever suggested. Upon his voluntary retirement from the bench of the Supreme Court in 1873, after a service of over twenty-seven years, the other justices bore unsought testimony to his "mature wisdom, large learning and sterling integrity," whilst a number of prominent lawyers, representing different sections and different parties, formally expressed their appreciation and admiration of his "learning, sagacity and integrity," his "elevated conception of justice and of right," and the "preeminent judicial qualities which distinguished his career on the bench." Such was the man to whose judgment the Southern people might have appealed to justify their attitude towards the negro governments put over them at the point of the bayonet.

The National Democratic party in its platform declared the Reconstruction measures to be "unconstitutional, revolutionary, null and void," and upon that platform stood Horatio Seymour, whose fidelity to the Union was never questioned, and Frank P. Blair, who had been a corps commander in Sherman's army. That platform was accepted and defended by some of the strongest jurists in the country—men, too, who had always stood by the Union.

As already shown every effort to have a decision of the Supreme Court of the United States upon the grave questions involved had failed—that tribunal in every instance dismissing the proceedings without an adjudication of any of such questions on its merits. In the absence of the judicial determination which they actively sought the Southern people were justified in holding to their opinion that the measures taken by Congress to enfranchise the negro were beyond the scope of its powers, revolutionary, null and void. Participation or even acquiescence in the establishment of a State Government under such measures could not fairly be expected; and such participation was surely not invited by the mode in which Congress undertook to enforce them—enforcement at the point of the bayonet.

Nor must it be forgotten that there was no choice left to the white people. The Reconstruction acts submitted the question of restoration not to the electorate established by that State Constitution (1790) of whose authority no doubt was suggested, but to the whole male population within given ages. Had the white electorate, left free to decide, rejected the propositions submitted the responsibility would have been theirs. The determination actually left by the very terms of the law to the negro voters, the responsibility became theirs exclusively.

In this connection it is only fair to note the fact that every objection of the white people of South Carolina to the establishment of the Constitution of 1868—every prediction of bad results to follow—was amply justified by the course of the negro government at various stages of its existence. Bad as it was, conditions would have been far worse but for the coolness, bravery and forbearance of the white people acting under the advice of wise and patriotic leaders.

It has been charged that the deliverance of South Carolina from negro rule and from the infamies continuously incident thereto was accomplished by unlawful means—by force or fraud or both. Whatever may be said of the methods alleged to have been used by the whites in the campaign of 1876, it must also be said that the conduct of the negroes, incited by their leaders, was quite as bad. Of actual intimidation there was much more visited upon colored

Democrats than upon colored Republicans. The effort was made to frighten the whole negro race by telling them that none of their rights would be safe under Democratic rule and that the white people would, if such a thing were possible, put them back in slavery. Instances of the brutal maltreatment of colored men who declared a purpose to vote the Hampton ticket were many enough to indicate a formed design, in every part of the State, to frighten the colored people into voting the Republican ticket. There was quite as much fraud in Beaufort or Charleston as there was in Edgefield or Laurens. A careful study of the whole situation—including the election returns—must bring the conclusion that if all the fraudulent or otherwise illegal votes had been eliminated Hampton would still have been elected, and the Democrats would still have had a majority in the House of Representatives and in joint assembly.

To those who may be fond of moralizing is left the question whether the casting of a fraudulent ballot is any more wicked or any more hurtful to any public interest or to the individual conscience than the crime of bribery—which, in the case of the official corrupted, involves the crime of perjury. There might also be interest in the question, Which is the worse—to maintain a corrupt, oppressive and inefficient government by a free ballot, or to establish an impartial, honest and efficient government by enforcing the supremacy of the white race?

CHARACTERISTICS OF NEGRO RULE.

The personnel of the convention held to organize the Republican party of South Carolina, as already given, was an index to that of every similar body assembled in that State during the period of negro rule—the Constitutional Convention, the General Assembly and every convention of that party. The ruling characteristic of each of these bodies was its irresponsibility. Dominated either by native whites conscious of having incurred the displeasure of their race or by "carpetbaggers" who never had any standing among that race, or by smart negroes most of whom were unscrupulous, or by all of these acting together, the constituency to which these bodies looked was the negro race exclusively—and this race incapable of forming any judgment upon the actions of men, naturally suspicious of their former masters and stirred to hostility to these latter by the vicious counsels of political tutors. From the passage of the resolution in the Convention, to allow themselves grossly excessive pay, up to the last performance of the Mackey body acting in defiance of the judgment of the Supreme Court, the pervading characteristic of the negro government and its agents was irresponsibility. There was accountability to none of the "tribunals" generally held to control the actions of public servants—neither to the law, to public opinion, to official obligation nor to an overlooking constituency.

Every reckless, vicious or corrupt act of those in places of power or opportunity under Republican rule in South Carolina had its inducement or its inception in the wrongdoer's belief that actually independent of public opinion he was by consequence above the reach of the law. That sense of safety prompted first excess, then recklessness, then robbery, then perjury—this whether the occasion lay in the waste of time, the misapplication of public money, the issue of fraudulent paper, the bribery of legislators or officials, the bartering of pardons, the packing of a jury or the effort to corrupt a judge.

The sense of irresponsibility naturally bred corruption—and it will have been observed that different agents of the negro government in South Carolina were corrupt from the time when, in the fall of 1868, some of them proposed to the superintendent of the penitentiary to discontinue their pursuit of him if he would share with them his income from his office, to the time when, in December, 1876, Corbin, a leading Republican high in the favor of the administration at Washington, fraudulently appropriated public money held in trust and used the same to bribe men unlawfully claiming to be members of the House of Representatives. The corruption was not confined to the buying or selling of votes or the issuance of fraudulent paper, but it extended to every branch of the Government—actually including the University, from whose officers came written reports making false showings of the state of the institution in order to secure large appropriations. Individuals who managed to keep aloof from actual thievery consciously connived at the crimes of others or consented to the misapplication of public funds, so manifestly unwarranted as to constitute a fraud upon the people. Another form of dishonesty was presented in the persistent election or appointment of grossly incompetent persons to public office. The public school system was for eight years tainted with this form of dishonesty—ignorant persons being elected to the office of school commissioner, these appointing others equally ignorant as trustees, and those others joining in the employment of grossly incompetent teachers. The administration of the educational system, from the University down through the humblest school, was one vast fraud upon the State and an imposition upon the people elsewhere who were frequently told of the achievements of the negro party in South Carolina in the work of enlightening the masses! In this connection must be noted the fact that some of the leaders in the schemes of robbery prided themselves on their culture.

Irresponsible, debased and corrupt, the negro government was confessedly weak—always relying upon the help of Federal bayonets to enforce its authority and, indeed, to keep it from falling to pieces. Backed by the power of the United States, this government constituted a tyranny. Every right of the white people was at the mercy of an irresponsible majority whose will was supreme and whose demands upon the National Executive always found ready response.

It was more than once suggested by the critics of the white people of South Carolina that their violent opposition to the State Government was chiefly because the negro had been clothed with all the rights of citizenship—that even had the negro government been administered honestly, effectively and economically the white people would not have acquiesced. The latter proposition is true. Indeed, no expression of policy or purpose by the white people of South Carolina ever went beyond the promise to recognize the negro's rights under the Constitution and give him equal protection under the law. There was never a promise of equal civil rights as demanded by negro leaders, never a promise of mixing the races in school or college, never an acknowledgment of the right of the negro race to rule the white. Negro domination was invariably repudiated and resisted. The flagrant blunder of the Republican party, acting through Federal legislation, consisted in the belief of its leaders that negro domination was possible—its principal crime was in the effort by the use of mere brute force to effect the subordination of the white race to the black. The criminal folly of the leading negroes was chiefly in their reliance upon the strength of numbers or the power of the bayonet—that reliance founded on their belief that an irresponsible majority could by the use of mere brute force hold in subjection a race which had hitherto dominated every part of the civilized world, and which in South Carolina actually constituted the commonwealth. No excuse can be found for the folly of these leaders. The explanation of their course lies in the fact that they were all corrupt.

REPUBLICAN REFORM.

Of the character of the Government of South Carolina during the administrations of Governors Scott and Moses there was scarcely any difference of opinion. It was generally accounted infamous. But the uprising of the white people in 1876 was thought by some unnecessary, by others unreasonable, because of the reforms instituted on the suggestion of Governor Chamberlain. In judging the course of the white people towards him it is only fair to consider the light in which they viewed him taken as one of the products of the Reconstruction period and as a leader of the negroes in South Carolina.

Mr. Chamberlain began his political career on one of the sea islands, near Charleston, where the negro population outnumbered the white quite ten to one. He selected his constituency—for he was not embarrassed by any ties incident to proprietorship. It was among these negroes that he started his political career—some of his harangues, by the way, being of a character well calculated to incite them to wrongdoing. By these negroes he was sent as a delegate to the Constitutional Convention. His course in that body was as a whole conservative, but he showed his purpose to make friends of the negroes as such by insisting upon some extreme measures, notably the requirement that all public schools, of whatsoever grade, should be open to negroes in common with whites. From this time till the last day of his occupancy of the State House his closest associates were from among the lowest products of the Reconstruction period. Always a partisan, he stuck to his party at every stage of its career.

Mr. Chamberlain very soon confessed that his party had disgraced itself and brought odium upon the State. In a letter (May 5, 1871) to William L. Trenholm of Charleston, referring to the condition of affairs, he wrote: "Three years have passed, and the result is—what? Incompetency, dishonesty, corruption in all its forms, 'have advanced their miscreated fronts,' have put to flight the small remnant that opposed them, and now rule the party which rules the State." This confession must be considered in connection with Mr. Chamberlain's active work in 1870 for the reelection of Governor Scott, and his boast in the Republican convention in April, 1876, of that work, saying that he had been commissioned to help to save the life of his party. His unquestioning allegiance continued through the term of Governor Moses, whose election he was never known to have opposed. He stated that he had during Moses' incumbency closely followed his profession, "taking no part whatever in public or political affairs."

It thus appears that Mr. Chamberlain actively assisted in the election of Scott and Moses. It further appears that from the writing of his letter to Colonel Trenholm to his inauguration he never raised his voice against his party—never once protested against the frauds that especially marked the State Government during the whole of Moses' term. This much is admitted even by Mr. Chamberlain's partisans. Without further examination of his course there would be enough to justify the belief of the white people of South Carolina that he never was a fit person for the office of Governor. But some review of his administration is necessary, to ascertain the extent to which it had any of the characteristics of preceding ones.

The partisan character of the Government continued. Governor Chamberlain conceded this much when in a party caucus he explicitly declared that in the election of a circuit judge three qualifications must be considered—"first, the candidate must be a Republican; second, he must be a man of ability, qualified to fill the position; and third, his character and integrity must be above suspicion." In his letter to Oliver P. Morton (January 13, 1876,) the Governor declared: "Never since 1868 were there ever so few Democrats in office in this State as since my administration." Republicanism recognized as the first prerequisite to the holding of office, it followed that there were not only in the Legislature but among Governor Chamberlain's appointees many who were incapable and quite as many who were corrupt. One case deserves particular mention because of its terrible consequences.

Trial Justice Prince Rivers, who issued the warrant for certain negro militiamen of Hamburg in July, 1876, was Governor Chamberlain's appointee. A careful reading of Attorney-General Wm. Stone's report of the disturbance must force the conclusion that Rivers so dallied with the trouble, so delayed proceedings, so "put on airs," as to anger the white men assembled—these already suspecting that the trial justice sympathized with the accused or at the best was trying to "show off." It is clear that in the hands of a firm, capable and incorrupt magistrate of either race the controversy could have been peaceably settled to the satisfaction of the complainants and in perfect justice to the accused. Rivers following his own course, the irritation increased and bloodshed resulted. When Rivers was appointed he was notoriously incompetent, corrupt, and disposed to make trouble between the races. The impartial seeker for the real causes of the dreadful affair in Hamburg must find the principal of these in Governor Chamberlain's appointment of Rivers, whose unfitness for his place was in fact quite as flagrant as was that of Whipper or Moses for the circuit bench—though, truth to tell, Governor Chamberlain regarded the act of voting for either or both of them quite consistent with personal integrity. Writing of Simon P. Coker, a colored man who lost his life in the Ellenton riot, the Governor referred to the deceased as "an honest, peaceful man," well known to himself as a member of the Legislature from Barnwell. Yet Coker had voted for both Whipper and Moses.

The attitude of Mr. Chamberlain, both before and after his election, towards the State University as a mixed school for whites and blacks, intended to establish actual social equality between them, evidenced his purpose to truckle to the demands of the worst men in his party and, when his own interests were at stake, stop short of no offense to the feelings or wishes of the white people. Besides, Governor Chamberlain knew that the University was a fraud upon the State, as well as an imposition upon the taxpaying whites whose sons were excluded from its advantages—excluded unless they should consent to associate upon terms of social equality with negroes, some of whom were of notoriously bad character.

It is plain that Governor Chamberlain's policy involved the condonation of the corrupt acts committed in previous administrations. Niles G. Parker was never prosecuted. Sued for money actually stolen from the State, he was adjudged by the court to make restitution. The judgment against him was never satisfied. He fled the State. It seems clear that Governor Chamberlain had no heart in the pursuit of Parker. One of Parker's lawyers (Hoge) said to his jury that "reform" in the State Government meant immunity to the wrongdoers.

It is certain that the evidence upon which the Democratic investigating committees in 1877 started their inquiries, resulting in a full exposure of the frauds, was easily accessible to Governor Chamberlain. In all his public career—first as Attorney-General and most significantly as Governor—he did nothing either to expose the robberies or to punish the thieves.

Full statement has been given of Governor Chamberlain's recommendations looking to retrenchment, and due comparison made between his figures and those of preceding administrations. Still his standards were totally unsuited to conditions in South Carolina, and especially to the ideas of the taxpaying whites. In his message of November 23, 1875, he urged that the tax levy for State purposes, not including two mills for schools, be fixed at seven and five-sixths mills —and this was two mills more than the highest levy under Democratic administration. He urged a reduction of legislative expenses to $125,000—the average cost per session under white rule has been less than $55,000. And it must be remembered that in the case of every supply act, every appropriation bill, passed during his incumbency, he set his approval to levies and expenditures far beyond the figures which he had declared to be amply sufficient.

Except in the refusal to commission Whipper and Moses there was no point at which Governor Chamberlain actually took issue with his party—his recommendations were all persuasively given, and no remonstrance of his ever ripened into protest. His partisanship was never modified sufficiently to cause any abatement of his servile submission to the behests of his party.

It has been made clear, by a simple narration of actual occurrences, that after his nomination in 1876 Governor Chamberlain made no pretense of objection to the support, the cooperation or the companionship, whether personal or political or both, of any man calling himself a Republican. Elliott, whom he afterwards confessed that he should have repudiated, was the candidate of Governor Chamberlain as fully as of the Republican party. For the election of Elliott—incompetent, depraved and disgraced—Governor Chamberlain did quite as much that, according to his own statements, required courage and conscience, as he did when he refused to commission Whipper and Moses, for whose elevation to the bench Elliott was responsible to a greater extent than any other individual. When there arose a question of fact in relation to a charge made against Hampton by Chamberlain, the latter called Elliott as a witness whose word should settle it. Daniel H. Chamberlain, in order to impeach Wade Hampton, called as his own witness a man who had been false to every trust, who was fairly reeking with corruption, whose personal conduct was disreputable, and who had taken to wife a strumpet!

REVIEW AND REFLECTIONS 511

Mr. Chamberlain's last act in his relations to public affairs in South Carolina evidenced his slavery to his party and his disregard for standards of right when its interests were involved. The self-appointed committee who in March, 1877, submitted a scheme for the adjustment, through a commission, of the troubles in South Carolina, consisted of Daniel H. Chamberlain, D. T. Corbin and John J. Patterson. The ex-Governor well knew the public record and the character of each of these his chosen and confidential friends. He knew, or should have known, that Corbin had used his place as United States Attorney as a means of persecution in order to swell his fees—that he had helped to pack the juries in the Kuklux trials—that in the course of those trials he had suborned some witnesses and was believed to have corrupted others—that in those trials he had taken advantage of his office to insult a clergyman and speak disrespectfully of a lady, and had made a false statement to the court—that he had on some occasions taken advantage of his Federal office to offend persons having business with the court—that he was without one aspiration of a gentleman and never rose to the plane of a reputable lawyer—and that as a final act (in aid of Mr. Chamberlain) he had fraudulently used money of the State to pay members of the Mackey body to vote for himself for the office of United States senator.

John J. Patterson's conduct—certainly his bribery of the Legislature to send him to the Senate—was notorious. It was as well known to Mr. Chamberlain as to the people to whom the press of the country gave ample information at the time of the infamous transactions.

Mr. Chamberlain explicitly declared that whatever the abuses and offenses prevailing in the negro government, there was, nevertheless, more of good than of evil in its administration. In the course of an interview, December 23, 1876, with the correspondent of the *Chicago Tribune,* the ex-Governor said:

It is quite too much the custom in speaking of what are called the "carpetbag" governments of the South to present only one side of the picture. I freely admit that there is one side which is to a large degree discreditable to the State Governments of South Carolina for some part of the time since 1867. And I have during my own administration considered it my duty, for the best interests of the State, of the Republican party, and especially ot both races of people living on this soil, without regard to party, to oppose and discountenance many of the practices that have grown up under our State Government since Reconstruction. In consequence of being engaged somewhat conspicuously in this work of correcting Republican abuses, it has been very erroneously supposed that I was a wholesale denouncer of the Government which has existed here since Reconstruction.

The fact is that I have never lost sight of the benefits the new order of things has conferred upon this State. And I say now, very deliberately, that in my judgment the so-called "carpetbag" governments of South Carolina have done more for the permanent prosperity and progress of South Carolina than any other agency which has ever existed in this State.

ATTITUDE OF THE FEDERAL GOVERNMENT.

When Congress passed the act readmitting South Carolina into the Federal Union that body "washed its hands of the whole business" of restoration. A civil government had been established, in which the negro race was dominant; and men of that race, guided by a few whites, were to work out the problems which the new situation plainly presented. The legislative power thus apparently exhausted, it was left to the Executive to give promised protection to the State Government from "domestic violence" and from any disturbance of the conditions wrought by the process of restoration according to the Congressional plan.

Towards the new State Government the attitude of the President was throughout that of dogged friendship. Upon the mere statement of the Governor troops were sent into the State. In election years, though there was neither sign nor suggestion of domestic violence, soldiers were sent to different polling-places just as the head of the negro government desired.

The legislation embodied in the Enforcement acts of 1870-71 gave new opportunities for the use of Federal troops. How the President used his powers—with what apparent flippancy he established martial law in several counties of South Carolina—has been sufficiently told.

The position of President Grant in sending soldiers into a Southern State was simple. The demand of the Governor, founded upon his mere allegation of domestic violence, was conclusive in every case. The character of the applicant was not considered. The word of Frank Moses or John Patterson or Cass Carpenter was taken against that of Kershaw or Conner or Bratton. There was no room for either explanation or remonstrance. What was most unfortunate for the people of South Carolina, what was chiefly dishonorable to President Grant, was the help he gave to the representatives of the negro government when there was no sign of domestic violence or purpose of resistance to the laws. Every Republican Governor—Scott, Moses, Chamberlain—was made to feel that without reference to justice or honesty or decency he could always rely upon the support of President Grant. John J. Patterson, notoriously corrupt, actually a criminal, always had the ear of the Executive. It will be remembered that it was after a visit from Honest John that the President in his treatment of the taxpayers' committee was guilty of the most unseemly acts ever done in the White House.

The Federal courts in South Carolina were in ill repute for quite twenty years after the Civil War. Judge Bryan, as early as 1867, thought it proper, in granting a motion to remand a case to the State court, to express his belief that the parties could have their rights protected and adjudicated as fairly in the Federal as in the State court—evidently realizing that many of the white people doubted the fairness of the Federal tribunals. In a very recent case Judge Pritchard, of the United States Circuit Court, in the course of a decree, referred to the feeling, once somewhat prevalent among the people of North Carolina, that the Federal court was "a foreign court, and as such hostile to the interests of the people of the State"—attributing that feeling to the unpopularity of the internal revenue laws. To this feeling reference was made by Judge Goff, in an opinion delivered in a South Carolina case in 1895.

Judge Bryan, in standing by the Constitution as he viewed it, in seeking to maintain the dignity and preserve the purity of the Federal courts in South Carolina, did his full part in saving them from the disrepute, not to say disgrace, which came upon them in some others of the Southern States. These efforts were especially useful in view of the character and purposes of the circuit judge, H. L. Bond. An outright partisan, hating the white people of the South, of small learning (though, truth to tell, fine intellect), a product of the bad times in Maryland in the early 'sixties, Judge Bond never rose above the plane of a pettifogger sitting in the seat of justice. In him the lowest of the fellows who were leaders in his party in South Carolina found always a hearty coadjutor. A careful reading of the story of the Kuklux trials must bring the conclusion that Judge Bond connived at much that was disgraceful. He was at every stage the partisan of the Government in the issues tried before him. He evidently sympathized with the palpable manipulation of the juries in the interest of the prosecution. He was offensive to lawyers and witnesses for the defense—on one occasion guilty of coarse behavior to a clergyman on the stand. He ruled a lawyer for contempt, heard argument, pocketed the case and never rendered a decision. Thus he went to his grave a self-convicted shyster, a self-convicted coward.

Of D. T. Corbin, the District Attorney, enough has been written to show how much he did to bring the Federal courts into disrepute.

The administration of the internal revenue laws was well calculated to destroy the white people's confidence in the Federal Government. Prosecutions were brought upon the flimsiest pretexts. Reputable citizens were arrested, recognized to appear at court, and then released on the payment of money. However innocent, they found it cheaper to pay the sum demanded than to go to trial in Charleston or Columbia. One instance of this corrupt extortion of money must be given to illustrate the style in which the revenue laws were administered. A merchant dealing in cigars had bought his license, and had it in his showcase where, first lying flat, it had rolled up. That merchant was arrested on the charge of not having his license "exposed," and was forced to settle at a cost of more than a hundred dollars. The deputy collector—the "informer"—who put up this job was John B. Hubbard, of whose doings enough has been told to give some idea of his character. For eight years he stood high in Republican circles.

The corrupt officials in South Carolina for more than eight years had the moral support of the Federal Government, the constant help of its courts and its administrative officers.

Such being the character of the negro government of South Carolina, such the motives and conduct of its agents, it naturally became a "stench in the nostrils of decent people" and a disgrace to the country. The Federal bayonets removed, the power of the thieves destroyed, the so-called government fell to pieces of its own imbecility, came to nought of its own all-pervading corruption. Negro domination had proven as well an injury to the black race as an offense to the white—an experiment always doomed to failure—the device of those who, in the name of freedom and justice, had inaugurated and sustained a government that was never worthy of the name.

INDEX.

A.

Aiken, D. Wyatt....21, 340, 342, 347, 352, 361	394
Aiken, Wm................12,	20
Aldrich, A. P....15, 22, 41, 69, 70, 101, 250, 325,	461
Allen, J. M............102, 106, 243,	482
Amnesty Proclamation.......	9
Andrews, T. C.................262,	299

B

Bank and Trust Co.—See Solomon.	
"Big Bonanza"........	317
"Black Code".............27, 33,	495
Blue Ridge Scrip........116, 159, 147, 239,	467
Boozer, L..........13, 15, 21, 62, 77, 86, 113,	127
Bowen, C. C........60, 77, 88, 104, 225, 286, 313, 366,	464
Bosemon, B. A..........107, 123, 225,	333
Bond, Hugh L............202, 209, 404, 406,	513
Bowley, James A...............236,	310
Bratton, John........15, 21, 250, 342, 351,	353
Bryan, George S.............34, 43, 44,	513
Burt, Armistead..............20, 43,	250
Butler, M. C., 22, 42, 100, 143, 157, 164, 250, 263, 272, 302, 340, 341, 345, 348, 350, 360, 433,	461
Buttz, C. W................314, 394,	461

C.

Campbell, James B..........	34
Canby, E. R. S...............69, 97,	98
Cardozo, F. L., ...77, 87, 123, 157, 224, 235, 247, 249, 296, 307, 366, 462,	485
Cain, R. H.,............77, 106, 109, 226,	394
Carpenter, R. B...............113, 143, 229,	362
Carpenter, L. Cass...............265,	476
Cainhoy massacre...........	378
Canvassers, State Board...............397,	401
Chamberlain, D. H., in Convention of '68, 77, 80; Attorney-General, 87; Republican elector, 102; Solicitor, 104; in taxpayers' convention, 164; in Kuklux trials, 202; for Governor in '72, 223; approves mixed schools, 234; university trustee, 236; on extravagance, 267; nominated for Governor, 276; elected Governor, 282; inaugural address, 287; on minority representation, 290; on deficiencies, 292;	

Chamberlain, D. H.—(*Continued.*)
    on trial justice system, 293; sustains Treasurer Cardozo, 298; generally commended, 300; on Solomon's bank, 306; second annual message, 314; denounces election of Whipper and Moses, 322, 323; extent of his reforms, 326; on "the Hamburg massacre," 346; appeals to the President, 347; on Democratic campaign methods, 360; carries April convention, 364; personal canvass, 364; renominated for Governor, 366; stands by the ticket, 367; letter to William Lloyd Garrison, 367; orders whites to "disperse," 381; answered by the Democracy, 383; address to the nation, 385; commends Board of Canvassers, 404; "inaugurated," 423; issues a pardon, 439; memorializes Congress, 443; proposes arbitration, 450; answers Stanley Matthews, 451; opposes withdrawal of troops, 454; formally surrenders, 457; leaves South Carolina, 462; in railroad schemes, 465; denies official misconduct, 468; and the Phosphate bill, 487; and the Whaley case, 492; standards of reform, 508; commends "carpetbag" governments......... 512

Charleston riots............374, 391
Civil rights act............48, 118, 125, 128, 291
Claflin University............ 125
Convention of 1865, 15-20; of 1868............74, 76, 84
Code Commissions............20, 24, 118
Conner, James............16, 43, 67, 340, 342, 348, 351, 406
Constitution of 1865, 17, 19; of 1868............81-83
Constitutional Amendments, (State)............173, 318
Compromise measures (Congress)............ 51
Corbin, D. T............106, 109, 113, 118, 202, 225, 314, 402, 434, 450, 461, 462
Constabulary............115, 138, 145
Conversion bonds............178, 239, 464
Cooke, Thompson H............229, 372
Cochran, John R............261, 322, 414
Conservative convention............ 279
Cothran, J. S............347, 349, 352
Contributions............ 436
Crews, Joseph............78, 108, 123, 132, 145, 261, 311

D

Dawkins, Thomas N............16, 23
Dawson, F. W............ 313
DeLarge, R. C............60, 77, 107, 123, 150, 491
Democratic conventions, 88, 100, 340; reorganization, 337; campaign methods............355, 503
Deaf and Dumb Asylum............237, 241
Dennis, John B............269, 310, 410, 411, 472, 479, 487, 489
Delany, Martin R............279, 378
Divorces............83, 173

INDEX

Dueling 83, 119
Dunn, Thomas C. 296, 366

E.

Elliott, R. B., ...77, 79, 107, 123, 150, 152, 226, 227, 286, 333, 366, 425, 462
Ellenton riot..................... 375
Electoral vote.................... 447
Enforcement acts 191
Euphradian Society 99
Evins, John H. 341, 342, 352, 394

F

Farmer, C. B. 22
Feeling among whites............. 98
Financial Board (see frauds)........115, 116
Fifteenth Amendment............120, 142, 354
Fourteenth Amendment 33, 34, 49, 51, 109, 354, 499
Freedmen's Bureau..............44, 47, 50
Fraser, Thomas B. 325, 342, 349, 358
Frauds, miscellaneous............. 486

G

Gary, M. W. 42, 101, 164, 264, 341, 343, 348, 360, 395
Garfield, James A. 497
General Order No. 10............65, 68, 69
Gillmore, Q. A. 4, 136
Gleaves, R. H. 59, 60, 224, 366, 460, 462
Gordon, John B. 402, 443
Graham, Robert F. 22, 102, 158
Grant, U. S. ...34, 35, 40, 196, 216, 263, 386, 388, 409, 440, 512
Green, John T. 113, 225, 279, 295
Greenville and Columbia Railroad........159, 465

H

Hampton, Wade, elected to Convention of '65, 16; to National Convention, 101; in State Convention, 348; position as to Governorship 350; nominated for Governor, 351; speech of acceptance, 352; urges self-control, 387; carries the State, 393; congratulates the people, 396; denounces the Board of Canvassers, 402; charges Ruger with bad faith, 416; inaugurated as Governor, 426; demands possession, 432; calls for contributions, 435; adjudged to be Governor, 437; memorializes Congress, 442; writes to Hayes and Tilden, 444; asks withdrawal of troops, 449; goes to Washington, 453; occupies State House, 460; assembles Legislature.................. 460
Haskell, A. C. 21, 341, 342, 348, 353, 410, 446, 451, 461
Hayne, I. W. 71, 89
Hayne, H. E. 78, 106, 224, 233, 241, 366, 401

518 ·RECONSTRUCTION IN SOUTH CAROLINA

Hagood, Johnson.................89, 250, 325, 342, 347, 349,   351
Habeas corpus suspended...   196
Harllee, W. W...341, 348,   349
Hamburg trouble   344
Hayes, R. B...............................442, 447, 449, 453,   456
Hoge, S. L............104, 112, 128, 202, 224, 237, 284,   462
Hoyt, James A.................................166, 250, 343, 347,   353
Hubbard, John B.................................114, 138, 467,   514
Humbert, J. L...   269
Hunter, H. H...   332
Hunkidori mob...418,   421
Hudson, J. H...   461

I.

Ignorance in official stations   120
Impeachment (frauds)...   470
Investigating committee (Republican)   176
Independent Republicans...   279

J.

Jillson, J. K........................60, 77, 87, 106, 123, 236,   237
Johnson, Andrew 6, 9, 12, 13, 26, 34, 35, 36, 37, 48, 55,   495
Johnson, Reverdy..39, 202, 212,   215
Jones, A. O.....................................154, 226, 286,   410

K.

Kennedy, John D.....................20, 102, 341, 342,   353
Kershaw, Joseph B.....................21, 143, 282, 342,   449
Kerrigan, James E..   152
Kimpton, H. H.................................115, 175, 270,   464
Kuklux, organization, 179, 217; legislation, 191; trials, 202; rewards,   216

L.

Land Commission...................119, 126, 135, 170,   490
Lesesne, H. D...16, 67,   105
Lee, Thomas B..   84
Lee, Samuel J........................107, 234, 236, 261, 462,   485
Leaphart, S. L..89,   351
Leslie, C. P.............................77, 106, 474, 484,   491
Legislative expenses................128, 160, 174, 231, 245,   485
Legislative workings...   330
Lincoln, Abraham..7,   495
"Little Bonanza"..   317
Lunatic asylum 123, 219, 241,   269

INDEX 519

M.

Manning, John L............21, 100, 250, 340, 342, 348,	349
Mackey, A. G..................................77, 79, 110,	123
Mackey, E. W. M............60, 78, 262, 284, 415, 419,	460
Mackey, Thomas J......172, 302, 304, 309, 321, 372, 447, 430, 449,	461
Maher, John J..172,	325
Matthews, Stanley 449,	451
Melton, Samuel W...127,	224
Merrill, Lewis 197,	216
Military interference...	39
Militia........26, 50, 119, 135, 136, 138, 182, 272, 301, 344, 374, 377, 379,	380
Minority representation...	166
Moses, F. J., Sr.,.............16, 21, 23, 68, 112, 157, 437,	439
Moses, F. J., Jr., in Constitutional Convention, 78; Adjutant-General, 87; expelled from college society, 99; speaker, 109, 154; university trustee, 123, 236; elected Governor, 225; inaugurated, 226; calls extra session, 238; approves mixed schools, 241; "the Robber Governor," 266; indicted for embezzlement, 269; elected judge, 322, 324; vagrant and criminal...............................	462
Moses, Montgomery...158,	320
Mobley, J. S. (June)...145, 183,	333
Moise, E. W..349,	351

Mc.

McAlily, Samuel..12,	89
McCaw, Wm. H..244,	250
McGowan, Samuel.........................15, 20, 89, 282, 284,	342
McIver, Henry...15, 143,	460

N.

Nash, W. Beverly......71, 78, 80, 85, 107, 123, 284, 366, 425, 462,	489
Negro troops (U. S.)..4,	7
Nelson, Samuel..44,	502
Neagle, J. L...78, 87, 123, 145,	462
Normal School (State).......................................230,	233
Northrop, L. C..236, 321,	461
Norris, Tilda...	438

O.

Orr, James L., in Convention of '65, 15; elected Governor, 20; inaugurated, 25; opposes Fourteenth Amendment, 33; in Philadelphia convention, 39; letter to General Sickles, 68; elected circuit judge, 114; for Scott and Ransier, 147; in Republican convention of '72, 223; leads Republican bolt...............................	225

O'Neale, R., Jr............................136, 348, 353
Orphan asylum (State)..........................118, 490

P.

Parker, Niles G....70, 79, 87, 172, 234, 244, 308, 465, 466, 468, 470, 474,
  479, 491, 493
Patterson, John J..........159, 175, 227, 270, 441, 443, 450, 467, 472, 484
Pay certificates (frauds) 483
Perry, B. F., provisional Governor, 12; on parish system, 18; elected
  U. S. Senator, 23; race for Congress, 226; in Convention of '76,
  342; delegate to National Convention............................. 342
Philadelphia Convention.. 37
Phosphate act 126
Pillsbury, G..60, 61, 77, 105, 213
Platt, Z..70, 113
Porter, Wm. D.................................25, 67, 89, 164, 245, 263, 342
Pope, Y. J..143, 341
Protest of whites...74, 90, 91, 93, 94
Pressley, B. C...324, 461
Public printing (frauds)... 473

R.

Randolph, B. F.......................................60, 61, 79, 102, 103
Rainey, J. H...61, 106, 150, 226, 284
Ransier, A. J..77, 107, 149, 226, 462
Reconstruction theories, 7-9; measures, 47-59; committee, 49; completed.. 96
Republican party organized....................................... 59
Republican conventions, 86, 102, 143, 222, 276, 362, 366; reply to taxpayers.. 253
Republican Printing Co...........................159, 162, 239, 293, 473
Reed, Jacob P..104, 295, 322
Revenue Bond Scrip...........................116, 159, 147, 239, 467
Rion, James H...15, 274, 348, 349, 402
Rifle Clubs...274, 382, 389, 440
Rivers, Prince R.......................................77, 107, 261, 345, 346, 508
Robertson, Thomas J......60, 78, 85, 99, 110, 111, 123, 157, 158, 218, 441, 449
Rutland, James M.......................................77, 106, 113
Ruger, Thomas H......................................409, 416, 417, 422

S.

Sawyer, F. A..78, 110, 111, 225
Scott, R. K., Commissioner of Freedmen's Bureau, 45-46; elected
  Governor, 93; appointed Governor, 97; inaugurated, 109; campaign plans, 135; arming the negroes, 135; renominated for

INDEX

Scott, R. K.—(*Continued.*)
    Governor, 143; reelected, 150; last message, 170; impeachment, 172, 470; candidate for U. S. Senate, 227; urges recognition of Hampton 449
Sheppard, J. C..246, 341, 342, 411
Shaw, A. J..104, 296, 461
Sims, R. M..15, 106, 250, 351
Simonton, C. H..............................22, 101, 245, 248, 263, 339, 340, 348, 349
Sickles, Daniel E..40, 41, 61, 66, 67, 68
Simpson, William D...104, 351, 432, 460
Sinking Fund Commission..269, 488
Smalls, Robert...................................77, 107, 262, 311, 366, 462, 493
Smyth, J. Adger..348, 353
Solomon, Hardy................................239, 305, 470, 477, 487, 488, 490
Soldiers, U. S., evacuate State House..456, 460
Stanbery, Henry..57, 58, 202, 205, 215
State debt.....................................155, 169, 170, 178, 219, 238, 463
State House evacuated by U. S. troops..456, 460
Stone, William...346, 435
Stevens, Thaddeus...9, 48, 497
Supplies (frauds)... 476
Swails, S. A........................78, 102, 107, 225, 226, 261, 286, 460, 462

T.

Taxpayers' Convention, 162, 170, 245; appeal to Congress......250, 263, 265
Tax Union (State)... 272
Thomson, Thomas...15, 21, 461
Thompson, James G.....................................16, 247, 249, 263, 294
Thompson, Hugh S... 351
Thomas, John P..23, 93, 94, 102, 166
Thomas, William M..................................113, 185, 195, 198
Thirteenth Amendment...23, 354
Third District investigation... 131
Tillman, George D..15, 21, 342, 348, 352, 361
Tomlinson, R...107, 119, 123, 224, 225
Township system... 115
Townsend, C. P.. 172

U.

Union League.. 62
Union Reform movement.. 139
University..118, 123, 229, 231, 241, 502

V.

Vernon, T. O. P..114, 151, 152

W.

Wardlaw, David L...15,	34
Wallace, A. S..............................104, 150, 226, 284,	365
Wallace, W. H...............143, 284, 342, 349, 410, 412, 419,	461
Wallace House.............................411, 412, 414, 419,	421
Whipper, W. J..........59, 77, 107, 118, 225, 295, 322, 324, 333,	462
Whittemore, B. F.........60, 61, 77, 87, 104, 106, 132, 144, 225, 462,	484
Winsmith, John..21,	87
Williams, George W..21,	113
Willard, A. J.......................................43, 113, 437,	460
Wiggin, Pierce L...322,	326
Wilson, Henry...	497
Woodruff, J..............................109, 154, 226, 286,	461
Worthington, H. G...............................152, 227,	472
Wright, J. J...........................61, 77, 106, 128, 437, 461,	485